The Guinness Book of
Olympic
FACTS AND FEATS

Stan Greenberg

GUINNESS PUBLISHING

Acknowledgements

I am much indebted to the original research by Olympic historians Erich Kamper (AUT) and Volker Kluge (formerly GDR). Other important work has been done by Bill Mallon (USA) and Ian Buchanan (GBR). My main sources were, in alphabetical order:

The Associated Press and Grolier – *Pursuit of Excellence, The Olympic Story* (1979)
Sandor Barcs (HUN) – *The Modern Olympics Story* (1964)
Pat Besford (GBR) – *Encyclopaedia of Swimming* (1976)
Ian Buchanan (GBR) – *British Olympians* (1991)
John Durant (USA) – *Highlights of the Olympics* (1961)
Erich Kamper (AUT) – *Enzyklopadie der Olympischen Spiele* (1972), *Lexicon der Olympischen Winter Spiele* (1964), and *Lexicon der 14, 000 Olympioniken* (1983)
Erich Kamper (AUT) and Bill Mallon (USA) – *The Golden Book of the Olympic Games* (1992)
Lord Killanin (IRE) and John Rodda (GBR) – *The Olympic Games* (1976)
Volker Kluge (ex GDR) – *Die Olympischen Spiele von 1896 bis 1980* (1981)
Volker Kluge (ex GDR) – *Winter Olympia Kompakt* (1992)
Bill Mallon (USA) and Ian Buchanan (GBR) – *Quest for Gold* (1984)
Bill Mallon (USA) – *The Olympic Record Book* (1988)
Peter Matthews (GBR) – *Track and Field Athletics, The Records* (1986)
Norris and Ross McWhirter (GBR) – *The Guinness Book of Olympic Records* (1980)
David Wallechinsky (USA) – *The Complete Book of the Olympics* (1984, 1988, 1992)
Melvyn Watman (GBR) – *The Encyclopaedia of Track and Field Athletics* (1981)

Other experts and organizations whose publications and personal help have been invaluable include:

Richard Ayling, Howard Bass, Harry Carpenter, Jim Coote, Peter Diamond (USA), Maurice Golesworthy, John Goodbody, Mark Heller, Richard Hymans, Peter Johnson, Ove Karlsson (SWE), Wolf Lyberg (SWE), Ferenc Mezo (HUN), Ron Pickering, Jack Rollin, Bob Sparks, Stuart Storey, Dave Terry, John Tidy, Lance Tingay, Martin Tyler, David Vine, Alan Weeks, Ture Widlund (SWE), Dorian Williams, Don Wood.

The Association of Track and Field Statisticians(ATFS) and its members, British Olympic Association, The International Society of Olympic Historians (ISOH), International Amateur Athletic Federation (IAAF), International Olympic Committee (IOC), International Weight-lifting Federation, National Ski Federation of Great Britain, National Union of Track Statisticians (NUTS) and its members, *New York Times*, *Sports Illustrated*, *The Times*, *Track and Field News*, and many national and international bodies and individuals.

I would particularly like to thank Keith Greenberg for his advice and help with my word processor, as well as some typing and checking, and Carole Greenberg for her good humour and understanding.

Where contradictions have been found in different sources I have invariably arrived at my own conclusion. The recent political upheavals of the former East European bloc has caused Olympic chroniclers some problems. I have taken my own attitude to such matters and made my own, perhaps unique, medal compilations. However, I have given all necessary data so that should readers have different views they can reconstruct tables to their own liking. After extensive recent research, new participation figures have been agreed by members of the International Society of Olympic Historians.

Stan Greenberg
London 1996

Reprint 10 9 8 7 6 5 4 3 2 1 0

Text design and layout: Mitchell Associates
Cover design: Ad Vantage Studios
Front cover: Sally Gunnell

Printed and bound in Great Britain by The Bath Press, Bath

'GUINNESS' is a registered trademark of Guinness Publishing Ltd

A catalogue record of this book is available from the British Library

ISBN 0-85112-639-1

Contents

Olympic attendance — by nation

Only five countries have never failed to be represented at celebrations of the Summer Games since 1896 (including 1906): Australia, France, Greece, Great Britain and Switzerland. (Prior to 1924 Irish competitors were members of the Great Britain team, and did not represent Ireland. In 1956 Switzerland only competed in the Stockholm segment of the Games). Of those five, only France, Great Britain and Switzerland have been present at all Winter Games as well. Only Great Britain also competed in the skating and ice hockey events of 1908 and 1920, the 'Winter' events included in those Summer Games.

Country		Summer Games Debut	Summer Games Number attended	Winter Games Debut	Winter Games Number attended
AFG	Afghanistan (a)	1936	9	-	
AHO	Netherlands Antilles	1952	9	1988	2
ALB	Albania	1972	2	-	
ALG	Algeria	1964	7	1992	1
AND	Andorra	1976	5	1976	6
ANG	Angola	1980	3	-	
ANT	Antigua	1976	4		
ARG	Argentina	1920	16	1908	13
ARM	Armenia	-		1994	1
ARU	Aruba	1988	2		
ASA	American Samoa	1988	2	1994	1
AUS	Australia (1)	1896	23	1936	13
AUT	Austria (2)	1896	22	1924	17
AZE	Azerbaijan	-			
BAH	Bahamas	1952	10	-	
BAN	Bangladesh	1984	3	-	
BAR	Barbados	1968	6	-	
BDI	Burundi	-			
BEL	Belgium	1900	21	1920	16
BEN	Benin (ex Dahomey)	1980	4	-	
BER	Bermuda	1936	12	1992	2
BHU	Bhutan	1984	3	-	
BIR	see Myanmar				
BIZ	Belize (ex British Honduras)	1968	6	-	
BLR	Belarus	-		1994	1
BOH	Bohemia (3)	-	-	-	
BOL	Bolivia	1936	8	1956	5
BOT	Botswana	1980	4	-	
BRA	Brazil	1920	16	1992	2
BRN	Bahrain	1976	4	-	
BRU	Brunei (a)	-	-	-	
BSH	Bosnia & Herzegovina	1992	1	1994	1
BUL	Bulgaria	1896	14	1936	14
BUR	Burkina Faso (ex Upper Volta)	1972	3	-	
CAF	Central African Republic	1968	4		
CAM	Cambodia (4)	1956	3		
CAN	Canada	1900	21	1920	18
CAY	Cayman Islands	1976	4	-	
CGO	Congo	1964	6		
CHA	Chad	1964	6		
CHI	Chile	1896	17	1948	11
CHN	China	1932	7	1980	5
CIV	Ivory Coast	1964	7		
CMR	Cameroon	1964	8	-	

(a) Brunei (1988) and Afghanistan (1992) only sent officials . . (1) Australia and New Zealand combined as Australasia 1908-1912
(2) Not invited in 1920 . . (3) Represented by Bohemia up to 1912 . . (4) Provisional recognition of current regime in Cambodia

Country		Summer Games		Winter Games	
		Debut	*Number attended*	*Debut*	*Number attended*
COK	Cook Islands	1988	2	-	
COL	Colombia	1932	13	-	
COM	Comoros Is	-			
CPV	Cape Verde Is	-			
CRC	Costa Rica	1936	9	1984	3
CRO	Croatia	1992	1	1992	2
CUB	Cuba	1900	14	-	
CYP	Cyprus	1980	4	1980	5
CZE	Czech Republic (3)	-		1994	1
DEN	Denmark	1896	22	1948	8
DJI	Djibouti	1984	3		
DMA	Dominica	-			
DOM	Dominican Republic	1964	8	-	
ECU	Ecuador	1924	8	-	
EGY	Egypt (5)	1906	17	1984	1
ESA	El Salvador	1968	5	-	
ESP	Spain	1900	17	1936	14
EST	Estonia (6)	1920	6	1928	4
ETH	Ethiopia	1956	7	-	
FIJ	Fiji	1956	8	1988	2
FIN	Finland	1906	20	1920	18
FRA	France	1896	23	1920	18
FRG	Federal Republic of Germany (7)	1968	5	1968	6
GAB	Gabon	1972	4	-	
GAM	Gambia	1984	3	-	
GBR	Great Britain	1896	23	1908	19
GDR	German Democratic Republic (7)	1968	5	1968	6
GEO	Georgia	-		1994	1
GEQ	Equatorial Guinea	1984	3	-	
GER	Germany (8)	1896	14	1908	10
GHA	Ghana (ex Gold Coast)	1952	8	-	
GNB	Guinea-Bissau	–		–	
GRE	Greece	1896	23	1936	13
GRN	Grenada	1984	3		
GUA	Guatemala	1952	8	1988	1
GUI	Guinea	1968	5	-	
GUM	Guam	1988	2	1988	1
GUY	Guyana (ex British Guiana)	1948	11	-	
HAI	Haiti	1900	10	-	
HKG	Hong Kong	1952	10	-	
HON	Honduras	1968	5	1992	1
HUN	Hungary	1896	21	1924	17
INA	Indonesia	1952	9	-	
IND	India	1900	18	1964	4
IRI	Iran	1948	10	1956	5
IRL	Ireland (9)	1924	15	1992	1
IRQ	Iraq	1948	8	-	
ISL	Iceland	1908	15	1948	12
ISR	Israel	1952	10	1994	1
ISV	Virgin Islands	1968	6	1984	4
ITA	Italy	1900	21	1924	17
IVB	British Virgin Islands	1984	3	-	
JAM	Jamaica (10)	1948	12	1988	3

(5) As United Arab Republic 1960-68 . . (6) Annexed by the Soviet Union in 1940; independent again from 1992
(7) Separate teams 1968-88; GDR part of combined German team 1956-64 . . (8) Not invited 1920, 1924 and 1948
(9) Part of Great Britain team until 1924 . . (10) Jamaica and Trinidad combined as Antilles in 1960

Country		Summer Games Debut	Number attended	Winter Games Debut	Number attended
JOR	Jordan	1980	4	-	
JPN	Japan	1912	6	1928	14
KAZ	Kazakstan	-		1994	1
KEN	Kenya	1956	8	-	
KGZ	Kirghizstan	-		1994	1
KOR	Korea (11)	1948	11	1948	12
KSA	Saudi Arabia	1976	4	-	
KUW	Kuwait	1968	7	-	
LAO	Laos	1980	3	-	
LAT	Latvia (6)	1924	5	1924	5
LBA	Libya	1968	5	-	
LBR	Liberia	1956	6	-	
LCA	St Lucia	-			
LES	Lesotho	1972	5	-	
LIB	Lebanon	1948	11	1948	12
LIE	Liechtenstein	1936	11	1936	13
LTU	Lithuania (6)	1924	3	1928	3
LUX	Luxembourg	1912	17	1928	5
MAD	Madagascar	1964	6	-	
MAR	Morocco	1960	8	1968	4
MAS	Malaysia (12)	1956	9	-	
MAW	Malawi	1972	4	-	
MDV	Maldives	1988	2	-	
MEX	Mexico	1924	16	1928	4
MGL	Mongolia	1964	7	1964	8
MKD	Macedonia	-			
MLD	Moldova	-		1994	1
MLI	Mali	1964	7	-	
MLT	Malta	1928	10	-	
MON	Monaco	1920	14	1984	4
MOZ	Mozambique	1980	4	-	
MRI	Mauritius	1984	3	-	
MTN	Mauretania	1984	3	-	
MYA	Myanmar (ex Burma)	1948	11		
NAM	Namibia	1992	1		
NCA	Nicaragua	1968	6		
NED	Netherlands	1900	21	1928	15
NEP	Nepal	1964	7	-	
NGR	Nigeria	1952	10		
NIG	Niger	1964	6		
NOR	Norway	1900	21	1920	18
NZL	New Zealand	1908	19	1952	10
OMA	Oman	1984	3	-	
PAK	Pakistan	1948	11	-	
PAN	Panama	1928	11	-	
PAR	Paraguay	1968	6	-	
PER	Peru	1936	12	-	
PHI	Philippines	1924	15	1972	3
PLE	Palestine	-			
PNG	Papua New Guinea	1976	4		
POL	Poland	1924	15	1924	17
POR	Portugal	1912	18	1952	3
PRK	Democratic People's Republic of Korea (11)	1972	4	1964	5
PUR	Puerto Rico	1948	12	1984	4

(11) Country partitioned in 1945, and separate regimes established in 1948
(12) Prior to 1964 Malaya and North Borneo (later Sabah) competed separately. Combined in 1964 with Sarawak and Singapore.

Country		Summer Games Debut	Number attended	Winter Games Debut	Number attended
QAT	Qatar	1984	3	-	
ROM	Romania	1924	14	1928	15
RSA	South Africa (13)	1904	14	1960	2
RUS	Russia (14)	1900	3	1908	2
RWA	Rwanda	1984	3	-	
SAM	Western Samoa	1984	3	-	
SAR	Saar (15)	1952	1	-	
SEN	Senegal	1964	8	1984	3
SEY	Seychelles	1980	3	-	
SIN	Singapore	1948	11		
SKN	St Kitts & Nevis	-			
SLE	Sierra Leone	1968	5		
SLO	Slovenia	1992	1	1992	2
SMR	San Marino	1960	7	1976	5
SOL	Solomon Islands	1984	3	-	
SOM	Somalia	1972	3		
SRI	Sri Lanka (ex Ceylon)	1948	11		
STP	Sao Tome & Principe				
SUD	Sudan	1960	6	-	
SUI	Switzerland (16)	1896	23	1920	18
SUR	Surinam	1968	6	-	
SVK	Slovakia	-		1994	1
SWE	Sweden	1896	22	1908	19
SWZ	Swaziland	1972	4	1992	1
SYR	Syria	1948	7	-	
TAN	Tanzania	1964	7	-	
TCH	Czechoslovakia (3)	1900	20	1920	17
TGA	Tonga	1984	3	-	
THA	Thailand	1952	10	-	
TJK	Tajikistan	-			
TKM	Turkmenistan	-			
TOG	Togo	1972	4		
TPE	Taipei (ex Formosa/Taiwan)	1956	8	1972	6
TRI	Trinidad & Tobago (10)	1948	12	1994	1
TUN	Tunisia	1960	8	-	
TUR	Turkey	1908	16	1936	11
UAE	United Arab Emirates	1984	3	-	
UGA	Uganda	1956	9	-	
UKR	Ukraine	-		1994	1
URS	Soviet Union (17)	1952	10	1956	10
URU	Uruguay	1924	15	-	
USA	United States	1896	22	1908	19
UZB	Uzbekistan	-		1994	1
VAN	Vanuatu	1988	2	-	
VEN	Venezuela	1948	12	-	
VIE	Vietnam (18)	1952	9	-	
VIN	St Vincent	1988	2	-	
YEM	Yemen (19)	1992	1	-	
YUG	Yugoslavia (20)	1912	18	1924	14
ZAI	Zaire	1968	4	-	
ZAM	Zambia (ex N Rhodesia)	1964	7	-	
ZIM	Zimbabwe (ex Rhodesia)	1928	7	-	

(13) Not invited 1960-88 . . (14) As Czarist Russia 1900-12; separately again in 1994 . . (15) Independent 1947-1957, then incorporated into Germany . . (16) Switzerland only in Stockholm in 1956 . . (17) Former Soviet republics (excluding Baltic states) competed in 1992 as the Unified Team (EUN) or Commonwealth of Independent States (CIS) . . (18) From 1952 to 1972 only a South Vietnamese team competed (19) The Republic of Yemen was formed in 1960 of the Yemen Arab Republic (which competed 1984/88) and the Yemen People's Democratic Republic (which competed in 1988) . . (20) Representatives of the Yugoslavia Serbs competed as Independent Olympic Participants (IOP) in the 1992 Games. In 1912 Serbia had competed as a separate entity.

Celebrations of the games

(New research on competitors has resulted in revised figures for participation in many celebrations of the Games)

Summer

	Year	Venue	Date	Nations	Women	Men	Total
I	1896	Athens, Greece	6-15 April(1)	14	-	c.211	211
II	1900	Paris, France	20 May-28 October	26	19	1206	1225
III	1904	St Louis, USA	1 July-23 November	13	6	681	687
*	1906	Athens, Greece	22 April-2 May	20	6	820	826
IV	1908	London, England	27 April-31 October	22	36	1999	2035
V	1912	Stockholm, Sweden	5 May-22 July	28	57	2490	2547
VI	1916	Berlin, Germany	Not held due to war	-	-	-	-
VII	1920	Antwerp, Belgium	20 April-12 September	29	77	2591	2668
VIII	1924	Paris, France	4 May-27 July	44	136	2956	3092
IX	1928	Amsterdam, Holland	17 May-12 August	46	290	2724	3014
X	1932	Los Angeles, USA	30 July-14 August	37	127	1281	1408
XI	1936	Berlin, Germany	1-16 August	49	328	3738	4066
XII	1940	Tokyo, then Helsinki	Not held due to war	-	-	-	-
XIII	1944	London	Not held due to war	-	-	-	-
XIV	1948	London, England	29 July-14 August	59	385	3714	4099
XV	1952	Helsinki, Finland	19 July-3 August	69	518	4407	4925
XVI	1956	Melbourne, Australia(2)	22 Nov-8 December	67	371	2813	3184
XVII	1960	Rome, Italy	25 Aug-11 September	83	610	4736	5346
XVIII	1964	Tokyo, Japan	10-24 October	93	683	4457	5140
XIX	1968	Mexico City, Mexico	12-27 October	112	781	4749	5530
XX	1972	Munich, FRG	26 Aug-10 September	121	1058	6065	7123
XXI	1976	Montreal, Canada	17 July-1 August	92	1247	4781	6028
XXII	1980	Moscow, Soviet Union	19 July-3 August	80	1124	4093	5217
XXIII	1984	Los Angeles, USA	28 July-12 August	140	1567	5230	6797
XXIV	1988	Seoul, Korea	17 Sep-2 October	159	2186	6279	8465
XXV	1992	Barcelona, Spain	25 July-9 August	169	2707	6657	9364
XXVI	1996	Atlanta, USA	19 July-4 August	-	-	-	-
XXVII	2000	Sydney, Australia	15 Sep-1 October (prov)	-	-	-	-

*This celebration (to mark the tenth anniversary of the modern Games) was officially intercalated, but not numbered.
(1) Actually 25 March-3 April by the Julian Calendar then in use in Greece
(2) Equestrian events held in Stockholm, Sweden, 10-17 June, with 158 competitors (of which 13 were women) from 29 countries.

Winter

	Year	Venue	Date	Nations	Women	Men	Total
I	1924	Chamonix, France	25 Jan-4 February	16	13	245	258
II	1928	St Moritz, Switzerland	11-19 February	25	26	438	464
III	1932	Lake Placid, USA	4-15 February	17	21	231	252
IV	1936	Garmisch-Partenkirchen, Germany	6-16 February	28	80	588	668
	1940	Sapporo, then St Moritz, then Garmisch-P	Not held due to war	-	-	-	-
	1944	Cortina d'Ampezzo, Italy	Not held due to war	-	-	-	-
V	1948	St Morotz, Switzerland	30 Jan-8 February	28	77	592	669
VI	1952	Oslo, Norway	14-25 February	30	109	585	694
VII	1956	Cortina d'Ampezzo, Italy	26 Jan-5 February	32	132	688	820
VIII	1960	Squaw Valley, USA	18-28 February	30	143	522	665
IX	1964	Innsbruck, Austria	29 Jan-9 February	36	200	891	1091
X	1968	Grenoble, France	6-18 February	37	211	947	1158
XI	1972	Sapporo, Japan	3-13 February	35	206	800	1006
XII	1976	Innsbruck, Austria	4-15 February	37	231	892	1123
XIII	1980	Lake Placid, USA	13-24 February	37	233	839	1072
XIV	1984	Sarajevo, Yugoslavia	8-19 February	49	274	1000	1274
XV	1988	Calgary, Canada	13-28 February	57	313	1110	1423
XVI	1992	Albertville, France	8-23 February	64	488	1313	1801
XVII	1994	Lillehammer, Norway	12-27 February	67	520	1217	1737
XVIII	1998	Nagano, Japan	7-22 February	-	-	-	-
XIX	2002	Salt Lake City, USA	-	-	-	-	-

Olympic records

Most Golds (Summer)
Men: 10 Ray Ewry (USA) 1900-1908 Athletics
Women: 9 Larissa Latynina (URS) 1956-64 Gymnastics
Men, in one Games: 7 Mark Spitz (USA) 1972 Swimming
Women, in one Games: 6 Kristin Otto (GDR) 1988 Swimming

Most Medals (Summer)
Men: 15 Nikolay Andrianov (URS) 1972-80 Gymnastics
Women: 18 Larissa Latynina (URS) 1956-64 Gymnastics
Men, in one Games: 8 Alexandr Dityatin (URS) 1980 Gymnastics
Women, in one Games: 7 Maria Gorokhovskaya (URS) 1952 Gymnastics

Most Golds (Winter)
Men: 5 Clas Thunberg (FIN) 1924-1928 Speed Skating, Eric Heiden (USA) 1980 Speed Skating, Bjorn Dählie (NOR) 1992-94 Nordic Skiing
Women: 6 Lydia Skoblikova (URS) 1960-1964 Speed Skating, Lyubov Yegorova (EUN-RUS) 1992-94 Nordic Skiing
Men, in one Games: 5 Eric Heiden (USA) 1980 Speed Skating
Women, in one Games: 4 Lydia Skoblikova (URS) 1964 Speed Skating

Most Medals (Winter)
Men: 9 Sixten Jernberg (SWE) 1956-1964 Nordic Skiing
Women: 10 Raisa Smetanina (URS) 1976-1992 Nordic Skiing
Men, in one Games: 5 Clas Thunberg (FIN) 1924 Speed Skating, Roald Larsen (NOR) 1924 Speed Skating, Eric Heiden (USA) 1980 Speed Skating
Women, in one Games: 5 Lyubov Yegorova (EUN-RUS) 1992 Nordic Skiing, Yelena Valbe (EUN-RUS) 1992 Nordic Skiing, Manuela di Centa (ITA) 1994 Nordic Skiing

Age Records (Summer)
Oldest Male Gold: 64y 258d Oscar Swahn (Swe) 1912 Shooting
Oldest Female Gold: 53y 277d Queenie Newall (GBR) 1908 Archery
Oldest Male Medallist: 72y 279d Oscar Swahn (Swe) 1920 Shooting
Oldest Female Medallist: 53y 277d Queenie Newall (GBR) 1908 Archery
Youngest Male Gold: 7-10y Unknown French boy 1900 Rowing
Youngest Female Gold: 13y 267d Marjorie Gestring (USA) 1936 Diving
Youngest Male Medallist: 7-10y Unknown French boy 1900 Rowing
Youngest Female Medallist: 12y 24d Inge Sörensen (Den) 1936 Swimming
Oldest Competitor (Male): 72y 279d Oscar Swahn (SWE) 1920 Shooting
Oldest Competitor (Female): 70y 5d Lorna Johnstone (GBR) 1972 Equestrianism
Youngest Competitor (Male): 7-10y Unknown boy (FRA) 1900 Rowing
Youngest Competitor (Female): 11y 328d Liana Vicens (PUR) 1968 Swimming

Age Records (Winter)
Oldest Male Gold: 48y 359d Jay O'Brien (USA) 1932 Bobsledding
Oldest Female Gold: 39y 354d Raisa Smetanina (EUN-RUS) 1992 Nordic Skiing

Oldest Male Medallist: 49y 278d Max Houben (BEL) 1948 Bobsledding
Oldest Female Medallist: 39y 354d Raisa Smetanina (EUN-RUS) 1992 Nordic Skiing
Youngest Male Gold: 16y 259d Toni Nieminen (FIN) 1992 Ski Jumping
Youngest Female Gold: 13y 83d Kim Yoon-Mi (KOR) 1994 Short-Track Speed Skating
Youngest Male Medallist: 14y 363d Scott Allen (USA) 1964 Figure Skating
Youngest Female Medallist: 13y 83d Kim Yoon-Mi (KOR) 1994 Short-Track Speed Skating
Oldest Competitor (Male): 53y 297d James Coats (GBR) 1948 Tobogganing
Oldest Competitor (Female): 45y 318d Edwina Chamier (CAN) 1936 Skiing
Youngest Competitor (Male): 12y 110d Jan Hoffmann (GDR) 1968 Figure Skating
Youngest Competitor (Female): 11y 73d Cecilia Colledge (GBR) 1932 Figure Skating

Most Games/Longest Span (Summer) – Men
8 Games: Raimondo d'Inzeo (ITA) 1948-76 Equestrianism, Piero d'Inzeo (ITA) 1948-76 Equestrianism, Hubert Raudaschl (AUT) 1964-92 Yachting, Durward Knowles (GBR/BAH) 1948-72, 88, Paul Elvström (DEN) 1948-60, 68-72, 84-88 all Yachting
40 yr: Ivan Osiier (DEN) 1908-48 Fencing, Magnus Konow (NOR) 1908-48 Yachting, Durward Knowles (GBR/BAH) 1948-1988 Yachting, Paul Elvström (DEN) 1948-1988 Yachting

Most Games/Longest Span (Summer) – Women
7 Games: Kerstin Palm (SWE) 1964-88 Fencing
28 yr: Anne Newberry-Ransehousen (USA) 1960-88 Equestrianism, Christilot Hanson-Boylen (CAN) 1964-92 Equestrianism

Most Games/Longest Span (Winter) – Men
6 Games: Colin Coates (AUS) 1968-1988 Speed Skating, Carl-Erik Eriksson (SWE) 1964-1984 Bobsledding
20 yr: John Heaton (USA) 1928-1948 Tobogganing, Max Houben (BEL) 1928-1948 Bobsledding, Richard Torriani (SUI) 1928-1948 Ice Hockey, Frank Stack (CAN) 1932-1952 Speed Skating, Stanislaw Marusarz (POL) 1932-1952 Nordic Skiing, James Bickford (USA) 1936-1956 Bobsledding, Sepp Bradl (AUT) 1936-1956 Ski Jumping, Carl-Erik Eriksson (SWE) 1964-1984 Bobsledding, Colin Coates (AUS) 1968-1988 Speed Skating

Most Games/Longest Span (Winter) – Women
6 Games: Marja-Liisa Hämäläinen-Kirvesniemi (FIN) 1976-94 Nordic Skiing
18yr: Marja-Liisa Hämäläinen-Kirvesniemi (FIN) 1976-94 Nordic Skiing

IOC Presidents

1894 - 1896	Demetrius Vikelas (Greece)
1896 - 1925	Baron Pierre de Coubertin (France)
1925 - 1942	Henri de Baillet-Latour (Belgium)
1942 - 1952	Sigfrid Edström (Sweden)
1952 - 1972	Avery Brundage (USA)
1972 - 1980	Lord Killanin (Ireland)
1980 -	Juan Antonio Samaranch (Spain)

Olympic medals — by nation

		Summer				Winter					Overall
		G	S	B	TOTAL	G	S	B	TOTAL		TOTAL
1	United States	789	602	523	1914 (1)	53	56	37	146	(3)	2060
2	Soviet Union [1]	485	395	354	1234 (2)	87	63	67	217	(1)	1451
3	Great Britain	176	225	219	620 (3)	7	4	12	23	(=17)	643
4	France	161	174	190	525 (4)	16	16	21	53	(12)	578
5	Sweden	132	148	171	451 (=5)	39	26	34	99	(7)	550
6	Germany [2]	131	163	157	451 (=5)	34	29	24	87	(8)	538
7	GDR [3]	153	130	127	410 (7)	39	36	35	110	(6)	520
8	Italy	153	126	130	409 (8)	25	21	21	67	(10)	476
9	Finland	98	78	112	288 (10)	36	45	42	123	(5)	411
10	Hungary	135	124	145	404 (9)	-	2	4	6	(=22)	410
11	Norway	44	38	35	117 (23)	73	77	64	214	(2)	331
12	Japan	90	83	93	266 (11)	3	8	8	19	(19)	285
13	Canada	46	66	83	195 (16)	19	20	25	64	(11)	259
14	Australia	78	76	99	253 (12)	-	-	1	1	(=34)	254
15	Switzerland	42	65	60	167 (=18)	27	29	29	85	(9)	252
16	FRG [4]	56	64	80	200 (15)	11	15	13	39	(14)	239
17	Romania	59	70	90	219 (13)	-	-	1	1	(=24)	220
18	Netherlands	45	52	71	168 (17)	14	19	17	50	(13)	218
19	Poland	43	62	105	210 (14)	1	1	2	4	(=24)	214
20	Austria	19	30	32	81 (29)	36	48	44	128	(4)	209
21	Czechoslovakia [5]	49	50	50	149 (21)	2	8	16	26	(15)	175
22	Bulgaria	40	69	58	167 (=18)	-	-	1	1	(=34)	168
23	Denmark	35	59	56	150 (20)	-	-	-	-		150
24	Belgium	35	48	47	130 (22)	1	1	2	4	(=24)	134
25	China	36	41	37	114 (24)	-	4	2	6	(=22)	120
26	Korea	31	27	41	99 (26)	6	2	2	10	(20)	109
27	Greece	24	38	44	106 (25)	-	-	-	-		106
28	Yugoslavia	26	30	30	86 (27)	-	3	1	4	(=24)	90
29	Cuba	36	25	23	84 (28)	-	-	-	-		84
30	New Zealand	27	10	28	65 (30)	-	1	-	1	(=34)	66
=31	South Africa	16	17	20	53 (=31)	-	-	-	-		53
=31	Turkey	26	15	12	53 (=31)	-	-	-	-		53
33	Spain	17	19	11	47 (=33)	1	-	1	2	(=29)	49
34	Argentina	13	19	15	47 (=33)	-	-	-	-		47
35	Mexico	9	13	18	40 (35)	-	-	-	-		40
36	Brazil	9	10	20	39 (36)	-	-	-	-		39
37	Kenya	13	13	13	39 (37)	-	-	-	-		39
38	Iran	4	12	17	33 (38)	-	-	-	-		33
39	Russia [6]	-	4	3	7 (=55)	12	8	4	24	(16)	31
40	Jamaica	4	13	9	26 (39)	-	-	-	-		26
=41	Estonia	7	6	10	23 (40)	-	-	-	-		23
=41	North Korea (PRK)	6	5	10	21 (41)	-	1	1	2	(=29)	23
43	Egypt	6	6	6	18 (42)	-	-	-	-		18
44	Ireland	5	5	5	15 (43)	-	-	-	-		15
45	India	8	3	3	14 (44)	-	-	-	-		14
=46	Portugal	2	4	7	13 (=45)	-	-	-	-		13
=46	Mongolia	-	5	8	13 (=45)	-	-	-	-		13
=46	Ethiopia	6	1	6	13 (=45)	-	-	-	-		13
49	Pakistan	3	3	4	10 (48)	-	-	-	-		10
=50	Liechtenstein	-	-	-	-	2	2	5	9	(21)	9
=50	Uruguay	2	1	6	9 (=49)	-	-	-	-		9
=50	Morocco	4	2	3	9 (=49)	-	-	-	-		9

[1] Including Unified Team of 1992
[2] Germany 1896-1964, 1992-1994
[3] GDR, EastGermany, 1968-1988
[4] FRG, WestGermany, 1968-1988
[5] Includes Bohemia
[6] Includes CzaristRussia

Rank	Nation	G	S	B	Total	(pos)	G	S	B	Total	(pos)	Total
=53	Venezuela	1	2	5	8	(=51)	-	-	-	-	-	8
=53	Chile	-	6	2	8	(=51)	-	-	-	-	-	8
=53	Philippines	-	1	7	8	(=51)	-	-	-	-	-	8
=53	Nigeria	-	4	4	8	(=51)	-	-	-	-	-	8
57	Trinidad & Tobago	1	2	4	7	(=55)	-	-	-	-	-	7
=58	Colombia	-	2	4	6	(=57)	-	-	-	-	-	6
=58	Latvia	-	4	2	6	(=57)	-	-	-	-	-	6
=58	Indonesia	2	3	1	6	(=57)	-	-	-	-	-	6
=61	Uganda	1	3	1	5	(=60)	-	-	-	-	-	5
=61	Tunisia	1	2	2	5	(=60)	-	-	-	-	-	5
=61	Puerto Rico	-	1	4	5	(=60)	-	-	-	-	-	5
=61	Slovenia	-	-	2	2	(=72)	-	-	3	3	(=27)	5
=65	Lebanon	-	2	2	4	(=63)	-	-	-	-	-	4
=65	Peru	1	3	-	4	(=63)	-	-	-	-	-	4
=65	Ghana	-	1	3	4	(=63	-	-	-	-	-	4
=65	Chinese Taipei	-	2	2	4	(=63)	-	-	-	-	-	4
=65	Thailand	-	1	3	4	(=63)	-	-	-	-	-	4
=65	Luxembourg	1	1	-	2	(=72)	-	2	-	2	(=29)	4
=65	Algeria	1	-	3	4	(=63)	-	-	-	-	-	4
=72	Bahamas	1	-	2	3	(=69)	-	-	-	-	-	3
=72	Croatia	-	1	2	3	(=69)	-	-	-	-	-	3
=72	Kazakstan	-	-	-	-	-	1	2	-	3	(=27)	3
=75	Tanzania	-	2	-	2	(=71)	-	-	-	-	-	2
=75	Cameroon	-	1	1	2	(=71)	-	-	-	-	-	2
=75	Haiti	-	1	1	2	(=71)	-	-	-	-	-	2
=75	Iceland	-	1	1	2	(=71)	-	-	-	-	-	2
=75	Panama	-	-	2	2	(=71)	-	-	-	-	-	2
=75	Israel	-	1	1	2	(=71)	-	-	-	-	-	2
=75	Lithuania	1	-	1	2	(=71)	-	-	-	-	-	2
=75	Surinam	1	-	1	2	(=71)	-	-	-	-	-	2
=75	Namibia	-	2	-	2	(=71)	-	-	-	-	-	2
=75	Belarus	-	-	-	-	-	-	2	-	2	(=29)	2
=75	Ukraine	-	-	-	-	-	1	-	1	2	(=29)	2
=86	Uzbekistan	-	-	-	-	-	1	-	-	1	(=34)	1
=86	Zimbabwe	1	-	-	1	(=82)	-	-	-	-	-	1
=86	CostaRica	-	1	-	1	(=82)	-	-	-	-	-	1
=86	IvoryCoast	-	1	-	1	(=82)	-	-	-	-	-	1
=86	Netherlands Antilles	-	1	-	1	(=82)	-	-	-	-	-	1
=86	Senegal	-	1	-	1	(=82)	-	-	-	-	-	1
=86	Singapore	-	1	-	1	(=82)	-	-	-	-	-	1
=86	SriLanka	-	1	-	1	(=82)	-	-	-	-	-	1
=86	Syria	-	1	-	1	(=82)	-	-	-	-	-	1
=86	Virgin Islands	-	1	-	1	(=82)	-	-	-	-	-	1
=86	Barbados	-	-	1	1	(=82)	-	-	-	-	-	1
=86	Bermuda	-	-	1	1	(=82)	-	-	-	-	-	1
=86	Djibouti	-	-	1	1	(=82)	-	-	-	-	-	1
=86	Dominican Republic	-	-	1	1	(=82)	-	-	-	-	-	1
=86	Guyana	-	-	1	1	(=82)	-	-	-	-	-	1
=86	Iraq	-	-	1	1	(=82)	-	-	-	-	-	1
=86	Niger Republic	-	-	1	1	(=82)	-	-	-	-	-	1
=86	Zambia	-	-	1	1	(=82)	-	-	-	-	-	1
=86	Malaysia	-	-	1	1	(=82)	-	-	-	-	-	1
=86	Qatar	-	-	1	1	(=82)	-	-	-	-	-	1

These totals (revised since the last edition in light of new research) include all first, second and third places, including those events no longer on the current (1996) schedule. The 1906 Games, which were officially staged by the International Olympic Committee (IOC), have also been included. However, medals won in the Art Competitions 1912-1948, have not been included. Note: Medals won in 1896, 1900, 1904, 1908 and 1912 by mixed teams from two countries have been counted twice, for both countries involved. The Unified teams of 1992 have been included in the Soviet Union figures. Medals won by IOP designated competitors in 1992 have been included in Yugoslavia figures. Figures in brackets denote a country's position in the medals tables for both the Summer and Winter Games respectively.

The ancient games

The Olympic Games originally evolved from legendary conflicts among the Greek Gods and the religious ceremonies held in their honour. Historical evidence dates the Games from about 900 BC, but there is good reason to believe that a similiar festival existed four centuries previously. Indeed the modern word 'athlete' derives from Aethlius, King of Elis. The area in which Olympia lies is in the plain of Elis, on the banks of the River Alpheios. It was a successor, Iphitus, who was instrumental in reviving the then faltering concept in the late 9th century BC. He also arranged for the truce between the continually warring states of the region which recognized the neutrality and sanctity of Olympia, and which lasted for the period of the Games. The first firm record dates from 776 BC, and the Games were numbered at four-yearly intervals from then.

At that time there was only one event, the stade race, and the winner, the first recorded Olympic champion, was Coroibis of Elis. The stade was 192.27m long, reputably 600 times the length of the god Heracles' (Hercules) foot. After thirteen Olympiads, in 724 BC, a race of two stade, the diaulus, was also contested, and in the following celebration the 24-stadia dolichus, about 4.5km in length, was instituted. In 708 BC came the pentathlon, consisting of running, jumping (with the aid of hand-held weights) throwing the discus and javelin, and wrestling. Eventually chariot racing, running in armour and boxing were included, and in 648 BC the pankration, a brutal mix of boxing and wrestling. Numerous variants of these sports appeared over the years, as did activities of a less sporting nature, such as contests for trumpeters.

Initially contestants wore simple shorts-like garments, but from about 720 BC they competed in the nude, and until 692 BC the Games only lasted for a single day. This was later increased to two days, and in 632 BC to a total of five days, of which the middle three were for actual competitions. For the next six centuries the fame of Olympia spread throughout the known world, and many famous people visited the Games. Victors, in those early days, won only a crown of wild olive leaves, but were often richly rewarded by their home states, and sometimes became very wealthy. Crowd figures were not published but archaeologists have estimated that the Stadium at Olympia could hold over 20,000 spectators.

For reasons not fully understood today women, and slaves, were strictly forbidden, under pain of death, even to attend the Games. An exception does appear to have been made for high ranking priestesses of the most important gods. However, it was possible for a woman to gain an Olympic prize. This was because in the chariot race the chaplet of olive leaves was awarded to the owner of the horses and not the drivers. One of the first women to win an Olympic title in this way was Belistike of Macedonia in 268 BC as owner of the champion 2-horse chariot. It is recorded that some women did defy the rules and disguised

Romanticised portrayal of an early Olympic race (Popperfoto)

themselves, but were thrown over a cliff to their deaths on discovery. There is a story, perhaps apocryphal, that Pherenice of Rhodes acted as a second to watch her son, Pisidores, win his event. In her excitement she gave herself away, but when it was realized that not only her son, but also her father and brothers had all been Olympic champions, she was pardoned.

Possibly the most famous champion of early times was Leonidas of Rhodes who won the three 'track' events on four consecutive occasions 164-152 BC, making a total of 12 victories which has not been surpassed since. The first recorded triple gold medallist at one Games was Phanas of Pellene in 512 BC, while the Spartan runner Chionis won the stade in three successive Games 664-656 BC. Other excellent champions included Theagenes of Thassos who won eight titles at boxing, wrestling and pankration from 468-456 BC, and Milon of Croton who won six wrestling titles 536-516 BC.

Eventually the very success of the Games led to its downfall. The importance of winning at Olympia, and the reflected glory it bestowed on the winner's birthplace, led cities to hire professionals and bribe judges. With the dawn of the Christian Era the religious and physical backgrounds of the Games were attacked. An irreversible decline set in under Roman influence, so much so that in AD 67 a drunken Emperor Nero was crowned victor of the chariot race despite the fact that there were no other entrants (who could blame them) and he did not even finish the course. In AD 393 the Roman Emperor Theodosius I issued a decree in Milan which prohibited the Games and within a few generations the ravages of foreign invaders, earthquakes and flooding had virtually obliterated the site of Olympia, and the world forgot the glory that once had been.

There was a resurgence of interest in Ancient Greece in the 17th & 18th centuries and references to the Olympic Games in the poems of Pindar and other Greek poets were noted. In Britain the Cotswold Olympic Games were inaugurated in the early 17th century, and in 1850 the Much Wenlock Olympic Society was founded by Dr William Penny Brookes. At the end of the 18th century, in Germany, the famed founder of modern gymnastics, Johann Guts Muths, had suggested the revival of the Olympic ideal. Some 50 years later a fellow-countryman, Ernst Curtius, who had done archaeological work at Olympia (started by

Pierre de Fredi, Baron de Coubertin, the founder of the modern Olympics (Allsport)

the French in 1829) reiterated the idea in a lecture he gave in Berlin in 1852. In Greece itself Major Evangelis Zappas organized a Pan-Hellenic sports festival in 1859 which attracted a great deal of public support, and which was revived at intervals over the next 30 years.

However, the true founder of the modern Olympic Games is commonly acknowledged to be Pierre de Fredi, Baron de Coubertin, of France. In 1889 a French government commission to study physical culture methods led him to meet with Dr Brookes of Much Wenlock, and at the end of his travels he formed his concept of a revived Games, which he first propounded publicly at a lecture in the Sorbonne, Paris, on 25 November 1892. The enthusiastic reception given to him gave him an impetus, as did his meeting with representatives of the top American universities in the following year. In June 1894 he convened an international conference, also in the Sorbonne, at which 12 countries were represented and another 21 sent messages of support. The outcome was a resolution on 23 June, calling for sports competitions along the lines of the Ancient Games to be held every fourth year.

The International Olympic Committtee (IOC) was inaugurated under the presidency of Demetrius Vikelas of Greece with de Coubertin as secretary-general. The Frenchman had hoped to herald the new century with the new Games in Paris in 1900, but the delegates were impatient. Budapest in Hungary was strongly mooted at first, but, at the instigation of Vikelas, Athens was finally selected and the date set as 1896. On 23 June 1994 the IOC celebrated its centenary, noting that the advances of Olympianism extended competition to all the continents, and access for all races, religions and languages.

1896

Ist Olympic Games – Athens, Greece
6 – 15 April (25 March – 3 April by the Julian Calendar)

Attended by representatives of 14 countries, comprising 211 competitors.

Although the Greek government were apparently not consulted, and were anyway beset with internal financial and political problems, the Greek public were very enthusiastic. However, it was not until Crown Prince Constantine set up a committee and began organizing and collecting funds that the project became feasible, and the prospect of Budapest getting the honour by default faded. The turning point came with the generosity of a Greek businessman, Georges Averoff (formerly Avykeris) who actually lived in Alexandria, Egypt. He offered to pay for the reconstruction of the Panathenean Stadium in Athens at a cost of 920,000 drachma (£36,500 at the 1896 exchange rate). The stadium had first been built in 330 BC by the orator Luycurgus, a disciple of Plato. It was rebuilt 500 years later by Herodes Atticus, but had gradually disintegrated and was covered up until 1870 when King George of Greece had arranged for its excavation by the German, Ziller. The new track measured 333.33m, had very sharp turns, and the competitors ran in a clockwise direction.

The opening of the Games coincided with the 75th anniversary of the declaration of Greek independence from Turkish rule. Over 40,000 spectators in the stadium, plus thousands more on the surrounding hills, saw the King, George I, formally open the proceedings. The great majority of the competitors were from Greece itself. Many athletes entered privately, including holidaymakers, and the British contingent included two employees of the Embassy in Athens. Yet another member of the British team was an Irishman, John Boland, who happened to be on holiday in Greece at the time and entered the tennis events. He won the singles and, partnering a German, also won the pairs. Another nice touch of the period was provided by the French sprinter who insisted on wearing his gloves as he was running before royalty.

Not for the last time a gymnast, Hermann Weingärtner (GER), was the most successful with three first places, two seconds and a third place. A Frenchman, Paul Masson, won three cycling events, but perhaps the most outstanding achievement was that of Carl Schuhmann of Germany who not only won three gymnastic events but also won the wrestling title. Another competitor to gain medals in two sports was gymnast Fritz Hofmann (GER) whose total of five placings included a silver medal in the 100 metres. In shooting John and Sumner Paine (USA) became the first brothers to win Olympic gold medals, in military pistol and free pistol respectively. Their father had successfully defended yachting's America's Cup some years before.

The first competition of the modern Olympic Games was heat one of the 100m, and it was won, in 12.5sec, by the American Francis Lane of Princeton University, thus carving a niche in history for himself. The first gold medallist of modern times was James Brendan Connolly (USA) who won the hop, step and jump (now known as the triple jump). In fact the American team, composed exclusively of college students, dominated events in the stadium, despite arriving only the day before the start of the competitions, having travelled by ship to France and then by train to Greece. Victors actually received a silver medal and a crown of olive leaves; runners-up were given bronze medals and a crown of laurel; no awards were made for third place.

Two new sporting events were introduced at these Games; the discus throw and the marathon. Both were based on Greek antiquity and the hosts were eager to win them. However, the former was taken by Robert Garrett (USA) who had inadvertently practised with an implement much larger and heavier than the one which was actually used at Athens. The marathon had been proposed by a Frenchman, Michel Bréal, to commemorate the legendary run of a Greek courier, possibly Pheidippides, with the news of a Greek victory over the Persians in 490 BC. He is supposed to have run from the site of the battle, and, after crying out "Rejoice! We conquer", collapsed and died. To the great delight of the hosts the race was won by a Greek shepherd, Spiridon 'Spyros' Louis, who was escorted into the stadium by Crown Prince Constantine and Prince George.

The oldest gold medallist was Georgios Orphanidis (GRE) in the free rifle contest, aged 36yr 102 days, while the youngest was swimmer Alfred Hajós (HUN) aged 18yr 70 days when he

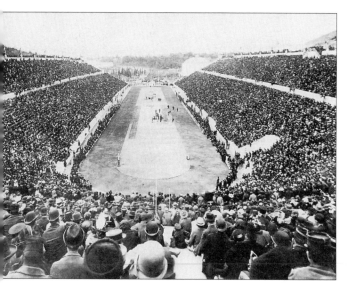

The Panathenean Stadium during the first Games of the modern era

won the 100m and 1200m freestyle events. A member of the Greek bronze medal team in gymnastics has been reported to be under 11 years of age, but some doubt exists about the veracity of this. In view of the modern saturation coverage of the Olympics by the media, it is noteworthy to record that the British press gave little space to reports from Athens, despite an earlier complaint in *The Times* about the lack of knowledge of the event in the country and Britain's inadequate representation. Nevertheless the Games had been a tremendous success and certainly Greece looked forward to the next celebration, which they also expected to host.

1896 MEDALS TABLE

	G	S	B
United States	11	7	1
Greece	10	19	18
Germany	7	5	2
France	5	4	2
Great Britain	3	3	1
Hungary	2	1	3
Austria	2	-	3
Australia	2	-	-
Denmark	1	2	4
Switzerland	1	2	-

G=Gold; S=Silver; B=Bronze

1900

IInd Olympic Games – Paris, France
20 May – 28 October

Attended by representatives of 26 countries, comprising 1225 competitors, of which 19 were women.

Despite strong Greek pressure for the exclusive rights to organize future Games, Baron de Coubertin won agreement to hold the 1900 Games in Paris, but made a serious mistake in making it part of the Fifth Universal Exposition also being held there. In the event the Games became merely a sideshow to the fair. Numerous internal rivalries within French sport left many of the sports without experienced officials or adequate venues. The track and field events were held on uneven turf at Croix-Catelan, in the Bois de Boulogne, where it is reported that the jumpers had to dig their own pits.

Many of the competitors, especially the Americans, had never run on a grass track before. Generally there were few spectators, and even these were nearly reduced in number when the 1896 discus champion despatched the implement into the crowd on all three throws. Cricket, croquet and golf made their appearance and amid the general confusion many competitors, even medal winners, were not aware until much later that they had been competing at the Olympic Games.

France, the host country, had a record-sized team numbering 884, the largest ever entered for the Games. The Americans were still represented by colleges and clubs, and the decision to have competition on Sunday upset many of those whose colleges were church controlled. Thus the long jump world record holder Myer Prinstein, a Jew but under the aegis of the University of Syracuse, a strong Methodist institution, gained a silver medal with his Saturday qualifying round jump (such performances then counted for medals), but had to withdraw from the Sunday final. The eventual winner Alvin Kraenzlein (USA) set a record of four individual gold medals, a feat never surpassed in track and field at one Games. Also much in evidence was America's Ray Ewry, the standing jump expert, at the start of his fabulous Olympic career, with three gold medals here. Behind him in the standing jumps was countryman Irving Baxter. He had already won the regular high jump and the pole vault, and reputedly became the first athlete of American Indian ancestry to win at the Olympic Games. In a similar vein, Norman Pritchard of India, later to become a successful actor in Hollywood silent films, won the first medals by an Asian sportsman with two silvers in the 200m flat and hurdles races.

Women were allowed to compete for the first time, but not in the major sports, and the first female Olympic

First ever female Olympic champion Charlotte Cooper (GBR), winner of the 1900 tennis title. Later Mrs Sterry, she died aged 96, one of the longest-lived Olympians ever (Allsport)

competitors (only recently researched) were Madame Brohy and Mademoiselle Ohnier (FRA) in the croquet competition on 28 June. The inaugural female Olympic champion was Britain's Charlotte Cooper, a Wimbledon champion, who won the tennis singles title on 9 July. Another unique record was set in the coxed pairs rowing final, in which a small French boy was drafted in at the last moment to cox the winning Dutch crew. His name was never recorded and he disappeared without trace afterwards, but he was no more than 10 years old, and possibly as young as 7, in either case the youngest ever Olympic gold medallist. The oldest gold medallist in 1900 was French-born Comte Hermann de Pourtales (SUI) in the 1-2 ton class yachting aged 53yr 55 days. The youngest female champion was Margaret Abbott (USA) in golf aged 20yr 110 days, while the oldest was Cooper aged 29yr 292 days.

Press coverage was barely apparent with many of the events not mentioned at all, and for years afterwards there was much confusion as to the names and nationalities of even the medallists. Thus it was that the first Olympic medals won by Canada, a gold and bronze gained by George Orton, were not 'discovered' for some years, as Orton had been entered by his American university and was billed as an American. Even more recently it has been found that the winner of the marathon, Michel Théato (FRA), was actually a Luxembourgeois – in this case the medal tables have not been altered.

1900 MEDALS TABLE

	G	S	B
France	27	39	33
United States	19	15	15
Great Britain	17	7	12
Switzerland	6	3	1
Belgium	5	5	4
Germany	3	2	2
Australia	2	-	4
Denmark	2	3	2
Italy	2	2	-
Netherlands	1	1	4
Hungary	1	2	2
Cuba	1	1	-
Canada	1	-	1
Sweden	1	-	1
Austria	-	3	3
Norway	-	2	3
Czechoslovakia	-	1	2
India	-	2	-

1904

IIIrd Olympic Games – St Louis, USA
1 July – 23 November

Attended by representatives of 13 countries, comprising 687 competitors, of which 6 were women.

For a time the third celebration seemed likely to go to Britain, and then to Philadelphia, but de Coubertin had favoured New York. The IOC finally designated Chicago for these Games, but at the request of President Theodore Roosevelt, also president of the US Olympic Committee, the venue was changed to St Louis to coincide with the World's Fair, held to celebrate the centenary of the Louisiana Purchase. Thus again they became merely a sideshow. The problems of distance and travel to the centre of the North American continent meant that there were few overseas entrants. Indeed, even de Coubertin did not attend. Thus 85 per cent of the competitors were from the host country, and, not surprisingly, they won 84 per cent of the medals. In fact the Games were a virtual college and club tournament with the New York AC beating the Chicago Athletic Association for the track and field team title (a points table was actually published). In swimming it was also noted that New York beat Germany and Hungary overall.

In such circumstances the Games degenerated into something of a farce, so that the cycling events, which had no foreign entrants at all and included a number of professional riders, were initially refused official Olympic status. However, recent scholarship suggests that they should be included in medal tables and results. Thus the unique achievement of Marcus Hurley in winning four cycling events should now be given due credit. Gymnast Anton Heida (USA) won 5 golds and 1 silver to be the most successful at these Games.

Under the rather loose controls imposed on most sports some strange things happened. In the 400m track race no heats were held and all 13 entrants ran in the final. Rowing events were held over a 1.5 mile course which entailed making a turn. The swimming events were held over Imperial distances, while the athletics track (in the grounds of Washington University, St Louis) measured one-third of a mile in circumference and had a 220 yard straightaway (i.e. no turns), which was quite an innovation for the visiting Europeans. In the track and field programme only two events went to non-Americans. The French-Canadian policeman Etienne Desmarteau won the 56lb (25.4kg) weight throw. He unfortunately died the following year of typhoid and a park was named after him in his home city of Montreal. The 10-event All-round competition, a forerunner of the decathlon, was won by one of the only two British entries, Thomas Kiely, who incidentally, like the silver medallist in the 2500m steeplechase, John Daly, was an Irishman. The unfortunate Myer Prinstein redressed his grievance of four years previously by taking the long jump title as well as winning the hop, step and jump. He also placed fifth in both the 60m and 400m finals. The ever liberal Prinstein here was representing the Greater New York Irish AA.

The 200m final, uniquely held on a straightaway, was won by Archie Hahn, with all three of his opponents given a one-yard (0.91m) handicap under the rules then governing false starts. Joseph Stadler won a silver medal in the standing high jump, while George Poage won bronzes in the 200m and 400m hurdle races. The significance of their performances was that they became the first black men to win medals in the Olympics. Despite the lack of foreign opposition the standard in many sports was very high, and the triple victories of Archie Hahn, Harry Hillman, James Lightbody, Ray Ewry and swimmer Charles Daniels were outstanding. Daniels, in winning the 220y, 440y and mile freestyle events, was the prototype of the American swimmers who were to dominate Olympic freestyle swimming for many years.

There was a scandal in the marathon when the first man out of the stadium, Fred Lorz (USA), was also the first man back, looking remarkably fresh. It later transpired that he had received a lift in a car after suffering cramp, and when the car itself broke down near the stadium he resumed running – as a joke, he claimed. He was banned for life (but was competing again after only a year) and the title awarded to British-born American Thomas Hicks who had finished in a daze due to being administered strychnine by his handlers as a stimulant – a practice then common and allowable. In ninth place was Lentauw (SAF), a Zulu in St Louis as part of a World's Fair exhibit, the first black African distance runner to compete in the Olympics.

The youngest gold medallist was golfer Robert Hunter (USA) aged 17yr 301 days, while the oldest was the Reverend Galen Spencer (USA), an archer, aged 64yr 2 days. Another American archer, Samuel Duvall, won a silver medal aged 68yr 194 days – the oldest American medallist ever. The oldest female champion was Lida Howell (USA) in archery aged 45yr 25 days. The youngest medallist was another archer, Henry Richardson (USA), aged 15yr 124 days. Yet another American, Frank Kungler, won a silver in wrestling, a bronze in tug-of-war, and two bronzes in weightlifting, to become the only Olympian to win medals at three different sports at a single Games.

A final insult to the Games were the Anthropology Days during which competitions were held, parodying the regular Olympic events, for aboriginal peoples, such as American Indians, African pygmies, Patagonians, Ainus from Japan, and the like. Finally in November, with the Association Football competition won by a Canadian college over two American teams, the IIIrd Olympic Games came to an end, and many in Europe wondered if the fledgling movement would recover.

1904 MEDALS TABLE

	G	S	B
United States	80	84	78
Germany	4	4	5
Canada	4	1	1
Cuba	4	-	-
Austria	2	1	1
Hungary	2	1	1
Great Britain	1	1	-
Greece	1	-	1
Switzerland	1	-	1
France	-	1	-

1906

The Interim or Intercalated Games – Athens, Greece
22 April – 2 May

Attended by representatives of 20 countries, comprising 826 competitors, of which 6 were women.

The remarkable Ray Ewry in 1906. Winner of a record 10 gold medals from 1900-08, he had suffered from polio as a child. Exercises to overcome this disability gave him tremendous strength in his legs (Popperfoto)

After two debacles something was needed to revive the flagging Olympic movement and de Coubertin, with some misgivings, agreed a series of four-yearly meetings, interspersed with the main Games, to be held in Athens. Although these had the blessing of the IOC, it was decided that the Interim games would not be numbered in sequence.

In the event only this meeting of the projected series was ever held. Again the Greeks showed their enthusiasm and large crowds, missing for the past 10 years, were in evidence. The marble stadium in Athens was full to capacity, and enthusiasm often helped to overcome organizational mishaps.

The 20 countries included the first 'official' American team, selected and sent by the US Olympic Committee, so ending the practice of colleges, clubs and private individuals entering. Also present was the first ever team from Finland, with the doyen of the famous Järvinen family, Werner, gaining his country's first ever Olympic gold medal. The programme of track and field events was altered by a reduction in the number of spring and hurdles races, and the addition of a pentathlon and the javelin throw.

There were some excellent performances, especially by some of the 1904 champions such as the perennial Ray Ewry and the New York policeman Martin Sheridan. Another American, with the apt name of Paul Pilgrim, had only been added to the team at the last moment after he had privately raised the money for the fare. He had won a gold medal in 1904 as a member of the New York AC relay team, but in Athens surprisingly won the 400m and 800m titles, a feat not to be equalled until 1976.

The new pentathlon event, consisting of a 192m run, standing long jump, discus and javelin throws, and Greco-Roman wrestling, was won by Hjalmar Mellander of Sweden. In third place was his countryman Erick Lemming who also gained bronze medals in the shot and tug-of-war as well as winning the first of three Olympic javelin titles. There was a real surprise in the 1500m walk, which was also the scene of a number of purely chauvinistic decisions by the various national judges. The American distance runner George Bonhag had disappointed in the 1500m and 5 mile runs, and had entered the walk, an entirely new event to him, in a last effort to win a medal. Owing mainly to the excessive number of disqualifications, with all the favourites ruled out, he won the gold. With all three previous Olympic marathons having been won by the host country, the Greeks were hopeful of continuing tradition, but despite half the entrants coming from Greece it was won by William Sherring of Canada by a massive margin of nearly 7 minutes. The most successful competitor at these Games was shooter Louis Richardet (SUI) who won three gold and three silver medals.

The oldest gold medallist was Maurice Lecoq (FRA) aged 52yr 31 days when he won the rapid fire pistol event. The youngest was the coxswain of the Italian fours crew, Giorgio Cesana, aged 14yr 12 days. The youngest female champion was Marie Décugis (FRA) in tennis aged 21yr 261 days. The oldest medallist was fencer Charles Newton-Robinson (GBR) at 52yr 195 days.

Despite the soft cinder track in the stadium, poor facilities for the swimmers in the sea at Phaleron, complaints about food and judging decisions, these Interim Games put the whole Olympic concept back on a path towards de Coubertin's ideal.

1906 MEDALS TABLE

	G	S	B
France	15	9	16
United States	12	6	6
Greece	8	13	13
Great Britain	8	11	5
Italy	7	6	3
Switzerland	5	6	4
Germany	4	6	5
Norway	4	2	-
Austria	3	3	2
Denmark	3	2	1
Sweden	2	5	7
Hungary	2	5	3
Belgium	2	2	3
Finland	2	1	1
Canada	1	1	-
Netherlands	-	1	2
Australia	-	-	3
Czechoslovakia	-	-	2
South Africa	-	-	1

1908

IVth Olympic Games – London, UK
27 April – 31 October

Attended by representatives of 22 countries, comprising 2035 competitors, of which 36 were women.

Originally awarded to Rome, the IVth Games were re-allocated to London when the Italian authorities informed the IOC during the Interim Games that they would have to withdraw due to financial problems. London formally accepted on 19 November 1906. Nevertheless, they were the most successful held so far and set the pattern for future Games. Drawing on the expertise of many British sporting governing bodies – such as the Amateur Swimming Association, founded in 1869, and the Amateur Athletic Association, founded in 1880 – the organizing committee under Lord Desborough went to work.

A 68,000 capacity stadium was built in West London, for a reported cost of £40,000. (That stated 'capacity' was apparently well exceeded on a number of occasions.) It contained an athletics track of three laps to the mile, inside a 660yd banked concrete cycle track. On the grass infield stood a giant 330ft x 50ft (100m x 15.24m) pool for the swimming events. Rowing was on the Thames at Henley, tennis was held at the All-England Club, Wimbledon, yachting at Ryde, Isle of Wight, and the new sport of motorboating was on Southampton Water. The main competitions took place in July, although the overall programme lasted from April to October. There were 21 sports in all, including four ice skating events. There was also a demonstration sport, bicycle polo, in which Ireland beat Germany 3-1.

Entries were only by nations, as opposed to individuals. This tended to emphasize the nationalism which undoubtedly caused some of the disputes which marred this first truly international sporting occasion. These problems started during the formal opening, by King Edward VII, at the White City stadium on 13 July. Sweden and the United States were upset that their flags had been inadvertently missed from those flying around the stadium. Then Ralph Rose, the American flag bearer and eventual winner of the shot, refused to dip the Stars and Stripes to King Edward in the march past. The Finnish team would not march behind the flag of Czarist Russia and came in without any banner. Later things got worse as complaints came from all sides, but especially from US officials. They complained about 'fixed' heats, illegal coaching, rule breaking and British chauvinism. The weather was also rather foul, even by British standards, and badly affected cycling and tennis in particular.

All the rancour came to a head in the 400m event final, in which three of the four finalists were Americans. They were accused of impeding the sole British runner, Lieut. Wyndham Halswelle, and a re-run was ordered for the next day, with the winner of the disputed race, Carpenter, being disqualified. The other Americans refused to appear and Halswelle gained the gold medal in the only walk-over in Games history. One of the runners involved was John Taylor who, as a member of the winning medley relay team, became the first black man to win an Olympic gold medal. A more imaginative resolution to a problem apparently came in the 110m hurdles. The favourite, Forrest Smithson, an American student of theology, protested against the official decision to run the final on a Sunday, and then proceeded to break the world record with 15.0sec, supposedly carrying a bible in his left hand. While uplifting, the only 'evidence' of this story is a photograph that was obviously staged after the event.

Finally the bitterness reached such a level that it was thought necessary to produce a booklet entitled 'Replies to Criticism of the Olympic Games', which, owing to its rather pompous tone, did little to alleviate the situation. One result of all this was the decision that future control of competitions should be in the hands of the various international governing bodies of the sports and not left solely to the host country.

The previous year the IOC had decided that medals should be awarded for the first three places in all events. There were many excellent performances throughout the Games, despite all the problems. The ubiquitous Ray Ewry, now 33 years old, won his record-breaking ninth and tenth gold medals in the standing jumps, while

John Flanagan (one of the so-called Irish-American 'Whales') won his third hammer title. Middle distance runner Mel Sheppard (USA) was a triple gold medallist, as was British swimmer Henry Taylor. Charles Daniels (USA) won the 100m freestyle to add to his three titles from the last two Games, and set a record of four individual event swimming gold medals that has not yet been beaten. The Hungarian swimmer Zoltán von Halmay increased his total medal haul to nine since 1900, a total unsurpassed in the sport until 1972.

The introduction of skating events gave the opportunity to Russia to win its first Olympic title, courtesy of Nikolai Panin (actually Kolomenkin) who four years later was a member of the fourth-placed revolver shooting team. Another Olympic first came in the London shooting programme when Oscar and Alfred Swahn of Sweden became the first father and son to win gold medals, with Oscar being the oldest gold medallist at these Games aged 60yr 265 days in the Running Deer event. The youngest champion was Daniel Carroll (AUS) in rugby aged 16yr 245 days, while the youngest female gold medallist was Gladys Eastlake-Smith (GBR) in tennis aged 24yr 273 days. The oldest female champion was archer Queenie Newall (GBR) aged 53yr 275 days.

Undoubtedly the most famous event in the IVth Games was the marathon. Originally the distance was to be about 25 miles, but the start was moved to Windsor Castle, an exact 26 miles. Then at the request of Princess Mary it was

Dorando Pietri being presented with a gold cup by Queen Alexandra as a consolation for his disqualification in the 1908 marathon. If the race distance had not been extended he might have won (Allsport)

moved again to start beneath the windows of the royal nursery in the Castle grounds, making a final distance of 26miles 385yds (42,195m). This arbitrarily arrived-at distance was later (1924) accepted worldwide as the standard marathon length. The race itself was run in intensely hot and humid conditions, quite the opposite of most of the preceding weather, and was watched by an estimated 250,000 people. The little Italian Dorando Pietri reached the stadium first in a state of near collapse, and fell five times on the last part-lap of the track. Over-zealous officials, reputedly including the famous author Sir Arthur Conan Doyle, helped him over the finish line. On behalf of the second finisher, Johnny Hayes, the Americans lodged a protest which was upheld and the Italian was disqualified. The wave of public sympathy found expression in the gift of Queen Alexandra to Pietri of a special gold cup.

Great Britain won the greatest number of medals overall, but the United States, as always, was well in front in the centrepiece of the Games, the track and field events. Two sportsmen, Ivan Osiier (DEN), a fencer, and Magnus Konow (NOR), a yachtsman, though unplaced in their events, began Olympic careers which continued until the next Games in London in 1948, setting a record-breaking span for Olympic competition of 40 years. Colonel Joshua Millner, winner of the 1000y Free Rifle, was, at a minimum age of 58yr 237 days, Britain's oldest ever Olympic gold medallist. The youngest British winner in 1908 was William Foster (GBR) in the 4 x 200m swimming relay, six days past his 18th birthday.

1908 MEDALS TABLE

	G	S	B
Great Britain	56	50	39
United States	23	12	12
Sweden	8	6	11
France	5	5	9
Germany	3	5	5
Hungary	3	4	2
Canada	3	3	10
Norway	2	3	3
Italy	2	2	-
Belgium	1	5	2
Australia*	1	2	1
Russia	1	2	-
Finland	1	1	3
South Africa	1	1	-
Greece	-	3	1
Denmark	-	2	3
Czechoslovakia	-	-	2
Netherlands	-	-	2
Austria	-	-	1
New Zealand*	-	-	1

Australia and New Zealand combined as Australasia

1912

Vth Olympic Games – Stockholm, Sweden
5 May – 22 July

Attended by representatives of 28 countries, comprising 2547 competitors, of which 57 were women.

Stockholm finally attained the honour that Sweden had wanted from the very beginning, and Torben Grut designed and built a 31,000 capacity stadium, with a 383m track laid out under the direction of Charles Perry, the Englishman responsible for the 1896 and 1908 tracks. Baron de Coubertin had insisted that the number of sports be cut, and now with only 14 there were high standards of performance and sportsmanship, with few arguments or protests. Boxing was not held, the last time that it was left out of the Olympic programme. The Games were opened officially by King Gustav V. One of the rare complaints at these Games was from the Finns, again about competing under the Russian flag. Indeed the triple gold medallist Hannes Kolehmainen stated that he almost wished he had not won rather than see the hated flag raised for his victories.

Various innovations included the first use of electrical timing equipment for the running events. Baron de Coubertin had asked for a new event to be introduced, the modern pentathlon, which consisted of five disciplines in different sports. It was dominated by the Swedes but in fifth place was one Lieut. George S. Patton (USA), later to become a controversial Second World War general. As previously, the American team lived on the liner that had brought them across the Atlantic, ironically named *Finland* – for this was the Games in which the first of the 'Flying Finns', Kolehmainen, made his appearance, winning the 5000m, 10,000m and 12,000m cross country. Thus began a domination which lasted into the 1940s. Kolehmainen's race with Jean Bouin of France in the 5000m was one of the most enthralling ever seen to that time with the Finn winning by a stride in 14:36.6, improving the world record by a margin of 24.6sec.

Other track stars were Ted Meredith (USA), gold medallist in the 800m in a new world mark, and Ralph Craig (USA) who took both sprints. Under current rules he would not have won as he was responsible for three of the seven false starts to the race. He reappeared at the Games, as a yachtsman, 36 years later, in London, when he was given the honour of carrying the US team flag.

In the swimming pool, the first of the great Hawaiian competitors, Duke Paoa Kahanamoku, won the 100m freestyle. The son of Hawaiian royalty, he received his first name as a mark of respect for the Duke of Edinburgh, Queen Victoria's second son, who was visiting the islands at the time of his birth. He competed in three more Games before becoming a film star. There was only one cycling event, but it was unique in that it was the longest road race ever held in the Games. It was won by Rudolph Lewis

Timekeepers and the electric 'timing apparatus' at Stockholm in 1912

(RSA), who took the 320km event in just short of 10.75 hours. A great impetus was given to the game of soccer at these Olympics, with 25,000 spectators present to see Great Britain beat Denmark 4-2 in the final. Gymnastics, which like wrestling was held outdoors, also gained new status.

In wrestling, problems were caused by the extreme length of some of the bouts. In the light-heavyweight final the judges called a halt after the bout had gone on for 9 hours and gave both wrestlers a silver medal, with no gold awarded. Even this was surpassed in the middleweight category where the tussle for the silver medal between Asikáinen (FIN) and Klein, an Estonian representing Russia, went on for 11hr 40min, a record for the sport. Klein finally triumphed. The first known twins to win Olympic gold medals were the Carlberg brothers, Vilhelm (3) and Eric (2), in shooting, while an even rarer sibling combination came in the 6m class yachting when the French winner *Mac Miche* was crewed by the three Thubé brothers.

However, the star of the Games was undoubtedly Jim Thorpe. Of Irish, French, but mainly American Indian ancestry, Thorpe won both of the newly constituted athletic pentathlon and decathlon events with consummate ease. Additionally he was fourth in the individual high jump and seventh in the long jump. Presenting him with his medals, King Gustav V called him 'the greatest athlete in the world'. Thorpe reportedly replied, 'Thanks, King.' Six months later, a sportswriter for the *Worcester Telegram* in Massachusetts, Roy Johnson, reported that Thorpe had played minor baseball for money. Owing to the violent amateur/professional dichotomy of the time, perhaps reinforced by American anti-Indian prejudice, Thorpe's medals were taken back and his performances removed from Olympic annals. It seems almost certain that he was ignorant of the amateur laws of the time, and the amount involved was very small. Twenty years after his death in

1953 the American Athletic Union reinstated him as an amateur, but the IOC stubbornly refused all entreaties on his behalf. It had been suggested that his cause was not helped by the fact that the President of the IOC from 1952-72 was Avery Brundage, a team-mate of Thorpe's in 1912 who had placed fifth (or sixth depending on your view) in the pentathlon. To their credit the runners-up to Thorpe, Hugo Wieslander (SWE) and Ferdinand Bie (NOR), initially refused to accept the gold medals when they were sent them, although their names were inscribed in Olympic annals as winners of the events. Finally, in October 1982 Thorpe, the man who had been voted in 1950 as the greatest athlete of the first half-century, was pardoned by the IOC and the medals presented to his family.

The oldest gold medallist at these Games was the ubiquitous Oscar Swahn (SWE) now aged 64 yr 258 days, while team-mate diver Greta Johansson was the youngest aged 17yr 186 days. Only 40 days older was Isabella Moore (GBR) in the winning freestyle swimming relay team, who became Britain's youngest ever female gold medallist. The youngest male champion was fencer Nedo Nadi (ITA) aged 18yr 30 days. British tennis player Edith Hannam was the oldest female gold medallist aged 33yr 171 days. The youngest medallist was swimmer Greta Rosenberg (GER) at 15yr 280 days.

At the Stockholm Games the Olympic movement finally 'came of age' and the marvellous efforts of the organizing committee under Viktor Balck, later deservedly President of the IOC, must take much of the credit. The only unfortunate incident at the Games was the collapse and death of Francisco Lazzaro (POR) during the marathon – ironically it was the first Games that his country had attended. Another new country was Japan, and the Games were beginning to achieve the worldwide support originally envisaged for them.

1912 MEDALS TABLE

	G	S	B
United States [1]	25	19	18
Sweden	24	24	16
Great Britain	10	15	16
Finland	9	8	9
France	7	4	3
Germany	5	13	7
South Africa	4	2	-
Norway	4	1	5
Hungary	3	2	3
Canada	3	2	2
Italy	3	1	2
Australia [2]	2	2	2
Belgium	2	1	3
Denmark	1	6	5
Greece	1	-	1
New Zealand [2]	1	-	1
Switzerland	1	-	-
Russia	-	2	3
Austria	-	2	2
Netherlands	-	-	3

[1] *Adjusted by reinstatement of Jim Thorpe in 1982*
[2] *Australia and New Zealand combined as Australasia*

1920

VIIth Olympic Games – Antwerp, Belgium
20 April – 12 September

Attended by representatives of 29 countries, comprising 2668 competitors, of which 77 were women.

When the venue of the VIth Games, due in 1916, came to be discussed in Stockholm, three cities were put forward as candidates – Budapest, Alexandria and Berlin. It is said that the latter was chosen in an attempt to avert the war that was then threatening Europe. With the outbreak of hostilities in 1914 hopes of holding the Games virtually disappeared, although the Germans still made preparations for them, believing that the war would not last very long. In 1920, although Antwerp was sorely affected by the human tragedy and economic ruin of the conflict, the organizing committee under Count Henri de Baillet-Latour, later IOC President, overcame all difficulties to put the Games on. The recent enemies, Germany, Austria, Hungary and Turkey were not invited, but still a record number of countries and competitors attended. These included New Zealand as a separate entity (previously it had been part of an Australasian team), Argentina and Brazil. The Games were opened by King Albert and the concept of the Olympic oath was introduced. This was taken by Victor Boin who had competed in two previous Games, winning medals at water polo; in Antwerp he gained another at fencing.

Another newcomer at these Games was the newly devised Olympic flag. It had been designed by Baron de Coubertin in 1913, based on a design depicted on an ancient Greek artefact, and consisted of five interlaced rings coloured blue, yellow, black, green and red, from left to right. The rings were meant to symbolize the friendship of mankind, with the colours, including the white background of the flag itself, representing all nations, as every national flag contains at least one of these colours. Unfortunately the 400m running track at the new 30,000-seat stadium was very poor (Charles Perry, the famous groundsman, had not been able to do much with it) and badly affected by the persistent rain. Due to the weather and the economic aftermath of the recent conflict, crowds generally were small. The competitors were housed in school buildings, which caused something of a revolt among the US team – though they were much more incensed by the intolerable conditions experienced aboard the old freighter which had brought them to Belgium.

For the first time Finland competed under its own flag, having gained independence in 1917, and the Finns celebrated the occasion by halting the American track and field juggernaut, winning as many athletic gold medals as the United States. The star of 1912, Hannes Kolehmainen, made a surprise return to win the marathon, but his mantle had been taken over by another outstanding Finnish runner, Paavo Nurmi. Although he lost his very first Olympic final, over 5000m to the gassed French war veteran Joseph Guillemot, he was at the start of a brilliant career in which he won a record 12 Olympic medals, 9 of them gold, and set 29 world records of one type or another. Also outstanding was 31-year-old Albert Hill of Great Britain, who, having fought throughout the war, here gained the 800m/1500m double, a feat not repeated for 44 years. Hill also gained a silver medal in the 3000m team race. Second in the 1500m was Philip Baker (GBR) who later in life, as Philip Noel-Baker MP, was the recipient of the 1959 Nobel Peace Prize – a unique achievement for an Olympian. Charley Paddock retained the 100m sprint title for the United States, delighting the spectators with his spectacular jump finish. A Second World War Marine Corps hero, he posthumously had a ship named after him. The most successful competitors were Willis Lee (USA) who won five golds, one silver and one bronze, and his team-mate Lloyd Spooner, who won four golds, one silver and two bronzes, both as shooting competitors. The shooting events also produced the first gold medal won by a South American country, when Guilherme Paraense (BRA) took the rapid-fire pistol title. Another shooter, the phenomenal Oscar Swahn (SWE), became the oldest ever Olympic medallist with a silver at the age of 72yr 280 days. Another outstanding competitor was fencer Nedo Nadi (ITA) who won two individual and three team golds. His younger brother, Aldo, added another three to the family total.

Returning to Olympic competition for the first time since 1906, when he had won two golds and a silver, archer Hubert van Innis (BEL) won four golds and two silvers, and was the oldest champion at these Games aged 54yr 187 days. The youngest gold medallist was tiny (1.43m) diver Aileen Riggin (USA) at 14yr 119 days. Indeed she was the youngest Olympic champion ever to that date, but almost lost the honour to Sweden's Nils Skoglund who finished a very close second in high-diving when three months younger. The youngest male gold medallist was Holland's Franciscus Hin in the yachting aged 14yr 163 days. Riggin won a diving silver four years later and, more unusually, a bronze in the 100m backstroke. The oldest female champion was Winifred McNair (GBR) in tennis at 43yr 15 days.

Swimming was dominated by two Americans who captured three gold medals each. Ethelda Bleibtrey, who had suffered from polio as a child, won all events open to her, in world record times. The previous year she had been arrested in America and charged, under local decency laws, with swimming 'nude' at a public beach, when all she had done was to remove her stockings. Norman Ross won the 400m, 1500m and was part of the winning relay team, and also figured in an unusual incident when he was disqualified in the 100m final for impeding an Australian swimmer. The race had been won by Duke Kahanamoku in world record time. The re-swim was also won by the Hawaiian but in a slower time. Another incident, of a more serious nature, occurred in the soccer final when Czechoslovakia were disqualified for leaving the field after 40 minutes play in protest at decisions by the British referee. Belgium were leading 2-0 at that point.

Daniel Carroll completed a unique double in the rugby final when he won a second gold medal as part of the US team. He had played in the victorious Australian team of 1908, but had emigrated in the meantime. The tennis events were the stage for one of the greatest players in the game, Suzanne Lenglen (FRA), eventually six times winner of the Wimbledon title. The winner of the single sculls and, teamed with his cousin, the double sculls was John Kelly.

The Philadelphia bricklayer John B Kelly won two gold medals at Antwerp in 1920 and another at Paris in 1924. His son John Jr won a bronze in 1956 (Popperfoto)

Earlier in the year the American had been refused entry to the Henley Regatta in England on the grounds that as a bricklayer he had an unfair advantage over 'gentlemen'. Ironically, after he had become a millionaire, his son John Jr won at Henley in 1947, and his daughter Grace, the film actress, became Princess of Monaco. Coincidentally, these were the first Games at which Monaco participated.

Two winter sports were also held, ice hockey and figure skating, attracting 73 men and 12 women from 10 countries. The latter witnessed the first gold medals won by a husband and wife, in the pairs champions Walter and German-born Ludowika Jakobsson of Finland. On this subject it may be that the first Olympic marriage was that of American diver Alice Lord and high jump champion Dick Landon soon after they returned home. While on the subject of matrimonial bliss, it was revealed after the competitions that the ladies skating champion, Magda Mauroy-Julin (SWE), was three months pregnant.

1920 MEDALS TABLE

	G	S	B
United States	41	27	27
Sweden	19	20	25
Finland	15	10	9
Great Britain	14	15	13
Belgium	13	11	11
Norway	13	9	9
Italy	13	5	5
France	9	19	13
Netherlands	4	2	5
Denmark	3	9	1
South Africa	3	4	3
Canada	3	3	3
Switzerland	2	2	7
Estonia	1	2	-
Brazil	1	1	1
Australia	-	2	1
Japan	-	2	-
Spain	-	2	-
Greece	-	1	-
Luxembourg	-	1	-
Czechoslovakia	-	-	2
New Zealand	-	-	1

1924

Ist Winter Games – Chamonix/Mont Blanc
25 January – 4 February

Attended by representatives of 16 countries, comprising 258 competitors, of which 13 were women.

After skating and ice hockey events were held in 1908 and 1920 as part of the Summer Games, it was finally decided to hold a separate Winter festival. Although initially opposed by the Scandinavian countries, who felt that Winter Olympics would detract from their own Nordic Games, an 'International Winter Sports Week' was held at Chamonix, France. In 1926 it was accorded the title of Winter Games retrospectively. The French Under Secretary for Physical Education, Gaston Vidal, formally opened the proceedings, and the oath was taken by all the flag bearers, that of France being by a skier, Camille Mandrillon. Seventeen countries marched in the opening ceremony, but Estonia did not have any competitors in the actual competitions.

The first ever official Olympic Winter gold medallist was Charles Jewtraw (USA) who won the 500m speed skating on 26 January, which also made it the earliest gold

At Chamonix in 1924 Clas Thunberg won five medals, a Winter Games record not equalled until 1980. He won another two golds at St Moritz in 1928 (Allsport)

medal ever won in an Olympic year. It was the only speed skating medal won by a competitor from other than Finland or Norway. Clas Thunberg (FIN) won three golds, one silver and a bronze (tied) to dominate the sport. In skiing, only the Nordic variety was held as Alpine skiing was still in its infancy. Norway's Thorleif Haug won three gold medals. He was also originally awarded the bronze in the special jumping event, but 50 years later a Norwegian sports historian, Jacob Vaage, discovered that the points had been added incorrectly and that the fourth-placed jumper, Anders Haugen, a Norwegian-born American, had beaten Haug. In place of her deceased father, Haug's daughter presented the bronze medal to the 86-year-old Haugen in 1974.

Canada retained its title from 1920 in ice hockey, scoring 110 goals to 3 in five matches. At figure skating Gillis Grafström (SWE) gained the second of his three gold medals. He was later to gain even more fame as coach of Sonja Henie (NOR) who, as an 11-year-old competitor in Chamonix, placed eighth and last in the women's skating. Aside from her Olympic successes she was to earn an estimated $47.5 million from her film and ice show activities, making her the richest ever female Olympian. The inaugural 4-man bobsleigh contest was won by the Swiss, the first of a record four titles they have won in this discipline. Curling and a military patrol were held as demonstration events.

The oldest champion was speed skater Julius Skutnabb (FIN) aged 34yr 229 days, and the youngest was Heinrich Schläppi, in Switzerland's 4-man bob, aged 18yr 279 days. The oldest medallist was pairs skater Walter Jakobsson (FIN) aged 41yr 357 days, although it is possible that Belgian bobsledder René Mortiaux was over 42. It is of note that Jakobsson and his partner/wife Ludowika, herself well over 39, are the oldest couple ever to win Olympic silver medals. Two days before the closing ceremony a meeting established the International Ski Federation (FIS).

1924 (Winter) MEDALS TABLE

	G	S	B
Norway	4	7	6
Finland	4	3	3
Austria	2	1	-
United States	1	2	1
Switzerland	1	-	1
Canada	1	-	-
Sweden	1	-	-
Great Britain	-	1	2
Belgium	-	-	1
France	-	-	1

1924

VIIIth Olympic Games – Paris, France
4 May – 27 July

Attended by representatives of 44 countries, comprising 3092 competitors, of which 136 were women.

De Coubertin requested that the Games, originally scheduled for Amsterdam, be transferred to Paris in the hope that the bad image acquired in 1900 could be eradicated. The IOC had taken steps to impose its authority on the staging of the Olympics so that never again could a host country add events as it wished. The Colombes stadium, with a 500m track built in 1909, was enlarged to hold 60,000 spectators. An Olympic village had been proposed but the idea was not carried through, although

Harold Abrahams (419, second from left) wins the 1924 100 metres from Scholz (274) and Porritt (dark vest)

competitors were housed in huts scattered around the main site. Four of the five 'enemy' countries in the war were included in the record number of nations accepting invitations, but Germany was still not present due to the particularly frosty relations between it and France. Among the newcomers were Ireland, competing separately from Britain for the first time, Romania and Poland. Polish sportsmen had competed previously but always in the teams of other countries. The Games were formally opened by the President of France, Gaston Doumergue, and were attended by well over 600,000 spectators in total. However, the chauvinism of the French supporters was outrageous at times. The weather was good, in fact too good at times – for the 10,000m cross-country event it was reported to be over 40 degrees and more than half the starters did not finish.

Despite, for the first time, all sports being organized by their international governing bodies and the instigation of Juries of Appeal, there were still many complaints of unfair decisions, notably in boxing. The newly instituted Olympic motto, *Citius, Altius, Fortius* (faster, higher, stronger), originally composed by Father Henri Didon in 1895, was taken to heart. Numerous records were set, sometimes unexpectedly. The long jump was won by William DeHart Hubbard (USA), with 7.44m. Another American, Robert LeGendre, had been left out of that event but entered in the athletic pentathlon in which he broke the world long jump record with 7.76m on the way to winning a bronze medal. Incidentally, Hubbard was the first black athlete to win a gold medal in an individual, as opposed to a team, event.

The track events were dominated by the resurgent Finns with their outstanding stars Paavo Nurmi and Ville Ritola. Nurmi won a then record five gold medals and the American-based Ritola four golds and two silvers. The remarkable Nurmi won the 1500m and 5000m title within 100 minutes on the same day – a unique performance. His

other victories came in the 3000m team race and the 10,000m cross-country team and individual events. In this latter event, run in record high temperatures, Nurmi beat Ritola by well over a minute. The statue of him which stands outside the Helsinki stadium was sculpted in 1925 to commemorate his Paris triumphs. It is interesting to note that the only viable opposition to the 'Flying Finns' came from Edvin Wide of Sweden, himself actually born in Finland. Two Britons scored upset wins when Harold Abrahams became the first European to win an Olympic sprint title and Eric Liddell set a world record in taking the 400m crown. Abrahams, coached by Sam Mussabini who had also trained Reggie Walker to victory in 1908, later recollected that there were no victory ceremonies and that he received his gold medal in the post some time later. Third in that 100m final was New Zealand's Arthur Porritt, who later became Governor-General of his country.

A unique double was achieved by Harold Osborn (USA) who won the decathlon title and the high jump. In the latter event, Osborn's habit of pressing the bar back against the uprights with his hand as he jumped, using the Western Roll technique, led to a change in the event's rules. The rules in another event resulted in a strange set of circumstances when the third finisher in the 400m hurdles was credited with a new Olympic record (also bettering the world mark). This happened because the winner, Frank Morgan Taylor (USA), had knocked down a hurdle, while the second finisher, Charles Brookins (USA), had been disqualified for leaving his lane. Thus the eventual silver medallist, third finisher Erik Vilén (FIN), claimed the record. In fourth place was Georges André (FRA) who had taken the oath at the opening ceremony, and who had won a silver medal in the 1908 high jump.

In the pool Johnny Weissmuller (USA) won three golds in freestyle swimming and a bronze at water polo. After

Winning his third gold medal in 1924, Johnny Weissmuller – later the most famous Tarzan of them all – takes the 100m freestyle. He also won a bronze at water polo (Popperfoto)

more medals four years later he turned to films and in the 1930s he became the most famous screen 'Tarzan' of them all. His team-mate in Paris Gertrude Ederle, who had become the youngest person ever to set a world record in 1919 at the age of 12yr 298 days, here won a gold in the relay, and two years later became the first woman to swim the English Channel. Incidentally, this Games was the first to introduce lane dividers in the pool. In rowing, another American later to gain fame elsewhere was Benjamin Spock, number 7 in the winning eight. He won renown as a best-selling writer and paediatrician. France came into her own in the fencing and cycling events. In the former Roger Ducret won three golds and one silver, while in the latter Armand Blanchonnet won the 188km road race by a near-record margin of over 9 minutes. A pointer to the future came in the soccer final as it was won by Uruguay, the first South American country to enter the Olympic football competition.

Now aged 45, Alfred Swahn (SWE) won his ninth shooting medal in four Games. His father, the incredible Oscar, had been picked for the team, but at 76 was too ill. However, he and Alfred won a family total of six golds, four silvers and five bronzes. The American shooter Carl Osburn gained another silver to raise his individual total since 1912 to 11, comprising five gold, four silver and two bronze. Tennis made its last appearance for 64 years, but had an all-star entry with all titles won by Wimbledon champions. One of them, Norris Williams, who partnered Hazel Wightman in the mixed doubles, was a survivor of the *Titanic* disaster in 1912. Rugby also disappeared from the Games, leaving the United States as reigning Olympic champions.

The oldest gold medallist at Paris was Allen Whitty (GBR) in the Running Deer shooting aged 58yr 78 days. The youngest winner at Paris was featherweight boxer Jackie Fields (USA) at 16yr 162 days. The youngest female winner was 400m freestyle champion Martha Norelius (USA) at 14yr 177 days (recent research confirming her as two years younger than originally thought). The oldest female gold medallist was Hazel Wightman (USA) in tennis aged 37yr 213 days. The United States won the major share of the medals at Paris, but a record number of 30 countries shared in the total.

1924 (Summer) MEDALS TABLE

	G	S	B
United States	45	27	27
Finland	14	13	10
France	13	15	10
Great Britain	9	13	12
Italy	8	3	5
Switzerland	7	8	10
Norway	5	2	3
Sweden	4	13	12
Netherlands	4	1	5
Belgium	3	7	3
Australia	3	1	2
Denmark	2	5	2
Hungary	2	3	4
Yugoslavia	2	-	-
Czechoslovakia	1	4	5
Argentina	1	3	2
Estonia	1	1	4
South Africa	1	1	1
Luxembourg	1	1	-
Greece	1	-	-
Uruguay	1	-	-
Austria	-	3	1
Canada	-	3	1
Ireland	-	1	1
Poland	-	1	1
Haiti	-	-	1
Japan	-	-	1
New Zealand	-	-	1
Portugal	-	-	1
Romania	-	-	1

1928

IInd Winter Games – St Moritz, Switzerland
11 – 19 February

Attended by representatives of 25 countries, comprising 464 competitors, of which 26 were women.

The decision that the same country should host both Summer and Winter editions of the Games had to be abandoned in 1928. The Games were officially declared open by the President of Switzerland, Edmund Schulthess, and the oath was taken by Hans Eidenbenz, a skier. Japan, Holland, Romania and Mexico were making their Winter debuts. Unseasonal weather threatened the programme – one of the speed skating events had to be cancelled and the bobsleigh had only two runs instead of four.

The cancellation of the 10,000m skating event by the Norwegian referee caused particularly bad feeling among the American team, as at that point Irving Jaffee (USA) was surprisingly leading and seemed likely to retain that lead. Despite vigorous protests by all nationalities, no medals were awarded. (Perhaps the unfortunate circumstances at Lake Placid four years later provided Jaffee with rough justice.) In the other events Clas Thunberg (FIN) added two more golds to his 1924 haul to amass a total of five gold, one silver and one bronze, a record for the sport. There was a unique occurrence in the 500m in which two men tied for first place and three men for third, with no silver medals awarded. Another uncommon happening was in the skeleton toboggan race conducted on the famous Cresta Run, where brothers Jennison and John Heaton (USA) gained the gold and silver respectively.

The bobsleigh, for the first and only time composed of 5-man teams, also went to the United States. The driver, William Fiske, was aged only 16yr 260 days, and was then the youngest ever male Winter gold medallist. Also in the team was the oldest gold medallist at these Games, Nion Tucker, aged 42yr 182 days. The youngest was Sonja Henie (NOR), taking the first of her three titles aged 15yr 316 days. She was the 'star' of the Games with her interpretation of *The Dying Swan*, which began a whole new era for figure skating. The youngest medallist at these Games was Thomas Doe (USA) in the bob aged 15yr 129 days, while the oldest was his team-mate Jay O'Brien at 44yr 361 days. Pair skating witnessed the last appearance of the 1920 champions, Ludowika and Walter Jakobsson (FIN), who were placed fifth, their combined ages totalling 89 years. The men's skating event gave Gillis Grafström (SWE) his third consecutive gold medal, an achievement unmatched to the present day.

In ski-jumping, the defending champion Jacob Tullin-Thams (NOR) was nearly killed crashing at the end of a 73m jump on a hill designed for jumps of considerably less. A true Olympian, he reappeared in 1936 to gain a silver medal at yachting. Johan Gröttumsbraaten (NOR) won the 18km race and the Nordic Combination title to match Thunberg's two wins. As was becoming a habit, the Canadians easily won the ice hockey tournament scoring a total of 38 goals to none against. The only demonstration event was a military patrol contest.

1928 (Winter) MEDALS TABLE

	G	S	B
Norway	6	4	5
United States	2	2	2
Sweden	2	2	1
Finland	2	1	1
Canada	1	-	-
France	1	-	-
Austria	-	3	1
Belgium	-	-	1
Czechoslovakia	-	-	1
Germany	-	-	1
Great Britain	-	-	1
Switzerland	-	-	1

1928

IXth Olympic Games – Amsterdam, Netherlands
17 May – 12 August

Attended by representatives of 46 countries, comprising 3014 competitors, of which 290 were women.

After unsuccessfully applying for the Games of 1916, 1920 and 1924, the Dutch finally were rewarded and built a new 40,000 capacity stadium on reclaimed land in Amsterdam. The size of the running track, 400m, encircled by a cycling track, was then standardized for future Games. The design of the stadium won the architect, Jan Wils, an Olympic prize in the architecture competition. One innovation was the erection of a large results board; others included the release of pigeons at the opening ceremony – to symbolize peace – and the burning of an Olympic flame throughout the period of competition. The formal opening was by HRH Prince Hendrik, the consort of Queen Wilhelmina who was on a state visit to Norway, although the Queen herself handed out medals at the end of the Games. The record number of countries included Rhodesia and Panama

Pairs skaters Ludowika and Walter Jakobsson competed in three Games with distinction, winning gold and silver medals in 1920 and 1924

for the first time. Germany made its return to the Summer Olympics in great strength.

After much argument in world sporting circles, and the opposition of Baron de Coubertin himself, women were allowed to compete in track and field, albeit in only five events. World records were set in all five, although there were such harrowing scenes of distress in the 800m that it was then omitted from the programme until 1964. In winning that 800m Lina Radke won the first ever Olympic track and field gold medal for Germany. Her team-mate, Anni Holdmann, became the first woman to win an Olympic track race by finishing first in heat 1 of the 100m on 30 July. Another first in the sport was a gold medal for Japan by Mikio Oda in the triple jump.

Ritola leads fellow Finn Nurmi and Wide (SWE) in the 1928 10,000 metres

The Finns again dominated the athletics, although the fabulous Nurmi only won one gold and two silvers. Looking far older than his 31 years, due to his increasing baldness, the dour Finn offered some light relief when he competed in the steeplechase. Unused to the event, he had problems with most of the barriers, and in his heat ignominiously fell into the water jump. A Frenchman, Lucien Duquesne, stopped and courteously helped him to his feet. Obviously grateful, Nurmi broke his long-standing rule and thanked him, and then proceeded to 'shepherd' the French runner for the rest of the race, even inviting him to break the tape first. This Duquesne, to his eternal credit, declined to do. Despite running his fifth distance race in seven days, Nurmi won the silver medal (behind a team-mate) in the final. It was later reported that the great Finn had damaged his famous stopwatch in the fall.

The unheralded Canadian youngster Percy Williams took both sprints, and with Lord Burghley becoming the first member of the British House of Lords to win an

Olympic athletic title and Douglas Lowe (GBR) successfully defending his 800m title, the Americans had a lean time. A pointer for the future was the victory in the marathon of Mohammed El Ouafi, representing France but an Algerian and the pathfinder for future great African distance runners. The US team was under the control of the President of the US Olympic Committee, Major-General Douglas MacArthur, later in command of the victorious Americans in the Pacific theatre of the Second World War. In the swimming pool another threat to United States dominance came in the form of the Japanese who won their first ever swimming medals in Amsterdam, giving an indication of things to come. American honour was saved by Johnny Weissmuller in the 100m and relay. Dorothy Poynton (USA) won a silver medal in springboard diving when only 24 days past her 13th birthday, one of the youngest medallists ever. She won gold medals at the next two Games. There was an unfortunate mix-up in the result of the men's high diving when Farid Simaika of Egypt was initially awarded the gold on the basis of his greater points score. The result was later reversed and the title given to Ulise 'Pete' Desjardins (USA) as more first-place decisions had been made in his favour by the judges. Canadian-born Desjardins had been the first Olympic diver to be awarded a score of 10, in the 1924 springboard event.

Another Egyptian, Ibrahim Moustafa, won the light-heavyweight wrestling title to become the first non-European to take a Greco-Roman event. Not for the first – nor last – time, boxing was beset with protests about the standard of officiating. In yachting, Crown Prince Olav, later King Olav V of Norway, gained the first Olympic victory by a member of a Royal house when he was a crew member of the 6m yacht *Norna*. (His son Crown Prince Harald also competed in Olympic yachting 1964-1972, but without his father's success.) In the soccer tournament Uruguay retained their title, beating another South American country, Argentina, in the final. India won the first of their six consecutive hockey gold medals, retaining the title until 1960. Their goalkeeper, Richard Allen, did not concede a single goal in the tournament.

A team-mate of the Crown Prince in *Norna*, Johan Anker, a gold medallist from 1912, was the oldest gold medallist in Amsterdam aged 57yr 44 days, while the youngest, also water-borne, was the Swiss pairs cox Hans Boúrquin aged 14yr 222 days. The youngest female champion was Elizabeth Robinson (USA) who won the 100m sprint aged 16yr 343 days, while the oldest woman to win a gold medal was Virginie Hériot (FRA) in the 8m yachting aged 38yr 15 days. The youngest medallist was Luigina Giavotti (ITA), silver in gymnastics aged 11yr 302 days.

1928 (Summer) MEDALS TABLE

	G	S	B
United States	22	18	16
Germany	10	7	14
Finland	8	8	9
Sweden	7	6	12
Italy	7	5	7
Switzerland	7	4	4
France	6	10	5
Netherlands	6	9	4
Hungary	4	5	-
Canada	4	4	7
Great Britain	3	10	7
Argentina	3	3	1
Denmark	3	1	2
Czechoslovakia	2	5	2
Japan	2	2	1
Estonia	2	1	2
Egypt	2	1	1
Austria	2	-	1
Australia	1	2	1
Norway	1	2	1
Poland	1	1	3
Yugoslavia	1	1	3
South Africa	1	-	2
India	1	-	-
Ireland	1	-	-
New Zealand	1	-	-
Spain	1	-	-
Uruguay	1	-	-
Belgium	-	1	2
Chile	-	1	-
Haiti	-	1	-
Philippines	-	-	1
Portugal	-	-	1

1932

IIIrd Winter Games – Lake Placid, USA
4 – 15 February

Attended by representatives of 17 countries, comprising 252 competitors, of which 21 were women.

Snow had to be brought over to the United States from Canada by lorries for some of the venues at Lake Placid, and a thaw caused the 4-man bob event to be held after the official closing ceremony on 13 February. The Games were opened by the Governor of New York State, Franklin D. Roosevelt, who became President of the United States the following year. Incidentally, Eleanor, his redoubtable wife, took a ride down the bob course. The oath was taken by Jack Shea, who won the 500m speed skating gold later in the day. An Olympic first was achieved in the opening ceremony by the British contingent when their flag was carried by a woman, skater Mollie Phillips. Innovatively, figure skating was held indoors and drew large crowds, and three speed skating events for women were given demonstration status – 28 years later such events were on the programme proper. Demonstrations were also given of curling and dog sled racing, the latter won by Emile St Goddard of Canada.

Not surprisingly the Scandinavians swept the Nordic skiing, but an upset occurred in the speed skating where the Americans and Canadians dominated. It is arguable whether this owed more to the abilities of the North Americans or to the change of rules that the organizing committee had invoked. Instead of the more usual European system of competition in pairs, with the fastest times deciding the medal places, American rules were in force, under which mass start races were held, similar to track running, with heats and finals. Lack of familiarity with the (often quite physical) tactics employed put the Europeans at a distinct disadvantage. Indeed Finland's four-time gold medallist Clas Thunberg did not even bother to appear at Lake Placid. The Canadians won the ice hockey title for the fourth consecutive time, but only on goal average after three periods of overtime against the United States in the final game.

In figure skating the peerless Sonja Henie (NOR) easily retained her title, but triple champion Gillis Grafström (SWE), now 38, was the victim of an unfortunate accident. During the compulsory figures he collided with a badly

Three great skating champions of the 1920s and 1930s: Sonja Henie (NOR) with Karl Schäfer (AUT, left) and the Swede Gillis Grafström (Popperfoto)

positioned movie camera and fell, suffering a mild concussion. It may well have cost him an unprecedented fourth title. The oldest competitor was Joseph Savage (USA) aged 52yr 144 days in the pairs skating. The winners of that title, Pierre and Andrée Brunet (FRA), became the first pair to win both as an unmarried and married couple. In so doing Andrée was the oldest female gold medal winner at Lake Placid aged 30yr 149 days. They later coached gold medallists Carol Heiss (1960), and Hayes (1956) and David (1960) Jenkins. In the ladies individual event Cecilia Colledge was Britain's youngest ever Olympic competitor at any sport aged 11yr 73 days. She was probably the youngest ever competitor in the Olympic Winter Games.

History of a different kind was made by Eddie Eagan (USA) in the 4-man bob as a late and virtually untried draftee. As part of the winning team he became the only man to win gold medals in both Summer and Winter celebrations – he was a 1920 boxing champion. The 2-man bob was won by brothers Curtis and Hubert Stevens (USA), and a third brother, Paul, won a silver medal in the 4-man event. The oldest gold medallist at Lake Placid was Eagan's bob team-mate Jay O'Brien aged 48yr 359 days, while Sonja Henie was again the youngest, now aged 19yr 308 days. The youngest male champion was ice hockey player Albert Duncansson (CAN) aged 20yr 134 days. O'Brien is still the oldest person to win a winter Olympics gold medal.

1932 (Winter) MEDALS TABLE

	G	S	B
Untied States	6	4	2
Norway	3	4	3
Sweden	1	2	-
Canada	1	1	5
Finland	1	1	1
Austria	1	1	-
France	1	-	-
Switzerland	-	1	-
Germany	-	-	2
Hungary	-	-	1

1932

Xth Olympic Games – Los Angeles, USA
30 July – 14 August

Attended by representatives of 37 countries, comprising 1408 competitors, of which 127 were women.

As early as 1920 the US delegation to the IOC, led by William May Garland, had applied for either the 1924 or 1928 Games to be held in Los Angeles. Despite trepidations felt over the memory of the 1904 'farce' at St Louis, in 1923 Los Angeles was awarded the 1932 Games. Against further worries about distance and cost of travel were set the

advantages of favourable weather and competitive conditions. The announcement by the organizing committee that they would subsidize transportation, housing and feeding costs helped greatly at a time of Depression, and did much to offset the critics.

One source of income was a new 3-cent postage stamp depicting a runner, for which the model was the anchor man of the 1924 gold medal relay team, Alfred Leconey. The concept of an Olympic 'village' came to fruition with the construction of 550 specially designed small houses for male competitors in the Baldwin Hills area. It was strictly guarded by cowboys who 'rode the fences' around the perimeter. Female competitors were put up separately in the Chapman Park Hotel on Wilshire Boulevard, and the strict rule preventing women in the village barred the Finnish team's lady cook. However, despite the strictures of Prohibition, the French team were allowed to bring in wine for their own consumption. After journeys often lasting two weeks, the visitors found excellent weather and facilities awaiting them.

The main stadium was the Los Angeles Coliseum which had begun construction in 1921 and opened two years later. In 1930 it had been enlarged to hold 101,000 seated spectators, and the track had a new crushed peat running surface. Also there was the 10,000 seat Swimming Stadium, the State Armory where fencing took place, and the Olympic Auditorium, seating 10,000 to watch boxing, wrestling and weightlifting events, while a specially built wooden track was erected in the famous Pasadena Rose Bowl for the cycling. Long Beach harbour was the venue for yachting, and Long Beach Marine Stadium hosted the rowing. The Los Angeles Museum of History, Science and Art was the home for the fine art competitions. The Games were formally opened by the Vice President of the United States, Charles Curtis, on behalf of President Hoover who was in the middle of an electioneering tour. The oath on behalf of the competitors was taken by an American fencer, Lieut. George Calnan of the US Navy, who died the following April when the dirigible *Akron* crashed into the Pacific Ocean. Although the number of teams, and total competitors, were lower than at Amsterdam, there were two countries making their Olympic debuts, Colombia and China, both with sole representatives, neither of whom achieved any success. However, another small team, Ireland with only eight men, finished well up the medal table with two golds.

At these Games new ideas included the use of photo-finish equipment – the Kirby Two-Eyed Camera – for track races. Although it could accurately provide times to one-hundredth of a second it was only used to decide close finishes, and only a few of the timings have ever come to light. Another innovation was the three-tiered victory stand, with medal awarding ceremonies involving the raising of national flags taking place at the end of each day's events. In boxing the system of having the referee in the ring with the boxers was introduced into the Games for the first time, although it did not settle all arguments in that sport.

As with all such international gatherings there were some unfortunate incidents, but in the main they were of minor importance. Prior to the arrival of the teams there was a major 'scandal' with the banning of the great Finnish runner Paavo Nurmi, under charges of professionalism – he was accused of accepting unduly large expenses on a German tour. Despite rigorous protests on his behalf, the Finnish Federation finally accepted the ruling, although he had already been selected for the marathon and, indeed, had arrived with the team in Los Angeles. It does not seem unreasonable to suggest that he would have finished a remarkable career with another gold medal. The Finns were also involved in another incident once the Games were underway when the runners in the 3000m steeplechase ran an extra lap due to a miscalculation by the lap counter. Happily the error did not appear to have altered the final medal placings.

Another minor irritant was the American habit of announcing all the field event results only in Imperial units of measurement, much to the annoyance, and bafflement, of the foreign competitors and spectators. But there were two

strange judgement made, for although Didrikson cleared the same height as her team-mate, Jean Shiley, and then tied in a jump-off, the judges decided that her 'Western Roll' style of jump had been performed illegally, with her head preceding her body over the bar, and illogically they placed her second. She later became the world's greatest female golfer under her married name of Zaharias.

Another curiosity occurred in the 400m hurdles where Irishman Bob Tisdall, who reportedly had spent most of the preceding days in bed recuperating from a long and tiring journey, won the gold medal in a time superior to the world record. However, because he knocked down the last hurdle the world record was given to the runner-up Glenn Hardin (USA). Uniquely, the first four finishers at Los Angeles were all gold medallists in the event – Tisdall (1932), Hardin (1936), Taylor (1924) and Burghley (1928). In the 200m final Ralph Metcalfe was inadvertently made to start about 1.5m before the correct place, thus almost certainly costing him a silver medal – but as Americans had placed 1-2-3, Metcalfe, later a US Congressman, declined the offered re-run. The Indian hockey team, while not looking quite so

The unbeatable Indian team in their record-breaking match against the United States at Los Angeles in 1932

more serious occurrences, one on the track and one in the swimming pool. The first was in the 5000m when the eventual winner, Lauri Lehtinen (FIN), deliberately blocked the American Ralph Hill twice in the final stages of the race, a not uncommon practice in Europe but one which drew loud booing from the partisan crowd. They were quickly quietened by the announcer Bill Henry, whose words, 'Remember please, these people are our guests,' have entered Olympic lore. The second incident was of a much more serious nature when the Brazilian water polo team, after losing 7-3 to Germany, lost their tempers and insulted the referee. They were disqualified from the tournament.

On the brighter side was the performance of the outstanding individual of the Games, Mildred 'Babe' Didrikson (since her death her family has insisted that the surname should be spelt with an 'e' not an 'o'). Much to her annoyance, she was only allowed to enter three events. She set Olympic records in each of them, winning the javelin and 80m hurdles and gaining a silver in the high jump. Thus she is the only athlete to win medals in individual running, jumping and throwing events. In the high jump there was a

invincible as previously, set a record-beating score by defeating the United States 24-1, with Roop Singh scoring 12 goals. Similarly, in the water polo competition, Hungary beat Japan with a record score of 18-0. Nevertheless, the Japanese were particularly noteworthy in swimming, highlighted by their superb 4 x 200m team breaking the world record by a remarkable 37.8 secs.

The oldest gold medallist at Los Angeles was yachtsman Pierpoint Davis (USA) aged 47yr 224 days, while the youngest was 1500m freestyle champion Kusuo Kitamura (JPN) aged 14yr 309 days. The youngest female champion was Claire Dennis (AUS) who won the 200m breaststroke aged 16yr 117 days. The oldest female winner was Lillian Copeland (USA) in the discus aged 27yr 251 days. The youngest medallist was diver Katharine Rawls (USA), 58 days past her 14th birthday. The oldest medallist was Hiram Tuttle (USA) in the dressage aged 49yr 231 days. As demonstration sports, the hosts provided American

*By winning the 1500m freestyle in 1932, 14-year-old
Kusuo Kitamura became the youngest ever male
Olympic swimming champion*

football and lacrosse. During the closing ceremony the
President of the IOC, Count Henri de Baillet-Latour,
presented Olympic Merit Awards for Alpinism to Franz and
Toni Schmid (GER) for the first climb of the north face of
the Matterhorn. Despite all the economic and
organizational misgivings the Xth Games were a great
success, attended by a total of 1.25 million spectators, and
realized a profit of about $1 million.

One last innovation at these Games was the use of two
sentences, attributed to Baron de Coubertin, but actually
based on words used by the Bishop of Central Pennsylvania,
Ethelbert Talbot, in a sermon at St Paul's Cathedral,
London on 19 July 1908. Displayed on the scoreboard at
every opening ceremony since, the words are: 'The most
important thing in the Olympic Games is not to win but to
take part, just as the most important thing in life is not the
triumph but the struggle. The essential thing is not to have
conquered but to have fought well.'

1932 (Summer) MEDALS TABLE

	G	S	B
United States	41	32	30
Italy	12	12	12
France	10	5	4
Sweden	9	5	9
Japan	7	7	4
Hungary	6	4	5
Finland	5	8	12
Germany	3	12	5
Great Britain	4	7	5
Australia	3	1	1
Argentina	3	1	-
Canada	2	5	8
Netherlands	2	5	-
Poland	2	1	4
South Africa	2	-	3
Ireland	2	-	-
Czechoslovakia	1	2	1
Austria	1	1	3
India	1	-	-
Denmark	-	3	3
Mexico	-	2	-
Latvia	-	1	-
New Zealand	-	1	-
Switzerland	-	1	-
Philippines	-	-	3
Spain	-	-	1
Uruguay	-	-	1

1936

IVth Winter Games – Garmisch-Partenkirchen, Germany
6 – 16 February

*Attended by representatives of 28 countries,
comprising 668 competitors, of which 80 were
women.*

It is not always remembered that when the Winter and
Summer Games of 1936 were awarded to Germany five
years previously, Adolf Hitler was virtually unknown.
However, by the year of the Games they were seen by many
as a test case of how the German Olympic Committee
would react to the demands of the National Socialist
government of Germany. There had been much heated
discussion around the world as to the advisability of
attending these Games, or the later Summer Olympics, at
all, due to the racialist policies of the host government. In
spite of this, a record entry included teams from Bulgaria,
Turkey, Australia, Spain and Liechtenstein for the first time.
The Games were declared open by Chancellor Hitler, and
Wilhelm Bogner, a skier, took the oath on behalf of the
competitors. By the end of the competitions, over 500,000
paying spectators had watched the six different sports.
These now included Alpine skiing, although the only event
was a combination one, for both men and women.

Birger Ruud (NOR) successfully defended his ski jump
title, and then caused a major surprise by winning the
downhill segment of the men's Alpine combination. By dint
of a 5.9sec margin of victory in the slalom segment, the title
went to Franz Pfnür (GER) and Ruud fell back to fourth
place. In the women's event there was a similar situation as
the downhill race was won by 16-year-old Laila Schou
Nilsen (NOR), who held five world speed skating records
but had entered the skiing in the absence of such events for
women. In the slalom Christl Cranz (GER), who was
eventually to win a record 12 world skiing championships,
won by the quite astounding margin of 11.3sec and took the
overall gold medal, Nilsen gaining the bronze.

The top medal winner was speed skater Ivar Ballangrud
(NOR) with three golds and a silver. In contrast to the Lake
Placid conditions of four years earlier, the racers competed

under European-style rules with pairs of skaters racing against the clock. Instead of four gold medals the Americans gained a solitary bronze. Sonja Henie (NOR) won her third consecutive figure skating title, to add to her ten world championships, and then went off to Hollywood, followed sometime later by the twelfth-placed British girl Gladys Jepson-Turner, who gained cinematic fame as Belita. The British caused a major upset by winning the ice hockey, albeit with a team containing some Anglo-Canadians. In this competition appeared Rudi Ball, one of only two athletes of Jewish origin selected by Germany in 1936. Ball, a bronze medallist from 1932, was especially requested to return from his exile in France – the hosts hoping to offset criticism of their attitude to Jewish competitors by this act.

A most unusual double nearly came the way of Ernst Baier (GER) who won the pairs skating with Maxi Herber but only came second in the men's singles. It was still the best such double placing ever. His pairs partner Herber was the youngest gold medallist aged 15yr 128 days, and sister and brother Ilse and Erik Pausin (AUT), the pairs silver medallists, were the youngest ever couple to gain a medal in the event, their ages totalling a mere 32yr 307 days. The oldest gold medallist was Carl Erhardt (GBR), one day past his 39th birthday in the ice hockey final. The demonstration events were German curling and the military patrol.

1936 (Winter) MEDALS TABLE

	G	S	B
Norway	7	5	3
Germany	3	3	-
Sweden	2	2	3
Finland	1	2	3
Austria	1	1	2
Switzerland	1	2	-
Great Britain	1	1	1
United States	1	-	3
Canada	-	1	-
France	-	-	1
Hungary	-	-	1

1936

XIth Olympic Games – Berlin, Germany
1 – 16 August

Attended by representatives of 49 countries, comprising 4066 competitors, of which 328 were women.

These Games were awarded to Berlin just prior to the rise to power of Adolf Hitler and the National Socialist (Nazi) Party. Abhorrence of Germany's policies under this government led many countries, not least the United States, to propose a boycott, but the President of the US Olympic Committee, Avery Brundage, was strongly in favour of

participation, and won the day. In Germany itself the notorious Heinrich Himmler was opposed to the Games being held, but Josef Goebbels convinced Hitler that they would present tremendous propaganda opportunities. Political overtones overshadowed the Games until the last moment when Spain withdrew owing to the outbreak of civil war there.

The original intention had been to enlarge the stadium that had been built for the aborted 1916 Games, but Hitler decreed that a brand new 100,000 capacity arena be built. The architect was Werner March, whose father had designed the 1916 stadium. Other fine stadia and halls were erected, plus a magnificent 'village' of 150 buildings for the competitors. Yachting events were held at Kiel on the north-west coast.

At the instigation of Carl Diem, the main organizer, a torch relay was inaugurated to bring the sacred Olympic flame from the Temple of Zeus at Olympia – 3,000 runners crossed seven countries in ten days. The sacred flame, lit by 'priestesses' Koula Pratsika and Aleka Katseli, was handed to a Greek runner, Kyril Kondylis. The last runner into the stadium to light the cauldron was athlete Fritz Schilgen. The Games were formally opened by Hitler, as a specially commissioned 16.5 ton bell was rung and thousands of pigeons set free. As the massive German contingent, 406 strong, entered, the giant airship *Hindenburg* flew over the stadium.

The German team, with full government backing, was probably the best prepared team ever in the Games. As a sop to foreign criticism it contained one athlete of Jewish origin, Heléne Mayer, persuaded to return from America with the promise of full 'Aryan' classification. Ironically she placed second in the foil to the Hungarian Jewess Ilona Elek, with another Jewish fencer in third. Perhaps even more ironic, at the opening ceremony the 1896 marathon victor, Spiridon Louis, attired in national dress, presented Hitler with an olive branch – signifying peace – from Olympia. In the march-past of teams, a number of them gave the Nazi salute, but the United States and Great Britain, to the annoyance of the crowd, merely made the traditional 'eyes right'. The music for the ceremony was conducted by the famous composer Richard Strauss. An indication of the future came with the first ever use of television at the Games, with a closed circuit system to special halls, operated by the Reich Rundfunkgesellschaft, and watched by 150,000 people at 28 venues around Berlin.

Very high standards were reached at these Games, and at the forefront of the record breaking were the ten black members of the US track and field team. Anathema to the German propaganda machine, which dubbed them 'Black Auxiliaries', they won seven gold, three silver and three bronze medals – more than any national team, including their own white team-mates. Outstanding among them was Jesse Owens with four gold medals, in the 100m, 200m, long jump, and as a member of the 4 x 100m relay team. The runner-up in the 200m was Mack Robinson, whose brother Jackie was the first black Major League baseball player. It

The immortal Jesse Owens, one of the greatest Olympians ever, won four gold medals in 1936 at Berlin (Popperfoto)

should be noted that the attitude of the German government to Owens was not shared by the majority of the fans – and he was in tremendous demand by autograph hunters.

Much has been written about Hitler refusing to meet and congratulate Owens and the other black gold medallists. In fairness, it should be realized that after Hitler had made a point of personally greeting the German victors on the first day, he was rebuked for the practice by the President of the IOC, Henri de Baillet-Latour, who informed him that only IOC-designated people performed such duties in an Olympic stadium. After that Hitler refrained from further congratulatory meetings, although it is reported that he met all German medallists in private. Thus, if he *did* snub anybody, it would have been not Owens but high jumper Corny Johnson, the only black winner on the first day.

Other track highlights included the superb sprinting of Helen Stephens (USA), the decathlon victory of team-mate Glenn Morris, later to be another screen Tarzan, and the 1500m world record by Jack Lovelock (NZL). This last event is considered by many to have been the highlight of the Games. The Finns took all three places in the 10,000m as well as the first two places in the 5000m and steeplechase, Volmari Iso-Hollo successfully defending his title in the latter. Outstanding in the pool were the Dutch women led by Hendrika Mastenbroek, who personally won three golds and a silver.

The winner of the women's springboard diving, Marjorie Gestring (USA), became the youngest ever female gold medallist, and the youngest ever individual event champion, aged 13yr 267 days. The oldest gold medallist at Berlin was Friedrich Gerhard (GER) in the dressage team aged 52yr 20 days. The youngest male champion was fencer Edoardo Mangiarotti (ITA) aged 17yr 124 days, while the

oldest female champion was gymnast Friedl Iby (GER) at 31yr 128 days.

Robert Charpentier (FRA) won three gold medals in cycling, where Toni Merkens (GER) won the 1000m sprint despite being fined, but not disqualified, for obstruction in the first race. In wrestling, Kristjan Palusalu of Estonia matched the achievement of Ivar Johansson (SWE) in 1932 by winning titles in both freestyle and Greco-Roman styles. Interestingly, the list of gold medallists at Berlin includes the famous name Nurmi, but in this case it is the name of the horse ridden by Ludwig Stubbendorff (GER) to his easy victory in the tough three-day event. Of the fourteen teams which started, only four finished with sufficient scorers. These included Britain, whose final placer, Capt. Richard Fanshawe, gained his team the bronze medal despite numerous penalty points incurred resulting from having to chase his horse for 4000m before remounting.

In the single-handed Olympia class yachting, the bronze medal went to Peter Markham Scott, son of the tragic Antarctic explorer, and later himself a world-famous naturalist. Canoeing and basketball made their official debuts, with the inventor of the latter, Dr James Naismith, on hand to see the US team begin its remarkable sequence of victories. At the end of the Games a magnificent film, *Olympische Spiele*, was produced by Leni Riefenstahl, which although criticized as propaganda, is still the best ever documentary record of an Olympic Games.

1936 (Summer) MEDALS TABLE

	G	S	B
Germany	33	26	30
United States	24	20	12
Hungary	10	1	5
Italy	8	9	5
Finland	7	6	6
France	7	6	6
Sweden	6	5	9
Japan	6	4	8
Netherlands	6	4	7
Great Britain	4	7	3
Austria	4	6	3
Czechoslovakia	3	5	-
Argentina	2	2	3
Estonia	2	2	3
Egypt	2	1	2
Switzerland	1	9	5
Canada	1	3	5
Norway	1	3	2
Turkey	1	-	1
India	1	-	-
New Zealand	1	-	-
Poland	-	3	3
Denmark	-	2	3
Latvia	-	1	1
Romania	-	1	-
South Africa	-	1	-

Yugoslavia . . . . - . . . . . 1 . . . . -
Mexico . . . . - . . . . . - 3
Belgium . . . . - . . . . . - 2
Australia . . . . - . . . . . - 1
Philippines . . . . - . . . . . - 1
Portugal . . . . - . . . . . - 1

1948

Vth Winter Games – St Moritz, Switzerland
30 January – 8 February

Attended by representatives of 28 countries, comprising 669 competitors, of which 77 were women.

In 1936 the Winter Games of 1940 were initially awarded to Sapporo, Japan, but as a consequence of the Sino-Japanese conflict they were reallocated to St Moritz. Due to some disagreements the IOC transferred them again in June 1939 to Garmisch-Partenkirchen, Germany, at the same time deciding that the 1944 meeting should be held at Cortina d'Ampezzo, Italy. The Second World War then upset these plans and in 1946 a postal vote of IOC members relocated the 1948 Games to St Moritz, as neutral Switzerland had been virtually untouched by the war. Chile, Denmark, Iceland, Korea and Lebanon competed for the first time in the Winter Games, but Germany and Japan were not invited, although Italy was. The oath was taken by ice hockey player Richard Torriani on behalf of the competitors, and Swiss President Enrico Celio formally declared the Games open. There were now six Alpine events, which attracted larger fields than the Nordic disciplines. Poor weather affected some of the competitions and there were a number of disputes.

The most medals were won by Henri Oreiller (FRA) with golds in the downhill (by a record margin of 4.1sec) and combination and a bronze in the slalom. Alpine skier Gretchen Fraser (USA) gained the first skiing title ever won by a non-European. In Nordic skiing the Swedes broke the Norwegian monopoly. They had the three medals and fifth place in the 18km, first two and fifth in the 50km, and won the 4 x 10km relay by a margin of nearly 9 minutes. They also won their first ever speed skating title when Ake Seyffarth took the 10km event. The athletic American figure skaters brought a new concept to figure skating as Dick Button gained an easy victory.

The ice hockey competition was the cause of a major row. Two American teams appeared in St Moritz. One represented the Amateur Hockey Association of the United States (AHA) and the other was picked by the US Olympic Committee. The AHA, while not affiliated to the USOC, was a member of the International Hockey Federation (IHF) which was the governing body of most of the other teams at the Games, and the IHF threatened to withdraw all the other teams if the AHA team were not allowed to play.

The USOC in turn threatened to withdraw its whole Olympic team if they were! Initially the IOC decided to bar both teams, but then agreed with the Swiss organizers and the IHF to allow the AHA team to compete. Strangely, however, the USOC team members marched in the opening ceremony. The AHA team eventually finished fourth, but a year later the AHA was disqualified for non-affiliation to the Olympic movement. The Canadians won the title once again, but only just. The title was decided on goal average, with the Czechs taking the silver. The Swiss in third place contained the man who had taken the oath, 'Bibi' Torriani thus adding another bronze medal to the one he had won 20 years earlier when he was just past his sixteenth birthday.

The US bobsleds were sabotaged prior to the competitions, but it did not prevent them from winning a gold and two bronzes. They have never won an Olympic bob event since. In the skeleton toboggan, which is only held when the Games are at St Moritz, on the Cresta Run, John Heaton (USA) won his second silver medal, 20 years after his first. The gold medal went to Nino Bibbia of Italy. He was a master of the Cresta Run and won many titles and championships over the next quarter of a century. The great Norwegian ski jumper Birger Ruud, nearly 37 years old and a survivor of a wartime concentration camp, ended his Olympic career with a silver medal to add to his golds from 1932 and 1936. He and his brother Sigmund had made the event a family preserve since 1928. A third brother, Asbjorn, was also in the 1948 team.

Gretchen Fraser (USA), the 1948 slalom gold medallist. Aged 29, she was one of the oldest ever female skiing champions (Allsport)

A record thirteen countries shared out the medals, and Italy and Belgium won their first ever Winter Games titles. There were two demonstration events: a military ski patrol and a winter pentathlon. This latter consisted of 10km cross-country skiing, pistol shooting, downhill skiing, fencing, and horse riding. No medals were awarded, but in second place was Capt. Willie Grut (SWE) of whom much more was to be heard 6 months later in London. The oldest gold medallist was Francis Tyler, in the US 4-man bob aged 43yr 58 days, while the youngest was skater Dick Button aged 18yr 202 days. The youngest female champion was skater Barbara-Ann Scott (CAN) aged 19yr 273 days, while the oldest female winner was Gretchen Fraser (USA) in the slalom aged 28yr 360 days. The youngest medallist was skater Suzanne Morrow (CAN) with a pairs bronze aged 17yr 55 days, while the oldest was bobsledder Max Houben (BEL) at 49yr 278 days.

1948 (Winter) MEDALS TABLE

	G	S	B
Norway	4	3	3
Sweden	4	3	3
Switzerland	3	4	3
United States	3	4	2
France	2	1	2
Canada	2	-	1
Austria	1	3	4
Finland	1	3	2
Belgium	1	1	-
Italy	1	-	-
Czechoslovakia	-	1	-
Hungary	-	1	-
Great Britain	-	-	2

1948

XIVth Olympic Games – London, Great Britain
29 July – 14 August

Attended by representatives of 59 countries, comprising 4099 competitors, of which 385 were women.

In 1936 the XIIth Games were awarded to Tokyo, to take place from 24 August–8 September 1940. When the Sino-Japanese war began in 1938 the Games were transferred to Helsinki, but the Soviet invasion of Finland then scuppered these plans. In June 1939, a very optimistic IOC awarded the XIIIth Games for 1944 to London, over competing claims from Detroit, Lausanne and Rome. A postal vote of IOC members called by the President, Sigfrid Edström of Sweden, in 1946 awarded the XIVth Games to London. In the meantime, Baron de Coubertin had died in 1937 and his heart was buried at Olympia in Greece.

Organized by the British Olympic Association, under

the Presidency of Lord Burghley, the 1948 Olympics were an austerity Games – after six years of war Britain still had rationing of food and clothing. Housing was very short due to wartime destruction, and competitors were housed at RAF and Army camps (for men) and colleges (for women). A temporary running track was laid at the 83,000 capacity Wembley Stadium, the home of British football. Other existing buildings were adapted. Rowing was held at Henley on the River Thames, and the yachting was at Torbay, Devon. The total expenditure amounted to no more than £600,000 and final accounts suggested that a profit of over £10,000 was made. The Games were opened by King George VI. Not surprisingly Germany and Japan were not invited, but a record 59 countries attended. These included the first entries by countries under Communist governments. Some of the hottest weather for years occurred on the opening days, but later it rained. Photo-finish equipment, as used on racecourses, was used for the track events, but only to decide places.

The undoubted star of the Games was Francina 'Fanny' Blankers-Koen (NED) who won four gold medals, a record for a woman. Now 30 years of age and a mother of two children, she had finished in sixth place in the 1936 high jump. In 1948 she held seven world records including those in the high and long jumps, neither of which she contested in London. The gap between her and the second girl in the 200m, 0.7sec, remains the largest margin of victory ever achieved in an Olympic sprint, by men or women. In the high jump Dorothy Tyler (née Odam) (GBR) placed second again, 12 years after her other silver medal – both times she had cleared the same height as the winner. Bob Mathias

The star of Wembley, Fanny Blankers-Koen, winning the 4x100m relay for Holland from Australia, Canada, Great Britain (Maureen Gardner) and Denmark (Popperfoto)

(USA) became the youngest ever male Olympic individual athletics champion when he won the decathlon aged 17yr

263 days. He retained the title in 1952, made a film of his life, and later was elected a US Congressman. Another athlete to catch the eye was Emil Zatopek (TCH), not so much by his easy win in the 10,000m, but by his remarkable last 300m sprint to narrowly lose the 5000m. An American, Harrison Dillard, acknowledged to be the world's best high hurdler, had fallen in the US trials and failed to make their team in his best event. In London he won his 'second-string' event, the 100m, and won another gold in the relay. Two of the debuting countries made their marks early in the Games. Duncan White of Ceylon (now Sri Lanka) gained the only medal his country has ever won with a silver in the 400m hurdles. Jamaica made an even bigger impact by collecting a gold, two silvers and two other finalists in the 200m, 400m and 800m. The marathon provided its usual drama: Etienne Gailly, a Belgian paratrooper, entered the stadium first but, exhausted, was passed by two runners before the tape.

An outstanding competitor in the modern pentathlon was Willie Grut of Sweden who won three disciplines of the five-sport event, and placed fifth and eighth in the others, to win by a large margin. He was the son of the designer of the 1912 Olympic stadium. Another exceptional champion was South African boxer George Hunter, who not only won the light-heavyweight title, but also the Val Barker Trophy as the best stylist in the whole competition. However, lack of experienced referees and judges resulted in much criticism of the boxing tournament. There were problems too at Herne Hill stadium where some of the cycling events finished in very poor light due to the lack of floodlighting.

There was an unfortunate turn of events in the equestrian competitions where the team dressage contest was won by the Swedes only for them to be disqualified the following year, and their medals taken away, when it was learned that one of their number, Gehnäll Persson, was not a commissioned officer as the rules then required. In fencing Ilona Elek (HUN) retained her 1936 title even though she was now over 41 years of age. Her sister Margit placed sixth. The 1932 champion Ellen Müller-Preis (AUT) gained the bronze medal. An even more outstanding veteran was 40-year-old Heikki Savolainen, the famous Finnish gymnast, who in his fourth Olympics won his first gold medal, on the pommel horse. The soccer gold medallists, Sweden, scored one of the strangest goals in the history of the sport in their semi-final against Denmark. Centre-forward Gunnar Nordahl, one of three brothers in the team, leapt into the Danish goalnet to avoid being offside during a Swedish attack. At the end of the move his inside-left headed the ball into the goal, where in the absence of the Danish keeper it was caught by Nordahl.

Yachting witnessed the end of one long Olympic career when Ralph Craig, the 1912 double sprint champion, reappeared in the American yachting team. Although he carried the US flag in the opening ceremony, he did not actually compete. Torbay was also the start of another exceptional career with the appearance of Durward Knowles, competing for Britain. He then competed in yachting events for the Bahamas in the next six Games, and

made it an eighth time in 1988. A rare happening at the yachting was the victory of the father/son combination Paul and Hilary Smart (USA) in the Star class. At the Empire Pool, US competitors won 12 of the 15 swimming events, excluding water polo. One of the rare non-American champions was Greta Andersen (DEN) in the 100m freestyle; sixteen years later she set a female record for swimming the English Channel. In diving, Vicki Draves (USA) won both titles, then a unique achievement.

The oldest gold medallist in London was Paul Smart (see above) in yachting aged 56yr 212 days, and the youngest was Thelma Kalama (USA) in the swimming sprint relay for women aged 17yr 135 days. Bob Mathias, the decathlon champion, was the youngest male champion (see above), while the oldest female winner was fencer Ilona Elek (HUN) aged 41yr 77 days.

1948 (Summer) MEDALS TABLE

	G	S	B
United States	38	27	19
Sweden	16	11	17
France	10	6	13
Hungary	10	5	12
Italy	8	12	9
Finland	8	7	5
Turkey	6	4	2
Czechoslovakia	6	2	3
Switzerland	5	10	5
Denmark	5	7	8
Netherlands	5	2	9
Great Britain	3	14	6
Argentina	3	3	1
Australia	2	6	5
Belgium	2	2	3
Egypt	2	2	1
Mexico	2	1	2
South Africa	2	1	1
Norway	1	3	3
Jamaica	1	2	-
Austria	1	-	3
India	1	-	-
Peru	1	-	-
Yugoslavia	-	2	-
Canada	-	1	2
Portugal	-	1	1
Uruguay	-	1	1
Ceylon (now Sri Lanka)	-	1	-
Cuba	-	1	-
Spain	-	1	-
Trinidad	-	1	-
Korea	-	-	2
Panama	-	-	2
Brazil	-	-	1
Iran	-	-	1
Poland	-	-	1
Puerto Rico	-	-	1

1952

VIth Winter Games – Oslo, Norway
14 – 25 February

Attended by representatives of 30 countries, comprising 694 competitors, of which 109 were women.

Until 1994 these Games were the only Winter Olympics to have been held in a Nordic country, even though Norway, Sweden and Finland between them had dominated the medals. There were enormous crowds in Oslo at all venues, including a record for any Olympic event at the ski jumping at Holmenkollen, estimated at 150,000. An innovation was the Olympic flame coming not from Olympia, but from Morgedal in southern Norway, the home of Sondre Nordheim, the father of modern skiing. The last relay 'runner' who brought the flame into the Bislet Stadium was Eigil Nansen, grandson of the renowned Polar explorer Fridtjof Nansen. The oath was taken by ski jumper Torbjörn Falkanger. All entrants from Commonwealth countries wore black armbands as the opening day coincided with the funeral of Britain's King George VI. Since King Haakon and the Crown Prince were therefore in London, the Games were opened by HRH Princess Ragnhild. Back in the Olympic fold were Germany and Japan, and for the first time in the Winter Games the entries included Portugal and New Zealand.

Bad weather conditions meant the women's giant slalom and the 2-man bob being started the day before the opening ceremony. Of the three Alpine events, the giant slalom and downhill races were held some 120km from Oslo, at Norefjell. In the men's giant slalom Stein Eriksen (NOR) became the first ever winner of an Alpine skiing event to come from a Nordic country; this did not happen again until 1980. The star of the Games was Hjalmar Andersen of the host country who won three speed skating gold medals. In winning the ladies figure skating title, Jeanette Altwegg won Britain's first skating gold medal since Madge Syers in 1908. Instead of turning professional, as did most of her predecessors and successors, she went to work at the famed village for orphan children, Pestalozzi in Switzerland. The men's title went to defending champion Dick Button (USA) with some of the most remarkable jumps ever seen in competition. Finishing sixth was Carlo Fassi (ITA), later to coach Olympic champions Peggy Fleming (USA), Dorothy Hamill (USA), John Curry (GBR) and Robin Cousins (GBR).

The basic running abilities required by cross-country skiers were highlighted in the Nordic skiing when the 18km gold medal was won by Hallgeir Brenden (NOR), who went on to win two national steeplechase titles. With him in the silver Norwegian relay team was Martin Stokken, who had placed fourth in the 1948 Olympic 10,000m run in London. By competing again at Helsinki in the summer he became one of the few men to compete in a Winter and Summer Games in the same year. For the first time there was a Nordic ski race for women, dominated by Finland with four of the first five places. Bandy, a distant relative of ice hockey, was played as a demonstration sport and won by Sweden.

The oldest gold medallist at Oslo was Franz Kemser in the German 4-man bob aged 41yr 103 days, and the

Giant slalom champion Andrea Mead Lawrence shares a drink with her husband – and team-mate – David, to celebrate her victory (Allsport)

youngest was slalom winner Andrea Mead Lawrence (USA) aged 19yr 301 days. The youngest male winner was Robert Dickson (CAN) in ice hockey aged 20yr 308 days, while the oldest female champion was Lydia Wideman (FIN) in the 10km cross-country aged 31yr 282 days. The youngest

British gold medallist Jeanette Altwegg (centre) with Erika Krafft (GER, left) and Jacqueline du Bief (FRA) (Allsport)

medallist was skater Tenley Albright (USA) with a silver aged 16yr 217 days. Albert Madörin (SUI) won a bronze in the 4-man bob aged 46yr 342 days.

1952 (Winter) MEDALS TABLE

	G	S	B
Norway	7	3	6
United States	4	6	1
Finland	3	4	2
Germany	3	2	2
Austria	2	4	2
Canada	1	-	1
Italy	1	-	1
Great Britain	1	-	-
Netherlands	-	3	-
Sweden	-	-	4
Switzerland	-	-	2
France	-	-	1
Hungary	-	-	1

1952

XVth Olympic Games – Helsinki, Finland
19 July – 3 August

Attended by representatives of 69 countries, comprising 4925 competitors, of which 518 were women.

One of the greatest Olympian countries, Finland, finally hosted the Games. President Juho Paasikivi formally opened the Games in the smallest city ever to be host, his capital Helsinki having a population of only 367,000. There were two dramatic moments during the ceremony. First, when a so-called 'Angel of Peace', an apparently mentally deranged German girl in a flowing white robe, ran around part of the track. More appropriate to the occasion was the moment when the last relay runner was due and the scoreboard indicated the first letter of his name. The stadium erupted to cheers as 55-year-old Paavo Nurmi, arguably the greatest ever distance runner, ran a lap and lit the flame in the stadium. He then pased the torch to 62-year-old Hannes Kolehmainen, who ascended the stadium tower by lift and lit another flame there.

After 40 years the Russians returned to the Olympics, now in the guise of the Soviet Union. Fears of confrontation between them and the United States team proved unfounded, as the competitors seemed to treat each other quite cordially, if somewhat coolly. Attending the Games for the first time were teams from the Bahamas, the Gold Coast (now Ghana), Guatemala, Dutch Antilles, Hong Kong, Indonesia, Israel, Nigeria, Thailand, Vietnam, and, for the only time ever, the Saar. Because mainland China had been invited, the Nationalist Chinese (Taiwan) had withdrawn. Although they all marched together, there were two Olympic villages; surprisingly the IOC allowed the Soviet bloc to set up their own at Otaniemi, while everybody else was at Kapyla.

The athlete of these Games was the Czech runner Emil Zatopek who won an unprecedented triple of the 5000m, 10,000m and marathon. To crown his achievements his wife Dana, born on the same day as Emil, also won a gold medal in the javelin within an hour of his 5000m victory. The outstanding female track athlete was Australia's Marjorie Jackson, who set world records winning the 100m and 200m but dropped the baton when certain to

The phenomenal Emil Zatopek leads from Chris Chataway (GBR) in their 5000m heat (Popperfoto)

win a third gold in the sprint relay. Incidentally she retrieved the baton and finished in fifth place. In the winning American team was Barbara Pearl Jones who became the youngest ever track and field gold medallist aged 15yr 123 days. However, the youngest gold medallist at Helsinki was French cox Bernard Malivoire at 14yr 94 days in the pairs event. Once again small nations did well, with Jamaican runners invincible over 400m and Josy Barthel causing the band some problems as they tried to find the anthem of his native Luxembourg when he scored an upset win in the 1500m.

The 1948 100m sprint champion Harrison Dillard (USA) was here back to his first love, winning the 110m hurdles and taking his fourth gold medal in the sprint relay. His team-mate Horace Ashenfelter gained America's first win in a distance run since 1908 when he set an inaugural official world record for the 3000m steeplechase. The Press had great fun with the fact that Ashenfelter, an FBI agent, was here 'followed home' by a Russian. The Soviet Union's first ever Olympic gold medal was won by Nina Romashkova in the women's discus. Highly questionable disqualifications by blatantly biased judges marred the 10,000m track walk, but did not stop the Swiss and Russian second and third place medallists literally running the last 30 metres to the line, outsprinting the judge who vainly tried to reach them to rule them out! The event was dropped from future Games. The winner of the high jump, Walt Davis (USA), was, at 2.04m, probably the tallest competitor ever to win an individual event at the Games.

In the swimming pool the Hungarians won four of the five events for women. Almost matching the Zatopeks were Eva Székely, who won the 200m breaststroke, and her husband Dezsö Gyarmati, a member of the victorious Hungarian water polo team four days later. Much media attention was gained by the 400m freestyle for men when the father of the winner, Jean Boiteux (FRA), jumped into the pool fully clothed to congratulate his son. In diving, tiny (1.56m tall) Dr Sammy Lee, an American of Korean origin, became the first man to successfully defend a diving title, in this case the highboard. He later coached the next man to achieve the feat, Bob Webster in 1960 and 1964.

The gymnastics competitions were dominated by the Soviet teams, led by Viktor Chukarin with four golds and two silvers, and his female counterpart Maria Gorokhovskaya with two golds and five silvers. The Finnish veteran Dr Heikki Savolainen, who had taken the oath at the opening ceremony, gained a team bronze, the fifth consecutive Games at which he had won a medal, just two months short of his 45th birthday. Other veterans did well in 1952. Ilona Elek (HUN) added a silver to her two fencing golds at the age of 45yr 71 days. In the dressage André Jousseaume (FRA) won an individual bronze medal two days after his 58th birthday, and 20 years after his gold medal at Los Angeles. In all he placed in the first five positions in five Games.

Another great sportsman, Károly Takács (HUN), won the rapid-fire pistol for the second time. Before the war he had won the European title as a right-handed shooter, but in 1938 he lost his right hand when a grenade exploded while he was holding it. He painstakingly taught himself to shoot with his left and won two Olympic titles. On a less uplifting note there was the disqualification of Ingemar Johannson (SWE) in the heavyweight boxing final for 'not trying'. His silver medal was withheld for 14 years. In 1959 he won the world professional title from the 1952 Olympic middleweight champion Floyd Patterson (USA).

The oldest gold medallist at these Games was Everard Endt (USA) in the 6m yachting aged 59yr 112 days. Another yachtsman, Ernst Westerlund (FIN), was the oldest medallist, 19 days older than Endt. The youngest male and female champions were Bernard Malivoire and Barbara Pearl Jones (see above). The oldest female winner was Sylvi Saimo (FIN) in the 500m kayak event aged 37yr 260 days. At the end of the Games a record 43 countries had won medals in Helsinki, and it was announced that

Avery Brundage (USA) had taken over the Presidency of the IOC from the retiring Sigfrid Edström.

1952 (Summer) MEDALS TABLE

	G	S	B
United States	40	19	17
Soviet Union	22	30	19
Hungary	16	10	16
Sweden	12	13	10
Italy	8	9	4
Czechoslovakia	7	3	3
France	6	6	6
Finland	6	3	13
Australia	6	2	3
Norway	3	2	-
Switzerland	2	6	6
South Africa	2	4	4
Jamaica	2	3	-
Belgium	2	2	-
Denmark	2	1	3
Turkey	2	-	1
Japan	1	6	2
Great Britain	1	2	8
Argentina	1	2	2
Poland	1	2	1
Canada	1	2	-
Yugoslavia	1	2	-
Romania	1	1	2
Brazil	1	-	2
New Zealand	1	-	2
India	1	-	-
Luxembourg	1	-	-
Germany	-	7	17
Netherlands	-	5	-
Iran	-	3	4
Chile	-	2	-
Austria	-	1	1
Lebanon	-	1	1
Ireland	-	1	-
Mexico	-	1	-
Spain	-	1	-
Korea	-	-	2
Trinidad	-	-	2
Uruguay	-	-	2
Bulgaria	-	-	1
Egypt	-	-	1
Portugal	-	-	1
Venezuela	-	-	1

1956

VIIth Winter Games – Cortina d'Ampezzo, Italy

26 January – 5 February

Attended by representatives of 32 countries, comprising 820 competitors, of which 132 were women.

Most of the money spent on these Games came from the Italian soccer Pools, but despite excellent facilities there were still problems with the weather. Once again snow needed to be 'imported' for some venues. The President of Italy, Giovanni Granchi, formally opened the Games. Giuliana Chenal-Minuzzo, who won the 1952 bronze medal in downhill skiing, became the first woman in Olympic history to pronounce the oath on behalf of all competitors. The last runner in the torch relay, speed skater Guido Caroli, fell as he completed a circuit of the arena but happily the flame did not go out. The entry of the Soviet Union provided the first Russian competitors in Olympic 'Winter' events since 1908. These were the first Winter Games to be televised, which undoubtedly resulted in smaller numbers of spectators than previously.

Lamberto Dalla Costa and Giacomo Conti in Italy's number one bob clocked the fastest times in each of the four runs at Cortina (Popperfoto)

Most attention was gained by the Austrian plumber Toni Sailer who gained a grand slam of all three Alpine titles, downhill, slalom and giant slalom, winning in treacherous conditions by outstanding margins of 3.5, 4.0

and 6.2sec respectively. Second in the slalom was Asia's first Winter medallist, Chiharu Igaya (JPN), an American college student, who had to wait anxiously while the jury investigated an unsubstantiated claim by Sweden and the United States that he had missed a gate. Madeleine Berthod (SUI) won the women's downhill by a record margin of 4.7sec which still stands.

The honour of most medals won at Cortina went to Sixten Jernberg (SWE) with one gold, two silvers and a bronze in Nordic skiing. Hallgeir Brenden (NOR) successfully defended his 1952 title, the distance now reduced from 18km to 15km. Using a new style, the Finns dominated the ski jumping and the Norwegians, who had won 15 of the 18 medals available in the sport since 1924, failed to place in the first six. Though Germany competed as a single team, the jumping bronze, won by Harry Glass, is claimed by the GDR as its first Olympic medal. The speed skating surface on Lake Misurina, at an altitude of 1755m, was considered to be the fastest ever, and witnessed a wholesale attack on the record book. The winner of the 500m title, Yevgeniy Grishin (URS), had been a member of the Soviet cycling team in Helsinki. In figure skating, Hayes (gold) and David (bronze) Jenkins were the first brothers to win medals in the same skating event. Their team-mate, ladies champion Tenley Albright, had been a victim of polio as a child.

A member of the winning Swiss 4-man bob, Franz Kapus, at 46yr 298 days was the oldest gold medallist at Cortina. The youngest champion was Elisabeth Schwarz (AUT) in pairs skating aged 19yr 260 days. The youngest male winner was Toni Sailer (AUT) in the giant slalom aged 20yr 73 days, and the oldest female champion was Siiri Rantanen (FIN) in the cross-country relay aged 31yr 49 days. The youngest medallist was skater Ingrid Wendl (AUT) with a bronze aged 15yr 260 days, and the youngest male medallist was speed skater Alv Gjestvang (NOR) at 18yr 137 days. The Soviet competitors won a total of 16 medals to head the unofficial medals table – a position they were rarely to concede in future Winter Games.

1956 (Winter) MEDALS TABLE

	G	S	B
Soviet Union	7	3	6
Austria	4	3	4
Finland	3	3	1
Switzerland	3	2	1
Sweden	2	4	4
United States	2	3	2
Norway	2	1	1
Italy	1	2	-
Germany	1	-	1
Canada	-	1	2
Japan	-	1	-
Hungary	-	-	1
Poland	-	-	1

The Olympic flag paraded in the Stockholm stadium for the 'Equestrian Games' of 1956 (Allsport)

1956

XVIth Summer Games –
(a) Stockholm, Sweden (10 – 17 June)
(b) Melbourne, Australia (22 November – 8 December)

Attended by (a) representatives of 29 countries, comprising 158 competitors, of which 13 were women; (b) representatives of 67 countries, comprising 3184 competitors, of which 371 were women.

In 1949 the IOC had decided on Melbourne by only one vote, and they were disquieted, to say the least, by first the Australians' apparent tardiness in completing the facilities, and second by their inability to hold the equestrian events because of their stringent animal quarantine laws. Thus for the first and only time, contrary to the Olympic Charter, a sport was detached from the main Games and held elsewhere, in Stockholm. Except for the cross-country section of the three-day event, the venue was the 1912 Olympic Stadium. The host country won three of the six titles, but there were strong accusations of chauvinism by the judges in the dressage competition, and the cross-country was thought to be too dangerous in the existing wet conditions.

The Games proper, the first ever celebration in the Southern Hemisphere, opened in Melbourne under a cloud of international ill-will occasioned by the Soviet invasion of Hungary and the Franco-British intervention in the Suez Canal dispute between Israel and Egypt. The Netherlands, Spain and Switzerland withdrew because of the former, and Egypt and Lebanon because of the latter. This time mainland China withdrew because of the presence of Taiwan. Perhaps surprisingly the Hungarians did compete, and with good effect. West and East Germany entered a combined team, and continued to do so until after 1964. In addition to Taiwan, Olympic debuts were made by teams from Ethiopia, Fiji, Kenya, Liberia, Uganda, Malaya and North Borneo (the two latter now combined as Malaysia). Cambodia's appearance in the Stockholm events was its first Olympic participation. HRH The Duke of Edinburgh opened the Games at the Melbourne Cricket Ground, the main venue. The final torch bearer was a 19-year-old Australian miler, Ron Clarke, destined to be one of the world's greatest runners.

The distance runs in Melbourne were dominated by the Soviet sailor Vladimir Kuts, with record-breaking victories at 5000m and 10,000m. Ireland won its first gold medal since 1932 when Ronnie Delaney took the 1500m with an exceptionally fast last 300 metres. In the sprints both Bobby-Joe Morrow (USA) and Betty Cuthbert (AUS) gained three gold medals, including the relays. Teamed with Cuthbert in the 4 x 100m was Shirley de la Hunty (née Strickland), who ended her three-Games career with an unbeaten total of seven medals (three gold, one silver, three bronze). A photo-finish picture, which was not unearthed for many years after the event, indicates that she was also placed third, not fourth, in the 200m in 1948 – but she made no official claim and the original result stands.

After placing second to Emil Zatopek in three Olympic races since 1948, Frenchman Alain Mimoun finally beat him into sixth place in taking the marathon – the oldest man to do so at only a month short of his 36th birthday. The 50km walk was won by Norman Read, representing his adopted country New Zealand. As a former English junior mile walk champion Read had watched the 1952 Games as a spectator (sitting next to the author). Another English-born competitor, Murray Rose (AUS), became the first male swimmer to win two individual freestyle events since 1924 and also won a third gold medal in the relay. Pat McCormick (USA) achieved a unique double 'double', retaining both her diving titles from Helsinki. Boxing too had its record-breaker when László Papp did his bit to raise Hungarian spirits by gaining an unprecedented third gold medal at boxing. Not surprisingly, bad feeling erupted in the water polo semi-final between Hungary and the Soviet Union. By a nice touch of irony the referee was from the perennially neutral Sweden, and with Hungary leading 4-0 he ended the game as it had degenerated into a 'boxing match under water'. However, by beating Yugoslavia in the soccer final on the last day, 8 December, the Soviet Union went into history as the winners of the latest gold medal ever won in an Olympic year.

John Kelly Jr, the son of the 1920 gold medallist, won a bronze in the single sculls where Vyacheslav Ivanov (URS) gained the first of his record three consecutive titles. At the shooting range Gerard Ouellette (CAN) won the prone small bore rifle competition with a world record 'maximum' of 600, only to have the record, but not the gold medal, disallowed because the range was found to be 1.5m short of the international distance of 50m. The oldest gold medallist in Melbourne was Henri St Cyr (SWE) in dressage aged 54yr 93 days, while the youngest was swimmer Sandra Morgan (AUS) in the 4 x 100m freestyle relay aged 14yr 183 days. The youngest male winner was Murray Rose (AUS) aged 17yr 332 days, while the oldest female champion was Hungarian gymnast Agnes Keleti at 35yr 331 days. Although not even a medallist, Gunhild Larking,

a beautiful Swedish high jumper, undoubtedly had more photographs taken of her than any of the more successful competitors. A member of the combined Germany team, Wolfgang Behrendt, was the GDR's first gold medallist taking the boxing bantamweight title.

At the closing ceremony, for the first time the athletes entered en masse, signifying the friendship of the Games. The idea for this had come from an Australian-born Chinese boy, John Wing, in a letter to the chairman of the organizing committee, the Hon W S Kent Hughes. A happy postscript to these Games occurred in Prague in March 1957 when the American hammer winner Harold Connolly married Olga Fikotova, the Czech Olympic discus champion. The best man at this 'Olympic' wedding was, appropriately, Emil Zatopek.

1956 (Summer) MEDALS TABLE

	G	S	B
Soviet Union	37	29	32
United States	32	25	17
Australia	13	8	14
Hungary	9	10	7
Italy	8	8	9
Sweden	8	5	6
Germany	6	13	7
Great Britain	6	7	11
Romania	5	3	5
Japan	4	10	5
France	4	4	6
Turkey	3	2	2
Finland	3	1	11
Iran	2	2	1
Canada	2	1	3
New Zealand	2	-	-
Poland	1	4	4
Czechoslovakia	1	4	1
Bulgaria	1	3	1
Denmark	1	2	1
Ireland	1	1	3
Norway	1	-	2
Mexico	1	-	1
Brazil	1	-	-
India	1	-	-
Yugoslavia	-	3	-
Chile	-	2	2
Belgium	-	2	-
Argentina	-	1	1
Korea	-	1	1
Iceland	-	1	-
Pakistan	-	1	-
South Africa	-	-	4
Austria	-	-	2
Bahamas	-	-	1
Greece	-	-	1
Switzerland	-	-	1
Uruguay	-	-	1

American diver Pat McCormick achieved a unique double 'double' with both platform and springboard titles in 1952 and 1956 (Allsport)

1960

VIIIth Winter Games – Squaw Valley, USA
18 – 28 February

Attended by representatives of 30 countries, comprising 665 competitors, of which 143 were women.

When the IOC voted narrowly, 32-30, to give the Games to Squaw Valley instead of Innsbruck, virtually nothing existed at the site. Thanks to the efforts of Alexander Cushing, who owned most of the area, it became the first purpose-built Winter Games venue. Despite initial delays, everything was ready for the the official opening, under the direction of Walt Disney. The formal opening was by Richard Nixon, then Vice-President of the United States. The last relay runner was Ken Henry, the 500m speed skating champion of 1952, and the oath was taken by figure skater Carol Heiss, who went on to win the ladies title.

Practising for Squaw Valley, four-time world champion Carol Heiss. She took the gold medal (Popperfoto)

There were a number of protests and problems. Bobsledding was dropped as the organizers would not accept the cost of building a run for what they considered would be a small entry. Artificial obstacles were built into the downhill runs to make them more difficult, and concern was expressed over the altitude (over 1900m) at which the Nordic skiing events were held. East and West Germany competed as one entity, with agreement reached on the popular theme from Beethoven's Ninth Symphony being played for any victory ceremonies, instead of their respective national anthems. A team from South Africa appeared, for the first time in the Winter Games, only to be banned thereafter. The biathlon and speed skating for women made Olympics debuts. The biathlon was the successor to the military patrol event which had been a demonstration event on four previous occasions.

The speed skating times in general were excellent, with Knut Johannesen (NOR) beating the 10,000m world record by 46.0sec, the greatest margin achieved this century. Yevgeniy Grishin (URS) equalled his own world mark to become the first man to successfully defend the 500m title. Helga Haase (GER) was the first ever women's Olympic champion in speed skating when she won the 500m. In figure skating David Jenkins kept the men's title in the family, and his brother Hayes, who had won in 1956, made the family even more Olympian by marrying Squaw Valley's lady champion Carol Heiss later.

There was a first in Nordic skiing when Georg Thoma, a German postman from the Black Forest who was often forced to deliver mail on skis in bad weather, achieved the first victory by a non-Scandinavian in the sport. The winner of the inaugural biathlon, Klas Lestander (SWE), was only 15th in the cross-country segment of the contest but scored a maximum possible 20 in the shooting. The Soviet Union's women dominated their 10,000m race, taking the first four places, but they lost the relay, a virtual certainty, when their first girl fell and broke a ski. A protest was made against the first Swedish girl, who was accused of deliberate fouling, but it was not upheld.

In Alpine skiing metallic skis were used in the Games for the first time. The medals were more widespread than usual, with no skier winning more than one event and only Penny Pitou (USA) winning more than one medal, with two silvers. The outstanding competitor was Anne Heggtveit (CAN) who won the women's slalom by a margin of 3.3sec. only ever bettered by the 1936 combination winner, Christl Cranz (GER).

The oldest gold medallist was Veikko Hakulinen (FIN) in the Nordic relay aged 35yr 52 days, and the youngest was Heidi Biebl (GER), the downhill champion, 3 days past her 19th birthday. The youngest male champion was American ice hockey player Thomas Williams aged 19yr 317 days. The oldest female gold medallist was Sonja Ruthström (SWE) in the Nordic relay aged 29yr 94 days. The youngest medallist was skier Traudl Hecher (AUT) with a downhill bronze aged 16yr 145 days.

1960 (Winter) MEDALS TABLE

	G	S	B
Soviet Union	7	5	9
Germany	4	3	1
United States	3	4	3
Norway	3	3	-
Sweden	3	2	2

Finland	2	3	3
Canada	2	1	1
Switzerland	2	-	-
Austria	1	2	3
France	1	-	2
Netherlands	-	1	1
Poland	-	1	1
Czechoslovakia	-	1	-
Italy	-	-	1

1960

XVIIth Olympic Games – Rome, Italy
25 August – 11 September

Attended by representatives of 83 countries, comprising 5346 competitors, of which 610 were women.

After its near miss in 1908, the Games finally went to Rome, the home city of the Emperor Theodosius who had ended the Ancient Games 1567 years before. A number of old Roman sites were utilized as well as a brand-new 100,000 capacity stadium. The Baths of Caracalla housed the gymnastics and the Basilica di Massenzio had the wrestling competitions. The marathon began at the Capitol Hill and finished on the Appian Way, near the Arch of Constantine. It was the first time that an Olympic marathon had not started or finished in the main Olympic stadium. Yachting was held in the bay of Naples under the shadow of Mt Vesuvius. The Games were opened by the President of Italy, Giovanni Gronchi, before 100,000 spectators. The oath was taken by the 1948 discus champion Adolfo Consolini. Morocco, Tunisia, Sudan and San Marino made their debuts. Nationalist China protested, but competed, when they were told by the IOC to appear under the name of Taiwan and not China. These Games were the first to have worldwide television coverage.

The extreme heat undoubtedly caused upsets but did nothing to hinder the successes of the Australasians in the middle-distance running events. Peter Snell (NZL) won the 800m, Herb Elliott (AUS) won the 1500m by a record margin of 2.8sec in world record time, and Murray Halberg (NZL), handicapped by a withered arm, won the 5000m. An unknown runner, Abebe Bikila, won the marathon barefoot and signalled the entry of Ethiopia onto the world distance running scene. The team from Taiwan was cheered up somewhat when their decathlete Chuan-Kwang Yang had a tremendous battle with Rafer Johnson (USA), a team-mate at the University of Southern California, and only lost the gold medal narrowly. The stadium was captivated by sprinter Wilma Rudolph (USA) who won three gold medals – she was one of 22 children and had suffered from polio as a child. Sisters Irina and Tamara Press (URS) won the 80m hurdles and shot respectively, while a countrywoman, Ludmila Shevtsova, won the first 800m event for women since 1928.

In the swimming pool the only one of the fifteen events not won by either Australia or the United States went to Anita Lonsbrough (GBR). The outstanding swimmer was America's Christine von Saltza, a descendant of Prussian/Swedish nobility, with three golds and a silver. The standard was very high, with Olympic records broken in every event. An unfortunate incident occurred in the men's 100m freestyle when Lance Larson (USA) was timed at one-tenth faster than John Devitt (AUS) but was placed second to him despite slow-motion film indicating that the American was first. In future Games full electronic timing was used. Only the second Royal gold medal in Olympic history was won by Crown Prince Constantine (later King Constantine II of Greece) in the Dragon class yachting. It is reported that he received the traditional winner's ducking, being pushed into the water by his mother, Queen Frederika. In the Flying Dutchman class Peder Lunde Jr (NOR) became the third generation of his family to win a medal, equalling his grandfather's gold of 1924, but going one better than his mother and father in 1952. Paul Elvström (DEN) won his fourth consecutive individual gold medal in dinghy sailing, the first sportsman from any sport to achieve this distinction. The canoeing, on Lake Albano, had a particularly distinguished spectator as Pope John apparently watched some of the competitions from his summer palace. In boxing the light-welter silver medallist Clement 'Ike' Quartey (GHA) was the first black African to win an Olympic medal.

The most medals won in Rome were the seven (4 gold, 2 silver, 1 bronze) gained by gymnast Boris Shakhlin (URS). Aladár Gerevich (HUN), at 50yr 178 days the oldest champion in Rome, won his sixth team sabre gold medal in as many Games – a feat unsurpassed by any other Olympic competitor. In the foil and épée events Edoardo Mangiarotti

Wilma Rudolph overcame childhood polio to become the fastest sprinter in the world and win three gold medals at Rome in 1960 (Popperfoto)

Soviet gymnast Boris Shakhlin won seven medals in Rome. Overall, in three Games, he totalled 13 medals including seven golds

(ITA) brought his total of fencing medals to a record 13 (6 gold, 5 silver, 2 bronze) in five Games, 1936-60. The light-heavyweight boxing title went to Cassius Clay (USA), who became a professional after the Games and later, as Muhammad Ali, amassed the greatest amount ever earned by a sportsman, $68 million. In soccer Yugoslavia won the gold medal after three consecutive runner-up placings. The first loss by India in Olympic hockey since they entered the competition in 1928 occurred when Pakistan beat them 1-0 in the final.

The youngest gold medallist was Klaus Zerta, cox of the German coxed pairs, aged 13yr 283 days, and the youngest female champion was swimmer Carolyn Wood (USA) in the freestyle relay aged 14yr 260 days. The oldest female winner was discus champion Nina Ponomaryeva (URS) at 31yr 131 days. The oldest medallist was yachtsman Manfred Metzger (SUI) at 55yr 104 days, while the oldest female medallist was Italian fencer Welleda Cesari at 40yr 201 days. A tragic note was struck by the collapse and death of cyclist Knut Jensen (DEN), originally diagnosed as being due to the excessive heat, but later revealed as the result of a drug overdose. At the end of the Games, a then record 44 countries had shared in the medals.

1960 (Summer) MEDALS TABLE

	G	S	B
Soviet Union	43	29	31
United States	34	21	16
Italy	13	10	13
Germany	12	19	11
Australia	8	8	6
Turkey	7	2	-
Hungary	6	8	7
Japan	4	7	7
Poland	4	6	11
Czechoslovakia	3	2	3
Romania	3	1	6
Great Britain	2	6	12
Denmark	2	3	1
New Zealand	2	-	1
Bulgaria	1	3	3
Sweden	1	2	3
Finland	1	1	3
Austria	1	1	-
Yugoslavia	1	1	-
Pakistan	1	-	1
Ethiopia	1	-	-
Greece	1	-	-
Norway	1	-	-
Switzerland	-	3	3
France	-	2	3
Belgium	-	2	2
Iran	-	1	3
Netherlands	-	1	2
South Africa	-	1	2
Argentina	-	1	1
Egypt (UAR)	-	1	1
Canada	-	1	-
Ghana	-	1	-
India	-	1	-
Morocco	-	1	-
Portugal	-	1	-
Singapore	-	1	-
Taiwan (Taipei)	-	1	-
Brazil	-	-	2
Jamaica*	-	-	2
Barbados*	-	-	1
Iraq	-	-	1
Mexico	-	-	1
Spain	-	-	1
Venezuela	-	-	1

* Double-counted, part of Antilles team

1964

IXth Winter Games – Innsbruck, Austria
29 January – 9 February

Attended by representatives of 36 countries, comprising 1091 competitors, of which 200 were women.

Awarded to Innsbruck in 1959, these Games were the most successful yet, with over one million spectators attending a now record 34 events. Among them were lugeing and a second ski jump. However, weather again was a problem, and snow had to be manhandled to some venues by the

Austrian Army. During practice before the Games began there were two tragic deaths, of a British tobogganist and an Australian skier. The official opening by the Austrian President, Dr Adolf Schärf, took place at the Bergisel ski jump in front of 60,000 people. The last relay runner who lit the flame was a skier, Joseph Rieder, and the oath was taken by a bobsledder, Paul Aste. Mongolia and India competed for the first time, while Korea was split into North and South teams. South Africa was now banned from the Olympics. An innovation was the use of computers officially to aid judging as well as provide electronic timing.

Lydia Skoblikova won an all-time speed skating record of six Olympic titles in 1960 and 1964 (Popperfoto)

The Games were dominated by the Soviet Union, and for the first and only time since, Switzerland failed to gain a single medal. Lydia Skoblikova (URS), a teacher from Siberia, won all four women's speed skating events to give her a total of six gold medals in two Games, a record for the sport. The Soviet husband and wife skating pair, Ludmila Belousova and Oleg Protopopov, brought a new concept, classical ballet, to the sport. The silver medal went for the second consecutive occasion to Marika Kilius and Hansjürgen Bäumler (GER), but two years later they were disqualified owing to professional activities which had then come to light. The women's individual skating title went to Sjouke Dijkstra, Holland's first ever Winter Games gold medal.

The first sisters to win gold medals at the same Games were Marielle and Christine Goitschel (FRA) who swapped first and second places in the Alpine slalom events. The re-introduced bobsleigh events were won, for the first time, by

countries which did not possess bob runs of their own. The victory by Tony Nash and Robin Dixon (GBR) in the 2-man bob was the first by a 'lowland' country, and owed much to a replacement bolt supplied by an Italian adversary, Eugenio Monti. He was later awarded the Pierre de Coubertin Fair Play Trophy for this action. Klaudia Boyarskikh (URS) won three gold medals in Nordic skiing, while Sixten Jernberg (SWE) brought his total to a record nine medals in three Games. A demonstration of German curling was also held.

The oldest gold medallist was Jernberg, winning his fourth gold medal two days after his 35th birthday. The youngest was Manfred Stengl (AUT) aged 17yr 310 days in the 2-man luge, with Marielle Goitschel (FRA) the youngest female winner in the giant slalom aged 18yr 128 days. The oldest female champion was Alevtina Koltschina (URS) in the Nordic relay at 33yr 88 days. Scott Allen (USA) was the youngest medallist with his bronze in the men's figure skating just two days short of his 15th birthday, while the oldest was Eugenio Monti (ITA) aged 36yr 15 days.

1964 (Winter) MEDALS TABLE

	G	S	B
Soviet Union	11	8	6
Austria	4	5	3
Norway	3	6	6
Finland	3	4	3
France	3	4	-
Sweden	3	3	1
Germany	3	2	3
United States	1	2	4
Canada	1	1	1
Netherlands	1	1	-
Great Britain	1	-	-
Italy	-	1	3
North Korea (PRK)	-	1	-
Czechoslovakia	-	-	1

1964

XVIIIth Olympic Games – Tokyo, Japan
10 – 24 October

Attended by representatives of 93 countries, comprising 5140 competitors, of which 683 were women.

Asia's first Games witnessed large crowds and a tremendous assault on the record books. Vast sums, estimated to be as much as $3 billion, had been spent not only on stadia but also on transport facilities. Teams from 14 countries made their first appearance at the Games, but South Africa no longer received an invitation. Also missing were Indonesia and North Korea whose athletes, having competed in the previous year's unsanctioned GANEFO Games (Games of the New Emergent Forces), were banned. Emperor Hirohito performed the formal opening, and the flame was brought into the stadium by a young runner who had been born near Hiroshima on the day the atom bomb was dropped there in 1945. The Olympic flag was raised to the top of a flagpole which measured 15.21m, the distance reached in the triple jump by Mikio Oda in 1928 when he won Japan's first Olympic gold medal.

The growth of the Games can be highlighted by distance runner Ron Clarke's remark after failing to gain the gold medal over 10,000m. Having 'dropped' all the known opposition, he looked over his shoulder and saw 'an Ethiopian, a North African Arab and an American Indian'. The last of these, Billy Mills, a part-Sioux Indian Marine officer, was America's first ever winner at the distance. In the marathon Bikila (ETH), only six weeks after having his appendix removed – and this time wearing shoes – became the first man to retain the title, and Peter Snell (NZL) won the rare 800/1500m double. The winner of the 100m, Bob Hayes, ran a phenomenal last leg in the 4 x 100m relay to regain the title that the USA had lost in Rome for the first time in 40 years. There is a story told that one of the beaten teams decried the US team to the effect that all they had was Hayes. This was met by the now famous rejoinder, 'Man, that's all we needed.' Britain won its first ever gold in women's athletics when Mary Rand took the long jump, and her room-mate Ann Packer added the 800m gold for good measure.

Britain's Ann Packer causes a surprise, winning the 1964 800 metres, her second-string event, in world record time (Popperfoto)

At the much admired pool, Australia and the United States won all the titles bar one. That was the women's 200m breaststroke, the event which had also prevented a clean sweep by the two swimming superpowers in Rome. Here it was won by Galina Prozumenshchikova (later Stepanova), the Soviet Union's first ever swimming gold medallist – she won a further two silver and two bronze at the next two Games. Don Schollander (USA) became the first swimmer to win four golds in a single Games. Close behind him came Sharon Stouder (USA) with three golds and a silver in the women's events. Australia's Dawn Fraser, just past her 27th birthday, won her third consecutive 100m title, a unique achievement in swimming, and added a relay silver to take her total haul to eight medals, a record for a female swimmer. Another competitor to complete a unique triple was Soviet rower Vyacheslav Ivanov by winning the single sculls once again. In the eights, the cox of the winning American crew, 46-year-old Robert Zimonyi, had been cox of the third-placed Hungarian pairs in 1948. In water polo the Hungarian veteran Dezsö Gyarmati won his third gold medal, his fifth medal in as many Games.

The most medals were won by gymnast Larissa Latynina (URS) with two golds, two silvers and two bronzes. Her team-mate Boris Shakhlin brought his total of golds since 1956 to seven, of which a record six were in individual events. In weightlifting Norbert Schemansky (USA) won a bronze to add to his previous gold, silver and bronze since 1948, giving him a record for his sport of four medals. Wrestler Imre Polyák (HUN) finally won gold in his fourth Games after an unprecedented three silvers. Of the two new sports – the other was volleyball – judo had been included at the express wish of the host country. It was considered to be a Japanese monopoly, and the whole country suffered a terrible shock when the Open class title went to the giant (1.98m) Dutchman Anton Geesink. Leading the United States basketball team to its sixth consecutive victory was Bill Bradley, later to become a member of the US Senate.

The oldest gold medallist in Tokyo was Australian 5.5m yachtsman William Northam aged 59yr 23 days, and the youngest was swimmer 'Pokey' Watson (USA) aged 14yr 96 days in the freestyle relay. The oldest female winner was Katalin Juhász-Nagy (HUN), a member of the foil team at 31yr 328 days, while the youngest male champion was swimmer Richard Roth (USA) in the 400m medley 18 days past his 17th birthday. Team-mate 1500m freestyler John Nelson was the youngest male medallist at 16yr 131 days.

1964 (Summer) MEDALS TABLE

	G	S	B
United States	36	26	28
Soviet Union	30	31	35
Japan	16	5	8
Germany	10	22	18
Italy	10	10	7
Hungary	10	7	5
Poland	7	6	10
Australia	6	2	10
Czechoslovakia	5	6	3
Great Britain	4	12	2
Bulgaria	3	5	2
Finland	3	-	2
New Zealand	3	-	2
Romania	2	4	6
Netherlands	2	4	4
Turkey	2	3	1
Sweden	2	2	4
Denmark	2	1	3
Yugoslavia	2	1	2
Belgium	2	-	1
France	1	8	6
Canada	1	2	1
Switzerland	1	2	1
Bahamas	1	-	-
Ethiopia	1	-	-
India	1	-	-
Korea	-	2	1
Trinidad	-	1	2
Tunisia	-	1	1
Argentina	-	1	-
Cuba	-	1	-
Pakistan	-	1	-
Philippines	-	1	-
Iran	-	-	2
Brazil	-	-	1
Ghana	-	-	1
Ireland	-	-	1
Kenya	-	-	1
Mexico	-	-	1
Nigeria	-	-	1
Uruguay	-	-	1

1968

Xth Winter Games – Grenoble, France
6 – 18 February

Attended by representatives of 37 countries, comprising 1158 competitors, of which 211 were women.

There were complaints that venues at Grenoble were very widespread, with some 40km distant, but the new 12,000 seat indoor ice stadium delighted everyone. For the first time sex tests for female competitors were held. The political split between East and West Germany was finally acknowledged, with separate teams accepted, and Morocco made its debut. The official opening was performed by President Charles de Gaulle, the last relay runner was Alain Calmat, the 1964 skating silver medallist, and the oath was taken by Leo Lacroix, a 1964 skiing silver medal winner. The IOC attempted to control the exploitation of the Games by commercial interests by banning the use of trade names on competitors' equipment. Following the threat of withdrawal by some leading skiers, who relied very heavily on ski company sponsorship, it was finally agreed that they need only remove the equipment before appearing in photographs or on television.

Grenoble hero Jean-Claude Killy (centre) after the giant slalom with runner-up Willy Favre (SUI, right) and bronze medallist Heinrich Messner (AUT) (Popperfoto)

The undoubted star of these Games was Jean-Claude Killy (FRA), who emulated Toni Sailer's 1956 record by winning all three Alpine skiing events. However, in the last of the three, the slalom, Karl Schranz (AUT) claimed that in his second round run he had been distracted by a policeman cutting across the course in front of him. He was allowed another run, which he accomplished in a faster time to become the overall winner. Then it was decided that on his first attempt he had already missed a gate before the policeman incident, and his rerun was disqualified. (He was to be even more unlucky four years later.) The best of the women Alpinists was Canada's Nancy Greene with a gold in the giant slalom and a silver in the slalom. The latter was won by Marielle Goitschel (FRA) to keep the title in the family – her sister had won in 1964.

The most successful Nordic skier was Finnish-born Toini Gustafsson (SWE) with two golds and a silver in the women's events. By winning the 30km race Franco Nones (ITA) became the first ever non-Scandinavian winner in cross-country skiing. Another shock to Scandinavian

Horst Floth (GER, left) and Eugenio Monti (ITA) initially tied for first place in the 2-man bob. The jury finally awarded the gold medal to Monti (Popperfoto)

1968 (Winter) MEDALS TABLE

	G	S	B
Norway	6	6	2
Soviet Union	5	5	3
France	4	3	2
Italy	4	-	-
Austria	3	4	4
Netherlands	3	3	3
FRG	2	2	3
United States	1	5	1
Finland	1	2	2
GDR	1	2	2
Czechoslovakia	1	2	1
Canada	1	1	1
Switzerland	-	2	4
Romania	-	-	1

sensibilities occurred in the two jumps and the combination event, when they only won a single bronze from the nine medals available. Yet another upset was in the women's luge, where the GDR girls, in first, second and fourth places, were disqualified for illegally heating their sled runners. The bob run at Alpe d'Huez, which was badly sited and considered to be very dangerous, was the scene of total triumph for the 'good sport' of Innsbruck four years previously, Eugenio Monti. The Italian, nine times a world champion bobsledder, won both Olympic gold medals. In the 2-man event the total times after four runs for Monti's bob and that of the German bob were equal. The tie was decided in the Italian's favour as he had the fastest single run. Aged 40yr 24 days, Monti was the oldest gold medallist at Grenoble.

The youngest champion was skater Peggy Fleming (USA) aged 19yr 198 days. The youngest male gold medallist was Wolfgang Schwarz, winning Austria's first skating title since 1936, aged 20yr 155 days. Ludmila and Oleg Protopopov (URS) retained their pairs title, with Ludmila the oldest female champion at 32yr 84 days. In 26th place in the men's figure skating was Jan Hoffmann (GDR) aged 12yr 110 days – the youngest ever male competitor in Olympic Winter Games. He won the silver medal twelve years later. The oldest female medallist was Nordic skier Alevtina Koltschina (URS) with a bronze in her fourth Games at 37yr 97 days.

For the only time to date no speed skater gained more than one victory. The women's 500m was reminiscent of the men's events of 1948 and 1964 as three women tied for the silver medal. Making this occasion unique was the fact that all three of them were from the same country, the United States. For the last time, Norway topped the medal table.

1968

XIXth Olympic Games – Mexico City, Mexico
12 – 27 October

Attended by representatives of 112 countries, comprising 5530 competitors, of which 781 were women.

From 1963, when these Games were awarded to Mexico City, there was a gradually increasing furore about the effects of its altitude, 2240m above sea level, on competitors in events which required endurance. Some medical authorities even forecast possible deaths. This extreme view turned out, thankfully, to be overly pessimistic, but many cases of severe exhaustion did occur. When Australian distance runner Ron Clarke developed serious heart problems in 1981, there was speculation that his condition had been aggravated by his efforts at Mexico City in 1968. Certainly standards were low in events which required over three minutes of continuous effort. However, the same conditions contributed to some startling performances in the 'explosive' events. Outstanding was the 8.90m long jump by Bob Beamon (USA) – a performance of 21st-century quality. The world records set in that long jump, and the 4 x 400m relay, lasted for over twenty years.

The thin air was not the only complaint heard prior to these Games. Some felt that the traditional 'mañana' attitude attributed to the Mexicans would result in incomplete facilities. In fact all were ready in good time. There was also the threat of a boycott by Black African nations over the readmission of South Africa earlier in the year. After 40 countries had indicated that they would withhold their teams, the IOC reversed its decision and South Africa was barred again. In August the Soviet Union and its allies invaded Czechoslovakia and international

One of the greatest sporting performances of all time – Bob Beamon jumps a prodigious 8.90m at Mexico City, adding 55cm to the world record (Allsport/Tony Duffy)

tension mounted. A few weeks before the Games began, serious student riots erupted at the University of Mexico which were ruthlessly suppressed, with dozens killed and hundreds injured. In America there was a move to get black athletes to boycott the US team to protest the treatment of blacks in general in the United States. When this appeared to get little support, its organizers implied that some type of demonstration would take place at the Games. Despite all these problems, President Gustavo Diaz Ordaz declared the formal opening to a record number of teams and athletes. Enriqueta Basilio, a hurdler, became the first woman to light the Olympic flame in the stadium.

Because of the conditions, the distance running events were dominated by athletes who lived and trained at high altitude, such as the Kenyans and Ethiopians. Exceptional performances abounded in the sprints and jumps. Beamon's jump was beyond the limits of the measuring device in use at the pit, and a steel tape had to be used. In the triple jump the existing Olympic record was beaten by seven men, and the world mark was improved on five occasions. The high jump winner, Dick Fosbury (USA), used the 'flop' style which he popularized and which was to revolutionize the event. Al Oerter (USA) won his record fourth consecutive discus title, and Wyomia Tyus (USA) was the first sprinter successfully to defend an Olympic 100m crown, other than Archie Hahn (USA) at the 1906 Intercalated Games.

The men's 100m final was unique, up to that time, in that all eight finalists were black. A more heralded expression of Black Power was the demonstration by Tommie Smith and John Carlos (USA) at the 200m victory ceremony. The Americans, who had come first and third respectively, raised black-gloved, clenched fists during the playing of their anthem. For this action they were suspended and expelled from the Olympic village. (Some old-timers noted that their action was no more, nor less, insulting than that of the numerous medallists who had given the Nazi salute in 1936.) The marathon was won for the third consecutive time by an Ethiopian, but on this occasion by Mamo Wolde after two-time champion Abebe Bikila withdrew at 17km. Tragically, Bikila was paralysed in a car accident the following year and died in 1973 at the age of 41.

Most medals were won, as usual, by gymnasts. Although Mikhail Voronin (URS) won seven medals (two gold, four silver, one bronze), the star of the sport was Vera Caslavska (TCH) with four golds and two silvers. Her floor exercises routine, to the music of the 'Mexican Hat Dance', was immensely popular. Soon after her events were over, but still during the Games, she married her countryman Josef Odlozil, the 1964 silver medallist at 1500m. Voronin's wife Sinaida won a gold, a silver and two bronze medals in the Soviet women's gymnastic team.

The outstanding swimmers were Charles Hickcox (USA) with three golds and a silver, and Debbie Meyer (USA) who, uniquely to that date, won three individual events. Six other swimmers won two gold medals each, including an 18-year-old American named Mark Spitz. Mexico's first ever swimming gold medal was won by Felipe Munoz in the 200m breaststroke. He was nicknamed Tibio, which means 'lukewarm' in English. This was no reflection on his determination, but was the result of his father coming from a town named Aguascalientes ('hot waters') and his mother from Rio Frio ('cold river').

Although eliminated in the fencing, Janice Romary (USA) became the first woman to compete in six consecutive Games and because of this also became the first woman to carry the flag for the United States in a Games opening ceremony. The 5.5m class yachting, held at the resort city of Acapulco, produced the unique result of triple gold medal siblings as the Swedish brothers Ulf, Peter and Jorgen Sundelin crewed *Wasa IV* to an easy victory. Behind them, skippering the second-placed Swiss boat *Toucan*, was Louis Noverraz, at 66yr 154 days the oldest medallist at these Games.

The oldest gold medallist was Josef Neckarmann (FRG) in the dressage team aged 56yr 141 days, while the youngest was Günther Tiersch (GDR), cox of the winning eight aged 14yr 172 days. The oldest female champion was Liselott Linsenhoff (FRG), also in the dressage team aged 41yr 58 days, while the youngest female gold medallist was swimmer Susan Pedersen (USA) in the medley relay the day after her 15th birthday. The oldest competitor at Mexico City was Roberto Soundy, a trapshooter from El Salvador aged 68yr 229 days, and the same country had the youngest male competitor in Ruben Guerrero, a medley relay swimmer aged 13yr 351 days. However, the youngest competitor of all was Liana Vicens of Puerto Rico, only 11yr 328 days in the women's 100m breaststroke. The oldest woman was Britain's Lorna Johnstone, who was 13th in the dressage at 66yr 51 days.

For the first time since they had entered the hockey competition in 1928, India failed to reach the final. In soccer, won for a record third time by Hungary, the surprise bronze medallists were Japan. They were the first, and to date only, Asian team to win a soccer medal, and the first non-European team to do so for 40 years.

1968 (Summer) MEDALS TABLE

	G	S	B
United States	45	28	34
Soviet Union	29	32	30
Japan	11	7	7
Hungary	10	10	12
GDR	9	9	7
France	7	3	5
Czechoslovakia	7	2	4
FRG	5	11	10
Australia	5	7	5
Great Britain	5	5	3
Poland	5	2	11
Romania	4	6	5
Italy	3	4	9
Kenya	3	4	2
Mexico	3	3	3
Yugoslavia	3	3	2
Netherlands	3	3	1
Bulgaria	2	4	3
Iran	2	1	2
Sweden	2	1	1
Turkey	2	-	-
Denmark	1	4	3
Canada	1	3	1
Finland	1	2	1
Ethiopia	1	1	-
Norway	1	1	-
New Zealand	1	-	2
Tunisia	1	1	1
Pakistan	1	1	-
Venezuela	1	-	-
Cuba	-	4	-
Austria	-	2	2
Switzerland	-	1	4
Mongolia	-	1	3
Brazil	-	1	2
Belgium	-	1	1
Korea	-	1	1
Uganda	-	1	1
Cameroon	-	1	-
Jamaica	-	1	-
Argentina	-	-	2
Greece	-	-	1
India	-	-	1
Taiwan (Taipei)	-	-	1

1972

XIth Winter Games – Sapporo, Japan
3 – 13 February

Attended by representatives of 35 countries, comprising 1006 competitors, of which 206 were women.

The Games finally came to Sapporo, 32 years after they were first awarded to the city but cancelled due to World War II. It was the most populous city, with one million inhabitants, ever to host the Winter Games. Some $555 million was spent on facilities over a five-year period, not least for the enormous number of media personnel who outnumbered competitors by two to one. Arguments between the IOC and sponsored skiers, which had caused problems in 1968, came to a head and resulted in Austria's star skier Karl Schranz being expelled. Although there was a list of 40 competitors apparently under threat of suspension, only he was banned. This led to an initial threat of withdrawal by the Austrian team, but at Schranz's urging this was averted. Another aspect of the amateur/professional debate was highlighted by Canada's refusal to compete at ice hockey against the state-sponsored players from the Eastern bloc. Their call for 'open' Olympic ice hockey was ignored.

The Games were formally opened by Emperor Hirohito. The flame was delivered by Hideki Takada, a speed skater, and another, Keichi Suzuki, took the oath. Teams from Taiwan and the Philippines competed for the first time. First ever Winter gold medals were won by Poland (ski jumping), Spain (slalom) and the host country (ski jumping). In the latter event, on the 70m hill, Japan had a unique grand slam of all three medals. To take only the second Olympic gold medal won by his country, Spanish skier Francisco Fernandez-Ochoa beat the Italian cousins Gustavo and Rolando Thoeni. The women's slalom was won by Barbara Cochran (USA) by the smallest margin ever in an Olympic Alpine event, 0.02sec. Her sister Marilyn and brother Bob were also in the US team.

Galina Kulakova (URS) won three gold medals in Nordic skiing, and this total was matched in the speed skating by Ard Schenk of Holland. The Dutchman might have had more, but he fell in the 500m event and finished 34th out of 37 competitors. East Germany (GDR) returned to total domination of the luge competitions. The women's event was won by Anna-Maria Müller, one of the three girls who had been disqualified for heating their runners at the previous Games. Austria's Trixie Schuba took the women's figure skating title despite a comparatively poor (7th placed) free skating segment – her compulsory figures were

Irina Rodnina and Alexey Ulanov won the pairs skating at Sapporo but then broke up. Rodnina won twice more with a new partner, later her husband (Popperfoto)

1972

XXth Olympic Games – Munich, FRG
26 August – 10 September

Attended by representatives of 121 countries, comprising 7123 competitors, of which 1058 were women.

Awarded the Games in 1966, Munich built a magnificent complex on the rubble of World War II bombing. Total costs were estimated at $650 million. Just prior to the opening day the IOC expelled Rhodesia under intense pressure from the Black African nations. A number of new electronic devices were used in the conduct of the Games, including a triangulation device to measure distances in the athletics throwing events. Archery and men's handball returned to the Olympic programme, and with additions to other sports there were a total of 195 gold medals available, the Soviet Union taking over a quarter of them. These Olympics became the most widely covered in history with over 4000 representatives of the world's media on hand. When German President Gustav Heinemann opened the Games in a colourful ceremony there was a television audience estimated at an all-time live viewing record of 1000 million. The oath was taken by athlete Heidi Schüller, the first woman ever to do so. An oath for judges was introduced at Munich. The record number of countries taking part included first timers Albania, Dahomey (later Benin), Lesotho, Malawi, Upper Volta (later Burkina Faso), Somalia, Swaziland, Togo and North Korea (South Korea sent a separate team).

The first week was dominated by swimmer Mark Spitz (USA) who smashed all records for a single Games by winning seven gold medals, four individual and three relays – there were world records in each of his events. With his medals from Mexico City he had a total of nine golds, one silver and a bronze. His female equivalent, Shane Gould (AUS), won three golds, a silver and a bronze, swimming in 12 races, itself a record for a female swimmer at the Games. The closest win in Olympic history came in the men's 400m medley when Gunnar Larsson (SWE) was given the decision over Tim McKee (USA) by two-thousandths of a second. This decision led to a change in the rules so that in future times and places would be decided only in hundredths.

Valeriy Borzov (URS) became the first European to win a men's sprint double on the track. In 1994 he became the IOC member for the Ukraine. Ulrike Meyfarth (FRG) equalled the world high jump record to win the gold medal aged 16yr 123 days, the youngest ever individual athletics event champion. In hockey, for the first time since 1920 a team from outside the Indian sub-continent won the title, as Germany defeated Pakistan in the final. However, the outstanding attraction of the first few days was gymnast Olga Korbut (URS) whose gamine qualities stole the show from her more illustrious colleague Ludmilla Tourischeva (who later married sprint champion Borzov). Virtually

excellent and at the time the two segments were scored on a 50-50 basis. Soon after the Games this method was changed in favour of free skating ability. An 'affaire de coeur' involving Alexey Ulanov (URS), who with Irina Rodnina won the skating pairs, and Ludmila Smirnova, his team-mate who placed second with her partner Andrey Suraikin, titillated the skating world. Later they married and competed internationally as a partnership, but never with the success they had attained with their original partners.

The oldest gold medallist was Jean Wicki (SUI) in the 4-man bob aged 38yr 239 days. The youngest was Anne Henning (USA) who won the 500m speed skating title aged 16yr 157 days. The oldest female winner was Christina Baas-Kaiser (NED) with her 3000m speed skating victory at 33yr 268 days, and the youngest male champion was Wojciech Fortuna (POL) who won the 90m ski jump aged 19yr 189 days. The youngest medallist was skater Manuela Gross (GDR), bronze in the pairs aged 15yr 10 days. In all, medals were won by a record 17 countries with 14 of them gaining gold.

1972 (Winter) MEDALS TABLE

	G	S	B
Soviet Union	8	5	3
GDR	4	3	7
Switzerland	4	3	3
Netherlands	4	3	2
United States	3	2	3
FRG	3	1	1
Norway	2	5	5
Italy	2	2	1
Austria	1	2	2
Sweden	1	1	2
Japan	1	1	1
Czechoslovakia	1	-	2
Poland	1	-	-
Spain	1	-	-
Finland	-	4	1
France	-	1	2
Canada	-	1	-

Though not the best gymnast even in her own team, Olga Korbut (URS) had 'star quality' and her performances captivated the spectators at Munich (Allsport)

overnight, with blanket media coverage, Korbut became a 'superstar', although she finished only 7th in the all-around competition.

On the morning of 5 September all the euphoria evaporated when a band of eight Arab terrorists broke into the Israeli team headquarters at 31 Connolly Strasse in the Olympic village. Two Israelis were killed immediately, and nine others held hostage, as German police and the world's press surrounded the area. After lengthy negotiations the terrorists and their hostages were allowed to go to the airport, where an abortive rescue attempt resulted in the murder of all nine Israelis and the death of some of their captors. The following morning the Games were suspended for a memorial service in a packed stadium, but with the agreement of most of the parties involved, including the Israeli officials, competitions were resumed later in the day. The overall feeling seemed to be that the Games should go on, although a number of individuals, notably from Holland, Norway and the Philippines, decided to withdraw. The Israeli team returned home immediately.

The Games continued with the United States suffering a number of misfortunes and reverses. Two prospective American medallists had missed the 100m second round heats due to a misreading, by their coach, of the starting time. The world 1500m record holder, Jim Ryun, was not seeded as his entry performance, a fast mile time, was mistakenly interpreted as a slow 1500m time. Then to add to his misfortune he fell in his heat and was eliminated. A pre-Games banning of the poles used by the American vaulters was probably responsible for ending their 13-Games winning streak. The US gold and silver medallists in the 400m were banned from further competition for a 'Black Power' protest, which meant that the Americans, the

favourites, could not field a 4 x 400m relay team. Since 1920 teams from the USA had always won a medal. In swimming, Rick DeMont was disqualified after winning the 400m freestyle when a dope test proved positive. If the US team officials had notified the IOC beforehand that he had to take a certain drug, containing a prohibited substance, to alleviate an asthma condition, he would have retained his title. Then to cap it all, the American basketball team were controversially defeated by the Soviet Union, ending a remarkable 63 consecutive victories in the Games since 1936. Another incident, with a happier conclusion, occurred when the 800m champion Dave Wottle, in his excitement at the victory ceremony, forgot to remove his lucky cap during the American national anthem. He was very embarrassed and proferred apologies to everyone who would listen.

On the track Kipchoge Keino (KEN) added the 3000m steeplechase title to the 1500m that he had won four years earlier. This made him the first runner since James Lightbody (USA) in 1904 to win Olympic titles at the two distances. Lasse Viren (FIN) won the 5000m/10,000m double, setting a world record in the latter despite falling over early in the race, and America's Frank Shorter won the marathon in the city of his birth. Romanian discus thrower Lia Manoliu competed in her record sixth Games (placing ninth with a performance superior to that which had won her the gold in Mexico City). In the women's pentathlon, silver medallist Heide Rosendahl (FRG) technically held the Olympic and world records for the event for 1.12sec, the difference between her winning time in the last discipline, the 200m, and that of the eventual overall champion, Mary Peters (GBR).

By winning the five-sport modern pentathlon individual title, Hungary's Andras Balczo brought his total medal haul since 1960 to an event record of three golds and two silvers. For the second consecutive Games the three medallists in skeet shooting all achieved the same score, the tie being broken by shooting another 25-bird round. The double cycling gold medallist from 1968, Daniel Morelon (FRA), added a third by retaining the sprint title, and Aleksandr Medved (URS) won his third wrestling title in a row (and his tenth world championship) after a disputed decision over the giant American Chris Taylor. Taylor, reportedly weighing 182kg or more, was the heaviest known man to have competed in the Olympic Games. Among serious doping disqualifications at these Games were those of Bakhaavaa Buidaa, who had won a wrestling silver medal for Mongolia, Jaime Huelamo (ESP), the bronze medallist in the cycling road race, and the Dutch four who had gained third place in the cycling team race.

The oldest gold medallist at Munich was Hans Günter Winkler (FRG) aged 46yr 49 days in the show-jumping team, and the youngest was Deena Deardurff (USA) aged 15yr 118 days in the swimming medley relay. The oldest female champion was Liselott Linsenhoff (FRG) in the dressage at 45yr 13 days, and she was also the first woman to win an individual equestrian event. In that competition

Britain's Lorna Johnstone set a record as the oldest ever female competitor in the Olympics when she reached the last 12 five days past her 70th birthday. A bronze medallist in this event was Maud Van Rosen (SWE), the oldest female medallist at these Games at 46yr 258 days. The youngest male gold medallist at Munich was Uwe Benter (FRG), cox of the winning fours at 16yr 276 days, although it should be noted that the unfortunate Rick DeMont was 143 days younger. The youngest medallist was swimmer Kornelia Ender (GDR) at 13yr 308 days. The tallest competitor at the Games, and the tallest medallist ever in the Olympics, was Tom Burleson (USA), the 2.23m basketball player. One of the runners in the torch relay bringing the Olympic flame to Munich was Edgar Fried, a former general-secretary of the Austrian Olympic Committee, who had been in the original torch relay in 1936 and was the only one to repeat in that of 1972, in his 78th year. At the end of the XXth Games a record 48 countries had won at least one medal.

1972 (Summer) MEDALS TABLE

	G	S	B
Soviet Union	50	27	22
United States	33	31	30
GDR	20	23	23
FRG	13	11	16
Japan	13	8	8
Australia	8	7	2
Poland	7	5	9
Hungary	6	13	16
Bulgaria	6	10	5
Italy	5	3	10
Sweden	4	6	6
Great Britain	4	5	9
Romania	3	6	7
Cuba	3	1	4
Finland	3	1	4
Netherlands	3	1	1
France	2	4	7
Czechoslovakia	2	4	2
Kenya	2	3	4
Yugoslavia	2	1	2
Norway	2	1	1
North Korea (PRK)	1	1	3
New Zealand	1	1	1
Uganda	1	1	-
Denmark	1	-	-
Switzerland	-	3	-
Canada	-	2	3
Iran	-	2	1
Belgium	-	2	-
Greece	-	2	-
Austria	-	1	2
Colombia	-	1	2
Argentina	-	1	-
Korea	-	1	-
Lebanon	-	1	-
Mexico	-	1	-
Mongolia	-	1	-
Pakistan	-	1	-
Tunisia	-	1	-
Turkey	-	1	-
Brazil	-	-	2
Ethiopia	-	-	2
Ghana	-	-	1
India	-	-	1
Jamaica	-	-	1
Niger Republic	-	-	1
Nigeria	-	-	1
Spain	-	-	1

1976

XIIth Winter Games – Innsbruck, Austria
4 – 15 February

Attended by representatives of 37 countries, comprising 1123 competitors, of which 231 were women.

These Games were originally awarded to Denver, Colorado, in 1970, but two years later a State referendum decided against providing the necessary finance. So in February 1973 Innsbruck became the first centre to be awarded the Winter Games for a second time. Most facilities were still available from 1964 and 'only' $44 million was required to refurbish and update. The Games were opened by the President of Austria, Dr Rudolf Kirchschläger, and uniquely two Olympic flames were lit, by Christl Haas, 1964 gold medal skier, and Josef Feistmantl, 1964 gold medal luger. The oath was taken by Werner Delle-Karth, a bobsledder. A total of 1.5 million spectators watched the 37-event schedule. There were 600 million television viewers around the world. Unfortunately an influenza outbreak affected some of the competitors. Two of the smallest states in the world, Andorra and San Marino, made their Winter Games debuts.

The outstanding competitor was Rosi Mittermaier (FRG) who by winning the downhill and slalom races, and taking second place in the giant slalom, set up the best series of performances ever by a female Alpine skier. She failed by a mere 0.13 sec, in the giant slalom, to match the male record of three golds held by Sailer and Killy. In taking the men's downhill on the Patscherkofel course, Austria's Franz Klammer achieved the then highest speed recorded in an Olympic downhill race, 102.828km/h. In Nordic skiing Galina Kulakova (URS) was disqualified from third place in the 5000m event when a banned drug was found present in a nasal spray she was using to combat influenza, but she was allowed to compete in other events and won a gold and another bronze. Her team-mate Raisa Smetanina won two golds and a silver to be the most successful Nordic skier. Particular attention, and some ridicule, was given to Bill Koch (USA) who used his newly developed 'skating' style of

Germany's Rosi Mittermaier wins her second gold medal at Innsbruck, in the slalom. She only just failed to win an historic third title (Popperfoto)

skiing. Rather more attention, and less ridicule, came when he won a silver medal in the 30km race, the only Nordic skiing medal ever by an American. However, the greatest tally of medals at these Games was two gold and two bronze by Tatyana Averina (URS) in speed skating. Preventing a clean sweep of those titles by the Soviet women was Sheila Young (USA) who took the 500m title, and later in the year won her second world cycling championship.

In figure skating the 'jilted' Irina Rodnina (URS) successfully defended her pairs skating title, but this time with a different partner, her new husband Aleksandr Zaitsev. The men's champion John Curry (GBR) brought balletic art to his event just as the Protopopovs had to the pairs in 1964 and 1968. His Italian/American coach, Carlo Fassi, became the first to train both individual champions at a single Games when Dorothy Hamill (USA) won the ladies title. In the new ice dancing event, Soviet couples were placed first, second and fourth. All five luge and bobsled events were won by GDR competitors.

The oldest gold medallist was Meinhard Nehmer (GDR) in the 2-man bob aged 35yr 25 days, and the youngest was skater Hamill aged 19yr 201 days. The youngest male gold medallist was Boris Aleksandrov (URS) in the champion ice hockey team aged 20yr 93 days, while the oldest female champion was Kulakova in the Nordic relay aged 33yr 289 days. Toni Innauer (AUT) won a silver in ski jumping aged 17yr 320 days, while the oldest medallist was Marjatta Kajosmaa (FIN) with a Nordic relay silver nine days after her 38th birthday. The oldest competitor at these Games was 46-year-old Carl Erik Eriksson (SWE) in the bob events, while the youngest was figure skater Yelena Voderzova (URS), only three months away from her 13th birthday.

1976 (Winter) MEDALS TABLE

	G	S	B
Soviet Union	13	6	8
GDR	7	5	7
United States	3	3	4
Norway	3	3	1
Germany (FRG)	2	5	3
Finland	2	4	1
Austria	2	2	2
Switzerland	1	3	1
Netherlands	1	2	3
Italy	1	2	1
Canada	1	1	1
Great Britain	1	-	-
Czechoslovakia	-	1	-
Liechtenstein	-	-	2
Sweden	-	-	2
France	-	-	1

1976

XXIst Olympic Games – Montreal, Canada
17 July – 1 August

Attended by representatives of 92 countries, comprising 6028 competitors, of which 1247 were women.

When the Games were initially awarded to Montreal, mainly due to the efforts of Mayor Jean Drapeau, it was estimated that they would cost $310 million. Because of planning errors, strikes, slowdowns, and, it has been suggested, widespread corruption, the final bill amounted to $1400 million. The stadium alone cost $485 million, and the projected 160m-high tower and suspended roof was never completed. In 1994 it was stated that the total debt remaining to the citizens of Quebec was $304 million. In the wake of the Munich disaster, security arrangements involving 16,000 police and soldiers cost $100 million. Six months before the Games it seemed that the main facilities would not be finished in time, but by the official opening pronounced by Queen Elizabeth II, all that was necessary was ready. The expected record number of entries was well down due to an eleventh-hour boycott by 20 Third World, mainly African, nations, protesting against the inclusion of New Zealand whose rugby union team had visited South Africa. Also withdrawing was Taiwan because Canada refused to recognize them under the title of Republic of China. The withdrawals, mostly only two days prior to the start of competitions, caused some problems with seeding arrangements and particularly affected the quality of boxing and some running events.

Efforts had been made by the IOC to prune the programme, and to this end the 50km walk, tandem

Kornelia Ender (GDR) displays the medals (four golds and a silver) she won in Montreal. She had previously won three silvers in 1972 at Munich (Popperfoto)

six silver and two bronze medals from three Games. In highboard diving, the Austrian-born Italian Klaus Dibiasi, competing in his fourth Games, became the first diver to gain three consecutive gold medals. A member of the Hungarian water polo team which won their country's record sixth victory in the sport was István Szivós, whose father had been in the winning 1952 and 1956 teams.

In the main stadium Lasse Viren, the latest 'Flying Finn', completed his double 'double' by successfully defending his 5000m and 10,000m titles. He attempted to emulate Zatopek's 1952 feat but finished fifth in the marathon. The Cuban Alberto Juantorena, nicknamed 'El Caballo' – The Horse – won a rare 400m/800m double (only America's Paul Pilgrim had previously achieved it, in the 1906 Interim Games). Irena Szewinska (POL), now aged 30, won the 400m in her fourth Games, to equal the record

Alberto Juantorena (CUB) wins the 800 metres at Montreal from Ivo Van Damme (BEL, 103) and Rick Wohlhuter (USA). The Cuban also took the 400m title (Allsport/Tony Duffy)

cycling, slalom canoeing, free rifle and three swimming events had been eliminated. However, with the addition of women's basketball and handball, four canoeing races and seven rowing events, of which six were for women, the total number of gold medals available was now 198 – three more than at Munich. The torch was brought into the stadium by two 15-year olds, a girl and a boy; Sandra Henderson of English descent and Stéphane Prefontaine of French stock, each with a hand on the torch, signifying Canada's joint heritage. In true storybook fashion, the pair were married some years later.

The star of Munich, gymnast Olga Korbut, was at Montreal, but she was overshadowed by a 14-year-old Romanian, Nadia Comaneci, who scored the first-ever maximum 10.00 marks achieved at the Olympics on the first day, and ended the Games with a total of seven maximums, having drawn a world record crowd for gymnastics of 18,000 to the finals of the women's events. Nelli Kim (URS) also scored two maximums. The men's individual champion, Nikolai Andrianov (URS), won the most medals at Montreal with four golds, two silvers and a bronze. In the swimming pool, Kornelia Ender (GDR) and John Naber (USA) each won four golds and a silver, with Ender and her team-mates failing to win only two of the thirteen women's swimming titles. The American men did better, only losing one of their thirteen events as David Wilkie won Britain's first men's swimming gold since 1908. Ender later married her team-mate, backstroke specialist Roland Matthes, giving them a family total of eight gold,

total of seven medals in athletics. The winner of the men's javelin with a new world record, Miklos Nemeth (HUN), was the son of 1948 hammer winner Imre. They remain the only father and son in track and field to win gold medals.

Three sets of brothers did very well in the Montreal rowing events. Frank and Alf Hansen (NOR) won the double sculls, while the Landvoigt twins, Jörg and Bernd (GDR), took the coxless pairs. Another set of GDR twins, Walter and Ullrich Diessner, were in the silver medal coxed four crew. Elsewhere the Flying Dutchman class yachting was won by another set of brothers, Jörg and Eckart Diesch (FRG). In women's fencing Elena Novikova-Belova (URS) won her record fourth gold medal in the team contest, while

Hungary's Ildikó Sagi-Retjö set an all-medal record of seven, comprising two golds, three silvers and two bronzes collected at five Games. America's Margaret Murdock became the first woman to win a shooting medal and was unlucky not to win the gold: initially she was declared the winner of the small-bore rifle (three positions) event, but an error was discovered which gave her a tie with her team-mate, Lanny Bassham. A closer examination of targets then relegated her down a place. Although unplaced, show jumpers Raimondo and Piero D'Inzeo (ITA) set an unprecedented record by competing in their eighth Games, 1948-76. Alwin Schockemöhle (FRG) became only the third rider in the history of the Games to win the jumping title without any faults.

The new Olympic sport of women's basketball produced the tallest known woman ever to compete in the Games. She was Iuliana Semenova (URS) who was unofficially reported to be 2.18m tall and weighed 129kg. Her team won the title, and she is one of tallest, including men, to win an Olympic gold medal. In weightlifting two Bulgarians and a Pole, all medallists, were later disqualified for failing dope tests. A far greater scandal occurred in the modern pentathlon when one of the favourites, Boris Onischenko (URS), was discovered to have tampered with his épée in the fencing segment of the competition. His disqualification eliminated the Soviet team and the team gold went to Great Britain. The revenge basketball match between the USA and USSR never materialized as the Soviets were beaten by Yugoslavia in the semi-finals. The United States regained the title, making their Olympic match record played 70, won 69.

The oldest gold medallist at Montreal was Harry Boldt (FRG) in the winning dressage team aged 46yr 157 days. The youngest was gymnast Nadia Comaneci who won her first gold medal aged 14yr 252 days. The youngest male champion was Brian Goodell (USA), aged 17yr 109 days when he won the 1500m freestyle, while the oldest female gold medallist was Ivanka Khristova (BUL) in the shot aged 34yr 255 days. The youngest medallist was Canadian swimmer Robin Corsiglia in the medley relay aged 13yr 341 days. The oldest medallist was Australian 3-day eventer Bill Roycroft aged 61yr 131 days. One of the youngest competitors ever in the Olympics was Spanish swimmer Antonia Real aged 12yr 310 days. At these Games Canada gained the unhappy distinction of being the only host country of a Summer Olympics not to win a single gold medal.

1976 (Summer) MEDALS TABLE

	G	S	B
Soviet Union	49	41	35
GDR	40	25	25
United States	34	35	25
Germany (FRG)	10	12	17
Japan	9	6	10
Poland	7	6	13
Bulgaria	6	9	7
Cuba	6	4	3
Romania	4	9	14
Hungary	4	5	13
Finland	4	2	-
Sweden	4	1	-
Great Britain	3	5	5
Italy	2	7	4
France	2	3	4
Yugoslavia	2	3	3
Czechoslovakia	2	2	4
New Zealand	2	1	1
Korea	1	1	4
Switzerland	1	1	2
Jamaica	1	1	-
North Korea (PRK)	1	1	-
Norway	1	1	-
Denmark	1	-	2
Mexico	1	-	1
Trinidad	1	-	-
Canada	-	5	6
Belgium	-	3	3
Netherlands	-	2	3
Portugal	-	2	-
Spain	-	2	-
Australia	-	1	4
Iran	-	1	1
Mongolia	-	1	-
Venezuela	-	1	-
Brazil	-	-	2
Austria	-	-	1
Bermuda	-	-	1
Pakistan	-	-	1
Puerto Rico	-	-	1
Thailand	-	-	1

1980

XIIIth Winter Games – Lake Placid, USA
13 -24 February

Attended by representatives of 37 countries, comprising 1072 competitors, of which 233 were women.

Lake Placid had been applying for the Games unsuccessfully since 1962 when they were finally rewarded in 1974. Most of the facilities used in 1932 had to be rebuilt, and new ones constructed, so that the budget for these Games was nearly 80 times the $1.1 million spent in 1932. Some complaints were voiced about the 'village', a building later to be used as a penal institution, but as a report noted, 'at least security would not be a problem'. Once the Games were underway the accommodation was found to be quite suitable and acceptable. One pre-Games worry which turned into a major problem was transport for the spectators and Press.

At times it was virtually impossible to reach and/or return from venues. The official opening was undertaken by Walter Mondale, the Vice-President of the United States. The last relay runner was Dr Charles Morgan Kerr, a psychiatrist, and the honour of taking the oath was given, with outstanding foresight, to speed skater Eric Heiden. The People's Republic of China and Cyprus made their debuts in the Winter Games.

The aforementioned Heiden (USA) stole all the headlines by gaining an unprecedented sweep of all five speed skating gold medals, all in Olympic record times. His sister Beth also won a bronze in the women's events. Her team-mate Leah Poulos-Mueller won two silver medals but could not match her husband Peter's gold performance of 1976. In Nordic skiing Nikolay Simyatov (URS) won a unique three golds in one Games, while team-mate Galina Kulakova, now over 37, raised her record total of medals over four Games to eight. Ulrich Wehling (GDR) won his third consecutive gold medal in the Nordic combination, while Aleksandr Tikhonov (URS) won a fourth consecutive gold in the biathlon relay. The closest ever result in Olympic Nordic skiing came in the men's 15km cross-country event when Thomas Wassberg (SWE) beat Juha Mieto (FIN) by one-hundredth of a second. Eight years previously the unlucky Finn had lost a bronze medal by only sixth-hundredths. However, he had won a gold in the 1976 relay.

Slalom specialist Ingemar Stenmark (SWE) won both of his races to become the most successful male Alpine skier at these Games, but Hanni Wenzel from tiny Liechtenstein won both women's slaloms and the silver medal in the downhill. Her brother Andreas added a silver to put their country in sixth place on the unofficial medal table. (Another sister, Petra, was also in the team of seven.) In winning the 90m ski jump Jouko Törmänen (FIN) made the longest jump attained to that time in Olympic competition when he cleared 117m. In the 70m event there was an unfortunate incident when after nine competitors had taken their jumps, the judges ruled that conditions were too dangerous. The start point was moved lower down to reduce take-off speed, and the competition begun again.

Irina Rodnina (URS) equalled the record of three gold medals by a figure skater when she and her husband Aleksandr Zaitsev retained the pairs title. By successfully defending the men's singles for Great Britain, Robin Cousins won his country's only medal of these Games. The bobsledding was a virtual replay of the 1976 rivalry between the Swiss and GDR teams. A member of the American 12th-placed 4-man bob was Willie Davenport, who had competed in the Summer Games from 1964 to 1976 and had won the 110m hurdles in 1968. By far the most popular win was that of the United States ice hockey team over the Soviet Union (their first defeat since 1964) on their way to the final. The celebrations which followed were described on American television as the biggest since the end of World War II. In the final the US then beat Finland.

The celebrations begin after the US ice hockey team's surprise victory over the Soviet Union, favourites for the gold medal (Allsport/Steve Powell)

The oldest gold medallist was Meinhard Nehmer (GDR) in the 4-man bob aged 39yr 42 days, and the youngest was his team-mate Karin Enke who won the 500m speed skating title aged 18yr 240 days. The youngest male winner was Mike Ramsey of the victorious US ice hockey team aged 19yr 83 days. The oldest female champion was Rodnina, aged 30yr 159 days. Special mention must be made of Marina Tcherkasova (URS), a silver medallist in pair skating only 93 days past her 15th birthday.

1980 (Winter) MEDALS TABLE

	G	S	B
Soviet Union	10	6	6
GDR	9	7	7
United States	6	4	2
Austria	3	2	2
Sweden	3	-	1
Liechtenstein	2	2	-
Finland	1	5	3
Norway	1	3	6
Netherlands	1	2	1
Switzerland	1	1	3
Great Britain	1	-	-
Germany (FRG)	-	2	3
Italy	-	2	-
Canada	-	1	1
Hungary	-	1	-
Japan	-	1	-
Bulgaria	-	-	1
Czechoslovakia	-	-	1
France	-	-	1

1980

XXIInd Olympic Games – Moscow, USSR
19 July – 3 August

Attended by representatives of 80 countries, comprising 5217 competitors, of which 1124 were women.

There had been only a little dissent when the IOC awarded these Games to Moscow in 1974. Tsarist Russia had competed in 1900 and from 1906 to 1912. Athletes from Lithuania, Estonia and Latvia, which had been provinces of Russia prior to 1918 and were taken over by the Soviet Union in 1940, had competed independently between 1920 and 1936. The Soviet Union had entered the Olympics in force in 1952, and was now the second highest medal scorer of all time – a remarkable achievement. However, in December 1979 the Soviet army invaded Afghanistan, and much of the non-Communist world, led by the United States, tried to impose a boycott on the Games (although not, it was noted, on trade or other economic activity). Not all countries supported the boycott, although individual sports within participating countries sometimes did. Because a number of countries which were unlikely to go to Moscow anyway for financial reasons found it politic to 'jump on the bandwagon', it is difficult to complete a definitive list of boycotting nations. The most reliable estimate is 45-50, of which the most important in sporting terms were the United States, the Federal Republic of Germany and Japan. When the Games were officially opened by Leonid Brezhnev, President of the USSR, there were eight first-time entries, not including Zimbabwe which had previously competed as Rhodesia.

Facilities in Moscow were excellent, including the 103,000 capacity Lenin Stadium, and large crowds attended most sports. It must be stated that although the Soviet spectators were, in the main, very knowledgeable, they left something to be desired in their treatment of foreign competitors, particularly those from other Eastern bloc countries. New competitions such as women's hockey, two extra judo classes, one extra weightlifting class, and various reintroduced events brought the total of gold medals available to a record 203 (barring ties). The heroine of Montreal, Nadia Comaneci (ROM), returned but was no longer the force she had been, and for the first time for many years the star of gymnastics was a male, Aleksandr Dityatin (URS). He won the greatest number of medals (8) ever won by a competitor at any sport at one Games, and was also awarded a 10.00 in the horse vault, the first maximum ever to a male gymnast in the Olympics. His team-mate Nikolay Andrianov brought his total of medals to a male record of 15 in three Games. This total has only ever been exceeded by Larissa Latynina, also a Soviet gymnast.

East African athletes dominated the distance runs, led by Miruts Yifter (ETH) with a 5000m/10,000m double. The

Steve Ovett took the gold in the 'wrong' event at Moscow, beating team-mate Seb Coe in the 800m but finishing third behind Coe in the 1500m (Allsport/Tony Duffy)

100m was the closest for 28 years, with Britain's Allan Wells given the verdict over Silvio Leonard of Cuba. Two other Britons each won the 'wrong' event, Steve Ovett and Sebastian Coe taking the 800m and 1500m respectively. Waldemar Cierpinski (GDR) became only the second man to successfully defend the marathon title, although he was over a minute slower than in 1976. In the triple jump Viktor Saneyev (URS) ended his remarkable career with a silver to add to his three gold medals since 1968. By repeating her Montreal successes in the 200m and relay, Bärbel Wöckel (GDR) equalled the female track and field record of four gold medals. In that relay Ludmila Maslakova of the silver medal Soviet team was running in her fourth consecutive relay final since 1968. Although only winning the pentathlon silver medal, Olga Rukavishnikova (URS) theoretically held the world record, albeit for only 0.4 sec, as she finished first in the last discipline, 800m. That gave her the shortest reign of any world record holder ever.

Once more the GDR girls dominated the swimming events, winning 26 of the available 35 medals. Highest medal scorers were Caren Metschuck with three golds and a silver, and Ines Diers with two golds, two silvers and a bronze. More unusually their team-mate Rica Reinisch won three gold medals, all in world record times. The inaugural women's hockey competition resulted in Zimbabwe gaining a gold medal in their debut at the games, while India were back to winning ways taking a record eighth title in the men's competition. In the yachting events held at Tallinn, the former capital of Estonia, the Finn class dinghy event was won appropriately enough by a Finn, Esko Rechardt.

Vladimir Parfenovich (URS) was the first canoeist to win three gold medals at the same Games, and the Cuban heavyweight Teofilo Stevenson became the only boxer to win the same event in three Games (the great Hungarian Laszlo Papp had won his three golds at two different weights). In rowing the Landvoigt twins, Jörg and Bernd (GDR), retained their coxless pairs title by beating the Soviet Pimenov twins, Yuriy and Nikolay. The other GDR twins, Ullrich and Walter Diessner, went one better than four years previously and won gold medals in the coxed fours. Yet another pair of twins won titles in wrestling when Anatoly and Sergey Beloglasov (URS) won the 52kg and 57kg freestyle events respectively.

The oldest gold medallist at Moscow, or rather Tallinn, was Valentin Mankin (URS) in the Star yachting, in his fourth Games, aged 41yr 346 days, while the youngest champion at these Games was swimmer Rica Reinisch (GDR), winning the first of her three golds aged 15yr 105 days. The oldest female winner was Anthea Stewart (ZIM) at 35yr 253 days in the hockey, while the youngest male gold medallist was the Hungarian backstroker Sandor Wladar, seven days over his seventeenth birthday. The youngest medallist was Zirvard Emirzyan (URS) with a silver in women's diving aged 14yr 52 days, while the oldest medallist was Petre Rosca (ROM) in the dressage at 57yr 283 days. The youngest competitor of all was Polish gymnast Anita Jokiel aged 13yr 232 days. In the same competition was Myong Hui Choe of North Korea, the smallest competitor of all at 1.35m tall and weighing 25kg. At the other end of the scale were the Soviet basketball player Vladimir Tkachenko, standing 2.20m tall, and the Greco-Roman wrestler Roman Codrean (ROM), who weighed 170kg. Despite the unfillable losses and gaps caused by the boycott, the standard of performance was very high throughout the Games.

1980 (Summer) MEDALS TABLE

	G	S	B
Soviet Union	80	69	46
GDR	47	37	42
Bulgaria	8	16	17
Cuba	8	7	5
Italy	8	3	4
Hungary	7	10	15
Romania	6	6	13
France	6	5	3
Great Britain	5	7	9
Poland	3	14	15
Sweden	3	3	6
Finland	3	1	4
Czechoslovakia	2	3	9
Yugoslavia	2	3	4
Australia	2	2	5
Denmark	2	1	− 2

Brazil	2	−	2
Ethiopia	2	−	2
Switzerland	2	−	−
Spain	1	3	2
Austria	1	2	1
Greece	1	−	2
Belgium	1	−	−
India	1	−	−
Zimbabwe	1	−	−
North Korea (PRK)	−	3	2
Mongolia	−	2	2
Tanzania	−	2	−
Mexico	−	1	3
Netherlands	−	1	2
Ireland	−	1	1
Uganda	−	1	−
Venezuela	−	1	−
Jamaica	−	−	3
Guyana	−	−	1
Lebanon	−	−	1

1984

XIVth Winter Games – Sarajevo, Yugoslavia
8 – 19 February

Attended by representatives of 49 countries, comprising 1274 competitors, of which 274 were women.

The first Winter Games to be held in Eastern Europe were awarded to Sarajevo in 1978. With a population of 500,000 it was the second largest city to host the Winter Games, and was previously famous only as the site of the assassination of Archduke Ferdinand on 28 June 1914 – an act which historians argue precipitated the First World War. There were a record 49 countries attending, including debuts by the British Virgin Islands, Egypt, Costa Rica, Puerto Rico and perhaps most unlikely, Senegal. The Games were opened by Mika Spiljak, the President of the Socialist Federal Republic of Yugoslavia. Sanda Dubravcic, who later placed tenth in the ladies figure skating, lit the flame after running up 94 steps in the Kosevo Stadium. The oath was taken by skier Bojan Krizaj, later seventh in the slalom. Actually the competitions had started the day before, with preliminary rounds of the ice hockey tournament.

Prior to the Games much had been made of the wolf mascot, Vucko, being depicted with its claws crossed – as though hoping for the best. In fact, although the weather caused various problems, the enthusiasm of the organizers and the local populace overcame most difficulties. Even the transport system worked. One of the few things that did cause hackles to rise was outside the control of the host city. This was the highly questionable, or at the very least confusing, judging of the figure skating – a problem not unique to Sarajevo in recent years. One 'cause celebre' just prior to the Games was the banning, as professionals, of the two defending champions in the men's and women's slalom races, Ingemar Stenmark (SWE) and Hanni Wenzel (LIE). There was one new event in the programme, a 20km Nordic skiing race for women.

slalom. By winning the women's downhill race, Michaela Figini (SUI) became the youngest ever Alpine skiing gold medallist aged 17yr 314 days, as well as being the youngest champion at Sarajevo. Unusually, in the Alpine events only one skier, Perrine Pelen (FRA), won more than one medal, and few begrudged the silver gained by Jure Branko in the

Jayne Torvill and Christopher Dean reached new standards in winning the gold medal for ice dance at Sarajevo in 1984 (Allsport/Trevor Jones)

The unheralded Bill Johnson (USA) achieved a record average speed of over 104 km/h in winning the 1984 downhill event (Allsport/David Cannon)

For the first time the GDR won more gold medals than the Soviet Union, although not total medals. However, in the men's luge, in which they had won 7 gold, 2 silver and 4 bronze medals in the last four Games, the East Germans only took a single bronze. The outstanding competitor, unusually, was a female Nordic skier, Marja-Liisa Hämäläinen (FIN), who won all three individual events and a bronze in the relay. However, Britain's Jayne Torvill and Christopher Dean gained the most media attention with their superb ice dancing – their artistic interpretation of Ravel's *Bolero* was awarded an unprecedented nine perfect sixes, with another three for technical merit. The ladies singles winner, Katarina Witt (GDR), was trained by Jutta Müller, who had not only coached her daughter, Gabriele Seyfert, to a silver in 1968, but had also been the driving force behind the 1980 champion, Anett Pötzsch.

Alpine skiers from the United States made a major impact with three titles. Bill Johnson, hardly a retiring personality, proved he was as good as he had been saying he was to anyone and everyone who would listen, and won the first Olympic downhill title by an American in a record average speed of 104.532km/h. His team-mates, twins Phil and Steve Mahre, took the gold and silver medals in the

giant slalom, the first Winter Games medal ever by Yugoslavia. One unusual feature of these events was the participation of Sam Guss, not because he was an Australian but because he stood 2.08m tall, possibly the tallest ever Alpine skier.

In speed skating Tomas Gustafsson (SWE) and Igor Malkov (URS) swapped medals over 5000m and 10,000m, in two of the closest races ever skated in the Games, unique over such distances. The Swede won the shorter race by 2/100ths of a second and Malkov the other by 5/100ths. The Soviet ice hockey team equalled Canada's record with a sixth gold medal. Just prior to the Games another eligibility controversy had arisen with the decision that an amateur for Olympic ice hockey purposes was someone who had not played in the National Hockey League of North America. One other bone of contention had been resolved before competitions began when the revolutionary rocket-shaped Soviet bobs were barred. The 90m ski jump was won by a young Finn, Matti Nykänen, by a record margin of 18.5 points, though he was to make a far greater impression four years later.

The oldest gold medallist at Sarajevo was the Soviet ice hockey goalminder Vladyslav Tretyak, in his fourth Games, aged 31yr 299 days, and the youngest was Figini. The youngest male champion was Malkov, just 9 days past his 19th birthday, while the oldest female gold medallist was Hämäläinen aged 28yr 161 days. The oldest competitor was Carl-Erik Eriksson (SWE) at 53yr 289 days, competing in his record sixth successive Olympic bobsleigh competition. The youngest was Babette Preussler (GDR) in pair skating aged 15yr 143 days. One of the victorious German pair in the luge, Hans Stanggassinger, had another distinction. He was reportedly the heaviest champion weighing 111kg.

1984 (Winter) MEDALS TABLE

	G	S	B
GDR	9	9	6
Soviet Union	6	10	9
United States	4	4	-
Finland	4	3	6
Sweden	4	2	2
Norway	3	2	4
Switzerland	2	2	1
Canada	2	1	1
Germany (FRG)	2	1	1
Italy	2	-	-
Great Britain	1	-	-
Czechoslovakia	-	2	4
France	-	1	2
Japan	-	1	-
Yugoslavia	-	1	-
Liechtenstein	-	-	2
Austria	-	-	1

1984

XXIIIrd Olympic Games – Los Angeles, USA

28 July – 12 August

Attended by representatives of 140 countries, comprising 6797 competitors, of which 1567 were women.

The IOC awarded the Games to Los Angeles (in 1978) only after protracted negotiations about the financial guarantees usually required from a host city. Various innovations to protect the city from a Montreal-like deficit were implemented – not least, widespread sponsorship by private corporations. Television rights alone amounted to $287 million – one of the largest TV audiences in history, some 2500 million, watched the Games – of which the great bulk came from the ABC network for US rights. The programme was expanded to 221 events, including an extra 12 for women, while baseball and tennis were demonstration sports. The Memorial Coliseum, main site for the 1932 Games, was fully refurbished and had a seating capacity of 92,607, while many other venues, often famous in their own right, were utilized. There were complaints that some of these venues were too far-flung, but the overall good weather and the enthusiasm, at times overwhelming, of the American crowds offset most problems.

The one, albeit major, disaster suffered by these Games was the last-minute boycott by the Soviet Union, which announced its non-participation on the very day, 8 May 1984, that the Olympic flame arrived in the United States to begin a nationwide torch relay. Within a week or so most of the Soviet bloc had also pulled out – with the notable exception of Romania. Additionally, but not surprisingly, Iran and Libya did not appear. However, of 159 invitations sent out, 140 countries accepted – beating the Munich record. A number of sports were very seriously affected, although standards were still generally high. In particular, canoeing, fencing, gymnastics, weightlifting, wrestling and women's athletics were diminished, both in numbers and quality.

The Games were formally opened by President Ronald Reagan, the first US incumbent ever to do so. The final runner on the torch relay was Gina Hemphill, a granddaughter of the great Olympian Jesse Owens. She had also run the first leg on American soil, jointly with Jim Thorpe's grandson Bill, and some years after the Games she married Henry Tillman who won the heavyweight boxing title at Los Angeles. In the stadium she handed over the torch to 1960 Olympic decathlon champion Rafer Johnson, who from a gantry lit the flame on the top of the stadium peristyle, by means of a 96-step hydraulic slip-stair. Apparently in rehearsals Johnson had developed a leg injury, and 1976 champion Bruce Jenner, one of the Olympic flag's escorts, stood by in case he had to replace him. The oath was taken, somewhat stumblingly, by 1976 400m hurdle champion Edwin Moses, who went on to win a second gold medal. There followed a three-hour Hollywood-style extravaganza featuring, among other things, marching bands and 85 pianos, which was arranged by film producer David Wolper.

Problems of smog and traffic congestion did not materialize to anything like the degree predicted, although one unfortunate phenomenon was the American chauvinism displayed, especially by the media. Attendances at all sports were quite remarkable, with a final attendance figure of 5.7 million, and a highest single figure of 101,799 for the final of the soccer tournament (France beat Brazil 2-0) in the Rose Bowl at Pasadena. One particular feature of these Games was the tremendous outlay made on security – some 7000 personnel and ancillary equipment costing as much as $100 million. The first gold medal of the Games, won by shooter Xu Haifeng, was China's first ever Olympic title.

Aided enormously by the absence of Soviet and East German opposition, the United States gained the lion's share of the medals. Leading their gold rush was sprinter/jumper Carl Lewis, who exactly equalled Jesse Owens's feat of 1936 with four gold medals in the 100m, 200m, long jump and relay. Another athlete, Valerie Brisco-Hooks, and five swimmers, all won three golds each. However, the most successful competitors were gymnasts

Carl Lewis wins the 200m at Los Angeles, the third of his four gold medals at those Games which matched the achievement of the legendary Jesse Owens (Popperfoto)

Ecaterina Szabo (ROM) with four golds and a silver and China's Li Ning with three golds, two silvers and a bronze. The introduction of consolation finals, for non-qualifiers to the regular finals, led to the unusual situation of an Olympic record being set in the men's 400m freestyle 'B' final, faster than the gold medallist had attained. The judo Open champion Yamashita (JPN) extended his winning streak to 198, despite being handicapped by a foot injury.

A number of families were particularly successful: twins Mark and David Schultz (USA) and Lou and Ed Banach (USA) all won wrestling gold medals; William Buchan (USA) and his son William Jr won yachting titles, but not together; British husband and wife Garry (silver, 4 x 400m) and Kathy Cook (bronze, 400m & 4 x 100m) won medals; Al Joyner (USA) and his sister Jackie won gold (triple jump) and silver (heptathlon) medals respectively; and brothers Carmine and Giuseppe Abbagnale (ITA) won the coxed pairs rowing event. In the dressage event, 48-year-old Reiner Klimke (FRG) won two gold medals in his fourth Games over a 20-year period, equalling his countryman Hans-Günter Winkler's equestrian record of five golds and seven medals. One of the few negative things at Los Angeles was the disqualification for doping offences of 12 competitors from weightlifting, wrestling, volleyball and athletics. Probably the most well-known of these was Martti Vainio (FIN) who finished second in the 10,000m on the track.

The oldest gold medallist at Los Angeles was William Buchan (USA) in the Star yachting aged 49yr 91 days (see above). The youngest was Romanian gymnast Simona Pauca in the team event aged 14yr 317 days; she also won the individual beam title four days later. The youngest male champion was Perica Bukic (YUG) in water polo aged 17yr 264 days, while the oldest female gold medallist was Linda Thom (CAN) who won the women's pistol aged 40yr 212 days. The oldest female medallist finished third in that same competition: Patricia Dench (AUS) at 52yr 143 days. The

oldest male medallist was another shooter, Ragnar Skanaker (SWE), aged 50yr 52 days. At the other end of the scale was Belgian coxswain Philippe Cuelenaere, the youngest competitor at Los Angeles a month short of his 13th birthday.

At the end of the Games – after another closing extravaganza featuring one of the greatest firework displays ever seen – the organizers reported a profit of $215 million, prompting the suggestion that perhaps the pendulum had swung too far the other way since Montreal. The whole thing was a triumphant vindication of the leadership of Peter Ueberroth, President of the Los Angeles Olympic Organizing Committee. Coincidentally, Ueberroth was born on the very day, 2 September 1937, that Baron de Coubertin had died.

1984 (Summer) MEDALS TABLE

	G	S	B
United States	83	61	30
Romania	20	16	17
FRG	17	19	23
China	15	8	9
Italy	14	6	12
Canada	10	18	16
Japan	10	8	14
New Zealand	8	1	2
Yugoslavia	7	4	7
Great Britain	5	11	21
France	5	7	16
Netherlands	5	2	6
Australia	4	8	12
Finland	4	2	6
Sweden	2	11	6
Mexico	2	3	1
Morocco	2	-	-
Brazil	1	5	2
Spain	1	2	2
Belgium	1	1	2
Austria	1	1	1
Kenya	1	-	2
Portugal	1	-	2
Pakistan	1	-	-
Switzerland	-	4	4
Denmark	-	3	3
Jamaica	-	1	2
Norway	-	1	2
Greece	-	1	1
Nigeria	-	1	1
Puerto Rico	-	1	1
Colombia	-	1	-
Egypt	-	1	-
Ireland	-	1	-
Ivory Coast	-	1	-
Peru	-	1	-
Syria	-	1	-
Thailand	-	1	-

1988

XVth Winter Games – Calgary, Canada
13 – 28 February

Attended by representatives of 57 countries, comprising 1423 competitors, of which 313 were women.

Having had three unsuccessful bids previously, Calgary was finally awarded these Games in 1981. Most of the venues were close together except for Mount Allan and Kenmore, some 90km away, where the Alpine and Nordic skiing took place. The programme was stretched to 16 days to include three weekends – particularly favourable for television coverage, for which ABC paid $309 million for the North American rights, over three times the sum for the Sarajevo Games. There were a number of new events: Nordic Combination for teams, Team Jumping, Alpine Combination, Super Giant Slaloms for men and women, and a 5000m speed skating event for women. In all there were 46 events, as well as the demonstration sports of curling, short track speed skating and freestyle skiing. Five teams made their Winter Games debuts: Fiji, Guam, Guatemala, Ireland and Jamaica.

The official opening was performed by the Governor-General of Canada, Jeanne Sauvé, on behalf of Queen Elizabeth II. The torch was brought into the stadium by a couple, speed skater Cathy Priestner and skier Ken Read, and then handed to a 12-year-old girl skater, Robyn Perry, who lit the flame. Incidentally, that flame was easily the highest ever as it was set at the top of the 626ft (191m) Calgary Tower. The oath was taken by Pierre Harvey, a Nordic skier who had also represented Canada at cycling in the 1984 Olympics. The facilities in the main were excellent, and the expected local transport problems were few and far between. Accommodation was at a premium with so many teams and competitors, and some officials were based in an establishment which had previously been a 'house of ill-repute'.

However, one unforeseen occurrence caused real problems, and that was a dramatic climatic change caused by the 'chinook' wind, which gave springlike weather and

strong winds, bringing havoc to the timetable. These conditions, which primarily affected the bob, luge and ski jumping events, resulted in some unexpected placings. The exposed ski jumps were very dangerous at times, and caused the Nordic Combination event, comprising jumping and cross-country skiing, to be contested all on one day. Nevertheless, there were many excellent performances, even if the 'star' of these Games was an unknown British ski jumper. Despite, or more likely because of, being totally inept by world standards, Michael 'Eddie the Eagle' Edwards stole the media attention from the great and famous, to the amusement of many and the chagrin of some. Britain's first Olympic entrant ever in this sport, he finished last in both jumps, albeit with a British record of 71m, over 20m behind the rest of the competitors.

The most successful competitors were Yvonne van Gennip (NED), who won three speed skating titles, and Matti Nykänen (FIN), who won all three gold medals open to him. The Finn totally dominated his sport and leapt to 118.5m on the 90m hill, the greatest distance ever achieved in the Games. In Alpine skiing both Vreni Schneider (SUI) and Alberto Tomba (ITA) won the slalom and giant slalom

Italian skiing star Alberto Tomba with his supporters at Calgary, the beginning of his illustrious Olympic slaloming career (Allsport/Mike Powell)

events. Frank-Peter Rötsch (GDR) became the first man to win both individual biathlon races in a single Games, while the Soviet Union won the relay for the sixth consecutive time. The Soviet women hardly made an error in the Nordic skiing, taking 7 of the 9 individual medals on offer as well as the relay. Although not in that relay, 35-year-old Raisa Smetanina gained a silver and a bronze to raise her total from four Games to a record nine medals for the sport.

After the shocks of Sarajevo, the GDR lugers were back winning all three golds, two silvers and a bronze. Steffi Walter (née Martin) was the first luger to retain an individual title, and led her team-mates to a clean sweep. Incidentally, one of the British competitors in this sport was Nick Ovett, whose older brother Steve had won the 1980 Olympic 800m. The bobsleigh course was likened to sandpaper after the winds blew so much dirt onto the track, and many of the top crews were upset. There was bitter rivalry between the Swiss and GDR 4-man crews with officials of both teams checking the legality of each other's sleds. The coach of the Swiss team was 1980 gold medallist Erich Schärer, while the GDR coach was Horst Hörnlein who had won gold in the 2-man luge in 1972. After the fourth and final run the Swiss were triumphant by 7/100ths of a second, the smallest margin ever in the event. The drama was heightened even further when the rather unlikely crew from Jamaica crashed badly, but fortunately no one was seriously hurt. Bogdan Musiol (GDR) with two silver medals raised his total to a record-equalling six. Placed 25th (of 41) in the 2-man bob was Prince Albert of Monaco, himself a Member of the IOC, partnered by a croupier from the Principality's Casino. The Prince's grandfather and uncle, both named John Kelly, had won Olympic rowing medals.

Katarina Witt (GDR) was the first individual skater since 1952 to retain a figure skating title, amid some criticism about her skimpy costumes which was not shared by the spectators. In third place Debi Thomas (USA) was the first black skater to win an Olympic medal. Speed skating was held indoors for the first time at the Olympics, in the superb $39 million Olympic Oval. It proved to be the fastest circuit in the world with world records set in seven of the nine events, and as many as 29 skaters bettering the world mark in the men's 5000m. Karin Kania (née Enke) (GDR) added two silvers and a bronze for a record medal haul of eight since 1980. Monika Holzner (FRG), the 1972 1000m champion, competed in her fifth Games, then a record number of appearances for a female Winter Olympics competitor. The Soviet Union moved past Canada in ice hockey with its seventh title, while the host nation and the United States, who won in 1980, failed to gain a medal. A small consolation prize for Canada was that the most prolific goalscorer, with 7, in the tournament was their Serge Boisvert. There was only one competitor in Calgary who failed a dope test, and he was a Polish ice hockey player.

The youngest gold medallist was Ekaterina Gordiyeva (URS) in the pairs skating aged 16yr 264 days, while the oldest was Ekkehard Fasser (SUI) in the 4-man bob aged 35yr 178 days. The youngest male champion was Ari Pekka Nikkola (FIN) in the 90m team ski jump at 18yr 284 days, and the oldest female gold medallist was Christa Rothenburger (GDR) who won the 1000m speed skating aged 28yr 84 days. Competitors' ages ranged from a 14-year-old North Korean girl skater to a bobsledder, 52-year-old Harvey Hook, from the US Virgin Islands.

1988 (Winter) MEDALS TABLE

	G	S	B
Soviet Union	11	9	9
GDR	9	10	6
Switzerland	5	5	5
Finland	4	1	2
Sweden	4	-	2
Austria	3	5	2
Netherlands	3	2	2
FRG	2	4	2
United States	2	1	3
Italy	2	1	2
France	1	-	1
Norway	-	3	2
Canada	-	2	3
Yugoslavia	-	2	1
Czechoslovakia	-	1	2
Japan	-	-	1
Liechtenstein	-	-	1

1988

XXIVth Olympic Games – Seoul, Korea
17 September – 2 October

Attended by representatives of 159 countries, comprising 8465 competitors of which 2186 were women.

The capital of Korea, Seoul had one of the largest populations of any city on earth, an estimated 9,000,000. Nearly all facilities for the Games were in situ by the end of 1986 when the Asian Games were held there. Most major installations were part of the sports complex on the banks of the Han River, and included a 100,000 spectator stadium. Once again the programme was expanded, with the reintroduction of tennis (for the first time since 1924), the addition of table tennis, and the inclusion of a number of extra events which brought the total to a record 237. Baseball, taekwondo and women's judo were the demonstration sports. American television companies offered incredible sums (up to $750 million) for the US rights – providing the major sports finals took place during American prime-time viewing. That would have required athletics finals to be held between 9 and 11am local time. This was opposed by the International Amateur Athletic Federation, and indeed by the IOC, although some compromise was finally agreed. The income from television sources was still immense, NBC acquiring the American rights alone for $300 million. There were an estimated 16,000 media personnel at these Games.

Prior to the opening ceremony the most tenacious problem was the claim of North Korea to host half the Games. Against IOC rules but nonetheless with their blessing, some sports were offered to North Korea, but they continued to be intransigent. They finally refused to attend and attempted to get the Eastern bloc to support them. However, only the hard-line Communist countries backed them, and the only other absentees were Albania, Cuba, Ethiopia, Madagascar, Nicaragua and the Seychelles. Against that there were a number of first-timers including American Samoa, Aruba, Burkina Faso (which had competed as Upper Volta in 1972), Cook Islands, Guam, the Maldives, St Vincent, Vanuatu and the Democratic Republic of Yemen. Also attending was Brunei, but only with an official, so that the officially claimed figure of 160 countries participating is not strictly correct.

The opening ceremony began on the Han River and transferred to the main stadium. The President of Korea, Roh Tae-Woo, declared the Games open, and the oath was taken by Huh Jae, a basketball player. One unusual feature of the ceremony was that as the Korean alphabet began with the letter G, the traditional first team, Greece, was then followed by Gabon and Ghana. A more entertaining occurrence in that march-past was the inclusion in the Thailand contingent of the reigning Miss Universe, a beautiful Thai girl, which delighted the spectators. Because the original 1920 Olympic flag had been fading away, a new one was presented to the IOC by the Seoul Organizing Committee and was flown for the first time on 17 September 1988. The torch was carried for part of the distance on the track by 76-year-old Sohn Kee-Chung (better known as Kitei Son), the 1936 marathon champion – a Korean who had been forced to run for Japan, the occupying power at the time. He passed it to the final runner, female athlete Lim Chun-Ae. The torch was raised to the top of the cauldron tower, and the flame was lit by three representatives of Science, Art and Sport (their names were Chiung Sun-Man, Kim Won-Tuk and Sohn Mi-Chung). Unfortunately, some of the pigeons which had been released during an earlier part of the ceremony had perched on the cauldron and were caught in the rush of flame.

The athlete who gained most attention at these Games was undoubtedly the Canadian sprinter Ben Johnson, initially for the best of reasons and then for the worst. Having looked somewhat out of form in the preliminary rounds of the 100m, he blasted away in the final to destroy a talented field, including arch-rival Carl Lewis, and clock an almost unbelievable world record of 9.79 sec. Three days later it was revealed that Johnson had failed a drug test and he was disqualified, with Lewis moving up to the gold medal with a very respectable 9.92sec. Another nine competitors, from weightlifting (4), modern pentathlon (2), judo, wrestling and shooting were disqualified for drug-related offences.

Although African men won everything on the track over 400m, the outstanding athlete at the Games was a woman, Florence Griffith-Joyner, who won three golds and a silver in the sprints and relays, running a total of 11 races. Her sister-in-law, Jackie Joyner-Kersee, won the heptathlon, as expected, and the long jump. Continuing the Olympic

tradition of successful families, Viktor Bryzgin (4 x 100m) and his wife Olga Bryzgina (400m, 4 x 400m) both won gold medals. In rowing, Carmine and Giuseppe Abbagnale (ITA) retained their coxed pair title from 1984, and a third brother, Agostino, was a member of the winning quadruple sculls crew.

The most successful competitor in Seoul was Kristin Otto (GDR) who not only won six gold medals (a record by

The outstanding competitor at Seoul, Kristin Otto (GDR) won an unprecedented six swimming gold medals (Allsport)

any woman, in any sport, at any Games) but also became the first swimmer to win titles at three different strokes at the same Games. America's Matt Biondi, saddled before the Games with the expectation of an impossible Mark Spitz-like scenario, nevertheless ended the Games with seven medals (5 gold, 1 silver, 1 bronze). Vladimir Salnikov (URS) became the only swimmer to regain a title eight years after winning it the first time. Greg Louganis (USA) gained the first double 'double' by a male diver when he successfully defended his two titles from Los Angeles, despite hitting his head on the board during a dive in the springboard preliminaries. Also in the pool, Anthony Nesty of Surinam became the first South American and first black swimmer to win a gold medal by taking the 100m butterfly. Similarly Kenny Monday (USA) was the first black competitor to win a wrestling gold.

A number of 'old-timers' reappeared on the Olympic scene. Fifty-two-year-old Reiner Klimke (FRG) won his sixth dressage gold medal and his eighth medal in five Games over a 24-year period, all records for his sport. His horse, *Ahlerich*, also set a record. One of Klimke's compatriots in the winning team was Ann-Kathrin Linsenhoff – remarkably her mother had been his team-mate in the gold medal team of 1968. Britain's David Broome returned after three Games out as a 'professional', 28 years after he first competed. The yachting events, held at Pusan, featured two of the greatest Olympians of all time. Quadruple gold medallist Paul Elvström (DEN), partnered by his daughter Trine, was competing in a record-equalling eighth Games, over a 40-year span. This was matched by yachtsman Durward Knowles (BAH), a 1964 gold medallist, also in his eighth celebration over a similar span.

By winning the silver medal in women's sprint cycling, the GDR's Christa Luding (nee Rothenburger) became the first competitor in Olympic history to win medals at a Summer and Winter celebration in the same year. She had won a speed skating gold and silver at Calgary. Because of the record number of entries in boxing, two rings were used simultaneously. Not surprisingly this caused some confusion. Also, not for the first time, the boxing competitions witnessed some 'bizarre', often home-town, decisions. One of the most scandalous in Olympic history occurred when Ray Jones (USA) was judged to have lost his light-middleweight bout against Park Si Hun of Korea. Pointedly, the International Amateur Boxing Association awarded Jones the Val Barker Cup as the best stylist at the Games. There were other disputed decisions and some of the judges were suspended. One of the Korean boxers, Byun Jong-Il, refused to leave the ring after the decision went against him in his bantamweight bout, and remained there, a solitary figure, for over an hour.

The oldest gold medallist at Seoul was Klimke, aged 52yr 255 days. The youngest was swimmer Krisztina Egerszegi (HUN) at 14yr 41 days. The oldest female champion was hockey player Elspeth Clement (AUS) aged 32yr 103 days, while the youngest male winner was Soviet cyclist Dmitri Nelyubin aged 17yr 229 days. The oldest medallist at Seoul was Romanian cox Ladislau Lovrenski aged 56yr 65 days. The youngest medallist was Egerszegi, three days before her gold, while the youngest male medallist was Xiong Ni (CHN) with a silver in diving aged 14yr 247 days. The oldest competitor was Knowles in Star class yachting aged 70yr 331 days, while the youngest was swimmer Nadia Cruz of Angola aged 13yr 73 days. The oldest female competitor was Inoue Kikuko (JPN) in the dressage, aged 63yr 297 days.

Thus, despite threats of boycotts, of North Korean terror, of student riots etc, the Games on the whole went very well, the good humour, flexibility and courtesy of the hosts overcoming most minor problems. A record 52 countries won medals, and some time after the Games ended it was reported that a record profit of $288 million had been made.

1988 (Summer) MEDALS TABLE

	G	S	B
Soviet Union	55	31	46
GDR	37	35	30
United States	36	31	27
Korea	12	10	11
FRG	11	14	15
Hungary	11	6	6
Bulgaria	10	12	13
Romania	7	11	6
France	6	4	6
Italy	6	4	4
China	5	11	12
Great Britain	5	10	9
Kenya	5	2	2
Japan	4	3	7
Australia	3	6	5
Yugoslavia	3	4	5
Czechoslovakia	3	3	2
New Zealand	3	2	8
Canada	3	2	5
Poland	2	5	9
Norway	2	3	-
Netherlands	2	2	5
Denmark	2	1	1
Brazil	1	2	3
Finland	1	1	2
Spain	1	1	2
Turkey	1	1	-
Morocco	1	-	2
Austria	1	-	-
Portugal	1	-	-
Surinam	1	-	-
Sweden	-	4	7
Switzerland	-	2	2
Jamaica	-	2	-
Argentina	-	1	1
Chile	-	1	-
Costa Rica	-	1	-
Indonesia	-	1	-
Iran	-	1	-
Netherlands Antilles	-	1	-
Peru	-	1	-
Senegal	-	1	-
Virgin Islands	-	1	-
Belgium	-	-	2
Mexico	-	-	2
Colombia	-	-	1
Djibouti	-	-	1
Greece	-	-	1
Mongolia	-	-	1
Pakistan	-	-	1
Philippines	-	-	1
Thailand	-	-	1

1992

XVIth Winter Games – Albertville, France
8 – 23 February

Attended by representatives of 64 countries, comprising 1801 competitors of which 488 were women.

In October 1986 the IOC awarded the Games to Albertville, in the Savoie region of France, ahead of six other sites in six other countries. The 1968 triple gold medallist, Jean-Claude Killy, was co-president of the organizing committee. With a population of less than 20,000 it was the smallest place ever to host an Olympic Games. The 13 different venues were very widespread, which gave rise to complaints that 'atmosphere and spirit' were lacking as compared to previous celebrations. Nevertheless, the Games were highly successful, with a record number of competitors and participating countries. These included such newcomers as Swaziland, Senegal, Ireland and the Virgin Islands. The political upheaval in Eastern Europe manifested itself in various ways. There was a combined German team for the first time since 1964. Latvia, Estonia and Lithuania competed independently again after 56 years, having been incorporated into the Soviet Union in 1940. Competing under the title of the Unified Team (EUN) were the NOCs of Russia, Belarus, Ukraine, Kazakstan and Uzbekistan – they used the Olympic flag, and Beethoven's Ninth Symphony for victory ceremonies. The break-up of Yugoslavia meant that Croatia and Slovenia competed separately for the first time.

As usual the world's media attended in force, trying to cope with the logistical problems caused by the multi-venued sports facilities. CBS paid some $243 million for the American television rights. There was a remarkable opening ceremony with the Games declared open by François Mitterand, the President of France. The flame was lit by soccer star Michel Platini and a local child, François-Syrille Grange, and skater Surya Bonaly (later placed fifth) took the oath. A record 57 events included the newly accepted sports of short-track speed skating and freestyle skiing. Overall, there were nine extra events added since the previous Games, plus demonstration sports of curling, speed skiing, and two forms of freestyle skiing not in the Games proper. Another change was that in figure skating compulsory exercises were eliminated.

Unusually, the Alpine skiers did not produce the stars as in the past. Italy's Alberto Tomba gained a lot of attention by becoming the first Alpinist to successfully defend a title, but no skier really dominated. Indeed, only Petra Kronberger of Austria won more than one event, and the sport's 30 available medals were spread among 25 skiers. Surprisingly, the Swiss won only a single bronze, while female skiers from Sweden and New Zealand won the first such medals from their areas. Nordic skiing made a big impact, and with good television coverage some of the cross-country competitors became stars. The Norwegians Vegard Ulvang and Björn Dählie received due recognition for winning three golds and a silver each. They made good media copy too, especially Dählie who deliberately skied backwards over the line for his last gold medal in the relay. But the most successful competitor at Albertville was their female equivalent, Lyubov Yegorova of the Unified Team, who won three golds and two silvers – a record total of medals in one winter Games. That was matched by her team-mate, Yelena Valbe, with four individual bronzes and a gold in the relay. The inclusion of women's biathlon events enabled Anfissa Reztsova (EUN) to become the first person to win gold medals in two separate sports – she had gained a gold in the 1988 cross-country relay.

A brilliant all-round skier, Austria's Petra Kronberger won both the Alpine Combined title and the slalom in 1992 (Popperfoto)

Austrian ski jumpers put up a surprising challenge to the Finns, especially in the team event, and it was mainly the superb jumping of the young Toni Nieminen which won the day. Another closely fought contest involving Austria came in the 4-man bob, when their team beat Germany by a mere 2/100ths of a second after four rounds, the smallest margin of victory ever. In lugeing, the Neuner sisters, also from Austria, took first and second places, matching the feat of the French Goitschel sisters in the 1964 Alpine skiing. By winning the ice hockey the Unified Team, in effect, extended the Soviet Union's victory tally to eight since they first entered the Games in 1956.

Despite the new rules most of the favourites won the medals in figure skating, with Viktor Petrenko (EUN) taking his country's first individual skating gold since 1908. In speed skating, both sprint titles were retained by the 1988 champions, Bonnie Blair (USA) and Uwe-Jens Mey (GER) respectively. However, the surprise here, and in the new short-track events, was the rise of Asia, whose skaters, from China, Japan and the Koreas, won 13 medals.

Nieminen, the Finnish gold medallist in the 120m ski jump individual and team events, was only 16yr 259 days of age when he gained his first title, thereby becoming the youngest ever male winter Olympics champion. A member of the Unified Team, Raisa Smetanina, was the oldest ever female gold medallist as a member of the 4 x 5km relay team just 12 days short of her 40th birthday. She set another record by winning medals in five consecutive Games, 1976-92, and said her secret was being really only 10 years old – born on 29 February. The oldest male champion was Fritz Fischer (GER) in the biathlon aged 35yr 146 days, while the oldest medallist was Maurilio De Zolt (ITA) with a silver in the 50km cross-country aged 41yr 150 days. The youngest medallist was Nikki Ziegelmeyer (USA) with a silver in the short-track speed skating relay, while the youngest competitor was figure skater Krisztina Czako (HUN), aged 13yr 66 days, whose father/coach Gyorgy had skated in the 1952 Games.

These were the last Winter Games to be held in the same year as the Summer celebration. In future the Winter Games would be held on the even-numbered years between editions of the Summer Games.

1992 (Winter) MEDALS TABLE

	G	S	B
Germany	10	10	6
Unified Team	9	6	8
Norway	9	6	5
Austria	6	7	8
United States	5	4	2
Italy	4	6	4
France	3	5	1
Finland	3	1	3
Canada	2	3	2
Korea	2	1	1
Japan	1	2	4
Netherlands	1	1	2
Sweden	1	-	3
Switzerland	1	-	2
China	-	3	-
Luxembourg	-	2	-
New Zealand	-	1	-
Czechoslovakia	-	-	3
North Korea (PRK)	-	-	1
Spain	-	-	1

NB: Two silvers in Women's Giant Slalom

1992

XXVth Olympic Games – Barcelona, Spain
25 July – 9 August

Attended by representatives of 169 countries, comprising 9364 competitors, of which 2707 were women.

After intense 'politicking' the 1992 Summer Games were awarded to Barcelona in October 1986. The city, the birthplace of the IOC President Juan Antonio Samaranch, had been promised the Games in 1924 but Baron de Coubertin had changed his mind and opted for Paris. Barcelona was then suggested for the 1936 celebration, but the spectre of civil war decided the IOC in favour of Berlin. The stadium intended for those Games, built in 1929 on Montjuic, was completely refurbished for 1992 and was the main venue. Most of the other venues were within the city limits, with only football (preliminary games), rowing, canoeing and road cycling sites at any great distance.

Television revenue set a new record with NBC paying $401 million for the American rights. As well as two new sports, baseball and badminton, being added to the official programme, there were also a number of extra events. These included seven for women in judo, a women's 10km walk, a dinghy sailing competition for women, and four canoe-slalom contests. There were 26 sports and the total number of medal events was a record 259 (with the distribution of 815 medals in all). An outbreak of African equine plague in Spain in 1989 originally cast considerable doubt as to whether the equestrian events would be held, but it was curtailed in time. There were three demonstration sports: pelota Basque, taekwondo and rink hockey.

Despite the fact that most sports now had their own world championships, which for some critics diluted the importance of the Olympic competitions, the world's sportsmen and women still considered an Olympic medal as the pinnacle of sporting achievement. For the first time in many Olympiads not a single nation boycotted the occasion, and there were a record number of countries and competitors, so much so that the IOC felt compelled to discuss the need for 'quotas' to limit numbers in future Games. The Baltic states were independent again and Germany competed as one team. However, Yugoslavia was split into Bosnia-Herzogovina, Croatia and Slovenia, with Serbia and Macedonia competing as Independent Olympic Participants (IOP). South Africa returned to the Olympic fold after 32 years. In total 170 countries marched in the parade, though Afghanistan actually had no competitors. Media representatives still outnumbered the competitors.

The Games were a tremendous success overall – many thought among the best ever – with the one sour note caused by transport shortcomings for fans billeted way out of town. Fears of terrorist activity proved to be unfounded, but security arrangements were reported to have cost $90 million. Tennis professionals were joined by others from basketball, and the appearance of the US 'Dream Team', containing NBA stars such as Magic Johnson, Michael Jordan, Larry Bird and Charles Barkley, was one of the highlights of the Games. Because of their presence, these sports received greatly increased television coverage even outside the United States. The disintegrating Soviet Union, known here as the Commonwealth of Independent States (CIS) or Unified Team (UT), made its last appearance.

King Juan Carlos, an Olympic yachtsman in 1972, declared the Games open during a colourful ceremony, and the oath was taken by Luis Doreste Blanco, who later won a gold medal in the Flying Dutchman class. He had won gold in the 470 class in 1984, while his brother José had won the 1988 Finn event. Incidentally the King's son Felipe placed 6th in the Barcelona Soling, and his daughter Christina had been in the 1988 Tornado class. Their uncle, Constantine of Greece, had been a yachting gold medallist in 1960. The flame on the stadium pedestal was spectacularly lit by paraplegic archer Antonio Rebollo symbolically shooting an arrow at the torch tower. Recent research indicates that Spain's first Olympic champion, Lucius Minicius, winner of the chariot race in 129 AD, was born in Barcelona, and his ghost must have been smiling as Spain gained a record number of medals, nearly doubling its total from the 16 previous Games. In all 64 countries won a medal, another record, and 37 of these won a gold. Although the heat did affect a number of sports adversely, the overall standard was very high, with perhaps the outstanding individual performances of the Games being the 1500m freestyle of 14:43.48 by swimmer Kieren Perkins of Australia, and the 400m hurdles in 46.78sec by Kevin Young (USA). In the swimming pool there was a fine swansong by the Unified Team as Alexander Popov won two golds and two silvers, and Yevgeni Sadovyi took three golds. The most successful competitor was their compatriot gymnast Vitali Shcherbo who won 6 gold medals. Although he only placed 20th in the Star yacht class, Hubert Raudaschl (AUT) equalled a record having competed in eight Games, 1964-92. Indonesian-born Christlot Hanson-Boylen (CAN), 12th in the dressage competition, in her sixth Olympic Games, equalled the record 28yr span of competition for women.

The youngest gold medallist/medallist was the diver Fu Mingxia (CHN) aged 13yr 345 days, while the youngest male winner was her diving team-mate Sun Shuwei at 16yr 185 days. The oldest gold medallist was Klaus Balkenhol (GER) in the dressage team aged 52yr 243 days, with the oldest female champion Gillian Rolton (AUS) in the 3-Day Event team at 36yr 88 days. The oldest medallist was the Swedish shooter Ragnar Skanakar (a gold medallist in 1972) in his sixth Games at 58yr 48 days, while the oldest female medallist was Carol Lavell (USA) in the dressage aged 49yr 118 days. The youngest competitor was rowing cox Carlos Barrera of Spain aged 11yr 256 days. The youngest female competitor was Hungarian swimmer Judit Kiss at 12yr 184 days.

Sporting superstar and two-time gold medallist Michael Jordan, part of the American basketball 'Dream Team' which dominated the 1992 tournament (Popperfoto)

1992 (Summer) MEDALS TABLE

	G	S	B
Unified Team	45	38	29
United States	37	34	37
Germany	33	21	28
China	16	22	16
Cuba	14	6	11
Spain	13	7	2
Korea	12	5	12
Hungary	11	12	7
France	8	5	16
Australia	7	9	11
Canada	7	4	7
Italy	6	5	8
Great Britain	5	3	12
Romania	4	6	8
Czechoslovakia	4	2	1
North Korea (PRK)	4	-	5
Japan	3	8	11
Bulgaria	3	7	6
Poland	3	6	10
Netherlands	2	6	7
Kenya	2	4	2
Norway	2	4	1
Turkey	2	2	2
Indonesia	2	2	1
Brazil	2	1	-
Greece	2	-	-
Sweden	1	7	4
New Zealand	1	4	5
Finland	1	2	2
Denmark	1	1	4
Morocco	1	1	1
Ireland	1	1	-
Ethiopia	1	-	2
Algeria	1	-	1
Estonia	1	-	1
Lithuania	1	-	1
Switzerland	1	-	-
Jamaica	-	3	1
Nigeria	-	3	1
Latvia	-	2	1
Austria	-	2	-
Namibia	-	2	-
South Africa	-	2	-
Belgium	-	1	2
Croatia	-	1	2
IOP	-	1	2
Iran	-	1	2
Israel	-	1	1
Chinese Taipei	-	1	-
Mexico	-	1	-
Peru	-	1	-
Slovenia	-	-	2
Mongolia	-	-	2
Argentina	-	-	1
Bahamas	-	-	1
Colombia	-	-	1
Ghana	-	-	1
Malaysia	-	-	1
Pakistan	-	-	1
Philippines	-	-	1
Puerto Rico	-	-	1
Qatar	-	-	1
Surinam	-	-	1
Thailand	-	-	1

1994

XVIIth Winter Games – Lillehammer, Norway

12 – 27 February

Attended by representatives of 67 countries, comprising 1737 competitors of which 520 were women.

It was in September 1988 during the Seoul Olympics that the IOC decided to award these Games to Lillehammer, a town of 23,000 people some 180km north of Oslo. Three other cities had made bids but the Norwegian town, which had lost out to Albertville in the 1992 vote, won the IOC's approval this time. This was the first Winter Games not held in the same year as a summer celebration. Lillehammer held one of the most successful Games, summer or winter, of all time, with excellent weather, eye-catching facilities, firm and deep snow, good organization, and enthusiastic but non-chauvinistic spectators. The only adverse items were the extremely cold temperatures, often below minus 20 degrees C, and the high cost of food and drink.

A spectacular opening ceremony, embodying traditional themes such as the mythical Vetter people, involved actress Liv Ullmann and 'Kon-Tiki' anthropologist Thor Heyerdahl. The Games were officially opened by King Harald V, himself a former Olympian. The torch was brought into the stadium by Stein Gruben, who leaped from the ski jump before handing it to Catherine Nottingnes. She, in turn, passed it to Crown Prince Haakon, who lit the flame. The oath was taken by the triple gold medallist skier Vegard Ulvang. There was a minute's silence for the plight of Sarajevo – a former Olympic site.

The record number of countries, including 14 first-timers, was boosted by the break-up of the former Soviet Union, and led to a record 22 countries winning medals. In ice hockey and figure skating, professionals were allowed to compete. In the latter, stricter rules were in force governing skimpy clothing, and there were a number of controversial judging decisions which drew strong criticism. Prior to the Games excessive media interest had been generated by the vicious attack on US skater Nancy Kerrigan and the alleged involvement of her team-mate Tonya Harding. A record

Norwegian speed skater Johan Olav Koss thrilled the Hamar amphitheatre with his three gold medals, all won in world record times (Allsport/Shaun Botterill)

83% sale of event tickets was evidenced by the enormous crowds, particularly at the Nordic skiing, despite the intense cold. There were a number of new events including aerials in the freestyle skiing, and men's 500m and women's 1000m in the short-track speed skating. A reported $295million was paid by CBS for the American television rights.

The most successful competitor at Lillehammer was Manuela di Centa (ITA) who won five medals (2 gold, 2 silver, 1 bronze) in cross-country skiing, equalling the best ever total for a single Games. However, fellow Nordic skier Lyubov Yegorova (RUS) won three golds and one silver, thus equalling the Winter Games record total of six gold medals. In bobsledding, Gustave Weder (SUI) became the only man to successfully defend the 2-man title, while Wolfgang Höppe (GER) uniquely was a medallist in four Games. Alpine skier Vreni Schneider (SUI) was the first woman to total three gold medals in her sport, as well as setting an all-time record of five medals. Alberto Tomba (ITA) uniquely made it medals at three consecutive Games in Alpine skiing, which featured some very small margins of victory. Remarkably, for the first time ever, no Alpine nation gained a medal in the men's downhill race.

American speed skaters Bonnie Blair, with a record third consecutive 500m title, and Dan Jansen, a very popular, emotional winner after a series of disasters in the previous three Games, could not take the spotlight away from Norway's Johann Olav Koss. He won three gold medals, all in world record times. The ice hockey competition witnessed shock exits for the United States and Russia, and resulted in the first win by Sweden.

Kim Yoon-Mi (KOR) became the youngest ever gold medallist at a Winter Games in the short-track skating women's relay, aged 13yr 83 days. She was also the youngest ever female Olympic champion, winter or summer. The youngest male gold medallist at these Games was Maurizio Carnino (ITA) in the short-track relay aged 18yr 356 days. The winner of the women's figure skating, Oksana Baiul (UKR), was the youngest to win that title since Sonja Henie (NOR) in 1928. The oldest gold medallist/medallist was Maurilio De Zolt (ITA) in the Nordic relay aged 43yr 150 days, in his fifth Games. The oldest female medallist was Marja-Liisa Kirvesniemi (FIN) at 38yr 167 days, in her record-equalling sixth Games. Lillehammer was also the scene for the greatest sibling performance in a Winter Games, by the four Huber brothers of Italy. Wilfried and Norbert won gold and silver, separately in the luge pairs, while Gunther got a bronze in the 2-man bob and Arnold placed fourth in the luge singles.

At the end of these Games it was estimated that, excluding multi-participation by athletes, some 85,000 competitors had attended the Modern Games since 1896.

1994 (Winter) MEDALS TABLE

	G	S	B
Russia	11	8	4
Norway	10	11	5
Germany	9	7	8
Italy	7	5	8
United States	6	5	2
Korea	4	1	1
Canada	3	6	4
Switzerland	3	4	2
Austria	2	3	4
Sweden	2	1	-
Japan	1	2	2
Kazakstan	1	2	-
Ukraine	1	-	1
Uzbekistan	1	-	-
Belarus	-	2	-
Finland	-	1	5
France	-	1	4
Netherlands	-	1	3
China	-	1	2
Slovenia	-	-	3
Great Britain	-	-	2
Australia	-	-	1

1996

XXVIth Olympic Games – Atlanta, USA
19 July – 4 August

As these Games would be the 100th anniversary of the rebirth of the Modern Olympics, Athens was thought to be the most likely venue, although there were strong rival bids from Atlanta, Belgrade, Manchester, Melbourne and Toronto. The surprising decision, made in September 1990, was in favour of Atlanta. It was immediately suggested that many in the IOC had been swayed by the financial support that the city would receive from American media and other corporate sponsors (US television rights were sold for a record $456 million).

Whatever, the team from Atlanta undoubtedly made an excellent presentation. The Games will be one of the most centralized of recent years with most of the sports held within the periphery of the city. However, yachting, designated to the Georgia coast at Savannah, was a source of problems owing to the lack of facilities for competitors and officials. For a time it was suggested that the venue be changed and Miami in Florida was mentioned as one possibility. There was also a possible threat to the importation of horses from the Georgia state agriculture department, and a major worry was the anticipated 90 degree heat for the marathon races.

Although ideas to cut back on the number of sports and events in the Games have been mooted, there will be a record 29 sports and 271 events at Atlanta, with a possible 933 medals available. Newcomers will include softball, beach volleyball, mountain bike racing, and soccer for women. However, it has been agreed that demonstration sports will no longer be held as part of this and future celebrations. Other changes include the holding of the modern pentathlon on only one day, and the replacement of the Flying Dutchman 2-man yachting class by a single-handed Laser class. Many new facilities have been built, including an 85,000 seat stadium and a remarkable centre for equestrian sports. The comparative high price of event tickets and hotels, however, threatened to deter many European fans from attending.

1998

XVIIIth Winter Games – Nagano, Japan (7 – 22 February)

Nagano was awarded these Games in 1991, winning the IOC vote against Val d'Aosta (Italy), Jaca (Spain), Ostersund (Sweden) and Salt Lake City (USA). In 1994 CBS paid a record $375 million for the US television rights, while the EBU paid $72 million, another record, for the European rights. Curling, snowboarding and women's ice hockey will be new medal events. In men's ice hockey an agreement has been reached to allow NHL players to compete. Nagano is the southernmost site for a Winter Games.

2000

XXVIIth Olympic Games – Sydney, Australia (15 September – 1 October)

In 1994 Sydney was awarded the first Games of the second millennium, beating bids from Beijing, Brasilia, Istanbul, Manchester and, tentatively, Berlin. Two new sports will be Taekwondo (with four classes each for men and women) and the Triathlon. This latter will consist of a 1500m swim, 40km cycle and a 10km run. It was announced in August 1995 that NBC had paid a staggering $1.27 billion for the US television rights for Sydney ($785 million) and for the Winter Games of 2002.

2002

XIXth Winter Games – Salt Lake City, USA

After four previous bids Salt Lake City was finally chosen by the IOC in June 1995. There were nine original bids, which was reduced to four by the IOC – the others being Quebec City (Canada), Ostersund (Sweden) and Sion (Switzerland).

2004

XXVIIIth Olympic Games

Formal bids have been made by 11 cities around the world including Athens, Buenos Aires, Cape Town, Istanbul, Lille, Rio de Janeiro, Rome, San Juan, Seville, Stockholm and St Petersburg. The final decision will be taken by the IOC in September 1997.

In December 1995 NBC obtained exclusive US television rights to the Games of 2004, 2006 and 2008 for $2.3 billion. A number of cities have already expressed interest in hosting the 2006 Winter Games, 2008 Summer Games, and 2012 Summer Games. Thus the future of the Olympic movement well into the 21st century seems to be assured.

The Sports

Only five sports have been on the programme of every Modern Games since 1896 – cycling, fencing, gymnastics, swimming and track & field athletics. (Rowing should have been included with them, but rough seas caused its cancellation in 1896 although it was actually on the programme of events.)

Archery

The sport made its first appearance in the 1900 Games in Paris with six events on the programme. Some Olympic historians consider that another, live pigeon shooting, was an official event, but the majority think not, and this book follows that opinion. The contests were held in Continental style, with each archer shooting a single arrow at a time in competition order, as against the British method of three arrows at each turn. The eligibility of the 1904 archery competitions is also disputed by some, particularly as only American archers took part. However, the majority of historians (and this author) accept them as Olympic events. The competitors in the 1904 women's contests were among the first women to compete in the Olympics, only the tennis players in 1900 having a prior claim.

The competitions of 1908 were accorded a much higher status than before, although only three nations took part. The men's York Round was won by William Dod (GBR), and his remarkable sister Charlotte took the silver behind Queenie Newall in the women's event. Lottie Dod, then over 36 years old, was one of the greatest sportswomen of her, or any other, generation. She had won the Wimbledon tennis singles five times, the British Ladies golf crown in 1904, and had represented England at hockey. She also excelled at skating and tobogganing. She and William were also the first brother and sister, in any sport, to win medals at the Olympic Games.

Archery was not included in the 1912 Games but, reflecting Belgium's great interest in the sport, there were ten events at Antwerp in 1920, all in the Belgian style of shooting. With only three countries present again, Hubert van Innis (BEL), now 54, brought his total of medals to a record six gold and three silver. The most successful woman has been Kim Soo-Nyung (KOR) with three gold medals and a silver in 1988-92. The sport was dropped from the Games until 1972 when events were standardized into contests over Double FITA Rounds for men and women. A FITA (Fédération Internationale de Tir à l'Arc) Round consists of 144 arrows, comprising 36 each over distances of 90m, 70m, 50m and 30m for men and 70m, 60m, 50m and 30m for women. From 1988 the medals were decided by the scores in the final round of 36 arrows. Also in 1988

Elegance personified, Queenie Newall in 1908

team competitions were introduced. In 1992, after a qualifying round of 144 arrows, the top 32 competitors competed in knock-out stages of 12-arrow contests.

The oldest gold medallist was the Rev Galen Spencer (USA) in the winning 1904 team, two days past his 64th birthday. The youngest champion was Yun Young-Sookh (KOR) aged 17yr 21 days in the winning 1988 women's team. The youngest male winner was Park Sung-Soo (KOR) in the 1988 team aged 18yr 135 days, while the oldest female champion was Queenie Newall in 1908 aged 53yr 277 days. The oldest ever medallist was Samuel Harding Duvall (USA), winning a silver in the 1904 team contest aged 68yr 194 days, while the youngest medallist was Denise Parker (USA) with a team bronze in 1988 aged 14yr 294 days. The youngest male medallist was Henry Richardson (USA) with a team bronze in 1904 aged 15yr 126 days. Hubert van Innis (BEL) won gold medals over a record span of 20 years (1900-20). The first paraplegic to compete in a normal Olympic event was Neroli Fairhall (NZL) who finished 35th, from her wheelchair, in the 1984 women's archery event.

ARCHERY MEDALS TABLE

	Men			Women			
	G	S	B	G	S	B	Total
United States	7	5	4	4	2	3	25
France	6	10	6	-	-	-	22
Belgium	10	6	3	-	-	-	19
Korea	1	2	-	5	2	2	12
Soviet Union	-	1	1	1	2	4	9
Great Britain	1	1	3	1	1	1	8
Finland	1	1	1	-	-	1	4
Japan	-	1	1	-	-	-	2
China	-	-	-	-	2	-	2
Italy	-	-	2	-	-	-	2
Netherlands	1	-	-	-	-	-	1
Spain	1	-	-	-	-	-	1
Indonesia	-	-	-	-	1	-	1
Poland	-	-	-	-	1	-	1
Sweden	-	1	-	-	-	-	1
	28[1]	28	21[2]	11	11	11[3]	110

[1] Only a gold medal awarded in two 1920 events
[2] No bronze medals in one 1900 and six 1920 events
[3] No bronze medal in 1904 team event

ARCHERY MEDAL RESULTS 1900—1920

	GOLD	SILVER	BRONZE
1900	*Au cordon doré –50m*		
	Henri Herouin (FRA)	Hubert van Innis (BEL)	Emile Fisseux (FRA)
	Au cordon doré – 33m		
	Hubert van Innis (BEL)	Victor Thibaud (FRA)	Charles Petit (FRA)
	Au chapelet – 50m		
	Eugène Mougin (FRA)	Henri Helle (FRA)	Emile Mercier (FRA)
	Au chapelet – 33m		
	Hubert van Innis (BEL)	Victor Thibaud (FRA)	Charles Petit (FRA)
	Sur la perche à la herse		
	Emmanuel Foulon (FRA)	Pierre Serrurier (FRA) Emile Druart Jr (BEL)	–
	Sur la perche à la pyramide		
	Emile Grumiaux (FRA)	Auguste Serrurier (FRA)	Louis Glineux (BEL)
1904	**Men**		
	Double York Round		
	Phillip Bryant (USA)	Robert Williams (USA)	William Thompson (USA)
	Double American Round		
	Philip Bryant (USA)	Robert Williams (USA)	William Thompson (USA)
	Team Round		
	Potomac Archers (USA)	Cincinnati Archery Club (USA)	Boston AA (USA)
	Women		
	Double National Round		
	Lida Howell (USA)	Jessie Pollack (USA)	Emma Cooke (USA)
	Double Columbia Round		
	Lida Howell (USA)	Emma Cooke (USA)	Jessie Pollack (USA)

1908   **Men**
        York Round
        William Dod (GBR)   RB Brooks-King (GBR)   Henry Richardson (USA)
        Continental Style
        EG Grisot (FRA)   Louis Vernet (FRA)   Gustave Cabaret (FRA)
        Women
        National Round
        Queenie Newall (GBR)   Charlotte Dod (GBR)   Hill-Lowe (GBR)

1920   *Fixed bird target – small birds – individual*
        Edmond van Moer (BEL)   Louis van de Perck (BEL)   Joseph Hermans (BEL)
        Fixed bird target – small birds – team
        Belgium   –   –
        Fixed bird target – large birds – individual
        Edouard Cloetens (BEL)   Louis van de Perck (BEL)   Firmin Flamand (BEL)
        Fixed bird target – large birds – team
        Belgium   –   –
        Moving bird target – 28m – individual
        Hubert van Innis (BEL)   Léonce Quentin (FRA)   –
        Moving bird target – 28m – team
        Netherlands   Belgium   France
        Moving bird target – 33m – individual
        Hubert van Innis (BEL)   Julien Brulé (FRA)   –
        Moving bird target – 33m – team
        Belgium   France   –
        Moving bird target – 50m – individual
        Julien Brulé (FRA)   Hubert van Innis (BEL)   –
        Moving bird target – 50m – team
        Belgium   France   –

ARCHERY MEDAL RESULTS 1972–1988

DOUBLE FITA ROUND *(Maximum possible score 2880 points)*

	GOLD	SILVER	BRONZE
Men			
1972	John Williams (USA) 2528 pts	Gunnar Jarvil (SWE) 2481 pts	Kyösti Laasonen (FIN) 2467 pts
1976	Darrell Pace (USA) 2571 pts	Hiroshi Michinaga (JPN) 2502 pts	Giancarlo Ferrari (ITA) 2495 pts
1980	Tomi Poikolainen (FIN) 2455 pts	Boris Isachenko (URS) 2452 pts	Giancarlo Ferrari (ITA) 2449 pts
1984	Darrell Pace (USA) 2616 pts *	Richard McKinney (USA) 2564 pts	Hiroshi Yamamoto (JPN) 2563 pts
1988	Jay Barrs (USA) 338 pts (2605)	Park Sung-Soo (KOR) 336 pts (2614)	Vladimir Yecheyev (URS) 335 pts (2600)
1992	Sebastien Flute (FRA)	Chung Jae-Hun (KOR)	Simon Terry (GBR)
Women			
1972	Doreen Wilber (USA) 2424 pts	Irena Szydlowska (POL) 2407 pts	Emma Gapchenko (URS) 2403 pts
1976	Luann Ryon (USA) 2499 pts	Valentina Kovpan (URS) 2460 pts	Zebeniso Rustamova (URS) 2407 pts
1980	Keto Losaberidze (URS) 2491 pts	Batalya Butuzova (URS) 2477 pts	Päivi Meriluoto (FIN) 2449 pts
1984	Seo Hyang-Soon (KOR) 2568 pts	Li Lingjuan (CHN) 2559 pts	Kim Jin-Ho (KOR) 2555 pts
1988	Kim Soo-Nyung (KOR) 344 pts (2683*)	Wang Hee-Kyung (KOR) 332 pts (2612)	Yung Young-Sook (KOR) 327 pts (2603)
1992	Cho Youn-Jeong (KOR)	Kim Soo-Nyung (KOR)	Natalia Valeeva (EUN)

*Olympic record

Team – Men					**Team – Women**			
1988	Korea	United States	Great Britain		1988	Korea	Indonesia	United States
1992	Spain	Finland	Great Britain		1992	Korea	China	Unified Team

Athletics

The track and field events have been the centre-piece of every Olympic Games since 1896. From 1920 until the International Amateur Athletics Federation (IAAF) inaugurated their first world title meeting in 1983, the Olympic events were also official world championships. In the early Games quite large numbers of entries per country were allowed in an event, e.g. 12 in 1908, but in 1928 that was limited to four and in 1932 to three. After Barcelona in 1992 a suggestion was made to reduce that to two, but has not been acted on to date.

The first champion in modern Olympic history was James Connolly (USA) who won the triple jump (then called the hop, step and jump) on 6 April 1896. He also won medals in the high and long jumps, and was later a novelist and war correspondent. The first winner of an Olympic event was Francis Lane (USA) who won the first heat of the 100m earlier the same day. Women's events were introduced in 1928, and the first female gold medallist was Halina Konopacka (POL) in the discus. The first winner of an Olympic women's event was Anni Holdmann (GER), again in the first heat of the 100m the day before.

A record 10 gold medals were won by Ray Ewry (USA) in the standing jumps from 1900 to 1908. It is a feat unsurpassed in any sport, and was achieved despite the fact that Ewry had contracted polio as a child. The Finnish distance runner Paavo Nurmi won a total of 12 medals from 1920 to 1928, comprising nine golds and three silvers. He won them in an unmatched seven different events, and his five golds in 1924 is a record for one Games. Ewry had uniquely won three of his titles on the same day in 1900.

However, the most individual titles at one Games is four by Alvin Kraenzlein (USA) in 1900. This total was equalled by Jesse Owens (USA) in 1936 and Carl Lewis (USA) in 1984, but they only gained three individual events – 100m, 200m and long jump – with the fourth gold medal in the relay. Nurmi's team-mate Ville Ritola won a record six medals in 1924, consisting of four golds and two silvers, running eight distance races in eight days. In 1912 the forerunner of all 'Flying Finns', Hannes Kohlemainen, had won six such races within nine days.

Four gold medals have been won by four women: Fanny Blankers-Koen (NED) in 1948, which is a female record for one Games, as is the three individual titles she won; Betty Cuthbert (AUS) in 1956 and 1964; Bärbel Wöckel (née Eckert) (GDR) in 1976 and 1980; and Evelyn Ashford (USA) from 1984 to 1992. Shirley Strickland (later de la Hunty) (AUS) won a record seven medals from 1948 to 1956, comprising three golds, one silver and three bronzes. This total was equalled by Irena Szewinska (née Kirszenstein) (POL) with three golds, two silvers and two bronzes from 1964 to 1976. Szewinska and Ashford are the only women to win medals at three successive Games – in Szewinska's case also in five different events. Study of photo-finish evidence indicates that in addition to the

Kevin Young (USA) set a new Olympic and world record mark in winning the 400m hurdles at Barcelona in 1992 (Allsport/Bob Martin)

medals she is credited with, Strickland also came third in the 200m of 1948, but no move has been made to change the result officially.

A unique track and field achievement, equalling that of yachting's Paul Elvström, was the four successive gold medals in the discus by Al Oerter (USA), 1956-68. Almost as worthy were the three golds and one silver won by Viktor Saneyev (URS) in the triple jump, 1968-1980. Mildred Didrikson (USA) – who later achieved golfing fame as Babe Zaharias – achieved a unique triple in 1932 when she won medals in a run (80m hurdles, gold), a jump (high jump, silver) and a throw (javelin, gold). Another unusual spread of medals went to Micheline Ostermeyer (FRA) in 1948 with golds in the shot and discus and a bronze in the high jump – perhaps even more unusual was the fact that she was a concert pianist. The best male equivalent was Robert Garrett (USA) with golds in the shot and discus, and silvers in the high and long jumps, in 1896. Stanley Rowley won bronze medals in the 60m, 100m and 200m in 1900 representing Australasia (he was Australian), then was drafted into the British team for the 5000m team race and won a gold medal, although he did not finish the race.

The oldest gold medallist was Patrick 'Babe' McDonald (USA) winning the 56lb weight throw in 1920 aged 42yr 23 days. The youngest gold medallist was Barbara Pearl Jones (USA) in the 1952 sprint relay aged 15yr 123 days, while the youngest individual event champion was Ulrike Meyfarth (FRG) who won the high jump in 1972 when exactly one year older. The youngest male champion was Robert Mathias (USA) who won the 1948 decathlon aged 17yr 263 days, and later (1966) became a US Congressman. The oldest female champion was Lia Manoliu (ROM) in the 1968 discus aged 36yr 176 days. She is also co-holder of another record, that of attending six Games (1952-72). The equivalent male record of five Games is held by nine men. Her 20-year span of competition matched the record of

ATHLETICS OLYMPIC RECORDS

Men

100m	9.92s	Carl Lewis (USA)	1988
200m	19.73s	Michael Marsh (USA)	1992
400m	43.50s	Quincy Watts (USA)	1992
800m	1m 43.00s	Joaquim Cruz (BRA)	1984
1500m	3m 32.53s	Sebastian Coe (GBR)	1984
5000m	13m 05.59s	Said Aouita (MAR)	1984
10,000m	27m 21.46s	Brahim Boutayeb (MAR)	1988
Marathon	2h 09m 21s	Carlos Lopez (POR)	1984
110m H	12.98s	Roger Kingdom (USA)	1988
400m H	46.78s	Kevin Young (USA)	1992
3000m St	8m 05.51s	Julius Kariuki (KEN)	1988
20km Walk	1h 19m 57s	Jozef Pribilinec (TCH)	1988
50km Walk	3h 38m 29s	Vyacheslav Ivanenko (URS)	1988
4 x 100m	37.40s	United States	1992
4 x 400m	2m 55.74s	United States	1992
High Jump	2.38m	Gennadi Avdeyenko (URS)	1988
Pole Vault	5.90m	Sergei Bubka (URS)	1988
Long Jump	8.90m	Bob Beamon (USA)	1968
Triple Jump	17.63m	Mike Conley (USA)	1992
	(18.17w	Mike Conley (USA)	1992)
Shot	22.47m	Ulf Timmermann (GDR)	1988
Discus	68.82m	Jurgen Schult (GDR)	1988
Hammer	84.80m	Sergei Litvinov (URS)	1988
Javelin	89.66m	Jan Zelezny (TCH)	1992
Decathlon	8847pts	Daley Thompson (GBR)	1984

Women

100m	10.62s*	Florence Griffith-Joyner (USA)	1988
	(10.54w	Florence Griffith-Joyner (USA)	1988
200m	21.34s	Florence Griffith-Joyner (USA)	1988
400m	48.65s	Olga Bryzgina (URS)	1988
800m	1m 53.43s	Nadyezda Olizarenko (URS)	1980
1500m	3m 53.96s	Paula Ivan (ROM)	1988
3000m	8m 26.53s	Tatyana Samolenko (URS)	1988
10,000m	31m 05.21s	Olga Bondarenko (URS)	1988
Marathon	2h 24m 52s	Joan Benoit (USA)	1984
100m H	12.38s	Yordanka Donkova (BUL)	1988
400m H	53.17s	Debbie Flintoff-King (AUS)	1988
4 x 100m	41.60s	GDR	1980
4 x 400m	3m 15.17s	USSR	1988
10km Walk	44m 32s	Chen Yueling (CHN)	1992
High Jump	2.03m	Louise Ritter (USA)	1988
Long Jump	7.40m	Jackie Joyner-Kersee (USA)	1988
Shot	22.41m	Ilona Slupianek (GDR)	1980
Discus	72.30m	Martina Hellmann (GDR)	1988
Javelin	74.68m	Petra Felke (GDR)	1988
Heptathlon	7291pts	Jackie Joyner-Kersee (USA)	1988

* In preliminary round

Dorothy Odam-Tyler (GBR) and Toyoko Yoshino-Nakamura (JPN), both 1936-56. This was also equalled by Francie Larrieu-Smith (USA), 1972-92. The greatest span of competition in Olympic athletics is 24 years by discus thrower Frantisek Janda-Suk of Bohemia and Czechoslovakia, 1900-24.

The oldest medallist was Tebbs Lloyd Johnson (GBR) in the 50km walk of 1948 aged 48yr 115 days, and the oldest female medallist was Dana Zatopkova (TCH) in the 1960 javelin aged 37yr 348 days. Barbara Pearl Jones (see above) was also the youngest medallist, while the youngest male medallist was Mikhel Dorizas (GRE) in the 1906 stone throw aged 16yr 11 days. The oldest competitor ever in Olympic athletics was Percy Wyer (CAN) aged 52yr 199 days when 30th in the 1936 marathon. The oldest female competitor was Joyce Smith (GBR) aged 46yr 282 days when placing 11th in the 1984 marathon.

The first brothers to win medals were Richard and Lewis Sheldon (USA) in the 1900 throws and jumps respectively. The first to gain medals in the same event were Platt and Ben Adams (USA) who won gold and silver in the 1912 standing high jump. The most successful siblings were the Press sisters (URS), Tamara with three golds and a silver, and Irina with two golds, in 1960 and 1964. The only twins to win medals were Patrick and Pascal Barré (FRA) in the bronze medal sprint relay team of 1980.

Father and son gold medallists are represented by two families. Werner Järvinen (FIN) won the 1906 Greek style discus, his son Matti won the javelin in 1932, and another son, Akilles, gained silver medals in the 1928 and 1932 decathlons. In 1948 Imre Nemeth (HUN) won the hammer, and 28 years later his son Miklos won the javelin with a world record throw. The most successful mother/daughter combination was Elisabeta Bagriantseva (URS) with a silver in the 1952 discus and Irina Nazarova with a gold in the 4 x 400m relay of 1980.

One of the more poignant Olympic stories relates to Marie Dollinger, who was one of the girls involved in dropping the baton in the 1936 sprint relay when the German girls 'couldn't lose'. One imagines the thoughts of her daughter, Brunhilde Hendrix, in the 1960 relay final – happily she won a silver medal. It has recently been suggested that the disaster which befell the usual machine-like precision changes of the 1936 German team was due to last-minute change in their order, to match similar changes to the American team's order.

The first married couple to win gold medals were Emil and Dana Zatopek (TCH), Dana winning her javelin title on the same afternoon as one of Emil's in 1952. They also shared the same date of birth. The only other such couple were Viktor Bryzgin (URS), in the 4 x 100m in 1988, and his wife Olga, in the 400m and 4 x 400m.

Frank Wykoff (USA) was the only sprinter to win gold medals in three Games, in relay teams from 1928-36, until he was equalled by Evelyn Ashford (USA), also in relay teams 1984-92, and Carl Lewis (USA), 1984-92.

The first Olympic athlete to be disqualified for contravening the drug regulations was Danuta Rosani (POL) in the 1976 discus, but by far the biggest uproar occurred with the positive testing of Ben Johnson (CAN) after he had won the 1988 100m title in an apparently fabulous new world record of 9.79sec. The repercussions on world attitudes to drug testing were immense.

The scrutiny of 'sex testing' for women was introduced into the Games in 1968, many years too late in the opinion of many. They had in mind the case of Dora Ratjen (GER) who placed fourth in the 1936 women's high jump and was later found to be a man posing as a woman. Less clear cut was the case of Stella Walasiewicz (later Walsh), Polish-born but later an American citizen, who won gold and silver medals in the women's 100m of 1932 and 1936 respectively but was reported, after her violent death in 1980, to have 'primary male characteristics'.

The shortest time that an athlete has held an Olympic record is 0.4sec by Olga Rukavishnikova (URS) in the 1980 pentathlon. That is the difference between her second-place time in the final event (800m) and the third-place time of Nadyezda Tkachenko (URS), whose overall points score exceeded her team-mate's by 146.

Only three athletes have lost a title and then won it back. Nina Romashkova-Ponomareva (URS) won the discus in 1952, came third in 1956, then won again in 1960. Similarly Ulrike Meyfarth (FRG) won the high jump in 1972, did not make the final in 1976, but won again in 1984. The only man to do so was Vladimir Golubnichiy (URS) in the 20km walk, winning in 1960, placing third in 1964 and then first again in 1968. He also placed second in 1972. Meyfarth's twelve years between gold medals is matched only by Al Oerter and Irina Szewinska.

The largest number of competitors in a single event was the 118 runners, of whom 98 finished, in the 1988 men's marathon.

A number of athletics medallists have later made their mark in Hollywood films. In particular, they have come from the ranks of the decathletes – Jim Thorpe, Glenn Morris, Bob Mathias, Rafer Johnson, CK Yang, Floyd Simmons and Bruce Jenner. The 1928 silver medallist in the shot, Herman Brix, changed his name to Bruce Bennett and had many serious roles after an initial 'Tarzan' appearance. Norman Pritchard (IND), a 1900 medallist, made many silent films, while more recent additions to the Hollywood scene have been 1952 sprint relay gold winner Dean Smith (USA) and 1968 pole vault champion Bob Seagren (USA). The film industries of other countries have welcomed Tapio Rautavaara (FIN), the 1948 javelin champion; Giuseppe Tosi (ITA), the 1948 discus silver medallist; Giuseppe Gentile (ITA), 1968 triple jump bronze medallist; and Adhemar Ferreira da Silva (BRA), the 1952 and 1956 triple jump champion.

Tug of War

This sport was part of the athletics programme from 1900 to 1920. Three men won a record two golds and one silver from 1908 to 1920: John Shepherd, Frederick Humphreys and Edwin Mills, all from Great Britain. The oldest gold medallist was Humphreys aged 42yr 204 days in 1920, while the youngest was Karl Staaf (SWE) aged 19yr 101 days in 1900. There were some strange team compositions in the early days: the winning 1900 team comprised three Swedes and three Danes, the 1904 competition was between American clubs, and the 1908 tournament between British Police Clubs, with London City beating their colleagues from Liverpool.

OLDEST & YOUNGEST ATHLETICS MEDALLISTS

Men

Event	Medal	Youngest Yrs/Dys	Name/Country/Date	Oldest Yrs/Dys	Name/Country/Date
100m	G	19-128	Reggie Walker (SAF) 1908	32-121	Linford Christie (GBR) 1992
	M	18-234	Donald Lippincott (USA) 1912	32-121	Linford Christie (GBR) 1992
200m	G	20-47	Percy Williams (CAN) 1928	28-30	Pietro Mennea (ITA) 1980
	M	17-287	Dwayne Evans (USA) 1976	30-170	Barney Ewell (USA) 1948
400m	G	19-135	Steve Lewis (USA) 1988	30-323	Mike Larrabee (USA) 1964
	M	19-135	Steve Lewis (USA) 1988	30-323	Mike Larrabee (USA) 1964
800m	G	20-237	Ted Meredith (USA) 1912	31-147	Albert Hill (GBR) 1920
	M	20-035	Earl Jones (USA) 1984	32-58	Arthur Wint (JAM) 1952
1500m	G	21-62	Peter Rono (KEN) 1988	31-149	Albert Hill (GBR) 1920
	M	21-62	Peter Rono (KEN) 1988	31-149	Albert Hill (GBR) 1920
5000m	G	20-321	Joseph Guillemot (FRA) 1920	36-78	Miruts Yifter (ETH) 1980 [1]
	M	19-237	Fita Bayissa (ETH) 1992	36-78	Miruts Yifter (ETH) 1980 [1]
10,000m	G	21-42	Brahim Boutayeb (MAR) 1988	36-73	Miruts Yifter (ETH) 1980 [1]
	M	20-104	Richard Chelimo (KEN) 1992	36-73	Miruts Yifter (ETH) 1980 [1]
Marathon	G	20-301	Juan Zabala (ARG) 1932	37-176	Carlos Lopez (POR) 1984
	M	19-178	Ernst Fast (SWE) 1900	40-90	Mamo Wolde (ETH) 1972

Event					
3000m St	G	20-33	Matthew Birir (KEN) 1992	32-211	Kip Keino (KEN) 1972
	M	20-33	Matthew Birir (KEN) 1992	32-211	Kip Keino (KEN) 1972
110m Hur	G	20-304	Fred Kelly (USA) 1912	30-237	Mark McKoy (CAN) 1992
	M	20-304	Fred Kelly (USA) 1912	33-50	Willie Davenport (USA) 1976
400m Hur	G	20-329	Ed Moses (USA) 1976	29-207	Roy Cochran (USA) 1948
	M	18-325	Eddie Southern (USA) 1956	33-252	Kriss Akabusi (GBR) 1992
4x100m	G	18-118	Johnny Jones (USA) 1976	31-38	Carl Lewis (USA) 1992
	M	17-229	Ture Perrson (SWE) 1912	33-292	Jocelyn Delecour (FRA) 1968
4x400m	G	19-100	Edgar Ablowich (USA) 1932	32-62	Arthur Wint (JAM) 1952
	M	17-+	Pal Simon (HUN) 1908	33-254	Kriss Akabusi (GBR) 1992
20km Walk	G	23-109	Maurizio Damilano (ITA) 1980	33-110	Peter Frenkel (GDR) 1972
	M	21-253	Noel Freeman (AUS) 1960	37-71	Peter Frenkel (GDR) 1976
50km Walk	G	25-103	Norman Read (NZL) 1956	38-128	Thomas Green (GBR) 1932
	M	25-26	Antal Róka (HUN) 1952	48-115	Tebbs Lloyd Johnson (GBR) 1948
High Jump	G	19-214	Jacek Wszola (POL) 1976	30-3	Con Leahy (GBR) 1906
	M	18-140	Valeriy Brumel (URS) 1960	32-85	Con Leahy (GBR) 1906
Pole Vault	G	17-360	Lee Barnes (USA) 1924	30-280	Bob Richards (USA) 1956
	M	17-360	Lee Barnes (USA) 1924	30-280	Bob Richards (USA) 1956
Long Jump	G	19-17	Randy Williams (USA) 1972	31-36	Carl Lewis (USA) 1992
	M	19-17	Randy Williams (USA) 1972	32-200	Larry Myricks (USA) 1988
Triple Jump	G	20-225	Gustaf Lindblom (SWE) 1912	31-195	Peter O'Connor (GBR) 1906
	M	20-38	Arnoldo Devonish (VEN) 1952	34-296	Viktor Saneyev (URS) 1980
Shot	G	19-167 [2]	Ralph Rose (USA) 1904	32-151	Wladyslaw Komar (POL) 1972
	M	19-167	Ralph Rose (USA) 1904	37-59	Denis Horgan (GBR) 1908
Discus	G	20-69	Al Oerter (USA) 1956	35-240	Ludvik Danek (TCH) 1972
	M	19-170	Ralph Rose (USA) 1904	37-46	John Powell (USA) 1984
Hammer	G	20-161	Jozsef Csermak (HUN) 1952	35-187	John Flanagan (USA) 1908
	M	19-165	Ralph Rose (USA) 1904	45-205	Matt McGrath (USA) 1924
Javelin	G	20-34	Erik Lundkvist (SWE) 1928	33-149	Tapio Rautavaara (FIN) 1948
	M	20-34 [3]	Erik Lundkvist (SWE) 1928	38-332	Jozsef Varszegi (HUN) 1948
Decathlon	G	17-263	Bob Mathias (USA) 1948	30-102 [4]	Helge Lovland (NOR) 1920
	M	17-263	Bob Mathias (USA) 1948	30-102	Helge Lovland (NOR) 1920

Women

Event					
100m	G	16-343	Elizabeth Robinson (USA) 1928	30-98	Fanny Blankers-Koen (HOL) 1948
	M	16-343	Elizabeth Robinson (USA) 1928	31-163	Evelyn Ashford (USA) 1988
200m	G	18-254	Betty Cuthbert (AUS) 1956	30-102	Fanny Blankers-Koen (HOL) 1948
	M	17-116	Raelene Boyle (AUS) 1968	32-98	Merlene Ottey (JAM) 1992
400m	G	19-340	Monika Zehrt (GDR) 1972	30-66	Irene Szewinska (POL) 1976
	M	18-152	Christina Brehner (GDR) 1976	30-66	Irene Szewinska (POL) 1976
800m	G	20-251	Madeline Manning (USA) 1968	27-223	Doina Melinte (ROM) 1984
	M	20-100	Inge Gentzel (SWE) 1928	33-205	Fita Lovin (ROM) 1984
1500m	G	24-29	Hassiba Boulmerka (ALG) 1992	29-47	Ludmila Bragina (URS) 1972
	M	19-227	Qu Yunxia (CHN) 1992	34-13	Maricica Puica (ROM) 1984
3000m	G	27-39	Tatyana Samolenko (URS) 1988	34-12	Maricica Puica (ROM) 1984
	M	23-357	Yvonne Murray (GBR) 1988	34-12	Maricica Puica (ROM) 1984
10,000m	G	20-139	Derartu Tulu (ETH) 1992	28-120	Olga Bondarenko (URS) 1988
	M	20-139	Derartu Tulu (ETH) 1992	32-28	Lynn Jennings (USA) 1992
Marathon	G	27-81	Joan Benoit (USA) 1984	30-86	Rosa Mota (POR) 1988
	M	25-228	Yuko Arimori (JPN) 1992	37-61	Lorraine Moller (NZL) 1992
80/100mH	G	17-19	Maureen Caird (AUS) 1968	31-133	Shirley Strickland (AUS) 1956
	M	17-19	Maureen Caird (AUS) 1968	34-95	Karin Balzer (GDR) 1972
400m Hur	G	22-115	Nawal El Moutawakel (MAR) 1984	28-161	Debbie Flintoff-King (AUS) 1988
	M	22-115	Nawal El Moutawakel (MAR) 1984	29-353	Sandra Farmer-Patrick (USA) 1992
4x100m	G	15-123	Barbara Jones (USA) 1952	35-115	Evelyn Ashford (USA) 1992
	M	15-123	Barbara Jones (USA) 1952	32-313	Evelyn Ashford (USA) 1982
4x400m	G	18-154 [5]	Christina Brehmer (GDR) 1976	30-235	Maria Pinigina (URS) 1988

	M	17-236	Mabel Fergerson (USA) 1972	30-235	Maria Pinigina (URS) 1988	
10km Walk	G	24-124	Chen Yueling (CHN) 1992	24-124	Chen Yueling (CHN) 1992	
	M	22-356	Li Chunxiu (CHN) 1992	26-184	Yelena Nikolayeva (CIS) 1992	
High Jump	G	16-123	Ulrike Meyfarth (FRG) 1972	30-225	Louise Ritter (USA) 1988	
	M	16-115	Dorothy Odam-Tyler (GBR) 1936	31-113	Sara Simeoni (ITA) 1984	
Long Jump	G	20-256	Tatyana Kolpakova (URS) 1980	29-67	Viorica Viscopoleanu (ROM) 1968	
	M	17-332	Willye White (USA) 1956	30-365	Tatyana Talysheva (URS) 1968	
Shot	G	21-186	Galina Zybina (URS) 1952	34-255	Ivanka Khristova (BUL) 1976	
	M	21-186	Galina Zybina (URS) 1952	35-244	Svetlana Krachevskaya (URS) 1980	
Discus	G	20-121	Evelin Schlaak (GDR) 1976	36-176	Lia Manoliu (ROM) 1968	
	M	20-100	Ruth Osburn (USA) 1932	36-176	Lia Manoliu (ROM) 1968	
Javelin	G	17-86	Mihaela Penes (ROM) 1964	33-190	Herma Bauma (AUT) 1948	
	M	17-86	Mihaela Penes (ROM) 1964	37-348	Dana Zatopkova (TCH) 1960	
Heptathlon	G	23-267	Glynis Nunn (AUS) 1984	30-152	Jackie Joyner-Kersee (USA) 1992	
	M	22-154	Jackie Joyner-Kersee (USA) 1984	30-344	Sabine John (GDR) 1988	

[1] *Questionable date of birth would result in revised age of 20 days less*
[2] *Michel Dorizas (GRE) was third in the 1906 Stone throw aged 16-11*
[3] *Michel Dorizas (GRE) was second in the 1908 Javelin (freestyle) aged 18-90*
[4] *Thomas Kiely (GBR) won the all-round title in 1904 aged 34-314*
[5] *Grit Breuer (GDR) only ran in heats of 1988 event, but received gold medal aged 16-228*

ATHLETICS MEDALS TABLE (Including Tug-of-War)

	Men			Women					Men			Women			
	G	S	B	G	S	B	Total		G	S	B	G	S	B	Total
United States [1]	251	188	159	36	24	14	672	Morocco	3	2	1	1	-	-	7
Soviet Union	37	37	42	34	29	35	214	Mexico	3	3	-	-	-	-	6
Great Britain	44	57	43	5	20	13	182	Spain	2	2	2	-	-	-	6
Finland	47	33	29	-	2	-	111	China	-	-	1	1	1	3	6
GDR	14	14	14	24	23	21	110	Ireland	4	1	-	-	-	-	5
Sweden	19	25	42	-	-	3	89	Argentina	2	2	-	-	1	-	5
Germany	7	22	24	-	7	12	13 ... 85	Portugal	1	1	1	1	-	1	5
Australia	6	9	12	11	8	12	58	Austria	-	-	1	1	3	-	5
France	7	21	18	4	1	3	54	Tunisia	1	2	1	-	-	-	4
Canada	10	10	17	2	5	7	51	Denmark	1	1	-	-	1	1	4
Italy	13	7	19	3	4	2	48	Trinidad	1	1	2	-	-	-	4
FRG	4	8	12	8	6	5	43	Nigeria	-	1	1	-	-	1	3
Poland	9	7	5	6	8	7	42	Chile	-	1	-	-	1	-	2
Hungary	6	13	16	3	1	2	41	India	-	2	-	-	-	-	2
Kenya	12	12	8	-	-	-	32	Tanzania	-	2	-	-	-	-	2
Greece	3	8	14	1	-	-	26	Yugoslavia	-	2	-	-	-	-	2
Czechoslovakia	8	7	3	3	2	2	25	Estonia	1	1	-	-	-	-	2
Romania	-	-	1	9	9	6	25	Latvia	1	1	-	-	-	-	2
Jamaica [2]	4	10	4	-	3	4	25	Taipei	-	-	-	-	1	1	2
Cuba	3	6	3	2	1	4	19	Namibia	-	2	-	-	-	-	2
New Zealand	7	1	7	1	-	2	18	Panama	-	-	2	-	-	-	2
Japan	4	5	6	-	2	-	17	Philippines	-	-	2	-	-	-	2
South Africa	4	4	4	1	2	1	16	Algeria	-	-	-	1	-	-	1
Bulgaria	1	-	-	1	2	7	5 ... 16	Korea	1	-	-	-	-	-	1
Netherlands	-	1	5	6	2	1	15	Lithuania	1	-	-	-	-	-	1
Ethiopia	5	1	6	1	-	-	13	Luxembourg	1	-	-	-	-	-	1
Norway	3	2	7	-	1	-	13	Uganda	1	-	-	-	-	-	1
Belgium	2	6	3	-	-	-	11	Haiti	-	1	-	-	-	-	1
Brazil	3	2	5	-	-	-	10	Iceland	-	1	-	-	-	-	1
Switzerland	-	6	2	-	-	-	8	Ivory Coast	-	1	-	-	-	-	1

[1] *Includes 2 additional golds awarded when Jim Thorpe was reinstated to 1912 decathlon/pentathlon titles*

	Men			Women			
	G	S	B	G	S	B	Total
Senegal	. . . . -	1	. . .	-	. . .	-	. . . . - 1
Sri Lanka	. . . . -	1	. . .	-	. . .	-	. . . . - 1
Bahamas	. . . . -	. .	. .	1	. . . . -	. . .	- 1
Barbados [2]	. . . . -	. .	. .	1	. . . . -	. . .	- 1
Colombia	. . . . -	. . .	-	. . .	-	. . .	1 1
Djibouti	. . . . -	. .	. .	1	. . . . -	. . .	- 1
Qatar	. . . . -	. .	. .	1	. . . . -	. . .	- 1
Turkey	. . . . -	. .	. .	1	. . . . -	. . .	- 1
Venezuela	. . . . -	. .	. .	1	. . . . -	. . .	- 1
	555	555	553	174	176	173	2186

[2] *Two bronzes counted for joint British West Indies 4 x 400m relay team in 1960*

Linford Christie became Britain's third Olympic 100m champion in 1992 (Allsport/Mike Powell)

ATHLETICS MEDAL RESULTS — MEN

Prior to 1972 automatic timings in the shorter distances to one-hundredths of a second are shown additionally, where known.

GOLD	SILVER	BRONZE

100 Metres

Year	GOLD	SILVER	BRONZE
1896	Thomas Burke (USA) 12.0	Fritz Hofmann (GER) 12.2	Alajos Szokolyi (HUN) 12.6
1900	Frank Jarvis (USA) 11.0	Walter Tewksbury (USA) 11.1	Stanley Rowley (AUS) 11.2
1904	Archie Hahn (USA) 11.0	Nathaniel Cartmell (USA) 11.2	William Hogenson (USA) 11.2
1906	Archie Hahn (USA) 11.2	Fay Moulton (USA) 11.3	Nigel Barker (AUS) 11.3
1908	Reginald Walker (RSA) 10.8	James Rector (USA) 10.9	Robert Kerr (CAN) 11.0
1912	Ralph Craig (USA) 10.8	Alvah Meyer (USA) 10.9	Donald Lippincott (USA) 10.9
1920	Charles Paddock (USA) 10.8	Morris Kirksey (USA) 10.8	Harry Edward (GBR) 11.0
1924	Harold Abrahams (GBR) 10.6	Jackson Scholz (USA) 10.7	Arthur Porritt (NZL) 10.8
1928	Percy Williams (CAN) 10.8	Jack London (GBR) 10.9	Georg Lammers (GER) 10.9
1932	Eddie Tolan (USA) 10.3 (10.38)	Ralph Metcalfe (USA) 10.3 (10.38)	Arthur Jonath (GER) 10.4 (10.50)
1936	Jesse Owens (USA) 10.3	Ralph Metcalfe (USA) 10.4	Martinus Osendarp (NED) 10.5
1948	Harrison Dillard (USA) 10.3	Norwood Ewell (USA) 10.4	Lloyd LaBeach (PAN) 10.4
1952	Lindy Remigino (USA) 10.4 (10.79)	Herb McKenley (JAM) 10.4 (10.80)	Emmanuel McD Bailey (GBR) 10.4 (10.83)
1956	Bobby Joe Morrow (USA) 10.5 (10.62)	Thane Baker (USA) 10.5 (10.77)	Hector Hogan (AUS) 10.6 (10.77)
1960	Armin Hary (GER) 10.2 (10.32)	David Sime (USA) 10.2 (10.35)	Peter Radford (GBR) 10.3 (10.42)
1964	Bob Hayes (USA) 10.0 (10.06) [1]	Enrique Figuerola (CUB) 10.2 (10.25)	Harry Jerome (CAN) 10.2 (10.27)
1968	James Hines (USA) 9.9 (9.95)	Lennox Miller (JAM) 10.0 (10.04)	Charles Greene (USA) 10.0 (10.07)
1972	Valeriy Borzov (URS) 10.14	Robert Taylor (USA) 10.24	Lennox Miller (JAM) 10.33
1976	Hasely Crawford (TRI) 10.06	Don Quarrie (JAM) 10.08	Valeriy Borzov (URS) 10.14
1980	Allan Wells (GBR) 10.25	Silvio Leonard (CUB) 10.25	Petar Petrov (BUL) 10.39
1984	Carl Lewis (USA) 9.99	Sam Graddy (USA) 10.19	Ben Johnson (CAN) 10.22
1988	Carl Lewis (USA) 9.92 [2]	Linford Christie (GBR) 9.97	Calvin Smith (USA) 9.99
1992	Linford Christie (GBR) 9.96	Frankie Fredericks (NAM) 10.02	Dennis Mitchell (USA) 10.04

[1] *Hayes ran a wind-assisted 9.91 in the semi-final.*
[2] *Ben Johnson (CAN) won in 9.79 but was later disqualified.*

200 Metres

Year	GOLD	SILVER	BRONZE
1900	Walter Tewksbury (USA) 22.2	Norman Pritchard (IND) 22.8	Stanley Rowley (AUS) 22.9
1904 [1]	Archie Hahn (USA) 21.6	Nathaniel Cartmell (USA) 21.9	William Hogenson (USA) d.n.a.
1908	Robert Kerr (CAN) 22.6	Robert Cloughen (USA) 22.6	Nathaniel Cartmell (USA) 22.7
1912	Ralph Craig (USA) 21.7	Donald Lippincott (USA) 21.8	Willie Applegarth (GBR) 22.0
1920	Allen Woodring (USA) 22.0	Charles Paddock (USA) 22.1	Harry Edward (GBR) 22.2
1924	Jackson Scholz (USA) 21.6	Charles Paddock (USA) 21.7	Eric Liddell (GBR) 21.9
1928	Percy Williams (CAN) 21.8	Walter Rangeley (GBR) 21.9	Helmut Kornig [2] (GER) 21.9

1932	Eddie Tolan (USA) 21.2 (21.12)	George Simpson (USA) 21.4	Ralph Metcalfe [3] (USA) 21.5
1936	Jesse Owens (USA) 20.7	Mack Robinson (USA) 21.1	Martinus Osendarp (NED) 21.3
1948	Mel Patton (USA) 21.1	Norwood Ewell (USA) 21.1	Lloyd LaBeach (PAN) 21.2
1952	Andrew Stanfield (USA) 20.7 (20.81)	Thane Baker (USA) 20.8 (20.97)	James Gathers (USA) 20.8 (21.08)
1956	Bobby Joe Morrow (USA) 20.7 (20.97)	Andrew Stanfield (USA) 20.9 (21.05)	Thane Baker (USA) 20.6 (20.75)
1960	Livio Berruti (ITA) 20.5 (20.62)	Lester Carney (USA) 20.6 (20.69)	Abdoulaye Seye (FRA) 20.7 (20.83)
1964	Henry Carr (USA) 20.3 (20.36)	Paul Drayton (USA) 20.5 (20.58)	Edwin Roberts (TRI) 20.6 (20.63)
1968	Tommie Smith (USA) 19.8 (19.83)	Peter Norman (AUS) 20.0 (20.06)	John Carlos (USA) 20.0 (20.10)
1972	Valeriy Borzov (URS) 20.00	Larry Black (USA) 20.19	Pietro Mennea (ITA) 20.30
1976	Don Quarrie (JAM) 20.23	Millard Hampton (USA) 20.29	Dwayne Evans (USA) 20.43
1980	Pietro Mennea (ITA) 20.19	Allan Wells (GBR) 20.21	Don Quarrie (JAM) 20.29
1984	Carl Lewis (USA) 19.80	Kirk Baptiste (USA) 19.96	Thomas Jefferson (USA) 20.26
1988	Joe DeLoach (USA) 19.75	Carl Lewis (USA) 19.79	Robson da Silva (BRA) 20.04
1992	Mike Marsh (USA) 20.01	Frankie Fredericks (NAM) 20.13	Michael Bates (USA) 20.38

[1] *Race over straight course. Hahn's three opponents were all given 2yd handicaps for false starting.*
[2] *Awarded bronze medal when Scholz (USA) refused to re-run after tie.*
[3] *Metcalfe's lane was later found to be 1.5m too long.*
1896, 1906 Event not held.

400 Metres

1896	Thomas Burke (USA) 54.2	Herbert Jamison (USA) 55.2	Fritz Hofmann (GER) 55.6
1900	Maxwell Long (USA) 49.4	William Holland (USA) 49.6	Ernst Schultz (DEN) 15m
1904	Harry Hillman (USA) 49.2	Frank Waller (USA) 49.9	Herman Groman (USA) 50.0
1906	Paul Pilgrim (USA) 53.2	Wyndham Halswelle (GBR) 53.8	Nigel Barker (AUS) 54.1
1908 [1]	Wyndham Halswelle (GBR) 50.0	–	–
1912	Charles Reidpath (USA) 48.2	Hanns Braun (GER) 48.3	Edward Lindberg (USA) 48.4
1920	Bevil Rudd (RSA) 49.6	Guy Butler (GBR) 49.9	Nils Engdahl (SWE) 50.0
1924	Eric Liddell (GBR) 47.6	Horatio Fitch (USA) 48.4	Guy Butler (GBR) 48.6
1928	Ray Barbuti (USA) 47.8	James Ball (CAN) 48.0	Joachim Büchner (GER) 48.2
1932	William Carr (USA) 46.2 (46.28)	Ben Eastman (USA) 46.4 (46.50)	Alexander Wilson (CAN) 47.4
1936	Archie Williams (USA) 46.5 (46.66)	Godfrey Brown (GBR) 46.7 (46.68)	James LuValle (USA) 46.8 (46.84)
1948	Arthur Wint (JAM) 46.2	Herb McKenley (JAM) 46.4	Mal Whitfield (USA) 46.6
1952	George Rhoden (JAM) 45.9 (46.09)	Herb McKenley (JAM) 45.9 (46.20)	Ollie Matson (USA) 46.8 (46.94)
1956	Charles Jenkins (USA) 46.7 (46.85)	Karl-Friedrich Haas (GER) 46.8 (47.12)	Voitto Hellsten (FIN) 47.0 (47.15)
			Ardalion Ignatyev (URS) 47.0 (47.15)
1960	Otis Davis (USA) 44.9 (45.07)	Carl Kaufmann (GER) 44.9 (45.08)	Mal Spence (RSA) 45.5 (45.60)
1964	Mike Larrabee (USA) 45.1 (45.15)	Wendell Mottley (TRI) 45.2 (45.24)	Andrzej Badenski (POL) 45.6 (45.64)
1968	Lee Evans (USA) 43.8 (43.86)	Lawrence James (USA) 43.9 (43.97)	Ron Freeman (USA) 44.4 (44.41)
1972	Vince Matthews (USA) 44.66	Wayne Collett (USA) 44.80	Julius Sang (KEN) 44.92
1976	Alberto Juantorena (CUB) 44.26	Fred Newhouse (USA) 44.40	Herman Frazier (USA) 44.95
1980	Viktor Markin (URS) 44.60	Rick Mitchell (AUS) 44.84	Frank Schaffer (GDR) 44.87
1984	Alonzo Babers (USA) 44.27	Gabriel Tiacoh (CIV) 44.54	Antonio McKay (USA) 44.71
1988	Steve Lewis (USA) 43.87	Harry Reynolds (USA) 43.93	Danny Everett (USA) 44.09
1992	Quincy Watts (USA) 43.50	Steve Lewis (USA) 44.21	Samson Kitur (KEN) 44.24

[1] *Re-run ordered after John Carpenter (USA) disqualified in first final. Only Halswelle showed up and 'walked over' for the title.*

800 Metres

1896	Edwin Flack (AUS) 2:11.0	Nandor Dáni (HUN) 2:11.8	Dimitrios Golemis (GRE) 2:28.0
1900	Alfred Tysoe (GBR) 2:01.2	John Cregan (USA) 2:03.0	David Hall (USA) d.n.a.
1904	James Lightbody (USA) 1:56.0	Howard Valentine (USA) 1:56.3	Emil Breitkreutz (USA) 1:56.4
1906	Paul Pilgrim (USA) 2:01.5	James Lightbody (USA) 2:01.6	Wyndham Halswelle (GBR) 2:03.0
1908	Mel Sheppard (USA) 1:52.8	Emilio Lunghi (ITA) 1:54.2	Hanns Braun (GER) 1:55.2
1912	James Meredith (USA) 1:51.9	Mel Sheppard (USA) 1:52.0	Ira Davenport (USA) 1:52.0
1920	Albert Hill (GBR) 1:53.4	Earl Eby (USA) 1:53.6	Bevil Rudd (RSA) 1:54.0
1924	Douglas Lowe (GBR) 1:52.4	Paul Martin (SUI) 1:52.6	Schuyler Enck (USA) 1:53.0
1928	Douglas Lowe (GBR) 1:51.8	Erik Bylehn (SWE) 1:52.8	Hermann Engelhardt (GER) 1:53.2
1932	Thomas Hampson (GBR) 1:49.7	Alexander Wilson (CAN) 1:49.9	Phil Edwards (CAN) 1:51.5

1936	John Woodruff (USA) 1:52.9	Mario Lanzi (ITA) 1:53.3	Phil Edwards (CAN) 1:53.6
1948	Mal Whitfield (USA) 1:49.2	Arthur Wint (JAM) 1:49.5	Marcel Hansenne (FRA) 1:49.8
1952	Mal Whitfield (USA) 1:49.2	Arthur Wint (JAM) 1:49.4	Heinz Ulzheimer (GER) 1:49.7
1956	Tom Courtney (USA) 1:47.7	Derek Johnson (GBR) 1:47.8	Audun Boysen (NOR) 1:48.1
1960	Peter Snell (NZL) 1:46.3	Roger Moens (BEL) 1:46.5	George Kerr [1] (BWI) 1:47.1
1964	Peter Snell (NZL) 1:45.1	Bill Crothers (CAN) 1:45.6	Wilson Kiprugut (KEN) 1:45.9
1968	Ralph Doubell (AUS) 1:44.3	Wilson Kiprugut (KEN) 1:44.5	Tom Farrell (USA) 1:45.4
1972	Dave Wottle (USA) 1:45.9	Yevgeniy Arzhanov (URS) 1:45.9	Mike Boit (KEN) 1:46.0
1976	Alberto Juantorena (CUB) 1:43.5	Ivo Van Damme (BEL) 1:34.9	Richard Wohlhuter (USA) 1:44.1
1980	Steve Ovett (GBR) 1:45.4	Sebastian Coe (GBR) 1:45.9	Nikolai Kirov (URS) 1:46.0
1984	Joaquim Cruz (BRA) 1:43.00	Sebastian Coe (GBR) 1:43.64	Earl Jones (USA) 1:43.83
1988	Paul Ereng (KEN) 1:43.45	Joaquim Cruz (BRA) 1:43.90	Saïd Aouita (MAR) 1:44.06
1992	William Tanui (KEN) 1:43.66	Nixon Kiprotich (KEN) 1:43.70	Johnny Gray (USA) 1:43.97

[1] *Kerr was a Jamaican in the combined Antilles team.*

1500 Metres

1896	Edwin Flack (AUS) 4:33.2	Arthur Blake (USA) 4:34.0	Albin Lermusiaux (FRA) 4:36.0
1900	Charles Bennett (GBR) 4:06.2	Henri Deloge (FRA) 4:06.6	John Bray (USA) 4:07.2
1904	James Lightbody (USA) 4:05.4	William Verner (USA) 4:06.8	Lacey Hearn (USA) d.n.a.
1906	James Lightbody (USA) 4:12.0	John McGough (GBR) 4:12.6	Kristian Hellström (SWE) 4:13.4
1908	Mel Sheppard (USA) 4:03.4	Harold Wilson (GBR) 4:03.6	Norman Hallows (GBR) 4:04.0
1912 [1]	Arnold Jackson (GBR) 3:56.8	Abel Kiviat (USA) 3:56.9	Norman Taber (USA) 3:56.9
1920	Albert Hill (GBR) 4:01.8	Philip Baker [1] (GBR) 4:02.4	Lawrence Shields (USA) 4:03.1
1924	Paavo Nurmi (FIN) 3:53.6	Willy Schärer (SUI) 3:55.0	Henry Stallard (GBR) 3:55.6
1928	Harri Larva (FIN) 3:53.2	Jules Ladoumègue (FRA) 3:53.8	Eino Purje (FIN) 3:56.4
1932	Luigi Beccali (ITA) 3:51.2	John Cornes (GBR) 3:52.6	Phil Edwards (CAN) 3:52.8
1936	Jack Lovelock (NZL) 3:47.8	Glenn Cunningham (USA) 3:48.4	Luigi Beccali (ITA) 3:49.2
1948	Henry Eriksson (SWE) 3:49.8	Lennart Strand (SWE) 3:50.4	Willem Slijkhuis (NED) 3:50.4
1952	Josef Barthel (LUX) 3:45.1	Bob McMillen (USA) 3:45.2	Werner Lueg (GER) 3:45.4
1956	Ron Delany (IRL) 3:41.2	Klaus Richtzenhain (GER) 3:42.0	John Landy (AUS) 3:42.0
1960	Herb Elliott (AUS) 3:35.6	Michel Jazy (FRA) 3:38.4	István Rózsavölgyi (HUN) 3:39.2
1964	Peter Snell (NZL) 3:38.1	Josef Odlozil (TCH) 3:39.6	John Davies (NZL) 3:39.6
1968	Kipchoge Keino (KEN) 3:34.9	Jim Ryun (USA) 3:37.8	Bodo Tümmler (FRG) 3:39.0
1972	Pekka Vasala (FIN) 3:36.3	Kipchoge Keino (KEN) 3:36.8	Rod Dixon (NZL) 3:37.5
1976	John Walker (NZL) 3:39.2	Ivo Van Damme (BEL) 3:39.3	Paul-Heinz Wellmann (FRG) 3:39.3
1980	Sebastian Coe (GBR) 3:38.4	Jürgen Straub (GDR) 3:38.8	Steve Ovett (GBR) 3:39.0
1984	Sebastian Coe (GBR) 3:32.53	Steve Cram (GBR) 3:33.40	Jose Abascal (ESP) 3:34.30
1988	Peter Rono (KEN) 3:35.96	Peter Elliott (GBR) 3:36.15	Jens-Peter Herold (GDR) 3:36.21
1992	Fermin Cacho (ESP) 3:40.12	Rachid El Basir (MAR) 3:40.62	Mohamed Suleiman (QAT) 3:40.69

[1] *Jackson later changed name to Strode-Jackson and Baker changed to Noel-Baker.*

5000 Metres

1912	Hannes Kolehmainen (FIN) 14:36.6	Jean Bouin (FRA) 14:36.7	George Hutson (GBR) 15:07.6
1920	Joseph Guillemot (FRA) 14:55.6	Paavo Nurmi (FIN) 15:00.0	Erik Backman (SWE) 15:13.0
1924 [1]	Paavo Nurmi (FIN) 14:31.2	Ville Ritola (FIN) 14:31.4	Edvin Wide (SWE) 15:01.8
1928	Ville Ritola (FIN) 14:38.0	Paavo Nurmi (FIN) 14:40.0	Edvin Wide (SWE) 14:41.2
1932	Lauri Lehtinen (FIN) 14:30.0	Ralph Hill (USA) 14:30.0	Lauri Virtanen (FIN) 14:44.0
1936	Gunnar Höckert (FIN) 14:22.2	Lauri Lehtinen (FIN) 14:25.8	Henry Jonsson [2] (SWE) 14:29.0
1948	Gaston Reiff (BEL) 14:17.6	Emil Zatopek (TCH) 14:17.8	Willem Slijkhuis (NED) 14:26.8
1952	Emil Zatopek (TCH) 14:06.6	Alain Mimoun (FRA) 14:07.4	Herbert Schade (GER) 14:08.6
1956	Vladimir Kuts (URS) 13:39.6	Gordon Pirie (GBR) 13:50.6	Derek Ibbotson (GBR) 13:54.4
1960	Murray Halberg (NZL) 13:43.4	Hans Grodotzki (GER) 13:44.6	Kazimierz Zimny (POL) 13:44.8
1964	Bob Schul (USA) 13:48.8	Harald Norpoth (GER) 13:49.6	Bill Dellinger (USA) 13:49.8
1968	Mohamed Gammoudi (TUN) 14:05.0	Kipchoge Keino (KEN) 14:05.2	Naftali Temu (KEN) 14:06.4
1972	Lasse Viren (FIN) 13:26.4	Mohamed Gammoudi (TUN) 13:27.4	Ian Stewart (GBR) 13:27.6
1976	Lasse Viren (FIN) 13:24.8	Dick Quax (NZL) 13:25.2	Klaus-Peter Hildenbrand (FRG) 13:25.4
1980	Miruts Yifter (ETH) 13:21.0	Suleiman Nyambui (TAN) 13:21.6	Kaarlo Maaninka (FIN) 13:22.0

1984	Saïd Aouita (MAR) 13:05.59	Markus Ryffel (SUI) 13:07.54	Antonio Leitao (POR) 13:09.20
1988	John Ngugi (KEN) 13:11.70	Dieter Baumann (FRG) 13:15.52	Hansjörg Kunze (GDR) 13:15.73
1992	Dieter Baumann (GER)	Paul Botok (13:12.52	

[1] *Nurmi won 5000m only 90 minutes after winning the 1500m.*
[2] *Jonsson later changed name to Kälarne.*
1896–1908 Event not held.

10,000 Metres

1906 [1]	Henry Hawtrey (GBR) 26:11.8	John Svanberg (SWE) 26:19.4	Edward Dahl (SWE) 26:26.2
1908 [1]	Emil Voigt (GBR) 25:11.2	Edward Owen (GBR) 25:24.0	John Svanberg (SWE) 25:37.2
1912	Hannes Kolehmainen (FIN) 31:20.8	Louis Tewanima (USA) 32:06.6	Albin Stenroos (FIN) 32:21.8
1920	Paavo Nurmi (FIN) 31:45.8	Joseph Guillemot (FRA) 31:47.2	James Wilson (GBR) 31:50.8
1924	Ville Ritola (FIN) 30:23.2	Edvin Wide (SWE) 30:55.2	Eero Berg (FIN) 31:43.0
1928	Paavo Nurmi (FIN) 30:18.8	Ville Ritola (FIN) 30:19.4	Edvin Wide (SWE) 31:00.8
1932	Janusz Kusocinski (POL) 30:11.4	Volmari Iso-Hollo (FIN) 30:12.6	Lauri Virtanen (FIN) 30:35.0
1936	Ilmari Salminen (FIN) 30:15.4	Arvo Askola (FIN) 30:15.6	Volmari Iso-Hollo (FIN) 30:20.2
1948	Emil Zatopek (TCH) 29:59.6	Alain Mimoun (FRA) 30:47.4	Bertil Albertsson (SWE) 30:53.6
1952	Emil Zatopek (TCH) 29:17.0	Alain Mimoun (FRA) 29:32.8	Aleksandr Anufriyev (URS) 29:48.2
1956	Vladimir Kuts (URS) 28:45.6	József Kovács (HUN) 28:52.4	Allan Lawrence (AUS) 28:53.6
1960	Pyotr Bolotnikov (URS) 28:32.2	Hans Grodotzki (GER) 28:37.0	David Power (AUS) 28:38.2 [2]
1964	Billy Mills (USA) 28:24.4	Mohamed Gammoudi (TUN) 28:24.8	Ron Clarke (AUS) 28:25.8
1968	Naftali Temu (KEN) 29:27.4	Mamo Wolde (ETH) 29:28.0	Mohamed Gammoudi (TUN) 29:34.2
1972	Lasse Viren (FIN) 27:38.4	Emiel Puttemans (BEL) 27:39.6	Miruts Yifter (ETH) 27:41.0
1976	Lasse Viren (FIN) 27:44.4	Carlos Lopes (POR) 27:45.2	Brendan Foster (GBR) 27:54.9
1980	Miruts Yifter (ETH) 27:42.7	Kaarlo Maaninka (FIN) 27:44.3	Mohammed Kedir (ETH) 27:44.7
1984	Alberto Cova (ITA) 27:47.54	Mike McLeod (GBR) 28:06.22 [3]	Mike Musyoki (KEN) 28:06.46
1988	Brahim Boutayeb (MAR) 27:21.46	Salvatore Antibo (ITA) 27:23.55	Kipkemboi Kimeli (KEN) 27:25.16
1992	Khalid Skah (MAR) 27:46.70	Richard Chelimo (KEN) 27:47.72	Addis Abebe (ETH) 28:00.07

[1] *5 miles (8046m).*
[2] *Recent investigation suggests 28:37.7.*
[3] *Martti Vainio (FIN) finished second but failed a drugs test.*
1896–1904 Event not held.

Marathon

The length of the marathon was standardized at the 1908 distance of 26 miles 385 yards (42,195 metres) from 1924.
Previously the distances had been: 1896 and 1904 – 40,000m, 1900 – 40,260m, 1906 – 41,860m, 1912 – 40,200m,
1920 – 42,750m.

1896	Spyridon Louis (GRE) 2h 58:50	Charilaos Vasilakos (GRE) 3h 06:03	Gyula Kellner (HUN) 3h 09:35
1900	Michel Theato [1] (FRA) 2h 59:45	Emile Champion (FRA) 3h 04:17	Ernst Fast (SWE) 3h 36:14
1904	Thomas Hicks (USA) 3h 28:35	Albert Coray [2] (FRA) 3h 34:52	Arthur Newton (USA) 3h 47:33
1906	William Sherring (CAN) 2h 51:23.6	John Svanberg (SWE) 2h 58:20.8	William Frank (USA) 3h 00:46.8
1908 [3]	John Hayes (USA) 2h 55:18.4	Charles Hefferon (RSA) 2h 56:06.0	Joseph Forshaw (USA) 2h 57:10.4
1912	Kenneth McArthur (RSA) 2h 36:54.8	Christian Gitsham (RSA) 2h 37:52.0	Gaston Strobino (USA) 2h 38:42.4
1920	Hannes Kolehmainen (FIN) 2h 32:35.8	Jüri Lossman (EST) 2h 32:48.6	Valerio Arri (ITA) 2h 36:32.8
1924	Albin Stenroos (FIN) 2h 41:22.6	Romeo Bertini (ITA) 2h 47:19.6	Clarence DeMar (USA) 2h 48:14.0
1928	Mohamed El Ouafi (FRA) 2h 32:57	Miguel Plaza (CHI) 2h 33:23	Martti Marttelin (FIN) 2h 35:02
1932	Juan Carlos Zabala (ARG) 2h 31:36	Sam Ferris (GBR) 2h 31:55	Armas Toivonen (FIN) 2h 32:12
1936	Sohn Kee-Chung [4] (JPN) 2h 29:19.2	Ernest Harper (GBR) 2h 31:23.2	Nam Seong-Yong [4] (JPN) 2h 31:42.0
1948	Delfo Cabrera (ARG) 2h 34:51.6	Tom Richards (GBR) 2h 35:07.6	Etienne Gailly (BEL) 2h 35:33.6
1952	Emil Zatopek (TCH) 2h 23:03.2	Reinaldo Gorno (ARG) 2h 25:35.0	Gustaf Jansson (SWE) 2h 26:07.0
1956	Alain Mimoun (FRA) 2h 25:00	Franjo Mihalic (YUG) 2h 26:32	Veikko Karvonen (FIN) 2h 27:47
1960	Abebe Bikila (ETH) 2h 15:16.2	Rhadi Ben Abdesselem (MAR) 2h 15:41.6	Barry Magee (NZL) 2h 17:18.2
1964	Abebe Bikila (ETH) 2h 12:11.2	Basil Heatley (GBR) 2h 16:19.2	Kokichi Tsuburaya (JPN) 2h 16:22.8
1968	Mamo Wolde (ETH) 2h 20:26.4	Kenji Kimihara (JPN) 2h 23:31.0	Michael Ryan (NZL) 2h 23:45.0
1972	Frank Shorter (USA) 2h 12:19.8	Karel Lismont (BEL) 2h 14:31.8	Mamo Wolde (ETH) 2h 15:08.4
1976	Waldemar Cierpinski (GDR) 2h 09:55.0	Frank Shorter (USA) 2h 10:45.8	Karel Lismont (BEL) 2h 11:12.6
1980	Waldemar Cierpinski (GDR) 2h 11:03	Gerard Nijboer (NED) 2h 11:20	Satymkul Dzhumanazarov (URS)

2h 11:35

1984	Carlos Lopes (POR) 2h 09:21	John Treacy (IRL) 2h 09:56	Charles Spedding (GBR) 2h 09:58
1988	Gelindo Bordin (ITA) 2h 10:32	Douglas Wakiihuri (KEN) 2h 10:47	Ahmed Saleh (DJI) 2h 10:59
1992	Hwang Young-cho (KOR) 2h13:23	Koichi Morishita (JPN) 2h13:45	Stephan Freigang (GER) 2h14:00

[1] *Recently found to have been of Luxembourg origin*

[2] *Usually shown as an American incorrectly.*

[3] *Dorando Pietri (ITA) finished first but was disqualified due to assistance by officials on last lap of the track.*

[4] *Then known as Kitei Son and Shoryu Nan – both from Korea.*

3000 Metres Steeplechase

1900 [1]	George Orton (CAN) 7:34.4	Sidney Robinson (GBR) 7:38.0	Jacques Chastanié (FRA) d.n.a.
1900 [2]	John Rimmer (GBR) 12:58.4	Charles Bennett (GBR) 12:58.6	Sidney Robinson (GBR) 12:58.8
1904 [3]	James Lightbody (USA) 7:39.6	John Daly (GBR) 7:40.6	Arthur Newton (USA) 25m
1908 [4]	Arthur Russell (GBR) 10:47.8	Archie Robertson (GBR) 10:48.4	John Eisele (USA) 20m
1920	Percy Hodge (GBR) 10:00.4	Patrick Flynn (USA) 100m	Ernesto Ambrosini (ITA) 30m
1924	Ville Ritola (FIN) 9:33.6	Elias Katz (FIN) 9:44.0	Paul Bontemps (FRA) 9:45.2
1928	Toivo Loukola (FIN) 9:21.8	Paavo Nurmi (FIN) 9:31.2	Ove Andersen (FIN) 9:35.6
1932 [5]	Volmari Iso-Hollo (FIN) 10:33.4	Tom Evenson (GBR) 10:46.0	Joseph McCluskey (USA) 10:46.2
1936	Volmari Iso-Hollo (FIN) 9:03.8	Kaarlo Tuominen (FIN) 9:06.8	Alfred Dompert (GER) 9:07.2
1948	Tore Sjöstrand (SWE) 9:04.6	Erik Elmsäter (SWE) 9:08.2	Göte Hagström (SWE) 9:11.8
1952	Horace Ashenfelter (USA) 8:45.4	Vladimir Kazantsev (URS) 8:51.6	John Disley (GBR) 8:51.8
1956	Chris Brasher (GBR) 8:41.2	Sándor Rozsnyói (HUN) 8:43.6	Ernst Larsen (NOR) 8:44.0
1960	Zdzslaw Krzyszkowiak (POL) 8:34.2	Nikolai Sokolov (URS) 8:36.4	Semyon Rzhischin (URS) 8:42.2
1964	Gaston Roelants (BEL) 8:30.8	Maurice Herriott (GBR) 8:32.4	Ivan Belyayev (URS) 8:33.8
1968	Amos Biwott (KEN) 8:51.0	Benjamin Kogo (KEN) 8:51.6	George Young (USA) 8:51.8
1972	Kipchoge Keino (KEN) 8:23.6	Benjamin Jipcho (KEN) 8:24.6	Tapio Kantanen (FIN) 8:24.8
1976	Anders Garderud (SWE) 8:08.0	Bronislaw Malinowski (POL) 8:09.1	Frank Baumgartl (GDR) 8:10.4
1980	Bronislaw Malinowski (POL) 8:09.7	Filbert Bayi (TAN) 8:12.5	Eshetu Tura (ETH) 8:13.6
1984	Julius Korir (KEN) 8:11.80	Joseph Mahmoud (FRA) 8:13.31	Brian Diemer (USA) 8:14.06
1988	Julius Kariuki (KEN) 8:05.51	Peter Koech (KEN) 8:06.79	Mark Rowland (GBR) 8:07.96
1992	Matthew Birir (KEN) 8:08.84	Patrick Sang (KEN) 8:09.55	William Mutwol (KEN) 8:10.74

[1] *2500m.*

[2] *4000m.*

[3] *2590m.*

[4] *3200m.*

[5] *3460m in final due to lap scoring error. Iso-Hollo clocked 9:14.6 in a heat.*
1896, 1906, 1912 Event not held.

110 Metres Hurdles

1896 [1]	Thomas Curtis (USA) 17.6	Grantley Goulding (GBR) 18.0	–
1900	Alvin Kraenzlein (USA) 15.4	John McLean (USA) 15.5	Fred Moloney (USA) 15.6
1904	Frederick Schule (USA) 16.0	Thadeus Shideler (USA) 16.3	Lesley Ashburner (USA) 16.4
1906	Robert Leavitt (USA) 16.2	Alfred Healey (GBR) 16.2	Vincent Duncker (RSA) [2] 16.3
1908	Forrest Smithson (USA) 15.0	John Garrells (USA) 15.7	Arthur Shaw (USA) 15.8
1912	Frederick Kelly (USA) 15.1	James Wendell (USA) 15.2	Martin Hawkins (USA) 15.3
1920	Earl Thomson (CAN) 14.8	Harold Barron (USA) 15.1	Frederick Murray (USA) 15.2
1924	Daniel Kinsey (USA) 15.0	Sydney Atkinson (RSA) 15.0	Sten Pettersson (SWE) 15.4
1928	Sydney Atkinson (RSA) 14.8	Stephen Anderson (USA) 14.8	John Collier (USA) 15.0
1932	George Saling (USA) 14.6 (14.57)	Percy Beard (USA) 14.7	Don Finlay (GBR) 14.8
1936	Forrest Towns (USA) 14.2	Don Finlay (GBR) 14.4	Fred Pollard (USA) 14.4
1948	William Porter (USA) 13.9	Clyde Scott (USA) 14.1	Craig Dixon (USA) 14.1
1952	Harrison Dillard (USA) 13.7 (13.91)	Jack Davis (USA) 13.7 (14.00)	Art Barnard (USA) 14.1 (14.40)
1956	Lee Calhoun (USA) 13.5 (13.70)	Jack Davis (USA) 13.5 (13.73)	Joel Shankle (USA) 14.1 (14.25)
1960	Lee Calhoun (USA) 13.8 (13.98)	Willie May (USA) 13.8 (13.99)	Hayes Jones (USA) 14.0 (14.17)
1964	Hayes Jones (USA) 13.6 (13.67)	Blaine Lindgren (USA) 13.7 (13.74)	Anatoliy Mikhailov (URS) 13.7 (13.78)
1968	Willie Davenport (USA) 13.3 (13.33)	Ervin Hall (USA) 13.4 (13.42)	Eddy Ottoz (ITA) 13.4 (13.46)

1972	Rod Milburn (USA) 13.24	Guy Drut (FRA) 13.34	Tom Hill (USA) 13.48
1976	Guy Drut (FRA) 13.30	Alejandro Casanas (CUB) 13.33	Willie Davenport (USA) 13.38
1980	Thomas Munkelt (GDR) 13.39	Alejandro Casanas (CUB) 13.40	Aleksandr Puchkov (URS) 13.44
1984	Roger Kingdom (USA) 13.20	Greg Foster (USA) 13.23	Arto Bryggare (FIN) 13.40
1988	Roger Kingdom (USA) 12.98	Colin Jackson (GBR) 13.28	Tonie Campbell (USA) 13.38
1992	Mark McKoy (CAN) 13.12	Tony Dees (USA) 13.24	Jack Pierce (USA) 13.26

[1] *Only two finalists.*

[2] *Recent research suggests he may have had German nationality at the time.*

400 Metres Hurdles

1900	Walter Tewksbury (USA) 57.6	Henri Tauzin (FRA) 58.3	George Orton (CAN) d.n.a.
1904 [1]	Harry Hillman (USA) 53.0	Frank Waller (USA) 53.2	George Poage (USA) 30m
1908	Charles Bacon (USA) 55.0	Harry Hillman (USA) 55.3	Leonard Tremeer (GBR) 57.0
1920	Frank Loomis (USA) 54.0	John Norton (USA) 54.3	August Desch (USA) 54.5
1924	Morgan Taylor (USA) 52.6 [2]	Erik Wilen (FIN) 53.8	Ivan Riley (USA) 54.2
1928	Lord Burghley (GBR) 53.4	Frank Cuhel (USA) 53.6	Morgan Taylor (USA) 53.6
1932	Bob Tisdall (IRL) 51.7 [2] (51.67)	Glenn Hardin (USA) 51.9 (51.85)	Morgan Taylor (USA) 52.0 (51.96)
1936	Glenn Hardin (USA) 52.4	John Loaring (CAN) 52.7	Miguel White (PHI) 52.8
1948	Roy Cochran (USA) 51.1	Duncan White (SRI) 51.8	Rune Larsson (SWE) 52.2
1952	Charlie Moore (USA) 50.8 (51.06)	Yuriy Lituyev (URS) 51.3 (51.51)	John Holland (NZL) 52.2 (52.26)
1956	Glenn Davis (USA) 50.1 (50.29)	Eddie Southern (USA) 50.8 (50.94)	Josh Culbreath (USA) 51.6 (51.74)
1960	Glenn Davis (USA) 49.3 (49.51)	Cliff Cushman (USA) 49.6 (49.77)	Dick Howard (USA) 49.7 (49.90)
1964	Rex Cawley (USA) 49.6	John Cooper (GBR) 50.1	Salvatore Morale (ITA) 50.1
1968	David Hemery (GBR) 48.1 (48.12)	Gerhard Hennige (FRG) 49.0 (49.02)	John Sherwood (GBR) 49.0 (49.03)
1972	John Akii-Bua (UGA) 47.82	Ralph Mann (USA) 48.51	David Hemery (GBR) 48.52
1976	Edwin Moses (USA) 47.64	Mike Shine (USA) 48.69	Yevgeniy Gavrilenko (URS) 49.45
1980	Volker Beck (GDR) 48.70	Vasiliy Arkhipenko (URS) 48.86	Gary Oakes (GBR) 49.11
1984	Edwin Moses (USA) 47.75	Danny Harris (USA) 48.13	Harald Schmid (FRG) 48.19
1988	Andre Phillips (USA) 47.19	Amadou Dia Ba (SEN) 47.23	Edwin Moses (USA) 47.56
1992	Kevin Young (USA) 46.78	Winthrop Graham (JAM) 47.66	Kriss Akabusi (GBR) 47.82

[1] *Hurdles only 2ft 6in (76.2cm) high instead of usual 3ft (91.4cm).*

[2] *Record not allowed because hurdle knocked down.*

1896, 1906, 1912 Event not held.

4 x 100 Metres Relay

1912 [1]	Great Britain 42.4	Sweden 42.6	–
1920	United States 42.2	France 42.6	Sweden 42.9
1924	United States 41.0	Great Britain 41.2	Netherlands 41.8
1928	United States 41.0	Germany 41.2	Great Britain 41.8
1932	United States 40.0 (40.10)	Germany 40.9	Italy 41.2
1936	United States 39.8	Italy 41.1	Germany 41.2
1948 [2]	United States 40.6	Great Britain 41.3	Italy 41.5
1952	United States 40.1 (40.26)	Soviet Union 40.3 (40.58)	Hungary 40.5 (40.83)
1956	United States 39.5 (39.60)	Soviet Union 39.8 (39.92)	Germany 40.3 (40.34)
1960 [3]	Germany 39.5 (39.66)	Soviet Union 40.1 (40.24)	Great Britain 40.2 (40.32)
1964	United States 39.0 (39.06)	Poland 39.3 (39.36)	France 39.3 (39.36)
1968	United States 38.2 (38.24)	Cuba 38.3 (38.40)	France 38.4 (38.43)
1972	United States 38.19	Soviet Union 38.50	FRG 38.79
1976	United States 38.33	GDR 38.66	Soviet Union 38.78
1980	Soviet Union 38.26	Poland 38.33	France 38.53
1984	United States 37.83	Jamaica 38.62	Canada 38.70
1988	Soviet Union 38.19	Great Britain 38.28	France 38.40
1992	United States 37.40	Nigeria 37.98	Cuba 38.00

[1] *German team finished second but was disqualified.*

[2] *United States disqualified but later reinstated.*

[3] *United States finished first (39.60) but disqualified.*

1896–1908 Event not held.

4 x 400 Metres Relay

1908 [1]	United States 3:29.4	Germany 3:32.4	Hungary 3:32.5
1912	United States 3:16.6	France 3:20.7	Great Britain 3:23.2
1920	Great Britain 3:22.2	South Africa 3:24.2	France 3:24.8
1924	United States 3:16.0	Sweden 3:17.0	Great Britain 3:17.4
1928	United States 3:14.2	Germany 3:14.8	Canada 3:15.4
1932	United States 3:08.2 (3:08.14)	Great Britain 3:11.2	Canada 3:12.8
1936	Great Britain 3:09.0	United States 3:11.0	Germany 3:11.8
1948	United States 3:10.4	France 3:14.8	Sweden 3:16.3
1952	Jamaica 3:03.9 (3.04.04)	United States 3:04.0 (3:04.21)	Germany 3:06.6 (3:06.78)
1956	United States 3:04.8	Australia 3:06.2 (3:06.19)	Great Britain 3:07.2 (3:07.19)
1960	United States 3:02.2 (3:02.37)	Germany 3:02.7 (3:02.84)	British West Indies [2] 3:04.0 (3:04.13)
1964	United States 3:00.7	Great Britain 3:01.6	Trinidad 3:01.7
1968	United States 3:56.1 (2:56.16)	Kenya 2:59.6 (2:59.64)	FRG 3:00.5 (3:00.57)
1972	Kenya 2:59.83	Great Britain 3:00.46	France 3:00.65
1976	United States 2:58.65	Poland 3:01.43	FRG 3:01.98
1980	Soviet Union 3:01.08	GDR 3:01.26	Italy 3:04.3
1984	United States 2:57.91	Great Britain 2:59.13	Nigeria 2:59.32
1988	United States 2:56.16	Jamaica 3:00.30	FRG 3:00.56
1992	United States 2:55.74	Cuba 2:59.51	Great Britain 2:59.73

[1] *Medley relay – 200m, 200m, 400m, 800m.*
[2] *Three from Jamaica, one from Barbados.*
1896–1906 Event not held.

20,000 Metres Road Walk

1956	Leonid Spirin (URS) 1h 31:27.4	Antonas Mikenas (URS) 1h 32:03.0	Bruno Junk (URS) 1h 32:12.0
1960	Vladimir Golubnichiy (URS) 1h 34:07.2	Noel Freeman (AUS) 1h 34:16.4	Stan Vickers (GBR) 1h 34:56.4
1964	Ken Matthews (GBR) 1h 29:34.0	Dieter Lindner (GER) 1h 31:13.2	Vladimir Golubnichiy (URS) 1h 31:59.4
1968	Vladimir Golubnichiy (URS) 1h 33:58.4	José Pedraza (MEX) 1h 34:00.0	Nikolai Smaga (URS) 1h 34:03.4
1972	Peter Frenkel (GDR) 1h 26:42.4	Vladimir Golubnichiy (URS) 1h 26:55.2	Hans Reimann (GDR) 1h 27:16.6
1976	Daniel Bautista (MEX) 1h 24:40.6	Hans Reimann (GDR) 1h 25:13.8	Peter Frenkel (GDR) 1h 25:29.4
1980	Maurizio Damilano (ITA) 1h 23:35.5	Pyotr Pochenchuk (URS) 1h 24:45.4	Roland Wieser (GDR) 1h 25:58.2
1984	Ernesto Canto (MEX) 1h 23:13	Raul Gonzalez (MEX) 1h 23:20	Maurizio Damilano (ITA) 1h 23:26
1988	Jozef Pribilinec (TCH) 1h 19:57	Ronald Weigel (GDR) 1h 20:00	Maurizio Damilano (ITA) 1h 20:14
1992	Daniel Plaza (ESP) 1h 21:45	Guillaume Leblanc (CAN) 1h 22:25	Giovanni de Benedictis (ITA) 1h 23:11

1896–1952 Event not held.

50,000 Metres Road Walk

1932	Thomas Green (GBR) 4h 50:10	Janis Dalinsh (LAT) 4h 57:20	Ugo Frigerio (ITA) 4h 59:06
1936	Harold Whitlock (GBR) 4h 30:41.1	Arthur Schwab (SUI) 4h 32:09.2	Adalberts Bubenko (LAT) 4h 32:42.2
1948	John Ljunggren (SWE) 4h 41:52	Gaston Godel (SUI) 4h 48:17	Tebbs Lloyd Johnson (GBR) 4h 48:31
1952	Giuseppe Dordoni (ITA) 4h 28:07.8	Josef Dolezal (TCH) 4h 30:17.8	Antal Tóka (HUN) 4h 31:27.2
1956	Norman Read (NZL) 4h 30:42.8	Yevgeniy Maskinov (URS) 4h 32:57.0	John Ljunggren (SWE) 4h 35:02.0
1960	Don Thompson (GBR) 4h 25:30.0	John Ljunggren (SWE) 4h 25:47.0	Abdon Pamich (ITA) 4h 27:55.4
1964	Abdon Pamich (ITA) 4h 11:12.4	Paul Nihill (GBR) 4h 11:31.2	Ingvar Pettersson (SWE) 4h 14:17.4
1968	Christoph Höhne (GDR) 4h 20:13.6	Antal Kiss (HUN) 4h 30:17.0	Larry Young (USA) 4h 31:55.4
1972	Bernd Kannenberg (FRG) 3h 56:11.6	Venjamin Soldatenko (URS) 3h 58:24.0	Larry Young (USA) 4h 00:46.0
1980	Hartwig Gauder (GDR) 3h 49:24	Jorge Llopart (ESP) 3h 51:25	Yevgeniy Ivchenko (URS) 3h 56:32
1984	Raul Gonzalez (MEX) 3h 47:26	Bo Gustafsson (SWE) 3h 53.19	Sandro Bellucci (ITA) 3h 53:45
1988	Vyacheslav Ivanenko (URS) 3h 38:29	Ronald Weigel (GDR) 3h 38:56	Hartwig Gauder (GDR) 3h 39:45
1992	Andrei Perlov (EUN) 3h50:13	Carlos Mercenario (MEX) 3h52:09	Ronald Weigel (GER) 3h 53:45

1896–1928, 1976 Event not held.

High Jump

Year			
1896	Ellery Clark (USA) 1.81m	James Connolly (USA) 1.65m	–
		Robert Garrett (USA) 1.65m	
1900	Irving Baxter (USA) 1.90m	Patrick Leahy (GBR) 1.78m	Lajos Gönczy (HUN) 1.75m
1904	Samuel Jones (USA) 1.80m	Garrett Serviss (USA) 1.77m	Paul Weinstein (GER) 1.77m
1906	Con Leahy (GBR) 1.77m	Lajos Gönczy (HUN) 1.75m	Herbert Kerrigan (USA) 1.72m
			Themistoklis Diakidis (GRE) 1.72m
1908	Harry Porter (USA) 1.905m	Con Leahy (GBR) 1.88m	–
		István Somodi (HUN) 1.88m	
		Georges André (FRA) 1.88m	
1912	Alma Richards (USA) 1.93m	Hans Liesche (GER) 1.91m	George Horine (USA) 1.89m
1920	Richmond Landon (USA) 1.94m	Harold Muller (USA) 1.90m	Bo Ekelund (SWE) 1.90m
1924	Harold Osborn (USA) 1.98m	Leroy Brown (USA) 1.95m	Pierre Lewden (FRA) 1.92m
1928	Robert King (USA) 1.94m	Ben Hedges (USA) 1.91m	Claude Ménard (FRA) 1.91m
1932	Duncan McNaughton (CAN) 1.97m	Robert Van Osdel (USA) 1.97m	Simeon Toribio (PHI) 1.97m
1936	Cornelius Johnson (USA) 2.03m	David Albritton (USA) 2.00m	Delos Thurber (USA) 2.00m
1948	John Winter (AUS) 1.98m	Björn Paulsen (NOR) 1.95m	George Stanich (USA) 1.95m
1952	Walt Davis (USA) 2.04m	Ken Wiesner (USA) 2.01m	Jose Telles da Conceicao (BRA) 1.98m
1956	Charlie Dumas (USA) 2.12m	Chilla Porter (AUS) 2.10m	Igor Kashkarov (URS) 2.08m
1960	Robert Shavlakadze (URS) 2.16m	Valeriy Brumel (URS) 2.16m	John Thomas (USA) 2.14m
1964	Valeriy Brumel (URS) 2.18m	John Thomas (USA) 2.18m	John Rambo (USA) 2.16m
1968	Dick Fosbury (USA) 2.24m	Ed Caruthers (USA) 2.22m	Valentin Gavrilov (URS) 2.20m
1972	Yuriy Tarmak (URS) 2.23m	Stefan Junge (GDR) 2.21m	Dwight Stones (USA) 2.21m
1976	Jacek Wszola (POL) 2.25m	Greg Joy (CAN) 2.23m	Dwight Stones (USA) 2.21m
1980	Gerd Wessig (GDR) 2.36m	Jacek Wszola (POL) 2.31m	Jörg Freimuth (GDR) 2.31m
1984	Dietmar Mögenburg (FRG) 2.35m	Patrik Sjöberg (SWE) 2.33m	Zhu Jianhua (CHN) 2.31m
1988	Gennadiy Avdeyenko (URS) 2.38m	Hollis Conway (USA) 2.36m	Rudolf Povarnitsin (URS) 2.36m
			Patrik Sjöberg (SWE) 2.36m
1992	Javier Sotormayor (CUB) 2.34m	Patrik Sjoberg (SWE) 2.34m	Hollis Conway (USA) 2.34m
			Tim Forsythe (AUS) 2.34m
			Artur Partyka (POL) 2.34m

Pole Vault

Year			
1896	William Hoyt (USA) 3.30m	Albert Tyler (USA) 3.20m	Ioannis Theodoropoulos (GRE) 2.60m
			Vasilios Xydas (GRE) 2.60m
			Evangelos Damaskos (GRE) 2.60m
1900	Irving Baxter (USA) 3.30m	Meredith Colkett (USA) 3.25m	Carl-Albert Andersen (NOR) 3.20m
1904	Charles Dvorak (USA) 3.50m	LeRoy Samse (USA) 3.43m	Louis Wilkins (USA) 3.43m
1906	Fernand Gonder (FRA) 3.50m	Bruno Söderstrom (SWE) 3.40m	Edward Glover (USA) 3.35m
1908	Edward Cooke (USA) 3.70m	–	Edward Archibald (CAN) 3.58m
	Alfred Gilbert (USA) 3.70m		Bruno Söderstrom (SWE) 3.58m
			Charles Jacobs (USA) 3.58m
1912	Harry Babcock (USA) 3.95m	Frank Nelson (USA) 3.85m	Bertil Uggla (SWE) 3.80m
		Marcus Wright (USA) 3.85m	William Happenny (CAN) 3.80m
			Frank Murphy (USA) 3.80m
1920	Frank Foss (USA) 4.09m	Henry Petersen (DEN) 3.70m	Edwin Meyers (USA) 3.60m
1924	Lee Barnes (USA) 3.95m	Glenn Graham (USA) 3.95m	James Brooker (USA) 3.90m
1928	Sabin Carr (USA) 4.20m	William Droegemuller (USA) 4.10m	Charles McGinnis (USA) 3.95m
1932	William Miller (USA) 4.31m	Shuhei Nishida (JPN) 4.30m	George Jefferson (USA) 4.20m
1936	Earle Meadows (USA) 4.35m	Shuhei Nishida (JPN) 4.25m	Sueo Oe (JPN) 4.25m
1948	Guinn Smith (USA) 4.30m	Erkki Kataja (FIN) 4.20m	Bob Richards (USA) 4.20m
1952	Bob Richards (USA) 4.55m	Don Laz (USA) 4.50m	Ragnar Lundberg (SWE) 4.40m
1956	Bob Richards (USA) 4.56m	Bob Gutowski (USA) 4.53m	Georgios Roubanis (GRE) 4.50m
1960	Don Bragg (USA) 4.70m	Ron Morris (USA) 4.60m	Eeles Landstrom (FIN) 4.55m
1964	Fred Hansen (USA) 5.10m	Wolfgang Reinhardt (GER) 5.05m	Klaus Lehnertz (GER) 5.00m
1968	Bob Seagren (USA) 5.40m	Claus Schiprowski (FRG) 5.40m	Wolfgang Nordwig (GDR) 5.40m
1972	Wolfgang Nordwig (GDR) 5.50m	Bob Seagren (USA) 5.40m	Jan Johnson (USA) 5.35m

1976	Tadeusz Slusarski (POL) 5.50m	Antti Kalliomaki (FIN) 5.50m	David Roberts (USA) 5.50m
1980	Wladislaw Kozakiewicz (POL) 5.78m	Tadeusz Slusarski (POL) 5.65m	–
		Konstantin Volkov (URS) 5.65m	
1984	Pierre Quinon (FRA) 5.75m	Mike Tully (USA) 5.65m	Earl Bell (USA) 5.60m
			Thierry Vigneron (FRA) 5.60m
1988	Sergey Bubka (URS) 5.90m	Rodion Gataullin (URS) 5.85m	Grigory Yegorov (URS) 5.80m
1992	Maksim Tarasov (EUN) 5.80m	Igor Trandenkov (EUN) 5.80m	Javier Garcia (ESP) 5.75m

Long Jump

1896	Ellery Clark (USA) 6.35m	Robert Garrett (USA) 6.18m	James Connolly (USA) 6.11m
1900	Alvin Kraenzlein (USA) 7.18m	Myer Prinstein (USA) 7.17m	Patrick Leahy (GBR) 6.95m
1904	Myer Prinstein (USA) 7.34m	Daniel Frank (USA) 6.89m	Robert Stangland (USA) 6.88m
1906	Myer Prinstein (USA) 7.20m	Peter O'Connor (GBR) 7.02m	Hugo Friend (USA) 6.96m
1908	Francis Irons (USA) 7.48m	Daniel Kelly (USA) 7.09m	Calvin Bricker (CAN) 7.08m
1912	Albert Gutterson (USA) 7.60m	Calvin Bricker (CAN) 7.21m	Georg Aberg (SWE) 7.18m
1920	William Pettersson (SWE) 7.15m	Carl Johnson (USA) 7.09m	Erik Abrahamsson (SWE) 7.08m
1924	William DeHart Hubbard (USA) 7.44m	Ed Gourdin (USA) 7.27m	Sverre Hansen (NOR) 7.26m
1928	Edward Hamm (USA) 7.73m	Silvio Cator (HAI) 7.58m	Alfred Bates (USA) 7.40m
1932	Ed Gordon (USA) 7.63m	Lambert Redd (USA) 7.60m	Chuhei Nambu (JPN) 7.44m
1936	Jesse Owens (USA) 8.06m	Luz Long (GER) 7.87m	Naoto Tajima (JPN) 7.74m
1948	Willie Steele (USA) 7.82m	Theodore Bruce (AUS) 7.55m	Herbert Douglas (USA) 7.54m
1952	Jerome Biffle (USA) 7.57m	Meredith Gourdine (USA) 7.53m	Odön Földessy (HUN) 7.30m
1956	Greg Bell (USA) 7.83m	John Bennett (USA) 7.68m	Jorma Valkama (FIN) 7.48m
1960	Ralph Boston (USA) 8.12m	Irvin Roberson (USA) 8.11m	Igor Ter-Ovanesyan (URS) 8.04m
1964	Lynn Davies (GBR) 8.07m	Ralph Boston (USA) 8.03m	Igor Ter-Ovanesyan (URS) 7.99m
1968	Bob Beamon (USA) 8.90m	Klaus Beer (GDR) 8.19m	Ralph Boston (USA) 8.16m
1972	Randy Williams (USA) 8.24m	Hans Baumgartner (FRG) 8.18m	Arnie Robinson (USA) 8.03m
1976	Arnie Robinson (USA) 8.35m	Randy Williams (USA) 8.11m	Frank Wartenberg (GDR) 8.02m
1980	Lutz Dombrowski (GDR) 8.54m	Frank Paschek (GDR) 8.21m	Valeriy Podluzhny (URS) 8.18m
1984	Carl Lewis (USA) 8.54m	Gary Honey (AUS) 8.24m	Giovanni Evangelisti (ITA) 8.24m
1988	Carl Lewis (USA) 8.72m	Mike Powell (USA) 8.49m	Larry Myricks (USA) 8.27m
1992	Carl Lewis (USA) 8.67m	Mike Powell (USA) 8.64m	Joe Greene (USA) 8.34m

Triple Jump
Formerly known as the Hop, step and jump

1896 [1]	James Connolly (USA) 13.71m	Alexandre Tuffere (FRA) 12.70m	Ioannis Persakis (GRE) 12.52m
1900	Myer Prinstein (USA) 14.47m	James Connolly (USA) 13.97m	Lewis Sheldon (USA) 13.64m
1904	Myer Prinstein (USA) 14.35m	Frederick Englehardt (USA) 13.90m	Robert Stangland (USA) 13.36m
1906	Peter O'Connor (GBR) 14.07m	Con Leahy (GBR) 13.98m	Thomas Cronan (USA) 13.70m
1908	Tim Ahearne (GBR) 14.92m	Garfield McDonald (CAN) 14.76m	Edvard Larsen (NOR) 14.39m
1912	Gustaf Lindblom (SWE) 14.76m	Georg Aberg (SWE) 14.51m	Erik Almlöf (SWE) 14.17m
1920	Vilho Tuulos (FIN) 14.50m	Folke Jansson (SWE) 14.48m	Erik Almlöf (SWE) 14.27m
1924	Anthony Winter (AUS) 15.52m	Luis Brunetto (ARG) 15.42m	Vilho Tuulos (FIN) 15.37m
1928	Miklo Oda (JPN) 15.21m	Levi Casey (USA) 15.17m	Vilho Tuulos (FIN) 15.11m
1932	Chuhei Nambu (JPN) 15.72m	Erik Svensson (SWE) 15.32m	Kenkichi Oshima (JPN) 15.12m
1936	Naoto Tajima (JPN) 16.00m	Masao Harada (JPN) 15.66m	John Metcalfe (AUS) 15.50m
1948	Arne Ahman (SWE) 15.40m	George Avery (AUS) 15.36m	Ruhi Sarialp (TUR) 15.02m
1952	Adhemar Ferreira da Silva (BRA) 16.22m	Leonid Shcherbakov (URS) 15.98m	Arnoldo Devonish (VEN) 15.52m
1956	Adhemar Ferreira da Silva (BRA) 16.35m	Vilhjalmur Einarsson (ISL) 16.26m	Vitold Kreyer (URS) 16.02m
1960	Jozef Schmidt (POL) 16.81m	Vladimir Goryayev (URS) 16.63m	Vitold Kreyer (URS) 16.43m
1964	Jozef Schmidt (POL) 16.85m	Oleg Fedoseyev (URS) 16.58m	Viktor Kravchenko (URS) 16.57m
1968	Viktor Saneyev (URS) 17.39m	Nelson Prudencio (BRA) 17.27m	Giuseppe Gentile (ITA) 17.22m
1972	Viktor Saneyev (URS) 17.35m	Jörg Drehmel (GDR) 17.31m	Nelson Prudencio (BRA) 17.05m
1976	Viktor Saneyev (URS) 17.29m	James Butts (USA) 17.18m	Joao de Oliveira (BRA) 16.90m
1980	Jaak Uudmae (URS) 17.35m	Viktor Saneyev (URS) 17.24m	Joao de Oliveira (BRA) 17.22m
1984	Al Joyner (USA) 17.26m	Mike Conley (USA) 17.18m	Keith Connor (GBR) 16.87m

| 1988 | Khristo Markov (BUL) 17.61m | Igor Lapshin (URS) 17.52m | Alexandr Kovalenko (URS) 17.42m |
| 1992 | Mike Conley (USA) 18.17m | Charles Simpkins (USA) 17.60m | Frank Rutherford (BAH) 17.36m |

[1] *Winner took two hops with his right foot, contrary to present rules.*

Shot Put

1896 [1]	Robert Garrett (USA) 11.22m	Miltiades Gouskos (GRE) 11.15m	Georgios Papasideris (GRE) 10.36m
1900 [1]	Richard Sheldon (USA) 14.10m	Josiah McCracken (USA) 12.85m	Robert Garrett (USA) 12.37m
1904 [1]	Ralph Rose (USA) 14.81m	Wesley Coe (USA) 14.40m	Leon Feuerbach (USA) 13.37m
1906	Martin Sheridan (USA) 12.32m	Mihály Dávid (HUN) 11.83m	Eric Lemming (SWE) 11.26m
1908	Ralph Rose (USA) 14.21m	Dennis Horgan (GBR) 13.61m	John Garrells (USA) 13.18m
1912	Patrick McDonald (USA) 15.34m	Ralph Rose (USA) 15.25m	Lawrence Whitney (USA) 13.93m
1920	Ville Pörhölä (FIN) 14.81m	Elmer Niklander (FIN) 14.155m	Harry Liversedge (USA) 14.15m
1924	Clarence Houser (USA) 14.99m	Glenn Hartranft (USA) 14.89m	Ralph Hills (USA) 14.64m
1928	John Kuck (USA) 15.87m	Herman Brix (USA) 15.75m	Emil Hirschfeld (GER) 15.72m
1932	Leo Sexton (USA) 16.00m	Harlow Rothert (USA) 15.67m	Frantisek Douda (TCH) 15.60m
1936	Hans Woellke (GER) 16.20m	Sulo Bärlund (FIN) 16.12m	Gerhard Stöck (GER) 15.66m
1948	Wilbur Thompson (USA) 17.12m	Jim Delaney (USA) 16.68m	Jim Fuchs (USA) 16.42m
1952	Parry O'Brien (USA) 17.41m	Darrow Hooper (USA) 17.39m	Jim Fuchs (USA) 17.06m
1956	Parry O'Brien (USA) 18.57m	Bill Nieder (USA) 18.18m	Jiri Skobla (TCH) 17.65m
1960	Bill Nieder (USA) 19.68m	Parry O'Brien (USA) 19.11m	Dallas Long (USA) 19.01m
1964	Dallas Long (USA) 20.33m	Randy Matson (USA) 20.20m	Vilmos Varju (HUN) 19.39m
1968	Randy Matson (USA) 20.54m	George Woods (USA) 20.12m	Eduard Gushchin (URS) 20.09m
1972	Wladyslaw Komar (POL) 21.18m	George Woods (USA) 21.17m	Hartmut Briesenick (GDR) 21.14m
1976	Udo Beyer (GDR) 21.05m	Yevgeniy Mironov (URS) 21.03m	Aleksandr Baryshnikov (URS) 21.00m
1980	Volodimir Kiselyev (URS) 21.35m	Aleksandr Baryshnikov (URS) 21.08m	Udo Beyer (GDR) 21.06m
1984	Alessandro Andrei (ITA) 21.26m	Michael Carter (USA) 21.09m	Dave Laut (USA) 20.97m
1988	Ulf Timmermann (GDR) 22.47m	Randy Barnes (USA) 22.39m	Werner Günthör (SUI) 21.99m
1992	Mike Stulce (USA) 21.70m	James Doehring (USA) 20.96m	Vyacheslav Lykho (EUN) 20.94m

[1] *From a 7ft (2.13m) square.*

Discus

1896 [1]	Robert Garrett (USA) 29.15m	Panoyotis Paraskevopoulos (GRE) 28.95m	Sotirios Versis (GRE) 28.78m
1900	Rudolf Bauer (HUN) 36.04m	Frantisek Janda-Suk (BOH) 35.25m	Richard Sheldon (USA) 34.60m
1904 [2]	Martin Sheridan (USA) 39.28m	Ralph Rose (USA) 39.28m	Nicolaos Georgantas (GRE) 37.68m
1906	Martin Sheridan (USA) 41.46m	Nicolaos Georgantas (GRE) 38.06m	Werner Jarvinen (FIN) 36.82m
1908	Martin Sheridan (USA) 40.89m	Merritt Giffin (USA) 40.70m	Marquis Horr (USA) 39.44m
1912	Armas Taipale (FIN) 45.21m	Richard Byrd (USA) 42.32m	James Duncan (USA) 42.28m
1920	Elmer Niklander (FIN) 44.68m	Armas Taipale (FIN) 44.19m	Augustus Pope (USA) 42.13m
1924	Clarence Houser (USA) 46.15m	Vilho Niittymaa (FIN) 44.95m	Thomas Lieb (USA) 44.83m
1928	Clarence Houser (USA) 47.32m	Antero Kivi (FIN) 47.23m	James Corson (USA) 47.10m
1932	John Anderson (USA) 49.49m	Henri Laborde (USA) 48.47m	Paul Winter (FRA) 47.85m
1936	Ken Carpenter (USA) 50.48m	Gordon Dunn (USA) 49.36m	Giorgio Oberweger (ITA) 49.23m
1948	Adolfo Consolini (ITA) 52.78m	Giuseppe Tosi (ITA) 51.78m	Fortune Gordien (USA) 50.77m
1952	Sim Iness (USA) 55.03m	Adolfo Consolini (ITA) 53.78m	James Dillion (USA) 52.38m
1956	Al Oerter (USA) 56.36m	Fortune Gordien (USA) 54.81m	Des Koch (USA) 54.40m
1960	Al Oerter (USA) 59.18m	Rink Babka (USA) 58.02m	Dick Cochran (USA) 57.16m
1964	Al Oerter (USA) 61.00m	Ludvik Danek (TCH) 60.52m	Dave Weill (USA) 59.49m
1968	Al Oerter (USA) 64.78m	Lothar Milde (GDR) 63.08m	Ludvik Danek (TCH) 62.92m
1972	Ludvik Danek (TCH) 64.40m	Jay Silvester (USA) 63.50m	Ricky Bruch (SWE) 63.40m
1976	Mac Wilkins (USA) 67.50m	Wolfgang Schmidt (GDR) 66.22m	John Powell (USA) 65.70m
1980	Viktor Rashchupkin (URS) 66.64m	Imrich Bugár (TCH) 66.38m	Luis Delis (CUB) 66.32m
1984	Rolf Danneberg (FRG) 66.60m	Mac Wilkins (USA) 66.30m	John Powell (USA) 65.46m
1988	Jürgen Schult (GDR) 68.82m	Romas Ubartas (URS) 67.48m	Rolf Danneberg (FRG) 67.38m
1992	Romas Ubartas (LTU) 65.12m	Jurgen Schult (GER) 64.94m	Roberto Moya (CUB) 64.12m

[1] *From 2.50m square.*

[2] *First place decided by a throw-off.*

Hammer

1900 [1]	John Flanagan (USA) 49.73m	Truxton Hare (USA) 49.13m	Josiah McCracken (USA) 42.46m
1904	John Flanagan (USA) 51.23m	John De Witt (USA) 50.26m	Ralph Rose (USA) 45.73m
1908	John Flanagan (USA) 51.92m	Matt McGrath (USA) 51.18m	Con Walsh (CAN) 48.50m
1912	Matt McGrath (USA) 54.74m	Duncan Gillis (CAN) 48.39m	Clarence Childs (USA) 48.17m
1920	Patrick Ryan (USA) 52.87m	Carl Lind (SWE) 48.43m	Basil Bennett (USA) 48.25m
1924	Fred Tootell (USA) 53.29m	Matt McGrath (USA) 50.84m	Malcolm Nokes (GBR) 48.87m
1928	Patrick O'Callaghan (IRL) 51.39m	Ossian Skjöld (SWE) 51.29m	Edmund Black (USA) 49.03m
1932	Patrick O'Callaghan (IRL) 53.92m	Ville Pörhölä (FIN) 52.27m	Peter Zaremba (USA) 50.33m
1936	Kerl Hein (GER) 56.49m	Erwin Blask (GER) 55.04m	Fred Warngard (SWE) 54.83
1948	Imre Németh (HUN) 56.07m	Ivan Gubijan (YUG) 54.27m	Bob Bennett (USA) 53.73m
1952	József Csermák (HUN) 60.34m	Karl Storch (GER) 58.86m	Imre Németh (HUN) 57.74m
1956	Harold Connolly (USA) 63.19m	Mikhail Krivonosov (URS) 63.03m	Anatoliy Samotsvetov (URS) 62.56m
1960	Vasiliy Rudenkov (URS) 67.10m	Gyula Zsivótzky (HUN) 65.79m	Tadeusz Rut (POL) 65.64m
1964	Romuald Klim (URS) 69.74m	Gyula Zsivótzky (HUN) 69.09m	Uwe Beyer (GER) 68.09m
1968	Gyula Zsivótzky (HUN) 73.36m	Romuald Klim (URS) 73.28m	Lázár Lovász (HUN) 69.78m
1972	Anatoliy Bondarchuk (URS) 75.50m	Jochen Sachse (GDR) 74.96m	Vasiliy Khmelevski (URS) 74.04m
1976	Yuriy Sedykh (URS) 77.52m	Aleksey Spiridonov (URS) 76.08m	Anatoliy Bondarchuk (URS) 75.48m
1980	Yuriy Sedykh (URS) 81.80m	Sergey Litvinov (URS) 80.64m	Juriy Tamm (URS) 78.96m
1984	Juha Tiainen (FIN) 78.08m	Karl-Hans Riehm (FRG) 77.98m	Klaus Ploghaus (FRG) 76.68m
1988	Sergey Litvinov (URS) 84.80m	Yuriy Sedykh (URS) 83.76m	Juriy Tamm (URS) 81.16m
1992	Andrei Abduvalyev (EUN) 82.54m	Igor Astapkovich (EUN) 81.96m	Igor Nikulin (EUN) 81.38m

[1] *From a 9ft (2.74m) circle.*
1896, 1906 Event not held.

Javelin

1906	Eric Lemming (SWE) 53.90m	Knut Lindberg (SWE) 45.17m	Bruno Söderström (SWE) 44.92m
1908	Eric Lemming (SWE) 54.82m	Arne Halse (NOR) 50.57m	Otto Nilsson (SWE) 47.09m
1912	Eric Lemming (SWE) 60.64m	Juho Saaristo (FIN) 58.66m	Mór Kóczán (HUN) 55.50m
1920	Jonni Myyrä (FIN) 65.78m	Urho Peltonen (FIN) 63.50m	Pekka Johansson (FIN) 63.09m
1924	Jonni Myyrä (FIN) 62.96m	Gunnar Lindström (SWE) 60.92m	Eugene Oberst (USA) 58.35m
1928	Erik Lundkvist (SWE) 66.60m	Béla Szepes (HUN) 65.26m	Olva Sunde (NOR) 63.97m
1932	Matti Järvinen (FIN) 72.71m	Matti Sippala (FIN) 69.79m	Eino Penttila (FIN) 68.69m
1936	Gerhard Stöck (GER) 71.84m	Yrjö Nikkanen (FIN) 70.77m	Kalervo Toivonen (FIN) 70.72m
1948	Tapio Rautavaara (FIN) 69.77m	Steve Seymour (USA) 67.56m	Joszef Várszegi (HUN) 67.03m
1952	Cyrus Young (USA) 73.78m	Bill Miller (USA) 72.46m	Toivo Hyytiainen (FIN) 71.89m
1956	Egil Danielsen (NOR) 85.71m	Janusz Sidlo (POL) 79.98	Viktor Tsibulenko (URS) 79.50m
1960	Viktor Tsibulenko (URS) 84.64m	Walter Krüger (GER) 79.36m	Gergely Kulcsár (HUN) 78.57m
1964	Pauli Nevala (FIN) 82.66m	Gergely Kulcsár (HUN) 82.32m	Janis Lusis (URS) 80.57m
1968	Janis Lusis (URS) 90.10m	Jorma Kinnunen (FIN) 88.58m	Gergely Kulcsár (HUN) 87.06m
1972	Klaus Wolfermann (FRG) 90.48m	Janis Lusis (URS) 90.46m	Bill Schmidt (USA) 84.42m
1976	Miklos Németh (HUN) 94.58m	Hannu Siitonen (FIN) 87.92m	Gheorghe Megelea (ROM) 87.16m
1980	Dainis Kula (URS) 91.20m	Aleksandr Makarov (URS) 89.64m	Wolfgang Hanisch (GDR) 86.72m
1984	Arto Härkonen (FIN) 86.76m	David Ottley (GBR) 85.74m	Kenth Eldebrink (SWE) 83.72m
1988 [1]	Tapio Korjus (FIN) 84.28m	Jan Zelezny (TCH) 84.12m	Seppo Räty (FIN) 83.26m
1992	Jan Zelezny (TCH) 89.66m	Seppo Raty (FIN) 86.60m	Steve Backley (GBR) 83.38m

[1] *New javelin introduced.*
1896–1904 Event not held.

Decathlon [1] [2]

1904 [3]	Thomas Kiely (GBR) 6036pts	Adam Gunn (USA) 5907pts	Truxton Hare (USA) 5813pts
1912 [4]	Hugo Wieslander (SWE) 5965pts	Charles Lomberg (SWE) 5721pts	Gösta Holmer (SWE) 5768pts
1920	Helge Lövland (NOR) 5803pts	Brutus Hamilton (USA) 5739pts	Bertil Ohlsson (SWE) 5639pts
1924	Harold Osborn (USA) 6476pts	Emerson Norton (USA) 6117pts	Alexander Klumberg (EST) 6056pts
1928	Paavo Yrjölä (FIN) 6587pts	Akilles Järvinen (FIN) 6645pts	Ken Doherty (USA) 6428pts
1932	Jim Bausch (USA) 6735pts	Akilles Järvinen (FIN) 6879pts	Wolrad Eberle (GER) 6661pts
1936	Glenn Morris (USA) 7254pts	Robert Clark (USA) 7063pts	Jack Parker (USA) 6760pts

1948	Bob Mathias (USA) 6628pts	Ignace Heinrich (FRA) 6559pts	Floyd Simmons (USA) 6531pts
1952	Bob Mathias (USA) 7592pts	Milt Campbell (USA) 6995pts	Floyd Simmons (USA) 6945pts
1956	Milt Campbell (USA) 7614pts	Rafer Johnson (USA) 7457pts	Vasiliy Kuznetsov (URS) 7337pts
1960	Rafer Johnson (USA) 7926pts	Yang Chuan-Kwang (TPE) 7839pts	Vasiliy Kuznetsov (URS) 7557pts
1964	Willi Holdorf (GER) 7794pts	Rein Aun (URS) 7744pts	Hans-Joachim Walde (GER) 7735pts
1968	Bill Toomey (USA) 8144pts	Hans-Joachim Walde (FRG) 8094pts	Kurt Bendlin (FRG) 8071pts
1972	Nikolai Avilov (URS) 8466pts	Leonid Litvinenko (URS) 7970pts	Ryszard Katus (POL) 7936pts
1976	Bruce Jenner (USA) 8634pts	Guido Kratschmer (FRG) 8407pts	Nikolai Avilov (URS) 8378pts
1980	Daley Thompson (GBR) 8522pts	Yuri Kutsenko (URS) 8369pts	Sergei Zhelanov (URS) 8135pts
1984	Daley Thompson (GBR) 8847pts	Jürgen Hingsen (FRG) 8695pts	Siegfried Wentz (FRG) 8416pts
1988	Christian Schenk (GDR) 8488pts	Torsten Voss (GDR) 8399pts	Dave Steen (CAN) 8328pts
1992	Robert Zmelik (TCH) 8611pts	Antonio Penalver (CUB) 8412	Dave Johnson (USA) 8309

[1] The decathlon consists of 100m, long jump, shot put, high jump, 400m, 110m hurdles, discus, pole vault, javelin and 1500m. The competition occupies two days, although in 1912 it took three days.

[2] The scores since 1912 given above have been recalculated on the current, 1984, scoring tables for purposes of comparison. (Note that in 1912, 1928, 1932 and 1948 the original medal order would have been different if these tables had been in force.

[3] Consisted of 100yd, 1 mile, 120yd hurdles, 880yd walk, high jump, long jump, pole vault, shot put, hammer and 56lb weight.

[4] Jim Thorpe (USA) finished first with 6564pts but was later disqualified for a breach of the then amateur rules. He was reinstated posthumously by the IOC in 1982, but only as joint first.

1896–1900, 1906–1908 Event not held.

ATHLETICS MEDAL RESULTS — WOMEN

The remarkable Florence Griffith-Joyner wins the 1988 100m in an outstanding time (Allsport/Mike Powell)

	GOLD	SILVER	BRONZE
100 Metres			
1928	Elizabeth Robinson (USA) 12.2	Fanny Rosenfeld (CAN) 12.3	Ethel Smith (CAN) 12.3
1932	Stanislawa Walasiewicz (POL) 11.9	Hilda Strike (CAN) 11.9	Wilhelmina von Bremen (USA) 12.0
1936	Helen Stephens (USA) 11.5	Stanislawa Walasiewicz (POL) 11.7	Kathe Krauss (GER) 11.9
1948	Fanny Blankers-Koen (NED) 11.9	Dorothy Manley (GBR) 12.2	Shirley Strickland (AUS) 12.2
1952	Marjorie Jackson (AUS) 11.5 (11.67)	Daphne Hasenjager (RSA) 11.8 (12.05)	Shirley Strickland (AUS) 11.9 (12.12)
1956	Betty Cuthbert (AUS) 11.5 (11.82)	Christa Stubnick (GER) 11.7 (11.92)	Marlene Matthews (AUS) 11.7 (11.94)
1960	Wilma Rudolph (USA) 11.0 (11.18)	Dorothy Hyman (GBR) 11.3 (11.43)	Giuseppina Leone (ITA) 11.3 (11.48)
1964	Wyomia Tyus (USA) 11.4 (11.49)	Edith Maguire (USA) 11.6 (11.62)	Ewa Klobukowska (POL) 11.6 (11.64)
1968	Wyomia Tyus (USA) 11.0 (11.08)	Barbara Ferrell (USA) 11.1 (11.5)	Irena Szewinska (POL) 11.1 (11.19)
1972	Renate Stecher (GDR) 11.07	Raelene Boyle (AUS) 11.23	Silvia Chivas (CUB) 11.24
1976	Annegret Richter (FRG) 11.08	Renate Stecher (GDR) 11.13	Inge Helten (FRG) 11.17
1980	Ludmila Kondratyeva (URS) 11.06	Marlies Göhr (GDR) 11.07	Ingrid Auerswald (GDR) 11.14
1984	Evelyn Ashford (USA) 10.97	Alice Brown (USA) 11.13	Merlene Ottey-Page (JAM) 11.16
1988 [1]	Florence Griffith-Joyner (USA) 10.54	Evelyn Ashford (USA) 10.83	Heike Drechsler (GDR) 10.85
1992	Gail Devers (USA) 10.82	Juliet Cuthbert (JAM) 10.83	Irina Privalova (EUN) 10.84

[1] Final was wind-assisted; 10.62 in preliminary round.

200 Metres

1948	Fanny Blankers-Koen (NED) 24.4	Audrey Williamson (GBR) 25.1	Audrey Patterson [1] (USA) 25.2
1952	Marjorie Jackson (AUS) 23.7 (23.89)	Bertha Brouwer (NED) 24.2 (24.25)	Nadyezda Khnykina (URS) 24.2 (24.37)
1956	Betty Cuthbert (AUS) 23.4 (23.55)	Christa Stubnick (GER) 23.7 (23.89)	Marlene Matthews (AUS) 23.8 (24.10)
1960	Wilma Rudolph (USA) 24.0 (24.13)	Jutta Heine (GER) 24.4 (24.58)	Dorothy Hyman (GBR) 24.7 (24.82)
1964	Edith Maquire (USA) 23.0 (23.05)	Irena Kirszenstein (POL) 23.1 (23.13)	Marilyn Black (AUS) 23.1 (23.18)
1968	Irena Szewinska (POL) 22.5 (22.58)	Raelene Boyle (AUS) 22.7 (22.74)	Jennifer Lamy (AUS) 22.8 (22.88)
1972	Renate Stecher (GDR) 22.40	Raelene Boyle (AUS) 22.45	Irena Szewinska (POL) 22.74
1976	Bärbel Eckert (GDR) 22.37	Annegret Richter (FRG) 22.39	Renate Stecher (GDR) 22.47
1980	Bärbel Wöckel (GDR) 22.03	Natalya Bochina (URS) 22.19	Merlene Ottey (JAM) 22.20
1984	Valerie Brisco-Hooks (USA) 21.81	Florence Griffith (USA) 22.04	Merlene Ottey-Page (JAM) 22.09
1988	Florence Griffith-Joyner (USA) 21.34	Grace Jackson (JAM) 21.72	Heike Drechsler (GDR) 21.95
1992	Gwen Torrence (USA) 21.81	Juliet Cuthbert (JAM) 22.02	Merlene Ottey (JAM) 22.09

[1] *A recently discovered photo-finish picture indicates that Shirley Strickland (AUS) was third.*
1928–1936 Event not held.

400 Metres

1964	Betty Cuthbert (AUS) 52.0 (52.01)	Ann Packer (GBR) 52.2 (52.20)	Judith Amoore (AUS) 53.4
1968	Colette Besson (FRA) 52.0 (52.03)	Lillian Board (GBR) 52.1 (52.12)	Natalya Burda (URS) 52.2 (52.25)
1972	Monika Zehrt (GDR) 51.08	Rita Wilden (FRG) 51.21	Kathy Hammond (USA) 51.64
1976	Irena Szewinska (POL) 49.29	Christina Brehmer (GDR) 50.51	Ellen Streidt (GDR) 50.55
1980	Marita Koch (GDR) 48.88	Jarmila Kratochvilova (TCH) 49.46	Christina Lathan (GDR) 49.66
1984	Valerie Brisco-Hooks (USA) 48.83	Chandra Cheeseborough (USA) 49.05	Kathy Cook (GBR) 49.43
1988	Olga Brzygina (URS) 48.65	Petra Muller (GDR) 49.45	Olga Nazarova (URS) 49.90
1992	Marie-Jose Perec (FRA) 48.83	Olga Bryzgina (EUN) 49.05	Ximena Restrepo (COL) 49.64

1928–1960 Event not held.

800 Metres

1928	Lina Radke (GER) 2:16.8	Kinuye Hitomi (JPN) 2:17.6	Inga Gentzel (SWE) 2:17.8
1960	Lyudmila Shevtsova (URS) 2:04.3	Brenda Jones (AUS) 2:04.4	Ursula Donath (GER) 2:05.6
1964	Ann Packer (GBR) 2:01.1	Maryvonne Dupureur (FRA) 2:01.9	Marise Chamberlain (NZL) 2:02.8
1968	Madeline Manning (USA) 2:00.9	Ilona Silai (ROM) 2:02.5	Maria Gommers (NED) 2:02.6
1972	Hildegard Falck (FRG) 1:58.6	Niole Sabaite (URS) 1:58.7	Gunhild Hoffmeister (GDR) 1:59.2
1976	Tatyana Kazankina (URS) 1:54.9	Nikolina Shtereva (BUL) 1:55.4	Elfi Zinn (GDR) 1:55.6
1980	Nadyezda Olizarenko (URS) 1:53.5	Olga Mineyeva (URS) 1:54.9	Tatyana Providokhina (URS) 1:55.5
1984	Doina Melinte (ROM) 1:57.60	Kim Gallagher (USA) 1:58.63	Fita Lovin (ROM) 1:58.83
1988	Sigrun Wodars (GDR) 1:56.10	Christine Wachtel (GDR) 1:56.64	Kim Gallagher (USA) 1:56.91
1992	Ellen van Langen (NED) 1:55.54	Lilia Nurutdinova (EUN) 1:55.99	Ana Quirot (CUB) 1:56.80

1932–1956 Event not held.

1500 Metres

1972	Lyudmila Brágina (URS) 4:01.4	Gunhild Hoffmeister (GDR) 4:02.8	Paola Cacchi-Pigni (ITA) 4:02.9
1976	Tatyana Kazankina (URS) 4:05.5	Gunhild Hoffmeister (GDR) 4:06.0	Ulrike Klapezynski (GDR) 4:06.1
1980	Tatyana Kazankina (URS) 3:56.6	Christiane Wartenberg (GDR) 3:57.8	Nadyezda Olizarenko (URS) 3:59.6
1984	Gabriella Dorio (ITA) 4:03.25	Doina Melinte (ROM) 4:03.76	Maricica Puica (ROM) 4:04.15
1988	Paula Ivan (ROM) 3:53.96	Laima Baikauskaite (URS) 4:00.24	Tatyana Samolenko (URS) 4:00.30
1992	Hassiba Boulmerka (ALG) 3:55.30	Lyudmila Rogacheva (EUN) 3:56.91	Qu Yunxia (CHN) 3:57.08

1928–1968 Event not held.

3000 Metres [1]

1984	Maricica Puica (ROM) 8:35.96	Wendy Sly (GBR) 8:39.47	Lynn Williams (CAN) 8:42.14
1988	Tatyana Samolenko (URS) 8:26.53	Paula Ivan (ROM) 8:27.15	Yvonne Murray (GBR) 8:29.02
1992	Yelena Romanova (EUN) 8:46.04	Tatyana Dorovskikh (EUN) 8:46.85	Angela Chalmers (CAN) 8:47.22

1928–1980 Event not held.
[1] *Replaced by 5000m in 1996.*

10,000 Metres

1988	Olga Bondarenko (URS) 31:05.21	Liz McColgan (GBR) 31:08.44	Yelena Zhupiyeva (URS) 31:19.82
1992	Derartu Tulu (ETH) 31:06.02	Elana Meyer (RSA) 31:11.75	Lynn Jennings (USA) 31:19.89

1928–1984 Event not held.

Marathon

1984	Joan Benoit (USA) 2h 24:52	Grete Waitz (NOR) 2h 26:18	Rosa Mota (POR) 2h 26:57
1988	Rosa Mota (POR) 2h 25:40	Lisa Martin (AUS) 2h 25:53	Kathrin Dörre (GDR) 2h 26:21
1992	Valentina Yegorova (EUN) 2h 32:41	Yuko Arimori (JPN) 2h 32:49	Lorraine Moller (NZL) 2h 33:59

1928–1980 Event not held.

100 Metres Hurdles

(Over 80m hurdles 1932–1968)

1932	Mildred Didrikson (USA) 11.7	Evelyne Hall (USA) 11.7	Marjorie Clark (RSA) 11.8
1936	Trebisonda Valla (ITA) 11.7 (11.75)	Anny Steuer (GER) 11.7 (11.81)	Elizabeth Taylor (CAN) 11.7 (11.81)
1948	Fanny Blankers-Koen (NED) 11.2	Maureen Gardner (GBR) 11.2	Shirley Strickland (AUS) 11.4
1952	Shirley de la Hunty (AUS) 10.8 (11.01)	Maria Golubnichaya (URS) 11.1 (11.24)	Maria Sander (GER) 11.1 (11.38)
1956	Shirley de la Hunty (AUS) 10.7 (10.96)	Gisela Köhler (GER) 10.9 (11.12)	Norma Thrower (AUS) 11.0 (11.25)
1960	Irina Press (URS) 10.8 (10.93)	Carol Quinton (GBR) 10.9 (10.99)	Gisela Birkemeyer (GER) 11.0 (11.13)
1964	Karin Balzer (GER) 10.5 (10.54)	Teresa Ciepla (POL) 10.5 (10.55)	Pam Kilborn (AUS) 10.5 (10.56)
1968	Maureen Caird (AUS) 10.3 (10.39)	Pam Kilborn (AUS) 10.4 (10.46)	Chi Cheng (TPE) 10.4 (10.51)
1972	Annelie Ehrhardt (GDR) 12.59	Valeria Bufanu (ROM) 12.84	Karin Balzer (GDR) 12.90
1976	Johanna Schaller (GDR) 12.77	Tatyana Anisimova (URS) 12.78	Natalya Lebedeva (URS) 12.80
1980	Vera Komisova (URS) 12.56	Johanna Klier (GDR) 12.63	Lucyna Langer (POL) 12.65
1984	Benita Fitzgerald-Brown (USA) 12.84	Shirley Strong (GBR) 12.88	Kim Turner (USA) 13.06
			Michele Chardonnet (FRA) 13.06
1988	Yordanka Donkova (BUL) 12.38	Gloria Siebert (GDR) 12.61	Claudia Zaczkiewicz (FRG) 12.75
1992	Paraskevi Patoulidou (GRE) 12.64	LaVonna Martin (USA) 12.69	Yordanka Donkova (BUL) 12.70

1928 Event not held.

400 Metres Hurdles

1984	Nawal El Moutawakel (MAR) 54.61	Judi Brown (USA) 55.20	Cristina Cojocaru (ROM) 55.41
1988	Debbie Flintoff-King (AUS) 53.17	Tatyana Ledovskaya (URS) 53.18	Ellen Fiedler (GDR) 53.63
1992	Sally Gunnell (GBR) 53.23	Sandra Farmer-Patrick (USA) 53.69	Janeene Vickers (USA) 54.31

1928–1980 Event not held.

4 x 100 Metres Relay

1928	Canada 48.4	United States 48.8	Germany 49.2
1932	United States 47.0 (46.86)	Canada 47.0	Great Britain 47.6
1936	United States 46.9	Great Britain 47.6	Canada 47.8
1948	Netherlands 47.5	Australia 47.6	Canada 47.8
1952	United States 45.9 (46.14)	Germany 45.9 (46.18)	Great Britain 46.2 (46.41)
1956	Australia 44.5 (44.65)	Great Britain 44.7 (44.70)	United States 44.9 (45.04)
1960	United States 44.5 (44.72)	Germany 44.8 (45.00)	Poland 45.0 (45.19)
1964	Poland 43.6 (43.69)	United States 43.9 (43.92)	Great Britain 44.0 (44.09)
1968	United States 42.8 (42.88)	Cuba 43.3 (43.36)	Soviet Union 43.4 (43.41)
1972	FRG 42.81	GDR 42.95	Cuba 43.36
1976	GDR 42.55	FRG 42.59	Soviet Union 43.09
1980	GDR 41.60	Soviet Union 41.20	Great Britain 42.43
1984	United States 41.65	Canada 42.77	Great Britain 43.11
1988	United States 41.98	GDR 42.09	Soviet Union 42.75
1992	United States 42.11	Unified Team 42.16	Nigeria 42.81

4 x 400 Metres Relay

1972	GDR 3:22.95	United States 3:35.15	FRG 3:26.51
1976	GDR 3:19.23	United States 3:22.81	Soviet Union 3:24.24
1980	Soviet Union 3:20.12	GDR 3:20.35	Great Britain 3:27.5

1984	United States 3:18.29	Canada 3:21.21	FRG 3:22.98
1988	Soviet Union 3:15.17	United States 3:15.51	GDR 3:18.29
1992	Unified Team 3:20.20	United States 3:20.92	Great Britain 3:24.23

1928–1968 Event not held.

10km Walk

| 1992 | Chen Yueling (CHN) 44.32 | Yelena Nikolayeva (EUN) 44.33 | Li Chunxiu (CHN) 44.41 |

Event not held

High Jump

1928	Ethel Catherwood (CAN) 1.59m	Carolina Gisolf (NED) 1.56m	Mildred Wiley (USA) 1.56m
1932	Jean Shiley (USA) 1.657m [1]	Mildred Didrikson (USA) 1.657m [1]	Eva Dawes (CAN) 1.60m
1936	Ibolya Csák (HUN) 1.60m	Dorothy Odam (GBR) 1.60m	Elfriede Kaun (GER) 1.60m
1948	Alice Coachman (USA) 1.68m	Dorothy Tyler (GBR) 1.68m	Micheline Ostermeyer (FRA) 1.61m
1952	Esther Brand (RSA) 1.67m	Sheila Lerwill (GBR) 1.65m	Aleksandra Chudina (URS) 1.63m
1956	Mildred McDaniel (USA) 1.76m	Thelma Hopkins (GBR) 1.67m	–
		Maria Pisaryeva (URS) 1.67m	
1960	Iolanda Balas (ROM) 1.85m	Jaroslawa Jozwiakowska (POL) 1.71m	–
		Dorothy Shirley (GBR) 1.71m	
1964	Iolanda Balas (ROM) 1.90m	Michelle Brown (AUS) 1.80m	Tasia Chenchik (URS) 1.78m
1968	Miloslava Rezkova (TCH) 1.82m	Antonina Okorokova (URS) 1.80m	Valentina Kozyr (URS) 1.80m
1972	Ulrike Meyfarth (FRG) 1.92m	Yordanka Blagoyeva (BUL) 1.88m	Ilona Gusenbauer (AUT) 1.88m
1976	Rosemarie Ackermann (GDR) 1.93m	Sara Simeoni (ITA) 1.91m	Yordanka Blagoyeva (BUL) 1.91m
1980	Sara Simeoni (ITA) 1.97m	Urszula Kielan (POL) 1.94m	Jutta Kirst (GDR) 1.94m
1984	Ulrike Meyfarth (FRG) 2.02m	Sara Simeoni (ITA) 2.00m	Joni Huntley (USA) 1.97m
1988	Louise Ritter (USA) 2.03m	Stefka Kostadinova (BUL) 2.01m	Tamara Bykova (URS) 1.99m
1992	Heike Henkel (GER) 2.02m	Galina Astafei (ROM) 2.00m	Ioamnet Quintero (CUB) 1.97m

[1] *Some sources suggest 1.66m.*

Long Jump

1948	Olga Gyarmati (HUN) 5.69m	Noemi Simonetto de Portela (ARG) 5.60m	Ann-Britt Leyman (SWE) 5.57m
1952	Yvette Williams (NZL) 6.24m	Aleksandra Chudina (URS) 6.14m	Shirley Cawley (GBR) 5.92m
1956	Elzbieta Krzesinska (POL) 6.35m	Willye White (USA) 6.09m	Nadyezda Dvalishvili (URS) 6.07m
1960	Vera Krepkina (URS) 6.37m	Elzbieta Krzesinska (POL) 6.27m	Hildrun Claus (GER) 6.21m
1964	Mary Rand (GBR) 6.76m	Irena Kirszenstein (POL) 6.60m	Tatyana Schelkanova (URS) 6.42m
1968	Viorica Viscopoleanu (ROM) 6.82m	Sheila Sherwood (GBR) 6.68m	Tatyana Talysheva (URS) 6.66m
1972	Heidemarie Rosendahl (FRG) 6.78m	Diana Yorgova (BUL) 6.77m	Eva Suranova (TCH) 6.67m
1976	Angela Voigt (GDR) 6.72m	Kathy McMillan (USA) 6.66m	Lidia Alfeyeva (URS) 6.60m
1980	Tatyana Kolpakova (URS) 7.06m	Brigitte Wujak (GDR) 7.04m	Tatyana Skatchko (URS) 7.01m
1984	Anisoara Stanciu (ROM) 6.96m	Vali Ionescu (ROM) 6.81m	Susan Hearnshaw (GBR) 6.80m
1988	Jackie Joyner-Kersee (USA) 7.40m	Heike Drechsler (GDR) 7.22m	Galina Chistiakova (URS) 7.11m
1992	Heike Dreschler (GER) 7.14m	Inessa Kravets (EUN) 7.12m	Jackie Joyner-Kersee (USA) 7.07m

1928–1936 Event not held.

Shot Put

1948	Micheline Ostermeyer (FRA) 13.75m	Amelia Piccinini (ITA) 13.09m	Ina Schäffer (AUT) 13.08m
1952	Galina Sybina (URS) 15.28m	Marianne Werner (GER) 14.57m	Klavdia Tochonova (URS) 14.50m
1956	Tamara Tyshkevich (URS) 16.59m	Galina Zybina (URS) 16.53m	Marianne Werner (GER) 15.61m
1960	Tamara Press (URS) 17.32m	Johanna Lüttge (GER) 16.61m	Earlene Brown (USA) 16.42m
1964	Tamara Press (URS) 18.14m	Renate Garisch (GDR) 17.61m	Galina Zybina (URS) 16.42m
1968	Margitta Gummel (GDR) 19.61m	Marita Lange (GDR) 18.78m	Nadyezda Chizhova (URS) 18.19m
1972	Nadyezda Chizhova (URS) 21.03m	Margitta Gummel (GDR) 20.22m	Ivanka Khristova (BUL) 19.35m
1976	Ivanka Khristova (BUL) 21.16m	Nadyezda Chizhova (URS) 20.96m	Helena Fibingerova (TCH) 20.67m
1980	Ilona Slupianek (GDR) 22.41m	Svetlana Krachevskaya (URS) 21.42m	Margitta Pufe (GDR) 21.20m
1984	Claudia Losch (FRG) 20.48m	Mihaela Loghin (ROM) 20.47m	Gael Martin (AUS) 19.19m
1988	Natalya Lisovskaya (URS) 22.24m	Kathrin Neimke (GDR) 21.07m	Li Meisu (CHN) 21.06m
1992	Svetlana Krivelyova (EUN) 21.06m	Huang Zhihong (CHN) 20.47m	Kathrin Neimke (GER) 19.78m

1928–1936 Event not held.

Tessa Sanderson's javelin victory in 1984 was the first throwing gold medal won by a British woman (Allsport/Tony Duffy)

Discus

1928	Helena Konopacka (POL) 39.62m	Lilian Copeland (USA) 37.08m	Ruth Svedberg (SWE) 35.92m
1932	Lilian Copeland (USA) 40.58m	Ruth Osburn (USA) 40.11m	Jadwiga Wajsacowna (POL) 38.73m
1936	Gisela Mauermayer (GER) 47.63m	Jadwiga Wajsówna (POL) 46.22m	Paula Mollenhauer (GER) 39.80m
1948	Micheline Ostermeyer (FRA) 41.92m	Edera Gentile (ITA) 41.17m	Jacqueline Mazeas (FRA) 40.47m
1952	Nina Romashkova (URS) 51.42	Elizaveta Bagryantseva (URS) 47.08m	Nina Dumbadze (URS) 46.29m
1956	Olga Fikotova (TCH) 53.69m	Irina Begiyakova (URS) 52.54m	Nina Ponomaryeva (URS) 52.02m [1]
1960	Nina Ponomaryeva (URS) 55.10m	Tamara Press (URS) 52.59m	Lia Manoliu (ROM) 52.36m
1964	Tamara Press (URS) 57.25m	Ingrid Lotz (GER) 57.21m	Lia Manoliu (ROM) 56.97m
1968	Lia Manoliu (ROM) 58.28m	Liesel Westermann (FRG) 57.76m	Jolán Kleiber (HUN) 54.90m
1972	Faina Melnik (URS) 66.62m	Argentina Menis (ROM) 65.06m	Vasilka Stoyeva (BUL) 64.34m
1976	Evelin Schlaak (GDR) 69.00m	Maria Vergova (BUL) 67.30m	Gabriele Hinzmann (GDR) 66.84m
1980	Evelin Jahl (GDR) 69.96m	Maria Petkova (BUL) 67.90m [2]	Tatyana Lesovaya (URS) 67.40m
1984	Ria Stalman (NED) 65.36m	Leslie Deniz (USA) 64.86m	Florenta Craciunescu (ROM) 63.64m
1988	Martina Hellmann (GDR) 72.30m	Diana Gansky (GDR) 71.88m	Tsvetanka Khristova (BUL) 69.74m
1992	Maritza Marten (CUB) 70.06m	Tsvetanka Khristova (BUL) 67.78m	Daniela Costian (AUS) 66.24m

[1] *Formerly Romashkova.*
[2] *Formerly Vergova.*

Javelin

1932	Mildred Didrikson (USA) 43.68m	Ellen Braumüller (GER) 43.49m	Tilly Fleischer (GER) 43.40m
1936	Tilly Fleischer (GER) 45.18m	Luise Krüger (GER) 43.29m	Marja Kwasniewska (POL) 41.80m
1948	Herma Bauma (AUT) 45.57m	Kaisa Parviainen (FIN) 43.79m	Lily Carlstedt (DEN) 42.08m
1952	Dana Zatopková (TCH) 50.47m	Aleksandra Chudina (URS) 50.01m	Yelena Gorchakova (URS) 49.76m
1956	Inese Jaunzeme (URS) 53.86m	Marlene Ahrens (CHI) 50.38m	Nadyezda Konyeyeva (URS) 50.28m
1960	Elvira Ozolina (URS) 55.98m	Dana Zatopková (TCH) 53.78m	Birute Kalediene (URS) 53.45m
1964	Mihaela Penes (ROM) 60.64m	Marta Rudas (HUN) 58.27m	Yelena Gorchakova (URS) 57.07m
1968	Angela Németh (HUN) 60.36m	Mihaela Penes (ROM) 59.92m	Eva Janko (AUT) 58.04m
1972	Ruth Fuchs (GDR) 63.88m	Jacqueline Todten (GDR) 62.54m	Kathy Schmidt (USA) 59.94m

1976	Ruth Fuchs (GDR) 65.94m	Marion Becker (FRG) 64.70m	Kathy Schmidt (USA) 63.96m
1980	Maria Colon (CUB) 68.40m	Saida Gunba (URS) 67.76m	Ute Hommola (GDR) 66.56m
1984	Tessa Sanderson (GBR) 69.56m	Tiina Lillak (FIN) 69.00m	Fatima Whitbread (GBR) 67.14m
1988	Petra Felke (GDR) 74.68m	Fatima Whitbread (GBR) 70.32m	Beate Koch (GDR) 67.30m
1992	Silke Renk (GER) 68.34m	Natalya Shikolenko (EUN) 68.26m	Karen Forkel (GER) 66.86m

1928 Event not held.

Pentathlon [1]

1964	Irina Press (URS) 5246pts	Mary Rand (GBR) 5035pts	Galina Bystrova (URS) 4956
1968	Ingrid Becker (FRG) 5098pts	Liese Prokop (AUT) 4966pts	Annamaria Tóth (HUN) 4959pts
1972 [2]	Mary Peters (GBR) 4801pts	Heidemarie Rosendahl (FRG) 4791pts	Burglinde Pollak (GDR) 4768pts
1976 [3]	Siegrun Siegl (GDR) 4745pts	Christine Laser (GDR) 4745pts	Burglinde Pollak (GDR) 4740pts
1980	Nadyezda Tkachenko (URS) 5083pts	Olga Rukivichnikova (URS) 4937pts	Olga Kuragina (URS) 4875pts

[1] *The pentathlon consisted of 100m hurdles, shot put, high jump, long jump and 200m from 1964 to 1976. In 1980 the 200m was replaced by 800m.*
[2] *New scoring tables were introduced in May 1971.*
[3] *Siegl finished ahead of Laser in three events.*
1928–1960 Event not held.

Heptathlon [4]

Replaced Pentathlon in 1984

1984	Glynis Nunn (AUS) 6387pts [5]	Jackie Joyner (USA) 6363pts	Sabine Everts (FRG) 6388pts
1988	Jackie Joyner-Kersee (US) 7291pts	Sabine John (GDR) 6897pts	Anke Behmer (GDR) 6858pts
1992	Jackie Joyner-Kersee (USA) 7044pts	Irina Belova (EUN) 6845	Sabine Braun (GER) 6649

[4] *The Heptathlon consists of 100m hurdles, high jump, shot, 200m on the first day; long jump, javelin and 800m on the second day.*
[5] *Re-calculated on 1984 tables.*

WOMEN WHO HAVE WON MEDALS UNDER BOTH THEIR MAIDEN AND MARRIED NAMES:

Becker – Mickler (FRG)
Brehmer – Lathan (GDR)
Eckert – Wöckel (GDR)
Foulds – Paul (GBR)
Kersee – Joyner (USA)
Khnykina – Dvalishvili (URS)
Kirszenstein – Szewinska (POL)
Köhler – Birkemeyer (GDR)
Manning – Jackson (USA)

Odam – Tyler (GBR)
Richter – Górecka (POL)
Romashkova – Ponomaryeva (URS)
Samolenko – Dorovskikh (URS)
Schaller – Klier (GDR)
Schlaak – Jahl (GDR)
Vergova – Petkova (BUL)
Wieczorek – Ciepla (POL)
Zharkova – Maslakova (URS)

DISCONTINUED EVENTS

GOLD	SILVER	BRONZE
60 Metres		
1900 ....Alvin Kraenzlein (USA) 7.0	Walter Tewksbury (USA) 7.1	Stanley Rowley (AUS) 7.2
1904 ....Archie Hahn (USA) 7.0	William Hogenson (USA) 7.2	Fay Moulton (USA) 7.2
3000 Team Race		
1912 ....United States 9pts	Sweden 13pts	Great Britain 23pts
1920 ....United States 10pts	Great Britain 20pts	Sweden 24pts
1924 ....Finland 8pts	Great Britain 14pts	United States 25pts

3 Miles Team Race

| 1908 | Great Britain 6pts | United States 19pts | France 32pts |

5000 Metres Team Race

| 1900 | Great Britain 26pts | France 29 pts | – |

4 Miles Team Race

| 1904 | United States 27pts | United States 28pts | – |

Individual Cross-Country

1912 [1]	Hannes Kolehmainen (FIN) 45:11.6	Hjalmar Andersson (SWE) 45:44.8	John Eke (SWE) 46:37.6
1920 [2]	Paavo Nurmi (FIN) 27:15.0	Erick Backman (SWE) 27:17.6	Heikki Liimatainen (FIN) 27:37.4
1924 [3]	Paavo Nurmi (FIN) 32:54.8	Ville Ritola (FIN) 34:19.4	Earle Johnson (USA) 35:21.0

[1] *12,000 metres.*
[2] *8000 metres.*
[3] *10,000 metres.*

Team Cross-Country

1912	Sweden 10pts	Finland 11pts	Great Britain 49pts
1920	Finland 10pts	Great Britain 21pts	Sweden 23pts
1924	Finland 11pts	United States 14pts	France 20pts

200 Metres Hurdles

| 1900 | Alvin Kraenzlein (USA) 25.4 | Norman Pritchard (IND) 26.6 | Walter Tewksbury (USA) n.t.a. |
| 1904 | Harry Hillman (USA) 24.6 | Frank Castleman (USA) 24.9 | George Poage (USA) n.t.a. |

1500 Metres Walk

| 1906 | George Bonhag (USA) 7:12.6 | Donald Linden (CAN) 7:19.8 | Konstantin Spetsiotis (GRE) 7:22.0 |

3000 Metres Walk

| 1906 | György Sztantics (HUN) 15:13.2 | Hermann Müller (GER) 15:20.0 | Georgios Saridakis (GRE) 15:33.0 |
| 1920 | Ugo Frigerio (ITA) 13:14.2 | George Parker (AUS) n.t.a. | Richard Remer (USA) n.t.a. |

3500 Metres Walk

| 1908 | George Larner (GBR) 14:55.0 | Ernest Webb (GBR) 15:07.4 | Harry Kerr (NZL) 15:43.4 |

10,000 Metres Walk

1912	George Goulding (CAN) 46:28.4	Ernest Webb (GBR) 46:50.4	Fernando Altimani (ITA) 47:37.6
1920	Ugo Frigerio (ITA) 48:06.2	Joseph Pearman (USA) n.t.a.	Charles Gunn (GBR) n.t.a.
1924	Ugo Frigerio (ITA) 47:49.0	Gordon Goodwin (GBR) 200m	Cecil McMaster (RSA) 300m
1948	John Mikaelsson (SWE) 45:13.2	Ingemar Johansson (SWE) 45:43.8	Fritz Schwab (SUI) 46:00.2
1952	John Mikaelsson (SWE) 45:02.8	Fritz Schwab (SUI) 45:41.0	Bruno Junk (URS) 45:41.2

1928–1936 Event not held.

10 Miles Walk

| 1908 | George Larner (GBR) 1h 15:57.4 | Ernest Webb (GBR) 1h 17:31.0 | Edward Spencer (GBR) 1h 21:20.2 |

Pentathlon

1906 [1]	Hjalmar Mellander (SWE) 24pts	Istvan Mudin (HUN) 25pts	Eric Lemming (SWE) 29pts
1912 [2]	Ferdinand Bie (NOR) 16pts [3]	James Donahue (USA) 24pts	Frank Lukeman (CAN) 24pts
1920 [2]	Eero Lehtonen (FIN) 14pts	Everett Bradley (USA) 24pts	Hugo Lahtinen (FIN) 26pts
1924 [2]	Eero Lehtonen (FIN) 14pts	Elemér Somfay (HUN) 16pts	Robert LeGendre (USA) 18pts

[1] *Consisted of standing long jump, discus (Greek style), javelin, one-lap race (192m), Greco-Roman wrestling.*
[2] *Consisted of long jump, javelin, 200m, discus, 1500m.*
[3] *Jim Thorpe (USA) finished first with 7 points but was subsequently disqualified. He was reinstated posthumously in 1982, but as joint first.*

Standing High Jump

1900	Ray Ewry (USA) 1.655m	Irving Baxter (USA) 1.525m	Lewis Sheldon (USA) 1.50m
1904	Ray Ewry (USA) 1.50m	James Stadler (USA) 1.45m	Lawson Robertson (USA) 1.45m
1906	Ray Ewry (USA) 1.565m	Martin Sheridan (USA) 1.50m	–
		Léon Dupont (BEL) 1.40m	
		Lawson Robertson (USA) 1.40m	
1908	Ray Ewry (USA) 1.575m	Konstantin Tsiklitiras (GRE) 1.55m	–
		John Biller (USA) 1.55m	
1912	Platt Adams (USA) 1.63m	Benjamin Adams (USA) 1.60m	Konstantin Tsiklitiras (GRE) 1.55m

Standing Long Jump

1900	Ray Ewry (USA) 3.21m	Irving Baxter (USA) 3.135m	Emile Torcheboeuf (FRA) 3.03m
1904	Ray Ewry (USA) 3.476m	Charles King (USA) 3.28m	John Biller (USA) 3.26m
1906	Ray Ewry (USA) 3.30m	Martin Sheridan (USA) 3.095m	Lawson Robertson (USA) 3.05m
1908	Ray Ewry (USA) 3.335m	Konstantin Tsiklitiras (GRE) 3.23m	Martin Sheridan (USA) 3.225m
1912	Konstantin Tsiklitiras (GRE) 3.37m	Platt Adams (USA) 3.36m	Benjamin Adams (USA) 3.28m

Standing Triple Jump

1900	Ray Ewry (USA) 10.58m	Irving Baxter (USA) 9.95m	Robert Garrett (USA) 9.50m
1904	Ray Ewry (USA) 10.55m	Charles King (USA) 10.16m	James Stadler (USA) 9.53m

Stone (6.40kg) Put

1906	Nicolaos Georgantas (GRE) 19.925m	Martin Sheridan (USA) 19.053m	Michel Dorizas (GRE) 18.585m

Shot (Both Hands)

Aggregate of throws with right and left hands.

1912	Ralph Rose (USA) 27.70m	Patrick McDonald (USA) 27.53m	Elmer Niklander (FIN) 27.14m

Discus (Both Hands)

Aggregate of throws with right and left hands.

1912	Armas Taipale (FIN) 82.86m	Elmer Niklander (FIN) 77.96m	Emil Magnusson (SWE) 77.37m

Discus (Greek Style)

1906	Werner Järvinen (FIN) 35.17m	Nicolaos Georgantas (GRE) 32.80m	Istvan Mudin (HUN) 31.91m
1908	Martin Sheridan (USA) 38.00m	Marquis Horr (USA) 37.325m	Werner Järvinen (FIN) 36.48m

Javelin (Both Hands)

Aggregate of throws with right and left hands.

1912	Julius Saaristo (FIN) 109.42m	Väinö Siikaniemi (FIN) 101.13m	Urho Peltonen (FIN) 100.24m

Javelin (Free Style)

1908	Eric Lemming (SWE) 54.445m	Michel Dorizas (GRE) 51.36m	Arne Halse (NOR) 49.73m

56-Pound (25.4kg) Weight Throw

1904	Etienne Desmarteau (CAN) 10.465m	John Flanagan (USA) 10.16m	James Mitchel (USA) 10.135m
1920	Patrick McDonald (USA) 11.265m	Patrick Ryan (USA) 10.965m	Carl Lind (SWE) 10.25m

TUG OF WAR MEDAL RESULTS

	GOLD	SILVER	BRONZE
1900	Sweden/Denmark	France	–
1904	United States	United States	United States
1906	Germany	Greece	Sweden
1908	Great Britain	Great Britain	Great Britain
1912	Sweden	Great Britain	–
1920	Great Britain	Netherlands	Belgium

Badminton

Introduced for the first time in 1992, badminton had been a demonstration sport in 1972 when the men's singles was won by Rudy Hartono of Indonesia. Because officials felt the necessity to control the number of entries, a mixed doubles competition was not included, but will be contested in 1996. The youngest gold medallist was Susi Susanti (INA), winning the women's singles aged 21yr 175 days, while the youngest male champion was her compatriot Alan Budi Kusuma at 25yr 128 days. The oldest champion was Kim Moon-Soo (KOR) in the 1992 doubles aged 28yr 219 days, and the oldest female winner was Hwang Hae-Young (KOR) at 26yr 19 days. The youngest medallist was Bang Soo-Hyun (KOR) in the 1992 women's singles at 19yr 326 days, while the oldest was Razif Sidek (MAS) at 30yr 66 days in the men's doubles. The youngest male medallist was Thomas Stuer-Lauridsen (DEN) aged 21yr 96 days, while the oldest female medallist was Guan Weizhen (CHN) at 28yr 62 days. Susanti's husband, Hermawan Susanto, won a bronze in the 1992 men's singles competition. Brothers Razif and Jalani Sidek won the bronze in the 1992 men's doubles, for Malaysia's first ever Olympic medal.

Indonesia's Alan Budi Kusuma was the inaugural male Olympic badminton champion at Barcelona (Popperfoto)

BADMINTON MEDALS TABLE

| | Men | | | Women | | | |
	G	S	B	G	S	B	Total
Indonesia	1	2	1	1	-	-	5
China	-	-	1	-	1	3	5
Korea	1	-	-	1	1	1	4
Denmark	-	-	1	-	-	-	1
Malaysia	-	-	1	-	-	-	1

BADMINTON MEDAL RESULTS

	GOLD	SILVER	BRONZE

Men
| 1992 | Alan Budi Kusuma (INA) | Ardy Wiranata (INA) | Thomas Stuer-Lauridsen (DEN) |
| | | | Hermawan Susanto (INA) |

1896-1988 Event not held

Women
| 1992 | Susi Susanti (INA) | Bang Soo-Hyun (KOR) | Huang Hua (CHN) |
| | | | Tang Jiuhong (CHN) |

1896-1988 Event not held

Men's Team
| 1992 | Korea | Indonesia | Malaysia |
| | | | China |

1896-1988 Event not held

Women's Team
| 1992 | Korea | China | Korea |
| | | | China |

1896-1988 Event not held

Baseball

There were six occasions when American baseball was demonstrated, plus an exhibition of Finnish baseball in 1952. In 1912 the USA team, containing many track & field medallists, beat Sweden 13-3. In 1936 a 'World Amateurs' team beat an American 'Olympic' team in front of 100,000 spectators in the Berlin Olympic Stadium. In 1956 an American Services team beat an Australian team 11-5 before an estimated 114,000 people, a record crowd for any baseball game anywhere. At Tokyo in 1964 a USA team beat two Japanese teams, and in 1984 Japan won an eight-nation tournament. In 1988 the USA also won an eight-nation tournament, beating Japan in the final. Finally in 1992 baseball became an official medal sport, with the inaugural title going to Cuba.

The greatest margin of victory, and the highest aggregate score, was the 20-0 victory by Chinese Taipei (Taiwan) over Spain in the 1992 competition. Koji Tokunaga (JPN) and Omar Linares Izquierdo (CUB) each scored 4 home runs in the 1992 competition. Victor Mesa Martinez (CUB) had the best batting average of .545, while Tomohito Ito (JPN) achieved 20 Strikeouts.

The oldest gold medallist/medallist was Lourdes Gurriel (CUB) aged 35yr 133 days, while the youngest winner was Giorge Diaz (CUB) at 21yr 324 days. Jong Yeu-Jeng (TPE) played for the silver medal team aged 18yr 217 days.

BASEBALL MEDALS TABLE

	G	S	B	Total
Cuba	1	-	-	1
Chinese Taipei	-	1	-	1
Japan	-	-	1	1

BASEBALL MEDAL RESULTS

1992	Cuba	Taiwan	Japan

1896-1988 Event not held

Basketball

The game made its official Olympic debut in 1936, although it was demonstrated in 1904 and the analogous Dutch game Korfball was demonstrated in 1928. The 1936 tournament was uniquely played outdoors, and the final score was very low due to a downpour which made the ground slippery and the ball slimy. Interestingly, one of the referees in that tournament was Avery Brundage (USA), later to become President of the IOC, while the man who had devised the modern game, Dr James Naismith, was among those who presented the medals.

The tournament was won by the United States, beginning a winning streak of seven titles and 63 victories. The run began with a walkover against Spain, whose team had returned home to fight in the civil war, and ended when they were beaten by the Soviet Union 51-50 in the much-disputed 1972 final, the Americans claiming that too much overtime was played. With one second to go, and the USA in the lead 50-49, the Soviet inbounds pass had been deflected and everyone thought the game was over. However, the Soviets were given another inbounds chance. They did not score and again the game seemed to be over, but Dr William Jones (GBR), Secretary-General of FIBA (Fédération Internationale de Basketball Amateur), stated that play had been incorrectly restarted at one second and that there should have been three seconds allowed. The clock was reset to three seconds and the Soviet Aleksandr Belov (who tragically died six years later) scored the winning basket. The US team protested vigorously and refused to accept the silver medals. Unbeaten again until another defeat by the Soviet Union in the 1988 semi-final, and unbeaten in 1992, the overall win-loss record of US teams is now 93-2.

After various changes and qualifying conditions since 1976, the IOC accepted 12 teams in both the men's and women's competitions at Atlanta. The Palacia de los Deportes in Mexico City in 1968 had a record capacity for an Olympic basketball game of 22,370 seats. The US players Bob Kurland (1948-52), Bill Hougland (1952-56), Burdette Haldorson (1956-60), Chris Mullin (1984-92), Patrick Ewing (1984-92) and Michael Jordan (1984-92) are the only men to win two gold medals. Two men have won medals at four Games: Gennadiy Volnov (URS) with a gold, two silvers and a bronze, 1960-72, and Sergei Belov (URS) with a gold and three bronzes, 1968-80. In April 1989 it was decided to allow professional players to compete in the Olympic tournaments. Thus the Americans were able to enter the 'Dream Team' for 1992, which included all-time NBA greats such as Earvin 'Magic' Johnson, Larry Bird, Michael Jordan, Patrick Ewing, Charles Barkley and David Robinson. This team averaged 117.25 points per game.

The oldest gold medallist was Larry Bird (USA) in 1992 aged 35yr 245 days, while the youngest was Spencer Haywood (USA) aged 19yr 186 days in 1968. The oldest medallist was Sergejus Jovaisa (LTU) in 1992 aged 37yr 235 days, while the youngest medallist was Vladimir Tkachenko (URS) in 1976 aged 18yr 311 days. The highest aggregate score in a game is 238 points when Brazil beat China 130-108 in 1988. In that same tournament Brazil also scored the highest total ever by a team in Olympic contests when they beat Egypt 138-85. The biggest margin of victory is 100 points, when Korea beat Iraq 120-20 and China beat Iraq 125-25, both in 1948. The highest score by an individual in a single game is 55 points by Oscar Schmidt (BRA) in a 1988 qualifying round encounter in which Spain beat Brazil 118-110. In Seoul he averaged a record 42.5 points a game. Teofilo Cruz (PUR) competed in a record five Olympic basketball tournaments, 1960-76.

The sensational final basketball match at Munich in 1972 when the Soviet Union beat the United States in disputed extra time, ending the Americans' 36-year winning streak (Popperfoto)

In the women's game Japan beat Canada 121-89 for an aggregate record of 210 points in 1976, while the highest total was 122 by the Soviet Union against Bulgaria (83) in 1980. The biggest margin was 66 points when the Soviet Union beat Italy 119-53 in 1980. Yevladia Stefanova (BUL) scored a record 39 points against Korea in 1988. The most successful female player has been Teresa Edwards (USA) with two gold medals and a silver, 1984-92. The oldest female gold medallist/medallist was Nadyezda Sakharova (URS) in 1976 aged 31yr 169 days, while the youngest was Edwards in 1984 aged 20yr 19 days. The youngest medallist was Zheng Haixia (CHN) in 1984 at 17yr 151 days. When the Soviet men's team beat the USA at Seoul their coach was Alexander Gomelsky, and when the Unified women's team beat the American women in Barcelona their coach was his brother Yevgeni.

The tallest ever player in Olympic basketball, and the tallest ever Olympic medallist in any sport, was Tommy Burleson (USA), silver medallist in 1972 at 2.23m (7ft 4in). Also reported in some quarters as the same height, but actually some 2cm shorter, was Arvidas Sabonis, who won gold in the 1988 Soviet team and bronze in the 1992 Lithuanian team. The tallest female player, and the tallest Olympic female gold medallist ever, was Iuliana Semenova (URS) at 2.18m (7ft 1¼ in) in 1976 and 1980. She was also the heaviest female gold medallist ever at 129kg 284lb. Incidentally, during the first tournament in 1936 there was a move to ban all players taller than 1.90m (6ft 2¾ in), but happily this was withdrawn.

BASKETBALL MEDALS TABLE

	Men			Women			
	G	S	B	G	S	B	Total
United States	10	1	1	2	1	1	16
Soviet Union	2	4	3	3	-	1	13
Yugoslavia	1	3	1	-	1	1	7
Brazil	-	-	3	-	-	-	3
Bulgaria	-	-	-	-	1	1	2
China	-	-	-	-	1	1	2
Uruguay	-	-	2	-	-	-	2
Canada	-	1	-	-	-	-	1
Croatia	-	1	-	-	-	-	1
France	-	1	-	-	-	-	1
Italy	-	1	-	-	-	-	1
Korea	-	-	-	-	1	-	1
Spain	-	1	-	-	-	-	1
Cuba	-	-	1	-	-	-	1
Lithuania	-	-	1	-	-	-	1
Mexico	-	-	1	-	-	-	1
	13	13	13	5	5	5	54

BASKETBALL MEDAL RESULTS

	GOLD	SILVER	BRONZE
Men			
1936	United States	Canada	Mexico
1948	United States	France	Brazil
1952	United States	Soviet Union	Uruguay
1956	United States	Soviet Union	Uruguay
1960	United States	Soviet Union	Brazil
1964	United States	Soviet Union	Brazil
1968	United States	Yugoslavia	Soviet Union
1972	Soviet Union	United States	Cuba
1976	United States	Yugoslavia	Soviet Union
1980	Yugoslavia	Italy	Soviet Union
1984	United States	Spain	Yugoslavia
1988	Soviet Union	Yugoslavia	United States
1992	USA	Croatia	Lithuania

1896–1932 Event not held

	GOLD	SILVER	BRONZE
Women			
1976	Soviet Union	United States	Bulgaria
1980	Soviet Union	Bulgaria	Yugoslavia
1984	United States	Korea	China
1988	United States	Yugoslavia	Soviet Union
1992	Unified Team	China	USA

1896–1972 Event not held

Boxing

Contests were included in the ancient Games in 688 BC, when competitors wore leather straps on their hands. As the status of the Games deteriorated in Roman times, metal studs were added. Later still, boxers wore metal 'knuckledusters'. One of the earliest known champions was Onomastos of Smyrna. The last known champion before the Games were abolished was Varazdetes (or Varastades), the winner in AD 369, who later became King of Armenia. This type of boxing should not be confused with the pankration event, which was a brutal combination of boxing and wrestling in which virtually anything was permitted. It is recorded that Arrachion of Phigalia was awarded that title in 564 BC, as his opponent 'gave up' - although Arrachion himself was by then lying dead in the arena.

Boxing was included in the modern Games in 1904 when the USA won all the titles. A pattern was set by the first heavyweight champion, Samuel Berger, when he turned professional after his victory. He was a member of the San Francisco Olympic Club which had also produced 'Gentleman Jim' Corbett, who won the world title in 1892. Over the years the weight limits for the various classes have been changed and new classes added. Bronze medals for losing semi-finalists were not awarded until 1952.

Two men have won three golds: László Papp (HUN), a southpaw, won the middleweight division in 1948 and the light-middleweight class in 1952 and 1956, while Teofilo Stevenson (CUB) won the same class, heavyweight, from 1972-80. In 1904 Oliver Kirk (USA) won two events at the same Games, also unique (though he only fought one bout in each class). The first boxer to defend a title successfully was Harry Mallin (GBR) who won the middleweight crown in 1920 and 1924. In those latter Games the standard of refereeing was highly suspect, not least because the European custom of seating the referees outside the ring was followed. Mallin was continually fouled by his French opponent in a preliminary bout, and ended the fight with teeth marks on his chest. Despite this, the outclassed

Frenchman was declared the winner. An immediate appeal, backed by a threat of the withdrawal of all English-speaking countries, was upheld. A strange occurrence was the disqualification of Ingemar Johansson (SWE) in the 1952 heavyweight final and the withholding of his silver medal due to 'inactivity in the ring'. In 1959 he won the world professional title, and thirty years after the Games, on his 50th birthday, he was finally presented with his medal.

The oldest gold medallist/medallist was Richard Gunn (GBR), the 1908 featherweight champion, aged 37yr 254 days. The youngest was Jackie Fields (né Jacob Finkelstein, USA) who won the 1924 featherweight crown aged 16yr 162 days. Both of these records can no longer be broken as current rules specify that boxers must be over 17 and under 37 prior to the start of the particular Games. Floyd Patterson (USA) won the 1952 middleweight title aged 17yr 211 days, and four years later was the youngest ever world professional heavyweight champion. The first black African to win a gold medal was Robert Wangila (KEN) in 1988. A number of brothers have won medals, but the only known father and son medallists are José Villanueva (PHI), bronze in the 1932 bantamweight, and Anthony Villanueva (PHI), silver in 1964 at featherweight.

Many Olympic boxing champions, and even more minor medallists, have won world professional titles. Only two, Joe Frazier (USA, 1964) and George Foreman (USA, 1968), won the Olympic heavyweight title and then became undisputed professional heavyweight champions. Perhaps more unusually the 1908 middleweight champion, John Douglas (GBR), later captained the England cricket team against Australia in 1911. Just as unusual was the fact that his opponent in the 1908 final, Reg 'Snowy' Baker, also competed in springboard diving and was a member of the Australian 4 x 200m swimming team which place fourth. Incidentally, over the years there has been an unsubstantiated story that their final bout was refereed by Douglas's father. Recent research indicates that the official in charge was Eugene Corri.

The Val Barker Cup is presented by the International Amateur Boxing Association (AIBA) – Barker was a former President – to the competitor adjudged the best stylist at the Games. First awarded in 1936, the winners have been:

1936	Louis Lauria (USA)	bronze	flyweight
1948	George Hunter (RSA)	gold	light-heavyweight
1952	Norvel Lee (USA)	gold	light-heavyweight
1956	Dick McTaggart (GBR)	gold	lightweight
1960	Giovanni Benvenuti (ITA)	gold	welterweight
1964	Valeriy Popentschenko (URS)	gold	middleweight
1968	Philip Waruinge (KEN)	bronze	featherweight
1972	Teofilo Stevenson (CUB)	gold	heavyweight
1976	Howard Davis (USA)	gold	lightweight
1980	Patrizio Oliva (ITA)	gold	light-welterweight
1984	Paul Gonzales (USA)	gold	light-flyweight
1988	Roy Jones (USA)	silver	light-middleweight
1992	Roberto Balado (CUB)	gold	super-heavyweight

In the 1988 tournament, because of a record 441 entries, two adjacent rings were used simultaneously. In 1992 elimination contests were held to limit entries to 32 per class. Despite pressure to drop boxing from the Olympic programme, the introduction of new gloves, safer protective helmets and three rounds of three minutes seems to have reprieved the sport, at least for the forseeable future. In 1992 an electronic scoring system was introduced, in which the judges had to simultaneously push a button to record a scoring point. Despite this innovation there was still considerable criticism of the scoring during the tournament, especially in the early bouts. The 1992 tournament was also noteworthy for the virtual eclipse of American boxers, with only one medal of each colour for the US - their worst ever showing - and the domination of the Cubans, who took 7 golds and 2 silvers from nine finals reached.

BOXING MEDALS TABLE

	G	S	B	Total
United States	46	21	29	96
Soviet Union	14	20	19	53
Great Britain	12	10	21	43
Poland	8	9	26	43
Italy	14	12	13	39
Cuba	19	10	5	34
Argentina	7	7	9	23
Germany	5	11	5	21
Romania	1	8	11	20
South Africa	6	4	9	19
Hungary	9	2	7	18
Canada	3	6	7	16
Korea	3	5	7	15
Finland	2	1	11	14
GDR	5	2	6	13
France	3	4	6	13
Bulgaria	3	3	7	13
Denmark	1	5	6	12
Yugoslavia	3	2	6	11
Mexico	2	3	6	11
Sweden	-	5	6	11
Ireland	1	3	5	9
Kenya	1	1	5	7
Czechoslovakia	3	1	2	6
North Korea (PRK)	2	2	2	6
Netherlands	1	1	4	6
FRG	1		5	6
Norway	1	2	2	5
Venezuela	1	2	2	5
Nigeria	-	3	2	5
Australia	-	2	3	5
Puerto Rico	-	1	4	5
Belgium	1	1	2	4
Uganda	-	3	1	4
Philippines	-	1	3	4
Thailand	-	1	3	4
Japan	1	-	2	3
Chile	-	1	2	3
Ghana	-	1	2	3
Algeria	-	-	3	3
Colombia	-	-	3	3
New Zealand	1	1	1	3
Cameroon	-	1	1	2
Spain	-	1	1	2
Mongolia	-	-	2	2
Morocco	-	-	2	2
Turkey	-	-	2	2
Estonia	-	1	-	1
Bermuda	-	-	1	1
Brazil	-	-	1	1
Dominican Republic	-	-	1	1
Egypt	-	-	1	1
Guyana	-	-	1	1
Niger	-	-	1	1
Pakistan	-	-	1	1
Tunisia	-	-	1	1
Uruguay	-	-	1	1
Zambia	-	-	1	1
	180	180	298	658

The official 1908 report only notes a single bronze medal awarded.

BOXING MEDAL RESULTS

	GOLD	SILVER	BRONZE

Light-Flyweight
Weight up to 48kg/105.8lb

	GOLD	SILVER	BRONZE
1968	Francisco Rodriguez (VEN)	Yong-ju Jee (KOR)	Harlan Marbley (USA)
			Hubert Skrzypczak (POL)
1972	György Gedo (HUN)	U Gil Kim (PRK)	Ralph Evans (GBR)
			Enrique Rodriguez (ESP)
1976	Jorge Hernandez (CUB)	Byong Uk Li (PRK)	Payao Pooltarat (THA)
			Orlando Maldonado (PUR)
1980	Shamil Sabirov (URS)	Hipolito Ramos (CUB)	Byong Uk Li (PRK)
			Ismail Moustafov (BUL)
1984	Paul Gonzales (USA)	Salvatore Todisco (ITA)	Keith Mwila (ZAM)
			Jose Bolivar (VEN)

1988	Ivailo Hristov (BUL)	Michael Carbajal (USA)	Robert Isaszegi (HUN)
			Leopoldo Serantes (PHI)
1992	Rogelio Marcelo (CUB)	Daniel Bojinov (BUL)	Roel Velasco (PHI)
			Jan Quast (GER)

1896–1964 Event not held

Flyweight

From 1948 the weight limit has been 51kg/112.5lb. In 1904 it was 105lb/47.6kg. From 1920 to 1936 112lb/50.8kg.

1904	George Finnegan (USA)	Miles Burke (USA)	–*
1920	Frank Di Gennara (USA)	Anders Petersen (DEN)	William Cuthbertson (GBR)
1924	Fidel LaBarba (USA)	James McKenzie (GBR)	Raymond Fee (USA)
1928	Antal Kocsis (HUN)	Armand Appel (FRA)	Carlo Cavagnoli (ITA)
1932	István Enekes (HUN)	Francisco Cabanas (MEX)	Louis Salica (USA)
1936	Willi Kaiser (GER)	Gavino Matta (ITA)	Louis Lauria (USA)
1948	Pascual Perez (ARG)	Spartaco Bandinelli (ITA)	Soo-Ann Han (KOR)
1952	Nathan Brooks (USA)	Edgar Basel (GER)	Anatoliy Bulakov (URS)
			William Toweel (RSA)
1956	Terence Spinks (GBR)	Mircea Dobrescu (ROM)	John Caldwell (IRL)
			René Libeer (FRA)
1960	Gyula Török (HUN)	Sergey Sivko (URS)	Kyoshi Tanabe (JPN)
			Abdelmoneim Elguindi (EGY)
1964	Fernando Atzori (ITA)	Artur Olech (POL)	Robert Carmody (USA)
			Stanislav Sorokin (URS)
1968	Ricardo Delgado (MEX)	Artur Olech (POL)	Servilio Oliveira (BRA)
			Leo Rwabwogo (UGA)
1972	Gheorghi Kostadinov (BUL)	Leo Rwabwogo (UGA)	Leszek Blazynski (POL)
			Douglas Rodriguez (CUB)
1976	Leo Randolph (USA)	Ramon Duvalon (CUB)	Leszek Blazynski (POL)
			David Torosyan (URS)
1980	Petar Lessov (BUL)	Viktor Miroshnichenko (URS)	Hugh Russel (IRL)
			Janos Varadi (HUN)
1984	Steve McCrory (USA)	Redzep Redzepovski (YUG)	Eyup Can (TUR)
			Ibrahim Bilali (KEN)
1988	Kim Kwang-Sun (KOR)	Andreas Tews (GDR)	Mario Gonzalez (MEX)
			Timofey Skriabin (URS)
1992	Choi Chol-su (PRK)	Raul Gonzalez (CUB)	Timothy Austin (USA)
			Istvan Kovacs (HUN)

1896–1900, 1906–1912 Event not held
*No third place.

Bantamweight

From 1948 the weight limit has been 54kg/119lb. In 1904 it was 115lb/52.16kg. In 1908 it was 116lb/52.62kg. From 1920 to 1936 118lb/53.52kg.

1904	Oliver Kirk (USA)	George Finnegan (USA)	–*
1908	Henry Thomas (GBR)	John Condon (GBR)	W Webb (GBR)
1920	Clarence Walker (RSA)	Christopher Graham (CAN)	James McKenzie (GBR)
1924	William Smith (RSA)	Salvadore Tripoli (USA)	Jean Ces (FRA)
1928	Vittorio Tamagnini (ITA)	John Daley (USA)	Harry Isaacs (RSA)
1932	Horace Gwynne (CAN)	Hans Ziglarski (GER)	José Villanueva (PHI)
1936	Ulderico Sergo (ITA)	Jack Wilson (USA)	Fidel Ortiz (MEX)
1948	Tibor Csik (HUN)	Giovanni Zuddas (ITA)	Juan Venegas (PUR)
1952	Pentti Hämäläinen (FIN)	John McNally (IRL)	Gennadiy Garbuzov (URS)
			Joon-Ho Kang (KOR)
1956	Wolfgang Behrendt (GER)	Soon-Chun Song (KOR)	Frederick Gilroy (IRL)
			Claudio Barrientos (CHI)
1960	Oleg Grigoryev (URS)	Primo Zamparini (ITA)	Brunoh Bendig (POL)
			Oliver Taylor (AUS)

1964	Takao Sakurai (JPN)	Shin Cho Chung (KOR)	Juan Fabila Mendoza (MEX)
			Washington Rodriguez (URU)
1968	Valeriy Sokolov (URS)	Eridadi Mukwanga (UGA)	Eiji Morioka (JPN)
			Kyou-Chull Chang (KOR)
1972	Orlando Martinez (CUB)	Alfonso Zamora (MEX)	George Turpin (GBR)
			Ricardo Carreras (USA)
1976	Yong Jo Gu (PRK)	Charles Mooney (USA)	Patrick Cowdell (GBR)
			Viktor Rybakov (URS)
1980	Juan Hernandez (CUB)	Bernardo Pinango (VEN)	Dumitru Cipere (ROM)
			Michael Anthony Parris (GUY)
1984	Maurizio Stecca (ITA)	Hector Lopez (MEX)	Dale Walters (CAN)
			Pedro Nolasco (DOM)
1988	Kennedy McKinney (USA)	Alexandar Hristov (BUL)	Jorge Julio Rocha (COL)
			Phajol Moolsan (THA)
1992	Joel Casamayor (CUB)	Wayne McCullough (IRL)	Li Gwang-sik (PRK)
			Mohamed Achik (MAR)

1896–1900, 1906, 1912 Event not held
No third place.

Featherweight

From 1952 the weight limit has been 57kg/126lb. In 1904 it was 125lb/56.70kg. From 1908 to 1936 it was 126lb/57.15kg. In 1948 it was 58kg.

1904	Oliver Kirk (USA)	Frank Haller (USA)	Fred Gilmore (USA)
1908	Richard Gunn (GBR)	CW Morris (GBR)	Hugh Roddin (GBr)
1920	Paul Fritsch (FRA)	Jean Gachet (FRA)	Edoardo Garzena (ITA)
1924	John Fields (USA)	Joseph Salas (USA)	Pedro Quartucci (ARG)
1928	Lambertus van Klaveren (NED)	Victor Peralta (ARG)	Harold Devine (USA)
1932	Carmelo Robledo (ARG)	Josef Schleinkofer (GER)	Carl Carlsson (SWE)
1936	Oscar Casanovas (ARG)	Charles Catterall (RSA)	Josef Miner (GER)
1948	Ernesto Formenti (ITA)	Denis Shepherd (RSA)	Aleksey Antkiewicz (POL)
1952	Jan Zachara (TCH)	Sergio Caprari (ITA)	Joseph Ventaja (FRA)
			Leonard Leisching (RSA)
1956	Vladimir Safronov (URS)	Thomas Nicholls (GBR)	Henryk Niedzwiedzki (POL)
			Pentti Hämäläinen (FIN)
1960	Francesco Musso (ITA)	Jerzy Adamski (POL)	William Meyers (RSA)
			Jorma Limmonen (FIN)
1964	Stanislav Stepashkin (URS)	Antony Villaneuva (PHI)	Charles Brown (USA)
			Heinz Schultz (GER)
1968	Antonio Roldan (MEX)	Albert Robinson (USA)	Philip Waruinge (KEN)
			Ivan Michailov (BUL)
1972	Boris Kuznetsov (URS)	Philip Waruinge (KEN)	Clemente Rojas (COL)
			András Botos (HUN)
1976	Angel Herrera (CUB)	Richard Nowakowski (GDR)	Juan Paredes (MEX)
			Leszek Kosedowski (POL)
1980	Rudi Fink (GDR)	Adolfo Horta (CUB)	Viktor Rybakov (URS)
			Krzysztof Kosedowski (POL)
1984	Meldrick Taylor (USA)	Peter Konyegwachie (NGR)	Turgut Aykac (TUR)
			Omar Peraza (VEN)
1988	Giovanni Parisi (ITA)	Daniel Dumitrescu (ROM)	Lee Jae-Hyuk (KOR)
			Abdelhak Achik (MAR)
1992	Andreas Tews (GER)	Faustino Reyes Lopez (ESP)	Hocine Soltani (ALG)
			Ramazi Paliani (EUN)

1896–1900, 1906, 1912 Event not held.

Lightweight
From 1952 the weight has been 60kg/132lb. In 1904 and from 1920 to 1936 it was 135lb/61.24kg. In 1908 it was 140lb/63.50kg. In 1948 it was 62kg/ 136.5lb.

1904	Harry Spanger (USA)	James Eagan (USA)	Russell Van Horn (USA)
1908	Frederick Grace (GBR)	Frederick Spiller (GBR)	HH Johnson (GBR)
1920	Samuel Mosberg (USA)	Gotfred Johansen (DEN)	Clarence Newton (CAN)
1924	Hans Nielsen (DEN)	Alfredo Coppello (ARG)	Frederick Boylstein (USA)
1928	Carlo Orlandi (ITA)	Stephen Halaiko (USA)	Gunnar Berggren (SWE)
1932	Lawrence Stevens (RSA)	Thure Ahlqvist (SWE)	Nathan Bor (USA)
1936	Imre Harangi (HUN)	Nikolai Stepulov (EST)	Erik Agren (SWE)
1948	Gerald Dreyer (RSA)	Joseph Vissers (BEL)	Svend Wad (DEN)
1952	Aureliano Bolognesi (ITA)	Aleksey Antkiewicz (POL)	Gheorge Fiat (ROM)
			Erkki Pakkanen (FIN)
1956	Richard McTaggart (GBR)	Harry Kurschat (GER)	Anthony Byren (IRL)
			Anatoliy Lagetko (URS)
1960	Kazimierz Pazdzior (POL)	Sandro Lopopoli (ITA)	Richard McTaggart (GBR)
			Abel Laudonio (ARG)
1964	Józef Grudzien (POL)	Vellikton Barannikov (URS)	Ronald Harris (USA)
			James McCourt (IRL)
1968	Ronald Harris (USA)	Józef Grudzien (POL)	Calistrat Cutov (ROM)
			Zvonimir Vujin (YUG)
1972	Jan Szczepanksi (POL)	László Orban (HUN)	Samuel Mbugua (KEN)
			Alfonso Perez (COL)
1976	Howard Davis (USA)	Simion Cutov (ROM)	Ace Rusevski (YUG)
			Vasiliy Solomin (URS)
1980	Angel Herrera (CUB)	Viktor Demianenko (URS)	Kazimierz Adach (POL)
			Richard Nowakowski (GDR)
1984	Pernell Whitaker (USA)	Luis Ortiz (PUR)	Martin Ebanga (CMR)
			Chun Chi-Sung (KOR)
1988	Andreas Zülow (GDR)	George Cramne (SWE)	Nerguy Enkhbat (MGL)
			Romallis Ellis (USA)
1992	Oscar de la Hoya (USA)	Marco Rudolph (USA)	Namjil Bayarsaikhan (MGL)
			Hong Sung-sik (KOR)

1896–1900, 1906, 1912 Event not held

Light-Welterweight
Weight up to 63.5kg/140lb

1952	Charles Adkins (USA)	Viktor Mednov (URS)	Erkki Mallenius (FIN)
			Bruno Visintin (ITA)
1956	Vladimir Yengibarvan (URS)	Franco Nenci (ITA)	Henry Loubscher (RSA)
			Constantin Dumitrescu (ROM)
1960	Bohumil Nemecek (TCH)	Clement Quartey (GHA)	Quincy Daniels (USA)
			Marian Kasprzvk (POL)
1964	Jerzy Kulej (POL)	Yegeniy Frolov (URS)	Eddie Blay (GHA)
			Habib Galhia (TUN)
1968	Jerzv Kulej (POL)	Enrique Regueiferos (CUB)	Arto Nilsson (FIN)
			James Wallington (USA)
1972	Ray Seales (USA)	Anghel Anghelov (BUL)	Zvonimir Vujin (YUG)
			Issaka Daborg (NIG)
1976	Ray Leonard (USA)	Andres Aldama (CUB)	Vladimir Kolev (BUL)
			Kazimierz Szczerba (POL)
1980	Patrizio Oliva (ITA)	Serik Konakbayev (URS)	Jose Aguilar (CUB)
			Anthony Willis (GBR)
1984	Jerry Page (USA)	Dhawee Umponmana (THA)	Mircea Fuger (ROM)
			Mirko Puzovic (YUG)
1988	Vyacheslav Janovski (URS)	Grahame Cheney (AUS)	Lars Myrberg (SWE)
			Reiner Gies (FRG)

| 1992 | Hector Vinent (CUB) | Marc Leduc (CAN) | Jyri Kjall (FIN) |
| | | | Leonard Doroftei (ROM) |

1896–1948 Event not held.

Welterweight
From 1948 the weight limit has been 67kg/148lb. In 1904 it was 14.75lb/65.27kg. From 1920 to 1936 it was 147lb/66.68kg.

1904	Albert Young (USA)	Harry Spanger (USA)	Joseph Lydon (USA)
			James Eagan (USA)
1920	Albert Schneider (CAN)	Alexander Ireland (GBR)	Frederick Colberg (USA)
1924	Jean Delarge (BEL)	Héctor Mendez (ARG)	Douglas Lewis (CAN)
1928	Edward Morgan (NZL)	Raul Landini (ARG)	Raymond Smillie (CAN)
1932	Edward Flynn (USA)	Erich Campe (GER)	Bruno Ahlberg (FIN)
1936	Sten Suvio (FIN)	Michael Murach (GER)	Gerhard Petersen (DEN)
1948	Julius Torma (TCH)	Horace Herring (USA)	Alessandro D'Ottavio (ITA)
1952	Zygmunt Chychla (POL)	Sergey Schtsherbakov (URS)	Victor Jörgensen (DEN)
			Günther Heidemann (GER)
1956	Nicholae Lince (ROM)	Frederick Tiedt (IRL)	Kevin Hogarth (AUS)
			Nicholas Gargano (GBR)
1960	Giovanni Benvenuti (ITA)	Yuriy Radonyak (URS)	Leszek Drogosz (POL)
			James Lloyd (GBR)
1964	Marian Kasprzyk (POL)	Ritschardas Tamulis (URS)	Pertti Perhonen (FIN)
			Silvano Bertini (ITA)
1968	Manfred Wolke (GDR)	Joseph Bessala (CMR)	Vladimir Musalinov (URS)
			Mario Guilloti (ARG)
1972	Emilio Correa (CUB)	Janos Kajdi (HUN)	Dick Murunga (KEN)
			Jesse Valdez (USA)
1976	Jochen Bachfeld (GDR)	Pedro Gamarro (VEN)	Reinhard Skricek (FRG)
			Victor Zilberman (ROM)
1980	Andrew Aldama (CUB)	John Mugabi (UGA)	Karl-Heinz Krüger (GDR)
			Kazimierz Szczerba (POL)
1984	Mark Breland (USA)	An Young-Su (KOR)	Joni Nyman (FIN)
			Luciano Bruno (ITA)
1988	Robert Wangila (KEN)	Laurent Boudouani (FRA)	Jan Dydak (POL)
			Kenneth Gould (USA)
1992	Michael Carruth (IRL)	Juan Hernandez (CUB)	Akrom Chenglai (THA)
			Anibal Acevedo (PUR)

1896–1900, 1906–1912 Event not held

Light-Middleweight
Weight up to 71kg/157lb.

1952	László Papp (HUN)	Theunis van Schalkwyk (RSA)	Boris Tishin (URS)
			Eladio Herrera (ARG)
1956	László Papp (HUN)	José Torres (USA)	John McCormack (GBR)
			Zbigniew Pietrzkowski (POL)
1960	Wilbert McClure (USA)	Carmelo Bossi (ITA)	Boris Lagutin (URS)
			William Fisher (GBR)
1964	Boris Lagutin (URS)	Josef Gonzales (FRA)	Nohim Maivegun (NGR)
			Jozef Grzesiak (POL)
1968	Boris Lagutin (URS)	Rolando Garbey (CUB)	John Baldwin (USA)
			Günther Meier (FRG)
1972	Dieter Kottysch (FRG)	Wieslaw Rudkowski (POL)	Alan Minter GBR)
			Peter Tiepold (GDR)
1976	Jerzy Rybicki (POL)	Tadija Kacar (YUG)	Roland Garbey (CUB)
			Viktor Savchenko (URS)
1980	Armando Martinez (CUB)	Aleksandr Koshkin (URS)	Jan Franck (TCH)
			Detlef Kastner (GDR)

1984	Frank Tate (USA)	Shawn O'Sullivan (CAN)	Manfred Zielonka (FRG)
			Christophe Tiozzo (FRA)
1988	Park Si-Hun (KOR)	Roy Jones (USA)	Richard Woodhall (GBR)
			Raymond Downey (CAN)
1992	Juan Carlos Lemus (CUB)	Orhan Delibas (NED)	Gyorgy Mizsei (HUN)
			Robin Reid (GBR)

1896–1948 Event not held

Middleweight
From 1952 the weight limit has been 75kg/165lb. From 1904 to 1908 it was 158lb/71.68kg. From 1920 to 1936 it was 160lb/72.57kg. In 1948 it was 73kg/161lb.

1904	Charles Mayer (USA)	Benjamin Spradley (USA)	–*
1908	John Douglas (GBR)	Reginald Baker (AUS/NZL)	W Philo (GBR)
1920	Harry Mallin (GBR)	Georges Prud'homme (CAN)	Moe Herscovitch (CAN)
1924	Harry Mallin (GBR)	John Elliott (GBR)	Joseph Beecken (BEL)
1928	Piero Toscani (ITA)	Jan Hermanek (TCH)	Léonard Steyaert (BEL)
1932	Carmen Barth (USA)	Amado Azar (ARG)	Ernest Pierce (RSA)
1936	Jean Despeaux (FRA)	Henry Tiller (NOR)	Raúl Villareal (ARG)
1948	László Papp (HUN)	John Wright (GBR)	Ivano Fontana (ITA)
1952	Floyd Patterson (USA)	Vasile Tita (ROM)	Boris Nikolov (BUL)
			Stig Sjolin (SWE)
1956	Gennadiy Schatkov (URS)	Ramon Tapia (CHI)	Gilbert Chapron (FRA)
			Victor Zalazar (ARG)
1960	Edward Crook (USA)	Tadeusz Walasek (POL)	Ion Monea (ROM)
			Yevgeniy Feofanov (URS)
1964	Valeriy Popentschenko (URS)	Emil Schultz (GER)	Franco Valle (ITA)
			Tadeusz Walasek (POL)
1968	Christopher Finnegan (GBR)	Aleksey Kisselyov (URS)	Agustin Zaragoza (MEX)
			Alfred Jones (USA)
1972	Vyatcheslav Lemechev (URS)	Reima Virtanen (FIN)	Prince Amartey (GHA)
			Marvin Johnson (USA)
1976	Michael Spinks (USA)	Rufat Riskiev (URS)	Alec Nastac (ROM)
			Luis Martinez (CUB)
1980	Jose Gomez (CUB)	Viktor Savchenko (URS)	Jerzy Rybicki (POL)
			Valentin Silaghi (ROM)
1984	Shin Joon-Sup (KOR)	Virgil Hill (USA)	Mohamed Zaoui (ALG)
			Aristides Gonzales (PUR)
1988	Henry Maske (GDR)	Egerton Marcus (CAN)	Chris Sande (KEN)
			Hussain Shaw Syed (PAK)
1992	Ariel Hernandez (CUB)	Chris Byrd (USA)	Chris Johnson (CAN)
			Lee Seung-bae (KOR)

1896–1900, 1906, 1912 Event not held
*No third place.

Light-Heavyweight
From 1952 the weight limit has been 81kg/178.5lb. From 1920 to 1936 it was 175lb/79.38kg. In 1948 it was 80kg/186.25lb.

1920	Edward Eagan (USA)	Sverre Sörsdal (NOR)	H Franks (GBR)
1924	Harry Mitchell (GBR)	Thyge Petersen (DEN)	Sverre Sörsdal (NOR)
1928	Victor Avendano (ARG)	Ernst Pistulla (GER)	Karel Miljon (NED)
1932	David Carstens (RSA)	Gino Rossi (ITA)	Peter Jörgensen (DEN)
1936	Roger Michelot (FRA)	Richard Vogt (GER)	Francisco Risiglione (ARG)
1948	George Hunter (RSA)	Donald Scott (GBR)	Maurio Cla (ARG)
1952	Norvel Lee (USA)	Antonio Pacenza (ARG)	Anotiliy Perov (URS)
			Harri Siljander (FIN)
1956	James Boyd (USA)	Gheorghe Negrea (ROM)	Carlos Lucas (CHI)
			Romualdas Murauskas (URS)

1960	Cassius Clay (USA)	Zbigniew Pietrzykowski (POL)	Anthony Madigan (AUS)
			Giulio Saraudi (ITA)
1964	Cosimo Pinto (ITA)	Aleksey Kisselyov (URS)	Aleksandr Nikolov (BUL)
			Zbigniew Pietrzykowski (POL)
1968	Dan Poznyak (URS)	Ion Monea (ROM)	Georgy Stankov (BUL)
			Stanislav Gragan (POL)
1972	Mate Parlov (YUG)	Gilberto Carrillo (CUB)	Isaac Ikhouria (NGR)
			Janusz Gortat (POL)
1976	Leon Spinks (USA)	Sixto Soria (CUB)	Costica Danifoiu (ROM)
			Janusz Gortat (POL)
1980	Slobodan Kacar (YUG)	Pavel Skrzecz (POL)	Herbert Bauch (GDR)
			Ricardo Rojas (CUB)
1984	Anton Josipovic (YUG)	Kevin Barry (NZL)	Mustapha Moussa (ALG)
			Evander Holyfield (USA)
1988	Andrew Maynard (USA)	Nourmagomed Chanavazov (URS)	Damir Skaro (YUG)
			Henryk Petrich (POL)
1992	Torsten May (GER)	Rostislav Zaoulitchyni (EUN)	Wojciech Bartnik (POL)
			Zoltan Beres (HUN)

1896–1912 Event not held.

Heavyweight
From 1984 the weight limit has been 91kg/200.5lb. From 1904 to 1908 it was over 158lb/71.67kg. From 1920 to 1936 it was over 175lb/79.38kg. In 1948 it was over 80kg/176.25kg. From 1952 to 1980 it was over 81kg/178.25lb.

1904	Samuel Berger (USA)	Charles Mayer (USA)	William Michaels (USA)
1908	AL Oldham (GBR)	SCH Evans (GBR)	Frederick Parks (GBR)
1920	Ronald Rawson (GBR)	Sören Petersen (DEN)	Xavier Eluère (FRA)
1924	Otto von Porat (NOR)	Sören Petersen (DEN)	Alfredo Porzio (ARG)
1928	Arturo Rodriguez Jurado (ARG)	Nils Ramm (SWE)	Jacob Michaelsen (DEN)
1932	Santiago Lovell (ARG)	Luigi Rovati (ITA)	Frederick Feary (USA)
1936	Herbert Runge (GER)	Guillermo Lovell (ARG)	Erling Nilsen (NOR)
1948	Rafael Iglesias (ARG)	Gunnar Nilsson (SWE)	John Arthur (RSA)
1952	Hayes Edward Sanders (USA)	Ingemar Johansson* (SWE)	Andries Nieman (RSA)
			Ilkka Koski (FIN)
1956	Peter Rademacher (USA)	Lev Mukhin (URS)	Daniel Bekker (RSA)
			Giacomo Bozzano (ITA)
1960	Franco de Piccoli (ITA)	Daniel Bekker (RSA)	Josef Nemec (TCH)
			Günter Siegmund (GER)
1964	Joe Frazier (USA)	Hans Huber (GER)	Guiseppe Ros (ITA)
			Vadim Yemelyanov (URS)
1968	George Foreman (USA)	Ionas Tschepulis (URS)	Giorgio Bambini (ITA)
			Joaquin Rocha (MEX)
1972	Teofilo Stevenson (CUB)	Ion Alexe (ROM)	Peter Hussing (FRG)
			Hasse Thomsen (SWE)
1976	Teofilo Stevenson (CUB)	Mircea Simon (ROM)	Johnny Tate (USA)
			Clarence Hill (BER)
1980	Teofilo Stevenson (CUB)	Pyotr Zayev (URS)	Jurgen Fanghanel (GDR)
			Istvan Levai (HUN)
1984	Henry Tillman (USA)	Willie Dewitt (CAN)	Angelo Musone (ITA)
			Arnold Vanderlijde (NED)
1988	Ray Mercer (USA)	Baik Hyun-Man (KOR)	Andrzej Golota (POL)
			Arnold Vanderlijde (NED)
1992	Felix Savon (CUB)	David Izonritei (NGR)	David Tua (NZL)
			Arnold van de Lijde (NED)

1896–1900, 1906, 1912 Event not held.
**Silver medal originally not awarded; Johansson disqualified but reinstated in 1982.*

British-born Lennox Lewis, representing Canada, won the 1988 super-heavyweight title beating Riddick Bowe (USA). He later became the professional WBC heavyweight champion in place of Bowe (Allsport)

Super-Heavyweight
From 1984 the class has been for those over 91kg/200.5lb.

1984	Tyrell Biggs (USA)	Francesco Damiani (ITA)	Robert Wells (GBR)
			Salihu Azis (YUG)
1988	Lennox Lewis (CAN)	Riddick Bowe (USA)	Alexandr Mirochnitchenko (URS)
			Jasz Zarenkiewicz (POL)
1992	Roberto Balado (CUB)	Richard Igbineghu (NGR)	Brian Nielsen (DEN)
			Svilen Roussinov (BUL)

1896–1980 Event not held.

Canoeing

Official canoeing competitions were first held in 1936, although kayak and Canadian events had been demonstrated in 1924. In 1972 at Munich four slalom events were held, and after a gap of 20 years slalom racing was reintroduced at Barcelona in 1992. The most successful canoeist has been Gert Fredriksson (SWE) with six golds, one silver and a bronze from 1948-60, all in kayaks. The most medals won by a woman is four golds and two silvers by Birgit Fischer-Schmidt, first representing GDR and then Germany, in 1980, 1988 and 1992. Two men, Vladimir Parfenovich in 1980 and Ian Ferguson (NZL) in 1984, have won three gold medals at one Games. The best by a woman at one Games is two golds and a silver, by Agneta Andersson (SWE) in 1984 and Birgit Fischer-Schmidt (GDR) in 1988.

The highest speed achieved in the Games over the standard 1000m course is 20.91km/h when the German K4 clocked 2:52.17 in a heat in 1992. In 1992 the Hungarian K4 team achieved an average speed of 21.94km/h over the first 250m, also in a heat. The fastest by a female crew over the 500m course is 19.37km/h when the Hungarian K4 clocked 1:32.94 in a heat in 1992. In another 1992 heat, the Swedish women's K4 achieved an average speed of 19.65km/h over the first 250m. The closest finish in an Olympic canoeing final occurred in the 1952 K2 1000m when the timekeepers were unable to separate the first and second placed pairs. The closest finish in women's canoeing was in the 1988 K1 500m when the winning margin was 0.12sec. This was equalled in the 1992 K2 final.

The oldest ever canoeing gold medallist/medallist was Gert Fredriksson (SWE) aged 40yr 292 days in the 1960 K2 over 1000m. The youngest was Bent Peder Rasch (DEN) in the C2 1000m in 1952 aged 18yr 58 days. The youngest female champion was Birgit Fischer (GDR) aged 18y 158 days in 1980, while the oldest was Sylvi Saimo (FIN) in 1952 aged 37yr 259 days. The youngest medallist was Francine Fox (USA), with a silver in 1964 at 15yr 220 days (incidentally, her partner was 20 years older). The youngest male medallist was Gábor Novák in 1952 aged 17yr 348 days, and the oldest woman to win a medal was Antonina Seredina (URS) in 1968 at 37yr 307 days. Ivar Patzaichin (ROM) won gold medals over a 16-year period, 1968-84, in the Canadian events.

When Philippe Renaud (FRA) won a bronze in the 1988 C2 500m, he was the latest success of an Olympic family - his brother Eric had won a canoe bronze in 1984, their father Marcel a canoe silver in 1956, and a great-uncle a cycling bronze in 1924.

CANOEING MEDALS TABLE

	Men			Women			Total
	G	S	B	G	S	B	
Soviet Union	22	12	6	8	2	3	53
Hungary	7	18	13	1	4	5	48
Germany	9	8	9	4	5	1	36
GDR	8	5	8	6	2	1	30
Romania	8	8	8	1	1	3	29
Sweden	11	8	2	2	2	1	26
France	1	6	13	-	-	-	14
United States	5	2	4	-	1	2	14
Bulgaria	3	1	6	1	2	1	14
Austria	3	4	4	-	1	1	13
Canada	3	5	3	-	1	1	13
Czechoslovakia	7	4	1	-	-	-	12
Denmark	2	4	4	1	-	1	12
Finland	4	2	3	1	-	-	10
Poland	-	3	4	-	-	3	10
Australia	1	2	4	-	1	-	8
Netherlands	-	1	3	-	2	2	8
New Zealand	5	1	1	-	-	-	7
FRG	1	1	1	1	2	1	7
Norway	1	2	3	-	-	-	6
Yugoslavia	2	2	1	-	-	-	5
Spain	-	2	2	-	-	-	4
Italy	1	1	1	-	-	-	3
Great Britain	-	1	-	-	-	-	1
Latvia	-	1	-	-	-	-	1
	104	104	104	26	26	26	390

CANOEING MEDAL RESULTS — MEN

GOLD	SILVER	BRONZE

500 Metres Kayak Singles (K1)

	GOLD	SILVER	BRONZE
1976	Vasile Diba (ROM) 1:46.41	Zoltan Szytanity (HUN) 1:46.95	Rüdiger Helm (GDR) 1:48.30
1980	Vladimir Parfenovich (URS) 1:43.43	John Sumegi (AUS) 1:44.12	Vasile Diba (ROM) 1:44.90
1984	Ian Ferguson (NZL) 1:47.84	Lars-Erik Möberg (SWE) 1:48.18	Bernard Bregeon (FRA) 1:48.41
1988	Zsolt Gyulay (HUN) 1:44.82	Andreas Stähle (GDR) 1:46.38	Paul McDonald (NZL) 1:46.46
1992	Mikko Kolehmainen (FIN) 1:40.34	Zsolt Gyulay (HUN) 1:40.64	Knut Holmann (NOR) 1:40.71

1896–1972 Event not held.

1000 Metres Kayak Singles (K1)

	GOLD	SILVER	BRONZE
1936	Gregor Hradetsky (AUT) 4:22.9	Helmut Cämmerer (GER) 4:25.6	Jacob Kraaier (NED) 4:35.1
1948	Gert Fredriksson (SWE) 4:33.2	Johann Kobberup (DEN) 4:39.9	Henri Eberhardt (FRA) 4:41.4
1952	Gert Fredriksson (SWE) 4:07.9	Thorvald Strömberg (FIN) 4:09.7	Louis Gantois (FRA) 4:20.1
1956	Gert Fredriksson (SWE) 4:12.8	Igor Pissaryev (URS) 4:15.3	Lajos Kiss (HUN) 4:16.2
1960	Erik Hansen (DEN) 3:53.00	Imre Szöllösi (HUN) 3:54.02	Gert Fredriksson (SWE) 3:55.89
1964	Rolf Peterson (SWE) 3:57.13	Mihály Hesz (HUN) 3:57.28	Aurel Vernescu (ROM) 4:00.77
1968	Mihály Hesz (HUN) 4:02.63	Aleksandr Shaparenko (URS) 4:03.58	Erik Hansen (DEN) 4:04.39
1972	Aleksandr Shaparenko (URS) 3:48.06	Rolf Peterson (SWE) 3:48.35	Geza Csapo (HUN) 3:49.38
1976	Rüdiger Helm (GDR) 3:48.20	Geza Csapo (HUN) 3:48.84	Vasile Diba (ROM) 3:49.65
1980	Rüdiger Helm (GDR) 3:48.77	Alain Lebas (FRA) 3:50.20	Ion Birladeanu (ROM) 3:50.49
1984	Alan Thompson (NZL) 3:45.73	Milan Janic (YUG) 3:46.88	Greg Barton (USA) 3:47.38
1988	Greg Barton (USA) 3:55.27	Grant Davies (AUS) 3:55.28	Andre Wohllebe (GDR) 3:55.55
1992	Clint Robinson (AUS) 3:37.26	Knut Holmann (NOR) 3:37.50	Greg Barton (USA) 3:37.93

1896–1932 Event not held.

10,000 Metres Kayak Singles (K1)

	GOLD	SILVER	BRONZE
1936	Ernst Krebs (GER) 46:01.6	Fritz Landertinger (AUT) 46:14.7	Ernest Riedel (USA) 47:23.9
1948	Gert Fredriksson (SWE) 50:47.7	Kurt Wires (FIN) 51:18.2	Ejvind Skabo (NOR) 51:35.4
1952	Thorvald Stromberg (FIN) 47.22.8	Gert Fredriksson (SWE) 47:34.1	Michel Scheuer (GER) 47:54.5
1956	Gert Fredriksson (SWE) 47:43.4	Ferenc Hatlaczky (HUN) 47:53.3	Michel Scheuer (GER) 48:00.3

1896–1932, 1960–1992 Event not held.

500 Metres Kayak Pairs (K2)

	GOLD	SILVER	BRONZE
1976	GDR 1:35.87	Soviet Union 1:36.81	Romania 1:37.43
1980	Soviet Union 1:32.38	Spain 1:33.65	GDR 1:34.00
1984	New Zealand 1:34.21	Sweden 1:35.26	Canada 1:35.41
1988	New Zealand 1:33.98	Soviet Union 1:34.15	Hungary 1:34.32
1992	Germany 1:28.27	Poland 1:29.84	Italy 1:30.00

1000 Metres Kayak Pairs (K2)

	GOLD	SILVER	BRONZE
1936	Austria 4:03.8	Germany 4:08.9	Netherlands 4:12.2
1948	Sweden 4:07.3	Denmark 4:07.5	Finland 4:08.7
1952	Finland 3:51.1	Sweden 3:51.1	Austria 3:51.4
1956	Germany 3:49.6	Soviet Union 3:51.4	Austria 3:55.8
1960	Sweden 3:34.7	Hungary 3:34.91	Poland 3:37.34
1964	Sweden 3:38.4	Netherlands 3:39.30	Germany 3:40.69
1968	Soviet Union 3:37.54	Hungary 3:38.44	Austria 3:40.71
1972	Soviet Union 3:31.23	Hungary 3:32.00	Poland 3:33.83
1976	Soviet Union 3:29.01	GDR 3:29.33	Hungary 3:30.56
1980	Soviet Union 3:26.72	Hungary 3:28.49	Spain 3:28.66
1984	Canada 3:24.22	France 3:25.97	Australia 3:26.80
1988	United States 3:32.42	New Zealand 3:32.71	Australia 3:33.76
1992	Germany 3:16.10	Sweden 3:17.70	Poland 3:18.86

1896–1932 Event not held.

10,000 Metres Kayak Pairs (K2)

1936	Germany 41:45.0	Austria 42:05.4	Sweden 43:06.1
1948	Sweden 46:09.4	Norway 46:44.8	Finland 46:48.2
1952	Finland 44:21.3	Sweden 44:21.7	Hungary 44:26.6
1956	Hungary 43:37.0	Germany 43:40.6	Australia 43:43.2

1896–1932, 1960–1992 Event not held.

1000 Metres Kayak Fours (K4)

1964	Soviet Union 3:14.67	Germany 3:15.39	Romania 3:15.51
1968	Norway 3:14.38	Romania 3:14.81	Hungary 3:15.10
1972	Soviet Union 3:14.02	Romania 3:15.07	Norway 3:15.27
1976	Soviet Union 3:08.69	Spain 3:08.95	GDR 3:10.76
1980	GDR 3:13.76	Romania 3:15.35	Bulgaria 3:15.46
1984	New Zealand 3:02.28	Sweden 3:02.81	France 3:03.94
1988	Hungary 3:00.20	Soviet Union 3:01.40	GDR 3:02.37
1992	Germany 2:54.18	Hungary 2:54.82	Australia 2:56.97

1896–1960 Event not held.

500 Meters Canadian Singles (C1)

1976	Aleksandr Rogov (URS) 1:59.23	John Wood (CAN) 1:59.58	Matija Ljubek (YUG) 1:59.60
1980	Sergey Postrekhin (URS) 1:53.37	Lubomir Lubenov (BUL) 1:53.49	Olaf Heukrodt (GDR) 1:54.38
1984	Larry Cain (CAN) 1:57.01	Henning Jakobsen (DEN) 1:58.45	Costica Olaru (ROM) 1:59.86
1988	Olaf Heukrodt (GDR) 1:56.42	Mikhail Slivinskiy (URS) 1.57.26	Martin Marinov (BUL) 1:57.27
1992	Nikolai Boukhalov (BUL) 1:51.15	Mikhail Slivinski (EUN) 1:51.40	Olaf Heukrodt (GER) 1:53.00

1896–1972 Event not held.

1000 Metres Canadian Singles (C1)

1936	Francis Amyot (CAN) 5:32.1	Bohuslav Karlik (TCH) 5:36.9	Erich Koschik (GER) 5:39.0
1948	Josef Holocek (TCH) 5:42.0	Douglas Bennet (CAN) 5:53.3	Robert Boutigny (FRA) 5:55.9
1952	Josef Holecek (TCH) 4:56.3	János Parti (Hun) 5:03.6	Olavi Ojanpera (FIN) 5:08.5
1956	Leon Rotman (ROM) 5:05.3	István Hernek (HUN) 5:06.2	Gennadiy Bukharin (URS) 5:12.7
1960	János Parti (HUN) 4:33.93	Alexsandr Silayev (URS) 4:34.41	Leon Rotman (ROM) 4:35.87
1964	Jürgen Eschert (GER) 4:35.14	Andrei Igorov (ROM) 4:37.89	Yevgeny Penyayev (URS) 4:38.31
1968	Tibor Tatai (HUN) 4:36.14	Detlef Lewe (FRG) 4:38.31	Vitaly Galkov (URS) 4:40.42
1972	Ivan Patzaichin (ROM) 4:08.94	Tamas Wichmann (HUN) 4:12.42	Detlef Lewe (FRG) 4:13.36
1976	Matija Ljubek (YUG) 4:09.51	Vasiliy Urchenko (URS) 4:12.57	Tamas Wichmann (HUN) 4:14.11
1980	Lubomir Lubenov (BUL) 4:12.38	Sergey Postrekhin (URS) 4:13.53	Eckhard Leue (GDR) 4:15.02
1984	Ulrich Eicke (FRG) 4:06.32	Larry Cain (CAN) 4:08.67	Henning Jakobsen (DEN) 4:09.51
1988	Ivan Klementyev (URS) 4:12.78	Jörg Schmidt (GDR) 4:15.83	Nikolay Boukhalov (BUL) 4:18.94
1992	Nikolai Boukhalov (BUL) 4:05.92	Ivans Klementjevs (LAT) 4:06.60	Gyorgy Zala (HUN) 4:07.35

1896–1932 Event not held.

10,000 Metres Canadian Singles (C1)

1948	Frantisek Capek (TCH) 62:05.2	Frank Havens (USA) 62:40.4	Norman Lane (CAN) 64:35.3
1952	Frank Havens (USA) 57:41.1	Gabor Novak (HUN) 57:49.2	Alfred Jindra (TCH) 57:53.1
1956	Leon Rotman (ROM) 56:41.0	János Parti (HUN) 57:11.0	Gennadiy Bukharin (URS) 57:14.5

1896–1936, 1960–1992 Event not held.

500 Metres Canadian Pairs (C2)

1976	Soviet Union 1:45.81	Poland 1:47.77	Hungary 1:48.35
1980	Hungary 1:43.39	Romania 1:44.12	Bulgaria 1:44.83
1984	Yugoslavia 1:43.67	Romania 1:45.68	Spain 1:47.71
1988	Soviet Union 1:41.77	Poland 1:43.61	France 1:43.81
1992	Unified Team 1:41.54	Germany 1:41.68	Bulgaria 1:41.94

1000 Metres Canadian Pairs (C2)

1936	Czechoslovakia 4:50.1	Austria 4:53.8	Canada 4:56.7

1948	Czechoslovakia 5:07.1	United States 5:08.2	France 5:15.2
1952	Denmark 4:38.3	Czechoslovakia 4:42.9	Germany 4:48.3
1956	Romania 4:47.4	Soviet Union 4:48.6	Hungary 4:54.3
1960	Soviet Union 4:17.94	Italy 4:20.77	Hungary 4:20.89
1964	Soviet Union 4:04.64	France 4:06.52	Denmark 4:07.48
1968	Romania 4:07.18	Hungary 4:08.77	Soviet Union 4:11.30
1972	Soviet Union 3:52.60	Romania 3:52.63	Bulgaria 3:58.10
1976	Soviet Union 3:52.76	Romania 3:54.28	Hungary 3:55.66
1980	Romania 3:47.65	GDR 3:49.93	Soviet Union 3:51.28
1984	Romania 3:40.60	Yugoslavia 3:41.56	France 3:48.01
1988	Soviet Union 3:48.36	GDR 3:51.44	Poland 3:54.33
1992	Germany 3:37.42	Denmark 3:39.26	France 3:39.51

1896–1932 Event not held.

10,000 Metres Canadian Pairs (C2)

1936	Czechoslovakia 50:33.5	Canada 51:15.8	Austria 51:28.0
1948	United States 55:55.4	Czechoslovakia 57:38.5	France 58:00.8
1952	France 54:08.3	Canada 54:09.9	Germany 54:28.1
1956	Soviet Union 54:02.4	France 54:48.3	Hungary 55:15.6

1896–1932, 1960–1992 Event not held

4 x 500 Metres Kayak Singles (K1) Relay

| 1960 | Germany 7:39.43 | Hungary 7:44.02 | Denmark 7:46.09 |

1896–1956, 1964–1992 Event not held

10,000 Metres Folding Kayak Singles (K1)

| 1936 | Gregor Hradetzky (AUT) 50:01.2 | Henri Eberhardt (FRA) 50:04.2 | Xaver Hörmann (GER) 50:06.5 |

1896–1932, 1948–1992 Event not held

10,000 Metres Folding Kayak Pairs (K2)

| 1936 | Sweden 45:48.9 | Germany 45:49.2 | Netherlands 46:12.4 |

1896–1932, 1948–1992 Event not held

SLALOM RACING – MEN

Not held 1896-1968, 1976-88

Kayak Singles (K1)

| 1972 | Siegbert Horn (GDR) 268.56pts | Norbert Sattler (AUT) 270.76pts | Harald Gimpel (GDR) 277.95pts |
| 1992 | Pierpaolo Ferrazzi (ITA) 106.89pts | Sylvain Curinier (FRA) 107.06pts | Jochen Lettmann (GER) 108.52pts |

Canadian Singles (C1)

| 1972 | Reinhard Eiben (GDR) 315.84pts | Reinhold Kauder (FRG) 327.89pts | Jamie McEwan (USA) 335.95pts |
| 1992 | Lukas Pollert (TCH) 113.69pts | Gareth Marriott (GBR) 116.48pts | Jacky Avril (FRA) 117.18pts |

Canadian Pairs (C2)

| 1972 | GDR 310.68 | FRG 311.90 | France 315.10 |
| 1992 | USA 122.41pts | Czechoslovakia 124.25pts | France 124.38pts |

CANOEING MEDAL RESULTS – WOMEN

	GOLD	SILVER	BRONZE
500 Metres Kayak Singles (K1)			
1948	Karen Hoff (DEN) 2:31.9	Alide Van de Anker-Doedans (NED) 3:32.8	Fritzi Schwingl (AUT) 2:32.9
1952	Sylvi Saimo (FIN) 2:18.4	Gertrude Liebhart (AUT) 2:18.8	Nina Savina (URS) 2:21.6
1956	Yelisaveta Dementyeva (URS) 2:18.9	Therese Zenz (GER) 2:19.6	Tove Söby (DEN) 2:22.3

1960	Antonina Seredina (URS) 2:08.08	Therese Zenz (GER) 2:08.22	Daniel Walkowiak (POL) 2:10.46
1964	Ludmila Khvedosyuk (URS) 2:12.87	Hilde Lauer (ROM) 2:15.35	Marcia Jones (USA) 2:15.68
1968	Ludmila Pinayeva (URS) 2:11.09	Renate Breuer (FRG) 2:12.71	Viorica Dumitru (ROM) 2:13.22
1972	Yulia Ryabchinskaya (URS) 2:03.17	Mieke Jaapies (NED) 2:04.03	Anna Pfeffer (HUN) 2:05.50
1976	Carola Zirzow (GDR) 2:01.05	Tatyana Korshunova (URS) 2:03.07	Klara Rajnai (HUN) 2:05.01
1980	Birgit Fischer (GDR) 1:57.96	Vanya Gheva (BUL) 1:59.48	Antonina Melnikova (URS) 1:59.66
1984	Agneta Andersson (SWE) 1:58.72	Barbara Schuttpelz (FRG)	Annemiek Derckx (NED) 2:00.11
1988	Vania Guecheva (BUL) 1:55.19	Birgit Schmidt (GDR) 1:55.31	Izabella Dylewska (POL) 1:57.38
1992	Birgit Schmidt (GER) 1:51.60	Rita Koban (HUN) 1:51.96	Izabella Dylewska (POL) 1:52.36

500 Metres Kayak Pairs (K2)

1960	Soviet Union 1:54.76	Germany 1:56.66	Hungary 1:58.22
1964	Germany 1:56.95	United States 1:59.16	Romania 2:00.25
1968	FRG 1:56.44	Hungary 1:58.60	Soviet Union 1:58.61
1972	Soviet Union 1:53.50	GDR 1:54.30	Romania 1:55.01
1976	Soviet Union 1:51.15	Hungary 1:51.69	GDR 1:51.81
1980	GDR 1:43.88	Soviet Union 1:46.91	Hungary 1:47.95
1984	Sweden 1:45.25	Canada 1:47.13	FRG 1:47.32
1988	GDR 1:43.46	Bulgaria 1:44.06	Netherlands 1:46.00
1992	Germany 1:40.29	Sweden 1:40.41	Hungary 1:40.81

1896–1956 Event not held

500 Metres Kayak Fours (K4)

1984	Romania 1:38.34	Sweden 1:38.87	Canada 1:39.40
1988	GDR 1:40.78	Hungary 1:41.88	Bulgaria 1:42.63
1992	Hungary 1:38.32	Germany 1:38.47	Sweden 1:39.79

1896–1980 Event not held

SLALOM RACING – WOMEN

Not held 1896-1968, 1976-88

Kayak Singles (K1)

1972	Angelika Bahmann (GDR) 364.50pts	Gisela Grothaus (FRG) 398.15pts	Magdalena Wunderlich (FRG) 400.50
1992	Elisabeth Micheler (GER) 126.41pts	Danielle Woodward (AUS) 128.27pts	Dana Chladek (USA) 131.75pts

Cycling

The first Olympic cycling champion was Léon Flameng (FRA), winner in 1896 of the 100km race, which was held on a 333.33m cement track and involved 300 circuits. Four men have won three gold medals: Paul Masson (FRA) in 1896, Francisco Verri (ITA) in 1906, Robert Charpentier (FRA) in 1936, and Daniel Morelon (FRA) in 1968 (two) and 1972. Of these only Morelon won a bronze as well. He also won a record seven world amateur titles. Although initially the 1904 cycling events were not considered official, recent thinking has 're-instated' them. Thus it should be noted that Marcus Hurley (USA) won a record four titles, plus a bronze medal, at that Games. His team-mate Burton Downing also set a 'record' at St Louis with six medals, comprising two golds, three silvers and a bronze. The only woman to win two gold medals is Erika Salumäe, who won the 1988 sprint representing the Soviet Union and the 1992 title for Estonia.

The first pair of brothers to win a medal were the Götze duo, Bruno and Max, of Germany with a tandem silver in 1906. The greatest family peformance in Olympic cycling was by the Pettersson brothers of Sweden: Gösta, Sture, Erik and Tomas. The first three, with Sten Hamrin, won a bronze in the 1964 team road race, and then in 1968, with their younger brother, won the silver.

One of the first modern cases of sporting drug-abuse occurred in the 1960 100km race when two Danish cyclists collapsed, and one, Knut Jensen, died from what was originally thought to be sunstroke. It transpired that they had both taken overdoses of a blood-circulation stimulant. Two other extremes of sportsmanship have been highlighted in Games cycling. In 1936 Charpentier beat his team-mate Guy Lapébie by 0.2 sec at the end of the 100km, the latter inexplicably slowing down just before the line. A photograph showed that Charpentier had pulled his rival back by

Olympic cycling records

Men

1000m Time-Trial

| 1m 02. 955s | Lothar Thoms (GDR) | 1980 |

4000m Individual Pursuit

| 4m 24.496s | Chris Boardman (GBR) | 1992 |

4000m Team Pursuit

| 4m 08.791s | Germany | 1992 |

Women

3000m Individual Pursuit

| 3m 41.753s | Petra Rossner (GER) | 1992 |

his shirt. More credit-worthy was another Frenchman, Flameng, who, when far ahead of his only opposition, a Greek, in 1896, stopped when the man's cycle broke down. After waiting for it to be replaced, Flameng still won by six laps. After the 1984 Games it was admitted that many of the US cycling team had indulged in 'blood-boosting' procedures – which were not illegal at the time. Those Games also witnessed numerous 'space-age' innovations, especially in the composition and construction of wheels.

Of the many excellent facilities that have been built for Olympic cycling programmes, one of the most remarkable sites was the magnificent Hachioji velodrome in Tokyo 1964. Built at a cost of $840,000, it was used for only four days during the Games, and within a year was demolished. Track cycling was held indoors for the first time in 1976.

The greatest speed ever achieved in Olympic cycling was in the altitude of Mexico City in 1968 when Daniel Morelon and Pierre Trentin (FRA) clocked 9.83 sec for the last 200m in the tandem race, an average of 73.24km/h. The greatest speed by an individual rider was 70.23km/h by Jens Fiedler (GER) in the elimination rounds at Barcelona in 1992 when he clocked 10.252 sec for the last 200m in the 1000m sprint. The fastest by a female rider was 63.05km/h

by Ingrid Haringa (NED), also in 1992, when she clocked 11.419 sec. The longest race ever held in the Games, at any sport, was the 1912 cycling road race over a distance of 320km.

Few future top professionals competed at the Games successfully as amateurs. Two of the three co-record holders in the Tour de France (five wins each), Eddy Merckx (BEL) and Jacques Anquetil (FRA), both finished twelfth in the Olympic race, in 1964 and 1952 respectively. However, the latter won a bronze in the team race. The only Olympic gold medallist to also win the Tour de France was Joop Zoetemelk (NED), a member of the winning quartet in the 1968 team time-trial. British rider Chris Boardman, riding a high-tech carbon-fibre machine with a revolutionary frame design, won the 1992 4km pursuit final by uniquely catching his opponent with a lap to go.

The youngest gold medallist was Dmitri Nelyubin (URS) in the 1988 team pursuit aged 17yr 229 days, while the oldest was Maurice Peeters (NED) aged 38yr 99 days in the 1920 1000m sprint. Winning a bronze four years later in the tandem, Peeters, at 42yr 83 days, was the oldest ever medallist as well. The oldest female champion was Erika Salumäe (EST) in 1992 aged 30yr 50 days, while the youngest gold medallist was Monique Knol (NED) in 1988 at 24yr 179 days. The oldest woman to win a medal was Jeannie Longo (FRA) in 1992 aged 33yr 269 days, while the youngest was Sandra Schumacher (FRG) in 1984 at 17yr 217 days. In 1984, the first race for women, a road race, was won by Connie Carpenter-Phinney (USA), whose husband Davis won a bronze in the 100km team event. She had competed in the 1972 Winter Games as a 14-year-old speed skater.

A number of changes have been made to the cycling programme for 1996, including the addition of a women's points race, and individual time trials for men and women. The men's team time trial has been deleted. Being held for the first time are mountain bike events for men and women.

CYCLING MEDALS TABLE

	Men			Women			
	G	S	B	G	S	B	Total
France	27	15	21	-	1	-	64
Italy	28	15	6	-	-	-	49
Great Britain	9	21	14	-	-	-	44
United States [1]	10	9	13	1	1	2	36
Netherlands	8	13	4	1	-	2	28
Soviet Union	10	4	8	1	-	1	24
Germany	6	8	8	1	1	-	24
Belgium	6	6	10	-	-	-	22
Australia	5	9	4	1	-	1	20
Denmark	6	6	8	-	-	-	20
GDR	6	5	4	-	1	-	16
FRG	4	4	4	-	1	1	14
Sweden	3	2	8	-	-	-	13
South Africa	1	4	3	-	-	-	8
Poland	-	5	3	-	-	-	8

Czechoslovakia	2	2	2	-	-	-	6
Switzerland	1	3	2	-	-	-	6
Greece	1	3	1	-	-	-	5
Canada	-	2	2	-	-	-	4
Austria	1	-	2	-	-	-	3
Norway	1	-	1	-	-	-	2
Estonia	-	-	-	1	-	-	1
Spain	1	-	-	-	-	-	1
Jamaica	-	-	1	-	-	-	1
Japan	-	-	1	-	-	-	1
Latvia	-	-	1	-	-	-	1
Mexico	-	-	1	-	-	-	1
New Zealand	-	-	1	-	-	-	1
	136	136	133 [2]	6	6	6	423

[1] *Includes 7 events in 1904 formerly excluded*
[2] *No bronzes in 1896 100km, 1972 road team trial and individual road race*

CYCLING MEDAL RESULTS — MEN

GOLD	SILVER	BRONZE

1000 Metres Time-Trial

1896 [1]	Paul Masson (FRA) 24.0	Stamatios Nikolopoulos (GRE) 25.4	Adolf Schmal (AUT) 26.6
1906 [1]	Francesco Verri (ITA) 22.8	Herbert Crowther (GBR) 22.8	Menjou (FRA) 23.2
1928	Willy Falck-Hansen (DEN) 1:14.4	Gerard Bosch van Drakestein (NED) 1:15.2	Edgar Gray (AUS) 1:15.6
1932	Edgar Gray (AUS) 1:13.0	Jacobus van Egmond (NED) 1:13.3	Charles Rampelberg (FRA) 1:13.4
1936	Arie van Vliet (NED) 1:12.0	Pierre Georget (FRA)1:12.8	Rudolf Karsch (GER) 1:13.2
1948	Jacques Dupont (FRA) 1:13.5	Pierre Nihant (BEL) 1:14.5	Thomas Godwin (GBR) 1:15.0
1952	Russell Mockridge (AUS) 1:11.1	Marino Morettini (ITA) 1:12.7	Raymond Robinson (RSA) 1:13.0
1956	Leandro Faggin (ITA) 1:09.8	Ladislav Foucek (TCH) 1:11.4	J Alfred Swift (RSA) 1:11.6
1960	Sante Gaiardoni (ITA) 1:07.27	Dieter Gieseler (GER) 1:08.75	Rotislav Vargashkin (URS) 1:08.86
1964	Patrick Sercu (BEL) 1:09.59	Giovanni Pettenella (ITA) 1:10.09	Pierre Trentin (FRA) 1:10.42
1968	Pierre Trentin (FRA) 1:03.91	Niels-Christian Fredborg (DEN) 1:04.61	Janusz Kierzkowski (POL) 1:04.63
1972	Niels-Christian Fredborg (DEN) 1:06.44	Daniel Clark (AUS) 1:06.87	Jürgen Schuetze (GDR) 1:07.02
1976	Klaus-Jürgen Grunke (GDR) 1:05.93	Michel Vaarten (BEL) 1:07.52	Niels-Christian Fredborg (DEN) 1:07.62
1980	Lothar Thoms (GDR) 1:02.955*	Aleksandr Pantilov (URS) 1:04.845	David Weller (JAM) 1:05.241
1984	Fredy Schmidtke (FRG) 1:06.10	Curtis Harnett (CAN) 1:06.44	Fabrice Colas (FRA) 1:06.65
1988	Alexandr Kiritchenko (URS) 1:04.499	Martin Vinnicombe (AUS) 1:04.784	Robert Lechner (FRG) 1:05.114
1992	Jose Manuel Moreno (ESP) 1:03.342	Shane Kelly (AUS) 1:04.288	Erin Hartwell (USA) 1:04.753

[1] *Held over 333.33 metres.*
Olympic record.
1908–1924 Event not held.

1000 Metres Sprint

1896 [1]	Paul Masson (FRA) 4:56.0	Stamatios Nikolopoulos (GRE)	Léon Flemeng (FRA)
1900 [1]	Georges Taillandier (FRA) 2:52.0	Fernand Sanz (FRA)	John Lake (USA)
1906	Francesco Verri (ITA) 1:42.2	HC Bouffler (GBR)	Eugène Debougnie (BEL)
1920	Maurice Peeters (NED) 1:38.3	H Thomas Johnson (GBR)	Harry Ryan (GBR)
1924 [2]	Lucien Michard (FRA) 12.8	Jacob Meijer (NED)	Jean Cugnot (FRA)
1928	René Beaufrand (FRA) 13.2	Antoine Mazairac (NED)	Willy Falck-Hansen (DEN)
1932	Jacobus van Egmond (NED) 12.6	Louis Chaillot (FRA)	Bruno Pellizzari (ITA)
1936	Toni Merkens (GER) 11.8	Arie van Vliet (NED)	Louis Chaillot (FRA)
1948	Mario Ghella (ITA) 12.0	Reginald Harris (GBR)	Axel Schandorff (DEN)
1952	Enzo Sacchi (ITA) 12.0	Lionel Cox (AUS)	Werner Potzernheim (GER)
1956	Michel Rousseau (FRA) 11.4	Guglielmo Pesenti (ITA)	Richard Ploog (AUS)

1960	Sante Gaiardoni (ITA) 11.1	Leo Sterckz (BEL)	Valentina Gasparella (ITA)
1964	Giovanni Pettenella (ITA) 13.69	Sergio Bianchetto (ITA)	Daniel Morelon (FRA)
1968	Daniel Morelon (FRA) 10.68	Giordano Turrini (ITA)	Pierre Trentin (FRA)
1972	Daniel Morelon (FRA) 11.25	John Nicholson (AUS)	Omarc Pchakadze (URS)
1976	Anton Tkac (TCH) 10.78	Daniel Morelon (FRA)	Hans-Jurgen Geschke (GDR)
1980	Lutz Hesslich (GDR) 11.40	Yave Cahard (FRA)	Sergey Kopylov (URS)
1984	Mark Gorski (USA) 10.49	Nelson Vails (USA)	Tsutomu Sakamoto (JPN)
1988	Lutz Hesslich (GDR)	Nikolay Kovche (URS)	Gary Neiwand (AUS)
1992	Jens Fiedler (GER)	Gary Neiwand (AUS)	Curtis Harnett (CAN)

1904, 1908[3]*–1912 Event not held.*

[1] *Held over 2000 metres. In 1900 Taillandier's last 200 was 13.0 sec.*

[2] *Since 1924 only times over the last 200 metres of the event have been recorded.*

[3] *There was a 1000 metres sprint event in the 1908 Games, but it was declared void because the riders exceeded the time limit, in spite of repeated warnings.*

4000 Metres Individual Pursuit

Note: Bronze medal times are set in a third place race, so can be faster than those set in the race for first and second place.

1964	Jiri Daler (TCH) 5:04.75	Giorgio Ursi (ITA) 5:05.96	Preben Isaksson (DEN) 5:01.90
1968	Daniel Rebillard (FRA) 4:41.71	Mogens Frey Jensen (DEN) 4:42.43	Xaver Kurmann (SUI) 4:39.42
1972	Knut Knudsen (NOR) 4:45.74	Xaver Kurmann (SUI) 4:51.96	Hans Lutz (FRG) 4:50.80
1976	Gregor Braun (FRG) 4:47.61	Herman Ponsteen (NED) 4:49.72	Thomas Huschke (GDR) 4:52.71
1980	Robert Dill-Bundi (SUI) 4:35.66*	Alain Bondue (FRA) 4:42.96	Hans-Henrik Orsted (DEN) 4:36.54
1984	Steve Hegg (USA) 4:39.35	Rolf Golz (FRG) 4:43.82	Leonard Nitz (USA) 4:44.03
1988	Gintaoutas Umaras (URS) 4:32.00	Dean Woods (AUS) 4:35.00	Bernd Dittert (GDR) 4:34.17
1992	Chris Boardman (GBR)	Jens Lehmann (GER)	Gary Anderson (NZL)

1896–1960 Event not held.

*Olympic record.

1992 Olympic pursuit champion Chris Boardman on his futuristic bicycle (Popperfoto)

4000 Metres Team Pursuit

Note: Bronze medal times are set in a third place race, so can be faster than those set in the race for first and second place.

1908 [1]	Great Britain 2:18.6	Germany 2:28.6	Canada 2:29.6
1920	Italy 5:20.0 [2]	Great Britain n.t.a.	South Africa n.t.a.
1924	Italy 5:15.0	Poland n.t.a.	Belgium n.t.a.
1928	Italy 5:01.8	Netherlands 5:06.2	Great Britain n.t.a.
1932	Italy 4:53.0	France 4:55.7	Great Britain 4:56.0
1936	France 4:45.0	Italy 4:51.0	Great Britain 4:52.6
1948	France 4:57.8	Italy 5:36.7	Great Britain 4:55.8
1952	Italy 4:46.1	South Africa 4:53.6	Great Britain 4:51.5
1956	Italy 4:37.4	France 4:39.4	Great Britain 4:42.2
1960	Italy 4:30.90	Germany 4:35.78	Soviet Union 4:34.05
1964	Germany 4:35.67	Italy 4:35.74	Netherlands 4:38.99
1968	Denmark 4:22.44 [3]	FRG 4:18.94	Italy 4:18.35
1972	FRG 4:22.14	GDR 4:25.25	Great Britain 4:23.78
1976	FRG 4:21.06	Soviet Union 4:27.15	Great Britain 4:22.41
1980	Soviet Union 4:15.70	GDR 4:19.67	Czechoslovakia [4]
1984	Australia 4:25.99	United States 4:29.85	FRG 4:25.60
1988	Soviet Union 4:13.31	GDR 4:14.09	Australia 4:16.02
1992	Germany 4:08.791	Australia 4:10.218	Denmark 4:15.860

1896–1906, 1912 Event not held.

[1] *Held over 1810.5 metres.*

[2] *Great Britain finished first but were relegated to second for alleged interference.*

[3] *Federal Republic of Germany finished first but were disqualified for illegal assistance. After the Games ended the International Cycling Federation awarded them the silver medal.*

[4] *Italy disqualified in third place race.*

2000 Metres Tandem

1906	Great Britain 2:57.0	Germany 2:57.2	Germany n.t.a.
1908	France 3:07.8	Great Britain n.t.a.	Great Britain n.t.a.
1920	Great Britain 2:94.4	South Africa n.t.a.	Netherlands n.t.a.
1924 [1]	France 12.6	Denmark	Netherlands
1928	Netherlands 11.8	Great Britain	Germany
1932	France 12.0	Great Britain	Denmark
1936	Germany 11.8	Netherlands	France
1948	Italy 11.3	Great Britain	France
1952	Australia 11.0	South Africa	Italy
1956	Australia 10.8	Czechoslovakia	Italy
1960	Italy 10.7	Germany	Soviet Union
1964	Italy 10.75	Soviet Union	Germany
1968	France 9.83	Netherlands	Belgium
1972	Soviet Union 10.52	GDR	Poland

1896–1904, 1912, 1976–1992 Event not held.

[1] *Since 1924 only times over last 200m have been recorded.*

Individual Points Race

1984	Roger Ilegems (BEL)	Uwe Messerschmidt (FRG)	Jose Youshimatz (MEX)
1988	Dan Frost (DEN)	Leo Peelen (NED)	Marat Ganeyev (URS)
1992	Giovanni Lombardi (ITA) 44pts	Leon van Bon (NED) 43pts	Cedric Mathy (BEL) 41pts

1896–1980 Event not held.

Team Road Race

(Consisting of the combined times of the best three – four 1912–20 – riders from each country in the individual race. In 1956 based on placings.)

1912	Sweden 44h 35:33.6	Great Britain 44h 44:39.2	United States 44h 47:55.5
1920	France 19h 16:43.2	Sweden 19h 23:10.0	Belgium 19h 28:44.4

1924 France 19h 30:14.0	Belgium 19h 46:55.4	Sweden 19h 59:41.6
1928 Denmark 15h 09:14.0	Great Britain 15h 14:49.0	Sweden 15h 27:49.0
1932 Italy 7h 27:15.2	Denmark 7h 38:50.2	Sweden 7h 39:12.6
1936 France 7h 39:16.2	Switzerland 7h 39:20.4	Belgium 7h 39:21.0
1948 Belgium 15h 58:17.4	Great Britain 16h 03:31.6	France 16h 08:19.4
1952 Belgium 15h 20:46.6	Italy 15h 33:27.3	France 15h 38:58.1
1956 France 22 points	Great Britain 23 points	Germany 27 points

Road Team Time-Trial
Over 100km except in 1964 (108.89km), 1968 (102km), 1980 (101km)

1960 Italy 2h 14:33.53	Germany 2h 16:56.31	Soviet Union 2h 18:41.67
1964 Netherlands 2h 26:31.19	Italy 2h 26:55.39	Sweden 2h 27:11.52
1968 Netherlands 2h 07:49.06	Sweden 2h 09:26.60	Italy 2h 10:18.74
1972 Soviet Union 2h 11:17.8	Poland 2h 11:47.5	*
1976 Soviet Union 2h 08:53.0	Poland 2h 09:13.0	Denmark 2h 12:20.0
1980 Soviet Union 2h 01:21.7	GDR 2h 02:53.2	Czechoslovakia 2h 02:53.9
1984 Italy 1h 58:28.0	Switzerland 2h 02:38.0	United States 2h 02:46.0
1988 GDR 1h 57:47.7	Poland 1h 57:54.2	Sweden 1h 59:47.3
1992 Germany 2h 01:39	Italy 2h 02:39	France 2h 05:25

1896–1908 Event not held.
*Netherlands finished in third place but their bronze medal was withdrawn following a drug test.

Individual Road Race

1896 Aristidis Konstantinidis (GRE) 3h 22:31.0	August Goedrich (GER) 3h 42:18.0	F Battel (GBR) d.n.a.
1906 Fernand Vast (FRA) 2h 41:28.0	Maurice Bardonneau (FRA) 2h 41:28.4	Edmund Lugnet (FRA) 2h 41:28.6
1912 Rudolph Lewis (RSA) 10h 42:39.0	Frederick Grubb (GBR) 10h 51:24.2	Carl Schutte (USA) 10h 52:38.8
1920 Harry Stenqvist (SWE) 4h 40:01.8	Henry Kaltenbrun (RSA) 4h 41:26.6	Fernand Canteloube (FRA) 4h 42.54.4
1924 Armand Blanchonnet (FRA) 6h 20:48.0	Henry Hoevenaers (BEL) 6h 30:27.0	René Hamel (FRA) 6h 40:51.6
1928 Henry Hansen (DEN) 4h 47:18.0	Frank Southall (GBR) 4h 55:06.0	Gösta Carlsson (SWE) 5h 00:17.0
1932 Attilio Pavesi (ITA) 2h 28:05.6	Guglielmo Segato (ITA) 2h 29:21.4	Bernhard Britz (SWE) 2h 29:45.2
1936 Robert Charpentier (FRA) 2h 33:05.0	Guy Lapebie (FRA) 2h 33:05.2	Ernst Nievergeit (SUI) 2h 33:05.8
1948 Jose Bevaert (FRA) 5h 18:12.6	Gerardus Voorting (NED) 5h 18:16.2	Lode Wouters (BEL) 5h 18:16.2
1952 Andre Nouvelle (BEL) 5h 06:03.4	Robert Grondelaers (BEL) 5h 06:51.2	Edi Ziegler (GER) 5h 07:47.5
1956 Ercole Baldini (ITA) 5h 21:17.0	Arnaud Gevre (FRA) 5h 23:16.0	Alan Jackson (GBR) 5h 23:16.0
1960 Viktor Kapitonov (URS) 4h 20:37.0	Livio Trape (ITA) 4h 20:37.0	Willy van den Berghen (BEL) 4h 20:57.0
1964 Mario Zanin (ITA) 4h 39:51.63	Kjell Rodian (DEN) 4h 39:51.65	Walter Godefroot (BEL) 4h 39:51.74
1968 Pierfranco Vianelli (ITA) 4h 41:25.24	Leif Mortensen (DEN) 4h 42:49.71	Gösta Pettersson (SWE) 4h 43:15.24
1972 Hennie Kuiper (NED) 4h 14:37.0	Kevin Sefton (AUS) 4h 15:04.0	*
1976 Bernt Johansson (SWE) 4h 46:52.0	Giuseppe Martinelli (ITA) 4h 47:23.0	Mieczyslaw Nowicki (POL) 4h 47:23.0
1980 Sergey Sukhoruchenkov (URS) 4h 48:28.9	Czeslaw Lang (POL) 4h 51:26.9	Yuriy Barinov (URS) 4h 51:26.9
1984 Alexi Grewal (USA) 4h 59:57.0	Steve Bauer (CAN) 4h 59:57.0	Dag Otto Lauritzen (NOR) 5h 00:18.0
1988 Olaf Ludwig (GDR) 4h 32:22.0	Bernd Gröne (FRG) 4h 32:25.0	Christian Henn (FRG) 4h 32:46.0
1992 Fabio Casartelli (ITA) 4h35:21	Hendrik Dekker (NED) 4h35:22	Dainis Ozols (LAT) 4h35:24

1900–1904, 1908 Event not held.
This event has been held over the following distances: 1896 – 87km; 1906 – 84km; 1912 – 320 km; 1920 – 175km; 1924 – 188km; 1928 – 168km; 1932 and 1936 – 100km; 1948 – 194.63km; 1952 – 190.4km; 1956 – 187.73km; 1960 – 175.38km; 1968 – 196.2km; 1972 – 182.4km; 1976 – 175km; 1980 – 189km; 1984 – 190km; 1988 – 196.8km; 1992 – 194km.
*Jaime Huelamo (ESP) finished third but medal withdrawn following a drug test.

DISCONTINUED EVENTS — MEN

GOLD	SILVER	BRONZE
440 yards Track (402.34m)		
1904 Marcus Hurley (USA) 31.8	Burton Downing (USA)	Edward Billingham (USA)

0.33 mile Track (536.45m)
1904   Marcus Hurley (USA) 43.8 — Burton Downing (USA) — Edward Billingham (USA)

660 yards Track (603.5m)
1908   Victor Johnson (GBR) 51.2 — Emile Demangel (FRA) close — Karl Neumer (GER) 1 length

880 yards Track (804.67m)
1904   Marcus Hurley (USA) 1:09.0 — Edward Billingham (USA) — Burton Downing (USA)

1 mile Track (1609.34m)
1904   Marcus Hurley (USA) 2:41.4 — Burton Downing (USA) — Edward Billingham (USA)

2 miles Track (3218.6m)
1904   Burton Downing (USA) 4:57.8 — Oscar Goerke (USA) — Marcus Hurley (USA)

5000m Track
1906   Francesco Verri (ITA) 8:35.0 — Herbert Crowther (GBR) — Fernand Vast (FRA)
1908   Benjamin Jones (GBR) 8:36.2 — Maurice Schilles (FRA) — Andre Auffray (FRA)

5 miles Track (8046.57m)
1904   Charles Schlee (USA) 13:08.2 — George Wiley (USA) — A Andrews (USA)

10,000m Track
1896   Paul Masson (FRA) 17:54.2 — Leon Flameng (FRA) — Adolf Schmal (AUT)

20,000m Track
1906   William Pett (GBR) 29:00.0 — Maurice Bardonneau (FRA) 29:30.0 — Fernand Vast (FRA) 29:32.0
1908   Charles Kingsbury (GBR) 34:13.6 — Benjamin Jones (GBR) — Joseph Werbrouck (BEL)

25 miles Track (40.225m)
1904   Burton Downing (USA) 1h 10:55.4 — A Andrews (USA) — George Wiley (USA)

50,000m Track
1920   Henry George (BEL) 1h 16:43.2 — Cyril Alden (GBR)* — Petrus Ikelaar (NED)
1924   Jacobus Willems (NED) 1:18:24 — Cyril Alden (GBR) — Frederick Wyld (GBR)
Most eyewitnesses considered that Ikelaar finished second.

100km Track
1896   Leon Flameng (FRA) 3h 08:19.2 — G. Kolettis (GRE) 6 laps — –*
1908   Charles Bartlett (GBR) 2h 41:48.6 — Charles Denny (GBR) — Octave Lapize (FRA)
Only two riders finished

12 hours Track
1896   Adolf Schmal (AUT) 314.997km — Frank Keeping (GBR) 314.664km — Georgios Paraskevopoulos (GRE) 313.330km

CYCLING MEDAL RESULTS — WOMEN

	GOLD	SILVER	BRONZE

Sprint
1988   Erika Saloumae (URS) — Christa Rothenburger-Luding (GDR) — Connie Young (USA)
1992   Erika Salumae (EST) — Annett Neumann (GER) — Ingrid Haringa (NED)
1896–1984 Event not held

3000m Individual Pursuit
1992   Petra Rossner (GER) — Kathryn Watt (AUS) — Rebecca Twigg (USA)
1896-1988 Event not held

Individual Road Race
1984   Connie Carpenter-Phinney (USA) 2h 11:14.0 — Rebecca Twigg (USA) 2h 11:14.0 — Sandra Schumacher (FRG) 2h 11:14.0
1988   Monique Knol (NED) 2h 00.52 — Jutta Niehaus (FRG) close — Laima Zilporiteye (URS) close
1992   Kathryn Watt (AUS) 2h 04:42 — Jeannie Longo-Ciprelli (FRA) 2h 05:02 — Monique Knol (NED) 2h 05:03
1896–1980 Event not held.
Event held over 79.2km in 1984; 82km in 1988; 81km in 1992.

Equestrianism

In the ancient Games the first known event using horses was a chariot race in 680BC. Horses with riders came into the Games in 648BC. The first equestrian gold medallist of the modern Olympics was Aimé Haegeman (BEL) on *Benton II* in the 1900 show jumping. In 1956 the equestrian events were held separately from the main Games, at Stockholm, due to the strict Australian quarantine laws.

The most gold medals won by a rider is six (one individual and five team events) by Reiner Klimke (FRG), 1964-88. Klimke's total of eight medals, comprising the six golds plus two bronzes, also constitutes a record for equestrianism, as does his feat of winning golds in five separate Games over a 24-year period (the medals won by Gustav-Adolf Boltenstern Jr (SWE) over a similar 24-year period, 1932-56, were not both gold).

The oldest gold medallist was Josef Neckarmann (FRG) in the 1968 dressage team aged 56yr 141 days. The oldest individual event winner was Ernst Linder (SWE) in the 1924 dressage aged 56yr 91 days. The youngest individual champion was Edmund Coffin (USA) in the 1976 three-day event aged 21yr 77 days. However, Mary Tauskey (USA) won a gold medal in the three-day team event in 1976 aged 20yr 235 days.

The d'Inzeo brothers of Italy, Raimondo and Piero, competed in a record eight Games, 1948-1976. Raimondo won a gold, two silver and three bronze medals, while Piero gained two silvers and four bronzes. The female record for participation is six Games by Christilot Hanson-Boylen (CAN), 1964-92. A Bulgarian, Kroum Lekarski, competed in the three-day event for a record period of 36 years between 1924 and 1960, but only competed in four Games. A record competition-span by a woman, 28 years, was set by British-born Anne Jessica Ransehousen (née Newberry, USA) in 1988 and Christilot Hanson-Boylen in 1992. Women first competed in 1952 and Lis Hartel (DEN) won the first female medal with a silver in the dressage, which she repeated in 1956. The most successful woman has been Nicole Uphoff (GER) with four golds, 1988-92. Since 1984 equestrianism has been the only Olympic sport in which men and women compete against each other in individual events.

The only horse to be ridden to medals in three Games was *Absent* in the Soviet dressage team, with a gold and two bronzes under Sergey Filatov in 1960 and 1964, and a silver with Ivan Kalita in 1968.

The most successful father and son have been Hans von Blixen-Finecke senior and junior (SWE), with the former winning a dressage team gold and individual bronze in 1912, and the latter the 3-day event individual and team golds 40 years later. Liselott Linsenhoff (FRG) won 2 dressage golds and a silver, 1968-72, and her daughter Ann-Kathrin won a gold in 1988. A unique equestrian participation record is that held by the family of William Roycroft (AUS), himself the oldest medallist in the sport at

61yr 130 days in 1976. His son Wayne won a bronze in the same team, as he also had in 1968, while two other sons, Clarke (1972) and Barry (1976 & 1988), also competed at a high level. In addition, Wayne's wife Vicki competed in 1984 and 1988, so that a Roycroft was in Australian teams from 1960 to 1988.

In 1936 Germany completed the only six-gold-medal 'clean sweep' in Games equestrian history. In the 1912 and 1920 individual dressage Sweden took the first three places both times, a unique occurrence.

Show Jumping

This was the first equestrian event to be included in the Games, along with high and long jumping contests, in 1900. From 1924 until 1968 teams comprised three members, all counting for the final score. This led to many teams not finishing, as in 1932 when no team medals were awarded at all, and in 1948 when only four of the 14 competing teams finished. Since 1972 teams have consisted of four riders with the best three scoring. The most gold medals won is five by Hans-Günter Winkler (FRG) 1956-72. His total of seven medals, including a silver and bronze, is also a record for the discipline, as is his feat of winning medals in six Games. Only Pierre Jonquères d'Oriola (FRA) has won the individual title twice. The first woman to win a medal was Pat Smythe (GBR) in the 1956 team event, while the first individual medallist was Marion Coakes (GBR) in 1968.

The oldest gold medallist was Winkler in 1972 aged 46yr 49 days, while the oldest individual champion was Jonquères d'Oriola aged 44yr 266 days in 1964. Bill Steinkraus (USA) won medals over a 20-year period from 1952-72, a record matched by Winkler, 1956-76. The youngest gold medallist was Jim Day (CAN) in the 1968 team aged 22yr 117 days.

The lowest score obtained by a winner is no faults by Frantisek Ventura (TCH) on *Eliot* in 1928, Jonquères d'Oriola (FRA) on *Ali Baba* in 1952, Alwin Schockemöhle (FRG) on *Warwick Rex* in 1976, and Ludger Beerbaum (GER) on *Classic Touch* in 1992. The most successful horse was Winkler's *Halla* with three golds in 1956 and 1960.

Dressage

The most successful rider was Reiner Klimke (GER), but Henri St Cyr (SWE), 1952-56, and Nicole Uphoff (GER), 1988-92, won the individual title twice. Remarkably, when Klimke won his last gold it was in the 1988 team event which included Ann-Kathrin Linsenhoff, the daughter of his gold-winning team partner of twenty years before. In all St Cyr won a record four golds, as did Nicole Uphoff. St Cyr's total would have been more but for his team being disqualified in 1948, having finished first, because one of its members, Gehnäll Persson, was not a fully commissioned officer - a requirement at that time. With the rules changed, Persson was in the 1952 and 1956 winning teams. This Swedish team of St Cyr, Persson and Gustav-Adolf

Boltenstern Jr uniquely finished in first place three times in a row, and can claim to be the most successful combination in Olympic history.

The first woman to win a medal was Lis Hartel (see above). Amazingly she was a polio victim who had to be helped on and off her horse. The first female gold medallist was Liselott Linsenhoff (FRG) in 1972. The silver medallist that year, Yelena Petushkova (URS), won gold in the team event and was, for a time, married to Valery Brumel, the 1964 Olympic high jump champion. The oldest gold medallist was Josef Neckarmann (see above), who was also the oldest medallist in 1972 aged 60yr 96 days. The oldest competitor in Olympic equestrian history was General Arthur von Pongracz (AUT) who began his Olympic career in 1924 aged 60 and finished it in 1936, just missing a bronze medal, aged 72 – one of the oldest ever Olympians. The oldest woman ever to compete in the Olympic Games, at any sport, was Lorna Johnstone (GBR) who placed twelfth in the 1972 dressage five days after her 70th birthday. The youngest rider to win a gold medal was Nicole Uphoff (FRG) in the 1988 team event aged 22yr 244 days. The most successful horse has been *Rembrandt*, ridden by Nicole Uphoff (GER) to four golds in 1988 and 1992.

Three-Day Event

Competitions actually last four days as the dressage segment now occupies two days.

Charles Pahud de Mortanges (NED) won the individual title twice, in 1928 and 1932, as did Mark Todd (NZL) in 1984 and 1988. However, the Dutchman also won a record total of four golds and a silver from 1924 to 1932. His Dutch team, including Gerard de Kruyff and Adolph van der Voort van Zijp, uniquely won two team titles with the same team members. The most appearances and the longest span of competition is 7 Games and 28 years by Mickey Plumb (USA) 1964-84. His Games total would have been a record-equalling 8 but for the US boycott of Moscow in 1980. The first female competitor was Helena Dupont (USA), 33rd in 1964, while the first female gold medallists were Mary Gordon-Watson and Bridget Parker (both GBR)

in 1972. The first individual medals won by women were in 1984 by Karen Stives (USA) and Virginia Holgate (GBR).

The oldest gold medallist was Derek Allhusen (GBR) aged 54yr 286 days in 1968, while the youngest was Mary Tauskey (USA) in 1976 aged 20yr 235 days. The oldest medallist was William Roycroft (AUS) with a bronze in 1976 aged 61yr 130 days, in the same team as his son Wayne. The youngest medallist was Charles Hough (USA) aged 18yr 92 days in 1952. The most successful horse was *Marcroix*, ridden by Charles Pahud de Mortanges (NED) to

Mark Todd (NZL) won two golds and a bronze riding Charisma, *here in 1984. In 1992, on another horse,* Welton Greyleg, *he won a team silver medal (Popperfoto)*

three golds and a silver in 1928 and 1932. *Silver Piece*, ridden by Voort van Zijp (NED) in 1924 and 1928, also won three golds.

The 1936 cross-country course was so tough that only four teams out of 14 finished. One of the members of that fourth-placed team, Otomar Bures of Czechoslovakia, had over 18,000 penalty points against him at the finish, due to having taken over 2¼ hours to catch his horse after a fall. Britain's Capt Richard Fanshawe, with a similar problem, gained over 8,000 penalty points, but had the satisfaction of finishing with a team bronze. In 1920 the dressage was excluded, with two cross-country runs, at 20km and 50km, added to the jumping.

EQUESTRIANISM MEDALS TABLE

	G	S	B	Total
Sweden	17	8	14	39
Germany	16	12	11	39
United States	8	15	11	34
France	11	12	9	32
FRG	11	5	9	25
Italy	7	9	7	23
Great Britain	5	7	9	21
Switzerland	4	8	7	19
Soviet Union	6	5	4	15
Netherlands	6	5	1	12
Belgium	4	2	6	12
Australia	4	1	2	7
Mexico	2	1	4	7
Poland	1	3	2	6
New Zealand	2	1	2	5
Denmark	-	4	1	5
Canada	1	1	2	4
Austria	1	1	1	3
Portugal	-	-	3	3
Spain	1	1	-	2
Chile	-	2	-	2
Romania	-	1	1	2
Czechoslovakia	1	-	-	1
Japan	1	-	-	1
Argentina	-	1	-	1
Bulgaria	-	1	-	1
Norway	-	1	-	1
Hungary	-	-	1	1
	109 [1]	107	107 [2]	323

[1] *Two golds in 1900 high jump*

[2] *No bronze in 1932 Three-day team event*

EQUESTRIAN MEDAL RESULTS

GOLD	SILVER	BRONZE
Grand Prix (Jumping)		
1900 Aime Haegeman (BEL) *Benton II*	Georges van de Poele (BEL) *Windsor Squire*	M de Champsvin (FRA) *Terpsichore*
1912 Jean Cariou (FRA) 186pts *Mignon*	Rabod von Kröcher (GER) 186 *Dohna*	Emanuel de Blomaert de Sove (BEL) 185 *Clonmore*
1920 Tommaso Lequio (ITA) 2 faults *Trebecco*	Alessandro Valerio (ITA) 3 *Cento*	Gustaf Lewenhaupt (SWE) 4 *Mon Coeur*
1924 Alphonse Gemuseus (SUI) 6 faults	Tommaso Lequio (ITA) 8.75 *Trebecco*	Adam Krolikiewicz (POL) 10 *Picador*
1928 Frantisek Ventura (TCH) no faults *Eliot*	Pierre Bertrand de Balanda (FRA) 2 *Papillon*	Charles Kuhn (SUI) 4 *Pepita*
1932 Takeichi Nishi (JPN) 8 pts *Uranus*	Harry Chamberlain (USA) 12 *Show Girl*	Clarence von Rosen Jr (SWE) 16 *Empire*
1936 Kurt Hasse (GER) 4 faults *Tora*	Henri Rang (ROM) 4 *Delius*	József von Platthy (HUN) 8 *Sellö*
1948 Humberto Mariles Cortés (MEX) 6.25 faults *Arete*	Rubén Uriza (MEX) 8 *Harvey*	Jean d'Orgeix (FRA) 8 *Sucre de Pomme*
1952 Pierre Jonquères d'Oriola (FRA) no faults *Ali Baba*	Oscar Cristi (CHI) 4 *Bambi*	Fritz Thiedemann (GER) 8 *Meteor*
1956 Hans Günter Winkler (GER) 4 faults *Halla*	Raimondo d'Inzeo (ITA) 8 *Merano*	Piero d'Inzeo (ITA) 11 *Uruguay*
1960 Raimondo d'Inzeo (ITA) 12 faults *Posillipo*	Piero d'Inzeo (ITA) 16 *The Rock*	David Broome (GBR) 23 *Sunslave*
1964 Pierre Jonquères d'Oriola (FRA) 9 faults *Lutteur*	Hermann Schridde (GER) 12.75 *Dozent*	Peter Robeson (GBR) 16 *Firecrest*
1968 William Steinkraus (USA) 4 faults *Snowbound*	Marian Coakes (GBR) 8 *Stroller*	David Broome (GBR) 12 *Mister Softee*
1972 Graziano Mancinelli (ITA) 8 faults *Ambassador*	Ann Moore (GBR) 8 *Psalm*	Neal Shapiro (USA) 8 *Sloopy*
1976 Alwin Schockemöhle (FRG) no faults *Warwick Rex*	Michael Vaillancourt (CAN) 12 *Branch County*	François Mathy (BEL) 12 *Gai Luron*
1980 Jan Kowalczyk (POL) 8 faults *Artemor*	Nikolai Korolkov (URS) 9.50 *Espadron*	Joaquin Perez Heras (MEX) 12 *Alymony*

1984 Joe Fargis (USA) 4 faults *Touch of Class*   Conrad Homfeld (USA) 4 *Abdullah*   Heidi Robbiani (SUI) 8 *Jessica V*
1988 Pierre Durand (FRA) 1.25 faults *Jappeloup*   Greg Best (USA) 4 *Gem Twist*   Karsten Huck (FRG) 4 *Nepomuk 8*
1992 Ludger Beerbaum (GER) 0.00pts *Classic Touch* Piet Raymakers (NED) 0.25 *Ratina Z*   Norman Dello Joio (USA) 4.75 *Irish*
1896, 1904–1908 Event not held.

Grand Prix (Jumping) Team

1912 Sweden 545pts	France 538	Germany 530
1920 Sweden 14 faults	Belgium 16.25	Italy 18.75
1924 Sweden 42.25 pts	Switzerland 50	Portugal 53
1928 Spain 4 faults	Poland 8	Sweden 10
1932 [1]	–	––
1936 Germany 44 faults	Netherlands 51.5	Portugal 56
1948 Mexico 34.25 faults	Spain 56.50	Great Britain 67
1952 Great Britain 40.75 faults	Chile 45.75	United States 52.25
1956 Germany 40 faults	Italy 66	Great Britain 69
1960 Germany 46.50 faults	United States 66	Italy 80.50
1964 Germany 68.50 faults	France 77.75	Italy 88.50
1968 Canada 102.75 faults	France 110.50	FRG 117.25
1972 FRG 32 faults	United States 32.25	Italy 48
1976 France 40 faults	FRG 44	Belgium 63
1980 Soviet Union 16 faults	Poland 32	Mexico 39.25
1984 United States 12 faults	Great Britain 36.75	FRG 39.25
1988 FRG 17.25 faults	United States 20.50	France 27.50
1992 Netherlands 12.00pts	Austria 16.75	France 24.75

1896–1908 Event not held.
[1] *There was a team competition but no nation had three riders complete the course.*

Grand Prix (Dressage)

1912 Carl Bonde (SWE) 15pts *Emperor*	Gustaf-Adolf Boltenstern Sr (SWE)21 *Neptun*	Hans von Blixen-Finecke (SWE) 32 *Maggie*
1920 Janne Lundblad (SWE) 27 237pts *Uno*	Bertil Sandström (SWE) 26 312 *Sabel*	Hans von Rosen (SWE) 15 125 *Running Sister*
1924 Ernst Linder (SWE) 276.4pts *Piccolomini*	Bertil Sandström (SWE) 275.8 *Sabel*	Xavier Lesage (FRA) 265.8 *Plumard*
1928 Carl von Langen (GER) 237.42pts *Draüfgänger*	Charles Marion (FRA) 231.00 *Linon*	Ragnar Olsson (SWE) 229.78 *Günstling*
1932 Xavier Lesage (FRA) 1031.25pts *Taine*	Charles Marion (FRA) 916.25 *Linon*	Hiram Tuttle (USA) 901.50 *Olympic*
1936 Heinz Pollay (GER) 1760pts *Kronos*	Friedrich Gerhard (GER) 1745.4 *Absinth*	Alois Podhajsky (AUT) 1721.5 *Nero*
1948 Hans Moser (SUI) 492.5pts *Hummer*	André Jousseaume (FRA) 480.0 *Harpagon*	Gustaf-Adolf Boltenstern Jr (SWE) 477.5 *Trumpf*
1952 Henri St Cyr (SWE) 561pts *Master Rufus*	Lis Hartel (DEN) 541.5 *Jubilee*	André Jousseaume (FRA) 541.0 *Harpagon*
1956 Henri St Cyr (SWE) 860pts *Juli*	Lis Hartel (DEN) 850 *Jubilee*	Liselott Linsenhoff (GER) 832 *Adular*
1960 Sergey Filatov (URS) 2144pts *Absent*	Gustav Fischer (SUI) 2087 *Wald*	Josef Neckermann (GER) 2082 *Asbach*
1964 Henri Chammartin (SUI) 1504 pts *Woermann*	Harry Boldt (GER) 1503 *Remus*	Sergey Filatov (URS) 1486 *Absent*
1968 Ivan Kizimov (URS) 1572pts *Ikhov*	Josef Neckermann (FRG) 1546 *Mariano*	Reiner Klimke (FRG) 1527 *Dux*
1972 Liselott Linsenhoff (FRG) 1229pts *Piaff*	Yelena Petuchkova (URS) 1185 *Pepel*	Josef Neckermann (FRG) 1177 *Venetia*
1976 Christine Stückelberger (SUI) 1486pts	Harry Boldt (FRG) 1435 *Woycek*	Reiner Klimke (FRG) 1395 *Mehmed*
1980 Elisabeth Theurer (AUT) 1370 pts *Mon Cherie*	Yuriy Kovshov (URS) 1300 *Igrok*	Viktor Ugryumov (URS) 1234 *Shkval*
1984 Reiner Klimke (FRG) 1504pts *Ahlerich*	Anne Grethe Jensen (DEN) 1442 *Marzog*	Otto Hofer (SUI) 1364 *Limandus*
1988 Nicole Uphoff (FRG) 1521pts *Rembrandt*	Margit Otto Crepin (FRA) 1462 *Corlandus*	Christine Stückelberger (SUI) 1417 *Gauguin De Lully*
1992 Nicole Uphoff (GER) 1626pts *Rembrandt*	Isabell Werth (GER) 1551 *Gigolo*	Klaus Balkenhol (GER) 1515 *Goldstern*

1896–1908 Event not held.

Grand Prix (Dressage Team)

1928 Germany 669.72pts	Sweden 650.86	Netherlands 642.96
1932 France 2828.75pts	Sweden 2678	United States 2576.75

1936 Germany 5074pts	France 4846	Sweden 4660.5
1948 [1] France 1269pts	United States 1256	Portugal 1182
1952 Sweden 1597.5pts	Switzerland 1759	Germany 1501
1956 Sweden 2475pts	Germany 2346	Switzerland 2346
1964 Germany 2558pts	Switzerland 2526	Soviet Union 2311
1968 FRG 2699pts	Soviet Union 2657	Switzerland 2547
1972 Soviet Union 5095pts	FRG 5083	Sweden 4849
1976 FRG 5155pts	Switzerland 4684	United States 4670
1980 Soviet Union 4383pts	Bulgaria 3580	Romania 3346
1984 FRG 4955pts	Switzerland 4673	Sweden 4630
1988 FRG 4302pts	Switzerland 4164	Canada 3969
1992 Germany 5224pts	Netherlands 4742	USA 4643

1896–1924, 1960 Event not held

[1] *Sweden were originally declared winners with 1366 pts but were subsequently disqualified one year later.*

Three-Day Event

1912 Axel Nordlander (SWE) 46.59pts *Lady Artist*	Friedrich von Rochow (GER) 46.42 *Idealist*	Jean Cariou (FRA) 46.32 *Cocotte*
1920 Helmer Mörner (SWE) 1775pts *Germania*	Age Lundström (SWE) 1738.75 *Yrsa*	Ettore Caffaratti (ITA) 1733.75 *Traditore*
1924 Adolph van der Voort van Zijp (NED) 1976pts *Silver Piece*	Fröde Kirkebjerg (DEN) 1853.5 *Meteor*	Sloan Doak (USA) 1845.5 *Pathfinder*
1928 Charles Pahud de Mortanges (NED) 1969.82pts *Marcroix*	Gerard de Kruyff (NED) 1967.26 *Va-t-en*	Bruno Neumann (GER) 1944.42 *Ilja*
1932 Charles Pahud de Mortanges (NED) 1813.83pts *Marcroix*	Earl Thomson (USA) 1811 *Jenny Camp*	Clarence von Rosen Jr (SWE) 1809.42 *Sunnyside Maid*
1936 Ludwig Stubbendorff (GER) 37.7 faults *Nurmi*	Earl Thomson (USA) 99.9 *Jenny Camp*	Hans Mathiesen Lunding (DEN) 102.2 *Jason*
1948 Bernard Chevallier (FRA) +4pts *Aiglonne*	Frank Henry (USA) −21 *Swing Low*	Robert Selfelt (SWE) −25 *Claque*
1952 Hans von Blixen-Finecke (SWE) 28.33 faults *Jubal*	Guy Lefrant (FRA) 54.50 *Verdun*	Wilhelf Büsing (GER) 55.50 *Hubertus*
1956 Petrus Kastenman (SWE) 66.53 faults *Illuster*	August Lütke-Westhues (GER) 84.87 *Trux von Kamax*	Frank Weldon (GBR) 85.48 *Kilbarry*
1960 Lawrence Morgan (AUS) +7.15pts *Salad Days*	Neale Lavis (AUS) −16.50 *Mirrabooka*	Anton Bühler (SUI) −51.21 *Gay Spark*
1964 Mauro Checcoli (ITA) 64.40pts *Surbean*	Carlos Moratorio (ARG) 56.40 *Chalan*	Fritz Ligges (GER) 49.20 *Donkosak*
1968 Jean-Jacques Guyon (FRA) 38.86pts *Pitou*	Derek Allhusen (GBR) 41.61 *Lochinvar*	Michael Page (USA) 52.31 *Faster*
1972 Richard Meade (GBR) 57.73pts *Laurieston*	Alessa Argenton (ITA) 43.33 *Woodland*	Jan Jonsson (SWE) 39.67 *Sarajevo*
1976 Edmund Coffin (USA) 114.99pts *Bally-Cor*	Michael Plumb (USA) 125.85 *Better & Better*	Karl Schultz (FRG) 129.45 *Madrigal*
1980 Federico Roman (ITA) 108.60pts *Rossinan*	Aleksandr Blinov (URS) 120.80 *Galzun*	Yuriy Salnikov (URS) 151.60 *Pintset*
1984 Mark Todd (NZL) 51.60pts *Charisma*	Karen Stives (USA) 54.20 *Ben Arthur*	Virginia Holgate (GBR) 56.80 *Priceless*
1988 Mark Todd (NZL) 42.60pts *Charisma*	Ian Stark (GBR) 52.80 *Sir Wattie*	Virginia Leng (GBR) 62.00 *Master Craftsman*
1992 Matthew Ryan (AUS) 70pts *Kibah Tic Toc*	Herbert Blocker (GER) 81.30 *Feine Dame*	Blyth Tait (NZL) 87.60 *Messiah*

1896–1908 Event not held

Three-Day Event Team

1912 Sweden 139.06pts	Germany 138.48	United States 137.33
1920 Sweden 5057.5pts	Italy 4735	Belgium 4560
1924 Netherlands 5297.5pts	Sweden 4743.5	Italy 4512.5
1928 Netherlands 5865.68pts	Norway 5395.68	Poland 5067.92
1932 United States 5038.08pts	Netherlands 4689.08	—[1]
1936 Germany 676.75pts	Poland 991.70	Great Britain 9195.90
1948 United States 161.50pts	Sweden 165.00	Mexico 305.25
1952 Sweden 221.49pts	Germany 235.49	United States 587.16
1956 Great Britain 355.48pts	Germany 475.61	Canada 572.72
1960 Australia 128.18pts	Switzerland 386.02	France 515.71
1964 Italy 85.80pts	United States 65.86	Germany 56.73
1968 Great Britain 175.93pts	United States 245.87	Australia 331.26
1972 Great Britain 95.53pts	United States 10.81	FRG −18.00

1976 United States 441.00pts
1980 Soviet Union 457.00pts
1984 United States 186.00pts
1988 FRG 225.95pts
1992 Australia 288.60pts
1896–1908 Event not held.
⁽¹⁾ *No other teams finished.*

FRG 584.60
Italy 656.20
Great Britain 189.20
Great Britain 256.80
New Zealand 290.80

Australia 599.54
Mexico 1172.85
FRG 234.00
New Zealand 271.20
Germany 300.30

DISCONTINUED EVENTS

GOLD	SILVER	BRONZE

Equestrian High Jump
1900 Dominique Gardères (FRA) 1.85m *Canela*
    Gian Giorgio Trissino (ITA) 1.85m *Oreste*

Georges van der Poele (BEL) 1.70
Ludlow

Equestrian Long Jump
1900 Constant van Langhendonck (BEL)
    6.10 *Extra Dry*

Gian Giorgio Trissino (ITA) *Oreste*

de Bellegarde (FRA) 5.30 *Tolla*

Figure Riding
(Only open to soldiers below the rank of NCO)
1920 Bouckaert (BEL) 30.5pts

Fiel (FRA) 29.5

Finet (BEL) 29.0

Teams
    Belgium

France

Sweden

The 1956 individual medallists in showjumping – Germany's Hans-Günter Winkler (centre) takes the gold from the Italians Raimondo (left) and Piero d'Inzeo, in second and third respectively (Popperfoto)

Fencing

This was one of the original sports held in 1896, when the first Olympic champion was Emile Gravelotte (FRA) in the foil. Until recently it was the only sport in which professionals had openly competed in the Games, special events for fencing masters having been held in 1896 and 1900. At the latter Games they even competed against other competitors, so that Albert Ayat (FRA) beat his pupil Ramon Fonst (CUB) in the épée. When Léon Pyrgos won the foil contest for fencing masters in 1896, he became the first Greek Olympic champion of modern times. A foil competition for women was introduced in 1924 and a team contest for them in 1960. In 1996, team and individual épée events for women are being introduced. Electronic scoring equipment was used for épée in 1936, for foil in 1956, and for the sabre in 1992.

Aladár Gerevich (HUN) won a record seven gold medals in the sabre between 1932 and 1960. The record for

One of the greatest ever Olympians, Hungarian Aladár Gerevich (centre), at the 1956 sabre team medal ceremony being congratulated by Yakov Rylsky (URS)

most medals is 13 by Edoardo Mangiarotti (ITA) in foil and épée, 1936-60, comprising six golds, five silvers and two bronzes. His elder brother Dario won a gold and two silvers, 1948-52. Nedo Nadi (ITA) won an unequalled five golds at one Games in 1920, and his younger brother Aldo added three more golds and a silver – a family record total for a Games. The most individual event gold medals won is three, achieved by Ramón Fonst (CUB) in 1900 and 1904 (two) and by Nedo Nadi in 1912 and 1920 (two).

The only man, in any sport, to win Olympic gold medals at six consecutive Games was Aladár Gerevich (see above); his medal-winning span of 28 years is also a record. Britain's Bill Hoskyns also competed at six Games, 1956-76, but only won two silver medals. The equal longest span of competition by any Olympic competitor is 40 years by Ivan Osiier (DEN) who fenced from 1908 to 1948, in a record 7 Games, during which time he won a silver medal in 1912, and became the oldest Olympic fencer, in 1948 aged 59yr 240 days. His wife Ellen won a gold medal in 1924.

Four fencers have won individual medals in all three disciplines at one Games. Both Nedo Nadi and his brother Aldo won golds in each of the team events in 1920. Roger Ducret (FRA) won foil and épée golds and a sabre silver in 1924. In the sparsely supported 1904 events, American-born Albertson Van Zo Post (CUB) won a foil silver and bronzes in the other two disciplines. The oldest gold medallist was Aladár Gerevich (HUN) in 1960 aged 50yr 178 days, while the youngest was Ramón Fonst (CUB) aged 16yr 289 days in 1900. The family of Gerevich has a unique position in Olympic fencing as he won seven golds, one silver and two bronzes; his wife Erna Bogen won a bronze in 1932; his father-in-law Albert Bogen won a silver in 1912; and Aladár's son Pal won bronze medals in 1972 and 1980.

Foil

Only Nedo Nadi (ITA), in 1912 and 1920, and Christian d'Oriola (FRA), in 1952 and 1956, have won two individual titles. In addition d'Oriola won two team golds and two silvers for a record six medals. The oldest gold medallist was Henri Jobier (FRA) who was over 44 years old in the winning 1924 team, while the youngest was Nedo Nadi in 1912 aged 18yr 29 days. In the 15 Games from 1920 to 1984, France only once failed to gain a team competition medal.

Épée

Ramón Fonst (CUB) was the only double winner of the individual title, but the most successful was Edoardo Mangiarotti (ITA) with five gold, one silver and two bronze medals, 1936-60. The oldest gold medallist was Fiorenzo Marini (ITA) aged 46yr 179 days in the 1960 team, and the youngest was Fonst (see above). Charles Newton-Robinson, a member of the silver-winning British team in 1906, was at 52yr 197 days the oldest ever Olympic fencing medallist.

Sabre

Jean Georgiadis (GRE), Jenö Fuchs (HUN), Rudolf Kárpáti (HUN), Viktor Krovopouskov (URS) and Jean François Lamour (FRA) have all won two individual titles. Gerevich (see above) won a record seven gold medals (only one individual) and was also the oldest gold medallist. The youngest was Mikhail Burtsev (URS) aged 20yr 36 days in the 1976 team event. Hungarians have dominated the discipline to an unparalleled extent, winning twelve gold, six silver and eight bronze individual medals. They won the individual title every year from 1908 to 1964, except in 1920 when they were not invited. They have won the team title eleven times, placed second once and third on three occasions, and won 46 consecutive contests from 1924 to 1964. Their 1960 team included Gerevich, Kárpáti and Pal Kovács, who between them amassed a total of 19 gold medals. The winning Hungarian teams of 1948 and 1952 comprised the same members. An interesting coincidence is that Karpati and IOC President Juan Antonio Samaranch were born on the same day.

Women's Foil

Only Ilona Elek (HUN) has won two individual titles, in 1936 and 1948, but Elena Novikova-Belova (URS) won a record four golds from 1968 to 1976. The record for most medals is seven by Ildikó Sagi-Retjö (formerly Ujlaki-Retjö) of Hungary in a record five Games, 1960-76. She was born deaf. Ellen Muller-Preis (AUT) competed over a record 24-year period,1932-56. This was matched by Kerstin Palm (SWE), 1964-88, and she notched up a record 7 Games - the most attended by any female Olympic competitor in any sport. The period of 24 years is also a record span of competition for any female fencer.

Elek was the oldest gold medallist in 1948 aged 41yr 77 days, and the oldest medallist four years later with a silver aged 45yr 71 days. The youngest champion/medallist was Helene Mayer (GER) in 1928 aged 17yr 225 days. When Gillian Sheen (GBR) won her gold medal in 1956 there were hardly any members of the British press corps on hand as they considered that fencing was a 'minor' sport, and anyway she had not been expected to achieve anything of note.

FENCING MEDALS TABLE

	Men			Women			
	G	S	B	G	S	B	Total
France	34	31	27	2	1	2	97
Italy	30	32	19	4	2	3	90
Hungary	27	13	19	5	6	5	75
Soviet Union	14	14	15	5	3	3	54
United States [1]	2	6	11	-	-	-	19
Poland	4	6	7	-	-	1	18
Germany	4	3	3	2	3	2	17
FRG	4	6	-	3	2	1	16
Belgium	5	3	5	-	-	-	13
Great Britain	-	6	-	1	-	3	10
Romania	1	-	2	-	2	4	9
Cuba [1]	5	2	1	-	-	-	8
Greece	3	3	2	-	-	-	8
Netherlands	-	1	7	-	-	-	8
Sweden	2	3	2	-	-	-	7
Austria	-	1	3	1	-	2	7
Denmark	-	1	1	1	1	2	6
Switzerland	-	2	3	-	-	-	5
Bohemia (Czech)	-	-	2	-	-	-	2
China	-	-	-	1	1	-	2
GDR	-	1	-	-	-	-	1
Mexico	-	-	-	-	1	-	1
Argentina	-	-	1	-	-	-	1
Portugal	-	-	1	-	-	-	1
	135	134	131	25	25	25	475

[1] *Double counting for 1904 foil team gold medal*

FENCING MEDAL RESULTS — INDIVIDUAL

GOLD	SILVER	BRONZE

Foil (Men)
Wins are assessed on both wins (2pts) and draws (1pt) so, as in 1928, the winner does not necessarily have most wins.

GOLD	SILVER	BRONZE
1896 Emile Gravelotte (FRA) 4 wins	Henri Callott (FRA) 3	Perikles Mavromichalis-Pierrakos (GRE) 2
1900 Emile Cost (FRA) 6 wins	Henri Masson (FRA) 5	Jacques Boulenger (FRA) 4

1904	Ramón Fonst (CUB) 3 wins	Albertson Van Zo Post [1] (USA)2	Charles Tatham [1] (USA)1
1906	Georges Dillon–Kavanagh (FRA) d.n.a.	Gustav Casmir (GER) d.n.a.	Pierre d'Hugues (FRA) d.n.a.
1912	Nedo Nadi (ITA) 7 wins	Pietro Speciale (ITA) 5	Richard Verderber (AUT) 4
1920	Nedo Nadi (ITA) 10 wins	Philippe Cattiau (FRA) 9	Roger Ducret (FRA) 9
1924	Roger Ducret (FRA) 6 wins	Philippe Cattiau (FRA) 5	Maurice van Damme (BEL) 4
1928	Lucien Gaudin (FRA) 9 wins	Erwin Casmir (GER) 9	Giulio Gaudini (ITA) 9
1932	Gustavo Marzi (ITA) 9 wins	Joseph Levis (USA) 6	Giulio Gaudini (ITA) 5
1936	Giulio Gaudini (ITA) 7 wins	Edouard Gardère (FRA) 6	Giorgio Bocchino (ITA) 4
1948	Jean Buhan (FRA) 7 wins	Christian d'Oriola (FRA) 5	Lajos Maszlay (HUN) 4
1952	Christian d'Oriola (FRA) 8 wins	Edoardo Mangiarotti (ITA) 6	Manlio di Rosa (ITA) 5
1956	Christian d'Oriola (FRA) 6 wins	Giancarlo Bergamini (ITA) 5	Antonio Spallino (ITA) 5
1960	Viktor Zhdanovich (URS) 7 wins	Yuriy Sissikin (URS) 4	Albert Axelrod (USA) 3
1964	Egon Franke (POL) 3 wins	Jean-Claude Magnan (FRA) 2	Daniel Revenu (FRA) 1
1968	Ion Drimba (ROM) 4 wins	Jenö Kamuti (HUN) 3	Daniel Revenu (FRA) 3
1972	Witold Woyda (POL) 5 wins	Jenö Kamuti (HUN) 4	Christian Nöel (FRA) 2
1976	Fabio Dal Zotto (ITA) 4 wins	Aleksandr Romankov (URS) 4	Bernard Talvard (FRA) 3
1980	Vladimir Smirnov (URS) 5 wins	Paskal Jolyot (FRA) 5	Aleksandr Romankov (URS) 5
1984	Mauro Numa (ITA)	Matthias Behr (FRG)	Stefano Cerioni (ITA)
1988	Stefano Cerioni (ITA)	Udo Wagner (GDR)	Alexandr Romankov (URS)
1992	Philippe Omnes (FRA)	Sergei Goloubiski (EUN)	Elvis Gregory (CUB)

1908 *Event not held.*

[1] *Van Zo Post and Tatham were American citizens wrongly reported as competing for Cuba.*

Sabre (Men)

1896	Jean Georgiadis (GRE) 4 wins	Telemachos Karakalos (GRE) 3	Holger Nielsen (DEN) 2
1900	Georges de la Falaise (FRA) d.n.a.	Léon Thiébaut (FRA) d.n.a.	Siegfried Flesch (AUT) d.n.a.
1904	Manuel Diaz (CUB) 4 wins	William Grebe (USA) 3	Albertson Van Zo Post [1] (USA) 2
1906	Jean Georgiadis (GRE) d.n.a.	Gustav Casmir (GER) d.n.a.	Federico Cesarano (ITA) d.n.a.
1908	Jeno Fuchs (HUN) 6 wins	Béla Zulavsky (HUN) 6	Vilem Goppold von Lobsdorf (BOH) 4
1912	Jeno Fuchs (HUN) 6 wins	Béla Békéssy (HUN) 5	Ervin Mészaros (HUN) 5
1920	Nedo Nadi (ITA) 11 wins	Aldo Nadi (ITA) 9	Adrianus EW de Jong (NED) 7
1924	Sándor Posta (HUN) 5 wins	Roger Ducret (FRA) 5	János Garai (HUN) 5
1928	Odön Tersztyanszky (HUN) 9 wins	Attila Petschauer (HUN) 9	Bino Bini (ITA) 8
1932	György Piller (HUN) 8 wins	Giulio Gaudini (ITA) 7	Endre Kabos (HUN) 5
1936	Endre Kabos (HUN) 7 wins	Gustavo Marzi (ITA) 6	Aladár Gerevich (HUN) 6
1948	Aladár Gerevich (HUN) 7 wins	Vincenzo Pinton (ITA) 5	Pál Kovács (HUN) 5
1952	Pál Kovács (HUN) 8 wins	Aladár Gerevich (HUN) 7	Tibor Berczelly (HUN) 5
1956	Rudolf Kárpáti (HUN) 6 wins	Jerzy Pawlowski (POL) 5	Lev Kuznyetsov (URS) 4
1960	Rudolf Kárpáti (HUN) 5 wins	Zoltán Horvath (HUN) 4	Wladimiro Calarese (ITA) 4
1964	Tibor Pézsa (HUN) 2 wins	Claude Arabo (FRA) 2	Umar Mavlikhanov (URS) 1
1968	Jerzy Pawlowski (POL) 4 wins	Mark Rakita (URS) 4	Tribor Pézsa (HUN) 3
1972	Viktor Sidiak (URS) 4 wins	Peter Maroth (HUN) 3	Vladimir Nazlimov (URS) 3
1976	Viktor Krovopouskov (URS) 5 wins	Vladimir Nazlimov (URS) 4	Viktor Sidiak (URS) 3
1980	Viktor Krovopouskov (URS) 5 wins	Mikhail Burtsev (URS) 4	Imre Gedovari (HUN) 3
1984	Jean François Lamour (FRA)	Marco Marin (ITA)	Peter Westbrook (USA)
1988	Jean François Lamour (FRA)	Janusz Olech (POL)	Giovanni Scalzo (ITA)
1992	Bence Szabo (HUN)	Marco Marin (ITA)	Jean-François Lamour (FRA)

[1] *See footnote to Foil above*

Épée (Men)

1900	Ramon Fonst (CUB)	Louis Perree (FRA)	Léon Sée (FRA)
1904	Ramon Fonst (CUB) 3 wins	Charles Tatham [1] (USA) 2	Albertson Van Zo Post [1] (USA)
1906	Georges de la Falaise (FRA) d.n.a.	Georges Dillon-Kavanagh (FRA) d.n.a.	Alexander van Blijenburgh (NED) d.n.d.
1908	Gaston Alibert (FRA) 5 wins	Alexandre Lippmann (FRA) 4	Eugène Olivier (FRA) 4
1912	Paul Anspach (BEL) 6 wins	Ivan Osiier (DEN) 5	Philippe Le Hardy de Beaulieu (BEL) 4
1920	Armand Massard (FRA) 9 wins	Alexandre Lippmann (FRA) 7	Gustave Buchard (FRA) 6
1924	Charles Delporte (BEL) 8 wins	Roger Ducret (FRA) 7	Nils Hellsten (SWE) 7

1928 Lucien Gaudin (FRA) 8 wins	Georges Buchard (FRA) 7	George Calnan (USA) 6
1932 Giancarlo Cornaggia-Medici (ITA) 8 wins	Georges Buchard (FRA) 7	Carlo Agostini (ITA) 7
1936 Franco Riccardi (ITA) 5 wins	Saverio Ragno (ITA) 6	Giancarlo Cornaggia-Medici (ITA) 6
1948 Luigi Cantone (ITA) 7 wins	Oswald Zappelli (SUI) 5	Edoardo Mangiarotti (ITA) 5
1952 Edoardo Mangiarotti (ITA) 7 wins	Dario Mangiarotti (ITA) 6	Oswald Zappelli (SUI) 6
1956 Carlo Pavesi (ITA) 5 wins	Giuseppe Delfino (ITA) 5	Edoardo Mangiarotti (ITA) 5
1960 Giuseppe Delfino (ITA) 5 wins	Allan Jay (GBR) 5	Bruno Khabarov (URS) 4
1964 Grigoriy Kriss (URS) 2 wins	William Hoskyns (GBR) 2	Guram Kostava (URS) 1
1968 Gyözö Kulcsár (HUN) 4 wins	Grigoriy Kriss (URS) 4	Gianluigi Saccaro (ITA) 4
1972 Csaba Fenyvesi (HUN) 4 wins	Jacques la Degaillerie (FRA) 3	Gyözö Kulcsár (HUN) 3
1976 Alexander Pusch (FRG) 3 wins	Jürgen Hehn (FRG) 3	Gyözö Kulcsár (HUN) 3
1980 Johan Harmenberg (SWE) 4 wins	Ernö Kolczonay (HUN) 3	Philippe Riboud (FRA) 3
1984 Philippe Boisse (FRA)	Bjorne Vaggo (SWE)	Philippe Riboud (FRA)
1988 Arnd Schmitt (FRG)	Philippe Riboud (FRA)	Andrey Chouvalov (URS)
1992 Eric Srecki (FRA)	Pavel Kolobkov (EUN)	Jean-Michel Henry (FRA)
1896 Event not held.		

[1] See footnote above

Women's Foil

1924 Ellen Osiier (DEN) 5 wins	Gladys Davis (GBR) 4	Grete Heckscher (DEN) 3
1928 Helène Mayer (GER) 7 wins	Muriel Freeman (GBR) 6	Olga Oelkers (GER) 4
1932 Ellen Preis (AUT) 9 wins	Heather Guinness (GBR) 8	Ena Bogen (HUN) 7
1936 Ilona Elek (HUN) 6 wins	Helène Mayer (GER) 5	Ellen Preis (AUT) 5
1948 Ilona Elek (HUN) 6 wins	Karen Lachmann (DEN) 5	Ellen Müller-Preis (AUT) 5
1952 Irene Camber (ITA) 5 wins	Ilona Elek (HUN) 5	Karen Lachmann (DEN) 4
1956 Gillian Sheen (GBR) 6 wins	Olga Orban (ROM) 6	Renée Garilhe (FRA) 5
1960 Heidi Schmid (GER) 6 wins	Valentina Rastvorova (URS) 5	Maria Vicol (ROM) 4
1964 Ildikó Ujlaki-Reitó (HUN) 2 wins	Helga Mees (GER) 2	Antonella Ragno (ITA) 2
1968 Elena Novikova (URS) 4 wins	Pilar Roldan (MEX) 3	Ildikó Ujlaki-Rejtó (HUN) 3
1972 Antonella Ragno-Lonzi (ITA) 4 wins	Ildikó Bóbis (HUN) 3	Galina Gorokhova (URS) 3
1976 Ildikó Schwarczenberger (HUN) 4 wins	Maria Collino (ITA) 4	Elena Novikova-Belova (URS) 3
1980 Pascale Trinquet (FRA) 4 wins	Magda Maros (HUN) 3	Barbara Wysoczanska (POL) 3
1984 Jujie Luan (CHN)	Cornelia Hanisch (FRG)	Dorina Vaccaroni (ITA)
1988 Anja Fichtel (FRG)	Sabine Bau (FRG)	Zita Funkenhauser (FRG)
1992 Giovanna Trillini (ITA)	Wang Huifeng (CHN)	Tatyana Sadovskaya (EUN)
1896–1920 Event not held.		

FENCING MEDAL RESULTS — TEAM

	GOLD	SILVER	BRONZE
Foil (Men)			
1904	Cuba/USA	United States	– [1]
1920	Italy	France	United States
1924	France	Belgium	Hungary
1928	Italy	France	Argentina
1932	France	Italy	United States
1936	Italy	France	Germany
1948	France	Italy	Belgium
1952	France	Italy	Hungary
1956	Italy	France	Hungary
1960	Soviet Union	Italy	Germany
1964	Soviet Union	Poland	France
1968	France	Soviet Union	Poland

1972	Poland	Soviet Union	France
1976	FRG	Italy	France
1980	France	Soviet Union	Poland
1984	Italy	FRG	France
1988	Soviet Union	FRG	Hungary
1992	Germany	Cuba	Poland

1896–1900, 1906–1912 Event not held.
[1] *No other teams entered.*

Women's Foil

1960	Soviet Union	Hungary	Italy
1964	Hungary	Soviet Union	Germany
1968	Soviet Union	Hungary	Romania
1972	Soviet Union	Hungary	Romania
1976	Soviet Union	France	Hungary
1980	France	Soviet Union	Hungary
1984	FRG	Romania	France
1988	FRG	Italy	Hungary
1992	Italy	Germany	Romania

1896–1956 Event not held

Sabre (Men)

1906	Germany	Greece	Netherlands
1908	Hungary	Italy	Bohemia
1912	Hungary	Austria	Netherlands
1920	Italy	France	Netherlands
1924	Italy	Hungary	Netherlands
1928	Hungary	Italy	Poland
1932	Hungary	Italy	Poland
1936	Hungary	Italy	Germany
1948	Hungary	Italy	United States
1952	Hungary	Italy	France
1956	Hungary	Poland	Soviet Union
1960	Hungary	Poland	Italy
1964	Soviet Union	Italy	Poland
1968	Soviet Union	Italy	Hungary
1972	Italy	Soviet Union	Hungary
1976	Soviet Union	Italy	Romania
1980	Soviet Union	Italy	Hungary
1984	Italy	France	Romania
1988	Hungary	Soviet Union	Italy
1992	Unified Team	Hungary	France

1896–1904 Event not held.

Épée (Men)

1906	France	Great Britain	Belgium
1908	France	Great Britain	Belgium
1912	Belgium	Great Britain	Netherlands
1920	Italy	Belgium	France
1924	France	Belgium	Italy
1928	Italy	France	Portugal
1932	France	Italy	United States
1936	Italy	Sweden	France
1948	France	Italy	Sweden
1952	Italy	Sweden	Switzerland
1956	Italy	Hungary	France
1960	Italy	Great Britain	Soviet Union

1964	Hungary	Italy	France
1968	Hungary	Soviet Union	Poland
1972	Hungary	Switzerland	Soviet Union
1976	Sweden	FRG	Switzerland
1980	France	Poland	Soviet Union
1984	FRG	France	Italy
1988	France	FRG	Soviet Union
1992	Germany	Hungary	Unified Team

1896–1904 Event not held.

DISCONTINUED EVENTS

Foil for Fencing Masters

| 1896 | Léon Pyrgos (GRE) | M Perronnet (FRA) | – |
| 1900 | Lucien Mérignac (FRA) | Alphonse Kirchhoffer (FRA) | Jean-Baptiste Mimiague (FRA) |

Épée for Fencing Masters

| 1900 | Albert Ayat (FRA) | Emile Bougnol (FRA) | Henri Laurent (FRA) |
| 1906 | Cyrille Verbrugge (BEL) | Carlo Gandini (ITA) | Ioannis Raissis (GRE) |

Épée for Amateurs and Fencing Masters

| 1900 | Albert Ayat (FRA) | Ramón Fonst (CUB) | Léon Sée (FRA) |

Sabre for Fencing Masters

| 1900 | Antonio Conte (ITA) | Italo Santelli (ITA) [1] | Milan Neralic (AUT) |
| 1906 | Cyrille Verbrugge (BEL) | Ioannis Raissis (GRE) | – |

[1] *Santelli actually lived in Hungary, hence some confusion as to his nationality*

Three Cornered Sabre

| 1906 | Gustav Casmir (GER) | George van Rossem (NED) | Péter Tóth (HUN) |

Single Sticks

| 1904 | Albertson Van Zo Post [1] (USA) | William Grebe (USA) | William O'Connor (USA) |

[1] *Van Zo Post was an American citizen wrongly reported as competing for Cuba.*

Football

Some sources refer to two exhibition matches at Athens in the first Games of 1896, when after two Greek towns had played an eliminator, the winner, Smyrna, was defeated by a Danish side 15-0. However, the Swedish Olympic expert Ture Widlund, after considerable research, considers these reports to be spurious. Although sometimes considered unofficial, the tournaments of 1900, 1904 and 1906 are usually counted in medal tables. Therefore soccer was the first team game to be included in the Olympics.

The first goal was scored by Great Britain (represented by Upton Park FC) versus France (4-0) in 1900. The 1904 tournament only had three entries, one Canadian and two American teams, while in 1906 a Danish team beat Smyrna (representing Greece). In that latter team were five Britons named Whittal, of which three were one set of brothers and the other two another set, the two lots being cousins. That must surely be some sort of Olympic record for siblings, and a family.

With the founding of FIFA in 1904, Olympic soccer came under their control and from 1908 the competition grew in stature. In 1920 came the first non-European entry (excepting the North Americans of 1904), from Egypt, and by 1924 there were 22 countries competing. That tournament and the next was won by Uruguay, who surprisingly never took part in Olympic soccer again after that. Two years after their 1928 victory, Uruguay won the inaugural World Cup with nine of their Olympic team playing. Only three other players, all Italian, have been in both Olympic (1936) and World Cup (1938) winning sides.

There has been considerable disillusionment with the interpretation of the term 'amateur' as applied to soccer at the Games, similar to the troubles in ice hockey. The arguments about 'pseudo-amateurs' were exacerbated with the entry of the Eastern European powers into the game after 1948. Great Britain, after three gold medals in the early days, did not enter in 1924 and 1928 due to disagreements between the Football Association (FA) and FIFA about broken-time payments to amateurs. In 1952, as entries increased, qualifying rounds were introduced to decide on the final 16 teams. In 1984 professionals were allowed to take part, but only those who had not yet participated in World Cup competition were eligible. Currently the only restriction on players is that they must be under 23 years of age.

The highest team score in Olympic soccer was the 17-1 defeat of France by Denmark in 1908, during which the Danish centre-forward Sophus Nielsen scored a record 10 goals. This mark was equalled by Gottfried Fuchs for Germany when they beat Russia 16-0 in 1912. The most goals scored by an individual in one tournament is 12 by Ferenc Bene (HUN) in 1964. The most scored in Olympic competition is 13 by Sophus Nielsen (DEN), 1908-12, and by Antal Dunai (HUN), 1968-72. The highest score in a final since the institution of 'proper' tournaments in 1908 has been the 4-2 defeat of Denmark by Great Britain in 1912. France's victory in 1984 was the first win by a Western European side since the outstanding Swedish team of 1948, and the first medal since the Swedish bronze of four years later. The 1968 final ended with only 18 players on the field, as three Bulgarians and a Hungarian had been sent off.

Top scorers at Olympic Games

1908	11	Sophus Nielsen (DEN)
1912	10	Gottfried Fuchs (FRG)
1920	7	Herbert Karlsson (SWE)
1924	8	Pedro Petrone (URU)
1928	7	Domingo Tarasconi (ARG)
1936	7	Annibale Frossi (ITA)
1948	7	Gunnar Nordahl (SWE)
		& Karl Aage Hansen (DEN)
1952	7	Branko Zebec (YUG) & Rajko Mitic (YUG)
1956	4	Dimiter Milanov (BUL)
		& Neville d'Souza (IND)
1960	7	Milan Galic (YUG) & Borivoje Kostic (YUG)
1964	12	Ferenc Bene (HUN)
1968	7	Kunishige Kamamoto (JPN)
1972	9	Kazimierz Deyna (POL)
1976	6	Andrzej Szarmach (POL)
1980	5	Sergey Andreyev (URS)
1984	5	Borislav Cvetkovic (YUG), Stjepan Deveric (YUG) & Daniel Xuereb (FRA)
1988	7	Romario Farias (BRA)
1992	7	Andrzej Juskowiak (POL)

There has only been one draw in an Olympic final. That was in 1928 between Uruguay and Argentina (1-1), and the replay was won by Uruguay, the defending champions, 2-1. Hungary is the only country to win on three occasions, and the team which won in Helsinki in 1952 was virtually the same line-up that 16 months later inflicted the first home defeat on England's professionals at Wembley Stadium.

The most successful player has been Dezsö Nowák (HUN) who added gold medals in 1964 and 1968 to the bronze he won in 1960. Of the ten other players to win two gold medals, only Arthur Berry and Vivian Woodward (both GBR) were not Uruguayans. Two of those, Antonio and Santos Urdinaran, became the first brothers to win soccer gold medals in 1924. This feat was surpassed by the Nordahl brothers, Bertil, Knut and Gunnar, in 1948. In 1908 two Danish brothers had gained silver medals in a team which included mathematician Harald Bohr, the brother of the famous atomic physicist Niels.

The oldest gold medallist was Rostislav Vaclavicek (TCH) aged 33yr 239 days in the 1980 final. The youngest was Pedro Petrone (URU), the highest scoring player of the 1924 tournament, who was just two days short of his 19th birthday in the final match. The youngest medallist was Osei Kuffour (GHA) in 1992 at 15yr 339 days, and the oldest Fyodor Cherenkov (URS) aged 41yr 92 days in 1980.

One of the most remarkable goals in international football involved the Swedish centre-forward Gunnar Nordahl in the 1948 semi-final against Denmark. Unexpectedly caught offside by a quick reversal of play, Nordahl realized that his team were attacking again. With lightning presence of mind he leapt into the back of the Danish goal, taking himself off the field of play, and duly caught the goalscoring header from his team-mate Henry Carlsson, with the goalkeeper on the ground five metres away. In the 1920 final between Belgium and Czechoslovakia the latter team walked off the field in protest against the referee before half-time when they were 2-0 down. The match was abandoned and the Czechs disqualified. The 1936 tournament resulted in many incidents, not least the withdrawal of the Peruvian team after their win over Austria in the second round was ordered to be replayed. Austria went on to reach the final.

After many years in the doldrums, Olympic soccer had a revival in 1980 when the 56 games of the tournament, played in Moscow, Leningrad, Minsk and Kiev, attracted nearly two million spectators – over a third of all spectators for the 1980 Games. This revival was unexpectedly reinforced at Los Angeles in 1984 when nearly 1.5 million watched the matches, including a record 101,799 audience for the final. In 1996 there will be an inaugural women's tournament.

Josep Guardiola Sala (SPA) shoots for goal during the host nation's 3-2 victory over Poland in the 1992 final at Barcelona (Popperfoto)

FOOTBALL MEDALS TABLE

	G	S	B	Total
Hungary	3	1	1	5
Soviet Union	2	-	3	5
Denmark	1	3	1	5
Yugoslavia	1	3	1	5
Great Britain	3	-	-	3
GDR	1	1	1	3
Poland	1	2	-	3
Sweden	1	-	2	3
Netherlands	-	-	3	3
Uruguay	2	-	-	2
Czechoslovakia	1	1	-	2
France	1	1	-	2
Belgium	1	-	1	2
Italy	1	-	1	2
Brazil	-	2	-	2
Bulgaria	-	1	1	2
Greece	-	1	1	2
Spain	1	1	-	2
United States	-	1	1	2
Canada	1	-	-	1
Argentina	-	1	-	1
Austria	-	1	-	1
Switzerland	-	1	-	1
FRG	-	-	1	1
Germany	-	-	1	1
Ghana	-	1	-	1
Japan	-	-	1	1
Norway	-	-	1	1
	21	21	22 [1]	64

[1] *Third place tie in 1972*

FOOTBALL MEDAL RESULTS

	GOLD	SILVER	BRONZE
1900	Great Britain	France	Belgium
1904	Canada	United States	United States
1906	Denmark	Greece	Greece
1908	Great Britain	Denmark	Netherlands
1912	Great Britain	Denmark	Netherlands
1920	Belgium	Spain	Netherlands
1924	Uruguay	Switzerland	Sweden
1928	Uruguay	Argentina	Italy
1936	Italy	Austria	Norway
1948	Sweden	Yugoslavia	Denmark
1952	Hungary	Yugoslavia	Sweden
1956	Soviet Union	Yugoslavia	Bulgaria

	GOLD	SILVER	BRONZE
1960	Yugoslavia	Denmark	Hungary
1964	Hungary	Czechoslovakia	Germany
1968	Hungary	Bulgaria	Japan
1972	Poland	Hungary	GDR [1]
			Soviet Union [1]
1976	GDR	Poland	Soviet Union
1980	Czechoslovakia	GDR	Soviet Union
1984	France	Brazil	Yugoslavia
1988	Soviet Union	Brazil	FRG
1992	Spain	Poland	Ghana

[1] *Tie declared after extra time played.*

1896, 1932 Event not held.

Gymnastics

In artistic gymnastics there are eight interlinked events for men and six for women. A team competition comes first, comprising one compulsory and one optional exercise for each separate discipline. For men these are floor exercises, pommel horse, rings, horse vault, parallel bars and horizontal bar; for women they are floor exercises, asymmetrical bars, horse vault and balance beam. Each competitor is marked out of 10.00 for both the compulsory and optional exercises at each discipline. The best total of five gymnasts per country decides the team competition.

The best 36 individuals (but only a maximum of three per country) then qualify for the individual all-round competition. They each complete a further optional exercise for each discipline, and are awarded new marks. Prior to 1992 these were added to the average of their previous best total from the team competition, but now they start from scratch. The best eight in each discipline go forward to the individual final for that event. With the exception of 1948, when scores were marked out of 20.00, points since 1936 are of some comparative value. After 1996 there will be no compulsory exercises. In 1984 an individual modern rhythmic event for women was introduced, and in 1996 there will be a team event.

The first gymnastics gold medal was won by the German team on the parallel bars event in 1896, and the first individual champion was Carl Schuhmann of that team in the vault. Due to the large number of disciplines, each with their own medals awarded, gymnasts are among the greatest collectors of Olympic medals. The most successful was Larissa Latynina (URS) who won a record 18 medals from 1956 to 1964, comprising nine golds (the most by any female Olympian), five silvers and four bronzes – unsurpassed in any sport. The most individual gold medals won is seven by Vera Caslavska (TCH) in 1964 and 1968. The male record for individual golds is six by Boris Shakhlin (URS) and Nikolay Andrianov (URS). The latter also holds the absolute Olympic record for most medals by a male competitor in any sport, with a total of fifteen. In 1980 Aleksandr Dityatin (URS) became the only male gymnast to gain medals in all eight events open to him at one Games, while in 1992 Vitali Shcherbo (EUN) uniquely won six gold medals at the one Games.

In recent years the sport has caught the imagination of the public due to a tremendous increase in media, especially television, coverage. In 1968 it was the attractive blonde Czech Vera Caslavska who drew the attention by defeating the Soviet women only two months after the invasion of her country. At Munich it was the elfin Olga Korbut (URS) who was the focus of all, even though she was outshone, technically, by her illustrious team-mate Ludmila Tourischeva. In 1976 the unsmiling Nadia Comaneci (ROM) deserved all the adulation as she scored the ultimate 10.00 on seven occasions, while the photogenic Nelli Kim (URS) attained that score twice. Aleksandr Dityatin stole the show from the girls in 1980 and also gained the first Olympic 10.00 by a man, in the horse vault. At Los Angeles the television cameras made a superstar of Mary Lou Retton (USA) in the absence of the main East Europeans.

The oldest gold medallist was Masao Takemoto (JPN) aged 40yr 344 days in the 1960 team event. Only 24 days younger was Heikki Savolainen (FIN) in the 1948 team event. He also competed in a record five Games over a record span of 24 years, 1928-52. The oldest male medallist was Lucien Démanet (FRA) at 45yr 266 days in 1920. The youngest champion was Nadia Comaneci (ROM) aged 14yr 252 days in 1976, while the oldest female champion was Agnes Keleti (HUN) in 1956 aged 35yr 331 days. The oldest medallist has been Ethel

Gymnastics multi-medal winners

		G	S	B
Larissa Latynina (URS)	1956-64	9	5	4
Sawao Kato (JPN)	1968-76	8	3	1
Nikolay Andrianov (URS)	1972-80	7	5	3
Boris Shakhlin (URS)	1956-64	7	4	2
Vera Caslavska (TCH)	1960-68	7	4	0
Viktor Chukarin (URS)	1952-56	7	3	1

The 18 medals won by gymnast Larissa Latynina (URS) in three Games is a record for any Olympic competitor at any sport (Allsport)

Seymour (GBR) in 1928 aged 46yr 222 days. The youngest male to win a gold medal was Harald Eriksen (NOR) in 1906 aged 17yr 292 days. The youngest medallist was Dimitrios Loundras (GRE) who gained a bronze in the parallel bars team event of 1896 aged 10yr 215 days. However, it must be said that some doubt exists about his exact age. Since 1984, male competitors must be a minimum of 16 years old and females 15 in the Games year. Recent revelations suggest that some countries in the Eastern bloc faked the ages of their young female performers, making them older than in fact they were.

The closest margin of victory in the individual all-round contest for men was 0.025pts in 1984 when Koji Gushiken (JPN) beat Peter Vidmar (USA). In 1992 there was a tremendous duel for the women's all-around title between Tatyana Gutsu (EUN) and Shannon Miller (USA) which resulted in the Ukrainian girl winning by the smallest ever margin of 0.012pts. There had been some controversy over the inclusion of Gutsu, who had failed to make the cut-off after the team competition but took part as a replacement for an (allegedly) injured team-mate.

On two occasions there has been a triple tie for a gold medal – both times in the pommel horse event, in 1948 and 1988. Since the Soviet Union entered Olympic competition in 1952 they have won the women's team title nine times (they were not present in 1984). In 1992 they (in the guise of the Unified Team) not only won for the tenth time, but as their swansong took the men's and women's individual and team titles plus the Rhythmic crown.

One of the most amazing competitors in Olympic history must be the American gymnast George Eyser who won six medals, including three golds, in the 1904 Games. He was well over 30 years of age, but even more remarkably had a wooden leg. Despite this he also competed in the all-round contest (the forerunner of the decathlon) in the track and field programme. In 1988 Vladimir Gogoladze (URS) performed a triple somersault in the team floor exercises – the first achieved in the Olympics. In the 1988 modern rhythmic competition, Marina Lobatch (URS) scored the maximum possible 60.00 points

The largest crowd to watch an Olympic gymnastic event was 18,000 at the Montreal Forum in 1976 for the final of the women's individual apparatus contests. In October 1994 Hjalmari Kivenheimo (FIN), silver medallist

in the 1912 team competition, died aged 105yr 34 days - the greatest known age ever reached by an Olympic medallist. Prior to 1928 it has been suggested that there were no individual medal events, merely competitors as part of the all-round title. However, the author has shown these in the tables of results and added them in the medal lists until more specific evidence comes to light.

GYMNASTICS MEDALS TABLE

	Men			Women			
	G	S	B	G	S	B	Total
Soviet Union	45	42	19	38	30	30	204
Japan	27	28	30	-	-	1	86
United States [1]	22	16	19	2	5	8	72
Switzerland	15	19	13	-	-	-	47
Romania	-	-	2	15	11	13	41
Hungary	6	5	4	7	6	10	38
GDR	3	3	10	3	10	7	36
Czechoslovakia	3	7	9	9	6	1	35
Germany	11	7	11	1	1	-	31
Italy	12	7	9	-	1	-	29
Finland	8	5	12	-	-	-	25
China	6	7	4	2	1	1	21
France	4	7	9	-	-	-	20
Yugoslavia	5	2	4	-	-	-	11
Sweden	4	1	-	1	1	1	8
Greece	3	2	3	-	-	-	8
Bulgaria	2	-	2	-	1	1	6
Norway	2	2	1	-	-	-	5
Denmark	1	3	1	-	-	-	5
Austria [1]	2	1	-	-	-	-	3
Great Britain	-	1	1	-	-	1	3
Belgium	-	1	1	-	-	-	2
Korea	-	-	2	-	-	-	2
Poland	-	1	-	-	-	1	2
FRG	-	-	1	-	-	1	2
Canada	-	-	-	1	-	-	1
Netherlands	-	-	-	1	-	-	1
NorthKorea (PRK)	1	-	-	-	-	-	1
Spain	-	-	-	-	1	-	1
	182	167	167	80	74	76	746

[1] *Double counting for 1904 men's team title*

GYMNASTICS MEDAL RESULTS — MEN

	GOLD	SILVER	BRONZE
Team			
1904	United States/Austria 374.43pts	United States 356.37	United States 349.69
1906	Norway 19.00pts	Denmark 18.00	Italy 16.71
1908	Sweden 438pts	Norway 425	Finland 405
1912	Italy 265.75pts	Hungary 227.25	Great Britain 184.50
1920	Italy 359.855pts	Belgium 346.745	France 340.100

1924	Italy 839.058pts	France 820.528	Switzerland 816.661
1928	Switzerland 1718.625pts	Czechoslovakia 1712.250	Yugoslavia 1648.750
1932	Italy 541.850pts	United States 522.275	Finland 509.995
1936	Germany 657.430pts	Switzerland 654.802	Finland 638.468
1948	Finland 1358.3pts	Switzerland 1356.7	Hungary 1330.35
1952	Soviet Union 575.4pts	Switzerland 567.5	Finland 564.2
1956	Soviet Union 568.25	Japan 566.40	Finland 555.95
1960	Japan 575.20pts	Soviet Union 572.70	Italy 559.05
1964	Japan 577.95pts	Soviet Union 575.45	Germany 565.10
1968	Japan 575.90pts	Soviet Union 571.10	GDR 557.15
1972	Japan 571.25pts	Soviet Union 564.05	GDR 559.70
1976	Japan 576.85pts	Soviet Union 576.45	GDR 654.65
1980	Soviet Union 589.60pts	GDR 581.15	Hungary 575.00
1984	United States 591.40pts	China 590.80	Japan 586.70
1988	Soviet Union 593.350pts	GDR 588.450	Japan 585.600
1992	Unified Team 585.450pts	China 580.375	Japan 578.250

1896–1900 Event not held.

Individual Combined Exercises

1900	Gustave Sandras (FRA) 302pts	Noël Bas (FRA) 295	Lucien Démanet (FRA) 293
1904	Julius Lenhart (AUT) 69.80pts	Wilhelm Weber (GER) 69.10	Adolf Spinnler (SUI) 67.99
1906 [2]	Pierre Paysse (FRA) 97pts	Alberto Braglia (ITA) 95	Georges Charmoille (FRA) 94
1906	Pierre Paysse (FRA) 116pts	Alberto Braglia (ITA) 115	Georges Charmoille (FRA) 113
1908	Alberto Braglia (ITA) 317.0pts	SW Tysal (GBR) 312.0	Louis Ségura (FRA) 297.0
1912	Alberto Braglia (ITA) 135.0pts	Louis Ségura (FRA) 132.5	Adolfo Tunesi (ITA) 131.5
1920	Giorgio Zampori (ITA) 88.35pts	Marco Torres (FRA) 87.62	Jean Gounot (FRA) 87.45
1924	Leon Stukelj (YUG) 110.340pts	Robert Prazák (TCH) 110.323	Bedrich Supcik (TCH) 106.930
1928	Georges Miez (SUI) 247.500pts	Herman Hänggi (SUI) 246.625	Leon Stukelj (YUG) 244.875
1932	Romeo Neri (ITA) 140.625pts	István Pelle (HUN) 134.925	Heikki Savolainen (FIN) 134.575
1936	Alfred Schwarzmann (GER) 113.100pts	Eugen Mack (SUI) 112.334	Konrad Frey (GER) 111.532
1948	Veikko Huhtanen (FIN) 229.7pts	Walter Lehmann (SUI) 229.0	Paavo Aaltonen (FIN) 228.8
1952	Viktor Chukarin (URS) 115.70pts	Grant Shaginyan (URS) 114.95	Josef Stalder (SUI) 114.75
1956	Viktor Chukarin (URS) 114.25pts	Takashi Ono (JPN) 114.20	Yuriy Titov (URS) 113.80
1960	Boris Shakhlin (URS) 115.95pts	Takashi Ono (JPN) 115.90	Yuriy Titov (URS) 115.60
1964	Yukio Endo (JPN) 115.95pts	Shuji Tsurumi (JPN) 115.40 Viktor Lisitsky (URS) 115.40 Boris Shakhlin (URS) 115.40	–
1968	Sawao Kato (JPN) 115.90pts	Mikhail Voronin (URS) 115.85	Akinori Nakayama (JPN) 115.65
1972	Sawao Kato (JNP) 114.650pts	Eizo Kenmotsu (JPN) 114.575	Akinori Nakayama (JPN) 114.325
1976	Nikolay Andrianov (URS) 116.650pts	Sawao Kato (JPN) 115.650	Mitsuo Tsukahara (JPN) 115.575
1980	Aleksandr Dityatin (URS) 118.650pts	Nikolay Andrianov (URS) 118.225	Stoyan Deltchev (BUL) 118.000
1984	Koji Gushiken (JPN) 118.700pts	Peter Vidmar (USA) 118.675	Li Ning (CHN) 118.575
1988	Vladimir Artemov (URS) 119.125pts	Valeriy Lyukhine (URS) 119.025	Dmitry Bilozertchev (URS) 118.975
1992	Vitali Shcherbo (EUN) 59.025pts	Grigori Misyutin (EUN) 58.925	Valeri Belenki (EUN) 58.625

[1] *Lenhart was a member of the Philadelphia Club, USA, which won the team event.*
[2] *Two competitions in 1906, one of five events and one of six.*
1896 Event not held.

Floor Exercises

1932	Istvan Pelle (HUN) 9.60	Georges Miez (SUI) 9.47	Mario Lertora (ITA) 9.23
1936	Georges Miez (SUI) 18.666	Josef Walter (SUI) 18.5	Konrad Frey (GER) 18.466 Eugen Mack (SUI) 18.466
1948	Ferenc Pataki (HUN) 38.7	János Mogyorosi-Klencs (HUN) 38.4	Zdenek Ruzicka (TCH) 38.1

1952	William Thoresson (SWE) 19.25	Tadao Uesako (JPN) 19.15	–
		Jerzy Jokiel (POL) 19.15	
1956	Valentin Muratov (URS) 19.20	Nobuyuki Aihara (JPN) 19.10	–
		Viktor Chukarin (URS) 19.10	
		William Thoresson (SWE) 19.10	
1960	Nobuyuki Aihara (JPN) 19.450	Yuriy Titov (URS) 19.325	Franco Menichelli (ITA) 19.275
1964	Franco Menichelli (ITA) 19.45	Viktor Lisitsky (URS) 19.35	–
		Yukio Endo (JPN) 19.35	
1968	Sawao Kato (JPN) 19.475	Akinori Nakayama (JPN) 19.400	Takeshi Kato (JPN) 19.275
1972	Nikolay Andrianov (URS) 19.175	Akinori Nakayama (JPN) 19.125	Shigeru Kasamatsu (JPN) 19.025
1976	Nikolay Andrianov (URS) 19.450	Vladimir Marchenko (URS) 19.425	Peter Kormann (USA) 19.300
1980	Roland Brückner (GDR) 19.750	Nikolay Andrianov (URS) 19.725	Aleksandr Dityatin (URS) 19.700
1984	Li Ning (CHN) 19.925	Yun Lou (CHN) 19.775	Koji Sotomura (JPN) 19.700
			Philippe Vatuone (FRA) 19.700
1988	Sergey Kharikov (URS) 19.925	Vladimir Artemov (URS) 19.900	Lou Yun (CHN) 19.850
			Yukio Iketani (JPN) 19.850
1992	Li Xiaosahuang (CHN) 9.925pts	Grigori Misyutin (EUN) 9.787	
		Yukio Iketani (JPN) 9.787	

Parallel Bars

1896	Alfred Flatow (GER) d.n.a.	Jules Zutter (SUI)	Hermann Weingartner (GER)
1904	George Eyser (USA) 44	Anton Heida (USA) 43	John Duha (USA) 40
1924	August Güttinger (SUI) 21.63	Robert Prazák (TCH) 21.61	Giorgio Zampori (ITA) 21.45
1928	Ladislav Vácha (TCH) 18.83	Josip Primozic (YUG) 18.50	Hermann Hänggi (SUI) 18.08
1932	Romeo Neri (ITA) 18.97	István Pelle (HUN) 18.60	Heikki Savolainen (FIN) 18.27
1936	Konrad Frey (GER) 19.067	Michael Reusch (SUI) 109.034	Alfred Schwarzmann (GER) 18.967
1948	Michael Reusch (SUI) 39.5	Veikkö Huhtanen (FIN) 39.3	Christian Kipfer (SUI) 39.1
			Josef Stalder (SUI) 39.1
1952	Hans Eugster (SUI) 19.65	Viktor Chukarin (URS) 19.60	Josef Stalder (SUI) 19.50
1956	Viktor Chukarin (URS) 19.20	Masami Kubota (JPN) 19.15	Takashi Ono (JPN) 19.10
			Masao Takemoto (JPN) 19.10
1960	Boris Shakhlin (URS)	Giovanni Carminucci (ITA) 19.375	Takashi Ono (JPN)19.350
1964	Yukio Endo (JPN) 19.675	Shuji Tsurumi (JPN) 19.450	Franco Menichelli (ITA) 19.350
1968	Akinori Nakayama (JPN) 19.475	Mikhail Voronin (URS) 19.425	Vladimir Klimenko (URS) 19.225
1972	Sawao Kato (JPN) 19.475	Shigeru Kasamatsu (JPN) 19.375	Eizo Kenmotsu (JPN) 19.25
1976	Sawao Kato (JPN) 19.675	Nikolay Andrianov (URS) 19.500	Mitsuo Tsukahara (JPN) 19.475
1980	Aleksandr Tkachev (URS) 19.775	Aleksandr Dityatin (URS) 19.750	Roland Brückner (GDR) 19.650
1984	Bart Conner (USA) 19.950	Nobuyuki Kajitani (JPN) 19.925	Mitchell Gaylord (USA) 19.850
1988	Vladimir Artemov (URS) 19.925	Valeriy Lyukhine (URS) 19.900	Sven Tippelt (GDR) 19.750
1992	Vitali Shcherbo (EUN) 9.900pts	Li Jing (CHN) 9.812	Guo Linyao (CHN) 9.800
			Igor Korobchinski (EUN) 9.800
			Masayuki Matsunaga (JPN) 9.800

1900, 1906–1920 Event not held.

Pommel Horse

1896	Jules Zutter (SUI) d.n.a.	Hermann Weingartner (GER)	Gyula Kakas (HUN)
1904	Anton Heida (USA) 42	George Eyser (USA) 33	William Merz (USA) 29
1924	Josef Wilhelm (SUI) 21.23	Jean Gutweiniger (SUI) 21.13	Antoine Rebetez (SUI) 20.73
1928	Hermann Hänggi (SUI) 1975	Georges Miez (SUI) 19.25	Heikki Savolainen (FIN) 18.83
1932	Istvan Pelle (HUN) 19.07	Omero Bonoli (ITA) 18.87	Frank Haubold (USA) 18.57
1936	Konrad Frey (GER) 19.333	Eugen Mack (SUI) 19.167	Albert Bachmann (SUI) 19.067
1948	Paavo Aaltonen (FIN) 38.7	Luigi Zanetti (ITA) 38.3	Guido Figone (ITA) 38.2
	Veikkö Huhtanen (FIN) 38.7		
	Heikki Savolainen (FIN) 38.7		
1952	Viktor Chukarin (URS) 19.50	Yevgeniy Korolkov (URS) 19.40	–
		Grant Shaginyan (URS) 19.40	
1956	Boris Shakhlin (URS) 19.25	Takashi Ono (JPN) 19.20	Viktor Chukarin (URS) 19.10

1960	Eugen Ekman (FIN) 19.375	–	Shuji Tsurumi (JPN) 19.150
	Boris Shakhlin (URS) 19.375		
1964	Miroslav Cerar (YUG) 19.525	Shuji Tsurumi (JPN) 19.325	Yuriy Tsapenko (URS) 19.200
1968	Miroslav Cerar (YUG) 19.325	Olli Laiho (FIN) 19.225	Mikhail Voronin (URS) 19.200
1972	Viktor Klimenko (URS) 19.125	Sawao Kato (JPN) 19.00	Eizo Kenmotsu (JPN) 18.950
1976	Zoltan Magyar (HUN) 19.700	Eizo Kenmotsu (JPN) 19.575	Nikolay Andrianov (URS) 19.525
1980	Zoltan Magyar (HUN) 19.925	Aleksandr Dityatin (URS) 19.800	Michael Nikolay (GDR) 19.775
1984	Li Ning (CHN) 19.950	–	Timothy Daggett (USA) 19.825
	Peter Vidmar (USA) 19.950		
1988	Lubomir Gueraskov (BUL) 19.950	–	–
	Zsolt Borkai (HUN) 19.950		
	Dmitry Bilozertchev (URS) 19.950		
1992	Vitali Shcherbo (EUN) 9.925pts	–	Andreas Wecker (GER) 9.887
	Pae Gil-su (PRK) 9.925		

1900, 1906–1920 Event not held.

Rings

1896	Ioannis Mitropoulos (GRE) d.n.a.	Hermann Weingartner (GER)	Petros Persakis (GRE)
1904	Herman Glass (USA) 45	William Merz (USA) 35	Emil Voight (USA) 32
1924	Franco Martino (ITA) 21.553	Robert Prazák (TCH) 21.483	Ladislav Vácha (TCH) 21.430
1928	Leon Skutelj (YUG) 19.25	Ladislav Vácha (TCH) 19.17	Emanuel Löffler (TCH) 18.83
1932	George Gulack (USA) 18.97	William Denton (USA) 18.60	Giovanni Lattuada (ITA) 18.50
1936	Alois Hudec (TCH) 19.433	Leon Skutelj (YUG) 18.867	Matthias Volz (GER) 18.667
1948	Karl Frei (SUI) 39.60	Michael Reusch (SUI) 39.10	Zdenek Ruzicka (TCH) 38.30
1952	Grant Shaginyan (URS) 19.75	Viktor Chukarin (URS) 19.55	Hans Eugster (SUI) 19.40
			Dimitriy Leonkin (URS) 19.40
1956	Albert Azaryan (URS) 1935	Valentin Muratov (URS) 19.15	Masao Takemoto (JPN) 19.10
			Masami Kubota (JPN) 19.10
1960	Albert Azaryan (URS) 19.725	Boris Shakhlin (URS) 19.500	Velik Kapsazov (BUL) 19.425
			Takashi Ono (JPN) 19.425
1964	Takuji Hayata (JPN) 19.475	Franco Menichelli (ITA) 19.425	Boris Shakhlin (URS) 19.400
1968	Akinori Nakayama (JPN) 19.450	Mikhail Voronin (URS) 19.325	Sawao Kato (JPN) 19.225
1972	Akinori Nakayama (JPN) 19.350	Mikhail Voronin (URS) 19.275	Mitsuo Tsukahara (JPN) 19.225
1976	Nikolay Andrianov (URS) 19.650	Alexandr Dityatin (URS) 19.550	Danut Grecu (ROM) 19.500
1980	Aleksandr Dityatin (URS) 19.875	Aleksandr Tkachev (URS) 19.725	Jiri Tabak (TCH) 19.600
1984	Koji Gushiken (JPN) 19.850	–	Mitchell Gaylord (USA) 19.825
	Li Ning (CHN) 19.850		
1988	Holger Behrendt (GDR) 19.925	–	Sven Tippelt (GDR) 19.875
	Dmitry Bilozertchev (URS) 19.925		
1992	Vitali Shcherbo (EUN) 9.937pts	Li Jing (CHN) 9.875	Li Xiaosahuang (CHN) 9.862
			Andreas Wecker (GER) 9.862

1900, 1906–1920 Event not held.

Horizontal Bar

1896	Hermann Weingartner (GER) d.n.a.	Alfred Flatow (GER)	unknown
1904	Anton Heida (USA) 40	–	George Eyser (USA) 39
	Edward Hennig (USA) 40		
1924	Leon Strukelj (YUG) 19.730	Jean Gutweniger (SUI) 19.236	André Higelin (FRA) 19.163
1928	Georges Miez (SUI) 19.17	Romeo Neri (ITA) 19.00	Eugen Mack (SUI) 18.92
1932	Dallas Bixler (USA) 18.33	Heikki Savolainen (FIN) 18.07	Einari Teräsvirta (FIN) 18.07 [1]
1936	Aleksanteri Saarvala (FIN) 19.367	Konrad Frey (GER) 19.267	Alfred Schwarzmann (GER) 19.233
1948	Josef Stalder (SUI) 39.7	Walter Lehmann (SUI) 39.4	Veikkö Huhtanen (FIN) 39.2
1952	Jack Günthard (SUI) 19.55	Josef Stalder (SUI) 19.50	–
		Alfred Schwarzmann (GER) 19.50	
1956	Takashi Ono (JPN) 19.60	Yuriy Titov (URS) 19.40	Masao Takemoto (JPN) 19.30
1960	Takashi Ono (JPN) 19.60	Masao Takemoto (JPN) 19.525	Boris Shakhlin (URS) 19.475
1964	Boris Shakhlin (URS) 19.625	Yuriy Titov (URS) 19.55	Miroslav Cerar (YUG) 19.50

1968	Mikhail Voronin (URS) 19.550 Akinori Nakayama (JPN) 19.550	–	Eizo Kenmotsu (JPN) 19.375
1972	Mitsuo Tsukahara (JPN) 19.725	Sawao Kato (JPN) 19.525	Shigeru Kasamatsu (JPN) 19.450
1976	Mitsuo Tsukahara (JPN) 19.675	Eizo Kenmotsu (JPN) 19.500	Eberhard Gienger (FRG) 19.475 Henry Boërio (FRA) 19.475
1980	Stoyan Deltchev (BUL) 19.825	Aleksandr Dityatin (URS) 19.750	Nikolay Andrianov (URS) 19.675
1984	Shinje Morisue (JPN) 20.00	Tong Fei (CHN) 19.955	Koji Gushiken (JPN) 19.950
1988	Vladimir Artemov (URS) 10.900 Valeriy Lyukhine (URS) 19.900	–	Holger Behrendt (GDR) 19.800 Marius Germann (ROM) 19.800
1992	Trent Dimas (USA) 9.875pts	Andreas Wecker (GER) 9.837 Grigori Misyutin (EUN) 9.837	

1900, 1906–1920 Event not held.
(1) *Teräsvirta conceded second place to Savolainen.*

Horse Vault

1896	Carl Schuhmann (GER) d.n.a.	Jules Zutter (SUI)	–
1904	Anton Heida (USA) 36 George Eyser (USA) 36	–	William Merz (USA) 31
1924	Frank Kriz (USA) 9.98	Jan Koutny (TCH) 9.97	Bohumil Morkovsky (TCH) 9.93
1928	Eugen Mack (SUI) 9.58	Emanuel Löffler (TCH) 9.50	Stane Derganc (YUG) 9.46
1932	Savino Guglielmetti (ITA) 18.03	Alfred Jochim (USA) 17.77	Edward Carmichael (USA) 17.53
1936	Alfred Schwarzmann (GER) 19.200	Eugen Mack (SUI) 18.967	Matthias Volz (GER) 18.467
1948	Paavo Aaltonen (FIN) 39.10	Olavi Rove (FIN) 39.00	János Mogyorosi-Klencs (HUN) 38.50 Ferenc Pataki (HUN) 38.50 Leos Sotornik (TCH) 38.50
1952	Viktor Chukarin (URS) 19.20	Masao Takemoto (JPN) 19.15	Tadao Uesako (JPN) 19.10 Takashi Ono (JPN) 19.10
1956	Helmuth Bantz (GER) 18.85 Valentin Muratov (URS) 18.85	–	Yuriy Titov (URS) 18.75
1960	Takashi Ono (JPN) 19.350 Boris Shakhlin (URS) 19.350	–	Vladimir Portnoi (URS) 19.225
1964	Haruhiro Yamashita (JPN) 19.600	Viktor Lisitsky (URS) 19.325	Hannu Rantakari (FIN) 19.300
1968	Mikhail Voronin (URS) 19.000	Yukio Endo (JPN) 18.950	Sergey Diomidov (URS) 18.925
1972	Klaus Koste (GDR) 18.850	Viktor Klimenko (URS) 18.825	Nikolay Andrianov (URS) 18.800
1976	Nikolay Andrianov (URS) 19.450	Mitsuo Tsukahara (JPN) 19.375	Hiroshi Kajiyama (JPN) 19.275
1980	Nikolay Andrianov (URS) 19.825	Aleksandr Dityatin (URS) 19.800	Roland Brückner (GDR) 19.775
1984	Lou Yun (CHN) 19.950	Li Ning (CHN) 19.825 Koji Gushiken (JPN) 19.825 Mitchell Gaylord (USA) 19.825 Shinje Morisue (JPN) 19.825	–
1988	Lou Yun (CHN) 19.875	Sylvio Kroll (GDR) 19.862	Park Jong-Hoon (KOR) 19.775
1992	Vitali Shcherbo (EUN) 9.856pts	Grigori Misyutin (EUN) 9.781	Yoo Ok-Youl (KOR) 9.762

1900, 1906–1920 Event not held.

GYMNASTICS MEDAL RESULTS — WOMEN

	GOLD	SILVER	BRONZE
Team			
1928	Netherlands 316.75pts	Italy 289.00	Great Britain 258.25
1936	Germany 506.50pts	Czechoslovakia 503.60	Hungary 499.00
1948	Czechoslovakia 445.45pts	Hungary 440.55	United States 422.63
1952	Soviet Union 527.03pts	Hungary 520.96	Czechoslovakia 503.32
1956	Soviet Union 444.80pts	Hungary 443.50	Romania 438.20
1960	Soviet Union 382.320pts	Czechoslovakia 373.323	Romania 372.053

1964	Soviet Union 380.890pts	Czechoslovakia 379.989	Japan 377.889
1968	Soviet Union 382.85pts	Czechoslovakia 382.20	GDR 379.10
1972	Soviet Union 380.50pts	GDR 376.55	Hungary 368.25
1976	Soviet Union 390.35pts	Romania 387.15	GDR 385.10
1980	Soviet Union 394.90pts	Romania 393.50	GDR 392.55
1984	Romania 392.20pts	United States 391.20	China 388.60
1988	Soviet Union 395.475pts	Romania 394.125	GDR 390.875
1992	Unified Team 395.666pts	Romania 395.079	USA 394.704

1896–1924, 1932 Event not held.

Individual Combined Exercises

1952	Maria Gorokhovskaya (URS) 76.78	Nina Bocharova (URS) 75.94	Margit Korondi (HUN) 75.82
1956	Larissa Latynina (URS) 74.933	Agnes Keleti (HUN) 74.633	Sofia Muratova (URS) 74.466
1960	Larissa Latynina (URS) 77.031	Sofia Muratova (URS) 76.696	Polina Astakhova (URS) 76.164
1964	Vera Caslavska (TCH) 77.564	Larissa Latynina (URS) 76.998	Polina Astakhova (URS) 76.965
1968	Vera Caslavska (TCH) 78.25	Zinaida Voronina (URS) 76.85	Natalya Muchinskaya (URS) 76.75
1972	Ludmila Tourischeva (URS) 77.025	Karin Janz (GDR) 76.875	Tamara Lazakovitch (URS) 76.850
1976	Nadia Comaneci (ROM) 79.275	Nelli Kim (URS) 78.675	Ludmila Tourischeva (URS) 78.625
1980	Yelena Davydova (URS) 79.150	Maxi Gnauck (GDR) 79.075 Nadia Comaneci (ROM) 79.075	–
1984	Mary Lou Retton (USA) 79.175	Ecaterina Szabo (ROM) 79.125	Simona Pauca (ROM) 78.675
1988	Yelena Chouchounova (URS) 79.662	Daniela Silivas (ROM) 79.637	Svetlana Bogunskaya (URS) 79.40
1992	Tatyana Gutsu (EUN) 39.737pts	Shannon Miller (USA) 39.725	Lavinia Milosovici (ROM) 39.687

Asymmetrical Bars

1952	Margit Korondi (HUN) 19.40	Maria Gorokhovskaya (URS) 19.26	Ágnes Keleti (HUN) 19.16
1956	Agnes Keleti (HUN) 18.966	Larissa Latynina (URS) 18.833	Sofia Muratova (URS) 18.800
1960	Polina Astakhova (URS) 19.616	Larissa Latynina (URS) 19.416	Tamara Lyukhina (URS) 19.399
1964	Polina Astakhova (URS) 19.332	Katalin Makray (HUN) 19.216	Larissa Latynina (URS) 19.199
1968	Vera Caslavska (TCH) 19.650	Karin Janz (GDR) 19.500	Zinaida Voronina (URS) 19.425
1972	Karin Janz (GDR) 19.675	Olga Korbut (URS) 19.450 Erika Zuchold (GDR) 19.450	–
1976	Nadia Comaneci (ROM) 20.00	Teodora Ungureanu (ROM) 19.800	Marta Egervari (HUN) 19.775
1980	Maxi Gnauck (GDR) 19.875	Emila Eberle (ROM) 19.850	Steffi Kräker (GDR) 19.775 Melita Rühn (ROM) 19.775 Maria Filatova (URS) 19.775
1984	Ma Yanhong (CHN) 19.950 Julianne McNamara (USA) 19.950	–	Mary Lou Retton (USA) 19.800
1988	Daniela Silivas (ROM) 20.00	Dagmar Kersten (GDR) 19.987	Yelena Chouchounova (URS) 19.962
1992	Li Lu (CHN) 10.000pts	Tatyana Gutsu (EUN) 9.975	Shannon Miller (USA) 9.962

1896–1948 Event not held.

Balance Beam

1952	Nina Bocharova (URS) 19.22	Maria Gorokhovskaya (URS) 19.13	Margit Korondi (HUN) 19.02
1956	Agnes Keleti (HUN) 18.80	Eva Bosáková (TCH) 18.63 Tamara Manina (URS) 18.63	–
1960	Eva Bosakova (TCH) 19.283	Larissa Latynina (URS) 19.233	Sofia Muratova (URS) 19.232
1964	Vera Caslavska (TCH) 19.449	Tamara Manina (URS) 19.399	Larissa Latynina (URS) 19.382
1968	Natalya Kuchinskaya (URS) 19.650	Vera Caslavska (TCH) 19.575	Larissa Petrik (URS) 19.250
1972	Olga Korbut (URS) 19.575	Tamara Lazakovitch (URS) 19.375	Karin Janz (GDR) 18.975
1976	Nadia Comaneci (ROM) 19.950	Olga Korbut (URS) 19.725	Teodora Ungureanu (ROM) 19.700
1980	Nadia Comaneci (ROM) 19.800	Yelena Davydova (URS) 19.750	Natalya Shaposhnikova (URS) 19.725
1984	Simona Pauca (ROM) 19.800 Ecaterina Szabo (ROM) 19.800	–	Kathy Johnson (USA) 19.650

| 1988 | Daniela Silivas (ROM) 19.924 | Yelena Chouchounova (URS) 19.875 | Gabriela Potorac (ROM) 19.837 Phoebe Mills (USA) 19.837 |
| 1992 | Tatyana Lyssenko (EUN) 9.975pts | Li Lu (CHN) 9.912 Shannon Miller (USA) 9.912 | – |

1896–1948 Event not held.

Floor Exercises

1952	Agnes Keleti (HUN) 19.36	Maria Gorokhovskaya (URS) 19.20	Margit Korondi (HUN) 19.00
1956	Larissa Latynina (URS) 18.733 Agnes Keleti (HUN) 18.733	–	Elena Leustean (ROM) 18.70
1960	Larissa Latynina (URS) 19.583	Polina Astakhova (URS) 19.532	Tamara Lyukhina (URS) 19.449
1964	Larissa Latynina (URS) 19.599	Polina Astakhova (URS) 19.500	Anikó Jánosi (HUN) 19.300
1968	Larissa Petrik (URS) 19.675 Vera Caslavska (TCH) 19.675	–	Natalya Kuchinskaya (URS) 19.650
1972	Olga Korbut (URS) 19.575	Ludmila Tourischeva (URS) 19.550	Tamara Lazakovitch (URS) 19.450
1976	Nelli Kim (URS) 19.850	Ludmila Tourischeva (URS) 19.825	Nadia Comaneci (ROM) 19.750
1980	Nelli Kim (URS) 19.875 Nadia Comaneci (ROM) 19.875	–	Natalya Shaposhnikova (URS) 19.825 Maxi Gnauck (GDR) 19.825
1984	Ecaterina Szabo (ROM) 19.975	Julianne McNamara (USA) 19.950	Mary Lou Retton (USA) 19.775
1988	Daniela Silivas (ROM) 19.937	Svetlana Bogunskaya (URS) 19.887	Diana Doudeva (BUL) 19.850
1992	Lavinia Milosovici (ROM) 10.000pts	Henrietta Onodi (HUN) 9.950	Tatyana Gutsu (EUN) 9.912 Christina Bontas (ROM) 9.912 Shannon Miller (USA) 9.912

1896–1948 Event not held

Horse Vault

1952	Yekaterina Kalinchuk (URS) 19.20	Maria Gorokhovskaya (URS) 19.19	Galina Minaitscheva (URS) 19.16
1956	Larissa Latynina (URS) 18.833	Tamara Manina (URS) 18.800	Ann-Sofi Colling (SWE) 18.733 Olga Tass (HUN) 18.733
1960	Margarita Nikolayeva (URS) 19.316	Sofia Muratova (URS) 19.049	Larissa Latynina (URS) 19.016
1964	Vera Caslavska (TCH) 19.483	Larissa Latynina (URS) 19.283 Birgit Radochla (GER) 19.283	–
1968	Vera Caslavska (TCH) 19.775	Erika Zuchold (GDR) 19.625	Zinaida Voronina (URS) 19.500
1972	Karin Janz (GDR) 19.525	Erika Zuchold (GDR) 19.275	Ludmila Tourischeva (URS) 19.250
1976	Nelli Kim (URS) 19.800	Ludmila Tourischeva (URS) 19.650 Carola Dombeck (GDR) 19.650	–
1980	Natalya Shaposhnikova (URS) 19.725	Steffi Kräker (GDR) 19.675	Melita Rühn (ROM) 19.650
1984	Ecaterina Szabo (ROM) 19.875	Mary Lou Retton (USA) 19.850	Lavinia Agache (ROM) 19.750
1988	Svetlana Bogunskaya (URS) 19.905	Gabriela Potorac (ROM) 19.830	Daniela Silivas (ROM) 19.818
1992	Lavinia Milosovici (ROM) 9.925pts Henrietta Onodi (HUN) 9.925pts	–	Tatyana Lyssenko (EUN) 9.912

1896–1948 Event not held.

Modern Rhythmic

1984	Lori Fung (CAN) 57.950	Doina Staiculescu (ROM) 57.900	Regina Weber (FRG) 57.700
1988	Marina Lobatch (URS) 60.00	Adriana Dounavska (BUL) 59.950	Alexandra Timochenko (URS) 59.875
1992	Aleksandra Timoshenko (EUN) 59.037 pts	Carolina Garcia (ESP) 58.100	Oksana Skaldina (EUN) 57.912

1896–1980 Event not held.

DISCONTINUED EVENTS

Parallel Bars (Men's Teams)

1896	Germany	Greece	Greece

Horizontal Bars (Men's Teams)

1896	Germany [1]

[1] *Walk-over.*

Rope Climbing (Men)

1896	Nicolaos Andriakopoulos (GRE) 23.4sec	Thomas Xenakis (GRE)	– [1]
1904	George Eyser (USA) 7.0sec	Charles Krause (USA) 7.8	Emil Voigt (USA) 9.8
1906	Georgios Aliprantis (GRE) 11.4sec	Béla Erödy (HUN) 13.8	Konstantinos Kozantis (GRE) 13.8
1924	Bedrich Supcik (TCH) 7.2sec	Albert Séguin (FRA)	August Güttinger (SUI) 7.8 Ladislav Vácha (TCH) 7.8
1932	Raymond Bass (USA) 6.7sec	William Galbraith (USA) 6.8	Thomas Connelly (USA) 7.0

[1] *Fritz Hofmann (GER) did not finish*

Club Swinging (Men)

1904	Edward Hennig (USA) 13pts	Emil Voigt (USA) 9	Ralph Wilson (USA) 5
1932	George Roth (USA) 8.97pts	Philip Erenberg (USA) 8.90	William Kuhlmeier (USA) 8.63

Tumbling (Men)

1932	Rowland Wolfe (USA) 18.90pts	Edward Gross (USA) 18.67	William Herrmann (USA) 19.37

Nine Event Competition (Men)

1904	Adolf Spinnler (SUI) 43.49pts	Julius Lenhart (AUT) 43.00	Wilhelm Weber (GER) 41.60

Triathlon (Men)
(Comprised 100 yards, long jump and shot put)

1904	Max Emmerich (USA) 35.70pts	John Grieb (USA) 34.00	William Merz (USA) 33.90

Four Event Competition (Men)

1904	Anton Heida (USA) 161 pts	George Eyser (USA) 152	William Merz (USA) 135

Sidehorse Vault (Men)

1924	Albert Séguin (FRA) 10.00pts	Jean Gounot (FRA) 9.93 François Gangloff (FRA) 9.93	–

Swedish System (Men's Teams)

1912	Sweden 937.46pts	Denmark 898.84	Norway 857.21
1920	Sweden 1364pts	Denmark 1325	Belgium 1094

Free System (Men's Teams)

1912	Norway 114.25pts	Finland 109.25	Denmark 106.25
1920 [1]	Denmark	Norway	–

[1] *Only two teams competed.*

Portable Apparatus (Women's Teams)

1952	Sweden 74.20pts	Soviet Union 73.00	Hungary 71.60
1956	Hungary 75.20pts	Sweden 74.20	Poland 74.00 Soviet Union 74.00

Handball

Magnus Wielander (SWE, 3) and his team-mates went down 22-20 to the Unified Team in a tough men's handball final at Barcelona (Allsport/Pascal Rondeau)

The sport was introduced in 1936 (appropriately, since it was a German invention) and played as an outdoor 11-a-side game. When reintroduced in 1972, it was as an indoor seven-a-side competition. Seven members of the Soviet women's team won gold medals in 1976 and 1980: Lyubov Odinkova, Zinaida Tourchina, Tatyana Kochergina, Ludmila Poradnik, Aldona Neneniene, Natalya Timoshkina and Larissa Karlova. Only Tourchina and Karlova also won a bronze, in 1988. Four male Romanian players have also won medals in three Games, but none of them was gold.

The oldest gold medallist was Yuriy Klimov (URS) aged 36yr 1 day in 1976, while the oldest female was Ludmila Poradnik (URS) in 1980 aged 34yr 200 days. Zinaida Tourchina (URS) won a bronze medal in 1988 aged 42yr 135 days. The youngest gold medallist/medallist was Larissa Karlova (URS) aged 17yr 356 days in 1976, while the youngest male winner was Günther Ortmann (GER) aged 19yr 257 days in 1936. Willy Hufschmid (SUI) won a bronze medal in 1936 aged 17yr 310 days.

The greatest margin of victory was 34 when Yugoslavia beat Kuwait 44-10 in 1980. The comparable margin among the women was 30 when Yugoslavia beat Congo 39-9 also in 1980. The greatest aggregate score was 62 when the FRG team beat Korea 37-25 in 1984. The comparable women's figure was 60 when Korea beat Czechoslovakia 33-27 in 1988. The record score by an individual in one game was 17

by Jasna Kolar-Merdan for the Yugoslavian women when they beat USA 33-20 in 1984. The male record is 13, by Istvan Varga (HUN) against the United States in 1972, and by Kenji Tamamura (JPN) against Hungary in 1988.

A member of the GDR winning team in 1980 was Hans-Georg Beyer, the brother of 1976 shot put champion Udo (who also won a bronze in 1980). To complete an outstanding family trio, their sister Gisela narrowly missed a bronze medal in the ladies discus in Moscow. Their countrywoman Roswitha Krause, a member of the silver medal handball team of 1976 and bronze medal team in 1980, had been a silver medallist in the 4 x 100m freestyle swimming quartet in 1968.

HANDBALL MEDALS TABLE

	Men			Women			
	G	S	B	G	S	B	Total
Soviet Union	3	1	-	2	-	2	8
Yugoslavia	2	-	1	1	1	-	5
Korea	-	1	-	2	1	-	4
Romania	-	1	3	-	-	-	4
GDR	1	-	-	-	1	1	3
Norway	-	-	-	-	2	-	2
Germany	1	-	-	-	-	-	1
Austria	-	1	-	-	-	-	1
Czechoslovakia	-	1	-	-	-	-	1
FRG	-	1	-	-	-	-	1
China	-	-	-	-	-	1	1
France	-	-	1	-	-	-	1
Hungary	-	-	-	-	-	1	1
Poland	-	-	1	-	-	-	1
Sweden	-	1	-	-	-	-	1
Switzerland	-	-	1	-	-	-	1
	7	7	7	5	5	5	36

HANDBALL MEDAL RESULTS

	GOLD	SILVER	BRONZE
Men			
1936[1]	Germany	Austria	Switzerland
1972	Yugoslavia	Czechoslovakia	Romania
1976	Soviet Union	Romania	Poland
1980	GDR	Soviet Union	Romania
1984	Yugoslavia	FRG	Romania
1988	Soviet Union	Korea	Yugoslavia
1992	Unified Team	Sweden	France

1896–1932, 1948–1968 Event not held.
[1] *Field handball played outdoors.*

	GOLD	SILVER	BRONZE
Women			
1976	Soviet Union	GDR	Hungary
1980	Soviet Union	Yugoslavia	GDR
1984	Yugoslavia	Korea	China
1988	Korea	Norway	Soviet Union
1992	Korea	Norway	Unified Team

1896–1972 Event not held

Hockey

The first Olympic hockey game was won by Scotland who beat Germany 4-0 in 1908, with the first goal scored by Iain Laing only two minutes after the start. In those Games, four of the six teams competing represented England, Ireland, Scotland and Wales. From 1928 Olympic hockey was

The Great Britain hockey team which took the gold medals in 1988 after a hiatus of 68 years (Allsport/David Cannon)

dominated by teams from the Indian sub-continent, with India winning eight times and Pakistan three. However, it should be noted that Great Britain, probably the world's strongest team at the time, did not participate in 1932 and 1936. The long-awaited meeting between them, the masters, and India, the pupils, came in the 1948 final which India won 4-0. In 1988, for the first time for 60 years, no team from the sub-continent won a medal.

Interestingly, after years of decline, in 1984 the Great Britain team, as a last-minute replacement for the boycotting Soviet Union, won the bronze – their first medal for 32 years. Then in 1988 the British won the gold medal again, after 68 years.

Several members of Indian teams have won a record three gold medals: Dhyan Chand 1928-36, Richard Allen 1928-36, Randhir Singh 1948-56, Balbir Singh 1948-56, Leslie Claudius 1948-56, Ranganandhan Francis 1948-56, and Udham Singh 1952-56 and 1964. Of these only Claudius and Udham Singh also won a silver each in 1960.

The oldest gold medallist/medallist was Dharam Singh (IND) in 1964 aged 45yr 278 days. The youngest winner was Russell Garcia (GBR) in 1988 aged 18yr 103 days, and the youngest medallist was Haneef Khan (PAK) at 17yr 26 days in 1976. The youngest female champion was Maider

Goni (ESP) in 1992 aged 19yr 24 days (Arlene Boxhall was under 19 as a member of the 1980 Zimbabwe women's team, but she did not actually play in the tournament). The oldest female gold medallist was the Zimbabwe player-coach Anthea Stewart, aged 35yr 253 days. Iveta Sramkova (TCH), in the 1980 silver medal team, was only 16yr 304 days of age.

The highest score ever achieved in international hockey was when India beat the United States 24-1 in 1932. The highest score in a final was also in 1932 when India beat Japan 11-1. Roop Singh (IND), brother of the team captain Dhyan Chand, scored a record 12 goals in the above-mentioned match against the US in 1932. The Indian goalkeepers did not concede a single goal during the 1928 tournament (five games), and only a total of three in 1932 (two games) and 1936 (five games). Over that period the Indians scored a total of 102 goals. The longest game in Olympic hockey lasted 2hr 25min (into the sixth period of extra time) when the Netherlands beat Spain 1-0 in Mexico on 25 October 1968.

Andreas Keller's gold medal in Germany's 1992 team capped a wonderful family achievement, in that his father Carsten won gold in 1972 and his grandfather Erwin silver in 1936. Keller's girlfriend, Anke Wild, also won a silver in the 1992 women's tournament. The 1988 Olympic competitions were particularly noteworthy for family achievements. Sisters Lee & Michelle Capes gained gold medals in the Australian women's team, and the Dutch siblings Marc and Carina Benninga gained bronze medals in their country's respective third placed teams.

HOCKEY MEDALS TABLE

| | Men | | | Women | | | |
	G	S	B	G	S	B	Total
India	8	1	2	-	-	-	11
Great Britain	3	2	4	-	-	1	10
Pakistan	3	3	2	-	-	-	8
Netherlands	-	2	3	1	-	1	7
Germany	1	1	2	-	1	-	5
Australia	-	3	1	1	-	-	5
FRG	1	2	-	-	1	-	4
Spain	1	1	1	-	-	-	3
Soviet Union	-	-	1	-	-	1	2
United States	-	-	1	-	-	1	2
New Zealand	1	-	-	-	-	-	1
Zimbabwe	-	-	-	1	-	-	1
Czechoslovakia	-	-	-	-	1	-	1
Denmark	-	1	-	-	-	-	1
Japan	-	1	-	-	-	-	1
Korea	-	-	-	-	1	-	1
Belgium	-	-	1	-	-	-	1
	17	17	18*	4	4	4	64

* Two bronzes in 1908

HOCKEY MEDAL RESULTS

	GOLD	SILVER	BRONZE
Men			
1908[1]	England	Ireland	Scotland [2]
			Wales [2]
1920	England [3]	Denmark	Belgium
1928	India	Netherlands	Germany
1932	India	Japan	United States
1936	India	Germany	Netherlands
1948	India	Great Britain	Netherlands
1952	India	Netherlands	Great Britain
1956	India	Pakistan	Germany
1960	Pakistan	India	Spain
1964	India	Pakistan	Australia
1968	Pakistan	Australia	India
1972	FRG	Pakistan	India
1976	New Zealand	Australia	Pakistan
1980	India	Spain	Soviet Union
1984	Pakistan	FRG	Great Britain
1988	Great Britain	FRG	Netherlands
1992	Germany	Australia	Pakistan

1896–1906, 1912, 1924 Event not held.

[1] *Great Britain had four teams entered.*

[2] *Tie for third place.*

[3] *Great Britain represented by England team.*

	GOLD	SILVER	BRONZE
Women			
1980	Zimbabwe	Czechoslovakia	Soviet Union
1984	Netherlands	FRG	United States
1988	Australia	Korea	Netherlands
1992	Spain	Germany	Great Britain

1896–1976 Event not held.

Judo

The sport was introduced at Tokyo in 1964 and appropriately the first gold medal was won by Japan's Takehide Nakatani in the lightweight class. However, one of the greatest upsets to a nation's sporting pride then occurred when the giant Dutchman Anton Geesink (1.98m) beat the Japanese favourite for the Open category title in front of 15,000 home supporters at the Nippon Budokan Hall.

Another Dutchman, Wilhelm Ruska, is the only man to win two gold medals at a single Games, with the over 93kg and Open classes in 1972. Hiroshi Saito (JPN) and Peter Seisenbacher (AUT) are the only men to successfully defend their titles, both in 1984 and 1988. Angelo Parisi won a record four medals, with a bronze in 1972 representing Great Britain and then gold and two silvers in 1980 and 1984 representing France. The winning of medals for two different countries at the Olympic Games is rare, but not unique. Parisi was born in Italy, went to Britain as a child and became a citizen, then married a French girl in 1973 and changed his nationality again. Robert Van de Walle (BEL) competed in a record five Olympic judo competitions from 1976 to 1992.

The oldest gold medallist was Ruska when he won the 1972 Open class aged 32yr 11 days, and the youngest was Antal Kovács (HUN) in the 1992 light-heavyweight division aged 20yr 61 days. The oldest medallist was Arthur Schnabel (FRG) with a bronze in the 1984 Open class aged 35yr 329 days, and the youngest medallist was Amiran Totikashvili (URS) with a bronze in the 1988 extra-lightweight class at 19yr 66 days. The fastest throw in Olympic competition was in 4 seconds by Akio Kaminaga (JPN) against Thomas Ong (PHI) in 1964.

The youngest female gold medallist was Kim Mi-Jung (KOR) aged 21yr 122 days while the oldest was Miriam Blasco Soto (ESP) at 28yr 232 days. The oldest medallist was Laetitia Meignan (FRA) aged 32yr 33 days, and the youngest was Ryoko Tamura (JPN) at 16yr 331 days (all the above in 1992, of course).

The biggest of many big men in Olympic judo was Jong Gil Pak (PRK) who was 2.13m tall and weighed 163kg in the 1976 Games. In 1972 the Mongolian lightweight silver medallist Bakhaavaa Buidaa became the first competitor ever to be disqualified for failing a dope test in any international judo competition. An amusing sidelight was provided by the 1976 lightweight gold medal winner Hector Rodriguez (CUB) who said he took up the sport when young in order to defend himself against his six older brothers!

The 1988 Games witnessed another astonishing upset for Japanese judo, with their competitors taking only one gold and three bronze medals. Women's events were contested as a demonstration sport in Seoul, and were added to the official programme in 1992. In 1996 a total limit of 400 competitors for the sport was imposed.

Yasuhiro Yamashita (JPN) enjoyed the highlight of his career with a gold medal at Los Angeles in 1984

JUDO MEDALS TABLE

	Men			Women			Total
	G	S	B	G	S	B	
Japan	16	3	8	-	3	2	32
Soviet Union	7	5	14	-	-	1	27
France	3	3	10	2	-	2	20
Korea	4	5	7	1	-	-	17
Great Britain	-	5	7	-	1	2	15
Cuba	1	3	1	1	1	2	9
GDR	1	2	6	-	-	-	9
FRG	1	4	3	-	-	-	8
Hungary	1	2	4	-	-	-	7
Netherlands	3	-	3	-	-	1	7
United States	-	3	4	-	-	-	7
Brazil	2	1	3	-	-	-	6
Poland	2	2	2	-	-	-	6
Italy	1	1	1	-	1	-	4
Germany	-	1	3	-	-	-	4
Austria	2	-	1	-	-	-	3
Belgium	1	-	1	-	1	-	3
Canada	-	1	2	-	-	-	3
China	-	-	-	1	2	-	3
Switzerland	1	1	1	-	-	-	3
Bulgaria	-	1	1	-	-	-	2
Israel	-	-	1	-	1	-	2
Mongolia	-	1	1	-	-	-	2
Romania	-	-	2	-	-	-	2
Spain	-	-	-	-	2	-	2
Yugoslavia	-	-	2	-	-	-	2
Egypt	-	1	-	-	-	-	1
Australia	-	-	1	-	-	-	1
Czechoslovakia	-	-	1	-	-	-	1
Iceland	-	-	1	-	-	-	1
North Korea (PRK)	-	-	1	-	-	-	1
Turkey	-	-	-	-	-	1	1
	46	45 [1]	92	7	7	14	211

[1] *1972 silver withheld due to disqualification*

JUDO MEDAL RESULTS — MEN

	GOLD	SILVER	BRONZE

Open Category *No Weight Limit*

Year	GOLD	SILVER	BRONZE
1964	Antonius Geesink (NED)	Akio Kaminaga (JPN)	Theodore Boronovskis (AUS) Klaus Glahn (GER)
1972	Willem Ruska (NED)	Vitaliy Kuznetsov (URS)	Jean-Claude Brondani (FRA) Angelo Parisi (GBR)
1976	Haruki Uemura (JPN)	Keith Remfry (GBR)	Shota Chochoshvili (URS) Jeaki Cho (KOR)
1980	Dietmar Lorenz (GDR)	Angelo Parisi (FRA)	András Ozsvar (HUN) Arthur Mapp (GBR)
1984	Yasuhiro Yamashita (JPN)	Mohamed Rashwan (EGY)	Mihai Cioc (ROM) Arthur Schnabel (FRG)

1968, 1988-92 Event not held.

Over 95kg

Year	GOLD	SILVER	BRONZE
1980	Angelo Parisi (FRA)	Dimitar Zaprianov (BUL)	Vladimir Kocman (TCH) Radomir Kovacevic (YUG)
1984	Hitoshi Saito (JPN)	Angelo Parisi (FRA)	Cho Yong-Chul (KOR) Mark Berger (CAN)
1988	Hitoshi Saito (JPN)	Henry Stöhr (GDR)	Cho Yong-Chul (KOR) Grigori Veritchev (URS)
1992	David Khakhaliashvili (EUN)	Naoya Ogawa (JPN)	David Douillet (FRA) Imre Csosz (HUN)

Up to 95kg

Year	GOLD	SILVER	BRONZE
1980	Robert Van de Walle (BEL)	Tengiz Khubuluri (URS)	Dietmar Lorenz (GDR) Henk Numan (NED)
1984	Ha Hyoung-Zoo (KOR)	Douglas Vieira (BRA)	Bjarni Fridriksson (ISL) Gunther Neureuther (FRG)
1988	Aurelio Miguel (BRA)	Marc Meiling (FRG)	Robert Van De Walle (BEL) Dennis Stewart (GBR)
1992	Antal Kovacs (HUN)	Ray Stevens (GBR)	Dmitri Sergeyev (EUN) Theo Meijer (NED)

Up to 86kg

Year	GOLD	SILVER	BRONZE
1980	Jürg Röthlisberger (SUI)	Isaac Azcuy Oliva (CUB)	Detlef Ultsch (GDR) Aleksandr Yatskevich (URS)
1984	Peter Seisenbacher (AUT)	Robert Berland (USA)	Seiki Nose (JPN) Walter Carmona (BRA)
1988	Peter Seisenbacher (AUT)	Vladimir Chestakov (URS)	Ben Spijkers (NED) Akinobu Osako (JPN)
1992	Waldemar Legien (POL)	Pascal Tayot (FRA)	Hirotaki Okada (JPN) Nicolas Gill (CAN)

Up to 78kg

Year	GOLD	SILVER	BRONZE
1980	Shota Khabaleri (URS)	Juan Ferrer La Hera (CUB)	Harald Heinke (GDR) Bernard Tchoullouyan (FRA)
1984	Frank Wieneke (FRG)	Neil Adams (GBR)	Michel Nowak (FRA) Mirces Fratica (ROM)
1988	Waldemar Legien (POL)	Frank Wieneke (FRG)	Torsten Brechot (GDR) Bachir Varayev (URS)
1992	Hidehiko Yoshida (JPN)	Jason Morris (USA)	Kim Byung-joo (KOR) Bertrand Damaisin (FRA)

Up to 71kg

	GOLD	SILVER	BRONZE
1980	Ezio Gamba (ITA)	Neil Adams (GBR)	Karl-Heinz Lehmann (GDR)
			Ravdan Davaadalai (MGL)
1984	Ahn Byeong-Keun (KOR)	Ezio Gamba (ITA)	Luis Onmura (BRA)
			Kerrith Brown (GBR)
1988	Marc Alexandre (FRA)	Sven Loll (GDR)	Michael Swain (USA)
			Guergui Tenadze (URS)
1992	Toshihiko Koga (JPN)	Bertalan Hajtos (HUN)	Chung Hoon (KOR)
			Shay Smadga (ISR)

Up to 65kg

1980	Nikolai Solodukhin (URS)	Tsendying Damdin (MGL)	Ilian Nedkov (BUL)
			Janusz Pawlowski (POL)
1984	Yoshiyuki Matsuoka (JPN)	Hwang Jung-Oh (KOR)	Josef Reiter (AUT)
			Marc Alexandre (FRA)
1988	Lee Kyung-Keun (KOR)	Janusz Pawlowski (POL)	Bruno Carabetta (FRA)
			Yosuke Yamamoto (JPN)
1992	Rogerio Sampaio (BRA)	Jozsef Csak (HUN)	Udo Quellmalz (GER)
			Israel Hernandez (CUB)

Up to 60kg

1980	Thierry Rey (FRA)	Rafael Carbonell (CUB)	Tibor Kincses (HUN)
			Aramby Emizh (URS)
1984	Shinji Hosokawa (JPN)	Kim Jae-Yup (KOR)	Edward Liddie (USA)
			Neil Eckersley (GBR)
1988	Kim Jae-Yup (KOR)	Kevin Asano (USA)	Shinji Hosokawa (JPN)
			Amiran Totikachvili (URS)
1992	Nazim Gousseinov (EUN)	Yoon Hyun (KOR)	Tadanori Koshino (JPN)
			Richard Trautmann (GER)

PREVIOUS WINNERS

Categories changed in 1980

	GOLD	SILVER	BRONZE
Over 93kg			
1964	Isao Inokuma (JPN)	AH Douglas Rogers (CAN)	Parnaoz Chikviladze (URS)
			Anzor Kiknadze (URS)
1972	Wilhelm Ruska (NED)	Klaus Glahn (FRG)	Givi Onashvili (URS)
			Motoki Nishimura (JPN)
1976	Sergey Novikov (URS)	Gunther Neureuther (FRG)	Sumio Endo (JPN)
			Allen Coage (USA)

1968 Event not held.

80kg to 93kg			
1972	Shota Chochoshvili (URS)	David Starbrook (GBR)	Chiaki Ishii (BRA)
			Paul Barth (FRG)
1976	Kazuhiro Ninomiya (JPN)	Ramaz Harshiladze (URS)	David Starbrook (GBR)
			Jürg Röthlisberger (SUI)

1964–1968 Event not held.

70kg to 80kg			
1964	Isao Okano (JPN)	Wolfgang Hofmann (GER)	James Bergman (USA)
			Eui Tae Kim (KOR)
1972	Shinobu Sekine (JPN)	Oh Seung-Lip (KOR)	Brian Jacks (GBR)
			Jean-Paul Coche (FRA)

| 1976 | Isamu Sonoda (JPN) | Valeriy Dvoinikov (URS) | Slavko Obadov (YUG) |
| | | | Park Youngchul (KOR) |

1968 Event not held.

63kg to 70kg

1972	Toyojazu Nomura (JPN)	Anton Zajkowski (POL)	Dietmar Hötger (GDR)
			Anatoliy Novikov (URS)
1976	Vladimir Nevzorov (URS)	Koji Kuramoto (JPN)	Patrick Vial (FRA)
			Marian Talaj (POL)

1964–1968 Event not held.

Up to 63kg

1964	Takehide Nakatani (JPN)	Eric Haenni (SUI)	Oleg Stepanov (URS)
			Aron Bogulubov (URS)
1972	Takao Kawaguchi (JPN)	– [1]	Kim Yong Ik (PRK)
			Jean-Jacques Mounier (FRA)
1976	Hector Rodriguez (CUB)	Chang Eunkyung (KOR)	Felice Mariani (ITA)
			Jozsef Tuncsik (HUN)

1968   Event not held.
[1] *Bakhaavaa Buidaa (MGL) disqualified after positive drug test.*

JUDO MEDALS — WOMEN

GOLD	SILVER	BRONZE

Up to 48kg

| 1992 | Cecile Nowak (FRA) | Ryoko Tamura (JPN) | Hulya Senyurt (TUR) |
| | | | Amarilis Savon (CUB) |

1964-88 Event not held

Up to 52kg

| 1992 | Almudena Munoz (ESP) | Noriko Mizoguchi (JPN) | Li Zhongyun (CHN) |
| | | | Sharon Rendle (GBR) |

1964-88 Event not held

Up to 56kg

| 1992 | Miriam Blasco (ESP) | Nicola Fairbrother (GBR) | Chiyori Tateno (JPN) |
| | | | Driulis Gonzalez (CUB) |

1964-88 Event not held

Up to 61kg

| 1992 | Catherine Fleury (FRA) | Yael Arad (ISR) | Zhang Di (CHN) |
| | | | Yelena Petrova (EUN) |

1964-88 Event not held

Up to 66kg

| 1992 | Odalis Reve (CUB) | Emanuela Pierantozzi (ITA) | Kate Howey (GBR) |
| | | | Heidi Rakels (BEL) |

1964-88 Event not held

Up to 72kg

| 1992 | Kim Mi-jung (KOR) | Yoko Tanabe (JPN) | Laetitia Meignan (FRA) |
| | | | Irene de Kok (NED) |

1964-88 Event not held

Over 72kg

| 1992 | Zhuang Xiaoyan (CHN) | Estela Rodriguez (CUB) | Yoko Sakaue (JPN) |
| | | | Natalia Lupino (FRA) |

1964-88 Event not held

Modern Pentathlon

The five events constituting the modern pentathlon are riding (over an 800m course), fencing (with epee), swimming (300m freestyle), shooting and cross-country running (4000m). Shooting until 1992 was with a rapid-fire pistol over 25m, but in 1996 it will be with an air pistol over 10m. Another change at Atlanta will be the elimination of the team event, and the individual competition will be completed in one day. In recent years it has been suggested that the Triathlon should replace the Modern Pentathlon in future Games, due to the fact that the latter is not practised in as many countries as the IOC would like.

The order of events has differed over the years, as has the points system. Prior to 1956 competitors were given points according to their placings in each event, ie, one point for first place, two points for second etc. Since 1956 points have been allocated according to an international scoring table. It is difficult therefore to compare performers under the two systems, but it is generally accepted that the margin of victory by Willie Grut (SWE) in 1948 was the greatest ever. In that competition, Grut, later the Secretary-General of the sport's governing body (UIPMB), placed first in riding, fencing and swimming, fifth in shooting, and eighth in running.

Captain Willie Grut (SWE) on his way to an overwhelming victory in the 1948 modern pentathlon, winning three of the five disciplines (Hulton-Deutsch)

The most gold medals have been won by András Balczó (HUN) with three, in 1960 (team), 1968 (team) and 1972 (individual). Only Lars Hall (SWE) has won two individual gold medals, in 1952 and 1956. Pavel Lednev (URS) won a record seven medals (two gold, two silver, three bronze), 1968-80, and was also the oldest gold medallist/medallist in 1980 aged 37yr 121 days. The youngest gold medallist/medallist was Aladár Kovácsi (HUN) in 1952 aged 19yr 227 days. Peter Macken of Australia competed in a record five Olympic contests, 1960-76.

Gustaf Dyrssen (SWE), who won the gold medal in 1920 and a silver in 1924, and Sven Thofelt (SWE), who won the gold in 1928, both won silver medals as members of the 1936 Swedish épée fencing team. Thofelt also won a bronze in the Swedish fencing team in 1948, while his son competed in the 1960 modern pentathlon. Dyrssen later became Sweden's IOC representative, and Thofelt became president of the UIPMB.

George Patton (USA), later a famous World War II general, was fifth in 1912 (with results that indicated he was not very good at shooting). Two men have scored maximums of 200 hits in shooting: Charles Leonard (USA) in 1936 and George Horvath (SWE) in 1980. The fastest time ever recorded in the 300m swimming event was 3:10.47 by Gintaras Staskevicius (LTU) in 1992. The other three disciplines are either not measurable or comparable. However, it is noteworthy that the fastest time recorded for the 4000m cross-country run is 12:09.50 by Adrian Parker (GBR) in 1976.

One of the biggest scandals in Olympic history occurred in the fencing segment of the 1976 competition when Boris Onischenko (URS), previous winner of a gold and two silver medals, was disqualified for using an illegal weapon. It transpired that he had tampered with his épée so that it registered a hit even when contact with an opponent had not taken place. Naturally the incident prompted speculation about whether he had used the implement in the 1972 Games, where his fencing victory over Jim Fox cost the Briton the individual bronze medal. By coincidence, Onischenko was also fencing against Fox when the Montreal incident came to light.

MODERN PENTATHLON MEDALS TABLE

	G	S	B	Total
Sweden	9	7	5	21
Hungary	8	7	3	18
Soviet Union	5	6	6	17
United States	-	5	3	8
Italy	2	2	3	7
Finland	-	1	4	5
Poland	3	-	-	3
Germany	1	-	1	2
Great Britain	1	-	1	2
Czechoslovakia	-	1	1	2
France	-	-	2	2
	29	29	29	87

MODERN PENTATHLON MEDAL RESULTS

	GOLD	SILVER	BRONZE

Individual

	GOLD	SILVER	BRONZE
1912	Gösta Lilliehöpök (SWE) 27	Gösta Asbrink (SWE) 28	Georg de Laval (SWE) 30
1920	Gustaf Dyrssen (SWE) 18	Erik de Laval (SWE) 23	Gösta Rüno (SWE) 27
1924	Bo Lindman (SWE) 18	Gustaf Dyrssen (SWE) 39.5	Bertil Uggla (SWE) 45
1928	Sven Thofelt (SWE) 47	Bo Lindman (SWE) 50	Helmuth Kahl (GER) 52
1932	Johan Gabriel Oxenstierna (SWE) 32	Bo Lindman (SWE) 35.5	Richard Mayo (USA) 38.5
1936	Gotthard Handrick (GER) 31.5	Charles Leonard (USA) 39.5	Silvano Abba (ITA) 45.5
1948	Willie Grut (SWE) 16	George Moore (USA) 47	Gösta Gärdin (SWE) 49
1952	Lars Hall (SWE) 32	Gábor Benedek (HUN) 39	István Szondi (HUN) 41
1956	Lars Hall (SWE) 4843	Olavi Nannonen (FIN) 4774.5	Väinö Korhonen (FIN) 4750
1960	Ferenc Németh (HUN) 5024	Imre Nagy (HUN) 4988	Robert Beck (USA) 4981
1964	Ferenc Török (HUN) 5116	Igor Novikov (URS) 5067	Albert Mokeyev (URS) 5039
1968	Björn Ferm (SWE) 4964	András Balczó (HUN) 4953	Pavel Lednev (URS) 4795
1972	András Balczó (HUN) 5412	Boris Onischenko (URS) 5335	Pavel Lednev (URS) 5328
1976	Janusz Pyciak-Peciak (POL) 5520	Pavel Lednev (URS) 5485	Jan Bartu (TCH) 5466
1980	Anatoliy Starostin (URS) 5568	Tamás Szombathelyi (HUN) 5502	Pavel Lednev (URS) 5282
1984	Daniel Massala (ITA) 5469	Svante Rasmuson (SWE) 5456	Carlo Massullo (ITA) 5406
1988	Janos Martinek (HUN) 5404	Carlo Massullo (ITA) 5379	Vakhtang Iagorachvili (URS) 5367
1992	Arkadiusz Skrzypaszek (POL) 5559	Attila Mizser (HUN) 5446	Edouard Zenovka (EUN) 5361

1896–1908 Event not held.

Team

	GOLD	SILVER	BRONZE
1952	Hungary 116	Sweden 182	Finland 213
1956	Soviet Union 13 690.5	United States 13 482	Finland 13 185.5
1960	Hungary 14 863	Soviet Union 14 309	United States 14 192
1964	Soviet Union 14 961	United States 14 189	Hungary 14 173
1968	Hungary 14 325	Soviet Union 14 248	France 13 289 [1]
1972	Soviet Union 15 968	Hungary 15 348	Finland 14 812
1976	Great Britain 15 559	Czechoslovakia 15 451	Hungary 15 395
1980	Soviet Union 16 126	Hungary 15 912	Sweden 15 845
1984	Italy 16 060	United States 15 568	France 15 565
1988	Hungary 15 886	Italy 15 571	Great Britain 15 276
1992	Poland 16 018	Unified Team 15 924	Italy 15 760

1896–1948 Event not held.

[1] *Sweden finished third in 1968 but were disqualified when a drug test indicated that a member of the team had an excessive level of alcohol.*

Rowing

Rowing for men was first held at the 1900 Games over a 1750m course on the river Seine in Paris. In 1904 the course measured 2 miles (3219m), in 1908 it was 1.5 miles (2414m) and in 1948 1 mile 300 yards (1883m). Women's rowing was introduced in 1976 over a 1000m course, but since 1988 both men and women have raced over a standard 2000m course. Even though in recent Games rowing has been held on still water, rather than flowing rivers as in the past, water and weather conditions vary too much to allow official Olympic records. It is worthy of note, however, that the fastest average speed achieved by a men's eight over the full course was 21.85km/h when the Canadian crew clocked 5:29.53 in 1992. In a 1992 heat the Romanian crew averaged 22.77km/h for the first 500m. The 1992 Canadian women's eight won the final in 6:02.62 averaging 19.85km/h. The 1988 GDR women's crew averaged 20.65km/h for the first 500m in a repechage. The narrowest winning margin in an Olympic final was 0.1sec in the 1924 pairs, although the 1932 coxed fours may actually have been closer. Since automatic timing was introduced, the smallest margin has been 0.14sec in the 1992 men's eights.

One of the first winning crews in the Games, the 1900 German four, contained three brothers, Oskar, Gustav and Carl Gossler, the latter as coxswain. This was the beginning of a tradition of sibling participation and success which reached a landmark at Moscow in 1980 when the Landvoigt twins (GDR) beat the Pimenov twins (URS) in the coxless pairs final – and caused problems at the medal ceremony. Similarly, in the 1992 coxed pairs, Jonathan and Greg Searle of Great Britain beat the Italian defending champions, Carmine and Giuseppe Abbagnale. When the latter pair won in 1988, their younger brother Agostino also won a gold in the quadruple sculls event. Fathers and sons have had great success in the sport, but usually independently of each other. The most famous are: the Beresfords (GBR) – Julius with a silver in 1912, and Jack with five medals (see below) in the next five Games; the Costellos (USA) – Paul winning three golds in the 1920s and son Bernard a silver in 1956; the Kellys (USA) – John Sr winning three gold medals (see below) and John Jr a bronze in 1956; and the Nickalls (GBR) – Guy Sr winning a gold in the 1908 eight and Guy Jr gaining two silvers in the 1920 and 1928 crews. However, the Burnells (GBR) – Charles (1908) and Richard (1948) – are the only father and son in Olympic rowing to both win gold medals.

Seven oarsmen have won a record three gold medals: John Kelly (USA) 1920-24; his cousin Paul Costello (USA) 1920-28; Jack Beresford (GBR) 1924, 1932-36; Vyacheslav Ivanov (URS) 1956-64; Siegfried Brietzke (GDR) 1972-80; Pertti Karppinen (FIN) 1976-84; and Steve Redgrave (GBR) 1984-92. Beresford also won two silvers, to be the most successful Olympic rower of all time. Ivanov and Karppinen are the only men to win three individual golds, while Beresford, again, is the only oarsman to win medals at five Games, 1920-36. Ivanov had an unfortunate experience after his first title win in Melbourne. He excitedly threw his medal into the air and lost it in the waters of Lake Wendouree. It was never recovered and later the IOC gave him a replacement.

The oldest gold medallist was Robert Zimonyi who coxed the United States eight in 1964 aged 46yr 180 days. In 1948 he had won a bronze coxing a pair from his native Hungary. The oldest actual oarsman to win a gold medal was Guy Nickalls (GBR) in the 1908 eight aged 41yr 261 days. His compatriot Julius Beresford won his silver medal (see above) aged 44yr 20 days. The youngest gold medal oarsman was Giliante D'Este (ITA) in 1928 aged 18yr 141 days, while the youngest medallist oarsman was Australian Walter Howell in 1956 at 16yr 346 days. The youngest gold medallist was the unknown French boy who coxed the winning Dutch pair in 1900. Believed to have been under 10 years of age, he was recruited at the last moment from the spectators to replace Hermanus Brockmann, their cox in the heats, who was considered to be too heavy. Incidentally, Brockmann coxed the Dutch fours to a silver medal and the eight to a bronze. Of the many other young winning coxes over the years, the youngest known for certain was another French boy, Noël Vandernotte, in the 1936 pairs and fours aged 12yr 232 days. The latter crew included his father and uncle.

In women's rowing the youngest gold medal oarswoman was Andrea Kurth (GDR) in 1976 aged 18yr 298 days, while the youngest medallist was Rodica Puscatu (ROM) at 18yr 83 days in 1980. The youngest female coxswain was Sabine Hess (GDR) in 1976 aged 17yr 297 days, and Lynn Silliman was 17yr 92 days old when she coxed the US eight to a bronze in 1976. The oldest female gold medallist oarswoman was Kay Worthington (CAN) in 1992 aged 32yr 225 days, and the oldest to win a medal was Antonina Zelikovich-Dumcheva, of the Unified team, in 1992 at 34yr 166 days. The oldest female coxswain to win a gold was Canadian Lesley Thompson in 1992 aged 32yr 317 days, while the oldest to win a medal was Ecaterina Oancia (ROM) at 34 yr 185 days in 1988.

The US oarsman Conn Findlay, winner of 2 golds and a bronze in coxed pairs 1956-64, also won a yachting bronze medal in 1976 in the Tempest class.

In 1996 several changes to the programme include the deletion of men's coxed pairs and fours, and women's coxless fours. New events include men's and women's lightweight double sculls and men's lightweight coxless fours.

ROWING MEDALS TABLE

	Men			Women			
	G	S	B	G	S	B	Total
United States	28	20	16	1	5	2	72
GDR	20	4	7	13	3	1	48
Soviet Union	11	14	6	1	6	5	43
Great Britain	18	15	6	-	-	-	39
Germany	15	10	8	2	1	2	38
Italy	12	11	9	-	-	-	32
Romania	2	4	2	8	6	5	27
Canada	4	6	9	3	2	2	26
France	4	13	9	-	-	-	26
Switzerland	4	7	9	-	-	-	20
Netherlands	4	4	6	-	1	1	16

							Total
Australia	5	4	4	-		1	14
FRG	4	4	4	-		2	14
Denmark	3	3	6	-		1	13
Czechoslovakia	2	2	7	-			11
New Zealand	3	2	5	-		1	11
Norway	1	4	6				11
Poland	-	1	9	-		1	11
Bulgaria	-		1	2	3	4	10
Belgium		6	1	-	1	1	9
Finland	3	3					6
Austria	-	3	2				5
Yugoslavia	1	1	3				5
Greece	1	2	1				4
Argentina	1	1					4
Uruguay	1		3				4
China				-	1	2	3
Hungary		1	2				3
Slovenia			2				2
Sweden		2					2
Spain		1					1
Russia	-	-	1				1
	146	146	149	30	30	30	531

ROWING MEDAL RESULTS — MEN

	GOLD	SILVER	BRONZE
Single Sculls			
1900	Henri Barrelet (FRA) 7:35.6	André Gaudin (FRA) 7:41.6	St George Ashe (GBR) 8:15.6
1904	Frank Greer (USA) 10:08.5	James Juvenal (USA) 2 lengths	Constance Titus (USA) 1 length
1906	Gaston Delaplane (FRA) 5:53.4	Joseph Larran (FRA) 6:07.2	–
1908	Harry Blackstaffe (GBR) 9:26.0	Alexander McCulloch (GBR) 1 length	Bernhard von Gaza (GER) d.n.a. / Károly Levitzky (HUN) d.n.a.
1912	William Kinnear (GBR) 7:47.6	Potydore Veirman (BEL) 1 length	Everard Butter (CAN) d.n.a. / Mikhail Kusik (RUS) d.n.a.
1920	John Kelly (USA) 7:35.0	Jack Beresford (GBR) 7:36.0	Clarence Hadfield d'Arcy (NZL) 7:48.0
1924	Jack Beresford (GBR) 7:49.2	William Garrett-Gilmore (USA) 7:54.0	Josef Schneider (SUI) 8:01.1
1928	Henry Pearce (AUS) 7:11.0	Kenneth Myers (USA) 7:20.8	David Collett (GBR) 7:19.8
1932	Henry Pearce (AUS) 7:44.4	William Miller (USA) 7:45.2	Guillermo Douglas (URU) 8:13.6
1936	Gustav Schäfer (GER) 8:21.5	Josef Hasenöhri (AUT) 8:25.8	Daniel Barrow (USA) 8:28.0
1948	Mervyn Wood (AUS) 7:24.4	Eduardo Risso (URU) 7:38.2	Romolo Catasta (ITA) 7:51.4
1952	Yuriy Tyukalov (URS) 8:12.8	Mervyn Wood (AUS) 8:14.5	Teodor Kocerka (POL) 8:19.4
1956	Vyacheslav Ivanov (URS) 8:02.5	Stuart Mackenzie (AUS) 8:07.0	John Kelly (USA) 8:11.8
1960	Vyacheslav Ivanov (URS) 7:13.96	Achim Hill (GER) 7:20.21	Teodor Kocerka (POL) 7:21.26
1964	Vyacheslav Ivanov (URS) 8:22.51	Achim Hill (GER) 8:26.34	Gottfried Kottmann (SUI) 8:29.68
1968	Henri Jan Wienese (NED) 7.47.80	Jochen Meissner (FRG) 7:52.00	Alberto Demiddi (ARG) 7:57.19
1972	Yuriy Malishev (URS) 7:10.12	Alberto Demiddi (ARG) 7:11.53	Wolfgang Gueldenpfennig (GDR) 7:14.45
1976	Pertti Karpinnen (FIN) 7:29.03	Peter Kolbe (FRG) 7: 31.67	Joachim Dreifke (GDR) 7:38.03
1980	Pertti Karpinnen (FIN) 7:09.61	Vasiliy Yakusha (URS) 7:11.66	Peter Kersten (GDR) 7:14.88
1984	Pertti Karppinen (FIN) 7:00.24	Peter Kolbe (FRG) 7:02.19	Robert Mills (CAN) 7:10.38
1988	Thomas Lange (GDR) 6:49.86	Peter Kolbe (FRG) 6:54.77	Eric Verdonk (NZL) 6:58.86
1992	Thomas Lange (GER) 6:51.40	Vaclav Chalupa (TCH) 6:52.93	Kajetan Broniewski (POL) 6:56.82

1896 Event not held.

Matthew Pinsent and Steven Redgrave (GBR), coxless pairs champions in 1992 (Allsport/David Cannon)

Double Sculls

1904	United States 10:03.2	United States d.n.a	United States d.n.a.
1920	United States 7:09.0	Italy 7:19.0	France 7:21.0
1924	United States 7:45.0	France 7:54.8	Switzerland d.n.a.
1928	United States 6:41.4	Canada 6:51.0	Austria 6:48.8
1932	United States 7:17.4	Germany 7:22.8	Canada 7:27.6
1936	Great Britain 7:20.8	Germany 7:26.2	Poland 7:36.2
1948	Great Britain 6:51.3	Denmark 6:55.3	Uruguay 7:12.4
1952	Argentina 7:32.2	Soviet Union 7:38.3	Uruguay 7:43.7
1956	Soviet Union 7:24.0	United States 7:32.2	Australia 7:37.4
1960	Czechoslovakia 6:47.50	Soviet Union 6:50.49	Switzerland 6:50.59
1964	Soviet Union 7:10.66	United States 7:13.16	Czechoslovakia 7:14.23
1968	Soviet Union 6:51.82	Netherlands 6:52.80	United States 6:54.21
1972	Soviet Union 7:01.77	Norway 7:02.58	GDR 7:05.55
1976	Norway 7:13.20	Great Britain 7:15.26	GDR 7:17.45
1980	GDR 6:24.33	Yugoslavia 6:26.34	Czechoslovakia 6:29.07
1984	United States 6:36.87	Belgium 6:38.19	Yugoslavia 6:39.59
1988	Netherlands 6:21.13	Switzerland 6:22.59	Soviet Union 6:22.87
1992	Australia 6:17.32	Austria 6:18.42	Netherlands 6:22.82

1896–1900, 1906–1912 Event not held.

Coxless Quadruple Sculls

1976	GDR 6:18.65	Soviet Union 6:19.89	Czechoslovakia 6:21.77
1980	GDR 5:49.81	Soviet Union 5:51.47	Bulgaria 5:52.38
1984	FRG 5:57.55	Australia 5:57.98	Canada 5:59.07
1988	Italy 5:53.37	Norway 5:55.08	GDR 5:56.13
1992	Germany 5:45.17	Norway 5:47.09	Italy 5:47.33

1896–1972 Event not held.

Coxless Pairs

1904	United States 10:57.0	United States d.n.a.	United States d.n.a.
1908	Great Britain 9:43.0	Great Britain 2.5 lengths	Canada
			Germany

1924	Netherlands 8:19.4	France 8:21.6	–
1928	Germany 7:06.4	Great Britain 7:08.08	United States 7:20.4
1932	Great Britain 8:00.0	New Zealand 8:02.4	Poland 8:08.2
1936	Germany 8:16.1	Denmark 8:19.2	Argentina 8:23.0
1948	Great Britain 7:21.1	Switzerland 7:23.9	Italy 7:31.5
1952	United States 8:20.7	Belgium 8:23.5	Switzerland 8:32.7
1956	United States 7:55.4	Soviet Union 8:03.9	Austria 8:11.8
1960	Soviet Union 7:02.01	Austria 7:03.69	Finland 7:03.80
1964	Canada 7:32.94	Netherlands 7:33.40	Germany 7:38.63
1968	GDR 7:26.56	United States 7:26.71	Denmark 7:31.84
1972	GDR 6:53.16	Switzerland 6:57.06	Netherlands 6:58.70
1976	GDR 7:23.31	United States 7:26.73	FRG 7:30.03
1980	GDR 6:48.01	Soviet Union 6:50.50	Great Britain 6:51.47
1984	Romania 6:45.39	Spain 6:48.47	Norway 6:51.81
1988	Great Britain 6:36.84	Romania 6:38.06	Yugoslavia 6:41.01
1992	Great Britain 6:27.72	Germany 6:32.68	Slovenia 6:33.43

1896–1906, 1912–1920 Event not held.

Coxed Pairs

1900	Netherlands 7:34.2	France I 7:34.4	France II 7:57.2
1906 [1]	Italy I 4:23.0	Italy II 4:30.0	France d.n.a.
1906 [2]	Italy 7:32.4	Belgium 8:03.0 [3]	France 8:08.6
1920	Italy 7:56.0	France 7:57.0	Switzerland d.n.a.
1924	Switzerland 8:39.0	Italy 8:39.1	United States 3m
1928	Switzerland 7:42.6	France 7:48.4	Belgium 7:59.4
1932	United States 8:25.8	Poland 8:31.2	France 8:41.2
1936	Germany 8:36.9	Italy 8:49.7	France 8:54.0
1948	Denmark 8:00.5	Italy 8:12.2	Hungary 8:25.2
1952	France 8:28.6	Germany 8:32.1	Denmark 8:34.9
1956	United States 8:26.1	Germany 8:29.2	Soviet Union 8:31.0
1960	Germany 7:29.14	Soviet Union 7:30.17	United States 7:34.58
1964	United States 8:21.23	France 8:23.15	Netherlands 8:23.42
1968	Italy 8:04.81	Netherlands 8:06.80	Denmark 8:08.07
1972	GDR 7:17.25	Czechoslovakia 7:19.57	Romania 7:21.36
1976	GDR 7:58.99	Soviet Union 8:01.82	Czechoslovakia 8:03.28
1980	GDR 7:02.54	Soviet Union 7:03.35	Yugoslavia 7:04.92
1984	Italy 7:05.99	Romania 7:11.21	United States 7:12.81
1988	Italy 6:58.79	GDR 7:00.63	Great Britain 7:01.95
1992	Great Britain 6:49.83	Italy 6:50.98	Romania 6:51.58

1896, 1904, 1908–1912 Event not held.
[1] *Over 1000m.*
[2] *Over 1600m.*
[3] *Greek cox*

Coxless Fours

1904	United States 9:05.8	United States d.n.a.	United States d.n.a.
1908	Great Britain 8:34.0	Great Britain 1.5 lengths	Netherlands
			Canada
1924	Great Britain 7:08.6	Canada 7:18.0	Switzerland 2 lengths
1928	Great Britain 6:36.0	United States 6:37.0	Italy 6:31.6
1932	Great Britain 6:58.2	Germany 7:03.0	Italy 7:04.0
1936	Germany 7:01.8	Great Britain 7:06.5	Switzerland 7:10.6
1948	Italy 6:39.0	Denmark 6:43.5	United States 6:47.7
1952	Yugoslavia 7:16.0	France 7:18.9	Finland 7:23.3
1956	Canada 7:08.8	United States 7:18.4	France 7:20.9
1960	United States 6:26.26	Italy 6:28.78	Soviet Union 6:29.62
1964	Denmark 6:59.30	Great Britain 7:00.47	United States 7:01.37

1968	GDR 6:39.18	Hungary 6:41.64	Italy 6:44.01
1972	GDR 6:24.27	New Zealand 6:25.64	FRG 6:28.41
1976	GDR 6:37.42	Norway 6:41.22	Soviet Union 6:42.52
1980	GDR 6:08.17	Soviet Union 6:11.81	Great Britain 6:16.58
1984	New Zealand 6.03.48	United States 6:06.10	Denmark 6:07.72
1988	GDR 6:03.11	United States 6:05.53	FRG 6:06.22
1992	Australia 5:55.04	USA 5:56.68	Slovenia 5:58.24

1896–1900, 1906, 1912–1920 Event not held.

Coxed Fours

1900 [1]	Germany 5:59.0	Netherlands 6:33.0	Germany 6:35.0
1900 [1]	France 7:11.0	France 7.18.0	Germany 7:18.2
1906	Italy 8:13.0	France d.n.a.	France d.n.a.
1912	Germany 6:59.4	Great Britain 2 lengths	Norway d.n.a.
			Denmark d.n.a.
1920	Switzerland 6:54.0	United States 6:58.0	Norway 7:02.0
1924	Switzerland 7:18.4	France 7:21.6	United States 1 length
1928	Italy 6:47.8	Switzerland 7:03.4	Poland 7:12.8
1932	Germany 7:19.0	Italy 7:19.2	Poland 7:26.8
1936	Germany 7:16.2	Switzerland 7:24.3	France 7:33.3
1948	United States 6:50.3	Switzerland 6:53.3	Denmark 6:58.6
1952	Czechoslovakia 7:33.4	Switzerland 7:36.5	United States 7:37.0
1956	Italy 7:19.4	Sweden 7:22.4	Finland 7:30.9
1960	Germany 6:39.12	France 6:41.62	Italy 6:43.72
1964	Germany 7:00.44	Italy 7:02.84	Netherlands 7:06.46
1968	New Zealand 6:45.62	GDR 6:48.20	Switzerland 6:49.04
1972	FRG 6:31.85	GDR 6:33.30	Czechoslovakia 6:35.64
1976	Soviet Union 6:40.22	GDR 6:42.70	FRG 6:46.96
1980	GDR 6:14.51	Soviet Union 6:19.05	Poland 6:22.52
1984	Great Britain 6:18.64	United States 6:20.28	New Zealand 6:23.68
1988	GDR 6:10.74	Romania 6:13.58	New Zealand 6:15.78
1992	Romania 5:59.37	Germany 6:00.34	Poland 6:03.27

1896, 1904, 1908 Event not held.
[1] *Two separate finals were held in 1900.*

Eights

1900	United States 6:09.8	Belgium 6:13.8	Netherlands 6:23.0
1904	United States 7:50.0	Canada d.n.a.	–
1908	Great Britain I 7:52.0	Belgium 2 lengths	Great Britain
			Canada
1912	Great Britain I 6:15.0	Great Britain II 6:19.0	Germany d.n.a.
1920	United States 6:02.6	Great Britain 6:05.0	Norway 6:36.0
1924	United States 6:33.4	Canada 6:49.0	Italy 0.75 length
1928	United States 6:03.2	Great Britain 6:05.6	Canada 6:03.8
1932	United States 6:37.6	Italy 6:37.8	Canada 6:40.4
1936	United States 6:25.4	Italy 6:26.0	Germany 6:26.4
1948	United States 5:56.7	Great Britain 6:06.9	Norway 6:10.3
1952	United States 6:25.9	Soviet Union 6:31.2	Australia 6:33.1
1956	United States 6:35.2	Canada 6:37.1	Australia 6:39.2
1960	Germany 5:57.18	Canada 6:01.52	Czechoslovakia 6:04.84
1964	United States 6:18.23	Germany 6:23.29	Czechoslovakia 6:25.11
1968	FRG 6:07.00	Australia 6:07.98	Soviet Union 6:09.11
1972	New Zealand 6:08.94	United States 6:11.61	GDR 6:11.67
1976	GDR 5:58.29	Great Britain 6:00.82	New Zealand 6.03.51
1980	GDR 5:49.05	Great Britain 5:51.92	Soviet Union 5:52.66
1984	Canada 5:41.32	United States 5:41.74	Australia 5:42.40
1988	FRG 5:46.05	Soviet Union 5:48.01	United States 5:48.26

| 1992 | Canada 5:29.53 | Romania 5:29.67 | Germany 5:31.00 |

1896, 1906 Event not held.

DISCONTINUED EVENTS

GOLD	SILVER	BRONZE

Naval Rowing Boats (200m)

| 1906 | Italy 10:45.0 | Greece d.n.a. | Greece d.n.a. |

16-Man Naval Rowing Boats (3000m)

| 1906 | Greece 16:35.0 | Greece 17:09.5 | Italy d.n.a. |

Coxed Fours (Inriggers)

| 1912 | Denmark 7:47.0 | Sweden 1 length | Norway d.n.a. |

ROWING MEDAL RESULTS — WOMEN

Women's rowing was introduced in 1976 over a course of 1000 metres. From 1988 it was over 2000m.

	GOLD	SILVER	BRONZE

Single Sculls

1976	Christine Scheiblich (GDR) 4:05.56	Joan Lind (USA) 4:06.21	Elena Antonova (URS) 4:10.24
1980	Sandra Toma (ROM) 3:40.69	Antonina Makhina (URS) 3:41.65	Martina Schröter (GDR) 3:43.54
1984	Valeria Racila (ROM) 3:40.68	Charlotte Geer (USA) 3:43.89	Ann Haesebrouck (BEL) 3:45.72
1988	Jutta Behrednt (GDR) 7:47.19	Anne Marden (USA) 7:50.28	Magdalene Gueorguieva (BUL) 7:53.65
1992	Elisabeta Lipa (ROM) 7:25.54	Annelies Bredael (BEL) 7:26.64	Silken Laumann (CAN) 7:28.85

Double Sculls

1976	Bulgaria 3:44.36	GDR 3:47.86	Soviet Union 3:49.93
1980	Soviet Union 3:16.27	GDR 3:17.63	Romania 3:18.91
1984	Romania 3:26.75	Netherlands 3:29.13	Canada 3:29.82
1988	GDR 7:00.48	Romania 7:04.36	Bulgaria 7:06.03
1992	Germany 6:49.00	Romania 6:51.47	China 6:55.16

Coxed Quadruple Sculls

1976	GDR 3:29.99	Soviet Union 3:32.49	Romania 3:32.76
1980	GDR 3:15.32	Soviet Union 3:15.73	Bulgaria 3:16.10
1984	Romania 3:14.11	United States 3:15.57	Denmark 3:16.02
1988*	GDR 6:21.06	Soviet Union 6:23.47	Romania 6:23.81
1992	Germany 6:20.18	Romania 6:24.34	Unified Team 6:25.07

Not coxed.

Coxless Pairs

1976	Bulgaria 4:01.22	GDR 4:01.64	FRG 4:02.35
1980	GDR 3:30.49	Poland 3:30.95	Bulgaria 3:32.39
1984	Romania 3:32.60	Canada 3:36.06	FRG 3:40.50
1988	Romania 7:28.13	Bulgaria 7:31.95	New Zealand 7:35.68
1992	Canada 7:06.22	Germany 7:07.96	USA 7:08.11

Coxed Fours

1976	GDR 3:45.08	Bulgaria 3:38.24	Soviet Union 3:49.38
1980	GDR 3:19.27	Bulgaria 3:20.75	Soviet Union 3:20.92
1984	Romania 3:19.30	Canada 3:21.55	Australia 3:23.29

| 1988 | GDR 6:56.00 | China 6:58.78 | Romania 7:01.13 |

1992 Event not held

Coxless Fours

| 1992 | Canada 6:30.85 | USA 6:31.86 | Germany 6:32.34 |

1976-88 Event not held

Eights

1976	GDR 3:33.32	Soviet Union 3:36.17	United States 3:38.68
1980	GDR 3:03.32	Soviet Union 3:04.29	Romania 3:05.63
1984	United States 2:59.80	Romania 3:00.87	Netherlands 3:02.92
1988	GDR 6:15.17	Romania 6:17.44	China 6:21.83
1992	Canada 6:02.62	Romania 6:06.26	Germany 6:07.80

Shooting

Baron de Coubertin, the founder of the modern Olympic Games, was a pistol shot of note in his youth, and this undoubtedly led to the sport being included in the first Games held in 1896. The first champion was Pantelis Karasevdas (GRE) who won the free rifle event over 200m on 9 April 1896. The number of events has varied considerably, especially in the early celebrations of the Games, from 21 in 1920 to only two in 1932. There were none at all in 1928. Since 1952 there has been some standardization. In 1984 three events for women were introduced, with another added in 1988. For 1996 mixed competition in the skeet and trap events was abolished, and at the same time double trap events for men and women were inaugurated. New regulations were introduced in 1988, in accordance with UIT rules. The leading eight competitors at the end of the designated number of rounds take part in a final shoot-out round, with the target sub-divided into tenths of a point for rifle and pistol shooting. For trap and skeet, each of the leading competitors has 25 extra shots.

The most successful competitor has been Carl Osburn (USA) who won a record 11 medals (five gold, four silver, two bronze) from 1912 to 1924. Six other men have won five gold medals: Konrad Stäheli (SUI) 1900-06; Louis Richardet (SUI) 1900-06; Alfred Lane (USA) 1912-20; Ole Lilloe-Olsen (NOR) 1920-24; Morris Fisher (USA) 1920-24; and Willis Lee (USA) all in 1920, a record for the sport.

However, the only man to win three individual gold medals at one Games was Gudbrand Skatteboe (NOR) in 1906. Lloyd Spooner (USA) competed in 12 events at the 1920 Games, a record in any sport in Olympic history. Lars Madsen (DEN) won gold medals over a record 20-year span, 1900-20. The only woman to win two gold medals was Marina Logvinenko-Dobrancheva of the Unified Team in 1992.

Women first competed, in men's events, in 1968 when three countries, Mexico, Peru and Poland, entered one each. Eulalia Rolinska (POL) and Gladys de Seminario (PER) were the first to compete, finishing 22nd and 31st respectively in the small-bore rifle, prone event. The first medallist was Margaret Murdock (USA) in the 1976 small-bore rifle (three positions). Initially she was listed the winner, but an error was discovered which placed her equal with her team-mate, Lanny Bassham. Then on the count-back rule she was placed second, to the embarrassment of Bassham, who pulled her up to the top of the victory rostrum at the medal ceremony.

The oldest gold medallist in Olympic history, in any sport, was the remarkable Oskar Swahn (SWE) in the 1912 Running Deer team aged 64yr 258 days (his son Alfred was also in the team). At Antwerp in 1920 he became the oldest medallist (72yr 280days) and, indeed, the oldest competitor at any sport in the Olympics ever, when he was again a member of the Swedish Running Deer silver medal team. He qualified for the 1924 Games in his 77th year, but illness prevented him from competing. He died three years later. The youngest winner of a gold medal was Konstantin Lukachik of the Unified Team in the 1992 free pistol aged 16yr 312 days. The oldest female champion was Linda Thom (USA), aged 40yr 212 days when winning the sport pistol in 1984. The youngest woman to win a gold was Yeo Kab-Soon (KOR) in the 1992 air rifle aged 18yr 80 days. The youngest medallists were Marcus Dinwiddie (USA), silver in the 1924 small-bore rifle, prone event, and Ulrike Holmer (FRG), silver in the 1984 standard rifle, both at 16yr 301 days.

John and Sumner Paine (USA) were the first brothers to win gold medals at the Olympic Games, in 1896, while the first twins to do so were Vilhelm and Eric Carlberg (SWE) in 1912. Károly Takács (HUN) was a European pistol champion in the 1930s using his right hand. In 1938, while he was on army training, a grenade blew up in his hand, destroying his right arm. After the war he won the rapid fire pistol event with his left hand at the 1948 and 1952 Games, one of only five shooters to have successfully defended an Olympic title.

The 1960 rapid fire pistol champion, William McMillan (USA), competed in his record sixth Games in 1976. Walter Winans (USA), who had won a gold medal in the 1908 Running Deer event, became the only man to win medals in both sport and artistic events at the same Games in 1912 when he gained a silver in shooting and a gold at sculpture. Winans was born in Russia to Dutch-American parents, and lived most of his life in England – he never set foot in America.

Gerald Ouellette (CAN) won the 1956 small-bore (prone) gold medal with a world record maximum possible score of 600, but it was not accepted as such, as the range was found to be 1.5m short of the regulation 50m distance. Miroslav Varga (TCH) also scored 600 in the 1988 event. When North Korean Li Ho Jun won the same event in 1972 with a score of 599, he was asked how he concentrated so well. He answered that he pretended that he was 'aiming at a capitalist'.

In 1992 Zhang Shan (CHN) became the first woman to win a gold medal in a mixed event and scored a maximum possible 200 in the preliminary round of skeet shooting. François La Fortuno Jr (BEL) competed in a record seven Games, 1952-76, while his father, François Sr, competed over a 36-year span, 1924-60. Philip Neame (GBR) is the only holder of the Victoria Cross to win an Olympic gold medal (1924 Running Deer, team).

One of the oddest occurrences in Olympic shooting came in the 1976 trap shooting event, when 65-year-old Paul Cerutti of Monaco was disqualified for using drugs, even though he had finished 43rd out of 44 competitors – he is the oldest competitor ever to be so penalized.

SHOOTING MEDALS TABLE

	Men [1]			Women			
	G	S	B	G	S	B	Total
United States	42	24	19	2	1	1	89
Soviet Union	18	16	15	4	1	3	57
Sweden	13	23	19	-	-	-	55
Great Britain	13	14	18	-	-	-	45
France	12	16	12	-	-	-	40
Norway	16	9	11	-	-	-	36
Switzerland	11	11	12	-	-	-	34
Greece	5	7	7	-	-	-	19
Italy	6	3	8	-	1	-	18
Finland	3	5	9	-	-	-	17
Denmark	3	8	5	-	-	-	16
GDR	3	8	5	-	-	-	16
Hungary	6	3	6	-	-	-	15
Romania	5	4	4	-	-	-	13
China	3	3	2	2	1	1	12
Germany	4	4	3	-	-	-	11
FRG	3	2	3	1	2	-	11
Canada	3	3	2	1	-	-	9
Czechoslovakia	4	3	2	-	-	-	9
Belgium	2	3	3	-	-	-	8
Bulgaria	1	1	2	-	3	1	8
Poland	2	1	3	-	-	1	7
Japan	1	1	3	-	1	-	6
Yugoslavia	1	-	1	1	1	2	6
Austria	1	1	3	-	-	-	5
Brazil	1	1	1	-	-	-	3
Korea	1	1	-	1	-	-	3
Peru	1	2	-	-	-	-	3
Colombia	-	2	-	-	-	-	2
Netherlands	-	1	1	-	-	-	2
Russia	-	1	1	-	-	-	2
Spain	-	1	1	-	-	-	2
Australia	-	-	1	-	-	1	2
North Korea (PRK)	1	-	-	-	-	-	1
Argentina	-	1	-	-	-	-	1
Chile	-	1	-	-	-	-	1
Latvia	-	1	-	-	-	-	1
Mexico	-	1	-	-	-	-	1

Portugal	-	1	-		-	1
South Africa	-	1	-		-	1
Cuba	-	-	1		-	1
Haiti	-	-	1		-	1
New Zealand	-	-	1		-	1
Mongolia	-	-	-		- 1	1
Venezuela	-	-	1	-	-	1
	185	187	187	12 [2]	11 11	593

[1] *Including female medallists prior to 1984*
[2] *Including female winner of 1992 open Skeet competition*

SHOOTING MEDAL RESULTS — MEN

GOLD	SILVER	BRONZE
Free Pistol (50 metres)		
1896 Sumner Paine (USA) 442	Holger Nielsen (DEN) 280	Nikolaos Morakis (GRE) d.n.a.
1900 Karl Röderer (SUI) 503	Achille Paroche (FRA) 466	Konrad Stäheli (SUI) 453
1906 Georgios Orphanidis (GRE) 221	Jean Fouconnier (FRA) 219	Aristides Rangavis (GRE) 218
1912 Alfred Lane (USA) 499	Peter Dolfen (USA) 474	Charles Stewart (GBR) 470
1920 Karl Frederick (USA) 496	Afranio da Costa (BRA) 489	Alfred Lane (USA) 481
1936 Torsten Ullmann (SWE) 559	Erich Krempel (GER) 544	Charles des Jammonières (FRA) 540
1948 Edwin Vazquez Cam (PER) 545	Rudolf Schnyder (SUI) 539	Torsten Ullmann (SWE) 539
1952 Huelet Benner (USA) 553	Angel Léon de Gozalo (ESP) 550	Ambrus Balogh (HUN) 549
1956 Pentti Linnosvuo (FIN) 556	Makhmud Oumarov (URS) 556	Offutt Pinion (USA) 551
1960 Aleksey Gushchin (URS) 560	Makhmud Oumarov (URS) 552	Yoshihisa Yoshikawa (JPN) 552
1964 Väinö Markkanen (FIN) 560	Franklin Green (USA) 557	Yoshihisa Yoshikawa (JPN) 554
1968 Grigory Kossykh (URS) 562	Heinz Mertel (FRG) 562	Harald Vollmar (GDR) 560
1972 Ragnar Skanakar (SWE) 567	Dan Iuga (ROM) 562	Rudolf Dollinger (AUT) 560
1976 Uwe Potteck (GDR) 573	Harald Vollmar (GDR) 567	Rudolf Dollinger (AUT) 560
1980 Aleksandr Melentyev (URS) 581	Harald Vollmar (GDR) 568	Lubcho Diakov (BUL) 565
1984 Xu Haifeng (CHN) 566	Ragnar Skanaker (SWE) 565	Wang Yifu (CHN) 564
1988 Sorin Babii (ROM) (566+94) 660	Ragnar Skanaker (SWE) (564+93) 657	Igor Bassinski (URS) (570+87) 657
1992 Konstantin Loukachik (EUN) 658	Wang Yifu (CHN) 657	Ragnar Skanaker (SWE) 657
1904, 1908, 1924–1932 Event not held.		
Rapid-Fire Pistol		
1896 Jean Phrangoudis (GRE) 344	Georgios Orphanidis (GRE) 249	Holger Nielsen (DEN) d.n.a.
1900 Maurice Larrouy (FRA) 58	Léon Moreaux (FRA) 57	Eugene Balme (FRA) 57
1906 Maurice Lecoq (FRA) 250	Léon Moreaux (FRA) 249	Aristides Rangavis (GRE) 245
1908 Paul van Asbroeck (BEL) 490	Réginald Storms (BEL) 487	James Gorman (USA) 485
1912 Alfred Lane (USA) 287	Paul Palén (SWE) 286	Johan von Holst (SWE) 283
1920 Guilherme Paraense (BRA) 274	Raymond Bracken (USA) 272	Fritz Zulauf (SUI) 269
1924 Paul Bailey (USA) 18	Vilhelm Carlberg (SWE) 18	Lennart Hannelius (FIN) 18
1932 Renzo Morigi (ITA) 36	Heinz Hax (GER) 36	Domenico Matteucci (ITA) 36
1936 Cornelius van Oyen (GER) 36	Heinz Hax (GER) 35	Torsten Ullmann (SWE) 34
1948 Károly Takács (HUN) 580	Carlos Diaz Sáenz Valiente (ARG) 571	Sven Lundqvist (SWE) 569
1952 Károly Takács (HUN) 579	Szilárd Kun (HUN) 578	Gheorghe Lichiardopol (ROM) 578
1956 Stefan Petrescu (ROM) 587	Evgeniy Shcherkasov (URS) 585	Gheorghe Lichiardopol (ROM) 581
1960 William McMillan (USA) 587	Penttii Linnosvuo (FIN) 587	Aleksandr Zabelin (URS) 587
1964 Penttii Linnosvuo (FIN) 592	Ion Tripsa (ROM) 591	Lubomir Nacovsky (TCH) 590
1968 Jozef Zapedzki (POL) 593	Marcel Rosca (ROM) 591	Renart Suleimanov (URS) 591
1972 Jozef Zapedzki (POL) 593	Ladislav Faita (TCH) 594	Victor Torshin (URS) 593
1976 Norbert Klaar (GDR) 597	Jurgen Wiefel (GDR) 596	Roberto Ferraris (ITA) 595
1980 Corneliu Ion (ROM) 596	Jurgen Wiefel (GDR) 596	Gerhard Petrisch (AUT) 596
1984 Takeo Kamachi (JPN) 595	Corneliu Ion (ROM) 593	Rauno Bies (FIN) 591
1988 Afanasi Kouzmine (URS) (598+100) 698	Ralf Schumann (GDR) (597+99) 696	Zoltan Kovacs (HUN) (594+99) 693
1992 Ralf Schumann (GER) 885pts	Afanasijs Kuzmins (LAT) 882	Vladimir Vokhmianine (EUN) 882
1904, 1928 Event not held.		

Small-Bore Rifle (Prone) [1]

1908 Arthur Carnell (GBR) 387	Harry Humby (GBR) 386	George Barnes (GBR) 385
1912 Frederick Hird (USA) 194	William Milne (GBR) 193	Harry Burt (GBR) 192
1920 Lawrence Nuesslein (USA) 391	Arthur Rothrock (USA) 386	Dennis Fenton (USA) 385
1924 Pierre Coquelin de Lisle (FRA) 398	Marcus Dinwiddie (USA) 396	Josias Hartmann (SUI) 394
1932 Bertil Rönnmark (SWE) 294	Gustavo Huet (MEX) 294	Zoltán Hradetsky-Soos (HUN) 293
1936 Willy Rögeberg (NOR) 300	Ralph Berzsenyi (HUN) 296	Wladyslaw Karás (POL) 296
1948 Arthur Cook (USA) 599	Walter Tomsen (USA) 599	Jonas Jonsson (SWE) 597
1952 Josif Sarbu (ROM) 400	Boris Andreyev (URS) 400	Arthur Jackson (USA) 399
1956 Gerald Ouellette (CAN) 600 [2]	Vasiliy Borissov (URS) 599	Gilmour Boa (CAN) 598
1960 Peter Kohnke (GER) 590	James Hill (USA) 589	Enrico Pelliccione (VEN) 587
1964 László Hammerl (HUN) 597	Lones Wigger (USA) 597	Tommy Pool (USA) 596
1968 Jan Kurka (TCH) 598	László Hammerl (HUN) 598	Ian Ballinger (NZL) 597
1972 Li Ho Jun (PRK) 599	Victor Auer (USA) 598	Nicolae Rotaru (ROM) 595
1976 Karlheinz Smieszek (FRG) 599	Ulrich Lind (FRG) 597	Gennadiy Lushchikov (URS) 595
1980 Karoly Varga (HUN) 599	Hellfried Heilfort (GDR) 599	Petar Zapianov (BUL) 598
1984 Edward Etzel (USA) 599	Michel Bury (FRA) 596	Michael Sullivan (GBR) 596
1988 Miroslav Varga (TCH) (600+103.9) 703.9	Cha Young-Chul (KOR) (598+104.8) 702.8	Attila Zahonyi (HUN) (597+104.9) 701.9
1992 Lee Eun-chul (KOR) 702.5pts	Harald Stenvaag (NOR) 701.4	Stefan Pletikosic (IOP) 701.1

[1] In 1908 and 1912 any position allowed; in 1920 it was a standing position.
[2] Range found to be marginally short – record not allowed.
1896–1906, 1928 Event not held

Small-Bore Rifle – Three Positions (Prone, Kneeling, Standing)

1952 Erling Kongshaug (NOR) 1164	Viho Ylönen (FIN) 1164	Boris Andreyev (URS) 1163
1956 Anatoliy Bogdanov (URS) 1172	Otakar Horinek (TCH) 1172	Nils Sundberg (SWE) 1167
1960 Viktor Shamburkin (URS) 1149	Marat Niyasov (URS) 1145	Klaus Zähringer (GER) 1139
1964 Lones Wigger (USA) 1164	Velitchko Khristov (BUL) 1152	László Hammerl (HUN) 1151
1968 Bernd Klingner (FRG) 1157	John Writer (USA) 1156	Vitaly Parkhimovich (URS) 1154
1972 John Writer (USA) 1166	Lanny Bassham (USA) 1157	Werner Lippoldt (GDR) 1153
1976 Lanny Bassham (USA) 1162	Margaret Murdock (USA) 1162	Werner Seibold (FRG) 1160
1980 Viktor Vlasov (URS) 1173	Bernd Hartstein (GDR) 1166	Sven Johansson (SWE) 1165

Malcolm Cooper (GBR) won the small-bore rifle event for the second time in 1988

1984 Malcolm Cooper (GBR) 1173 | Daniel Kipkow (SUI) 1163 | Alister Allan (GBR) 1162

1988 Malcolm Cooper (GBR) (1180+99.3) 1279.3 Alister Allan (GBR) (1181+94.6) 1275.6 Kirill Ivanov (URS) (1173+102) 1275.0

1992 Gratchia Petikiane (EUN) 1267.4 | Robert Foth (USA) 1266.6 | Ryohei Koba (JPN) 1265.9

1896–1948 Event not held.

Running Game Target

1900 Louis Debray (FRA) 20	P Nivet (FRA) 20	Comte de Lambert (FRA) 19
1972 Lakov Zhelezniak (URS) 569	Hanspeter Bellingrodt (COL) 565	John Kynoch (GBR) 562
1976 Aleksandr Gazov (URS) 579	Aleksandr Kedyarov (URS) 576	Jerzy Greszkiewicz (POL) 571
1980 Igor Sokolov (URS) 589	Thomas Pfeffer (GDR) 589	Aleksandr Gasov (URS) 587
1984 Li Yuwei (CHN) 587	Helmut Bellingrodt (COL) 584	Shiping Huang (CHN) 581
1988 Tor Heiestad (NOR) (591+98) 689	Huang Shiping (CHN) (589+98) 686	Gennadiy Avramenko (URS) (591+95) 685

1896, 1904–1968, 1992 Event not held.

10m Running Target

1992 Michael Jakosits (GER) 673pts | Anatoliy Asrabayev (EUN) 672 | Lubos Racansky (TCH) 670

1896-1988 Event not held

Olympic Trap Shooting

1900 Roger de Barbarin (FRA) 17	René Guyot (FRA) 17	Justinien de Clary (FRA) 17
1906 [1] Gerald Merlin (GBR) 24	Ioannis Peridis (GRE) 23	Sidney Merlin (GBR) 21
1906 [2] Sidney Merlin (GBR) 15	Anastasios Metaxas (GRE) 13	Gerald Merlin (GBR) 12
1908 Walter Ewing (CAN) 72	George Beattie (CAN) 60	Alexander Maunder (GBR) 57 Anastasios Metaxas (GRE) 57
1912 James Graham (USA) 96	Alfred Goeldel-Bronikowen (GER) 94	Harry Blau (URS) 91
1920 Marke Arie (USA) 95	Frank Troeh (USA) 93	Frank Wright (USA) 87
1924 Gyula Halasy (HUN) 98	Konrad Huber (FIN) 98	Frank Hughes (USA) 97
1952 George Généreux (CAN) 192	Knut Holmquist (SWE) 191	Hans Liljedahl (SWE) 191
1956 Galliano Rossini (ITA) 195	Adam Smelczynski (POL) 190	Alessandro Ciceri (ITA) 188
1960 Ion Dumitrescu (ROM) 192	Galliano Rossini (ITA) 191	Sergey Kalinin (URS) 190
1964 Ennio Mattarelli (ITA) 198	Pavel Senichev (URS) 194	William Morris (USA) 194
1968 Robert Braithwaite (GBR) 198	Thomas Garrigus (USA) 196	Kurt Czekalla (GDR) 196
1972 Angelo Scalzone (ITA) 199	Michel Carrega (FRA) 198	Silvano Basagni (ITA) 195
1976 Don Haldeman (USA) 190	Armando Marques (POR) 189	Ubaldesco Baldi (ITA) 189
1980 Luciano Giovanetti (ITA) 198	Rustam Yambulatov (URS) 196	Jorg Damme (GDR) 196
1984 Luciano Giovanetti (ITA) 192	Francisco Boza (PER) 192	Daniel Carlisle (USA) 192
1988 Dmitriy Monakov (URS) (197+25) 222	Miloslav Bednarik (TCH) (197+25) 222	Frans Peeters (BEL) (195+24) 219
1992 Petr Hrdilicka (TCH) 219	Kazumi Watanabe (JPN) 219	Marco Venturini (ITA) 218

[1] *Single shot.*
[2] *Double shot.*
1896, 1904, 1928–1948 Event not held.

Skeet Shooting

1968 Evgeny Petrov (URS) 198	Romano Garagnani (ITA) 198	Konrad Wirnhier (FRG) 198
1972 Konrad Wirnhier (FRG) 195	Evgeny Petrov (URS) 195	Michael Buchheim (GDR) 195
1976 Josef Panacek (TCH) 198	Eric Swinkels (NED) 198	Wieslaw Gawlikowski (POL) 196
1980 Hans Kjeld Rasmussen (DEN) 196	Lars-Goran Carlsson (SWE) 196	Roberto Garcia (CUB) 196
1984 Matthew Dryke (USA) 198	Ole Rasmussen (DEN) 196	Luca Scribani Rossi (ITA) 196
1988 Axel Wegner (GDR) (198+24) 222	Alfonso de Iruarrizaga (CHI) (198+23) 221	Jorge Guardiola (ESP) (196+24) 220
1992 Zhang Shan [1] (CHN) 233pts	Juan Jorge Giha (PER) 222	Bruno Rossetti (ITA) 222

1896–1964 Event not held.

[1] *First female to win an Olympic mixed shooting event*

Air Pistol

1988	Taniou Kiriakov (BUL) (585+102.9) 687.9	Erich Buljung (USA) (590+97.9) 687.9	Xu Haifeng (CHN) (584+100.5) 684.5
1992	Wang Yifu (CHN) 684.8	Sergei Pyzhanov (EUN) 684.1	Sorin Babii (ROM) 684.1

1896–1964 Event not held.

Air Rifle

1984	Philippe Herberle (FRA) 589	Andreas Kronthaler (AUT) 587	Barry Dagger (GBR) 587
1988	Goran Maksimovic (YUG) (594+101.6) 695.6	Nicolas Berthelot (FRA) (593+101.2) 694.2	Johann Riederer (FRG) (592+102) 694.0
1992	Yuri Fedkine (EUN) 695.3	Franck Badiou (FRA) 691.9	Johann Riederer (GER) 691.7

1896–1980 Event not held.

DISCONTINUED EVENTS

	GOLD	SILVER	BRONZE

Free Rifle (Three Positions)

1896	Georgios Orphanidis (GRE) 1583	Jean Phrangoudis (GRE) 1312	Viggo Jensen (DEN) 1305
1906	Gudbrand Skatteboe (NOR) 977	Konrad Stäheli (SUI) 943	Jean Reich (SUI) 933
1908	Albert Helgerud (NOR) 909	Harry Simon (USA) 887	Ole Saether (NOR) 883
1912	Paul Colas (FRA) 987	Lars Madsen (DEN) 981	Niels Larsen (DEN) 962
1920	Morris Fisher (USA) 997	Niels Larsen (DEN) 985	Östen Östensen (NOR) 980
1924	Morris Fisher (USA) 95	Carl Osrubn (USA) 95	Niels Larsen (DEN) 93
1948	Emil Grunig (SUI) 1120	Pauli Janhonen (FIN) 1114	Willy Rögeberg (NOR) 1112
1952	Anatoliy Bogdanov (URS) 1123	Robert Bürchler (SUI) 1120	Lev Vainschtein (URS) 1109
1956	Vasiliy Borissov (URS) 1138	Allan Erdman (URS) 1137	Vilho Ylönen (FIN) 1128
1960	Hubert Hammerer (AUT) 1129	Hans Spillmann (SUI) 1127	Vasiliy Borissov (URS) 1127
1964	Gary Anderson (USA) 1153	Shota Kveliashvili (URS) 1144	Martin Gunnarsson (USA) 1136
1968	Gary Anderson (USA) 1157	Vladimir Kornev (URS) 1151	Kurt Müller (SUI) 1148
1972	Lones Wigger (USA) 1155	Boris Melnik (URS) 1155	Lajos Papp (HUN) 1149

1900–1904, 1928–1936 Event not held.

Free Rifle

1896 [1]	Pantelis Karasevdas (GRE) 2320	Paulas Pavlidis (GRE) 1978	Nicolaos Tricoupes (GRE) 1718
1906 [2]	Marcel de Stadelhofen (SUI) 243	Konrad Stäheli (SUI) 238	Léon Moreaux (FRA) 234
1906 [3]	Gudbrand Skatteboe (NOR) 339	Louis Richardet (SUI) 332	Konrad Stäheli (SUI) 328
1906 [4]	Konrad Stäheli (SUI) 340	Louis Richardet (SUI) 338	Jean Reich (SUI) 320
1906 [5]	Gudbrand Skatteboe (NOR) 324	Julius Braathe (NOR) 310	Albert Helgerud (NOR) 305
1908 [6]	Jerry Millner (GBR) 98	Kellogg Casey (USA) 93	Maurice Blood (GBR) 92

[1] *Over 200m.*
[2] *Any position (300m).*
[3] *Prone (300m).*
[4] *Kneeling (300m).*
[5] *Standing (300m).*
[6] *Over 1000 yards.*
1900–1904 Event not held.

Free Rifle (Team)

1906	Switzerland 4596	Norway 4534	France 4511
1908	Norway 5055	Sweden 4711	France 4652
1912	Sweden 5655	Norway 5605	Denmark 5529
1920	United States 4876	Norway 4741	Switzerland 4698
1924	United States 676	France 646	Haiti 646

1896–1904 Event not held.

Military Rifle

1900 [1]	Emil Kellenberger (SUI) 930	Anders Nielsen (DEN) 921	Ole Östmo (NOR) 917
1900 [2]	Lars Madsen (DEN) 305	Ole Östmo (NOR) 299	Charles du Verger (BEL) 298
1900 [3]	Konrad Stäheli (SUI) 324	Emil Kellenberger (SUI) 314	–
		Anders Nielsen (DEN) 314	
1900 [4]	Achille Paroche (FRA) 332	Anders Nielsen (DEN) 330	Ole Östmo (NOR) 329
1906 [5]	Léon Moreaux (FRA) 187	Louis Richardet (SUI) 187	Jean Reich (SUI) 183
1906 [6]	Louis Richardet (SUI) 238	Jean Reich (SUI) 234	Raoul de Boigne (FRA) 232
1912 [1]	Sándor Prokopp (HUN) 97	Carl Osburn (USA) 96	Embret Skogen (NOR) 95
1912 [7]	Paul Colas (FRA) 94	Carl Osburn (USA) 94	Joseph Jackson (USA) 93
1920 [4]	Otto Olsen (NOR) 60	Léon Johnson (FRA) 59	Fritz Kuchen (SUI) 59
1920 [2]	Carl Osburn (USA) 56	Lars Madsen (DEN) 55	Lawrence Nuesslein (USA) 54
1920 [8]	Hugo Johansson (SWE) 58	Mauritz Eriksson (SWE) 56	Lloyd Spooner (USA) 56

1908 Event not held.

Military Rifle (Team)

1900	Switzerland 4399	Norway 4290	France 4278
1908	United States 2531	Great Britain 2497	Canada 2439
1912	United States 1687	Great Britain 1602	Sweden 1570
1920 [2]	Denmark 266	United States 255	Sweden 255
1920 [4]	United States 289	France 283	Finland 281
1920 [8]	United States 287	South Africa 287	Sweden 287
1920 [9]	United States 573	Norway 565	Switzerland 563

[1] *Three positions (300m).*
[2] *Standing (300m).*
[3] *Kneeling (300m).*
[4] *Prone (300m).*
[5] *Standing or kneeling (200m).*
[6] *Standing or kneeling (300m).*
[7] *Any position (600m).*
[8] *Prone (600m).*
[9] *Prone (300m and 600m).*
1896, 1904 Event not held.

Small Bore Rifle

1908 [1]	AF Fleming (GBR) 24	MK Matthews (GBR) 24	WB Marsden (GBR) 24
1908 [2]	William Styles (GBR) 45	HI Hawkins (GBR) 45	Edward Amoore (GBR) 45
1912 [2]	Wilhelm Carlberg (SWE) 242	Johan von Holst (SWE) 233	Gustaf Ericsson (SWE) 231

[1] *Moving target.*
[2] *Disappearing target.*

Small Bore Rifle (Team)

1908	Great Britain 771	Sweden 737	France 710
1912 [1]	Sweden 925	Great Britain 917	United States 881
1912 [2]	Great Britain 762	Sweden 748	United States 744
1920	United States 1899	Sweden 1873	Norway 1866

[1] *Over 25m.*
[2] *Over 50m.*

Live Pigeon Shooting

1900	Léon de Lunden (BEL) 21	Maurice Faure (FRA) 20	Donald MacIntosh (AUS) 18
			Crittenden Robinson (USA) 18

Clay Pigeons (Team)

1908	Great Britain 407	Canada 405	Great Britain 372
1912	United States 532	Great Britain 511	Germany 510
1920	United States 547	Belgium 503	Sweden 500
1924	United States 363	Canada 360	Finland 360

Running Deer Shooting

1908 [1]	Oscar Swahn (SWE) 25	Ted Ranken (GBR) 24	Alexander Rogers (GBR) 24
1908 [2]	Walter Winans (USA) 46	Ted Ranken (GBR) 46	Oscar Swahn (SWE) 38
1912 [1]	Alfred Swahn (SWE) 41	Ake Lundeberg (SWE) 41	Nestori Toivonen (FIN) 41
1912 [2]	Ake Lundeberg (SWE) 79	Edvard Benedicks (SWE) 74	Oscar Swahn (SWE) 72
1920 [1]	Otto Olsen (NOR) 43	Alfred Swahn (SWE) 41	Harald Natwig (NOR) 41
1920 [2]	Ole Lilloe-Olsen (NOR) 82	Fredrik Landelius (SWE) 77	Einar Liberg (NOR) 71
1924 [1]	John Boles (USA) 40	Cyril Mackworth-Praed (GBR) 39	Otto Olsen (NOR) 39
1924 [2]	Ole Lilloe-Olsen (NOR) 76	Cyril Mackworth-Praed (GBR) 72	Alfred Swahn (SWE) 72

[1] *Single shot.*
[2] *Double shot.*

Running Deer Shooting (Team)

1908	Sweden 86	Great Britain 85	–
1912	Sweden 151	United States 132	Finland 123
1920 [1]	Norway 178	Finland 159	United States 158
1920 [2]	Norway 343	Sweden 336	Finland 284
1924 [1]	Norway 160	Sweden 154	United States 158
1924 [2]	Great Britain 263	Norway 262	Sweden 250

[1] *Single shot.*
[2] *Double shot.*

Running Deer Shooting (Single & Double Shot)

1952	John Larsen (NOR) 413	Per Olof Sköldberg (SWE) 409	Tauno Mäki (FIN) 407
1956	Vitaliy Romanenko (URS) 441	Per Olof Sköldberg (SWE) 432	Vladimir Sevrugin (URS) 429

Military Revolver

1896	John Paine (USA) 442	Sumner Paine (USA) 380	Nikolaos Morakis (GRE) 205
1906	Louis Richardet (SUI) 253	Alexandros Theophilakis (GRE) 250	Georgios Skotadis (GRE) 240
1906 [1]	Jean Fouconnier (FRA) 219	Raoul de Boigne (FRA) 219	Hermann Martin (FRA) 215

[1] *Model 1873.*
1900–1904 Event not held.

Duelling Pistol

1906 [1]	Léon Moreaux (FRA) 242	Cesare Liverziani (ITA) 233	Maurice Lecoq (FRA) 231
1906 [2]	Konstantinos Skarlatos (GRE) 133	Johann von Holst (SWE) 115	Wilhelm Carlberg (SWE) 115

[1] *Over 20m.*
[2] *Over 25m.*
1896–1904 Event not held.

Team Event

1900	Switzerland 2271	France 2203	Netherlands 1876
1908	United States 1914	Belgium 1863	Great Britain 1817
1912 [1]	United States 1916	Sweden 1849	Great Britain 1804
1912 [2]	Sweden 1145	Russia d.n.a.	Great Britain d.n.a.
1920 [1]	United States 2372	Sweden 2289	Brazil 2264
1920 [2]	United States 1310	Greece 1285	Switzerland 1270

[1] *Over 50m.*
[2] *Over 30m.*
1904–1906 Event not held.

SHOOTING MEDAL RESULTS — WOMEN

Introduced in 1984

	GOLD	SILVER	BRONZE
Sport Pistol			
1984	Linda Thom (CAN) 585	Ruby Fox (USA) 585	Patricia Dench (AUS) 583
1988	Nino Saloukvadze (URS) (591+99) 690	Tomoko Hasegawa (JPN) (587+99) 686	Jasna Sekaric (YUG) (591+95) 686
1992	Marina Logvinenko (EUN) 684	Li Duihong (CHN) 680	Dorzhsuren Munkhbayar (MGL) 679
Small-Bore Rifle – Three positions			
1984	Wu Xiaoxuan (CHN) 581	Ulrike Holmer (FRG) 578	Wanda Jewell (USA) 578
1988	Silvia Sperber (FRG) (590+95.6) 685.6	Vessela Letcheva (BUL) (583.100.2) 683.2	Valentina Tcherkassova (URS) (586+95.4) 681.4
1992	Launi Meili (USA) 684.3	Nonka Matova (BUL) 682.7	Malgorzata Ksiazkiewicz (POL) 681.5
Air Pistol			
1988	Jasna Sekaric (YUG) (389+100.5) 489.5	Nino Saloukvadze (URS) (390+97.9) 487.9	Marina Dobrantcheva (URS) (385+100.2) 485.2
1992	Marina Logivinenko (EUN) 486.4	Jasna Sekaric (IOP) 486.4	Maria Grusdeva (BUL) 481.6

1984 Event not held.

	GOLD	SILVER	BRONZE
Air Rifle			
1984	Pat Spurgin (USA) 393	Edith Gufler (ITA) 391	Wu Xiaoxuan (CHN) 389
1988	Irina Chilova (URS) (395+103.5) 498.5	Silvia Sperber (FRG) (393+104.5) 497.5	Anna Maloukhina (URS) (394+101.8) 495.8
1992	Yeo Kab-soon (KOR) 498.2	Vesela Letcheva (BUL) 495.3	Aranka Binder (IOP) 495.1

Softball

Invented as an indoor version of baseball in 1887, the sport did not become known as softball until 1920. Originally a ten-a-side game, it is now played with nine per side and is governed by the International Softball Federation (ISF), formed in 1950. Pitching is done underarm, and there are fast-pitch and slow-pitch forms. A game lasts for seven innings. The fast-pitch variety for women will be introduced as an official Olympic medal sport in 1996 – despite never having been a demonstration sport – with eight teams.

Swimming

The sport has been an integral part of the Games since 1896 when it was held in the Bay of Zea near Piraeus. The first champion was Alfred Hajos (né Guttmann) (HUN) who won the 100m freestyle in freezing water. The first female champion (women's events were introduced in 1912) was Australia's Fanny Durack, also in the 100m freestyle. The first Olympic competition in a pool was in 1908, in a 100m long tank constructed inside the track at the White City Stadium, London. The first 50m pool was in 1924, outdoors, and the first one indoors was at Wembley, London in 1948. Emil Rausch (GER), in 1904, was the last to win an Olympic title using the side-stroke technique.

The most successful swimmer was Mark Spitz (USA) with nine gold medals plus a silver and bronze, 1968-72.

His feat of seven golds at one Games (1972) is unmatched in any sport. The most individual event golds won is four by Charles Daniels (USA) 1904-08, Roland Matthes (GDR) 1968-72, Spitz 1972, Kirstin Otto (GDR) 1988, Janet Evans (USA) 1988-92 and Krisztina Egerszegi (HUN) 1988-92. Otto's final tally of six golds at Seoul set female records for most all-time and most at a single Games. Otto is also the only swimmer to win Olympic titles in three different strokes – freestyle, backstroke and butterfly. Dawn Fraser (AUS) is the only swimmer, male or female, to win the same event (100m freestyle) three times. Matt Biondi (USA) equalled the record of 11 medals by Spitz, but his comprised 'only' eight golds, two silvers and a bronze, 1984-92. Three women have won a record eight medals: Fraser, 1956-64,

Olympic Records

Men

50m free	21. 91s	Alexander Popov (EUN)	1992
100m free	48. 63s	Matt Biondi (USA)	1988
200m free	1m 46.70s	Yevgeny Sadovyi (EUN)	1992
400m free	3m 45.00s	Yevgeny Sadovyi (EUN)	1992
1500m free	14m 43.38s	Kieren Perkins (AUS)	1992
4 x 100m free	3m 16.53s	United States	1988
4 x 200m free	7m 11.95s	Unified Team	1992
100m breast	1m 01.50s	Nelson Diebel (USA)	1992
200m breast	2m 10.16s	Mike Barrowman (USA)	1992
100m back	53. 86s*	Jeff Rouse (USA)	1992
200m back	1m 58.47s	Martin Lopez-Zubero (ESP)	1992
100m butterfly	53. 00s	Anthony Nesty (SUR)	1988
200m butterfly	1m 56.26s	Mel Stewart (USA)	1992
200m medley	2m 00.17s	Tamas Darnyi (HUN)	1988
400m medley	4m 14.23s	Tamas Darnyi (HUN)	1992
4 x 100m medley	3m 36.93s	United States	1988

* First leg in medley relay

Women

50m free	24. 79s	Yang Wenyi (CHN)	1992
100m free	54. 64s	Zhuang Yong (CHN)	1992
200m free	1m 57.65s	Heike Friedrich (GDR)	1988
400m free	4m 03.85s	Janet Evans (USA)	1988
800m free	8m 20.20s	Janet Evans (USA)	1988
4 x 100m free	3m 39.46s	United States	1992
100m breast	1m 07.95s	Tania Dangalakova (BUL)	1988
200m breast	2m 26.65s	Kyoko Iwasaki (JPN)	1992
100m back	1m 00.68s	Krisztina Egerzegi (HUN)	1992
200m back	2m 07.06s	Krisztina Egerzegi (HUN)	1992
100m butterfly	58. 62s	Qian Hong (CHN)	1992
200m butterfly	2m 06.90s	Mary Meagher (USA)	1984
200m medley	2m 11.65s	Li Lin (CHN)	1992
400m medley	4m 36.29s	Petra Schneider (GDR)	1980
4 x 100m medley	4m 02.54s	United States	1992

and Kornelia Ender (GDR), 1972-76, both with four golds and four silvers; and Shirley Babashoff (USA), who won two gold and uniquely six silver medals in 1972-76. Both Spitz and Babashoff set an endurance record of sorts, in 1972 and 1976 respectively, by taking part in 13 races within eight days.

The first to defend an Olympic swimming title successfully was Charles Daniels (USA) in the 100m freestyle in 1908. The first woman to do so was Martha Norelius (USA) in 1928 in the 400m freestyle. She was born in Sweden and her father, Charles, had been a member of the 1906 Swedish Olympic swimming team, while an uncle, Benkt, had won gold in the 1912 gymnastics. Later her first husband was the 1928 Canadian silver medallist oarsman Joseph Wright.

The oldest gold medallist was Cecil Healy (AUS) in the 1912 800m relay team aged 30yr 229 days. The oldest female champion/medallist was Ursula Happe (GER) in the 1956 200m breaststroke aged 30yr 41 days. The oldest medallist was William Henry (GBR), a last-minute replacement in the 1906 relay, aged 46yr 301 days. The youngest gold medallist was Kyoko Iwasaki (JPN) in the 1992 women's 200m breaststroke at 14yr 6 days. The youngest male champion/medallist was Kusuo Kitamura (JPN) in the 1500m in 1932 aged 14yr 309 days, while the youngest known medallist in any sport at the Games was Inge Sörensen (DEN), aged 12yr 24 days when she took bronze in the 200m breaststroke of 1936. The youngest known competitor, excepting rowing coxes, in any Summer Games sport was swimmer Liana Vicens of Puerto Rico in 1968 aged 11yr 328 days.

The first dead heat in Games swimming came in the 1984 women's 100m freestyle final when Carrie Steinseifer

An unmatched total of seven gold medals was achieved by Mark Spitz (USA) at Munich in 1972 (Allsport/Tony Duffy)

and Nancy Hogshead (both USA) gained a gold medal each. Also in those Games there was a strange situation when the winner of the 400m freestyle 'B' final, Thomas Fahrner (FRG), set an Olympic record, faster than the winner of the 'A' final. The closest to a dead heat in the men's events was in the 1972 400m medley when Gunnar Larsson (SWE) was given the decision over Tim McKee (USA). The margin was two-thousandths of a second or about 3 millimetres (estimated to be the length grown by a fingernail in 3 weeks). Happily, timings and placings are now decided to hundredths only, and the above would now be given as a dead heat. Another controversial decision occurred in the 1960 100m freestyle when Lance Larson (USA) was timed (manually) at one-tenth faster than John Devitt (AUS), but the judges placed the Australian first – and that is how the result remained, despite protests.

In the 1912 100m competition, the three best American swimmers missed the semi-finals because they had been told there would not be any. Following protests it was agreed that if they were timed, in a special race, at faster than the slowest qualifier from those semis then they would go forward to the final. The outstanding Hawaiian swimmer Duke Kahanamoku was so incensed that he broke the world record, and then won the final. At the next Games, in 1920, the final was re-swum after the Australian William Herald complained that he was impeded by Norman Ross (USA) – this was before lane dividers were used. The original winner, Kahanamoku, won again, in a slower time than before, but his first time of 60.4 secs was recognized as a world record. Kahanamoku, the first of the great Hawaiian swimmers, was born into the Hawaiian Royal Family, and was named 'Duke' after the Duke of Edinburgh, Queen Victoria's second son, who was visiting the Palace at the time. He was a pioneer of surfing, made many movies in Hollywood, and was the oldest individual event champion in 1920 when 5 days past his 30th birthday. His brother Sammy won a bronze in the 1924 100m freestyle.

Hollywood has attracted a number of Olympian swimmers: Johnny Weissmuller (USA), born in what is now Romania, won five gold medals, 1924-28, and then became the most famous 'Tarzan' of them all; Clarence 'Buster' Crabbe (USA), the 1932 400m champion, became 'Flash Gordon' and 'Buck Rogers' in children's serials; while Aileen Riggin (USA), the 1920 diving champion, and Eleanor Holm (USA), the 1932 backstroke champion, both took their good looks into movies. Holm was also in a Tarzan movie, in 1938 as Jane to the hero played by 1936 decathlon champion Glenn Morris.

Gertrude Ederle (USA) and Greta Andersen (DEN), gold medallists in 1924 and 1948 respectively, both later set Channel swimming records (the first Olympian to swim the Channel, in 1934, was Edward Temme (GBR), who was in the fourth-placed British water polo team in 1928). A change to the rules allowed female swimmers to wear two-piece costumes in competition – but only a few competitors took advantage of this, notably the Italians.

Oldest & Youngest Medallists by Event

Men

Event	Medal	Youngest Yrs/Dys	Name/Country/Date	Oldest Yrs/Dys	Name/Country/Date
50m Free	G	20-157	Alexander Popov (RUS) 1992	23-8	Zoltan Van Halmay (HUN) 1904
	M	19-166	Charles Davies (USA) 1904 [1]	27-298	Tom Jager (USA) 1992
100m Free	G	15-297	Yasuji Miyazaki (JPN) 1932	30-5	Duke Kahanamoku (USA) 1920
	M	15-297	Yasuji Miyazaki (JPN) 1932	33-330	Duke Kahanamoku (USA) 1924
200m Free	G	18-342	Mike Wenden (AUS) 1968	22-201	Mark Spitz (USA) 1972
	M	18-219	Antti Kasvio (FIN) 1992	24-72	Andrei Krylov (URS) 1980
400m Free	G	16-134	Otto Scheff (AUT) 1906	24-118	Norman Ross (USA) 1920
	M	16-134	Otto Scheff (AUT) 1906	34-62	John Jarvis (GBR) 1906

Event					
1500m Free	G	14-309	Kusuo Kitamura (JPN) 1932	28-127	Vladimir Salnikov (URS) 1988
	M	14-309	Kusuo Kitamura (JPN) 1932	34-60	John Jarvis (GBR) 1906
4x100m Free	G	18-167	Don Schollander (USA) 1964	27-297	Tom Jager (USA) 1992
	M	16-338	Peter Bruch (GDR) 1972	27-321	Dirk Richter (GDR) 1992
4x200m Free	G	15-299	Yasuji Miyazaki (JPN) 1932	30-229	Cecil Healy (AUS) 1912
	M	15-299	Yasuji Miyazaki (JPN) 1932	46-301	William Henry (GBR) 1906 [2]
100m Breast	G	21-73	Nobutaka Taguchi (JPN) 1972	24-117	Adrian Moorhouse (GBR) 1988
	M	18-93	John Hencken (USA) 1972	25-236	Vladimir Kosinsky (URS) 1968
200m Breast	G	17-226	Ian O'Brien (AUS) 1964	28-286	Yoshiyuki Tsoruta (JPN) 1932
	M	16-245	Reizo Koike (JPN) 1932	38-25	William Robinson (GBR) 1908
100m Back	G	16-173	Warren Kealoha (USA) 1920	24-290	Walter Brack (GER) 1904 [3]
	M	16-173	Warren Kealoha (USA) 1920	28-15	Herbert Haresnape (GBR) 1908
200m Back	G	17-7	Sandor Wladar (HUN) 1980	23-96	Martin Lopez-Zubero (ESP) 1992
	M	17-7	Sandor Wladar (HUN) 1980	24-185	Frank Baltrusch (GDR) 1988
100m Butt	G	19-48	Matt Vogel (USA) 1976	27-235	Pablo Morales (USA) 1992
	M	18-254	Mark Spitz (USA) 1968	27-235	Pablo Morales (USA) 1992
200m Butt	G	17-345	Jon Sieben (AUS) 1984	24-97	Michael Gross (FRG) 1988
	M	16-275	Neville Hayes (AUS) 1960	27-324	Gyorgy Tumpek (HUN) 1956
200m Med	G	20-105	Alex Baumann (CAN) 1984	25-58	Tamas Darnyi (HUN) 1992
	M	18-41	Attila Czene (HUN) 1992	25-58	Tamas Darnyi (HUN) 1992
400m Med	G	17-18	Richard Roth (USA) 1964	25-54	Tamas Darnyi (HUN) 1992
	M	16-166	Andras Hargitay (HUN) 1972	25-54	Tamas Darnyi (HUN) 1992
4x100m Med	G	18-2	Neil Brooks (AUS) 1980	27-239	Pablo Morales (USA) 1992
	M	16-274	Neville Hayes (AUS) 1960	30-94	Horst-Gunter Gregor (GDR) 1968

Women

Event					
50m Free	G	20-202	Yang Wenyi (CHN) 1992	22-231	Kristin Otto (GDR) 1988
	M	15-252	Katrin Meissner (GDR) 1988	27-121	Jill Sterkel (USA) 1988
100m Free	G	16-162	Sandra Nielson (USA) 1972	27-39	Dawn Fraser (AUS) 1964
	M	14-112	Franziska Van Almsick (GER) 1992	27-136	Frances Schroth (USA) 1920
200m Free	G	15-283	Shane Gould (AUS) 1972	21-17	Barbara Krause (GDR) 1980
	M	14-113	Franziska Van Almsick (GER) 1992	22-234	Kerstin Kielglass (GER) 1992
400m Free	G	15-281	Shane Gould (AUS) 1972	22-219	Dagmar Hase (GER) 1992
	M	14-156	Sylvia Ruuska (USA) 1956	27-139	Frances Schroth (USA) 1920 [4]
800m Free	G	15-190	Keena Rothhammer (USA) 1972	20-337	Janet Evans (USA) 1992
	M	15-70	Maria Teresa Ramirez (MEX) 1968	20-337	Janet Evans (USA) 1992
4x100m Free	G	14-96	Lilian 'Pokey' Watson (USA) 1964	27-140	Frances Schroth (USA) 1920
	M	13-310	Kornelia Ender (GDR) 1972	28-253	Eva Riise-Arndt (DEN) 1948
100m Breast	G	18-61	Petra Van Staveren (NED) 1984	24-85	Tonya Dangalakova (BUL) 1988
	M	16-8	Anita Nall (USA) 1992	24-85	Tonya Dangalakova (BUL) 1988
200m Breast	G	14-6	Kyoko Iwasaki (JPN) 1992	30-41	Ursula Happe (GER) 1956
	M	12-24	Inge Sorensen (DEN) 1936	30-41	Ursula Happe (GER) 1956
100m Back	G	15-112	Rica Reinisch (GDR) 1980	23-259	Karen Harup (DEN) 1948
	M	14-38	Krisztina Egerszegi (HUN) 1988	23-259	Karen Harup (DEN) 1948
200m Back	G	14-41	Krisztina Egerszegi (HUN) 1988	20-299	Jolanda de Rover (NED) 1984
	M	14-41	Krisztina Egerszegi (HUN) 1988	22-222	Dagmar Hase (GER) 1992
100m Butt	G	15-342	Sharon Stouder (USA) 1964	22-234	Kristin Otto (GDR) 1988
	M	15-75	Andrea Pollack (GDR) 1976	24-17	Catherine Plewinski (FRA) 1992
200m Butt	G	15-72	Andrea Pollack (GDR) 1976	22-274	Kathleen Nord (GDR) 1988
	M	15-72	Andrea Pollack (GDR) 1976	23-334	Mary Meagher (USA) 1988
200m Med	G	15-279	Shane Gould (AUS) 1972	21-295	Lin Li (CHN) 1992
	M	13-308	Kornelia Ender (GDR) 1972	22-108	Nancy Hogshead (USA) 1984
400m Med	G	17-29	Gail Neall (AUS) 1972	21-200	Tracey Caulkins (USA) 1984
	M	16-99	Sabine Steinbach (GDR) 1968	21-291	Lin Li (CHN) 1992
4x100m Med	G	15-1	Susan Pedersen (USA) 1968	22-12	Silke Horner (GDR) 1988
	M	13-314	Kornelia Ender (GDR) 1972	23-302	Margaret Kelly (GBR) 1980 [5]

[1] 50 yards [2] 4x250m [3] 100y [4] 300m [5] Mary Meagher only swam in heat in 1988 aged 23-333

SWIMMING MEDALS

	Men			Women			
	G	S	B	G	S	B	Total
United States	97	73	51	68	46	40	375
Australia (1)	24	20	28	14	13	13	112
GDR	6	7	5	32	25	17	92
Soviet Union	14	17	18	4	7	9	69
Great Britain	10	12	13	4	9	12	60
Hungary	12	13	11	8	6	3	53
Germany	9	11	9	3	7	11	50
Japan	12	17	11	3	1	1	45
Canada	6	7	6	1	5	10	35
Netherlands	-	-	2	9	13	10	34
Sweden	7	9	10	-	2	2	30
FRG	3	4	7	-	1	7	22
France	2	5	9	-	1	3	20
China	-	-	-	4	8	1	13
Denmark	-	2	1	2	3	3	11
Austria	2	4	4	-	-	1	11
Greece	1	3	3	-	-	-	7
Italy	-	-	3	-	1	2	6
Brazil	-	2	3	-	-	-	5
New Zealand (1)	1	1	2	-	-	1	5
South Africa	-	-	-	1	-	3	4
Bulgaria	-	-	-	1	1	1	3
Belgium	-	1	1	-	-	1	3
Spain	1	-	2	-	-	-	3
Poland	-	1	1	-	-	1	3
Romania	-	-	-	-	1	2	3
Finland	-	-	3	-	-	-	3
Argentina	1	-	-	-	1	-	2
Yugoslavia	-	-	-	1	1	-	2
Mexico	1	-	-	-	1	-	2
Surinam	1	-	1	-	-	-	2
Philippines	-	-	2	-	-	-	2
Costa Rica	-	-	-	1	-	-	1
Switzerland	-	-	1	-	-	-	1
Venezuela	-	-	1	-	-	-	1
	210 (1)	209	208 (2)	155 (3)	153	155 (4)	1090

(1) *Double counting of Australia/NZ relay team in 1912*
(2) *Third place in 1896 100m not known*
(3) *Two golds in 1984 100m freestyle*
(4) *Two bronzes in 1988 50m freestyle*

Diving

Men's diving was introduced into the Games in 1904, and for women in 1912. For 1996 new rules came into operation providing for three rounds instead of two, but with fewer dives in each round. The most successful diver has been Greg Louganis (USA) with four golds (a double 'double') in 1984-88, and a silver in 1976. Austrian-born Klaus Dibiasi (ITA) won three gold and two silver medals, 1964-76, uniquely winning the same event three times and gaining medals in four Games. Pat McCormick (USA) set a female record of four golds in 1952-56. Her daughter Kelly won a silver in 1984 and a bronze in 1988. Dorothy Poynton-Hill (USA), 1928-36, and Paula Myers-Pope (USA), 1952-60, both won medals in three separate Games. Isabella White (GBR), 1912-28, and Juno Stover-Irwin (USA), 1948-60, competed in four Games. White won a bronze medal and Stover-Irwin a silver and a bronze.

The oldest gold medallist was Hjalmar Johansson (SWE) aged 34yr 186 days in the plain diving at London in 1908; he was also the oldest ever medallist four years later in Stockholm with a silver aged 38yr 173 days. The oldest female champion was Micki King (USA) in 1972 aged 28yr 33 days, while the oldest female medallist was Ninel Krutova (URS) in 1960 at 33yr 293 days. The youngest champion, and the youngest individual Olympic champion at any sport, was Marjorie Gestring (USA) who won the 1936 springboard title aged 13yr 267 days. The youngest male diving champion was Sun Shuwei (CHN) in 1992 aged 16yr 185 days. Dorothy Poynton-Hill (USA) was the youngest medallist in 1928 aged 13yr 23 days, while the youngest male medallist was Nils Skoglund (SWE) aged 14yr 10 days, also in 1920. Greg Louganis (USA) won both diving titles in 1984 by the biggest margins ever recorded at the Games.

Four divers, three women and a man, have won medals at swimming as well as diving. The most successful was Aileen Riggin (USA) with gold and silver diving medals in 1920 and 1924 and a bronze in the backstroke at Paris. She is thought to be the smallest ever US Olympic champion at 1.42m. Georg Hoffmann (GER) won silvers in 1904 at diving and the 100m backstroke; Katherine Rawls (USA) won a silver in the 1936 springboard and a bronze in the relay; Hjördis Töpel (SWE) won bronzes at diving and the relay in 1924. The most successful husband and wife team were Clarence and Elizabeth (née Becker) Pinkston (USA), who between them won three golds, two silvers and two bronzes from 1920 to 1928. Elizabeth won her second gold medal, in 1928, on the second birthday of her twin children. Two male divers, Franco Cagnotto (ITA), 1964-80, and Niki Stajkovic (AUT), 1972-80 and 1988-92, have competed at five Games.

Synchronized Swimming

Introduced in the Games in 1984, there were solo and duet events until 1996. At Atlanta they will be replaced by a single team event, consisting of teams of eight women. Compulsory figures will be replaced with a technical programme.

The most successful women have been Tracie Ruiz-Conforto (USA) and Carolyn Waldo (CAN), both with two golds and one silver, 1984-88. The youngest gold medallist was Candy Costie (USA) in the 1984 duet aged 21yr 150 days, while the oldest were Karen and Sarah Josephson (USA) in the 1992 duet aged 28yr 210 days. The latter are among the most successful twins ever in Olympic swimming, with their gold medal in 1992 to add to the silver from 1988. In 1992 the second place went to another set of twins, Penny and Vicky Vilagos of Canada, who are the oldest medallists at 29yr 112 days.

In the 1992 solo event a mistake by a judge deprived Sylvie Fréchette (CAN) from sharing the gold medal. In December 1993 the result was revised.

Water Polo

The first Olympic contest was won by the Osborne Swimming Club, Manchester, representing Great Britain in 1900. Five players have won three gold medals each; George Wilkinson (GBR) 1900, 1908-12; Paul Radmilovic and Charles Smith (both GBR) 1908-20; Dezsö Gyarmati and György Kárpáti (HUN) 1952-56 and 1964. Of these, Radomilovic, Welsh-born of a Greek father and Irish mother, also won a gold in the 4 x 200m team in 1908. He (1908-28), Gyarmati (1948-64) and Gianni De Magistris (ITA, 1968-84) all competed in a record five Olympic tournaments. However, the Hungarian is the mossuccessful player outright, adding a silver in 1948 and a bronze in 1960, and becoming one of the few Olympians in any sport to win medals in five Games. Gyarmati also heads a fine Olympic family, as his wife Eva Székely won a gold (1952) and a silver (1956) in the 200m breaststroke, and their daughter Andrea won silver and bronze medals in the 1972 backstroke and butterfly events respectively. She then added to the family total of medals by marrying Mihaly Hesz (HUN), a canoeist with a gold (1968 K1) and a silver (1964 K1). The oldest gold medallist was Charles Smith (GBR) aged 41yr 217 days in 1920, while the youngest was György Kárpáti (HUN) in 1952 aged 17yr 40 days.

The oldest medallist was also Smith, while the youngest was Paul Vasseur (FRA) in 1900 aged 15yr 305 days. The first brothers to win gold medals in the same team were Ferenc and Alajos Keserü (HUN) in 1932, and they were matched by Tulio and Franco Pandolfini (ITA) in 1948. Georgi Mshvenieradze (URS) won a gold medal in 1980, going one better than his father Piotr who had gained a silver (1960) and a bronze (1956). A number of men have won medals at both swimming and water polo, the most notable being Johnny Weissmuller (USA) who gained a bronze in 1924 on the same day that he won two freestyle golds. Tim Shaw (USA), who won a silver medal in the 1976 400m freestyle, won another in the 1984 water polo competition.

The highest score by any team was by the GDR, 19-2 against UAE in 1968, and Spain, beating Brazil 19-12 in the aggregate record game of 1984. The most goals scored by an individual in one game is 9, by Zoran Jankovic of Yugoslavia against Japan in 1968 and by Manuel Estiarte for Spain against Brazil in 1984.

A member of the winning Hungarian teams of 1932 and 1936, Olivér Halassy, had had a leg amputated below the knee as a child.

DIVING MEDALS TABLE

	Men			Women			
	G	S	B	G	S	B	Total
United States	27	20	19	19	20	20	125
Sweden	4	5	4	2	3	3	21
Germany	3	5	5	3	1	2	19
SovietUnion	2	1	4	2	5	3	17
China	1	4	3	5	1	-	14
Italy	3	4	2	-	-	-	9
Mexico	1	3	4	-	-	-	8
GDR	1	-	-	1	2	3	7
Great Britain	-	-	2	-	1	2	5
Czechoslovakia	-	-	-	1	1	-	2
Canada	-	-	-	1	-	1	2
Denmark	-	-	-	1	-	1	2
Egypt	-	1	1	-	-	-	2
Australia	1	-	-	-	-	-	1
France	-	-	-	-	1	-	1
Austria	-	-	1	-	-	-	1
	43	43	45 [1]	35	35	35	236

[1] *Two bronzes awarded in a 1904 and a 1908 event*

SYNCHRONIZED SWIMMING MEDALS

	G	S	B	Total
Canada	3	3	-	6
United States	4	2	-	6
Japan	-	-	6	6
	7 [1]	5	6	18

[1] *Tie for gold in 1992*

WATER POLO MEDALS TABLE

	G	S	B	Total
Hungary	6	3	3	12
United States	1	4	3	8
Soviet Union	2	2	4	8
Yugoslavia	3	4	-	7
Belgium	-	4	2	6
Italy	3	1	1	5
Great Britain	4	-	-	4
France	1	-	3	4
Germany	1	2	-	3
Sweden	-	1	2	3
Netherlands	-	-	2	2
Spain	-	1	-	1
FRG	-	-	1	1
	21	22*	21*	64

* *Two bronzes 1900; two silvers, no bronze 1904*

Representing the Unified Team, Aleksandr Popov won the 50m and 100m freestyle races in 1992 (Allsport/Bob Martin)

SWIMMING MEDAL RESULTS — MEN

	GOLD	SILVER	BRONZE

50 Metres Freestyle

1904 [1]   Zóltán Halmay (HUN) 28.0   Scott Leary (USA) 28.6   Charles Daniels (USA) n.t.a.
1988   Matt Biondi (USA) 22.14   Thomas Jager (USA) 22.36   Gennadiy Prigoda (URS) 22.71
1992   Aleksandr Popov (EUN) 21.91   Matt Biondi (USA) 22.09   Tom Jager (USA) 22.30
1896–1900, 1906-84 Event not held.
[1] *50 yards. Race reswum after judges disagreed on result of first race*

100 Metres Freestyle

1896 [1]   Alfred Hajos (HUN) 1:22.2   Otto Herschmann (AUT) 1:23.0   -
1904 [2]   Zóltán Halmay (HUN) 1:02.8   Charles Daniels (USA) d.n.a.   Scott Leary (USA) d.n.a.
1906   Charles Daniels (USA) 1:13.4   Zóltán Halmay (HUN) 1:14.2   Cecil Healy (AUS) d.n.a.
1908   Charles Daniels (USA) 1:05.6   Zóltán Halmay (HUN) 1:06.2   Harald Julin (SWE) 1:08.0
1912   Duke Kahanamoku (USA) 1:03.4   Cecil Healy (AUS) 1:04.6   Kenneth Huszagh (USA) 1:05.6
1920   Duke Kahanamoku (USA) 1:01.4   Pua Kealoha (USA) 1:02.2   William Harris (USA) 1:03.0
1924   Johnny Weissmuller (USA) 59.0   Duke Kahanamoku (USA) 1:01.4   Sam Kahanamoku (USA) 1:01.8
1928   Johnny Weissmuller (USA) 58.6   István Bárány (HUN) 59.8   Katsuo Takaishi (JPN) 1:00.0
1932   Yasuji Miyazaki (JPN) 58.2   Tatsugo Kawaishi (JPN) 58.6   Albert Schwartz (USA) 58.8
1936   Ferenc Csik (HUN) 57.6   Masanori Yusa (JPN) 57.9   Shigeo Arai (JPN) 58.0
1948   Walter Ris (USA) 57.3   Alan Ford (USA) 57.8   Géza Kádas (HUN) 58.1
1952   Clarke Scholes (USA) 57.4   Hiroshi Suzuki (JPN) 57.4   Göran Larsson (SWE) 58.2
1956   Jon Henricks (AUS) 55.4   John Devitt (AUS) 55.8   Gary Chapman (AUS) 56.7
1960   John Devitt (AUS) 55.2   Lance Larson (USA) 55.2   Manuel dos Santos (BRA) 55.4
1964   Don Schollander (USA) 53.4   Bobbie McGregor (GBR) 53.5   Hans-Joachim Klein (GER) 54.0
1968   Mike Wenden (AUS) 52.2   Ken Walsh (USA) 52.8   Mark Spitz (USA) 53.0
1972   Mark Spitz (USA) 51.22   Jerry Heidenreich (USA) 51.65   Vladimir Bure (URS) 51.77
1976   Jim Montgomery (USA) 49.99   Jack Babashoff (USA) 50.81   Peter Nocke (FRG) 51.31
1980   Jörg Woithe (GDR) 50.40   Per Holmertz (SWE) 50.91   Per Johansson (SWE) 51.29

1984	Ambrose Gaines (USA) 49.80	Mark Stockwell (AUS) 50.24	Per Johansson (SWE) 50.31
1988	Matt Biondi (USA) 48.63	Chris Jacobs (USA) 49.08	Stephan Caron (FRA) 49.62
1992	Aleksandr Popov (EUN) 49.02	Gustavo Borges (BRA) 49.43	Stephan Caron (FRA) 49.50

[1] *Some confusion exists about the second and third finishers*
[2] *100 yards.*
1900 Event not held.

200 Metres Freestyle

1900	Frederick Lane (AUS) 2:25.2	Zóltán Halmay (HUN) 2:31.4	Karl Ruberl (AUT) 2:32.0
1904 [1]	Charles Daniels (USA) 2:44.2	Francis Gailey (USA) 2:46.0	Emil Raush (GER) 2:56.0
1968	Mike Wenden (AUS) 1:55.2	Don Schollander (USA) 1:55.8	John Nelson (USA) 1:58.1
1972	Mark Spitz (USA) 1:52.78	Steven Genter (USA) 1:53.73	Werner Lampe (FRG) 1:53.99
1976	Bruce Furniss (USA) 1:50.29	John Naber (USA) 1:50.50	Jim Montgomery (USA) 1:50.58
1980	Sergey Kopliakov (URS) 1:49.81	Andrej Krylov (URS) 1:50.76	Graeme Brewer (AUS) 1:51.60
1984	Michael Gross (FRG) 1:47.44	Michael Heath (USA) 1:49.10	Thomas Fahrner (FRG) 1:49.69
1988	Duncan Armstrong (AUS) 1:47.25	Anders Holmertz (SWE) 1:47.89	Matt Biondi (USA) 1:47.99
1992	Yevgeni Sadovyi (EUN) 1:46.70	Anders Holmertz (SWE) 1:46.86	Antti Kasvio (FIN) 1:47.63

[1] *220 yards.*
1896, 1906–1964 Event not held.

400 Metres Freestyle

1896 [1]	Paul Neuman (AUT) 8:12.6	Antonios Pepanos (GRE) 30m	Efstathios Choraphas (GRE) d.n.a.
1904 [2]	Charles Daniels (USA) 6:16.2	Francis Gailey (USA) 6:22.0	Otto Wahle (AUT) 6:39.0
1906	Otto Scheff (AUT) 6:23.8	Henry Taylor (GBR) 6:24.4	John Jarvis (GBR) 6:27.2
1908	Henry Taylor (GBR) 5:36.8	Frank Beaurepaire (AUS) 5:44.2	Otto Scheff (AUT) 5:46.0
1912	George Hodgson (CAN) 5:24.4	John Hatfield (GBR) 5:25.8	Harold Hardwick (AUS) 5:31.2
1920	Norman Ross (USA) 5:26.8	Ludy Langer (USA) 5:29.2	George Vernot (CAN) 5:29.8
1924	Johnny Weissmuller (USA) 5:04.2	Arne Borg (SWE) 5:05.6	Andrew Charlton (AUS) 5:06.6
1928	Alberto Zorilla (ARG) 5:01.6	Andrew Charlton (AUS) 5:03.6	Arne Borg (SWE) 5:04.6
1932	Buster Crabbe (USA) 4:48.4	Jean Taris (FRA) 4:48.5	Tautomu Oyokota (JPN) 4:52.3
1936	Jack Medica (USA) 4:44.5	Shumpei Uto (JPN) 4:45.6	Shozo Makino (JPN) 4:48.1
1948	William Smith (USA) 4:41.0	James McLane (USA) 4:43.4	John Marshall (AUS) 4:47.7
1952	Jean Boiteux (USA) 4:30.7	Ford Konno (USA) 4:31.3	Per-Olof Ostrand (SWE) 4:35.2
1956	Murray Rose (AUS) 4:27.3	Tsuyoshi Yamanaka (JPN) 4:30.4	George Breen (USA) 4:32.5
1960	Murray Rose (AUS) 4:18.3	Tsuyoshi Yamanaka (JPN) 4:21.4	John Konrads (AUS) 4:21.8
1964	Don Schollander (USA) 4:12.2	Frank Wiegand (GER) 4:14.9	Allan Wood (AUS) 4:15.1
1968	Mike Burton (USA) 4:09.0	Ralph Hutton (CAN) 4:11.7	Alain Mosconi (FRA) 4:13.3
1972	Brad Cooper (AUS) 4:00.27	Steven Genter (USA) 4:01.94	Tom McBeen (USA) 4:02.64
1976	Brian Goodell (USA) 3:51.93	Tim Shaw (USA) 3:52.54	Vladimir Raskatov (URS) 3:55.76
1980	Vladimir Salnikov (URS) 3:51.31	Andrej Krylov (URS) 3:53.24	Ivar Stukolkin (URS) 3:53.95
1984	George DiCarlo (USA) 3:51.23	John Mykkanen (USA) 3:51.49	Justin Lemberg (AUS) 3:51.79
1988	Uwe Dassler (GDR) 3:46.95	Duncan Armstrong (AUS) 3:47.15	Artur Wojdat (POL) 3:47.34
1992	Yeygeni Sadovyi (EUN) 3:45.00	Kieren Perkins (AUS) 3:45.16	Anders Holmertz (SWE) 3:46.77

[1] *500m.*
[2] *440 yards.*
1900 Event not held.

1500 Metres Freestyle

1896 [1]	Alfred Hajós (HUN) 18:22.2	Jean Andreou (GRE) 21:03.4	Efstathios Choraphas (GRE) d.n.a.
1900 [2]	John Jarvis (GBR) 13:40.2	Otto Wahle (AUT) 14:53.6	Zóltán Halmay (HUN) 15:16.4
1904 [3]	Emil Rausch (GER) 27:18.2	Géza Kiss (HUN) 28:28.2	Francis Gailey (USA) 28:54.0
1906 [3]	Henry Taylor (GBR) 28:28.0	John Jarvis (GBR) 30:13.0	Otto Scheff (AUT) 30:59.0
1908	Henry Taylor (GBR) 22:48.4	Sydney Battersby (GBR) 22:51.2	Frank Beaurepaire (AUS) 22:56.2
1912	George Hodgson (CAN) 22:00.0	John Hatfield (GBR) 22:39.0	Harold Hardwick (AUS) 23:15.4
1920	Norman Ross (USA) 22:23.2	George Vernot (CAN) 22:36.4	Frank Beaurepaire (AUS) 23:04.0
1924	Andrew Charlton (AUS) 20:06.6	Arne Borg (SWE) 20:41.4	Frank Beaurepaire (AUS) 21:48.4
1928	Arne Borg (SWE) 19:51.8	Andrew Charlton (AUS) 20:02.6	Buster Crabbe (USA) 20:28.8

1932	Kusuo Kitamura (JPN) 19:12.4	Shozo Makino (JPN) 19:14.1	James Christy (USA) 19:39.5
1936	Noboru Terada (JPN) 19:13.7	Jack Medica (USA) 19:34.0	Shumpei Uto (JPN) 19:34.5
1948	James McLane (USA) 19:18.5	John Marshall (AUS) 19:31.3	György Mitro (HUN) 19:43.2
1952	Ford Konno (USA) 18:30.0	Shiro Hashizune (JPN) 18:41.4	Tetsuo Okamoto (BRA) 18:51.3
1956	Murray Rose (AUS) 17:58.9	Tsuyoshi Yamanaka (JPN) 18:00.3	George Breen (USA) 18:08.2
1960	John Konrads (AUS) 17:19.6	Murray Rose (AUS) 17:21.7	George Breen (USA) 17:30.6
1964	Bob Windle (USA) 17:01.7	John Nelson (USA) 17:03.0	Allan Wood (AUS) 17:07.7
1968	Mike Burton (USA) 16:38.9	John Kinsella (USA) 16:57.3	Greg Brough (AUS) 17:04.7
1972	Mike Burton (USA) 15:52.58	Graham Windeatt (AUS) 15:58.48	Doug Northway (USA) 16:09.25
1976	Brian Goodell (USA) 15:02.40	Bobby Hackett (USA) 15:03.91	Steve Holland (AUS) 15:04.66
1980	Vladimir Salnikov (URS) 14:58.27	Aleksandr Chaev (URS) 15:14.30	Max Metzker (AUS) 15:14.49
1984	Michael O'Brien (USA) 15:05.20	George DiCarlo (USA) 15:10.59	Stefan Pfeiffer (FRG) 15:12.11
1988	Vladimir Salnikov (URS) 15:00.40	Stevan Pfeiffer (FRG) 15:02.69	Uwe Dassler (GDR) 15:06.15
1992	Kieren Perkins (AUS) 14:43.48	Glen Houseman (AUS) 14:55.29	Jörg Hoffmann (GER) 15:02.29

[1] *1200m.*
[2] *1000m.*
[3] *1 mile.*

100 Metres Breaststroke

1968	Don McKenzie (USA) 1:07.7	Vladimir Kossinsky (URS) 1:08.0	Nikolai Pankin (URS) 1:08.0
1972	Nobutaka Taguchi (JPN) 1:04.94	Tom Bruce (USA) 1:05.43	John Hencken (USA) 1:05.61
1976	John Hencken (USA) 1:03.11	David Wilkie (GBR) 1:03.43	Arvidas Iuozaytis (URS) 1:04.23
1980	Duncan Goodhew (GBR) 1:03.34	Arsen Miskarov (URS) 1:03.92	Peter Evans (AUS) 1:03.96
1984	Steve Lundquist (USA) 1:01.65	Victor Davis (CAN) 1:01.99	Peter Evans (AUS) 1:02.97
1988	Adrian Moorhouse (GBR) 1:02.04	Karoly Guttler (HUN) 1:02.05	Dmitry Volkov (URS) 1:02.20
1992	Nelson Diebel (USA) 1:01.50	Norbert Rozsa (HUN) 1:01.68	Phil Rogers (AUS) 1:01.76

1896–1964 Event not held.

200 Metres Breaststroke

1908	Frederick Holman (GBR) 3:09.2	William Robinson (GBR) 3:12.8	Pontus Hansson (SWE) 3:14.6
1912	Walter Bathe (GER) 3:01.8	Wilhelm Lützow (GER) 3:05.2	Kurt Malisch (GER) 3:08.0
1920	Häken Malmroth (SWE) 3:04.4	Thor Henning (SWE) 3:09.2	Arvo Aaltonen (FIN) 3:12.2
1924	Robert Skelton (USA) 2:56.5	Joseph de Combe (BEL) 2:59.2	William Kirschbaum (USA) 3:01.0
1928	Yoshiyuki Tsuruta (JPN) 2:48.8	Erich Rademacher (GER) 2:50.6	Teofilo Ylidefonzo (PHI) 2:56.4
1932	Yoshiyuki Tsuruta (JPN) 2:45.4	Reizo Koike (JPN) 2:46.4	Teofilo Ylidefonzo (PHI) 2:47.1
1936	Tetsuo Hamuro (JPN) 2:42.5	Erwin Sietas (GER) 2:42.9	Reizo Koike (JPN) 2:44.2
1948	Joseph Verdeur [1] (USA) 2:39.3	Keith Carter (USA) 2:40.2	Robert Sohl (USA) 2:43.9
1952	John Davies [1] (AUS) 2:34.4	Bowen Stassforth (USA) 2:34.7	Herbert Klein (GER) 2:35.9
1956	Masaru Furukawa [2] (JPN) 2:34.7	Masahiro Yoshimura (JPN) 2:36.7	Charis Yunitschev (URS) 2:36.8
1960	William Mulliken (USA) 2:37.4	Yoshihiko Osaki (JPN) 2:38.0	Wieger Mensonides (NED) 2:39.7
1964	Ian O'Brien (AUS) 2:27.8	Georgy Prokopenko (URS) 2:28.2	Chester Jastremski (USA) 2:29.6
1968	Felipe Munoz (MEX) 2:28.7	Vladimir Kossinsky (URS) 2:29.2	Brian Job (USA) 2:29.9
1972	John Hencken (USA) 2:21.55	David Wilkie (GBR) 2:23.67	Nobutaka Taguchi (JPN) 2:23.88
1976	David Wilkie (GBR) 2:15.11	John Hencken (USA) 2:17.26	Rick Colella (USA) 2:19.20
1980	Robertas Shulpa (URS) 2:15.85	Alban Vermes (HUN) 2:16.93	Arsen Miskarov (URS) 2:17.28
1984	Victor Davis (CAN) 2:13.34	Glenn Beringen (AUS) 2:15.79	Etienne Dagon (SUI) 2:17.41
1988	Jozsef Szabo (HUN) 2:13.52	Nick Gillingham (GBR) 2:14.12	Sergio Lopez (ESP) 2:15.21
1992	Mike Barrowman (USA) 2:10.16	Norbert Rozsa (HUN) 2:11.23	Nick Gillingham (GBR) 2:11.29

[1] *Used then permissible butterfly stroke.*
[2] *Used then permissible underwater technique.*
1896–1906 Event not held.

100 Metres Backstroke

1904 [1]	Walter Brack (GER) 1:16.8	Georg Hoffmann (GER) 1:18.0	Georg Zacharias (GER) 1:19.6
1908	Arno Bieberstein (GER) 1:24.6	Ludvig Dam (DEN) 1:26.6	Herbert Haresnape (GBR) 1:27.0
1912	Harry Hebner (USA) 1:21.2	Otto Fahr (GER) 1:22.4	Paul Kellner (GER) 1:24.0
1920	Warren Kealoha (USA) 1:15.2	Ray Kegeris (USA) 1:16.2	Gérard Blitz (BEL) 1:19.0

Having retired after Seoul, Pablo Morales came back to win the 100m butterfly in 1992 (Allsport/Bob Martin)

1924	Warren Kealoha (USA) 1:13.2	Paul Wyatt (USA) 1:15.4	Károly Bartha (HUN) 1:17.8
1928	George Kojac (USA) 1:08.2	Walter Laufer (USA) 1:10.0	Paul Wyatt (USA) 1:12.0
1932	Masaji Kiyokawa (JPN) 1:08.6	Toshio Irie (JPN) 1:09.8	Kentaro Kawatsu (JPN) 1:10.0
1936	Adolf Kiefer (USA) 1:05.9	Albert Van de Weghe (USA) 1:07.7	Masaji Kiyokawa (JPN) 1:08.4
1948	Allen Stack (USA) 1:06.4	Robert Cowell (USA) 1:06.5	Georges Vallerey (FRA) 1:07.8
1952	Yoshinobu Oyakawa (USA) 1:05.4	Gilbert Bozon (FRA) 1:06.2	Jack Taylor (USA) 1:06.4
1956	David Theile (AUS) 1:02.2	John Monckton (AUS) 1:03.2	Frank McKinney (USA) 1:04.5
1960	David Theile (AUS) 1:01.9	Frank McKinney (USA) 1:02.1	Robert Bennett (USA) 1:02.3
1968	Roland Matthes (GDR) 58.7	Charles Hickcox (USA) 1:00.2	Ronnie Mills (USA) 1:00.5
1972	Roland Matthes (GDR) 56.58	Mike Stamm (USA) 57.70	John Murphy (USA) 58.35
1976	John Naber (USA) 55.49	Peter Rocca (USA) 56.34	Roland Matthes (GDR) 57.22
1980	Bengt Baron (SWE) 56.53	Viktor Kuznetsov (URS) 56.99	Vladimir Dolgov (URS) 57.63
1984	Richard Carey (USA) 55.79	David Wilson (USA) 56.35	Mike West (CAN) 56.49
1988	Daichi Suzuki (JPN) 55.05	David Berkoff (USA) 55.18	Igor Polianski (URS) 55.20
1992	Mark Tewksbury (CAN) 53.98	Jeff Rouse (USA) 54.04	David Berkoff (USA) 54.78

[1] *100 yards.*
1896–1900, 1906, 1964 Event not held.

200 Metres Backstroke

1900	Ernst Hoppenberg (GER) 2:47.0	Karl Ruberl (AUT) 2:56.0	Johannes Drost (NED) 3:01.0
1964	Jed Graef (USA) 2:10.3	Gary Dilley (USA) 2:10.5	Robert Bennett (USA) 2:13.1
1968	Roland Matthes (GDR) 2:09.6	Mitchell Ivey (USA) 2:10.6	Jack Horsley (USA) 2:10.9
1972	Roland Matthes (GDR) 2:02.82	Mike Stamm (USA) 2:04.09	Mitchell Ivey (USA) 2:04.33
1976	John Naber (USA) 1:59.19	Peter Rocca (USA) 2:00.55	Don Harrigan (USA) 2:01.35
1980	Sandor Wladar (HUN) 2:01.93	Zóltán Verraszto (HUN) 2:02.40	Mark Kerry (AUS) 2:03.14
1984	Richard Carey (USA) 2:00.23	Frederic Delcourt (FRA) 2:01.75	Cameron Henning (CAN) 2:02.37
1988	Igor Polianski (URS) 1:59.37	Frank Baltrusch (GDR) 1:59.50	Paul Kingsman (NZL) 2:00.48
1992	Martin Lopez-Zubero (ESP) 1:58.47	Vladimir Selkov (EUN) 1:58.87	Stefano Battistelli (ITA) 1:59.40

1896, 1904–1960 Event not held.

100 Metres Butterfly

1968	Doug Russell (USA) 55.9	Mark Spitz (USA) 56.4	Ross Wales (USA) 57.2
1972	Mark Spitz (USA) 54.27	Bruce Robertson (CAN) 55.56	Jerry Heidenreich (USA) 55.74
1976	Matt Vogel (USA) 54.35	Joe Bottom (USA) 54.50	Gary Hall (USA) 54.65
1980	Pär Arvidsson (SWE) 54.92	Roger Pyttel (GDR) 54.94	David Lopez (ESP) 55.13
1984	Michael Gross (FRG) 53.08	Pablo Morales (USA) 53.23	Glenn Buchanan (AUS) 53.85
1988	Anthony Nesty (SUR) 53.00	Matt Biondi (USA) 53.01	Andy Jameson (GBR) 53.30
1992	Pablo Morales (USA) 53.32	Rafal Szukala (POL) 53.35	Anthony Nesty (SUR) 53.41

1896–1964 Event not held.

200 Metres Butterfly

1956	William Yorzyk (USA) 2:19.3	Takashi Ishimoto (JPN) 2:23.8	György Tumpek (HUN) 2:23.9
1960	Mike Troy (USA) 2:12.8	Neville Hayes (AUS) 2:14.6	David Gillanders (USA) 2:15.3
1964	Kevin Berry (AUS) 2:06.6	Carl Robie (USA) 2:07.5	Fred Schmidt (USA) 2:09.3
1968	Carl Robie (USA) 2:08.7	Martyn Woodroffe (GBR) 2:09.0	John Ferris (USA) 2:09.3
1972	Mark Spitz (USA) 2:00.70	Gary Hall (USA) 2:02.86	Robin Backhaus (USA) 2:03.23
1976	Mike Bruner (USA) 1:59.23	Steven Gregg (USA) 1:59.54	William Forrester (USA) 1:59.96
1980	Sergey Fesenko (URS) 1:59.76	Phil Hubble (GBR) 2:01.20	Roger Pyttel (GDR) 2:01.39
1984	Jon Sieben (AUS) 1:57.04	Michael Gross (FRG) 1:57.40	Rafael Castro (VEN) 1:57.51
1988	Michael Gross (FRG) 1:56.94	Benny Nielsen (DEN) 1:58.24	Anthony Mosse (NZL) 1:58.28
1992	Mel Stewart (USA) 1:56.26	Danyon Loader (NZL) 1:57.93	Franck Esposito (FRA) 1:58.51

1896–1952 Event not held.

200 Metres Individual Medley

1968	Charles Hickcox (USA) 2:12.0	Greg Buckingham (USA) 2:13.0	John Ferris (USA) 2:13.3
1972	Gunnar Larsson (SWE) 2:07.17	Tim McKee (USA) 2:08.37	Steve Furniss (USA) 2:08.45
1984	Alex Baumann (CAN) 2:01.42	Pablo Morales (USA) 2:03.05	Neil Cochran (GBR) 2:04.38
1988	Tamás Darnyi (HUN) 2:00.17	Patrick Kühl (GDR) 2:01.61	Vadim Yarochtchouk (URS) 2:02.40
1992	Tamas Darnyi (HUN) 2:00.76	Gregory Burgess (USA) 2:00.97	Attila Czene (HUN) 2:01.00

1896–1964, 1976–1980 Event not held.

400 Metres Individual Medley

1964	Richard Roth (USA) 4:45.4	Roy Saari (USA) 4:47.1	Gerhard Hetz (GER) 4:51.0
1968	Charles Hickcox (USA) 4:48.4	Gary Hall (USA) 4:48.7	Michael Holthaus (FRG) 4:51.4
1972	Gunnar Larsson (SWE) 4:31.98	Tim McKee (USA) 4:31.98	András Hargitay (HUN) 4:32.70
1976	Rod Strachan (USA) 4:23.68	Tim McKee (USA) 4:24.62	Andrei Smirnov (URS) 4:26.90
1980	Aleksandr Sidorenko (URS) 4:22.89	Sergey Fesenko (URS) 4:23.43	Zóltán Verraszto (HUN) 4:24.24
1984	Alex Baumann (CAN) 4:17.41	Ricardo Prado (BRA) 4:18.45	Robert Woodhouse (AUS) 4:20.50
1988	Tamás Darnyi (HUN) 4:14.75	David Wharton (USA) 4:17.36	Stefano Battistelli (ITA) 4:18.01
1992	Tamás Darnyi (HUN) 4:14.23	Erik Namesnik (USA) 4:15.57	Luca Sacchi (ITA) 4:16.34

1896–1960 Event not held.

4 x 100 Metres Freestyle Relay

1964	United States 3:33.2	Germany 3:37.2	Australia 3:39.1
1968	United States 3:31.7	Soviet Union 3:34.2	Australia 3:34.7
1972	United States 3:26.42	Soviet Union 3:29.72	GDR 3:32.42
1984	United States 3:19.03	Australia 3:19.68	Sweden 3:22.69
1988	United States 3:16.53	Soviet Union 3:18.33	GDR 3:19.82
1992	United States 3:16.74	Unified Team 3:17.56	Germany 3:17.90

1896–1960, 1976–1980 Event not held.

4 x 200 Metres Freestyle Relay

1906 [1]	Hungary 16:52.4	Germany 17:16.2	Great Britain n.t.a.
1908	Great Britain 10:55.6	Hungary 10:59.0	United States 11:02.8
1912	Australasia [2] 10:11.6	United States 10:20.2	Great Britain 10:28.2
1920	United States 10:04.4	Australia 10:25.4	Great Britain 10:37.2
1924	United States 9:53.4	Australia 10:02.2	Sweden 10:06.8
1928	United States 9:36.2	Japan 9:41.4	Canada 9:47.8
1932	Japan 8:58.4	United States 9:10.5	Hungary 9:31.4
1936	Japan 8:51.5	United States 9:03.0	Hungary 9:12.3
1948	United States 8:46.0	Hungary 8:48.4	France 9:08.0
1952	United States 8:31.1	Japan 8:33.5	France 8:45.9
1956	Australia 8:23.6	United States 8:31.5	Soviet Union 8:34.7
1960	United States 8:10.2	Japan 8:13.2	Australia 8:13.8
1964	United States 7:52.1	Germany 7:59.3	Japan 8:03.8
1968	United States 7:52.3	Australia 7:53.7	Soviet Union 8:01.6
1972	United States 7:35.78	FRG 7:41.69	Soviet Union 7:45.76

1976	United States 7:23.22	Soviet Union 7:27.97	Great Britain 7:32.11
1980	Soviet Union 7:23.50	GDR 7:28.60	Brazil 7:29.30
1984	United States 7:15.69	FRG 7:16.73	Great Britain 7:24.78
1988	United States 7:12.51	GDR 7:13.68	FRG 7:14.35
1992	Unified Team 7:11.95	Sweden 7:15.51	United States 7:16.23

[1] 4 x 250 metres.
[2] Composed of three Australians and a New Zealander.
1896–1904 Event not held.

4 x 100 Metres Medley Relay

1960	United States 4:05.4	Australia 4:12.0	Japan 4:12.2
1964	United States 3:38.5	Germany 4:01.6	Australia 4:02.3
1968	United States 3:54.9	GDR 3:57.5	Soviet Union 4:00.7
1972	United States 3:48.16	GDR 3:52.12	Canada 3:52.26
1976	United States 3:42.22	Canada 3:45.94	FRG 3:47.29
1980	Australia 3:45.70	Soviet Union 3:45.92	Great Britain 3:47.71
1984	United States 3:39.30	Canada 3:43.23	Australia 3:43.25
1988	United States 3:36.93	Canada 3:39.28	Soviet Union 3:39.96
1992	United States 3:36.93	Unified Team 3:38.56	Canada 3:39.66

1896–1956 Event not held.

DIVING MEDAL RESULTS — MEN

	GOLD	SILVER	BRONZE

Springboard Diving

1908	Albert Zurner (GER) 85.5	Kurt Behrens (GER) 85.3	George Gaidzik (USA) 80.8 Gottlob Walz (GER) 80.8
1912	Paul Günther (GER) 79.23	Hans Luber (GER) 76.78	Kurt Behrens (GER) 73.73
1920	Louis Kuehn (USA) 675.4	Clarence Pinkston (USA) 655.3	Louis Balbach (USA) 649.5
1924	Albert White (USA) 696.4	Pete Desjardins (USA) 693.2	Clarence Pinkston (USA) 653
1928	Pete Desjardins (USA) 185.04	Michael Galitzen (USA) 174.06	Farid Simaika (EGY) 172.46
1932	Michael Galitzen (USA) 161.38	Harold Smith (USA) 158.54	Richard Degener (USA) 151.82
1936	Richard Degener (USA) 163.57	Marshall Wayne (USA) 159.56	Al Greene (USA) 146.29
1948	Bruce Harlan (USA) 163.64	Miller Anderson (USA) 157.29	Samuel Lee (USA) 145.52
1952	David Browning (USA) 205.29	Miller Anderson (USA) 199.84	Robert Clotworthy (USA) 184.92
1956	Robert Clotworthy (USA) 159.56	Donald Harper (USA) 156.23	Joaquin Capilla Pérez (MEX) 150.69
1960	Gary Tobian (USA) 170.00	Samuel Hall (USA) 167.08	Juan Botella (MEX) 162.30
1964	Kenneth Sitzberger (USA) 159.90	Francis Gorman (USA) 157.63	Larry Andreasen (USA) 143.77
1968	Bernard Wrightson (USA) 170.15	Klaus Dibiasi (ITA) 159.74	James Henry (USA) 158.09
1972	Vladimir Vasin (URS) 594.09	F Giorgio Cagnotto (ITA) 591.63	Craig Lincoln (USA) 577.29
1976	Philip Boggs (USA) 619.05	F Giorgio Cagnotto (ITA) 570.48	Aleksandr Kosenkov (URS) 567.24
1980	Aleksandr Portnov (URS) 905.025	Carlos Giron (MEX) 892.140	F Giorgio Cagnotto (ITA) 871.500
1984	Greg Louganis (USA) 754.41	Tan Liangde (CHN) 662.31	Ronald Merriott (USA) 661.32
1988	Greg Louganis (USA) 730.80	Tan Liangde (CHN) 704.88	Li Deliang (CHN) 665.28
1992	Mark Lenzi (USA) 676.530pts	Tan Liangde (CHN) 645.570	Dmitri Saotine (EUN) 627.780

1896–1906 Event not held.

Highboard Diving

1904 [1]	George Sheldon (USA) 12.66	Georg Hoffmann (GER) 11.66	Frank Kehoe (USA) 11.33 Alfred Braunschweiger (GER) 11.33
1906	Gottlob Walz (GER) 156.00	Georg Hoffmann (GER) 150.20	Otto Satzinger (AUT) 147.40
1908	Hjalmar Johansson (SWE) 83.75	Karl Malmström (SWE) 78.73	Arvid Spangberg (SWE) 74.00
1912	Erik Adlerz (SWE) 73.94	Albert Zürner (GER) 72.60	Gustaf Blomgren (SWE) 69.56
1920	Clarence Pinkston (USA) 100.67	Erik Adlerz (SWE) 99.08	Haig Prieste (USA) 93.73
1924	Albert White (USA) 97.46	David Fall (USA) 97.30	Clarence Pinkston (USA) 94.60
1928	Pete Desjardins (USA) 98.74	Farid Simaika (EGY) 99.58	Michael Galitzen (USA) 92.34

1932	Harold Smith (USA) 124.80	Michael Galitzen (USA) 124.28	Frank Kurtz (USA) 121.98
1936	Marshall Wayne (USA) 113.58	Elbert Root (USA) 110.60	Hermann Stork (GER) 110.31
1948	Samuel Lee (USA) 130.05	Bruce Harlan (USA) 122.30	Joaquin Capilla Pérez (MEX) 113.52
1952	Samuel Lee (USA) 156.28	Joaquin Capilla Pérez (MEX) 145.21	Günther Haase (GER) 141.31
1956	Joaquin Capilla Pérez (MEX) 152.44	Gary Tobian (USA) 152.41	Richard Connor (USA) 149.79
1960	Robert Webster (USA) 165.56	Gary Tobian (USA) 165.25	Brian Phelps (GBR) 157.13
1964	Robert Webster (USA) 148.58	Klaus Dibiasi (ITA) 147.54	Thomas Gompf (USA) 146.57
1968	Klaus Dibiasi (ITA) 164.18	Alvaro Gaxiola (MEX) 154.49	Edwin Young (USA) 153.93
1972	Klaus Dibiasi (ITA) 504.12	Richard Rydze (USA) 480.75	F Giorgio Cagnotto (ITA) 475.83
1976	Klaus Dibiasi (ITA) 600.51	Greg Louganis (USA) 576.99	Vladimir Aleynik (URS) 548.61
1980	Falk Hoffmann (GDR) 835.650	Vladimir Aleynik (URS) 819.705	David Ambartsumyan (URS) 817.440
1984	Greg Louganis (USA) 710.91	Bruce Kimball (USA) 643.50	Li Kongzheng (CHN) 638.28
1988	Greg Louganis (USA) 638.61	Ni Xiong (CHN) 637.47	Jesus Mena (MEX) 594.39
1992	Sun Shuwei (CHN) 677.310	Scott Donie (USA) 633.630	Xiong Ni (CHN) 600.150

[1] *Combined springboard and highboard event.*
1896–1900 Event not held.

SWIMMING MEDAL RESULTS — WOMEN

	GOLD	SILVER	BRONZE
50 Metres Freestyle			
1988	Kristin Otto (GDR) 25.49	Yang Wenyi (CHN) 25.64	Katrin Meissner (GDR) 25.71
			Jill Sterkel (USA) 25.71
1992	Yang Wenyi (CHN) 24.79	Zhuang Yong (CHN) 25.08	Angel Martino (USA) 25.23

1896–1984 Event not held.

100 Metres Freestyle			
1912	Fanny Durack (AUS) 1:22.2	Wilhelmina Wylie (AUS) 1:25.4	Jennie Fletcher (GBR) 1:27.0
1920	Ethelda Bleibtrey (USA) 1:13.6	Irene Guest (USA) 1:17.0	Frances Schroth (USA) 1:17.2
1924	Ethel Lackie (USA) 1:12.4	Mariechen Wehselau (USA) 1:12.8	Gertrude Ederle (USA) 1:14.2
1928	Albina Osipowich (USA) 1:11.0	Eleanor Garatti (USA) 1:11.4	Joyce Cooper (GBR) 1:13.6
1932	Helene Madison (USA) 1:06.8	Willemijntje den Ouden (NED) 1:07.8	Eleanor Garatti-Saville (USA) 1:08.2
1936	Henrika Mastenbroek (NED) 1:05.9	Jeanette Campbell (ARG) 1:06.4	Gisela Arendt (GER) 1:06.6
1948	Greta Andersen (DEN) 1:06.3	Ann Curtis (USA) 1:06.5	Marie-Louise Vaessen (NED) 1:07.6
1952	Katalin Szöke (HUN) 1:06.8	Johanna Termeulen (NED) 1:07.0	Judit Temes (HUN) 1:07.1
1956	Dawn Fraser (AUS) 1:02.0	Lorraine Crapp (AUS) 1:02.3	Faith Leech (AUS) 1:05.1
1960	Dawn Fraser (AUS) 1:01.2	Chris von Saltza (USA) 1:02.8	Natalie Steward (GBR) 1:03.1
1964	Dawn Fraser (AUS) 59.5	Sharon Stouder (USA) 59.9	Kathleen Ellis (USA) 1:00.8
1968	Jan Henne (USA) 1:00.0	Susan Pedersen (USA) 1:00.3	Linda Gustavson (USA) 1:00.3
1972	Sandra Neilson (USA) 58.59	Shirley Babashoff (USA) 59.02	Shane Gould (AUS) 59.06
1976	Kornelia Ender (GDR) 55.65	Petra Priemer (GDR) 56.49	Enith Brigitha (NED) 56.65
1980	Barbara Krause (GDR) 54.79	Caren Metschuck (GDR) 55.16	Ines Diers (GDR) 55.65
1984	Carrie Steinseifer (USA) 55.92	–	Annemarie Verstappen (NED) 56.08
	Nancy Hogshead (USA) 55.92		
1988	Kristin Otto (GDR) 54.93	Zhuang Yong (CHN) 55.47	Catherine Plewinski (FRA) 55.49
1992	Zhuang Yong (CHN) 54.64	Jenny Thompson (USA) 54.84	Franziska van Almsick (GER) 54.94

1896–1908 Event not held.

200 Metres Freestyle			
1968	Debbie Meyer (USA) 2:10.5	Jan Henne (USA) 2:11.0	Jane Barkman (USA) 2:11.2
1972	Shane Gould (AUS) 2:03.56	Shirley Babashoff (USA) 2:04.33	Keena Rothhammer (USA) 2:04.92
1976	Kornelia Ender (GDR) 1:59.26	Shirley Babashoff (USA) 2:01.22	Enith Brigitha (NED) 2:01.40
1980	Barbara Krause (GDR) 1:58.33	Ines Diers (GDR) 1:59.64	Carmela Schmidt (GDR) 2:01.44
1984	Mary Wayte (USA) 1:59.23	Cynthia Woodhead (USA) 1:59.50	Annemarie Verstappen (NED) 1:59.69
1988	Heike Friedrich (GDR) 1:57.65	Silvia Poll (CRC) 1:58.67	Manuela Stellmach (GDR) 1:59.01
1992	Nicole Haislett (USA) 1:57.90	Franziska van Almsick (GER) 1:58.00	Kerstin Kielgass (GER) 1:59.67

1896–1964 Event not held.

400 Metres Freestyle

1920 [1]	Ethelda Bleibtrey (USA) 4:34.0	Margaret Woodbridge (USA) 4:42.8	Frances Schroth (USA) 4:52.0
1924	Martha Norelius (USA) 6:02.2	Helen Wainwright (USA) 6:03.8	Gertrude Ederle (USA) 6:04.8
1928	Martha Norelius (USA) 5:42.8	Marie Braun (NED) 5:57.8	Josephine McKim (USA) 6:00.2
1932	Helene Madison (USA) 5:28.5	Lenore Kight (USA) 5:28.6	Jennie Maakal (RSA) 5:47.3
1936	Henrika Mastenbroek (NED) 5:26.4	Ragnhild Hveger (DEN) 5:27.5	Lenore Kight-Wingard (USA) 5:29.0
1948	Ann Curtis (USA) 5:17.8	Karen Harup (DEN) 5:21.2	Cathy Gibson (GBR) 5:22.5
1952	Valeria Gyenge (HUN) 5:12.1	Eva Novak (HUN) 5:13.7	Evelyn Kawamoto (USA) 5:14.6
1956	Lorraine Crapp (USA) 4:54.6	Dawn Fraser (AUS) 5:02.5	Sylvia Ruuska (USA) 5:07.1
1960	Chris von Saltza (USA) 4:50.6	Jane Cederquist (SWE) 4:53.9	Catharina Lagerberg (NED) 4:56.9
1964	Virginia Duenkel (USA) 4:43.3	Marilyn Ramenofsky (USA) 4:44.6	Terri Stickles (USA) 4:47.2
1968	Debbie Meyer (USA) 4:31.8	Linda Gustavson (USA) 4:35.5	Karen Moras (AUS) 4:37.0
1972	Shane Gould (AUS) 4:19.04	Novella Calligaris (ITA) 4:22.44	Gudrun Wegner (GDR) 4:23.11
1976	Petra Thuemer (GDR) 4:09.89	Shirley Babashoff (USA) 4:10.46	Shannon Smith (CAN) 4:14.60
1980	Ines Diers (GDR) 4:08.76	Petra Schneider (GDR) 4:09.16	Carmela Schmidt (GDR) 4:10.86
1984	Tiffany Cohen (USA) 4:07.10	Sarah Hardcastle (GBR) 4:10.27	June Croft (GBR) 4:11.49
1988	Janet Evans (USA) 4:03.85	Heike Friedrich (GDR) 4:05.94	Anke Möhring (GDR) 4:06.62
1992	Dagmar Hase (GER) 4:07.18	Janet Evans (USA) 4:07.37	Hayley Lewis (AUS) 4:11.22

[1] *300 metres.*
1896–1912 Event not held.

800 Metres Freestyle

1968	Debbie Meyer (USA) 9:24.0	Pamela Kruse (USA) 9:35.7	Maria Ramirez (MEX) 9:38.5
1972	Keena Rothhammer (USA) 8:53.68	Shane Gould (AUS) 8:56.39	Novella Calligaris (ITA) 8:57.46
1976	Petra Thuemer (GDR) 8:37.14	Shirley Babashoff (USA) 8:37.59	Wendy Weinberg (USA) 8:42.60
1980	Michelle Ford (AUS) 8:28.9	Ines Diers (GDR) 8:32.55	Heike Dähne (GDR) 8:33.48
1984	Tiffany Cohen (USA) 8:24.95	Michele Richardson (USA) 8:30.73	Sarah Hardcastle (GBR) 8:32.60
1988	Janet Evans (USA) 8:20.20	Astrid Strauss (GDR) 8:22.09	Julie McDonald (AUS) 8:22.93
1992	Janet Evans (USA) 8:25.52	Hayley Lewis (AUS) 8:30.34	Jana Henke (GER) 8:30.99

1896–1964 Event not held.

100 Metres Breaststroke

1968	Djurdjica Bjedov (YUG) 1:15.8	Galina Prozumenschchikova [1] (URS) 1:15.9	Sharon Wichman (USA) 1:16.1
1972	Catherine Carr (USA) 1:13.58	Galina Stepanova (URS) 1:14.99	Beverley Whitfield (AUS) 1:15.73
1976	Hannelore Anke (GDR) 1:11.16	Lubov Rusanova (URS) 1:13.04	Marina Kosheveya (URS) 1:13.30
1980	Ute Geweniger (GDR) 1:10.22	Elvira Vasilkova (URS) 1:10.41	Susanne Nielsson (DEN) 1:11.16
1984	Petra Van Staveren (NED) 1:09.88	Anne Ottenbrite (CAN) 1:10.69	Catherine Poirot (FRA) 1:10.70
1988	Tania Dangalakova (BUL) 1:07.95	Antoaneta Frankeva (BUL) 1:08.74	Silke Hörner (GDR) 1:08.83
1992	Yelena Rudkovskaya (EUN) 1:08.00	Anita Nall (USA) 1:08.17	Samantha Riley (AUS) 1:09.25

[1] *Later Stepanova.*
1896–1964 Event not held.

200 Metres Breaststroke

1924	Lucy Morton (GBR) 3:33.2	Agnes Geraghty (USA) 3:34.0	Gladys Carson (GBR) 3:35.4
1928	Hilde Schrader (GER) 3:12.6	Mietje Baron (NED) 3:15.2	Lotte Mühe (GER) 3:17.6
1932	Claire Dennis (AUS) 3:06.3	Hideko Maehata (JPN) 3:06.4	Else Jacobsen (DEN) 3:07.1
1936	Hideko Maehata (JPN) 3:03.6	Martha Genenger (GER) 3:04.2	Inge Sörensen (DEN) 3:07.8
1948	Petronella van Vliet (NED) 2:57.2	Nancy Lyons (AUS) 2:57.7	Eva Novák (HUN) 3:00.2
1952	Eva Székely [1] (HUN) 2:51.7	Eva Novák (HUN) 2:54.4	Helen Gordon (GBR) 2:57.6
1956	Ursula Happe [2] (GER) 2:53.1	Eva Székely (HUN) 2:54.8	Eva-Maria ten Elsen (GER) 2:55.1
1960	Anita Lonsbrough (GBR) 2:49.5	Wiltrud Urselmann (GER) 2:50.0	Barbara Göbel (GER) 2:53.6
1964	Galina Prozumenshchikova (URS) 2:46.4	Claudia Kolb (USA) 2:47.6	Svetlana Babanina (URS) 2:48.6
1968	Sharon Wichman (USA) 2:44.4	Djurdjica Bjedov (YUG) 2:46.4	Galina Prozumenshchikova (URS) 2:47.0
1972	Beverly Whitfield (AUS) 2:41.7	Dana Schoenfield (USA) 2:42.05	Galina Stepanova (URS) 2:42.36

1976	Marina Kosheveya (URS) 2:33.35	Marina Yurchenia (URS) 2:36.08	Lubov Rusanova (URS) 2:36.22
1980	Lina Kachushite (URS) 2:29.54	Svetlana Varganova (URS) 2:29.61	Yulia Bogdanova (URS) 2:32.39
1984	Anne Ottenbrite (CAN) 2:30.38	Susan Rapp (USA) 2:31.15	Ingrid Lempereur (BEL) 2:31.40
1988	Silke Hörner (GDR) 2:26.71	Huang Xiaomin (CHN) 2:27.49	Antoaneta Frankeva (BUL) 2:28.34
1992	Kyoko Iwasaki (JPN) 2:26.65	Li Lin (CHN) 2:26.85	Anita Nall (USA) 2:26.88

(1) *Used then permitted butterfly stroke.*
(2) *Used then permitted underwater technique.*
1896–1920 Event not held.

100 Metres Backstroke

1924	Sybil Bauer (USA) 1:23.2	Phyllis Harding (GBR) 1:27.4	Aileen Riggin (USA) 1:28.2
1928	Marie Braun (NED) 1:22.0	Ellen King (GBR) 1:22.2	Joyce Cooper (GBR) 1:22.8
1932	Eleanor Holm (USA) 1:19.4	Philomena Mealing (AUS) 1:21.3	Valerie Davies (GBR) 1:22.5
1936	Dina Senff (NED) 1:18.9	Hendrika Mastenbroek (NED) 1:19.2	Alice Bridges (USA) 1:19.4
1948	Karen Harup (DEN) 1:14.4	Suzanne Zimmermann (USA) 1:16.0	Judy Davies (AUS) 1:16.7
1952	Joan Harrison (RSA) 1:14.3	Geertje Wielema (NED) 1:14.5	Jean Stewart (NZL) 1:15.8
1956	Judy Grinham (GBR) 1:12.9	Carin Cone (USA) 1:12.9	Margaret Edwards (GBR) 1:13.1
1960	Lynn Burke (USA) 1:09.3	Natalie Steward (GBR) 1:10.8	Satoko Tanaka (JPN) 1:11.4
1964	Cathy Ferguson (USA) 1:07.7	Cristine Caron (FRA) 1:07.9	Virginia Duenkel (USA) 1:08.0
1968	Kaye Hall (USA) 1:06.2	Elaine Tanner (CAN) 1:06.7	Jane Swaggerty (USA) 1:08.1
1972	Melissa Belote (USA) 1:05.78	Andrea Gyarmati (HUN) 1:06.26	Susie Atwood (USA) 1:06.34
1976	Ulrike Richter (GDR) 1:01.83	Birgit Treiber (GDR) 1:03.41	Nancy Garapick (CAN) 1:03.71
1980	Rica Reinisch (GDR) 1:00.86	Ina Kleber (GDR) 1:02.07	Petra Reidel (GDR) 1:02.64
1984	Theresa Andrews (USA) 1:02.55	Betsy Mitchell (USA) 1:02.63	Jolanda De Rover (NED) 1:92.91
1988	Kristin Otto (GDR) 1:00.89	Krisztina Egerszegi (HUN) 1:01.56	Cornelia Sirch (GDR) 1:01.57
1992	Krisztina Egerszegi (HUN) 1:00.68	Tunde Szabo (HUN) 1:01.14	Lea Loveless (USA) 1:01.43

1896–1920 Event not held.

200 Metres Backstroke

1968	Lillian Watson (USA) 2:24.8	Elaine Tanner (CAN) 2:27.4	Kaye Hall (USA) 2:28.9
1972	Melissa Belote (USA) 2:19.19	Susie Atwood (USA) 2:20.38	Donna Marie Gurr (CAN) 2:23.22
1976	Ulrike Richter (GDR) 2:13.43	Birgit Treiber (GDR) 2:14.97	Nancy Garapick (CAN) 2:15.60
1980	Rica Reinisch (GDR) 2:11.77	Cornelia Polit (GDR) 2:13.75	Birgit Treiber (GDR) 2:14.14
1984	Jolanda De Rover (NED) 2:12.38	Amy White (USA) 2:13.04	Aneta Patrascoiu (ROM) 2:13.29
1988	Krisztina Egerszegi (HUN) 2:09.29	Kathrin Zimmermann (GDR) 2:10.61	Cornelia Sirch (GDR) 2:11.45
1992	Krisztina Egerszegi (HUN) 2:07.06	Dagmar Hase (GER) 2:09.46	Nicole Stevenson (AUS) 2:10.20

1896–1964 Event not held.

100 Metres Butterfly

1956	Shelley Mann (USA) 1:11.0	Nancy Ramey (USA) 1:11.9	Mary Sears (USA) 1:14.4
1960	Carolyn Schuler (USA) 1:09.5	Marianne Heemskerk (NED) 1:10.4	Janice Andrew (AUS) 1:12.2
1964	Sharon Stouder (USA) 1:04.7	Ada Kok (NED) 1:05.6	Kathleen Ellis (USA) 1:06.0
1968	Lynette McClements (AUS) 1:05.5	Ellie Daniel (USA) 1:05.8	Susan Shields (USA) 1:06.2
1972	Mayumi Aoki (JPN) 1:03.34	Roswitha Beier (GDR) 1:03.61	Andrea Gyarmati (HUN) 1:03.73
1976	Kornelia Ender (GDR) 1:00.13	Andrea Pollack (GDR) 1:00.98	Wendy Boglioli (USA) 1:01.17
1980	Caren Metschuck (GDR) 1:00.42	Andrea Pollack (GDR) 1:00.90	Christiane Knacke (GDR) 1:01.44
1984	Mary Meagher (USA) 59.26	Jenna Johnson (USA) 1:00.19	Karin Seick (FRG) 1:00.36
1988	Kristin Otto (GDR) 59.00	Birte Weigang (GDR) 59.45	Qian Hong (CHN) 59.52
1992	Qian Hong (CHN) 58.62	Chrissy Ahmann-Leighton (USA) 58.74	Catherine Plewinski (FRA) 59.01

1896–1952 Event not held.

200 Metres Butterfly

1968	Ada Kok (NED) 2:24.7	Helga Lindner (GDR) 2:24.8	Ellie Daniel (USA) 2:25.9
1972	Karen Moe (USA) 2:15.57	Lynn Colella (USA) 2:16.34	Ellie Daniel (USA) 2:26.74
1976	Andrea Pollack (GDR) 2:11.41	Ulrike Tauber (GDR) 2:12.50	Rosemarie Gabriel (GDR) 2:12.86
1980	Ines Geissler (GDR) 2:10.44	Sybille Schönrock (GDR) 2:10.45	Michelle Ford (AUS) 2:11.66
1984	Mary Meagher (USA) 2:06.90	Karen Phillips (AUS) 2:10.56	Ina Beyermann (FRG) 2:11.91

1988	Kathleen Nord (GDR) 2:09.51	Birte Weigang (GDR) 2:09.91	Mary Meagher (USA) 2:10.80
1992	Summer Sanders (USA) 2:08.67	Wang Xiaohong (CHN) 2:09.01	Susan O'Neill (AUS) 2:09.03

1896–1964 Event not held.

200 Metres Individual Medley

1968	Claudia Kolb (USA) 2:24.7	Susan Pedersen (USA) 2:28.8	Jan Henne (USA) 2:31.4
1972	Shane Gould (AUS) 2:23.07	Kornelia Ender (GDR) 2:23.59	Lynn Vidali (USA) 2:24.06
1984	Tracy Caulkins (USA) 2:12.64	Nancy Hogshead (USA) 2:15.17	Michele Pearson (AUS) 2:15.92
1988	Daniela Hunger (GDR) 2:12.59	Yelena Dendeberova (URS) 2:13.31	Noemi Ildiko Lung (ROM) 2:14.85
1992	Li Lin (CHN) 2:11.65	Summer Sanders (USA) 2:11.91	Daniela Hunger (GER) 2:13.92

1896–1964, 1976–1980 Event not held.

400 Metres Individual Medley

1964	Donna De Varona (USA) 5:18.7	Sharon Finneran (USA) 5:24.1	Martha Randall (USA) 5:24.1
1968	Claudia Kolb (USA) 5:08.5	Lynn Vidali (USA) 5:22.2	Sabine Steinbach (GDR) 5:25.3
1972	Gail Neall (AUS) 5:02.97	Leslie Cliff (CAN) 5:03.57	Novella Calligaris (ITA) 5:03.99
1976	Ulrike Tauber (GDR) 4:42.77	Cheryl Gibson (CAN) 4:48.10	Becky Smith (CAN) 4:50.48
1980	Petra Schneider (GDR) 4:36.29	Sharron Davies (GBR) 4:46.83	Agnieszka Czopek (POL) 4:48.17
1984	Tracy Caulkins (USA) 4:39.24	Suzanne Landells (AUS) 4:48.30	Petra Zindler (FRG) 4:48.57
1988	Janet Evans (USA) 4:37.76	Noemi Ildiko Lung (ROM) 4:39.46	Daniela Hunger (GDR) 4:39.76
1992	Krisztina Egerszegi (HUN) 4:36.54	Li Lin (CHN) 4:36.73	Summer Sanders (USA) 4:37.58

1896–1960 Event not held.

4 x 100 Metres Freestyle Relay

1912	Great Britain 5:52.8	Germany 6:04.6	Austria 6:17.0
1920	United States 5:11.6	Great Britain 5:40.8	Sweden 5:43.6
1924	United States 4:58.8	Great Britain 5:17.0	Sweden 5:35.6
1928	United States 4:47.6	Great Britain 5:02.8	South Africa 5:13.4
1932	United States 4:38.0	Netherlands 4:47.5	Great Britain 4:52.4
1936	Netherlands 4:36.0	Germany 4:36.8	United States 4:40.2
1948	United States 4:29.2	Denmark 4:29.6	Netherlands 4:31.6
1952	Hungary 4:24.4	Netherlands 4:29.0	United States 4:30.1
1956	Australia 4:17.1	United States 4:19.2	South Africa 4:25.7
1960	United States 4:08.9	Australia 4:11.3	Germany 4:19.7
1964	United States 4:03.8	Australia 4:06.9	Netherlands 4:12.0
1968	United States 4:02.5	GDR 4:05.7	Canada 4:07.2
1972	United States 3:55.19	GDR 3:55.55	FRG 3:57.93
1976	United States 3:44.82	GDR 3:45.50	Canada 3:48.81
1980	GDR 3:42.71	Sweden 3:48.93	Netherlands 3:49.51
1984	United States 3:43.43	Netherlands 3:44.40	FRG 3:45.56
1988	GDR 3:40.63	Netherlands 3:43.39	United States 3:44.25
1992	United States 3:39.46	China 3:40.12	Germany 3:41.60

1896–1908 Event not held.

4 x 100 Metres Medley Relay

1960	United States 4:41.1	Australia 4:45.9	Germany 4:47.6
1964	United States 4:33.9	Netherlands 4:37.0	Soviet Union 4:39.2
1968	United States 4:28.3	Australia 4:30.0	FRG 4:36.4
1972	United States 4:20.75	GDR 4:24.91	FRG 4:26.46
1976	GDR 4:07.95	United States 4:14.55	Canada 4:15.22
1980	GDR 4:06.67	Great Britain 4:12.24	Soviet Union 4:13.61
1984	United States 4:08.34	FRG 4:11.97	Canada 4:12.98
1988	GDR 4:03.74	United States 4:07.90	Canada 4:10.49
1992	United States 4:02.54	Germany 4:05.19	Unified Team 4:06.44

1896–1956 Event not held.

DIVING MEDAL RESULTS – WOMEN

Springboard Diving

1920	Aileen Riggin (USA) 539.9	Helen Wainwright (USA) 534.8	Thelma Payne (USA) 534.1
1924	Elizabeth Becker (USA) 474.5	Aileen Riggin (USA) 460.4	Caroline Fletcher (USA) 434.4
1928	Helen Meany (USA) 78.62	Dorothy Poynton (USA) 75.62	Georgia Coleman (USA) 73.78
1932	Georgia Coleman (USA) 87.52	Katherine Rawls (USA) 82.56	Jane Fauntz (USA) 82.12
1936	Marjorie Gestring (USA) 89.27	Katherine Rawls (USA) 88.35	Dorothy Poynton-Hill (USA) 82.36
1948	Victoria Draves (USA) 108.74	Zoe Ann Olsen (USA) 108.23	Patricia Elsener (USA) 101.30
1952	Patricia McCormick (USA) 147.30	Madeleine Moreau (FRA) 139.34	Zoe Ann Jensen (USA) 127.57
1956	Patricia McCormick (USA) 142.36	Jeanne Stunyo (USA) 125.89	Irene Macdonald (CAN) 121.40
1960	Ingrid Krämer (GER) 155.81	Paula Myers-Pope (USA) 141.24	Elizabeth Ferris (GBR) 139.09
1964	Ingrid Krämer-Engel (GER) 145.00	Jeanne Collier (USA) 138.36	Mary Willard (USA) 138.18
1968	Sue Gossick (USA) 150.77	Tamara Pogozheva (URS) 145.30	Keala O'Sullivan (USA) 145.23
1972	Micki King (USA) 450.03	Ulrika Knape (SWE) 434.19	Marina Janicke (GDR) 430.92
1976	Jennifer Chandler (USA) 506.19	Christa Kohler (GDR) 469.41	Cynthia McIngvale (USA) 466.83
1980	Irina Kalinina (URS) 725.910	Martina Proeber (GDR) 698.895	Karin Guthke (GDR) 685.245
1984	Sylvie Bernier (CAN) 530.70	Kelly McCormick (USA) 527.46	Christina Seufert (USA) 517.62
1988	Gao Min (CHN) 580.23	Li Qing (CHN) 534.33	Kelly Anne McCormick (USA) 533.19
1992	Gao Min (CHN) 572.400pts	Irina Lachko (EUN) 514.140	Brita Baldus (GER) 503.070

1896–1912 Event not held.

Highboard Diving

1912	Greta Johansson (SWE) 39.9	Lisa Regnell (SWE) 36.0	Isabelle White (GBR) 34.0
1920	Stefani Fryland-Clausen (DEN) 34.6	Eileen Armstrong (GBR) 33.3	Eva Ollivier (SWE) 33.3
1924	Caroline Smith (USA) 10.5	Elizabeth Becker (USA) 11.0	Hjördis Töpel (SWE) 15.5
1928	Elizabeth Pinkston (USA) 31.6	Georgia Coleman (USA) 30.6	Lala Sjöqvist (SWE) 29.2
1932	Dorothy Poynton (USA) 40.26	Georgia Coleman (USA) 35.56	Marion Roper (USA) 35.22
1936	Dorothy Poynton-Hill (USA) 33.93	Velma Dunn (USA) 33.63	Käthe Köhler (GER) 33.43
1948	Victoria Draves (USA) 68.87	Patricia Elsener (USA) 66.28	Birte Christoffersen (DEN) 66.04
1952	Patricia McCormick (USA) 79.37	Paula Myers (USA) 71.63	Juno Irwin (USA) 70.49
1956	Patricia McCormick (USA) 84.85	Juno Irwin (USA) 81.64	Paula Myers (USA) 81.58
1960	Ingrid Krämer (GER) 91.28	Paula Myers-Pope (USA) 88.94	Ninel Krutova (URS) 86.99
1964	Lesley Bush (USA) 99.80	Ingrid Krämer-Engel (GER) 98.45	Galina Alekseyeva (URS) 97.60
1968	Milena Duchkova (TCH) 109.59	Natalia Lobanova (URS) 105.14	Ann Peterson (USA) 101.11
1972	Ulrika Knape (SWE) 390.00	Milena Duchkova (TCH) 370.92	Marina Janicke (GDR) 360.54
1976	Elena Vaytsekhovskaya (URS) 406.59	Ulrika Knape (SWE) 402.60	Deborah Wilson (USA) 401.07
1980	Martina Jäschke (GDR) 596.250	Servard Emirzyan (URS) 576.465	Liana Tsotadze (URS) 575.925
1984	Zhou Jihong (CHN) 435.51	Michele Mitchell (USA) 431.19	Wendy Wyland (USA) 422.07
1988	Xu Yanmei (CHN) 445.20	Michele Mitchell (USA) 436.95	Wendy Williams (USA) 400.44
1992	Fu Mingxia (CHN) 461.430	Yelena Mirochina (EUN) 411.630	Mary Ellen Clark (USA) 401.910

1896–1908 Event not held.

SYNCHRONISED SWIMMING MEDAL RESULTS

	GOLD	SILVER	BRONZE

Solo

1984	Tracie Ruiz (USA) 198.467	Carolyn Waldo (CAN) 195.300	Miwako Motoyoshi (JPN) 187.050
1988	Carolyn Waldo (CAN) 200.150	Tracie Ruiz-Conforto (USA) 197.633	Mikako Kotani (JPN) 191.850
1992	Kristen-Babb Sprague (USA) 191.848pts – Sylvia Frechette (CAN)		Fumiko Okuno (JPN) 187.056

1896–1980 Event not held.

Duet

1984	United States 195.584	Canada 194.234	Japan 187.992
1988	Canada 197.717	United States 197.284	Japan 190.159
1992	United States 192.175pts	Canada 189.394	Japan 186.868

1896–1980 Event not held.

DISCONTINUED EVENTS

GOLD   SILVER   BRONZE

100 Metres Freestyle (Sailors)
1896   Ioannis Malokinis (GRE) 2:20.4   Spiridon Khasapis (GRE) n.t.a.   Dimitrios Drivas (GRE) n.t.a.

200 Metres Obstacle Event
1900   Frederick Lane (AUS) 2:38.4   Otto Wahle (AUT) 2:40.0   Peter Kemp (GBR) 2:47.4

400 Metres Breaststroke
1904	Georg Zacharias (GER) 7:23.6	Walter Brack (GER) 20m	Jamison Handy (USA) d.n.a.
1912	Walter Bathe (GER) 6:29.6	Thor Henning (SWE) 6:35.6	Percy Courtman (GBR) 6:36.4
1920	Hakan Malmroth (SWE) 6:31.8	Thor Henning (SWE) 6:45.2	Arvo Aaltonen (FIN) 6:48.0

880 Yards Freestyle
1904   Emil Rausch (GER) 13:11.4   Francis Gailey (USA) 13:23.4   Géza Kiss (HUN) n.t.a.

4000 Metres Freestyle
1900   John Jarvis (GBR) 58:24.0   Zoltán Halmay (HUN) 1:08:55.4   Louis Martin (FRA) 1:13:08.4

Underwater Swimming
1900   Charles de Vendeville (FRA) 188.4   A Six (FRA) 185.4   Peder Lykkeberg (DEN) 147.0

Plunge for Distance
1904   Paul Dickey (USA) 19.05m   Edgar Adams (USA) 17.53m   Leo Goodwin (USA) 17.37m

200 Metres Team Swimming
1900   Germany 32pts   France 51   France 61

4 x 50 Yards Relay
1904   United States (New York AC) 2:04.6   United States (Chicago AC) n.t.a.   United States (Missouri AC) n.t.a.

Plain High Diving
1912	Erik Adlerz (SWE) 40.0	Hjalmar Johansson (SWE) 39.3	John Jansson (SWE) 39.1
1920	Arvid Wallmann (SWE) 183.5	Nils Skoglund (SWE) 183.0	John Jansson (SWE) 175.0
1924	Richmond Eve (AUS) 160.0	John Jansson (SWE) 157.0	Harold Clarke (GBR) 158.0

WATER POLO MEDAL RESULTS

1900 [1]	Great Britain	Belgium	France
1904 [1]	United States	United States	United States
1908	Great Britain	Belgium	Sweden
1912	Great Britain	Sweden	Belgium
1920	Great Britain	Belgium	Sweden
1924	France	Belgium	United States
1928	Germany	Hungary	France
1932	Hungary	Germany	United States
1936	Hungary	Germany	Belgium
1948	Italy	Hungary	Netherlands

1952	Hungary	Yugoslavia	Italy
1956	Hungary	Yugoslavia	Soviet Union
1960	Italy	Soviet Union	Hungary
1964	Hungary	Yugoslavia	Soviet Union
1968	Yugoslavia	Soviet Union	Hungary
1972	Soviet Union	Hungary	United States
1976	Hungary	Italy	Netherlands
1980	Soviet Union	Yugoslavia	Hungary
1984	Yugoslavia	United States	FRG
1988	Yugoslavia	United States	Soviet Union
1992	Italy	Spain	Unified Team

[1] *Entries were from clubs not international teams*
1896, 1906 Event not held

Sweden's Jan-Ove Waldner improved from 8th place in 1988 to win the men's table tennis gold in 1992 (Allsport/Chris Cole)

Table Tennis

Recognized as an Olympic sport by the IOC in 1977, table tennis was first included at the 1988 Seoul Games as a medal sport, never having been a demonstration sport. There are 64 men and 32 women, selected by an agreed international formula, competing in men's and women's singles and doubles events.

The most successful player has been Hyun Jung-Hwa (KOR) with a gold, silver and bronze in women's events, 1988-92, while the most successful male was Yoo Nam-Kyu (KOR) with a gold and two bronzes, 1988-92. Only Deng Yaping (CHN) has won two gold medals, both in the 1992 women's events. The youngest gold medallist was Hyun Jung-Hwa in the 1988 women's doubles aged 18yr 360 days, while the youngest male champion was Yoo Nam-Kyu who won the 1988 singles aged 20yr 119 days. The oldest gold medallist/medallist was Jan-Ove Waldner (SWE), winner of the 1992 men's singles aged 26yr 308 days, while the oldest female champion was Yang Young-Ja (KOR) in the women's doubles aged 24yr 86 days. The youngest female medallist was Jasna Fazlic (YUG) in the 1988 women's doubles aged 17yr 285 days, and the youngest male medallist was Zoran Primorac (YUG) in 1988 at 19yr 143 days. The oldest female medallist was Gordana Perkucin (YUG) in 1988 aged 26yr 147 days.

TABLE TENNIS MEDALS TABLE

| | Men | | | Women | | | |
	G	S	B	G	S	B	Total
China	2	-	1	3	4	1	11
Korea	1	1	4	1	-	2	9
Sweden	1	-	1	-	-	-	2
North Korea (PRK)	-	-	-	-	-	2	2
Yugoslavia	-	1	-	-	-	1	2
France	-	1	-	-	-	-	1
Germany	-	1	-	-	-	-	1
	4	4	6*	4	4	6*	28

* Two bronze medals in 1992

TABLE TENNIS MEDAL RESULTS

Introduced in 1988

	GOLD	SILVER	BRONZE
Men's Singles			
1988	Yoo Nam-Kyu (KOR)	Kim Ki-Taik (KOR)	Erik Lindh (SWE)
1992	Jan-Ove Waldner (SWE)	Jean Philippe Gatien (FRA)	Ma Wenge (CHN)
			Kim Taek-soo (KOR)
Men's Doubles			
1988	China	Yugoslavia	Korea
1992	China	Germany	Korea
			Korea
Women's Singles			
1988	Chen Jing (CHN)	Li Huifen (CHN)	Jiao Zhimin (CHN)
1992	Deng Yaping (CHN)	Qiao Hong (CHN)	Hyung Jung-hwa (KOR)
			Li Bun-hui (PRK)
Women's Doubles			
1988	Korea	China	Yugoslavia
1992	China	China	Korea
			PRK

Tennis

The inclusion of tennis in the Games was suspended from 1924 until 1988, although it was a demonstration sport in 1968 and 1984. The first gold medallist was Irish-born John Pius Boland (GBR) in the 1896 singles. He happened to be in Athens, visiting the famous German archaeologist Heinrich Schliemann, and entered the Games at the last minute. The ladies' singles champion in 1900, Charlotte Cooper (GBR), became the first woman to win an Olympic title in any sport. In the early years a number of medal-winning pairs were composed of players from two countries; thus Boland combined with a German to win the first mixed doubles title. The most successful player was Max Décugis (FRA) with a total of six medals comprising four golds, one silver and a bronze between 1900 and 1920. Britain's Kitty McKane won a record total for a woman of five (one gold, two silvers and two bronzes) in 1920 and 1924.

The oldest gold medallist was George Hillyard (GBR) in the 1908 men's doubles aged 44yr 160 days. The oldest female champion was Winifred McNair (GBR) aged 43yr 14 days in the women's doubles of 1920. She was also the oldest British female competitor to win a gold medal in any sport. The youngest gold medallist/medallist in tennis was Jennifer Capriati (USA), winner of the 1992 singles aged 16yr 132 days, while the youngest male was Fritz Traun (GER), Boland's partner in 1896, aged 20yr 13 days. The youngest male medallist was Max Decugis (FRA) in 1900 aged 17yr 290 days. Six years later, he and his wife Marie won the mixed title, while brothers Reggie and Laurie Doherty (GBR) added the 1900 Olympic title to the eight Wimbledon doubles championships they won. Steffi Graf (FRG), in 1988, is the only Grand Slam winner also to win an Olympic title.

Many of the greatest names in tennis have played in the Games and there have been 27 gold medal winners who were also successful at Wimbledon. One of the most remarkable of these was Swiss-born Norris Williams (USA), who survived the sinking of the *Titanic* in 1912 swimming in icy water for over an hour, won the Croix de Guerre and the Legion d'Honneur in the First World War, a Wimbledon title in 1920, an Olympic gold medal in 1924, and died aged 77. In 1996 a bronze medal match will be instituted.

TENNIS MEDALS TABLE

	G	S	B	Total
Great Britain	16	13	16	45
United States	11	5	7	23
France	8	7	6	21
Greece	1	5	3	9
Czechoslovakia	1	1	6	8
Germany	3	3	1	7
Sweden	-	2	5	7
South Africa	3	2	-	5
Spain	-	3	1	4
Australia	-	-	3	3
FRG	1	-	1	2
Japan	-	2	-	2
Argentina	-	1	1	2
Croatia	-	-	2	2
Soviet Union	-	-	2	2
Switzerland	1	-	-	1
Austria	-	1	-	1
Denmark	-	1	-	1
Bulgaria	-	-	1	1
Hungary	-	-	1	1
Italy	-	-	1	1
Netherlands	-	-	1	1
New Zealand	-	-	1	1
Norway	-	-	1	1
	45	46	60	151 [1]

[1] *Two-country pairs counted as two medals*

TENNIS MEDAL RESULTS

	GOLD	SILVER	BRONZE
Men's Singles			
1896 [1]	John Boland (GBR)	Demis Kasdaglis (GRE)	Momcilo Tapavica (HUN)
			K Paspatis (GRE)
1900 [1]	Hugh Doherty (GBR)	Harold Mahoney (GBR)	Reginald Doherty (GBR)
			AB Norris (GBR)
1904 [1]	Beals Wright (USA)	Robert LeRoy (USA)	Edgar Leonard (USA)
			Alphonzo Bell (USA)
1906	Max Décugis (FRA)	Maurice Germot (FRA)	Zdenek Zemla (BOH)
1908	Josiah Ritchie (GBR)	Otto Froitzheim (GER)	Wilberforce Eves (GBR)
1908 [2]	Wentworth Gore (GBR)	George Caridia (GBR)	Josiah Ritchie (GBR)
1912	Charles Winslow (RSA)	Harold Kitson (RSA)	Oscar Kreuzer (GER)
1912 [2]	André Gobert (FRA)	Charles Dixon (GBR)	Anthony Wilding (NZL)

1920	Louis Raymond (RSA)	Ichiya Kumagae (JPN)	Charles Winslow (GBR)
1924	Vincent Richards (USA)	Henri Cochet (FRA)	Umberto De Morpurgo (ITA)
1988 [1]	Miloslav Mecir (TCH)	Tim Mayotte (USA)	Stefan Edberg (SWE)
			Brad Gilbert (USA)
1992 [1]	Marc Rosset (SUI)	Jordi Arrese (ESP)	Goran Ivanisevic (CRO)
			Andrey Cherkasov (EUN)

[1] *Two bronze medals.*
[2] *Indoor tournaments.*

Men's Doubles

1896	GBR/Germany	Greece	Great Britain/Australia
1900 [1]	Great Britain	USA/France	France
			Great Britain
1904 [1]	United States	United States	United States
			United States
1906	France	Greece	Bohemia
1908	Great Britain	Great Britain	Great Britain
1908 [2]	Great Britain	Great Britain	Sweden
1912	South Africa	Austria	France
1912 [2]	France	Sweden	Great Britain
1920	Great Britain	Japan	France
1924	United States	France	France
1988 [1]	United States	Spain	Czechoslovakia
			Sweden
1992 [1]	Germany	South Africa	Croatia
			Argentina

[1] *Two bronze medals.*
[2] *Indoor tournaments.*

Mixed Doubles

1900 [1]	Great Britain	France/GBR	Bohemia/GBR
			United States/GBR
1906	France	Greece	Greece
1912	Germany	Sweden	France
1912 [2]	Great Britain	Great Britain	Sweden
1920	France	Great Britain	Czechoslovakia
1924	United States	United States	Netherlands

[1] *Two bronze medals.* [2] *Indoor tournament.*
1928–1992 Event not held.

Women's Singles

1900 [1]	Charlotte Cooper (GBR)	Hélène Prévost (FRA)	Marion Jones (USA)
			Hedwiga Rosenbaumova (BOH)
1906	Esmee Simiriotou (GRE)	Sophia Marinou (GRE)	Euphrosine Paspati (GRE)
1908	Dorothea Chambers (GBR)	Dorothy Boothby (GBR)	Joan Winch (GBR)
1908 [2]	Gwen Eastlake-Smith (GBR)	Angela Greene (GBR)	Märtha Adlerstrahle (SWE)
1912	Marguerite Broquedis (FRA)	Dora Köring (GER)	Molla Bjurstedt (NOR)
1912 [2]	Ethel Hannam (GBR)	Thora Castenschiold (DEN)	Mabel Parton (GBR)
1920	Suzanne Lenglen (FRA)	Dorothy Holman (GBR)	Kitty McKane (GBR)
1924	Helen Wills (USA)	Julie Vlasto (FRA)	Kitty McKane (GBR)
1988 [1]	Steffi Graf (FRG)	Gabriela Sabatini (ARG)	Zina Garrison (USA)
			Manuela Maleyeva (BUL)
1992 [1]	Jennifer Capriati (USA)	Steffi Graf (GER)	Mary-Jo Fernandez (USA)
			Arantxa Sanchez-Vicario (ESP)

[1] *Two bronze medals.*
[2] *Indoor tournaments.*
1928–1984 Event not held.

Jennifer Capriati (USA) beat favourite Steffi Graf (GER) 3-6, 6-3, 6-4 in the 1992 women's tennis final at Barcelona to emulate fellow American Helen Wills in 1924 (Allsport/Chris Cole)

Women's Doubles

1920	Great Britain	Great Britain	France
1924	United States	Great Britain	Great Britain
1988 [1]	United States	Czechoslovakia	Australia
			FRG
1992 [1]	United States	Spain	Australia
			Unified Team

[1] *Two bronze medals.*
1928–1984 Event not held.

Volleyball

Introduced into the Games in 1964 for men and women, volleyball has been dominated by Soviet teams. Their men played 51 matches, losing only ten, from 1964 to 1992 (when they failed to medal for the first time) and their women played 37 matches, losing only five, in the same period.

The most successful player was Inna Ryskal (URS) with two gold and two silver medals, 1964-76. The best by a male player was two golds and a silver by Yuriy Poyarkov (URS), 1964-72. Ryskal has competed in a record four Games in the women's sport, which is matched in the men's game by Katsutoshi Nekoda (JPN), Antonio Moreno and Amauri Ribiero (both BRA).

The oldest gold medallist was Georgi Mondsolevski (URS) aged 34yr 274 days in 1968, and the oldest female winner/medallist was Ludmila Buldakova (URS) aged 34yr 105 days in 1972. The youngest gold medallist was Regla Herrera (CUB) in 1992 aged 17yr 177 days, and the youngest male champion was Marcelo Negrao (BRA) aged 19yr 303 days in 1992. The oldest medallist was Bohumil Golián (TCH) who won a bronze in 1968 aged 37yr 215 days, while the youngest was Yevgeniya Artamonova of the Unified Team in 1992 at 17yr 22 days. The youngest male medallist was Alexander Savin (URS) in 1976 aged 19yr 29 days.

In 1996 separate beach volleyball tournaments for men (24 teams) and women (16 teams) will be introduced.

VOLLEYBALL MEDALS TABLE

	Men			Women			
	G	S	B	G	S	B	Total
Soviet Union	3	2	1	4	3	-	13
Japan	1	1	1	2	2	1	8
United States	2	-	1	-	1	1	5
Poland	1	-	-	-	-	2	3
China	-	-	-	1	-	1	2
GDR	-	1	--	-	1	-	2
Brazil	1	1	-	-	-	-	2
Bulgaria	-	1	-	-	-	1	2
Cuba	-	-	1	-	1	-	2
Czechoslovakia	-	1	1	-	-	-	2
Peru	-	-	-	-	1	-	1
Argentina	-	-	1	-	-	-	1
Italy	-	-	1	-	-	-	1
Netherlands	-	1	-	-	-	-	1
Korea	-	-	-	-	-	1	1
North Korea (PRK)	-	-	-	-	-	1	1
Romania	-	-	1	-	-	-	1
	8	8	8	8	8	8	48

VOLLEYBALL MEDAL RESULTS

Men

	GOLD	SILVER	BRONZE
1964	Soviet Union	Czechoslovakia	Japan
1968	Soviet Union	Japan	Czechoslovakia
1972	Japan	GDR	Soviet Union
1976	Poland	Soviet Union	Cuba
1980	Soviet Union	Bulgaria	Romania
1984	United States	Brazil	Italy
1988	United States	Soviet Union	Argentina
1992	Brazil	Netherlands	USA

1896–1960 Event not held.

VOLLEYBALL MEDAL RESULTS — WOMEN

	GOLD	SILVER	BRONZE
1964	Japan	Soviet Union	Poland
1968	Soviet Union	Japan	Poland
1972	Soviet Union	Japan	North Korea
1976	Japan	Soviet Union	South Korea
1980	Soviet Union	GDR	Bulgaria
1984	China	United States	Japan
1988	Soviet Union	Peru	China
1992	Cuba	Unified Team	USA

1896–1960 Event not held.

Weightlifting

Two events were held in 1896, consisting of one-arm and two-arm lifts. The first Olympic weightlifting champion was Viggo Jensen (DEN) who won the two-arm competition from Launceston Eliot (GBR); both had lifted the same weight but the Briton had moved one of his feet. The positions were reversed in the other event. Jensen was one of the first great all-rounders, as he also won silver and bronze medals at pistol and rifle shooting, and placed fourth in the rope climb.

An amusing incident occurred in 1896 when an attendant was having great trouble moving one of the weights, and Prince George of Greece, a member of the

The 'mighty atom', Naim Suleymanoglu, has given Turkey two gold medals, in 1988 and 1992, a return on the $1 million reportedly paid to Bulgaria for allowing his emigration (Allsport/Simon Bruty)

organizing committee and an immensely big and strong man, bent down and easily lifted it aside. Weightlifting was not included in the Games of 1900, 1908 or 1912.

In 1920 the contests were decided on the aggregate of a one-hand snatch, a one-hand jerk, and a two-hands jerk. In 1924 an additional two lifts were included, two-hands press and snatch. From 1928 to 1972 the result depended on the aggregate of three two-handed lifts: the press, snatch, and clean and jerk. In 1976 the press was eliminated, owing to difficulty in judging it correctly, and the total now is for the snatch and the clean and jerk. At the suggestion of the IOC, the forerunner of the International Weightlifting Federation was formed in 1920 to control the sport.

Of the 12 men to win two gold medals, only Tommy Kono (USA) and Norair Nurikyan (BUL) have won them in different categories. Kono won the 67.5 kg (1952) and the 82.5kg (1956), while more unusually Nurikyan moved down from the 60kg (1972) to the 56kg (1976). Norbert Schemansky (USA) has won the most medals, with one gold, one silver and two bronzes from 1948 to 1964.

The oldest gold medallist was Rudolf Plukfelder (URS) in the 82.5kg class of 1964 aged 36yr 40 days, while Schemansky was the oldest medallist in 1964 aged 40yr 141 days. The youngest gold medallist was Zeng Guoqiang (CHN) who won the 52kg class in 1984 aged 19yr 133 days, and the youngest ever medallist was Andrei Socaci (ROM) who won a 1984 silver in the 67.5kg category aged 18yr 43 days. The oldest known competitor was 56-year-old Teunist Jonck (RSA) in 1952, and the youngest known was 13-year-old M Djemal (TUR) in 1924. Imre Földi (HUN) competed in five Games, 1960-76.

The only brothers to win medals in the same event at the same Games were Yoshinobu and Yoshiyuki Miyake (JPN) who won gold and bronze respectively in the 60kg in 1968. Yoshinobu also won another gold and a silver, but Peter and James George (USA) hold the family record for medals with one gold, three silvers and a bronze from 1948 to 1960.

The silver medallist in the 82.5kg class in 1948, Harold Sakata (USA), later gained fame portraying 'Oddjob' in the James Bond film *Goldfinger*. Incidentally the margin of victory, 37.5kg, of the winner in that event, Stanley Stanczyk (USA), was a record for Olympic competition. In the 1988 featherweight class (up to 60kg) Naim Suleymanoglu (TUR) – for whose emigration the Turkish government is reported to have paid $1 million to Bulgaria – set an Olympic record equalling that for the next weight class.

Disqualifications for use of drugs have affected this sport more than most, with the first cases, gold medallist Zbigniew Kaczmarek (POL) and silver medallist Blagoi Blagoyev (BUL), being disqualified in 1976. At the end of 1992 the old weight classes were abolished by the IWF and replaced by new ones, in an attempt to replace any old records which might have been set by drug users prior to the introduction of strict controls.

WEIGHTLIFTING MEDALS TABLE

	G	S	B	Total
Soviet Union	44	25	2	71
United States	15	16	10	41
Bulgaria	10	13	5	28
Poland	4	3	18	25
Hungary	2	7	9	18
Germany	5	3	10	18
France	9	2	4	15
Italy	5	5	5	15
China	4	5	6	15
Japan	2	2	8	12
Austria	4	5	2	11
GDR	1	4	6	11
Romania	2	6	2	10
Egypt	5	2	2	9
Iran	1	3	5	9
Czechoslovakia	3	2	3	8
FRG	2	2	3	7
Estonia	1	3	3	7
Great Britain	1	3	3	7
Greece	3	-	3	6
Korea	1	1	4	6
Belgium	1	2	1	4
Switzerland	-	2	2	4
Sweden	-	-	4	4
Denmark	1	2	-	3
Australia	1	1	1	3
Cuba	1	1	1	3
Finland	1	-	2	3
Trinidad	-	1	2	3
North Korea (PRK)	-	1	2	3
Netherlands	-	-	3	3
Turkey	2	-	-	2
Canada	-	2	-	2
Argentina	-	1	1	2
Norway	1	-	-	1
Lebanon	-	1	-	1
Luxembourg	-	1	-	1
Singapore	-	1	-	1
Iraq	-	-	1	1
Taipei	-	-	1	1
	132 [1]	128	134 [2] [3] [4]	394

[1] *Tie for gold in 1928 and 1936 lightweight class*
[2] *Four-way tie for bronze in 1896*
[3] *Triple tie for bronze in 1906 heavyweight class*
[4] *No bronze in 1992 light-heavyweight class*

WEIGHTLIFTING MEDAL RESULTS

	GOLD	SILVER	BRONZE

Flyweight

(Up to 52kg 1972-92; up to 54kg 1996)

	GOLD	SILVER	BRONZE
1972	Zygmunt Smalcerz (POL) 337.5kg	Lajos Szuecs (HUN) 330kg	Sandor Holczreiter (HUN) 327.5kg
1976	Aleksandr Voronin (URS) 242.5kg	Gyorgy Koszegi (HUN) 237.5kg	Mohammad Nassiri (IRN) 235kg
1980	Kanybek Osmonoliev (URS) 245kg	Bong Chol Ho (PRK) 245kg	Gyond Si Han (PRK) 245kg
1984	Zeng Guoqiang (CHN) 235kg	Zhou Peishujn (CHN) 235kg	Kazushito Manabe (JPN) 232.5kg
1988	Sevdalin Marinov (BUL) 270kg	Chun Byung-Kwan (KOR) 260kg	He Zhuogiang (CHN) 257.5kg
1992	Ivan Ivanov (BUL) 265kg	Lin Qisheng (CHN) 262.5kg	Traian Ciharean (ROM) 252.5

1896–1968 Event not held.

Bantamweight

(Up to 56kg 1948-92; up to 59kg 1996)

	GOLD	SILVER	BRONZE
1948	Joseph de Pietro (USA) 307.5kg	Julian Creus (GBR) 297.5kg	Richard Tom (USA) 295kg
1952	Ivan Udodov (URS) 315kg	Mahmoud Namdjou (IRN) 307.5kg	Ali Mirzai (IRN) 300kg
1956	Charles Vinci (USA) 342.5kg	Vladimir Stogov (URS) 337.5kg	Mahmoud Namdjou (IRN) 332.5kg
1960	Charles Vinci (USA) 345kg	Yoshinobu Miyake (JPN) 337.5kg	Esmail Khan (IRN) 330kg
1964	Aleksey Vakhonin (URS) 357.5kg	Imre Földi (HUN) 355kg	Shiro Ichinoseki (JPN) 347.5kg
1968	Mohammad Nassiri (IRN) 367.5kg	Imre Földi (HUN) 367.5kg	Henryk Trebicki (POL) 357.5kg
1972	Imre Földi (HUN) 377.5kg	Mohammad Nassiri (IRN) 370kg	Gennadiy Chetin (URS) 367.5kg
1976	Norair Nurikyan (BUL) 262.5kg	Grzegorz Cziura (POL) 252.5kg	Kenkichi Ando (JPN) 250kg
1980	Daniel Nunez (CUB) 275kg	Yurik Sarkisian (URS) 270kg	Tadeusz Dembonczyk (POL) 265kg
1984	Wu Shude (CHN) 267.5kg	Lai Runming (CHN) 265kg	Masahiro Kotaka (JPN) 252.5kg
1988	Oksen Mirzoyan (URS) 292.5kg [1]	He Yingqiang (CHN) 287.5kg	Liu Shoubin (CHN) 267.5kg
1992	Chun Byung-kwan (KOR) 287.5kg	Liu Shoubin (CHN) 277.5kg	Luo Jianming (CHN) 277.5kg

[1] *Mitko Grablev (BUL) finished in first place with 297.5kg, but was subsequently disqualified.*
1896–1936 Event not held.

Featherweight

(Up to 60kg 1920-92; up to 64kg 1996)

	GOLD	SILVER	BRONZE
1920	Frans de Haes (BEL) 220kg	Alfred Schmidt (EST) 212.5kg	Eugène Ryther (SUI) 210kg
1924 [1]	Pierino Gabetti (ITA) 402.5kg	Andreas Stadler (AUT) 385kg	Arthur Reinmann (SUI) 382.5kg
1928	Franz Andrysek (AUT) 287.5kg	Pierino Gabetti (ITA) 282.5kg	Hans Wölpert (GER) 282.5kg
1932	Raymond Suvigny (FRA) 287.5kg	Hans Wölpert (GER) 282.5kg	Anthony Terlazzo (USA) 280kg
1936	Anthony Terlazzo (USA) 312.5kg	Saleh Mohammed Soliman (EGY) 305kg	Ibrahim Shams (EGY) 300kg
1948	Mahmoud Fayad (EGY) 332.5kg	Rodney Wilkes (TRI) 317.5kg	Jaffar Salmassi (IRN) 312.5kg
1952	Rafael Chimishkyan (URS) 337.5kg	Nikolai Saksonov (URS) 332.5kg	Rodney Wilkes (TRI) 332.5kg
1956	Isaac Berger (USA) 352.5kg	Yevgeniy Minayev (URS) 342.5kg	Marian Zielinski (POL) 335kg
1960	Yevgeniy Minayev (URS) 372.5kg	Isaac Berger (USA) 362.5kg	Sebastiano Mannironi (ITA) 352.5kg
1964	Yoshinobu Miyake (JPN) 397.5kg	Isaac Berger (USA) 382.5kg	Mieczyslaw Nowak (POL) 377.5kg
1968	Yoshinobu Miyake (JPN) 392.5kg	Dito Shanidze (URS) 387.5kg	Yoshiyuki Miyake (JPN) 385kg
1972	Norair Nurikyan (BUL) 402.5kg	Dito Shanidze (URS) 400kg	Janos Benedek (HUN) 390kg
1976	Nikolai Kolesnikov (URS) 285kg	Georgi Todorov (BUL) 280kg	Kazumasa Hirai (JPN) 275kg
1980	Viktor Mazin (URS) 290kg	Stefan Dimitrov (BUL) 287.5kg	Marek Seweryn (POL) 282.5kg
1984	Chen Weiqiang (CHN) 282.5kg	Gelu Radu (ROM) 280kg	Tsai Wen-Yee (TPE) 272.5kg
1988	Naim Suleymanoglu (TUR) 342.5kg	Stefan Topourov (BUL) 312.5kg	Ye Huanming (CHN) 287.5kg
1992	Naim Suleymanoglu (TUR) 320kg	Nikolai Peshalov (BUL) 305kg	He Yingqiang (CHN) 295kg

[1] *Aggregate of five lifts.*
1896–1912 Event not held.

Lightweight

(Up to 67.5kg 1920-92; up to 70kg 1996)

	GOLD	SILVER	BRONZE
1920	Alfred Neuland (EST) 257.5kg	Louis Williquet (BEL) 240kg	Florimond Rooms (BEL) 230kg
1924 [1]	Edmond Decottignies (FRA) 440kg	Anton Zwerina (AUT) 427.5kg	Bohumil Durdis (TCH) 425kg

1928 [2]	Kurt Helbig (GER) 322.5kg Hans Haas (AUT) 322.5kg	–	Fernand Arnout (FRA) 302.5kg
1932	René Duverger (FRA) 325kg	Hans Haas (AUT) 307.5kg	Gastone Pierini (ITA) 302.5kg
1936 [2]	Anwar Mohammed Mesbah (EGY) 342.5kg Robert Fein (AUT) 342.5kg		Karl Jansen (GER) 327.5kg
1948	Ibrahim Shams (EGY) 360kg	Attia Hamouda (EGY) 360kg	James Halliday (GBR) 340kg
1952	Tommy Kono (USA) 362.5kg	Yevgeniy Lopatin (URS) 350kg	Verne Barberis (AUS) 350kg
1956	Igor Rybak (URS) 380kg	Ravil Khabutdinov (URS) 372.5kg	Chang-Hee Kim (KOR) 370kg
1960	Viktor Bushuyev (URS) 397.5kg	Howe-Liang Tan (SIN) 380kg	Abdul Wahid Aziz (IRQ) 380kg
1964	Waldemar Baszanowski (POL) 432.5kg	Vladimir Kaplunov (URS) 432.5kg	Marian Zielinski (POL) 420kg
1968	Waldemar Baszanowski (POL) 437.5kg	Parviz Jalayer (IRN) 422.5kg	Marian Zielinski (POL) 420kg
1972	Mukharbi Kirzhinov (URS) 460kg	Mladen Koutchev (BUL) 450kg	Zbigniev Kaczmarek (POL) 437.5kg
1976 [3]	Pyotr Korol (URS) 305kg	Daniel Senet (FRA) 300kg	Kazimierz Czarnecki (POL) 295kg
1980	Yanko Rusev (BUL) 342.5kg	Joachin Kunz (GDR) 335kg	Mintcho Pachov (BUL) 325kg
1984	Yao Jingyuan (CHN) 320kg	Andrei Socaci (ROM) 312.5kg	Jouni Gronman (FIN) 312.5kg
1988	Joachim Kunz (GDR) 340kg	Israil Militossian (URS) 337.5kg	Li Jinhe (CHN) 325kg
1992	Israil Militossian (EUN) 337.5kg	Yoto Yotov (BUL) 327.5	Andreas Behm (GER) 320

[1] *Aggregate of five lifts.*
[2] *Tie-breaker rule relating to bodyweight not yet introduced.*
[3] *Zbigniev Kaczmarek (POL) finished in first place with 307.5kg but was subsequently disqualified.*
1896–1912 Event not held.

Middleweight
(Up to 75kg 1920-92; up to 76kg 1996)

1920	Henri Gance (FRA) 245kg	Pietro Bianchi [1] (ITA) 237.5kg	Albert Pettersson (SWE) 237.5kg
1924 [2]	Carlo Galimberti (ITA) 492.5kg	Alfred Neuland (EST) 455kg	Jaan Kikas (EST) 450kg
1928	Roger Francois (FRA) 335kg	Carlo Galimberti (ITA) 332.5kg	August Scheffer (NED) 327.5kg
1932	Rudolf Ismayr (GER) 345kg	Carlo Galimberti (ITA) 340kg	Karl Hipfinger (AUT) 337.5kg
1936	Khadr El Thouni (EGY) 387.5kg	Rudolf Ismayr (GER) 352.5kg	Adolf Wagner (GER) 352.5kg
1948	Frank Spellman (USA) 390kg	Peter George (USA) 382.5kg	Sung-Jip Kim (KOR) 380kg
1952	Peter George (USA) 400kg	Gerard Gratton (CAN) 390kg	Sung-Jip Kim (KOR) 382.5kg
1956	Fyodor Bogdanovski (URS) 420kg	Peter George (USA) 412.5kg	Ermanno Pignatti (ITA) 382.5kg
1960	Aleksandr Kurinov (URS) 437.5kg	Tommy Kono (USA) 427.5kg	Gyözö Veres (HUN) 405kg
1964	Hans Zdrazila (TCH) 445kg	Viktor Kurentsov (URS) 440kg	Masashi Ouchi (JPN) 437.5kg
1968	Viktor Kurentsov (URS) 475kg	Masashi Ouchi (JPN) 455kg	Károly Bakos (HUN) 440kg
1972	Yordan Bikov (BUL) 485kg	Mohamed Trabulsi (LIB) 472.5kg	Anselmo Silvino (ITA) 470kg
1976	Yordan Mitkov (BUL) 335kg	Vartan Militosyan (URS) 330kg	Peter Wenzel (GDR) 327.5kg
1980	Asen Zlatev (BUL) 360kg	Aleksandr Pervy (URS) 357.5kg	Nedeltcho Kolev (BUL) 345kg
1984	Karl-Heinz Radschinsky (FRG) 340kg	Jacques Demers (CAN) 335kg	Dragomir Cioroslan (ROM) 332.5kg
1988	Borislav Guidikov (BUL) 375kg	Ingo Steinhöfel (GDR) 360kg	Alexandr Varbanov (BUL) 357.5kg
1992	Fedor Kassapu (EUN) 357.5kg	Pablo Lara (CUB) 357.5kg	Kim Myong-nam (PRK) 352.5kg

[1] *Bianchi and Pettersson drew lots for the silver medal.*
[2] *Aggregate of five lifts.*
1896–1912 Event not held.

Light-Heavyweight
(Up to 82.5kg 1920-92; up to 83kg 1996)

1920	Ernest Cadine (FRA) 290kg	Fritz Hünenberger (SUI) 275kg	Erik Pettersson (SWE) 272.5kg
1924 [1]	Charles Rigoulot (FRA) 502.5kg	Fritz Hünenberger (SUI) 490kg	Leopold Friedrich (AUT) 490kg
1928	Said Nosseir (EGY) 355kg	Louis Hostin (FRA) 352.5kg	Johannes Verheijen (NED) 337.5kg
1932	Louis Hostin (FRA) 372.5kg	Svend Olsen (DEN) 360kg	Henry Duey (USA) 330kg
1936	Louis Hostin (FRA) 372.5kg	Eugen Deutsch (GER) 365kg	Ibrahim Wasif (EGY) 360kg
1948	Stanley Stanczyk (USA) 417.5kg	Harold Sakata (USA) 380kg	Gösta Magnussen (SWE) 375kg
1952	Trofim Lomakin (URS) 417.5kg	Stanley Stanczyk (USA) 415kg	Arkadiy Vorobyev (URS) 407.5kg

1956	Tommy Kono (USA) 447.5kg	Vassily Stepanov (URS) 427.5kg	James George (USA) 417.5kg
1960	Ireneusz Palinski (POL) 442.5kg	James George (USA) 430kg	Jan Bochenek (POL) 420kg
1964	Rudolf Plukfelder (URS) 475kg	Géza Toth (HUN) 467.5kg	Gyözö Veres (HUN) 467.5kg
1968	Boris Selitsky (URS) 485kg	Vladimir Belyayev (URS) 485kg	Norbert Ozimek (POL) 472.5kg
1972	Leif Jenssen (NOR) 507.5kg	Norbert Ozimek (POL) 497.5kg	György Horvath (HUN) 495kg
1976 [2]	Valeriy Shary (URS) 365kg	Trendachil Stoichev (BUL) 360kg	Peter Baczako (HUN) 345kg
1980	Yurik Vardanyan (URS) 400kg	Blagoi Blagoyev (BUL) 372.5kg	Dusan Poliacik (TCH) 367.5kg
1984	Petre Becheru (ROM) 355kg	Robert Kabbas (AUS) 342.5kg	Ryoji Isaoka (JPN) 340kg
1988	Israil Arsamakov (URS) 377.5kg	Istvan Messzi (HUN) 370kg	Lee Hyung-Kun (KOR) 367.5kg
1992	Pyrros Dimas (GRE) 370kg	Krzysztof Siemion (POL) 370	– [3]

[1] Aggregate of five lifts.
[2] Blagoi Blagoyev (BUL) finished in second place with 362.5kg but was subsequently disqualified.
[3] Ibraghim Samadov (EUN) placed third but disqualified. No bronze medal awarded.
1896–1912 Event not held.

Middle-Heavyweight
(Up to 90kg 1952-92; up to 91kg 1996)

1952	Norbert Schemansky (USA) 445kg	Grigoriy Nowak (URS) 410kg	Lennox Kilgour (TRI) 402.5kg
1956	Arkadiy Vorobyev (URS) 462.5kg	David Sheppard (USA) 442.5kg	Jean Debuf (FRA) 425kg
1960	Arkadiy Vorobyev (URS) 472.5kg	Trofim Lomakin (URS) 457.5kg	Louis Martin (GBR) 445kg
1964	Vladimir Golovanov (URS) 487.5kg	Louis Martin (GBR) 475kg	Ireneusz Palinski (POL) 467.5kg
1968	Kaarlo Kangasniemi (FIN) 517.5kg	Jan Talts (URS) 507.5kg	Marek Golab (POL) 495kg
1972	Andon Nikolov (BUL) 525kg	Atanas Chopov (BUL) 517.5kg	Hans Bettembourg (SWE) 512.5kg
1976	David Rigert (URS) 382.5kg	Lee James (USA) 362.5kg	Atanas Chopov (BUL) 360kg
1980	Peter Baczako (HUN) 377.5kg	Rumen Alexandrov (BUL) 375kg	Frank Mantek (GDR) 375kg
1984	Nicu Vlad (ROM) 392.5kg	Dumitru Petre (ROM) 360kg	David Mercer (GBR) 352.5kg
1988	Anatoly Khrapatiy (URS) 412.5kg	Nail Moukhamediarov (URS) 400kg	Slawomir Zawada (POL) 400kg
1992	Kakhi Kakhiashvili (EUN) 412.5	Sergei Syrtsov (EUN) 412.5	Sergiusz Wolczaniecki (POL) 392.5

1896–1948 Event not held.

Up to 100kg
(1980-92; up to 99kg 1996)

1980	Ota Zaremba (TCH) 395kg	Igor Nikitin (URS) 392.5kg	Alberto Blanco (CUB) 385kg
1984	Rolf Milser (FRG) 385kg	Vasile Gropa (ROM) 382.5kg	Pekka Niemi (FIN) 367.5kg
1988	Pavel Kuznetsov (URS) 425kg	Nicu Vlad (ROM) [1] 402.5kg	Peter Immesberger (FRG) 395kg
1992	Viktor Tregubov (EUN) 410kg	Timur Taimazov (EUN) 402.5kg	Waldemar Malak (POL) 400kg

[1] Andor Szanyi (HUN) finished second with 407.5kg, but was subsequently disqualified.
1896–1976 Event not held.

Heavyweight
(1920-48 class over 82.5kg; 1952-68 class over 90kg; 1972-92 class up to 110kg; 1996 up to 108kg)

1896 [1]	Launceston Eliot (GBR) 71kg	Viggo Jensen (DEN) 57.2kg	Alexandros Nikolopoulos (GRE) 57.2kg
1896 [2]	Viggo Jensen (DEN) 111.5kg	Launceston Eliot (GBR) 111.5kg	Sotirios Versis (GRE) 90kg
			Momcilo Tapavica (HUN) 90kg
			Carl Schuhmann (GER) 90kg
			Alexandros Nikolopoulos (GRE) 90kg
1904 [3]	Oscar Osthoff (USA) 48pts	Frederick Winters (USA) 45pts	Frank Kungler (USA) 10pts
1904 [2]	Perikles Kakousis (GRE) 111.58kg	Oscar Osthoff (USA) 84.36kg	Frank Kungler (USA) 79.83kg
1906 [1]	Josef Steinbach (AUT) 76.55kg	Tullio Camilotti (ITA) 73.75kg	Heinrich Schneidereit (GER) 70.75kg
1906 [2]	Dimitrios Tofalos (GRE) 142.5kg	Josef Steinbach (AUT) 136.5kg	Alexandre Maspoli (FRA) 129.5kg
			Heinrich Rondl (GER) 129.5kg
			Heinrich Schneidereit (GER) 129.5kg
1920	Filippo Bottino (ITA) 270kg	Joseph Alzin (LUX) 225kg	Louis Bernot (FRA) 250kg

1924 [4]	Giuseppe Tonani (ITA) 517.5kg	Franz Aigner (AUT) 515kg	Harald Tammer (EST) 497.5kg
1928	Josef Strassberger (GER) 372.5kg	Arnold Luhaäär (EST) 360kg	Jaroslav Skobla (TCH) 357.5kg
1932	Jaroslav Skobla (TCH) 380kg	Václav Psenicka (TCH) 377.5kg	Josef Strassberger (GER) 377.5kg
1936	Josef Manger (GER) 410kg	Václav Psenicka (TCH) 402.5kg	Arnold Luhaäär (EST) 400kg
1948	John Davis (USA) 452.2kg	Norbert Schemansky (USA) 425kg	Abraham Charité (NED) 412.5kg
1952	John Davis (USA) 460kg	James Bradford (USA) 437.5kg	Humberto Selvetti (ARG) 432.5kg
1956	Paul Anderson (USA) 500kg	Humberto Selvetti (ARG) 500kg	Alberto Pigaiani (ITA) 452.5kg
1960	Yuriy Vlasov (URS) 537.5kg	James Bradford (USA) 512.5kg	Norbert Schemansky (USA) 500kg
1964	Leonid Zhabotinsky (URS) 572.5kg	Yuriy Vlasov (URS) 570kg	Norbert Schemansky (USA) 537.5kg
1968	Leonid Zhabotinsky (URS) 572.5kg	Serge Reding (BEL) 555kg	Joseph Dube (USA) 555kg
1972	Jan Talts (URS) 580kg	Alexandre Kraitchev (BUL) 562.5kg	Stefan Grützner (GDR) 555kg
1976 [5]	Yuriy Zaitsev (URS) 385kg	Krastio Semerdiev (BUL) 385kg	Tadeusz Rutkowski (POL) 377.5kg
1980	Leonid Taranenko (URS) 422.5kg	Valentin Christov (BUL) 405kg	György Szalai (HUN) 390kg
1984	Norberto Oberburger (ITA) 390kg	Stefan Tasnadi (ROM) 380kg	Guy Carlton (USA) 377.5kg
1988	Yuriy Zakharevich (URS) 455kg	Jozsef Jacso (HUN) 427.5kg	Ronny Weller (GDR) 425kg
1992	Ronny Weller (GER) 432.5kg	Artur Akoyev (EUN) 430kg	Stefan Botev (BUL) 417.5kg

[1] One-hand lift.
[2] Two-hand lift.
[3] Dumbell lift.
[4] Aggregate of five lifts.
[5] Valentin Christov (BUL) finished in first place with 400kg but was subsequently disqualified.
1900, 1908–1912 Event not held.

Super-Heavyweight
(Over 110kg 1972-92; over 108kg 1996)

1972	Vasiliy Alexeyev (URS) 640kg	Rudolf Mang (FRG) 610kg	Gerd Bonk (GDR) 572.5kg
1976	Vasiliy Alexeyev (URS) 440kg	Gerd Bonk (GDR) 405kg	Helmut Losch (GDR) 387.5kg
1980	Sultan Rakhmanov (URS) 440kg	Jürgen Heuser (GDR) 410kg	Tadeusz Rutkowski (POL) 407.5kg
1984	Dinko Lukin (AUS) 412.5kg	Mario Martinez (USA) 410kg	Manfred Nerlinger (FRG) 397.5kg
1988	Aleksandr Kurlovich (URS) 462.5kg	Manfred Nerlinger (FRG) 430kg	Martin Zawieja (FRG) 415kg
1992	Aleksandr Kurlovich (EUN) 450kg	Leonid Taranenko (EUN) 425kg	Manfred Nerlinger (GER) 412.5kg

1896–1968 Event not held.

*Vasiliy Alexeyev (URS) – undefeated from
1970 to 1978 and twice Olympic champion,
he also set 80 world records in all (Allsport)*

Wrestling

Wrestling was the most popular sport in the ancient Games with victors recorded from 708 BC. The most famous was Milon of Kroton, a five-time winner.

Greco-Roman wrestling was included in the 1896 Games and freestyle in 1904; basically, holds are unlimited in freestyle but in Greco-Roman holds below the waist are

Germany's Wilfried Dietrich won five medals at four Games (1956-68) in both styles of wrestling (Allsport)

barred. There was no bodyweight limit in Athens and it was won, surprisingly, by the gymnastics triple gold medallist Carl Schuhmann (GER), who was only 1.63m (5ft 4in) tall;

he defeated Games weightlifting champion Launceston Eliot (GBR) in the preliminaries.

Until a time-limit was set in 1924, bouts often lasted for remarkable lengths of time. The most extreme was when Martin Klein, an Estonian representing Russia, and Alfred 'Alpo' Asikäinen (FIN) in the 1912 Greco-Roman middleweight class, wrestled for 11 hours 40 minutes. Klein won, but was too exhausted to challenge for the gold medal. In the light-heavy final that year Anders Ahlgren (SWE) and Ivar Böhling (FIN) were declared equal second after 9 hours without a decision, and no gold medal was awarded.

Three men have won three gold medals: Carl Westergren (SWE), Ivar Johansson (SWE) and Aleksandr Medved (URS). Johansson in 1932 and Kristjan Palusala (EST) in 1936 are the only men to win titles in both styles at the same Games, although Kaarle Anttila (FIN) had achieved this distinction previously over a two Games period, 1920-24.

Wilfried Dietrich (GER/FRG) won most medals with one gold, two silvers and two bronzes at both styles from 1956 to 1968. Dietrich (1956-72), Mario Tovar Gonzalez (MEX, 1952-68), Khorloo Baianmunkh (MGL, 1964-80), Czeslaw Kwiecinski (POL, 1964-80) and George Mackenzie (GBR, 1908-28) competed at a record five Games, Mackenzie over a record span of 20 years.

Although a number of brothers have each won gold medals, uniquely two pairs of brothers, Ed and Lou Banach and Dave and Mark Schultz, all from the United States, won titles in 1984. The only twins to win gold medals were Anatoliy and Sergey Beloglazov (URS) in 1980 and Ed and Lou Banach (USA) in 1984. Kustaa and Hermanni Pihlajamaki (FIN), who won three golds, one silver and a bronze between 1924 and 1936, were not brothers, as often thought, but cousins.

The first black champion was Kenny Monday (USA) in the 1988 freestyle welterweight division. The only Greek to win a gold medal in Greco-Roman wrestling was Stylianos Mygiakis in 1980. The oldest gold medallist/medallist was Adolf Lindfors (FIN) in 1920 aged 41yr 199 days. The youngest champion was Saban Trstena (YUG) in 1984 aged 19yr 222 days, and the youngest medallist was Nasser Givechi (IRN) in 1952 aged 16yr 254 days. The heaviest competitor ever in any Olympic event was the 1972 super-heavyweight bronze medallist Chris Taylor (USA) who weighed between 182kg (401lb) and 190kg (419lb).

When Osamu Watanabe (JPN) won the 1964 freestyle featherweight title it was his 186th successive victory in the sport.

WRESTLING MEDALS TABLE

	Freestyle			Greco-Roman			
	G	S	B	G	S	B	Total
Soviet Union	31	17	15	37	19	13	132
United States	41	32	21	2	2	3	101
Finland	8	7	10	19	20	18	82
Sweden	8	10	8	19	16	18	79
Bulgaria	6	15	9	8	14	7	59
Hungary	3	4	7	15	9	11	49
Turkey	15	11	6	9	4	2	47
Japan	16	9	7	4	4	2	42
Romania	1	-	4	6	8	13	32
Germany	1	3	2	4	12	7	29
Iran	3	8	11	-	1	1	24
Korea	4	4	6	3	1	5	23
Italy	1	-	-	5	4	9	19
Poland	-	1	3	2	7	5	18
Great Britain	3	4	10	-	-	-	17
Yugoslavia	1	1	2	3	5	4	16
Czechoslovakia	-	1	3	1	6	4	15
Switzerland	4	4	5	-	-	1	14
Denmark	-	-	-	2	3	7	12
France	2	2	3	1	1	2	11
Estonia	2	1	-	3	-	4	10
Canada	4	5	-	-	-	-	9
FRG	1	3	-	1	3	1	9
Greece	-	-	1	1	3	4	9
Mongolia	-	4	4	-	-	-	8
GDR	-	2	1	2	1	1	7
North Korea (PRK)	2	2	2	-	-	-	6
Cuba	1	-	1	1	-	2	5
Austria	-	-	1	1	2	1	5
Egypt (UAR)	-	-	-	1	2	2	5
Norway	-	1	-	2	1	1	5
Belgium	-	3	-	-	-	1	4
Australia	-	1	2	-	-	-	3
Russia	-	-	-	-	3	-	3
Lebanon	-	-	-	-	1	2	3
Latvia	-	-	-	-	1	-	1
Mexico	-	-	-	-	1	-	1
Syria	-	1	-	-	-	-	1
China	-	-	-	-	-	1	1
India	-	-	1	-	-	-	1
Pakistan	-	-	1	-	-	-	1
	153	153	154 [1]	152 [2]	154	152 [3]	918

[1] *Two bronzes in 1920 heavyweight class*
[2] *No gold in 1912 light-heavyweight class*
[3] *No bronze in 1906 all-around class*

WRESTLING MEDAL RESULTS

The contemporary descriptions of some bodyweight classes have varied during the history of the Games. Current descriptions are used in the lists below.

	GOLD	SILVER	BRONZE

Free-Style – Light Flyweight
(Weight up to 48kg)

Year	GOLD	SILVER	BRONZE
1904	Robert Curry (USA)	John Heim (USA)	Gustav Thiefenthaler (USA)
1972	Roman Dmitriev (URS)	Ognian Nikolov (BUL)	Ebrahim Javadpour (IRN)
1976	Khassan Issaev (BUL)	Roman Dmitriev (URS)	Akira Kudo (JPN)
1980	Claudio Pollio (ITA)	Se Hong Jang (PRK)	Sergey Kornilayev (URS)
1984	Robert Weaver (USA)	Takashi Irie (JPN)	Son Gab-Do (KOR)
1988	Takashi Kobayashi (JPN)	Ivan Tzonov (BUL)	Sergey Karamtchakov (URS)
1992	Kim Il (PRK)	Kim Jong-shin (KOR)	Vougar Oroudzhov (EUN)

1896–1900, 1906–1968 Event not held.

Free-Style – Flyweight
Note: 1904 weight up to 115lb (52.16kg). From 1948 weight up to 52kg.

Year	GOLD	SILVER	BRONZE
1904	George Mehnert (USA)	Gustave Bauer (USA)	William Nelson (USA)
1948	Lennart Viitala (FIN)	Halit Balamir (TUR)	Thure Johansson (SWE)
1952	Hasan Gemici (TUR)	Yushu Kitano (JPN)	Mahmoud Mollaghassemi (IRN)
1956	Mirian Tsalkalamanidze (URS)	Mohamad-Ali Khojastenpour (IRN)	Hüseyin Akbas (TUR)
1960	Ahmet Bilek (TUR)	Masayuki Matsubara (JPN)	Mohamad Saifpour Saidabadi (IRN)
1964	Yoshikatsu Yoshida (JPN)	Chang-sun Chang (KOR)	Said Aliaakbar Haydari (IRN)
1968	Shigeo Nakata (JPN)	Richard Sanders (USA)	Surenjav Sukhbaatar (MGL)
1972	Kiyomi Kato (JPN)	Arsen Alakhverdiev (URS)	Hyong Kim Gwong (PRK)
1976	Yuji Takada (JPN)	Aleksandr Ivanov (URS)	Jeon Hae-Sup (KOR)
1980	Anatoliy Beloglazov (URS)	Wladyslaw Stecyk (POL)	Nermedin Selimov (BUL)
1984	Saban Trstena (YUG)	Kim Jong-Kyu (KOR)	Yuji Takada (JPN)
1988	Mitsuru Sato (JPN)	Saban Trstena (YUG)	Vladimir Togouzov (URS)
1992	Li Hak-son (PRK)	Larry Lee Jones (USA)	Valentin Jordanov (BUL)

1896–1900, 1906–1936 Event not held.

Free-Style – Bantamweight
Note: The weight limit for this event has been: 1904, 125lb (56.70kg); 1908, 119lb (54kg); 1924–1936, 56kg and from 1948, 57kg.

Year	GOLD	SILVER	BRONZE
1904	Isidor Niflot (USA)	August Wester (USA)	ZB Strebler (USA)
1908	George Mehnert (USA)	William Press (GBR)	Aubert Coté (CAN)
1924	Kustaa Pihlajamaki (FIN)	Kaarlo Mäkinen (FIN)	Bryant Hines (USA)
1928	Kaarlo Mäkinen (FIN)	Edmond Spapen (BEL)	James Trifunov (CAN)
1932	Robert Pearce (USA)	Odön Zombori (HUN)	Aatos Jaskari (FIN)
1936	Odön Zombori (HUN)	Ross Flood (USA)	Johannes Herbert (GER)
1948	Nasuk Akar (TUR)	Gerald Leeman (USA)	Charles Kouyov (FRA)
1952	Shohachi Ishii (JPN)	Rashid Mamedbekov (URS)	Kha-Shaba Jadav (IND)
1956	Mustafa Dagistanli (TUR)	Mohamad Yaghoubi (IRN)	Mikhail Chakhov (URS)
1960	Terrence McCann (USA)	Nejdet Zalev (BUL)	Tadeusz Trojanowski (POL)
1964	Yojiro Uetake (JPN)	Hüseyin Akbas (TUR)	Aidyn Ibragimov (URS)
1968	Yojiro Uetake (JPN)	Donald Behm (USA)	Abutaleb Gorgori (IRN)
1972	Hideaki Yanagide (JPN)	Richard Sanders (USA)	László Klinga (HUN)
1976	Vladimir Yumin (URS)	Hans-Dieter Brüchert (GDR)	Masao Arai (JPN)
1980	Sergey Beloglazov (URS)	Li Ho Pyong (PRK)	Dugarsuren Ouinbold (MGL)
1984	Hideyaki Tomiyama (JPN)	Barry Davis (USA)	Kim Eui-Kon (KOR)
1988	Sergey Beloglazov (URS)	Askari Mohammadian (IRN)	Noh Kyung-Sun (KOR)
1992	Alejandro Puerto Diaz (CUB)	Sergei Smal (EUN)	Kim Yong-sik (PRK)

1896–1900, 1906, 1912–1920 Event not held.

Free-Style – Featherweight

Note: The weight limit for this event has been: 1904, 135lb (61.24kg); 1908, 133lb (60.30kg); 1920, 60kg; 1924–1936, 61kg; 1948–1960, and 1972 62kg; 1964–1968, 63kg; 1984, 62kg.

1904	Benjamin Bradshaw (USA)	Theodore McLear (USA)	Charles Clapper (USA)
1908	George Dole (USA)	James Slim (GBR)	William McKie (GBR)
1920	Charles Ackerly (USA)	Samuel Gerson (USA)	PW Bernard (GBR)
1924	Robin Reed (USA)	Chester Newton (USA)	Katsutoshi Naito (JPN)
1928	Allie Morrison (USA)	Kustaa Pihlajamaki (FIN)	Hans Minder (SUI)
1932	Hermanni Pihlajamaki (FIN)	Edgar Nemir (USA)	Einar Karlsson (SWE)
1936	Kustaa Pihlajamaki (FIN)	Francis Millard (USA)	Gösta Jönsson (SWE)
1948	Gazanfer Bilge (TUR)	Ivar Sjölin (SWE)	Adolf Müller (SUI)
1952	Bayram Sit (TUR)	Nasser Guivehtchi (IRN)	Josiah Henson (USA)
1956	Shozo Sasahara (JPN)	Joseph Mewis (BEL)	Erkki Penttilä (FIN)
1960	Mustafa Dagistanli (TUR)	Stantcho Ivanov (BUL)	Vladimir Rubashbili (URS)
1964	Osamu Watanabe (JPN)	Stantcho Ivanov (BUL)	Nodar Khokhashvili (URS)
1968	Masaaki Kaneko (JPN)	Enyu Todorov (BUL)	Shamseddin Seyed-Abbassi (IRN)
1972	Zagalav Abdulbekov (URS)	Vehbi Akdag (TUR)	Ivan Krastev (BUL)
1976	Yang Jung-Mo (KOR)	Zeveg Oidov (MGL)	Gene Davis (USA)
1980	Magomedgasan Abushev (URS)	Mikho Doukov (BUL)	Georges Hadiioannidis (GRE)
1984	Randy Lewis (USA)	Kosei Akaishi (JPN)	Lee Jung-Keun (KOR)
1988	John Smith (USA)	Stepan Sarkissian (URS)	Simeon Chterev (BUL)
1992	John Smith (USA)	Askari Mohammadian (IRN)	Lazaro Reinoso (CUB)

1896–1900, 1906, 1912 Event not held.

Free-Style – Lightweight

Note: The weight limit for this event has been: 1904, 145lb (65.77kg); 1908, 146.75lb (66.60kg); 1920 67.5kg; 1924 to 1936, 66kg; 1948 to 1960, 67kg; 1964 and 1968, 70kg and from 1972, 68kg.

1904	Otton Roehm (USA)	Rudolph Tesing (USA)	Albert Zirkel (USA)
1908	George de Relwyskow (GBR)	William Wood (GDR)	Albert Gingell (GBR)
1920	Kalle Anttila (FIN)	Gottfrid Svensson (SWE)	Peter Wright (GBR)
1924	Russell Vis (USA)	Volmart Wickström (FIN)	Arvo Haavisto (FIN)
1928	Osvald Käpp (EST)	Charles Pacome (FRA)	Eino Leino (FIN)
1932	Charles Pacome (FRA)	Károly Kárpáti (HUN)	Gustaf Klarén (SWE)
1936	Károly Kárpáti (HUN)	Wolfgang Ehrl (GER)	Hermanni Pihlajamaki (FIN)
1948	Celál Atik (TUR)	Gösta Frandfors (SWE)	Hermann Baumann (SUI)
1952	Olle Anderberg (SWE)	Thomas Evans (USA)	Djahanbakte Tovfighe (IRN)
1956	Emamali Habibi (IRN)	Shigeru Kasahara (JPN)	Alimberg Bestayev (URS)
1960	Shelby Wilson (USA)	Viktor Sinyavskiy (URS)	Enyu Dimov (BUL)
1964	Enyu Valtschev [1] (BUL)	Klaus-Jürgen Rost (GER)	Iwao Horiuchi (JPN)
1968	Abdollah Movahed Ardabili (IRN)	Enyu Valtschev[1] (BUL)	Sereeter Danzandarjaa (MGL)
1972	Dan Gable (USA)	Kikuo Wada (JPN)	Ruslan Ashuraliev (URS)
1976	Pavel Pinigin (URS)	Lloyd Keaser (USA)	Yasaburo Sagawara (JPN)
1980	Saipulla Absaidov (URS)	Ivan Yankov (BUL)	Saban Sejdi (YUG)
1984	You In-Tak (KOR)	Andrew Rein (USA)	Jukka Rauhala (FIN)
1988	Arsen Fadzayev (URS)	Park Jang-Soon (KOR)	Nate Carr (USA)
1992	Arsen Fadzayev (EUN)	Valentin Getzov (BUL)	Kosei Akaishi (JPN)

[1] *Valtschev competed as Dimov in 1960.*
1896–1900, 1906, 1912 Event not held.

Free-Style – Welterweight

Note: The weight limit for this event has been: 1904, 158lb (71.67kg); 1924 to 1936, 72kg; 1948 to 1960, 73kg; from 1972, 74kg.

1904	Charles Erikson (USA)	William Beckmann (USA)	Jerry Winholtz (USA)
1924	Hermann Gehri (SUI)	Eino Leino (FIN)	Otto Müller (SUI)
1928	Arvo Haavisto (FIN)	Lloyd Appleton (USA)	Maurice Letchford (CAN)
1932	Jack van Bebber (USA)	Daniel MacDonald (CAN)	Eino Leino (FIN)
1936	Frank Lewis (USA)	Ture Andersson (SWE)	Joseph Schleimer (CAN)

1948	Yasar Dogu (TUR)	Richard Garrard (AUS)	Leland Merrill (USA)
1952	William Smith (USA)	Per Berlin (SWE)	Abdullah Modjtabavi (IRN)
1956	Mitsuo Ikeda (JPN)	Ibrahim Zengin (TUR)	Vakhtang Balavadze (URS)
1960	Douglas Blubaugh (USA)	Ismail Ogan (TUR)	Mohammed Bashir (PAK)
1964	Ismail Ogan (TUR)	Guliko Sagaradze (URS)	Mohamad-Ali Sanatkaran (IRN)
1968	Mahmut Atalay (TUR)	Daniel Robin (FRA)	Dagvasuren Purev (MGL)
1972	Wayne Wells (USA)	Jan Karlsson (SWE)	Adolf Seger (FRG)
1976	Jiichiro Date (JPN)	Mansour Barzegar (IRN)	Stanley Dziedzic (USA)
1980	Valentin Raitchev (BUL)	Jamtsying Davaajav (MGL)	Dan Karabin (TCH)
1984	David Schultz (USA)	Martin Knosp (FRG)	Saban Sejdi (YUG)
1988	Kenneth Monday (USA)	Adlan Varayev (URS)	Rakhmad Sofiadi (BUL)
1992	Park Jang-soon (KOR)	Kenneth Monday (USA)	Amir Khadem (IRN)

1896–1900, 1906–1920 Event not held.

Freestyle – Middleweight

Note: The weight limit for this event has been: 1908, 161lb (73kg); 1920, 165.25lb (75kg); 1924 to 1960, 79kg; 1964 and 1968, 87kg; from 1972, 82kg.

1908	Stanley Bacon (GBR)	George de Relwyskow (GBR)	Frederick Beck (GBR)
1920	Eino Leino (FIN)	Väinö Penttala (FIN)	Charles Johnson (USA)
1924	Fritz Hagmann (SUI)	Pierre Ollivier (BEL)	Vilho Pekkala (FIN)
1928	Ernst Kyburz (SUI)	Donald Stockton (CAN)	Samuel Rabin (GBR)
1932	Ivar Johansson (SWE)	Kyösti Luukko (FIN)	József Tunyogi (HUN)
1936	Emile Poilvé (FRA)	Richard Voliva (USA)	Ahmet Kireicci (TUR)
1948	Glen Brand (USA)	Adil Candemir (TUR)	Erik Lindén (SWE)
1952	David Tsimakuridze (URS)	Gholamheza Takhti (IRN)	György Gurics (HUN)
1956	Nikola Stantschev (BUL)	Daniel Hodge (USA)	Georgiy Skhirtladze (URS)
1960	Hasan Güngör (TUR)	Georgiy Skhirtladze (URS)	Hans Antonsson (SWE)
1964	Prodan Gardschev (BUL)	Hasan Güngör (TUR)	Daniel Brand (USA)
1968	Boris Gurevitch (URS)	Munkbat Jigjid (MGL)	Prodan Gardschev (BUL)
1972	Leven Tediashvili (URS)	John Peterson (USA)	Vasile Jorga (ROM)
1976	John Peterson (USA)	Viktor Novoshilev (URS)	Adolf Seger (FRG)
1980	Ismail Abilov (BUL)	Magomedhan Aratsilov (URS)	Istvan Kovacs (HUN)
1984	Mark Schultz (USA)	Hideyuki Nagashima (JPN)	Chris Rinke (CAN)
1988	Han Myung-Woo (KOR)	Necmi Gencalp (TUR)	Josef Lohyna (TCH)
1992	Kevin Jackson (USA)	Elmadi Zhabraylov (EUN)	Razul Khadem (IRN)

1896–1906, 1912 Event not held.

Free-Style – Light-Heavyweight

Note: The weight limit for this event has been: 1920, 82.5kg; 1924 to 1960, 87kg; 1964 and 1968, 97kg; from 1972, 90kg.

1920	Anders Larsson (SWE)	Charles Courant (SUI)	Walter Maurer (USA)
1924	John Spellman (USA)	Rudolf Svensson (SWE)	Charles Courant (SUI)
1928	Thure Sjöstedt (SWE)	Anton Bögli (SUI)	Henri Lefèbre (FRA)
1932	Peter Mehringer (USA)	Thure Sjöstedt (SWE)	Eddie Scarf (AUS)
1936	Knut Fridell (SWE)	August Neo (EST)	Erich Siebert (GER)
1948	Henry Wittenberg (USA)	Fritz Stöckli (SUI)	Bengt Fahlkvist (SWE)
1952	Wiking Palm (SWE)	Henry Wittenberg (USA)	Adil Atan (TUR)
1956	Gholam Reza Tahkti (IRN)	Boris Kulayev (URS)	Peter Blair (USA)
1960	Ismet Atli (TUR)	Cholam Reza Tahkti (IRN)	Anatoliy Albul (URS)
1964	Aleksandr Medved (URS)	Ahmet Ayik (TUR)	Said Mustafafov (BUL)
1968	Ahmet Ayik (TUR)	Shota Lomidze (URS)	József Csatári (HUN)
1972	Ben Peterson (USA)	Gennadiy Strakhov (URS)	Karoly Bajko (HUN)
1976	Levan Tediashvili (URS)	Ben Peterson (USA)	Stelica Morcov (ROM)
1980	Sanasar Oganesyan (URS)	Uwe Neupert (GDR)	Aleksandr Cichon (POL)
1984	Ed Banach (USA)	Akira Ota (JPN)	Noel Loban (GBR)
1988	Makharbek Khadartsev (URS)	Akira Ota (JPN)	Kim Tae-Woo (KOR)
1992	Makharbek Khadartsev (EUN)	Kenan Simsek (TUR)	Christopher Campbell (USA)

1896–1912 Event not held.

Free-Style – Heavyweight

Note: The weight limit for this event has been: 1904, over 158lb (71.6kg); 1908, over 73kg; 1920, over 82.5kg; 1924 to 1960, over 87kg; 1964 and 1968, over 97kg; from 1972, up to 100kg.

1904	Bernhuff Hansen (USA)	Frank Kungler (USA)	Fred Warmbold (USA)
1908	George O'Kelly (GBR)	Jacob Gundersen (NOR)	Edmond Barrett (GBR)
1920	Robert Roth (SUI)	Nathan Pendleton (USA)	Ernst Nilsson (SWE)
			Frederick Meyer (USA)
1924	Harry Steele (USA)	Henry Wernli (SUI)	Andrew McDonald (GBR)
1928	Johan Richthoff (SWE)	Aukusti Sihovla (FIN)	Edmond Dame (FRA)
1932	Johan Richthoff (SWE)	John Riley (USA)	Nikolaus Hirschl (AUT)
1936	Kristjan Palusalu (EST)	Josef Klapuch (TCH)	Hjalmar Nyström (FIN)
1948	Gyula Bóbis (HUN)	Bertil Antonsson (SWE)	Joseph Armstrong (AUS)
1952	Arsen Mekokishvili (URS)	Bertil Antonsson (SWE)	Kenneth Richmond (GBR)
1956	Hamit Kaplan (TUR)	Hussein Mekhmedov (BUL)	Taisto Kangasniemi (FIN)
1960	Wilfried Dietrich (GER)	Hamit Kaplan (TUR)	Savkus Dzarassov (URS)
1964	Aleksandr Ivanitsky (URS)	Liutvi Djiber (BUL)	Hamit Kaplan (TUR)
1968	Aleksandr Medved (URS)	Osman Duraliev (BUL)	Wilfried Dietrich (FRG)
1972	Ivan Yaragin (URS)	Khorloo Baianmunkh (MGL)	József Csatári (HUN)
1976	Ivan Yaragin (URS)	Russell Hellickson (USA)	Dimo Kostov (BUL)
1980	Ilya Mate (URS)	Slavtcho Tchervenkov (BUL)	Julius Strnisko (TCH)
1984	Lou Banach (USA)	Joseph Atiyeh (SYR)	Vasile Pascasu (ROM)
1988	Vasile Puscasu (ROM)	Leri Khabelov (URS)	William Scherr (USA)
1992	Leri Khabelov (EUN)	Heiko Balz (GER)	Ali Kayali (TUR)

[1] *Tie for third place.*
1896–1900, 1906, 1912 Event not held.

Free-Style – Super-Heavyweight

(Weight over 100kg)

1972	Aleksandr Medved (URS)	Osman Duraliev (BUL)	Chris Taylor (USA)
1976	Soslan Andiev (URS)	Jozsef Balla (HUN)	Ladislau Simon (ROM)
1980	Soslan Andiev (URS)	Jozsef Balla (HUN)	Adam Sandurski (POL)
1984	Bruce Baumgartner (USA)	Bob Molle (CAN)	Ayhan Taskin (TUR)
1988	David Gobedjichvili (URS)	Bruce Baumgartner (USA)	Andreas Schröder (GDR)
1992	Bruce Baumgartner (USA)	Jeff Thue (CAN)	David Gobedjhichvili (EUN)

1896–1968 Event not held.

Greco-Roman – Light-Flyweight

(Weight up to 48kg)

1972	Gheorghe Berceanu (ROM)	Rahim Ahabadi (IRN)	Stefan Anghelov (BUL)
1976	Aleksey Shumakov (URS)	Gheorghe Berceanu (ROM)	Stefan Anghelov (BUL)
1980	Zaksylik Ushkempirov (URS)	Constantin Alexandru (ROM)	Ferenc Seres (HUN)
1984	Vincenzo Mzenza (ITA)	Markus Scherer (FRG)	Ikuzo Saito (JPN)
1988	Vincenzo Maenza (ITA)	Andrzej Glab (POL)	Bratan Tzenov (BUL)
1992	Oleg Kutcherenko (EUN)	Vincenzo Maenza (ITA)	Wilber Sanchez (CUB)

1896–1968 Event not held.

Greco-Roman – Flyweight

(Weight up to 52kg)

1948	Pietro Lombardi (ITA)	Kenan Olcay (TUR)	Reino Kangasmäki (FIN)
1952	Boris Gurevich (URS)	Ignazio Fabra (ITA)	Leo Honkala (FIN)
1956	Nikolai Solovyov (URS)	Ignazio Fabra (ITA)	Durum Ali Egribas (TUR)
1960	Dumitru Pirvulescu (ROM)	Osman Sayed (UAR)	Mohamad Paziraye (IRN)
1964	Tsutomu Hanahara (JPN)	Angel Kerezov (BUL)	Dumitru Pirvulescu (ROM)
1968	Petar Kirov (BUL)	Vladimir Bakulin (URS)	Miroslav Zeman (TCH)
1972	Petar Kirov (BUL)	Koichiro Hirayama (JPN)	Giuseppe Bognanni (ITA)
1976	Vitaliy Konstantinov (URS)	Nicu Ginga (ROM)	Koichiro Kirayama (JPN)
1980	Vakhtang Blagidze (URS)	Lajos Racz (HUN)	Mladen Mladenov (BUL)

1984	Atsuji Miyahara (JPN)	Daniel Aceves (MEX)	Bang Dae-Du (KOR)
1988	Jon Ronningen (NOR)	Atsuji Miyahara (JPN)	Lee Jae-Suk (KOR)
1992	Jon Ronningen (NOR)	Alfred Ter-Mkrttchian (EUN)	Min Kyung-kap (KOR)

1896–1936 Event not held.

Greco-Roman – Bantamweight

Note: The weight limit for this event has been: 1924 to 1928, 58kg; 1932 to 1936, 56kg; since 1948, 57kg.

1924	Eduard Pütsep (EST)	Anselm Ahlfors (FIN)	Väinö Ikonen (FIN)
1928	Kurt Leucht (GER)	Jindrich Maudr (TCH)	Giovanni Gozzi (ITA)
1932	Jakob Brendel (GER)	Marcello Nizzola (ITA)	Louis François (FRA)
1936	Márton Lörincz (HUN)	Egon Svensson (SWE)	Jakob Brendel (GER)
1948	Kurt Pettersén (SWE)	Aly Mahmoud Hassan (EGY)	Habil Kaya (TUR)
1952	Imre Hódos (HUN)	Zakaria Chihab (LIB)	Artem Teryan (URS)
1956	Konstantin Vyrupayev (URS)	Evdin Vesterby (SWE)	Francisco Horvat (ROM)
1960	Oleg Karavayev (URS)	Ion Cernea (ROM)	Petrov Dinko (BUL)
1964	Masamitsu Ichiguchi (JPN)	Vladlen Trostiansky (URS)	Ion Cernea (ROM)
1968	János Varga (HUN)	Ion Baciu (ROM)	Ivan Kochergin (URS)
1972	Rustem Kazakov (URS)	Hans-Jürgen Veil (FRG)	Risto Björlin (FIN)
1976	Pertti Ukkola (FIN)	Iván Frgic (YUG)	Farhat Mustafin (URS)
1980	Shamil Serikov (URS)	Jozef Lipien (POL)	Benni Ljungbeck (SWE)
1984	Pasquale Passarelli (FRG)	Masaki Eto (JPN)	Haralambos Holidis (GRE)
1988	Andras Sike (HUN)	Stoyan Balov (BUL)	Haralambos Holidis (GRE)
1992	An Han-bong (KOR)	Rifat Yildiz (GER)	Sheng Zetian (CHN)

1896–1920 Event not held.

Greco-Roman – Featherweight

Note: The weight limit for this event has been: 1912 to 1920, 60kg; 1924 to 1928, 1948 to 1960 and since 1972, 62kg; 1932 to 1936, 61kg; 1964 to 1968, 63kg.

1912	Kaarlo Koskelo (FIN)	Georg Gerstacker (GER)	Otto Lasanen (FIN)
1920	Oskari Friman (FIN)	Hekki Kähkönen (FIN)	Fridtjof Svensson (SWE)
1924	Kalle Antila (FIN)	Aleksanteri Toivola (FIN)	Erik Malmberg (SWE)
1928	Voldemar Väli (EST)	Erik Malmberg (SWE)	Giacomo Quaglia (ITA)
1932	Giovanni Gozzi (ITA)	Wolfgang Ehrl (GER)	Lauri Koskela (FIN)
1936	Yasar Erkan (TUR)	Aarne Reini (FIN)	Einar Karlsson (SWE)
1948	Mehmet Oktav (TUR)	Olle Anderberg (SWE)	Ferenc Tóth (HUN)
1952	Yakov Punkin (URS)	Imre Polyák (HUN)	Abdel Rashed (EGY)
1956	Rauno Mäkinen (FIN)	Imre Polyák (HUN)	Roman Dzneladze (URS)
1960	Muzahir Sille (TUR)	Imre Pllyák (HUN)	Konstantin Vyrupayev (URS)
1964	Imre Polyak (HUN)	Roman Rurua (URS)	Branko Martinovic (YUG)
1968	Roman Rurua (URS)	Hideo Fujimoto (JPN)	Simeon Popescu (ROM)
1972	Gheorghi Markov (BUL)	Heinz-Helmut Wehling (GDR)	Kazimierz Lipien (POL)
1976	Kazimierz Lipien (POL)	Nelson Davidian (URS)	Laszlo Reczi (HUN)
1980	Stilianos Migiakis (GRE)	Istvan Toth (HUN)	Boris Kramorenko (URS)
1984	Kim Weon-Kee (KOR)	Kent-Olle Johansson (SWE)	Hugo Dietsche (SUI)
1988	Kamandar Madjidov (URS)	Jivko Vanguelov (BUL)	An Dae-Hyun (KOR)
1992	Akif Pirim (TUR)	Sergei Martynov (EUN)	Juan Maren (CUB)

1896–1908 Event not held.

Greco-Roman – Lightweight

Note: The weight limit for this event has been: 1906, 75kg; 1908, 66.6kg; 1912 to 1928, 67.5kg; 1932 to 1936, 66kg; 1948 to 1960, 67kg; 1964 to 1968, 70kg; since 1972, 68kg.

1906	Rudolf Watzl (AUT)	Karl Karlsen (DEN)	Ferenc Holuban (HUN)
1908	Enrico Porro (ITA)	Nikolav Orlov (URS)	Avid Lindén-Linko (FIN)
1912	Eemil Wäre (FIN)	Gustaf Malmström (SWE)	Edvin Matiasson (SWE)
1920	Eemil Wäre (FIN)	Taavi Tamminen (FIN)	Fritjof Andersen (NOR)
1924	Oskari Friman (FIN)	Lajos Keresztes (HUN)	Kalle Westerlund (FIN)
1928	Lajos Keresztes (HUN)	Eduard Sperling (GER)	Eduard Westerlund (FIN)

1932	Erik Malmberg (SWE)	Abraham Kurland (DEN)	Eduard Sperling (GER)
1936	Lauri Koskela (FIN)	Josef Herda (TCH)	Voldemar Väli (EST)
1948	Gustaf Freij (SWE)	Aage Eriksen (NOR)	Károly Ferencz (HUN)
1952	Shazam Safin (URS)	Gustaf Freij (SWE)	Mikulás Athanasov (TCH)
1956	Kyösti Lentonen (FIN)	Riza Dogan (TUR)	Gyula Tóth (HUN)
1960	Avtandil Koridza (URS)	Branislav Martinovic (YUG)	Gustaf Freij (SWE)
1964	Kazim Avvaz (TUR)	Valeriu Bularca (ROM)	David Gvantseladze (URS)
1968	Munji Mumemura (JPN)	Stevan Horvat (YUG)	Petros Galaktopoulos (GRE)
1972	Shamil Khisamutdinov (URS)	Stoyan Apostolov (BUL)	Gian Matteo Ranzi (ITA)
1976	Suren Nalbandyan (URS)	Stefan Rusu (ROM)	Heinz-Helmut Wehling (GDR)
1980	Stefan Rusu (ROM)	Andrzej Supron (POL)	Lars-Erik Skiold (SWE)
1984	Vlado Lisjak (YUG)	Tapio Sipila (FIN)	James Martinez (USA)
1988	Levon Djoulfalakian (URS)	Kim Sung-Moon (KOR)	Tapio Sipila (FIN)
1992	Attila Repka (HUN)	Islam Dougutchyev (EUN)	Rodney Smith (USA)

1896–1904 Event not held.

Greco-Roman – Welterweight
Note: The weight limit for this event has been: 1932 to 1936, 72kg; 1948 to 1960, 73kg; 1964 to 1968, 78kg; since 1972, 74kg.

1932	Ivar Johansson (SWE)	Väinö Kajander (FIN)	Ercole Gallegatti (ITA)
1936	Rudolf Svedberg (SWE)	Fritz Schäfer (GER)	Eino Virtanen (FIN)
1948	Gösta Andersson (SWE)	Miklós Szilvási (HUN)	Henrik Hansen (DEN)
1952	Miklós Szilvási (HUN)	Gösta Andersson (SWE)	Khalil Taha (LIB)
1956	Mithat Bayrak (TUR)	Vladimir Maneyev (URS)	Per Berlin (SWE)
1960	Mithat Bayrak (TUR)	Günther Maritschnigg (GER)	René Schiermeyer (FRA)
1964	Anatoliy Kolesov (URS)	Cyril Todorov (BUL)	Bertil Nyström (SWE)
1968	Rudolf Vesper (GDR)	Daniel Robin (FRA)	Károly Bajkó (HUN)
1972	Vitezslav Macha (TCH)	Petros Galaktopoulos (GRE)	Jan Karlsson (SWE)
1976	Anatoliy Bykov (URS)	Vitezslav Macha (TCH)	Karlheinz Helbing (FRG)
1980	Ferenc Kocsis (HUN)	Anatoliy Bykov (URS)	Mikko Huhtala (FIN)
1984	Jonko Salomaki (FIN)	Roger Tallroth (SWE)	Stefan Rusu (ROM)
1988	Kim Young-Nam (KOR)	Daoulet Tourlykhanov (URS)	Jozef Tracz (POL)
1992	Mnatsakan Iskandarian (EUN)	Jozef Tracz (POL)	Torbjorn Kornbakk (SWE)

1896–1928 Event not held.

Greco-Roman – Middleweight
Note: The weight limit for this event has been: 1906, 85kg; 1908, 73kg; 1912 to 1928, 75kg; 1932 to 1960, 79kg; 1964 to 1968, 87kg; since 1972, 82kg.

1906	Verner Weckman (FIN)	Rudolf Lindmayer (AUT)	Robert Bebrens (DEN)
1908	Frithiof Mårtensson (SWE)	Mauritz Andersson (SWE)	Anders Andersen (DEN)
1912	Claes Johansson (SWE)	Martin Klein (URS)	Alfred Asikainen (FIN)
1920	Carl Westergren (SWE)	Artur Lindfors (FIN)	Matti Perttila (FIN)
1924	Eduard Westerlund (FIN)	Artur Lindfors (FIN)	Roman Steinberg (EST)
1928	Väinö Kokkinen (FIN)	László Papp (HUN)	Albert Kusnetz (EST)
1932	Väinö Kokkinen (FIN)	Jean Földeák (GER)	Axel Cadier (SWE)
1936	Ivar Johansson (SWE)	Ludwig Schweikert (GER)	József Palotás (HUN)
1948	Axel Grönberg (SWE)	Muhlis Tayfur (TUR)	Ercole Gallegatti (ITA)
1952	Axel Grönberg (SWE)	Kalervo Rauhala (FIN)	Nikolai Belov (URS)
1956	Givi Kartiziya (URS)	Dimiter Dobrev (BUL)	Rune Jansson (SWE)
1960	Dimiter Dobrev (BUL)	Lothar Metz (GER)	Ion Taranu (ROM)
1964	Branislav Simic (YUG)	Jiri Kormanik (TCH)	Lothar Metz (GER)
1968	Lothar Metz (GDR)	Valentin Olenik (URS)	Branislav Simic (YUG)
1972	Csaba Hegedus (HUN)	Anatoliy Nazarenko (URS)	Milan Nenadic (YUG)
1976	Momir Petkovic (YUG)	Vladimir Cheboksarov (URS)	Ivan Kolev (BUL)
1980	Gennadiy Korban (URS)	Jan Polgowicz (POL)	Pavel Pavlov (BUL)
1984	Ion Draica (ROM)	Dimitrios Thanapoulos (GRE)	Soren Claeson (SWE)
1988	Mikhail Mamiachvili (URS)	Tibor Komaromi (HUN)	Kim Sang-Kyu (KOR)
1992	Peter Farkas (HUN)	Piotr Stepien (POL)	Daoulet Tourlykhanov (EUN)

1896–1904 Event not held.

Greco-Roman – Light-Heavyweight

Note: The weight limit in this event has been: 1908, 93kg; 1912 to 1928, 82.5kg; 1932 to 1960, 87kg; 1964 to 1968, 97kg; since 1972, 90kg.

1908	Verner Weckman (FIN)	Yrjö Saarela (FIN)	Carl Jensen (DEN)
1912	– [1]	Anders Ahlgren (SWE)	Béla Varga (HUN)
		Ivor Böhling (FIN)	
1920	Claes Johansson (SWE)	Edil Rosenqvist (FIN)	Johannes Eriksen (DEN)
1924	Carl Westergren (SWE)	Rudolf Svensson (SWE)	Onni Pellinen (FIN)
1928	Ibrahim Moustafa (EGY)	Adolf Rieger (GER)	Onni Pellinen (FIN)
1932	Rudolf Svensson (SWE)	Onni Pellinen (FIN)	Mario Gruppioni (ITA)
1936	Axel Cadier (SWE)	Edwins Bietags (LAT)	August Néo (EST)
1948	Karl-Erik Nilsson (SWE)	Kaelpo Gröndahl (FIN)	Ibrahim Orabi (EGY)
1952	Kaelpo Gröndahl (FIN)	Shalva Shikhladze (URS)	Karl-Erik Nilsson (SWE)
1956	Valentin Nikolayev (URS)	Petko Sirakov (BUL)	Karl-Erik Nilsson (SWE)
1960	Tevfik Kis (TUR)	Krali Bimbalov (BUL)	Givi Kartoziya (URS)
1964	Boyan Radev (BUL)	Per Svensson (SWE)	Heinz Kiehl (GER)
1968	Boyan Radev (BUL)	Nikolai Yakovenko (URS)	Nicolae Martinescu (ROM)
1972	Valeriy Rezantsev (URS)	Josip Corak (YUG)	Czeslaw Kwiecinski (POL)
1976	Valeriy Rezantsev (URS)	Stoyan Ivanov (BUL)	Czeslaw Kwiecinski (POL)
1980	Norbert Nottny (HUN)	Igor Kanygin (URS)	Petre Disu (ROM)
1984	Steven Fraser (USA)	Ilie Matei (ROM)	Frank Andersson (SWE)
1988	Atanas Komchev (BUL)	Harri Koskela (FIN)	Vladimir Popov (URS)
1992	Maik Bullmann (GER)	Hakki Basar (TUR)	Gogui Kogouachvili (EUN)

[1] *Ahlgren and Böhling declared equal second after 9 hours of wrestling.*
1896–1906 Event not held.

Greco-Roman – Heavyweight

Note: The weight limit for this event has been: 1896, open; 1906, over 85kg; 1908, over 93kg; 1912 to 1928, over 82.5kg; 1932 to 1960, over 81kg; 1964 to 1968, over 91kg; since 1972, up to 100kg.

1896	Carl Schuhmann (GER)	Georgios Tsitas (GRE)	Stephanos Christopoulos (GRE)
1906	Sören Jensen (DEN)	Henri Baur (AUT)	Marcel Dubois (BEL)
1908	Richard Weisz (HUN)	Aleksandr Petrov (URS)	Sören Jensen (DEN)
1912	Yrjö Saarela (FIN)	Johan Olin (FIN)	Sören Jensen (DEN)
1920	Adolf Lindfors (FIN)	Poul Hansen (DEN)	Martti Nieminen (FIN)
1924	Henri Deglane (FRA)	Edil Rosenqvist (FIN)	Raymund Badó (HUN)
1928	Rudolf Svensson (SWE)	Hjalmar Nyström (FIN)	Georg Gehring (GER)
1932	Carl Westergren (SWE)	Josef Urban (TCH)	Nikolaus Hirschl (AUT)
1936	Kristjan Palusalu (EST)	John Nyman (SWE)	Kurt Hornfischer (GER)
1948	Ahmet Kireçci (TUR)	Tor Nilsson (SWE)	Guido Fantoni (ITA)
1952	Johannes Kotkas (URS)	Josef Ruzicka (TCH)	Tauno Kovanen (FIN)
1956	Anatoliy Parfenov (URS)	Wilfried Dietrich (GER)	Adelmo Bulgarelli (ITA)
1960	Ivan Bogdan (URS)	Wilfried Dietrich (GER)	Bohumil Kubat (TCH)
1964	István Kozma (HUN)	Anatoliy Roschin (URS)	Wilfried Dietrich (GER)
1968	István Kozma (HUN)	Anatoliy Roschin (URS)	Petr Kment (TCH)
1972	Nicolae Martinescu (ROM)	Nikolai Yakovenko (URS)	Ferenc Kiss (HUN)
1976	Nikolai Bolboshin (URS)	Kamen Goranov (BUL)	Andrzej Skrzylewski (POL)
1980	Gheorghi Raikov (BUL)	Roman Bierla (POL)	Vasile Andrei (ROM)
1984	Vasile Andrei (ROM)	Greg Gibson (USA)	Jozef Tertelje (YUG)
1988	Andrzej Wronski (POL)	Gerhard Himmel (FRG)	Dennis Koslowski (USA)
1992	Hector Milian (CUB)	Dennis Koslowski (USA)	Sergei Demiachkievich (EUN)

1900–1904 Event not held.

Greco-Roman – Super-Heavyweight

(Weight over 100kg)

1972	Anatoliy Roschin (URS)	Alexandre Tomov (BUL)	Victor Dolipschi (ROM)
1976	Aleksandr Kolchinsky (URS)	Alexandre Tomov (BUL)	Roman Codreanu (ROM)
1980	Aleksandr Kolchinsky (URS)	Alexandre Tomov (BUL)	Hassan Bchara (LIB)

1984	Jeffrey Blatnick (USA)	Refik Memisevic (YUG)	Victor Dolipschi (ROM)
1988	Aleksandr Kareline (URS)	Ranguel Guerovski (BUL)	Tomas Johansson (SWE)
1992	Aleksandr Kareline (EUN)	Tomas Johansson (SWE)	Ioan Grigoras (ROM)

1896–1968 Event not held.

DISCONTINUED EVENT

Greco-Roman All-around

| 1896 | Sören Jensen (DEN) | Verner Weckmann (FIN) | – |

Yachting

The first Olympic regatta should have been on the Bay of Salamis, but it was cancelled due to bad weather. Since 1900 the classes have been changed regularly, although recently some measure of standardization has been imposed. The current classes, for 1996, are as follows: Finn, 470 (men), 470 (women), Tornado, Star, Soling, Laser, Europe (women), Mistral (boardsailing, men), Mistral (boardsailing, women). In each class there are seven races over a prescribed course in which the fastest time wins. Yachts count their six best results. The only event which has been a permanent fixture is the Olympic monotype, ie one-man dinghy, albeit represented by different classes of boat prior to 1952 (now the Finn).

The most successful yachtsman is Paul Elvström (DEN) who won four successive Olympic monotype titles from 1948 to 1960 – the first man to achieve such a run in any sport. He competed again in the 1968 Star (fourth), 1972 Soling (thirteenth), 1984 Tornado (fourth), and 1988 Tornado (fifteenth) – in the last two partnering his daughter Trine. Frances Clytie Rivett-Carnac (GBR) was the first female gold medallist in the 7m class of 1908 with her husband, and she was the first woman to win in an event not restricted to women or mixed pairs in any sport. She and her husband were the first married couple to win gold medals in the Olympic Games.

The oldest gold medallist was Everard Endt (USA) in the 1952 6m class aged 59yr 112 days, while the oldest in a single-handed event was Leon Huybrechts (BEL) aged 47yr 215 days in 1924. The oldest female winner and medallist was Virginie Heriot (FRA) in the 1928 8m class aged 38yr 16 days. The youngest gold medallist/medallist was Franciscus Hin (NED), in the 1920 12-foot dinghy event with his brother Johannes, aged 14yr 163 days. The youngest female champion was Linda Andersen (NOR) in the 1992 Europe class aged 23yr 49 days, while the youngest female medallist was Natalia Via Dufresne (ESP), second in the same event at 19yr 54 days. The oldest medallist was Louis Noverraz (SUI) in the 5.5m category in 1968 aged 66yr 154 days.

Outstanding family achievements have occurred in Olympic yachting. In 1920 four Norwegian brothers, Henrik, Jan, Ole and Kristian Östervold, won gold medals in the 12m (1907 rating) class. The full crew of the winning 5.5m in 1968 were brothers Ulf, Jörgen and Peter Sundelin (SWE), and the winning 6m in 1912 was crewed by Amédée, Gaston and Jacques Thubé (FRA). The only twins to win gold were Sumner and Edgar White (USA) in the 5.5m of 1952. The first father and son to win together were Emile and Florimond Cornellie (BEL) in the 6m (1907 rating) in 1920.

However, the greatest Olympic yachting family must be the Norwegians, Lunde: Eugen won a gold in the 1924 6m class, his son Peder and daughter-in-law Vibeke along with Vibeke's brother won a silver in the 5.5m in 1952, and grandson Peder Jr won a gold in the 1960 Flying Dutchman contest.

Rodney Pattisson and Iain Macdonald-Smith (GBR) scored the lowest number of penalty points (three) ever achieved in Olympic yachting when they won the 1968 Flying Dutchman class with five wins, a second place and a disqualification (finished first) in their seven starts. Their boat *Superdocius* is now in the National Maritime Museum, Greenwich. The only boat to win two gold medals in the same Games was *Scotia*, crewed by Lorne Currie and John Gretton for

Paul Elvström (DEN, centre) with Peder Lunde and Björn Bergvall (NOR) in 1960 (Allsport)

Great Britain, in the 0.5-1 ton and Open classes in 1900. The United States yacht *Llanoria* won the 6m class in 1948 and 1952, skippered both times by Herman Whiton.

In 1948 Magnus Konow (NOR) equalled the longest span of Olympic competition when he took part in the 6m event 40 years after his debut in the 8m class of 1908. He won two golds and a silver in 1912, 1920 and 1936, the only other Games he attended.

Durward Knowles competed in a record eight Games, all in the Star class, from 1948 when he competed for Great Britain. He then represented the Bahamas in the next six celebrations, and again in 1988 (aged 71, probably the oldest Olympic yachtsman ever). The aforementioned Paul Elvström also made it eight Games in 1988, and both he and Knowles matched the 40-year span record. In 1992 Hubert Raudaschl (AUT) equalled the eight Games record, 1964-92. Tore Holm (SWE) won medals over a record span of 28 years (1920-48), and, more unusual, Hans Fogh won medals 24 years apart (1960-84), first for Denmark and then for Canada.

Russell Coutts (NZL), who won the 1984 Finn event, was the skipper of *Black Magic 1* which won the America's Cup in 1995. The helmsman of the third placed Tempest in 1976 was Dennis Conner (USA), who had won the America's Cup for the United States in 1980, lost it in 1983, and regained it in 1987. His Montreal partner, Conn Findlay, had won rowing golds in 1956 and 1964. A number of other Olympic yachtsmen later competed in the America's Cup competitions. In the 1984 Games all 13 members of the United States team won either gold or silver medals, a unique team achievement. The greatest number of boats in an Olympic regatta was the 201 (plus 68 sailboards) at Barcelona in 1992. The greatest entry in just one event was 45 in the 1988 men's sailboard competition.

An attempt has been made to bring some method of comparison to the Olympic results, made particularly difficult due to the wide variety of classes and types of boat used over the years. Where boats have been superseded by those of similar type, they have been listed in the same table. Purists may be unhappy but the general reader will find it easier to follow.

YACHTING MEDALS TABLE

	G	S	B	Total
United States	16	19	14	49
Great Britain	14	10	9	33
Sweden	9	11	9	29
Norway	16	11	1	28
France	12	6	9	27
Denmark	9	8	4	21
Netherlands	4	4	5	13
New Zealand	6	3	3	12
Soviet Union	4	5	3	12
Spain	7	2	1	10
Australia	3	1	6	10
Germany	2	3	3	8
Italy	2	1	5	8
Finland	1	1	6	8
Canada	-	2	6	8
Belgium	2	3	2	7
FRG	2	2	3	7
Brazil	2	1	4	7
GDR	2	2	2	6
Greece	1	1	1	3
Switzerland [1]	1	1	1	3
Austria [1]	-	3	-	3
Portugal	-	2	1	3
Bahamas	1	-	1	2
Argentina	-	2	-	2
Estonia	-	-	2	2
China	-	1	-	1
Cuba	-	1	-	1
Ireland	-	1	-	1
Netherlands Antilles	-	1	-	1
Virgin Islands	-	1	-	1
Hungary [1]	-	-	1	1
Russia	-	-	1	1
	116	109 [2]	103 [2]	328

[1] *It is worth noting that Austria, Hungary and Switzerland have no direct access to the sea.*

[2] *Some events in the early Games had no silver and/or bronze medals.*

Olympic Yachting Venues

1900 River Seine at Meulan (10-20 tonners at Le Havre)
1908 Cowes, Isle of Wight, and the Clyde
1912 Nyhashamn
1920 Ostend
1924 River Seine at Meulan (6m and 8m at Le Havre)
1928 Zuider-Zee
1932 San Pedro Bay
1936 Kiel
1948 Torbay, Devon
1952 Harmaja

1956 Port Phillip Bay
1960 Bay of Naples
1964 Sagami Bay
1968 Acapulco Bay
1972 Kiel
1976 Kingston, Lake Ontario
1980 Tallinn
1984 Long Beach
1988 Pusan
1992 Barcelona

YACHTING MEDAL RESULTS — MEN

	GOLD	SILVER	BRONZE
Olympic Monotype			
1920 [1]	Netherlands	Netherlands	–
	Franciscus Hin	Arnoud van der Biesen	
	Joahannes Hin	Petrus Beikers	
1924 [2]	Léon Huybrechts (BEL)	Henrik Robert (NOR)	Hans Dittmar (FIN)
1928 [3]	Sven Thorell (SWE)	Henrik Robert (NOR)	Bertil Broman (FIN)
1932 [4]	Jacques Lebrun (FRA)	Adriaan Maas (NED)	Santiago Cansino (ESP)
1936 [5]	Daniel Kagchelland (NED)	Werner Krogmann (GER)	Peter Scott (GBR)
1948 [6]	Paul Elvström (DEN)	Ralph Evans (USA)	Jacobus de Jong (NED)
1952 [7]	Paul Elvström (DEN)	Charles Currey (GBR)	Rickard Sarby (SWE)
1956	Paul Elvström (DEN)	André Nelis (BEL)	John Marvin (USA)
1960	Paul Elvström (DEN)	Aleksandr Chuchelov (URS)	André Nelis (BEL)
1964	Willi Kuhweide (GER)	Peter Barrett (USA)	Henning Wind (DEN)
1968	Valentin Mankin (URS)	Hubert Raudaschl (AUT)	Fabio Albarelli (ITA)
1972	Serge Maury (FRA)	Ilias Hatzipavlis (GRE)	Viktor Potapov (URS)
1976	Jochen Schümann (GDR)	Andrei Balashov (URS)	John Bertrand (AUS)
1980	Esko Rechardt (FIN)	Wolfgang Mayrhofer (AUT)	Andrei Balashov (URS)
1984	Russell Coutts (NZL)	John Bertrand (USA)	Terry Neilson (CAN)
1988	Jose Luis Doreste (ESP)	Peter Holmberg (ISV)	John Cutler (NZL)
1992	Jose Maria van der Ploeg (ESP) 33.40pts	Brian Ledbetter (USA) 54.70	Craig Monk (NZL) 64.70

[1] *12-foot dinghy (note two-handed), no bronze medal.*
[2] *Meulan class, 12-foot dinghy.*
[3] *International 12-foot class.*
[4] *Snowbird class.*
[5] *International Olympia class.*
[6] *Firefly class.*
[7] *Since 1952 Finn class.*
1896–1912 Event not held.

Sailboard Class

1984	Steve Van Den Berg (NED)	Randall Steele (USA)	Bruce Kendall (NZL)
1988	Bruce Kendall (NZL)	Jan Boersma (AHO)	Michael Gebhardt (USA)
1992	Franck David (FRA) 70.70pts	Michael Gebhardt (USA) 71.10	Lars Kleppich (AUS) 98.70

1896–1980 Event not held.

International Soling

1972	United States	Sweden	Canada
1976	Denmark	United States	GDR
1980	Denmark	Soviet Union	Greece
1984	United States	Brazil	Canada
1988	GDR	United States	Denmark
1992	Denmark	United States	Great Britain

1896–1968 Event not held.

International 470

1976	FRG	Spain	Australia
1980	Brazil	GDR	Finland
1984	Spain	United States	France
1988	France	Soviet Union	United States
1992	Spain 50.00pts	United States 66.70	Estonia 68.70

1896–1972 Event not held.

International Tornado

1976	Great Britain	United States	FRG
1980	Brazil	Denmark	Sweden
1984	New Zealand	United States	Australia
1988	France	New Zealand	Brazil
1992	France 40.40pts	United States 42.00	Australia 44.40

1896–1972 Event not held.

International Star

1932	United States	Great Britain	Sweden
1936	Germany	Sweden	Netherlands
1948	United States	Cuba	Netherlands
1952	Italy	United States	Portugal
1956	United States	Italy	Bahamas
1960	Soviet Union	Portugal	United States
1964	Bahamas	United States	Sweden
1968	United States	Norway	Italy
1972	Australia	Sweden	FRG
1980	Soviet Union	Austria	Italy
1984	United States	FRG	Italy
1988	Great Britain	United States	Brazil
1992	United States 31.40pts	New Zealand 58.40	Canada 62.70

1896–1928, 1976 Event not held.

Flying Dutchman

1956 [1]	New Zealand	Australia	Great Britain
1960	Norway	Denmark	Germany
1964	New Zealand	Great Britain	United States
1968	Great Britain	FRG	Brazil
1972	Great Britain	France	FRG
1976	FRG	Great Britain	Brazil
1980	Spain	Ireland	Hungary
1984	United States	Canada	Great Britain
1988	Denmark	Norway	Canada
1992	Spain 29.70pts	United States 32.70	Denmark 37.70

[1] *Sharpie class.*
1896–1952 Event not held.

YACHTING MEDAL RESULTS — WOMEN

Sailboard Class

1992	Barbara-Anne Kendall (NZL) 47.80pts	Zhang Xiaodong (CHN) 65.80	Dorien de Vries (NED) 68.70

1896-1988 Event not held.

International 470

1988	United States	Sweden	Soviet Union
1992	Spain 29.70	New Zealand 36.70	United States 40.70

1896–1984 Event not held.

Europe Class

1992	Linda Andersen (NOR) 48.70	Natalia Dufresne (ESP) 57.40	Julia Trotman (USA) 62.70

1896-1988 Event not held.

DISCONTINUED EVENTS

Swallow

1948	Great Britain	Portugal	United States

International Tempest

1972	Soviet Union	Great Britain	United States
1976	Sweden	Soviet Union	United States

Dragon

1948	Norway	Sweden	Denmark
1952	Norway	Sweden	Germany
1956	Sweden	Denmark	Great Britain
1960	Greece	Argentina	Italy
1964	Denmark	Germany	United States
1968	United States	Denmark	GDR
1972	Australia	GDR	United States

30 Square Metres

1920	Sweden	–	–

40 Square Metres

1920	Sweden	Sweden	–

5.5 Metres

1952	United States	Norway	Sweden
1956	Sweden	Great Britain	Australia
1960	United States	Denmark	Switzerland
1964	Australia	Sweden	United States
1968	Sweden	Switzerland	Great Britain

6 Metres

1908	Great Britain	Belgium	France
1912	France	Denmark	Sweden
1920	Norway	Belgium	–
1924	Norway	Denmark	Netherlands
1928	Norway	Denmark	Estonia
1932	Sweden	United States	Canada
1936	Great Britain	Norway	Sweden
1948	United States	Argentina	Sweden
1952	United States	Norway	Finland

6 Metres (1907 Rating)

1920	Belgium	Norway	Norway

6.5 Metres

1920	Netherlands	France	–

7 Metres

1908	Great Britain	–	–
1920	Great Britain	–	–
1912 Event not held.			

8 Metres

1908	Great Britain	Sweden	Great Britain
1912	Norway	Sweden	Finland
1920	Norway	Norway	Belgium
1924	Norway	Great Britain	France
1928	France	Netherlands	Sweden
1932	United States	Canada	–
1936	Italy	Norway	Germany

8 Metres (1907 Rating)

1920	Norway	Norway

10 Metres

1912	Sweden	Finland	Russia

10 Metres (1907 Rating)

1920	Norway	–	–

10 Metres (1919 Rating)

1920	Norway	–	–

12 Metres

1908	Great Britain	Great Britain	–
1912	Norway	Sweden	Finland

12 Metres (1907 Rating)

1920	Norway	–	–

12 Metres (1919 Rating)

1920	Norway	–	–

0.5 Ton Class

1900	France	France	France

0.5–1 Ton Class

1900	France	Great Britain	France

1–2 Ton Class

1900	Switzerland	France	France

2–3 Ton Class

1900	Great Britain	France	France

3–10 Ton Class

1900	France	Netherlands	France
			Great Britain

10–20 Ton Class

1900	France	France	Great Britain

Open Class

1900	Great Britain	Germany	France

Over 20 Ton Class

1900	Great Britain	Great Britain	United States

Discontinued Sports

In the early celebrations of the Games there were a number of sports included, often of a purely local interest to the host country. The last of these was polo, which had its final outing in 1936. Below are listed all the medallists in these sports.

Cricket

On the only occasion that cricket was played at the Games, in 1900, Great Britain, represented by the Devon Wanderers CC, beat a French team consisting of mainly expatriate Britons. In a 12-a-side match Great Britain made 117 and 145 for five declared, against the French totals of 78 and 26.

Croquet

Contested only in 1900 when all the competitors were French. In the singles (simple à la boule), the medals went to Aumoitte, Johin and Waydelich respectively, and in the singles (simple à deux boules) they went to Waydelich, Vignerot and Sautereau. Only a gold medal was awarded in the doubles, won by Aumoitte and Johin.

Golf

George Lyon (CAN) was 46yr 59 days when he won the 1904 title, while the most medals were won by Chandler Egan (USA) with a team gold and individual silver in 1904.

	Gold	Silver	Bronze
Men's Singles			
1900	Charles Sands (USA)	Walter Rutherford (GBR)	David Robertson (GBR)
1904	George Lyon (CAN)	Chandler Egan (USA)	Burt McKinnie (USA)
Men's Team			
1904	United States	United States	-
Women's Singles			
1904	Margaret Abbott (USA)	Pauline Whittier (USA)	Daria Pratt (USA)

Jeu de Paume

Held only in 1908, it was a demonstration sport in 1928. The medals in 1908 were won by Jay Gould (USA), Eustace Mills (GBR) and Neville Lytton (GBR).

Lacrosse

Held in 1904 and 1908; won by Canada on both occasions, with the silvers going to the United States and Great Britain respectively. In 1904 a Mohawk Indian team, representing Canada, won the bronze, but in 1908 only two teams competed. The highest score was when Canada beat Great Britain 14-10 in 1908. Demonstrations were held in 1928, 1932 and 1948.

Motorboating

Only held in 1908, when only one boat finished in each of the three classes. The Open class was won by France, the 60-foot and 8-metre classes by Great Britain.

Polo

Only Sir John Wodehouse (GBR), the 3rd Earl of Kimberley, won a silver (1908) to add to a gold (1920). The oldest gold medallist was Manuel Andrada (ARG) in 1936 aged 46yr 211 days, and the youngest was his team-mate Roberto Cavanagh aged 21yr 269 days. The biggest winning margin was 16-2 by Argentina v Spain and Great Britain v France, both in 1924, and by Mexico v Hungary in 1936. A number of Americans played for Great Britain in 1900.

	Gold	Silver	Bronze
1900	Great Britain	Great Britain	France
1908	Great Britain	Great Britain	Great Britain
1920	Great Britain	Spain	United States
1924	Argentina	United States	Great Britain
1936	Argentina	Great Britain	Mexico

Roque

Only held in 1904 with all competitors from the United States. The medals were won by Charles Jacobus, Smith Streeter and Charles Brown respectively.

Rackets

Only held in 1908, the singles went to Evan Noel (GBR), from Henry Leaf (GBR) and John Jacob Astor (GBR), with Great Britain also gaining all three medals in the doubles event.

Rugby Union

Only six countries competed in the four tournaments held – Australia, France, Germany, Great Britain, Romania and the United States. The 1908 title was won by Australia while they were on their first tour of Britain – in the final the Wallabies defeated Cornwall, the English county champions.

Five American players won two gold medals in 1920 and 1924: Charles Doe, John O'Neil, Colby Slater, John Patrick and Rudolph Scholz. Additionally, Daniel Carroll won his second gold with the 1920 US team, having been in the 1908 Australian squad aged only 16yr 245 days. This makes him the youngest player ever to represent his country at the sport, although 'purists' have never considered the Olympic matches to be 'full' internationals. The highest score was when France beat Romania 61-3 in 1924.

	Gold	Silver	Bronze
1900	France	Germany	Great Britain
1908	Australia	Great Britain	-
1920	United States	France	-
1924	United States	France	Romania

In 1920, sprint relay gold medallist Morris Kirksey, also runner-up in the 100m, won another gold in the winning US rugby team.

It always comes as a shock to enthusiasts to realize that the United States are the reigning Olympic champions at rugby. After their Paris victory the United States teamplayed in Britain and were beaten by the Harlequins and Blackheath club teams.

Demonstration Sports

It was decided by the IOC that after 1992 there would no longer be any demonstration sports held at the Games. Since 1904 there had been a variety of such demonstrations held, though not as official events eligible for medals. Some of them later became official sports and have been mentioned elsewhere. Other than those, there have also been the following:

American Football
In 1932 two teams representing the East and West of America played an exhibition which the West won 7-6.

Australian Rules Football
Two amateur Australian teams played an exhibition in 1956 which resulted in a 250-135 score.

Bandy
A tournament was included in the 1952 Winter Games. Final placings were decided on goal average with Sweden winning from Norway and Finland.

Budo
Exhibitions of Japanese archery, wrestling and fencing were given in 1964.

Dog Sled Racing
A race for twelve sled teams, seven dogs to a sled, was held in 1932. There were actually two races of approximately 25 miles (40km) each, with the aggregate times added together. Emile St Goddard (CAN) won easily, finishing first both times in a combined 4hr 23min 12.5sec, nearly eight minutes ahead of Lennard Seppala (USA).

Gliding
Fourteen countries took part in an exhibition in 1936, but the main demonstrations were by German gliders.

Korfball
A demonstration event in 1920 when a team representing South Holland beat Amsterdam 2-0.

Military Patrol
Held at four Winter Games, it is considered to be the forerunner of the official biathlon contests introduced in 1960. Switzerland won in 1924 and 1948, Norway won in 1928, and Italy took the 1936 title.

Pelota Basque
Demonstrated in 1924 by teams from Spain and France, and again in 1968. It was seen a third time in 1992.

Roller Hockey
This was demonstrated for the first time in 1992.

Speed Skiing
Demonstrated in 1992 when world records were set in both men's – 229.299km/h by Mikael Prufer (FRA) – and women's – 219.245km/h by Tarja Mulari (FIN) – events. Second in the men's competition was Philippe Goitschel (FRA), nephew of the sisters who had won golds in the 1964 Alpine events. Davina Galica (GBR) competed in the women's event 28 years after her first Olympic appearance as an Alpine skier, aged 47yr 189 days.

Taekwondo
This was demonstrated in 1988 and 1992, and will become a medal sport in the 2000 Games.

Water Skiing
Held in Kiel in 1972 with 36 competitors from 20 countries, with many of the best skiers in the world. Events were won by Roby Zucchi (ITA), Ricky McCormick (USA), Willy Stöhle (NED), Liz Allan-Shetter (USA) and Sylvie Maurial (FRA).

Winter Pentathlon
Held in 1948 and comprising a 10km cross-country skiing race, a pistol shoot, fencing, downhill skiing and horse-riding over a distance of 3500m. Gustaf Lindh (SWE) came first, with his team-mate Willie Grut second. Grut later that year won the modern pentathlon in the Summer Games by a record margin. In sixth place was Derek Allhusen (GBR) who 20 years later in his 55th year won an equestrian gold medal at Mexico City.

Alpine Skiing

Separate Alpine skiing events were first introduced into the Games in 1948, but this style was held in 1936 as an Alpine combination event consisting of an aggregate of points scored in a downhill and a slalom race. Toni Sailer (AUT) in 1956 and Jean-Claude Killy (FRA) in 1968 both won a record three gold medals. Vreni Schneider (SUI) is the first woman to win three golds (1988 and 1994), and set an all-time record of 5 medals (3 gold, 1 silver, 1 bronze). This total of five medals was equalled by Kjetil André Aamodt (NOR) 1992-94 (1 gold, 2 silver, 2 bronze), and Alberto Tomba (ITA) 1988-94 (3 gold, 2 silver), the latter also becoming the first Alpine skier to win medals in three consecutive Games (Tomba's coach, Gustavo Thoeni, won the 1972 giant slalom). There were a record 131 competitors in the 1992 giant slalom, representing a record 46 countries.

The oldest gold medallist was Zeno Colo (ITA) who won the 1952 downhill aged 31yr 231 days, while the youngest was Michela Figini (SUI) aged 17yr 314 days when winning the 1984 downhill. The youngest male winner was Sailer (see above) aged 20yr 73 days in the 1956 slalom, and the oldest female champion was Ossi Reichert (GER) in the 1956 giant slalom aged 30yr 33 days. Heinrich Messner (AUT) was the oldest medallist with the downhill bronze in 1972 aged 32yr 159 days, and the youngest medallist was Gertraud 'Traudl' Hecher (AUT) aged 16yr 145 days with the bronze in the 1960 downhill race. The youngest male medallist was Alfred Matt (AUT) with the 1968 slalom bronze aged 19yr 281 days, and the oldest female medallist was Dorothea Hochleitner (AUT) aged 30yr 201 days when she won the 1956 giant slalom bronze.

Vreni Schneider winning the slalom in 1994 on the way to her record total of five Alpine skiing medals (Allsport/Nathan Bilow)

The highest average speed attained in an Olympic downhill race was 104.532km/h (64.953 mph) by Bill Johnson (USA) in 1984. The highest in the women's event was 99.598km/h (61.887 mph) by Annemarie Moser-Pröll (AUT) in 1980. *(Appended below is a table of average speeds in Olympic downhill races since 1936)*

The greatest margin of victory in downhill was 4.7sec by Madeleine Berthod (FRA) in 1956, while the best in the male race was 4.1 sec by Henri Oreiller (FRA) in 1948. The smallest margin was 0.04sec in the 1994 men's race, while that for women is 0.05sec in the 1984 event. The greatest margin in slalom was 11.3sec by Cristl Cranz (GER) in the 1936 combination event, when that in the men's equivalent was 5.9sec by Franz Pfnür (GER). Since then Toni Sailer (AUT) has won by 4.0sec in 1956 and Anne Heggtveit (CAN) the 1960 women's race by 3.3sec. The smallest margin was 0.02sec in the 1972 women's event, which was equalled in the 1994 men's race. The tie for silver in the 1992 women's slalom was the first ever such tie since the introduction of automatic timing.

In the giant slalom the biggest margin was 6.2 sec by Sailer in 1956, while that for women was 2.64sec by Nancy Greene (CAN) in 1968. The smallest margin was 0.1sec (before electronic timing) by Yvonne Rüegg (SUI) in 1960, and 0.12sec by Kathy Kreiner (CAN) in 1976. The smallest for men was 0.20sec by Heini Hemmi (SUI) in 1976.

Year	**Men** km/h	Winner	**Women** km/h	Winner
1936	47.599	Ruud (NOR)	39.031	Schou-Nilsen (NOR)
1948	66.034	Oreiller (FRA)	43.695	Schlunegger (SUI)
1952	57.629	Colo (ITA)	50.420	Jochum-Beiser (AUT)
1956	72.356	Sailer (AUT)	55.484	Berthod (SUI)
1960	88.429	Vuarnet (FRA)	67.426	Biebl (GER)
1964	81.297	Zimmermann (AUT)	74.496	Haas (AUT)
1968	86.808	Killy (FRA)	77.080	Pall (AUT)
1972	85.291	Russi (SUI)	78.568	Nadig (SUI)
1976	102.828	Klammer (AUT)	85.286	Mittermaier (FRG)
1980	102.677	Stock (AUT)	99.598	Moser-Proell (AUT)
1984	104.532	Johnson (USA)	96.428	Figini (SUI)
1988	94.702	Zurbriggen (SUI)	93.836	Kiehl (FRG)
1992	99.418	Ortlieb (AUT)	88.600	Lee-Gartner (CAN)
1994	103.319	Moe (USA)	99.109	Seizinger (GER)

ALPINE SKIING MEDALS TABLE (excluding Freestyle skiing)

	Men G	S	B	**Women** G	S	B	Total
Austria	12	12	14	9	11	9	67
Switzerland	6	10	8	10	7	6	47
France	8	4	7	3	7	6	35
United States	3	4	1	6	9	3	26
Italy	7	5	2	3	1	4	22
Germany	3	2	1	4	4	4	18
Norway	4	3	5	-	-	1	13
Canada	-	-	2	4	1	3	10
FRG	-	1	-	3	4	1	9
Liechtenstein	-	1	3	2	1	2	9
Sweden	2	-	3	2	-	-	7
Slovenia	-	-	1	-	-	2	3
Luxembourg	-	-2-		-	-	-	2
Spain	1	-	-	-	-	1	2
Yugoslavia	-	1	-	-	1	-	2
Japan	-	1	-	-	-	-	1
New Zealand	-	-	-	-	1	-	1
Russia	-	-	-	-	1	-	1
Czechoslovakia	-	-	-	-	-	1	1
Soviet Union	-	-	-	-	1	-	1
	46	46	47 [1]	46	48 [2]	44	277

[1] *Two bronzes in 1948 downhill*
[2] *Two silvers in 1964 and 1992 giant slalom*

ALPINE SKIING MEDAL RESULTS — MEN

	GOLD	SILVER	BRONZE

Downhill

1948	Henri Oreiller (FRA) 2:55.0	Franz Gabl (AUT) 2:59.1	Karl Molitor (SUI) 3:00.3
			Rolf Olinger (SUI) 3:00.3
1952	Zeno Colo (ITA) 2:30.8	Othmar Schneider (AUT) 2:32.0	Christian Pravda (AUT) 2:32.4
1956	Anton Sailer (AUT) 2:52.2	Raymond Fellay (SUI) 2:55.7	Andreas Molterer (AUT) 2:56.2
1960	Jean Vuarnet (FRA) 2:06.0	Hans-Peter Lanig (GER) 2:06.5	Guy Perillat (FRA) 2:06.9
1964	Egon Zimmermann (AUT) 2:18.16	Leo Lacroix (FRA) 2:18.90	Wolfgang Bartels (GER) 2:19.48
1968	Jean-Claude Killy (FRA) 1:59.85	Guy Périllat (FRA) 1:59.93	Jean-Daniel Dätwyler (SUI) 2:00.32
1972	Bernhard Russi (SUI) 1:51.43	Roland Collombin (SUI) 1:52.07	Heinrich Messner (AUT) 1:52.40
1976	Franz Klammer (AUT) 1:45.73	Bernhard Russi (SUI) 1:46.06	Herbert Plank (ITA) 1:46.59
1980	Leonhard Stock (AUT) 1:45.50	Peter Wirnsberger (AUT) 1:46.12	Steve Podborski (CAN) 1:46.62
1984	Bill Johnson (USA) 1:45.59	Peter Müller (SUI) 1:45.86	Anton Steiner (AUT) 1:45.95
1988	Pirmin Zurbriggen (SUI) 1:59.63	Peter Müller (SUI) 2:00.14	Franck Piccard (FRA) 2:01.24
1992	Patrick Ortlieb (AUT) 1:50.37	Franck Piccard (FRA) 1:50.42	Gunther Mader (AUT) 1:50.47
1994	Tommy Moe (USA) 1:45.75	Kjetil-Andre Aamodt (NOR) 1:45.79	Edward Podivinsky (CAN) 1:45.87

1924-36 Event not held.

Slalom

1948	Edi Reinalter (SUI) 2:10.3	James Couttet (FRA) 2:10.8	Henri Oreiller (FRA) 2:12.8
1952	Othmar Schneider (AUT) 2:00.0	Stein Eriksen (NOR) 2:01.2	Guttorm Berge (NOR) 2:01.7
1956	Anton Sailer (AUT) 3:14.7	Chiharu Igaya (JPN) 3:18.7	Stig Sollander (SWE) 3:20.2
1960	Ernst Hinterseer (AUT) 2:08.9	Matthias Leitner (AUT) 2:10.3	Charles Bozon (FRA) 2:10.4
1964	Josef Stiegler (AUT) 2:21.13	William Kidd (USA) 2:21.27	James Hengu (USA) 2:21.52
1968	Jean-Claude Killy (FRA) 1:39.73	Herbert Huber (AUT) 1:39.82	Alfred Matt (AUT) 1:40.09
1972	Francisco Fernandez Ochoa (ESP) 1:49.27	Gustavo Thoeni (ITA) 1:50.28	Rolando Thoeni (ITA) 1:50.30
1976	Piero Gros (ITA) 2:03.29	Gustavo Thoeni (ITA) 2:03.73	Willy Frommelt (LIE) 2:04.28
1980	Ingemar Stenmark (SWE) 1:44.26	Phil Mahre (USA) 1:44.76	Jacques Lüthy (SUI) 1:45.06
1984	Phil Mahre (USA) 1:39.21	Steve Mahre (USA) 1:39.62	Didier Bouvet (FRA) 1:40.20
1988	Alberto Tomba (ITA) 1:39.47	Frank Wörndl (FRG) 1:39.53	Paul Frommelt (LIE) 1:39.84
1992	Finn Christian Jagge (NOR) 1:44.39	Alberto Tomba (ITA) 1:44.67	Michael Tritscher (AUT) 1:44.85
1994	Thomas Stanggassinger (AUT) 2:02.02	Alberto Tomba (ITA) 2:02.17	Jure Kosir (SLO) 2:02.53

1924-36 Event not held.

Giant Slalom

1952	Stein Eriksen (NOR) 2:25.0	Christian Pravda (AUT) 2:26.9	Toni Spiss (AUT) 2:28.8
1956	Anton Sailer (AUT) 3:00.1	Andreas Molterer (AUT) 3:06.3	Walter Schuster (AUT) 3:07.2
1960	Roger Staub (SUI) 1:48.3	Josef Stiegler (AUT) 1:48.7	Ernst Hinterseer (AUT) 1:49.1
1964	François Bonlieu (FRA) 1:46.71	Karl Schranz (AUT) 1:47.09	Josef Stiegler (AUT) 1:48.05
1968	Jean-Claude Killy (FRA) 3:29.28	Willy Favre (SUI) 3:31.50	Heinrich Messner (AUT) 3:31.83
1972	Gustavo Thoeni (ITA) 3:09.62	Edmund Bruggmann (SUI) 3:10.75	Werner Mattle (SUI) 3:10.99
1976	Heini Hemmi (SUI) 3:26.97	Ernst Good (SUI) 3:27.17	Ingemar Stenmark (SWE) 3:27.41
1980	Ingemar Stenmark (SWE) 2:40.74	Andreas Wenzel (LIE) 2:41.49	Hans Enn (AUT) 2:42.51
1984	Max Julen (SUI) 2:41.18	Juriy Franko (YUG) 2:41.41	Andreas Wenzel (LIE)
1988	Alberto Tomba (ITA) 2:06.37	Hubert Strolz (AUT) 2:07.41	Pirmin Zurbriggen (SUI) 2:08.39
1992	Alberto Tomba (ITA) 2:06.98	Marc Girardelli (LUX) 2:07.30	Kjetil-Andre Aamodt (NOR) 2:07.82
1994	Markus Wasmeier (GER) 2:52.46	Urs Kaelin (SUI) 2:52.48	Christian Mayer (AUT) 2:52.58

1924-48 Event not held.

Super Giant Slalom

1988	Franck Piccard (FRA) 1:39.66	Helmut Mayer (AUT) 1:40.96	Lars-Börje Eriksson (SWE) 1:41.08
1992	Kjetil-Andre Aamodt (NOR) 1:13.04	Marc Girardelli (LUX) 1:13.77	Jan Einar Thorsen (NOR) 1:13.83
1994	Markus Wasmeier (GER) 1:32.53	Tommy Moe (USA) 1:32.61	Kjetil-Andre Aamodt (NOR) 1:32.93

1924-84 Event not held.

Alpine Combination (Downhill and Slalom)

1936	Franz Pfnür (GER) 99.25pts	Gustav Lantschner (GER) 96.26pts	Emile Allais (FRA) 94.69pts
1948	Henri Oreiller (FRA) 3.27pts	Karl Molitor (SUI) 6.44pts	James Couttet (FRA) 6.95pts
1988	Hubert Strolz (AUT) 36.55pts	Bernhard Gstrein (AUT) 43.45pts	Paul Accola (SUI) 48.24pts
1992	Josef Polig (ITA) 14.58pts	Gianfranco Martin (ITA) 14.90pts	Steve Locher (SUI) 18.16pts
1994	Lasse Kjus (NOR) 3:17.53	Kjetil-Andre Aamodt (NOR) 3:18.55	Harald Strand Nielsen (NOR) 3:19.14

1924-32, 1952–1984 Event not held.

ALPINE SKIING MEDAL RESULTS — WOMEN

Downhill

1948	Hedy Schlunegger (SUI) 2:28.3	Trude Beiser (AUT) 2:29.1	Resi Hammerer (AUT) 2:30.2
1952	Trude Jochum-Beiser (AUT) 1:47.1	Annemarie Buchner (GER) 1:48.0	Giuliana Minuzzo (ITA) 1:49.0
1956	Madeleine Berthod (SUI) 1:40.7	Freida Dänzer (SUI) 1:45.4	Lucile Wheeler (CAN) 1:45.9
1960	Heidi Biebl (GER) 1:37.6	Penelope Pitou (USA) 1:38.6	Traudl Hecher (AUT) 1:38.9
1964	Christl Haas (AUT) 1:55.39	Edith Zimmerman (AUT) 1:56.42	Traudl Hecher (AUT) 1:56.66
1968	Olga Pall (AUT) 1:40.87	Isabelle Mir (FRA) 1:41.33	Christl Haas (AUT) 1:41.41
1972	Marie-Thérèse Nadig (SUI) 1:36.68	Annemarie Pröll (AUT) 1:37.00	Susan Corrock (USA) 1:37.68
1976	Rosi Mittermaier (FRG) 1:46.16	Brigitte Totschnig (AUT) 1:46.68	Cindy Nelson (USA) 1:47.50
1980	Annemarie Moser-Pröll (AUT) 1:37.52	Hanni Wenzel (LIE) 1:38.22	Marie-Thérèse Nadig (SUI) 1:38.36
1984	Michela Figini (SUI) 1:13.36	Maria Walliser (SUI) 1:13.41	Olga Chartova (TCH) 1:13.53
1988	Marina Kiehl (FRG) 1:25.86	Brigitte Oertli (SUI) 1:26.61	Karen Percy (CAN) 1:26.62
1992	Kerrin Lee-Gartner (CAN) 1:52.55	Hilary Lindh (USA) 1:52.61	Veronika Wallinger (AUT) 1:52.64
1994	Katya Seizinger (GER) 1:35.93	Picabo Street (USA) 1:36.59	Isolde Kostner (ITA) 1:36.85

1924-36 Event not held.

Slalom

1948	Gretchen Fraser (USA) 1:57.2	Antoinette Meyer (SUI) 1:57.7	Erika Mahringer (AUT) 1:58.0
1952	Andrea Mead-Lawrence (USA) 2:10.6	Ossi Reichert (GER) 2:11.4	Annemarie Buchner (GER) 2:13.3
1956	Renée Colliard (SUI) 1:52.3	Regina Schöpf (AUT) 1:55.4	Jevginija Sidorova (URS) 1:56.7
1960	Anne Heggtveit (CAN) 1:49.6	Betsy Snite (USA) 1:52.9	Barbi Henneberger (GER) 1:56.6
1964	Christine Goitschel (FRA) 1:29.86	Marielle Goitschel (FRA) 1:30.77	Jean Saubert (USA) 1:31.36
1968	Marielle Goitschel (FRA) 1:25.86	Nancy Greene (CAN) 1:26.15	Annie Famose (FRA) 1:27.89
1972	Barbara Cochran (USA) 1:31.24	Danielle Debernard (FRA) 1:31.26	Florence Steurer (FRA) 1:32.69
1976	Rosi Mittermaier (FRG) 1:30.54	Claudia Giordani (ITA) 1:30.87	Hanni Wenzel (LIE) 1:32.20
1980	Henni Wenzel (LIE) 1:25.09	Christa Kinshofer (FRG) 1:26.50	Erika Hess (SUI) 1:27.89
1984	Paolette Magoni (ITA) 1:36.47	Perrine Pelen (FRA) 1:37.38	Ursula Konsett (LIE) 1:37.50
1988	Vreni Schneider (SUI) 1:36.69	Mateja Svet (YUG) 1:38.37	Christa Kinshofer-Gütlein (FRG) 1:38.40
1992	Petra Kronberger (AUT) 1:32.68	Annelise Coberger (NZL) 1:33.10	Blanca Fernandez-Ochoa (ESP) 1:33.35
1994	Vreni Schneider (SUI) 1:56.01	Elfi Eder (AUT) 1:56.36	Katja Koren (SLO) 1:56.61

1924-36 Event not held.

Giant Slalom

1952	Andrea Mead-Lawrence (USA) 2:06.8	Dagmar Rom (AUT) 2:09.0	Annemarie Buchner (GER) 2:10.0
1956	Ossi Reichert (GER) 1:56.5	Josefine Frandl (AUT) 1:57.8	Dorothea Hochleitner (AUT) 1:58.2
1960	Yvonne Rüegg (SUI) 1:39.9	Penelope Pitou (USA) 1:40.0	Giuliana Chenal-Minuzzo (ITA) 1:40.2
1964	Marielle Goitschel (FRA) 1:52.24	Christine Goitschel (FRA) 1:53.11 Jean Saubert (USA) 1:53.11	–
1968	Nancy Greene (CAN) 1:51.97	Annie Famose (FRA) 1:54.61	Fernande Bochatay (SUI) 1:54.74
1972	Marie-Thérèse Nadig (SUI) 1:29.90	Annemarie Pröll (AUT) 1:30.75	Wiltrud Drexel (AUT) 1:32.35
1976	Kathy Kreiner (CAN) 1:29.13	Rosi Mittermaier (FRG) 1:29.25	Danielle Debernard (FRA) 1:29.95
1980	Hanni Wenzel (LIE) 2:41.66	Irene Epple (FRG) 2:42.12	Perrine Pelen (FRA) 2:42.41
1984	Debbie Armstrong (USA) 2:20.98	Christin Cooper (USA) 2:21.38	Perrine Pelen (FRA) 2:21.40
1988	Vreni Schneider (SUI) 2:06.49	Christa Kinshofer-Gütlein (FRG) 2:07.42	Maria Walliser (SUI) 2:07.72
1992	Pernilla Wiberg (SWE) 2:12.74	Diann Roffe (USA) 2:13.71 Anita Wachter (AUT) 2:13.71	–
1994	Deborah Compagnoni (ITA) 2:30.97	Martina Ertl (GER) 2:32.19	Vreni Schneider (SUI) 2:32.97

1924-48 Event not held.

Super Giant Slalom

1988	Sigrid Wolf (AUT) 1:19.03	Michela Figini (SUI) 1:20.03	Karen Percy (CAN) 1:20.29
1992	Deborah Compagnoni (ITA) 1:21.22	Carole Merle (FRA) 1:22.63	Katja Seizinger (GER) 1:23.19
1994	Diann Roffe (USA) 1:22.15	Svetlana Gladischeva (RUS) 1:22.44	Isolde Kostner (ITA) 1:22.45

1924-84 Event not held.

Alpine Combination (Downhill and Slalom)

1936	Christel Cranz (GER) 97.06pts	Käthe Grasegger (GER) 95.26pts	Laila Schou Nilsen (NOR) 93.48pts
1948	Trude Beiser (AUT) 6.58pts	Gretchen Fraser (USA) 6.95pts	Erika Mahringer (AUT) 7.04pts
1988	Anita Wachter (AUT) 29.25pts	Brigitte Oertli (SUI) 29.48pts	Maria Walliser (SUI) 51.28pts
1992	Petra Kronberger (AUT) 2.55pts	Anita Wachter (AUT) 19.39pts	Florence Masnada (FRA) 21.38pts
1994	Pernilla Wiberg (SWE) 3:05.16	Vreni Schneider (SUI) 3:05.29	Alenka Dovzan (SLO) 3:06.64

1924-32, 1952-84 Event not held

Bobsledding

A bob competition for 4-man sleds was first held in 1924. The rules allowed for 4- or 5-men teams in 1924 and 1928. The 2-man event was introduced in 1932. Both competitions have been held ever since except for 1960 when the Squaw Valley Organizing Committee refused to build a run. In 1952 a situation arose which led to changes in the rules governing the overall weight of teams and bobs. The Germans combined their heaviest men from their two vehicles into one 4-man sled averaging over 118kg per man, and won easily. Resulting complaints led to rules currently stipulating that the maximum weight of the bobs, with crews, must not exceed 390kg (2-man) and 630kg (4-man), but that extra weights may be added within those limits. In 1994 Gustave Weder (SUI) was the first to retain a 2-man title, and Wolfgang Hoppe (GER) became the only man to win medals in four winter Games.

The most gold medals won by an individual is three by Bernhard Germeshausen (GDR) and Meinhard Nehmer (GDR), both 1976-80. The most medals won is seven by Bogdan Musiol (GDR), 1 gold, 5 silver and 1 bronze 1980-92. The oldest gold medallist was Jay O'Brien (USA) in the 4-man in 1932 aged 48yr 359 days, which also makes him the oldest gold medallist in Winter Games history. The youngest champion was William Fiske (USA) who piloted the winning 5-man bob in 1928 aged 16yr 260 days. The youngest medallist was Thomas Doe Jr (USA) aged 15yr 127 days in the 1928 silver medal bob. The oldest medallist, and indeed the oldest in winter Games history, was Max Houben (BEL) aged 49yr 278 days in the 1948 4-man event. He had been a member of the sprint relay squad at Antwerp in 1920.

That 1932 American 4-man team had eventful lives outside bobsledding. Fiske had the distinction of being the first

American to join the RAF in the Second World War – he was killed in the Battle of Britain. O'Brien married silent film star Mae Murray. British-born Clifford 'Tippy' Gray was a songwriter and composed "If you were the only girl in the world", and Eddie Eagan was the only man to win medals in Summer and Winter Games. The tallest gold medallist was Edy Hubacher (SUI) in the 1972 4-man bob at 2.01m (6ft 7in). He also competed in the 1968 Summer Games shot put event. Carl-Erik Eriksson (SWE) was the first Olympic competitor to compete in six Games, 1964-84.

The first brothers to win gold medals were Alfred and Heinrich Schlappi (SUI) in the 4-man bob of 1924, while the inaugural 2-man event of 1932 was won by Hubert and Curtis Stevens (USA). The closest finish in Olympic bobsledding occurred in the 2-man of 1968 when Italy I and FRG I had identical aggregate times after the four runs. The title went to Italy, driven by the 40-year-old Eugenio Monti, as they had the fastest single run. The smallest margin in 4-man was 0.02sec after 4 runs in 1992.

BOBSLEDDING MEDALS TABLE

	G	S	B	Total
Switzerland	9	8	8	25
United States	5	4	5	14
GDR	5	5	3	13
Italy	3	4	3	10
Germany	3	2	4	9
FRG	1	3	2	6
Great Britain	1	1	1	3
Soviet Union	1	-	2	3
Austria	1	2	-	3
Belgium	-	1	1	2
Canada	1	-	-	1
Romania	-	-	1	1
	30	30	30	90

In 1994 Gustav Weder (front) drove the Swiss 4-man bob to a silver medal after winning the 2-man event (Popperfoto)

BOBSLEDDING MEDAL RESULTS

	GOLD	SILVER	BRONZE
2-Man Bob			
1932	United States I 8:14.14	Switzerland II 8:16.28	United States II 8:29.15
1936	United States I 5:29.29	Switzerland II 5:30.64	United States II 5:33.96
1948	Switzerland II 5:29.2	Switzerland I 5:30.4	United States II 5:35.3
1952	Germany I 5:24.54	United States I 5:26.89	Switzerland I 5:27.71
1956	Italy I 5:39.14	Italy II 5:31.45	Switzerland I 5:37.46
1964	Great Britain I 4:21.90	Italy II 4:22.02	Italy I 4:22.63
1968	Italy I 4:41.54	FRG I 4:41.54	Romania 4:44.46
1972	FRG II 4:47.07	FRG I 4:58.84	Switzerland I 4:59.33
1976	GDR II 3:44.42	FRG I 3:44.99	Switzerland I 3:45.70
1980	Switzerland II 4:09.36	GDR II 4:10.93	GDR I 4:11.08
1984	GDR II 3:28.56	GDR I 3:26.04	Soviet Union II 3:26.16
1988	Soviet Union I 3:53.48	GDR I 3:54.19	GDR II 3:54.64
1992	Switzerland I 4:03.26	Germany I 4:03.55	Germany II 4:03.63
1994	Switzerland I 3:30.81	Switzerland II 3:30.86	Italy I 3:31.01

1924-28, 1960 Event not held.

4-Man Bob

	GOLD	SILVER	BRONZE
1924	Switzerland I 5:45.54	Great Britain II 5:48.63	Belgium I 6:02.29
1928 [1]	United States II 3:20.5	United States I 3:21.0	Germany II 3:21.9
1932	United States I 7:53.68	United States II 7:55.70	Germany I 8:00.04
1936	Switzerland II 5:19.85	Switzerland I 5:22.73	Great Britain I 5:23.41
1952	Germany 5:07.84	United States I 5:10.48	Switzerland I 5:11.70

1956	Switzerland I 5:10.44	Italy II 5:12.10	United States I 5:12.39
1964	Canada 4:14.46	Austria 4:15.48	Italy II 4:15.60
1968 [2]	Italy I 2:17.39	Austria I 2:17.48	Switzerland I 2:18.04
1972	Switzerland 4:43.07	Italy I 4:43.83	FRG I 4:43.92
1976	GDR I 3:40.43	Switzerland II 3:40.89	FRG I 3:41.37
1980	GDR I 3:59.92	Switzerland I 4:00.87	GDR II 4:00.97
1984	GDR I 3:20.22	GDR II 3:20.78	Switzerland I 3:21.39
1988	Switzerland I 3:47.51	GDR I 3:47.58	Soviet Union II 3:48.26
1992	Austria I 3:53.90	Germany I 3:53.92	Switzerland I 3:54.13
1994	Germany II 3:27.78	Switzerland I 3:27.84	Germany I 3:28.01

1960 Event not held.

[1] *Five-man team in 1928; aggregate of two runs.*

[2] *Aggregate of two runs.*

Curling

After many appearances as a demonstration sport curling will finally become a medal sport at Nagano in 1998. A three-country contest was held in 1924, won by Great Britain from Sweden and France. In 1932 there were four Canadian Provincial and four American club teams. The Canadians took the first four places with the title won by Manitoba. In 1936 eight teams from Austria (3), Germany (3) and Czechoslovakia (2) competed in a specialized version of the game, German curling, with the Austrian number one team from the Tyrol, winning. The Austrians demonstrated the game in 1964 at Innsbruck, and it was a demonstration sport again in 1988 and 1992.

Figure Skating

Ice skating had been included in the original programme of events for the 1900 Games, but was not held. Thus, the first Olympic title at a winter Games event was won by Ulrich Salchow (SWE) in 1908 at the Prince's Rink, London. Salchow gave his name to one of the most popular jumps. In those 1908 Games there was also a special figures event which was won by a Russian (Czarist variety), Nikolai Panin, who had been too ill to compete in the main event. The first women's title went to Madge Syers (GBR), who six years previously had entered the World Championships, ostensibly for men only, and had placed second to Salchow. The most gold medals won by a figure skater is three by Gillis Grafström (SWE) 1920-1928, Sonja Henie (NOR) 1928-1936, and Irina Rodnina (URS) in the pairs 1972-1980. Of these only Grafström also won a silver, in 1932 aged 38, and thus is the only skater to win medals in four Games. No skater has doubled completely successfully in singles and pairs at the Games. The best have been Ernst Baier (GER) with the pairs gold and a singles silver in 1936, and Madge Syers (GBR) with a singles gold and a pairs bronze in 1908. The oldest gold medallist was Walter Jakobsson (FIN) who won the 1920 pairs with his German-born wife Ludowika aged 38yr 80 days. Ludowika became the oldest ever female winner aged 35yr 276 days. The youngest was Maxi Herber (GER) aged 15yr 128 days in the 1936 pairs with Baier, whom she later married.

The youngest male champion was Richard Button (USA) aged 18yr 202 days winning the 1948 singles. Sonja Henie (NOR) was remarkably 50 days short of her 16th birthday when she won her first title in 1928, after some last minute coaching by Britain's Alex Adams. She had been eighth and last in 1924 when still under 12 years of age. However, the youngest ever Winter Games competitor was her rival of 1936, Cecilia Colledge (GBR), who had been 11yr 73 days at the 1932 Games. The youngest male competitor was Jan Hoffmann (GDR) aged 12yr 110 days in 1968. Twelve years later he gained the silver medal. The youngest medallist was Scott Allen (USA) 2 days short of his 15th birthday taking the 1964 singles bronze, while the youngest female medallist was Manuela Gross (GDR) just ten days past her 15th birthday in the 1972 bronze-winning pair. The oldest medallist was Martin Stixrud (NOR) with the 1920 singles bronze aged 44yr 78 days, while the oldest female medallist was Ludowika Jacobsson (FIN) with a pairs silver in 1924 aged 39yr 189 days.

Sonja Henie won three Olympic, six European and ten World titles before turning professional and making an estimated $47 million in ice shows and films. The film world has attracted a number of other Olympic skaters. Down the field (16th) in 1936 was Gladys Jepson-Turner (GBR) who had a Hollywood career as Belita, and Vera Hruba (TCH), one place behind the British girl, who married the head of Republic Pictures and starred in many films as Vera Hruba Ralston.

Sonja Henie is usually credited with introducing jumps into the women's event, but in 1920 Theresa Weld (USA), the bronze medal winner, included a salchow in her programme, which brought a reprimand from the judges and a threat that she would be penalized if she continued with such 'unfeminine behaviour'. In the 1992 Games Surya Bonaly (FRA) attempted the first ever quadruple jump, in competition, by a woman.

A change of marking in the sport was brought about by Trixie Schuba (AUT) winning the 1972 title primarily on the basis of her excellent set figures (she was only placed seventh in free skating). At that time the marks had been divided 50-50 between sections, but they were changed to give greater emphasis to free skating. Set figures were skated for the last time at Calgary in 1988, and will no longer be included in Olympic competition. On the subject of marks, Jayne Torvill and Christopher Dean (GBR) were awarded a maximum nine sixes for their artistic impression in the 1984 ice dancing event, as well as another three sixes for technical merit – unsurpassed marking at the Games. In 1994 stricter rules governing skimpy clothing were introduced.

In 1972, although Irina Rodnina and Aleksey Ulanov (URS) won the pairs it was the latter's dalliance with Ludmila Smirnova, silver medallist with Andrey Suraikin, which caught the media interest. The result was a break-up of the top Soviet pair. Rodnina then teamed with Aleksandr Zaitsev, while Ulanov and Smirnova got married. In the World Championships the Rodnina/Zaitsev partnership beat the other pair and, getting married themselves in 1975, they went went on to win two Olympic titles, the second less than a year after the birth of a son.

FIGURE SKATING MEDALS TABLE

	G	S	B	Total
United States	11	12	14	37
Soviet Union	13	10	6	29
Austria	7	9	4	20
Canada	2	6	9	17
Great Britain	5	3	7	15
Sweden	5	3	2	10
GDR	3	3	4	10
France	2	2	5	9
Germany	4	4	-	8
Russia	4	2	-	6
Norway	3	2	1	6
Hungary	-	2	4	6
Czechoslovakia	1	1	3	5
Netherlands	1	2	-	3
Finland	1	1	-	2
Belgium	1	-	1	2
Switzerland	-	1	1	2
FRG	-	-	2	2
Ukraine	1	-	-	1
Japan	-	1	-	1
China	-	-	1	1
	64	64	64	192

FIGURE SKATING MEDAL RESULTS

	GOLD	SILVER	BRONZE
Men			
1908 [1]	Nikolai Panin (URS) 219pts	Arthur Cumming (GBR) 164pts	George Hall-Say (GBR) 104pts
1908	Ulrich Salchow (SWE) 1886.5pts	Richard Johansson (SWE) 1826.0pts	Per Thorén (SWE) 1787.0pts
1920	Gillis Gräfström (SWE) 2838.5pts	Andreas Krogh (NOR) 2634pts	Martin Stixrud (NOR) 2561.5pts
1924	Gillis Gräfström (SWE) 2757.2pts	Willy Böckl (AUT) 2518.75pts	Georges Gautschi (SUI) 2233.5pts
1932	Karl Schäfer (AUT) 2602.0pts	Gillis Gräfström (SWE) 2514.5pts	Montgomery Wilson (CAN) 2448.3pts
1936	Karl Schäfer (AUT) 2959.0pts	Ernst Baier (GER) 2805.3pts	Felix Kaspar (AUT) 2801.0pts
1948	Richard Button (USA) 1720.6pts	Hans Gerschwiler (SUI) 1630.1pts	Edi Rada (AUT) 1603.2pts

Katarina Witt (GDR) captured the women's title at Sarajevo in 1984 and retained it four years later (Popperfoto)

1952	Richard Button (USA) 1730.3pts	Helmut Seibt (AUT) 1621.3pts	James Grogan (USA) 1627.4pts
1956	Hayes Alan Jenkins (USA) 1497.95pts	Ronald Robertson (USA) 1492.15pts	David Jenkins (USA) 1465.41pts
1960	David Jenkins (USA) 1440.2pts	Karol Divin (TCH) 1414.3pts	Donald Jackson (CAN) 1401.0pts
1964	Manfred Schnelldorfer (GER) 1916.9pts	Alain Calmat (FRA) 1876.5pts	Scott Allen (USA) 1873.6pts
1968	Wolfgang Schwarz (AUT) 1894.1pts	Tim Woods (USA) 1891.6pts	Patrick Péra (FRA) 1864.5pts
1972	Ondrej Nepela (TCH) 2739.1pts	Sergey Tchetveroukhin (URS) 2672.4pts	Patrick Péra (FRA) 2653.1pts
1976	John Curry (GBR) 192.74pts	Vladimir Kovalev (URS) 187.64pts	Toller Cranston (CAN) 187.38pts
1980	Robin Cousins (GBR) 189.48pts [2]	Jan Hoffmann (GDR) 189.72pts [2]	Charles Tickner (USA) 187.06pts
1984	Scott Hamilton (USA) 3.4pl	Brian Orser (CAN) 5.6pl	Jozef Sabovtchik (TCH) 7.4pl
1988	Brian Boitano (USA) 3.0pl	Brian Orser (CAN) 4.2pl	Viktor Petrenko (URS) 7.8pl
1992	Viktor Petrenko (EUN) 1.5	Paul Wylie (USA) 3.5	Petr Barna (TCH) 4.0
1994	Alexei Urmanov (RUS) 1.5	Elvis Stojko (CAN) 3.0	Philippe Candeloro (FRA) 6.5

[1] *Special Figures competition.*
[2] *The majority of judges were in favour of Cousins. Since then, all medals have been decided by judges' placements.*
1912 Event not held.

The Ukraine's first ever gold medal as Oksana Baiul wins at Lillehammer, the youngest to win the figure skating title since Sonja Henie in 1928 (Popperfoto)

Women

1908	Madge Syers (GBR) 1262.5pts	Elsa Rendschmidt (GER) 1055.0pts	Dorothy Greenhough-Smith (GBR) 960.5pts
1920	Magda Mauroy-Julin (SWE) 913.5pts	Svea Norén (Swe) 887.75pts	Theresa Weld (USA) 898.0pts
1924	Herma Planck-Szabo (AUT) 2094.25pts	Beatrix Loughran (USA) 1959.0pts	Ethel Muckelt (GBR) 1750.50pts
1928	Sonja Henie (NOR) 2452.25pts	Fritzi Burger (AUT) 2248.50pts	Beatrix Loughran (USA) 2254.50pts
1932	Sonja Henie (NOR) 2302.5pts	Fritzi Burger (AUT) 2167.1pts	Maribel Vinson (USA) 2158.5pts
1936	Sonja Henie (NOR) 2971.4pts	Cecilia Colledge (GBR) 2926.8pts	Vivi-Anne Hultén (SWE) 2763.2pts
1948	Barbara Scott (CAN) 1467.7pts	Eva Pawlik (AUT) 1418.3pts	Jeanette Altwegg (GBR) 1405.5pts
1952	Jeanette Altwegg (GBR) 1455.8pts	Tenley Albright (USA) 1432.2pts	Jacqueline du Bief (FRA) 1422.0pts
1956	Tenley Albright (USA) 1866.39pts	Carol Heiss (USA) 1848.24pts	Ingrid Wendl (AUT) 1753.91pts
1960	Carol Heiss (USA) 1490.1pts	Sjoukje Dijkstra (NED) 1424.8pts	Barbara Roles (USA) 1414.8
1964	Sjoukje Dijkstra (NED) 2018.5pts	Regine Heitzer (AUT) 1945.5pts	Petra Burka (CAN) 1940.0pts
1968	Peggy Fleming (USA) 1970.5pts	Gabrielle Seyfert (GDR) 1882.3pts	Hana Maskova (TCH) 1828.8pts
1972	Beatrix Schuba (AUT) 2751.5pts	Karen Magnussen (CAN) 2763.2pts	Janet Lynn (USA) 2663.1pts
1976	Dorothy Hamill (USA) 193.80pts	Dianne De Leeuw (NED) 190.24pts	Christine Errath (GDR) 188.16pts
1980	Anett Pötzsch (GDR) 189.00pts	Linda Fratianne (USA) 188.30pts	Dagmar Lurz (FRG) 183.04pts
1984	Katarina Witt (GDR) 3.2pl	Rosalyn Sumners (USA) 4.6pl	Kira Ivanova (URS) 9.2pl
1988	Katarina Witt (GDR) 4.2pl	Elizabeth Manley (CAN) 4.6pl	Debra Thomas (USA) 6.0pl
1992	Kristi Yamaguchi (USA) 1.5	Midori Ito (JPN) 4.0	Nancy Kerrigan (USA) 4.0
1994	Oksana Baiul (UKR) 2.0	Nancy Kerrigan (USA) 2.5	Lu Chen (CHN) 5.0

1912 Event not held.

Pairs

1908	Germany 56.0pts	Great Britain 51.5pts	Great Britain 48.0pts
1920	Finland 80.75pts	Norway 72.75pts	Great Britain 66.25pts
1924	Austria 74.50pts	Finland 71.75pts	France 69.25pts
1928	France 100.50pts	Austria 99.25pts	Austria 93.25pts
1932	France 76.7pts	United States 77.5pts	Hungary 76.4pts

1936	Germany 103.3pts	Austria 102.7pts	Hungary 97.6pts
1948	Belgium 123.5pts	Hungary 122.2pts	Canada 121.0pts
1952	Germany 102.6pts	United States 100.6pts	Hungary 97.4pts
1956	Austria 101.8pts	Canada 101.9pts	Hungary 99.3pts
1960	Canada 80.4pts	Germany 76.8pts	United States 76.2pts
1964 [1]	Soviet Union 104.4pts	Germany 103.6pts	Canada 98.5pts
1968	Soviet Union 315.2pts	Soviet Union 312.3pts	FRG 304.4pts
1972	Soviet Union 420.4pts	Soviet Union 419.4pts	GDR 411.8pts
1976	Soviet Union 140.54pts	GDR 136.35pts	GDR 134.57pts
1980	Soviet Union 147.26pts	Soviet Union 143.80pts	GDR 140.52pts
1984	Soviet Union 1.4pl	United States 2.8pl	Soviet Union 3.8pl
1988	Soviet Union 1.4pl	Soviet Union 2.8pl	United States 4.2pl
1992	Unified Team 1.5	Unified Team 3.0	Canada 4.5
1994	Russia 1.5	Russia 3.0	Canada 4.5

[1] *Marika Kilius and Hansjürgen Bäumler (GER) finished second, were subsequently disqualified, then reinstated.*
1912 Event not held.

Ice Dance

1976	Soviet Union 209.92pts	Soviet Union 204.88pts	United States 202.64pts
1980	Soviet Union 205.48pts	Hungary 204.52pts	Soviet Union 201.86pts
1984	Great Britain 2.0pl	Soviet Union 4.0pl	Soviet Union 7.0pl
1988	Soviet Union 2.0pl	Soviet Union 4.0pl	Canada 6.0pl
1992	Unified Team 2.0	France 4.4	Unified Team 5.6
1994	Russia 3.4	Russia 3.8	Great Britain 4.8

1908–1972 Event not held.

Freestyle Skiing

Freestyle skiing, for men and women, was a demonstration sport in 1988 comprising ballet, aerials and mogul events. The mogul events were won by competitors from Sweden (men) and FRG (women). Mogul events became an Olympic medal sport in 1992, with aerials added in 1994. Marking is complicated but can best be compared to diving as each manouevre has a degree of difficulty which affects the final marks.

The most successful competitors have been Edgar Grospiron (FRA), with a gold and a bronze 1992-94, and Stine Lise Hattestad (NOR) equalling him in the women's events. Hattestad was also the oldest female champion aged 27yr 292 days winning the 1994 moguls; the oldest male winner was Andreas Schönbächler (SUI) who won the 1994 aerials just six days older than the Norwegian. The youngest winner, of the 1994 moguls, was Jean-Luc Brassard (CAN) aged 21yr 176 days, while the youngest medallist was Yelizaveta Kozhevnikova (EUN-RUS) in the 1992 moguls aged 19yr 48 days. Elizabeth McIntyre (USA) was the oldest medallist in the 1994 moguls aged 28yr 287 days.

Moguls expert Edgar Grospiron (FRA) won the inaugural event in 1992 and followed up with a bronze at Lillehammer (Popperfoto)

FREESTYLE SKIING MEDALS TABLE

	Men			Women			
	G	S	B	G	S	B	Total
Canada	1	1	1	-	-	-	3
France	1	1	1	-	-	-	3
United States	-	-	1	1	1	-	3
Norway	-	-	-	1	-	2	3
Russia	-	1	-	-	-	1	2
Switzerland	1	-	-	-	-	-	1
Uzbekistan	-	-	-	1	-	-	1
Soviet Union	-	-	-	-	1	-	1
Sweden	-	-	-	-	1	-	1
	3	3	3	3	3	3	18

FREESTYLE SKIING MEDAL RESULTS — MEN

	GOLD	SILVER	BRONZE

Moguls

	GOLD	SILVER	BRONZE
1992	Edgar Grospiron (FRA) 25.81pts	Olivier Allamand (FRA) 24.87	Nelson Carmichael (USA) 24.82
1994	Jean-Luc Brassard (CAN) 27.24	Sergei Shoupletsov (RUS) 26.90	Edgar Grospiron (FRA) 26.64

1924-88 Event not held

Aerials

	GOLD	SILVER	BRONZE
1994	Andreas Schonbachler (SUI) 234.67	Philippe Laroche (CAN) 228.23	Lloyd Langlois (CAN) 222.44

1924-92 Event not held

FREESTYLE SKIING MEDAL RESULTS — WOMEN

Moguls

	GOLD	SILVER	BRONZE
1992	Donna Weinbrecht (USA) 23.69pts	Yelizaveta Kozhevnikova (EUN) 23.50	Stine Lise Hattestad (NOR) 23.04
1994	Stine Lise Hattestad (NOR) 25.97	Elizabeth McIntyre (USA) 25.89	Yelizaveta Kozhevnikova (RUS) 25.81

1924-88 Event not held

Aerials

	GOLD	SILVER	BRONZE
1994	Lina Cherjasova (UZB) 166.84pts	Marie Lindgren (SWE) 165.88	Hilde Synnove Lid (NOR) 164.13

1924-92 Event not held

Patrik Juhlin (SWE) and Ken Lovsin (CAN, left) fight for the puck in the 1994 final won by Sweden (Popperfoto)

Ice Hockey

The game was introduced in 1920 as part of the Summer Games. The tournament was won by Canada, the first of a run of six victories only interrupted by Great Britain in 1936. However, the record number of wins is eight by the Soviet Union/Russia between 1956 and 1992, although in 1994 they did not win a medal for the first time since they entered in 1956. In the early days the Canadians were always represented by a club side, not a national side, so that the first Olympic champions were actually the Winnipeg Falcons. Since 1948 the tournament has been decided on a championship format and not, as previously, on a knock-out basis – thus there is no Olympic final as such. The game has been the centre of much bitter argument about amateur/professional status, and in 1972 Canada withdrew in protest against the alleged 'professionalism' of the Eastern European teams in particular. Happily they returned in 1980. In 1994 professionals were allowed to compete.

In 1948 there was a strange situation when two teams turned up to represent the United States, one from the Amateur Hockey Association (AHA) and the other picked by the US Olympic Committee. The AHA, while not affiliated to the USOC, was a member of the International Hockey Federation (IHF), the governing body of most of the other teams present in St Moritz. The IHF threatened to withdraw all the other teams if the AHA team did not play, while the USOC threatened to withdraw the whole Olympic team if the AHA team did play. Initially the IOC barred both teams, but then agreed to allow the AHA team to compete. They eventually finished fourth, but a year later were disqualified for non-affiliation to the Olympic movement. Strangely the USOC hockey team members marched in the opening ceremony. Six Soviet players have won a record three gold medals, but only goalminder Vladislaw Tretyak, 1972-1984, also won a silver. Richard 'Bibi' Torriani (SUI) won a bronze in 1928 and another in

1948, for a record 20 year span. The oldest gold medallist was Carl Erhardt (GBR) in 1936 on the day after his 39th birthday. The youngest was John Kilpatrick (GBR) in 1936 aged 18yr 224 days, while the youngest medallist was Richard Torriani (SUI) at 16yr 141 days in 1928. The oldest medallist was also Carl Erhardt in 1936. The first brothers to win gold were Herbert, Hugh and Rogers Plaxton along with Frank and Joseph Sullivan in the 1928 Canadian team. The only twins were Boris and Yevgeniy Maiorov (URS) in 1964. The only known father and son gold medallists were Bill and David Christian (USA) who won in 1960 and 1980 respectively. Another distinction for Bill is that he and his brother Roger, were one of two sets of brothers, the other was Bill and Bob Cleary, who helped the USA to win its first ice hockey gold in 1960.

The highest score and aggregate in Olympic ice hockey was the 33-0 victory by Canada over Switzerland in 1924. In that tournament the Canadians totalled 110 goals in five matches with only three against. In the 1980 tournament the American goalminder, James Craig, stopped 163 of 178 shots at his goal (91.6%), including 39 in the match against the Soviet Union. When the Czechs won the 1948 silver medal a member of the team was 1954 Wimbledon tennis champion Jaroslav Drobny.

ICE HOCKEY MEDALS TABLE

	G	S	B	Total
Canada	6	4	2	12
Soviet Union	8	1	1	10
United States	2	6	1	9
Czechoslovakia	-	4	4	8
Sweden	1	2	4	7
Great Britain	1	-	1	2
Finland	-	1	1	2
Switzerland	-	-	2	2
FRG	-	-	1	1
Germany	-	-	1	1
	18	18	18	54

ICE HOCKEY MEDAL RESULTS

	GOLD	SILVER	BRONZE
1920	Canada	United States	Czechoslovakia
1924	Canada	United States	Great Britain
1928	Canada	Sweden	Switzerland
1932	Canada	United States	Germany
1936	Great Britain	Canada	United States
1948	Canada	Czechoslovakia	Switzerland
1952	Canada	United States	Sweden
1956	Soviet Union	United States	Canada
1960	United States	Canada	Soviet Union
1964	Soviet Union	Sweden	Czechoslovakia
1968	Soviet Union	Czechloslovakia	Canada
1972	Soviet Union	United States	Czechoslovakia
1976	Soviet Union	Czechoslovakia	FRG [1]
1980	United States	Soviet Union	Sweden
1984	Soviet Union	Czechoslovakia	Sweden
1988	Soviet Union	Finland	Sweden
1992	Unified Team	Canada	Czechoslovakia
1994	Sweden	Canada	Finland

[1] Three-way tie for bronze with the United States and Finland decided on goal average.

Lugeing

In 1928 and 1948 there were one-man skeleton sled races held on the famous Cresta Run at St Moritz. In those events the contestants laid face down. Luge racing, in which contestants sit up or lie back, was introduced in 1964. Speeds of over 130km/h are achieved. The most successful lugers have been Thomas Kohler (GDR), with two gold medals and a silver in 1964 and 1968, and Georg Hackl (GER), with golds in 1992-94 and a silver in 1988. Hackl is the only man to successfully defend the singles title. Hans Rinn (GDR) won the 2-man event twice (with Norbert Hahn), in 1976-80, and a bronze in the 1976 singles. The most successful woman was Steffi Martin-Walter (GDR) with two golds in 1984 and 1988.

The oldest gold medallist was Paul Hildgartner (ITA) aged 31yr 249 days in the 1984 singles, while the youngest was Manfred Stengl (AUT) in the 2-man in 1964 aged 17yr 310 days. The youngest female winner was Ortrun Enderlein (GER) aged 20yr 65 days in 1964, and the oldest was Steffi Martin-Walter (GDR) in 1988 was aged 25yr 153 days. The youngest medallist has been Ute Rührold (GDR) aged 17yr 60 days gaining the silver in 1972. The oldest medallist in luge was Fritz Nachmann (FRG) in 1968 aged 38yr 186 days, but John Crammond (GBR) was 41yr 213 days when he took the bronze in the 1948 skeleton event. The oldest female medallist was Ute Weiss-Oberhoffner (GDR) aged 26yr 155 days in 1988. Probably the heaviest winner of a luge title was Hans Stanggassinger (FRG) in the 2-man of 1984 at a weight of 111kg/244lb. The Heaton brothers (USA) deserve mention for their exploits on the skeleton sleds as well as on bobs. Jennison won the 1928 skeleton event and a silver in the 5-man bob that year. Brother John was second in the 1928 skeleton, won a bronze in the 1932 2-man bob and then returned in 1948, in his 40th year, to win another skeleton silver. Seventh in that 1948 competition was Lt Col James Coats (GBR), holder of the Military Cross and at 53yr 297 days, the oldest ever competitor in the winter Olympic Games.

The smallest winning margin ever was in the 1994 men's singles when Georg Hackl (GER) beat Markus Prock (AUT), for the second successive Games, by only 0.013sec. In 1968 a scandal shook the Games when the first, second and fourth placed women from the GDR were all disqualified for illegally heating the runners of their sleds. The leading girl, Ortrun Enderlein, would have been the only female luger to retain her title, to that time.

LUGEING (and Skeleton Sled) MEDALS TABLE

	Men			Women			
	G	S	B	G	S	B	Total
GDR	9	3	5	4	5	3	29
Austria	2	4	3	1	1	2	13
Germany	4	2	2	1	2	1	12
Italy	4	3	3	2	-	-	12
FRG	1	3	3	-	1	2	10
Soviet Union	-	2	2	1	-	1	6
United States	1	2	-	-	-	-	3
Great Britain	-	-	2	-	-	-	2
	21	19	20	9	9	9	87

Two golds in 1972 2-man event

LUGEING MEDAL RESULTS — MEN

	GOLD	SILVER	BRONZE
1964	Thomas Köhler (GER) 3:26.77	Klaus Bonsack (GER) 3:27.04	Hans Plenk (GER) 3:30.15
1968	Manfred Schmid (AUT) 2:52.48	Thomas Köhler (GDR) 2:52.66	Klaus Bonsack (GDR) 2:55.33
1972	Wolfgang Scheidel (GDR) 3:27.58	Harald Ehrig (GDR) 3:28.39	Wolfram Fiedler (GDR) 3:28.73
1976	Detlef Günther (GDR) 3:27.688	Josef Fendt (FRG) 3:28.196	Hans Rinn (GDR) 3:28.574
1980	Bernhard Glass (GDR) 2:54.796	Paul Hildgartner (ITA) 2:55.372	Anton Winkler (FRG) 2:56.545
1984	Paul Hildgartner (ITA) 3:04.258	Sergey Danilin (URS) 3:04.962	Valeriy Dudin (URS) 3:05.012
1988	Jens Müller (GDR) 3:05.548	Georg Hackl (FRG) 3:05.916	Yuriy Khartchenko (URS) 3:06.274
1992	Georg Hackl (GER) 3:02.363	Markus Prock (AUT) 3:02.669	Markus Schmidt (AUT) 3:02.942
1994	Georg Hackl (GER) 3:21.571	Markus Prock (AUT) 3:21.584	Armin Zoggeler (ITA) 3:21.833

1924-60 Event not held.

2-Man

1964	Austria 1:41.62	Austria 1:41.91	Italy 1:42.87
1968	GDR 1:35.85	Austria 1:36.34	FRG 1:37.29
1972	Italy 1:28.35	–	GDR 1:29.16
	GDR 1:28.35		
1976	GDR 1:25.604	FRG 1:25.889	Austria 1:25.919
1980	GDR 1:19.331	Italy 1:19.606	Austria 1:19.795
1984	FRG 1:23.620	Soviet Union 1:23.660	GDR 1:23.887
1988	GDR 1:31.940	GDR 1:32.039	FRG 1:32.274
1992	Germany 1:32.053	Germany 1:32.239	Italy 1:32.298
1994	Italy 1:36.720	Italy II 1:36.769	Germany 1:36.945

1924-60 Event not held.

LUGEING MEDAL RESULTS – WOMEN

Singles

1964	Ortrun Enderlein (GER) 3:24.67	Ilse Geisler (GER) 3:27.42	Helene Thurner (AUT) 3:29.06
1968	Erica Lechner (ITA) 2:28.66	Christa Schmuck (FRG) 2:29.37	Angelika Dünhaupt (FRG) 2:29.56
1972	Anna-Maria Müller (GDR) 2:59.18	Ute Rührold (GDR) 2:59.49	Margit Schumann (GDR) 2:59.54
1976	Margit Schumann (GDR) 2:50.621	Ute Rührold (GDR) 2:50.846	Elisabeth Demleitner (FRG) 2:51.056
1980	Vera Sosulya (URS) 2:36.537	Melitta Sollmann (GDR) 2:37.657	Ingrida Amantova (URS) 2:37.817
1984	Steffi Martin (GDR) 2:46.570	Bettine Schmidt (GDR) 2:46.873	Ute Weiss (GDR) 2:47.248
1988	Steffi Martin-Walter (GDR) 3:03.973	Ute Weiss-Oberhoffner (GDR) 3:04.105	Cerstin Schmidt (GDR) 3:04.181
1992	Doris Neuner (AUT) 3:06.696	Angelika Neuner (AUT) 3:06.769	Susi Erdmann (GER) 3:07.115

1924-60 Event not held.

DISCONTINUED EVENT

Tobogganing – Skeleton Sled

1928 [1]	Jennison Heaton (USA) 3:01.8	John Heaton (USA) 3:02.8	Earl of Northesk (GBR) 3:05.1
1948 [2]	Nino Bibbia (ITA) 5:23.2	John Heaton (USA) 5:24.6	John Crammond (GBR) 5:25.1

[1] *Aggregate of three runs.*
[2] *Aggregate of six runs.*

Kurt Brugger and Wilfried Huber, Italian gold medallists in the 2-man luge at Lillehammer (Allsport/Mike Powell)

Enthusiastic crowds cheered the home favourite Bjorn Dählie (NOR) to his 15km gold medal in 1994 (Allsport/Chris Cole)

Nordic Skiing

Cross-country

This was the first form of skiing in the Olympics. The most successful competitor was Raisa Smetanina (URS-EUN) with four golds, five silvers and a bronze (a record total of ten medals) from 1976 to 1992. The best by a male was nine by Sixten Jernberg (SWE) with four gold, three silver and two bronze medals, from 1956 to 1964. Only Jernberg has won individual titles in three successive Games. Lyubov Yegorova (EUN-RUS) equalled the Winter Games record by a woman of six gold medals with 3 gold and 2 silver in 1992 and 3 gold and 1 silver in 1994, while Bjorn Dählie (NOR) equalled the male Winter Games record five golds in 1992-94. Dählie also won 3 silvers to become the most successful Winter Games competitor. Yegorova and team-mate Yelena Valbe, both in 1992, set a new female record of five medals in a single Games. Marja-Liisa Hämäläinen (later Kirvesniemi) of Finland won a record three individual gold medals at one Games in 1984. Kirvesniemi has competed in a record 6 Games, racing a total of 185km. Sixten Jernberg raced a record 315km in his 3 Games.

The oldest gold medallist/medallist was Maurilo De Zolt (ITA), aged 43yr 150 days in the 1994 relay, and the youngest was Gunde Swan (SWE) who won the 15km race in 1984 aged 22yr 32 days. The youngest was Ivar Formo (NOR) in the 1972 relay aged 20yr 234 days. The oldest female gold medallist and medallist in the Winter Games was Smetanina as a member of the 1992 relay team aged 39yr 354 days. She is also the only competitor to win medals in 5 Games. The youngest female champion was Carola Anding (GDR) aged 19yr 54 days in the 1980 relay, while the youngest female medallist was Marjo Matikainen (FIN) in the 1984 relay aged 19yr 12 days. Uniquely in 1994 a brother and sister won medals when Giorgio Vanzetta (ITA) took gold in the 4 x 10km relay and Bice gained a bronze in the 4 x 5km.

The 1928 50km race was won by Per Erik Hedlund (SWE) with a remarkable margin of 13min 27sec over the second man, whereas in the 1980 15km a mere 0.01sec separated first and second. Certain of the races are designated as freestyle events ie the 'skating' technique may be used. Otherwise only the classical 'stride and glide' is allowed. The shock silver medal won by Bill Koch (USA) in the 1976 50km was credited to his development of the former style.

Nordic Combination

The event was the 'blue riband' of Nordic skiing in the early Games. The all-round title, comprising a cross-country race and a jump, was won three successive times by Ulrich Wehling (GDR) 1972-1980. The oldest winner and medallist was Simon Slattvik (NOR) who won the title in 1952 aged 34yr 209 days. The youngest champion was Wehling in 1972 aged 19yr 212 days, and the youngest medallist was Stefan Kreiner (AUT) with a team bronze in 1992 aged 18yr 110 days.

Up until 1952 the cross-country segment was held first, but at Oslo the order of events was reversed, and has remained so.

Biathlon

The combination of skiing and shooting was introduced for men in 1960, and for women in 1992. Aleksandr Tikhonov (URS) set a Winter Games record by winning a gold medal in the relay on four successive occasions 1968-1980. The most successful women have been Myriam Bédard (CAN) and Anfissa Reztsova (EUN-RUS), both of whom won 2 golds and a bronze in 1992-94. However, Antje Misersky-Harvey (GER) has won a total of four medals (1 gold, 3 silver). The oldest gold medallist/medallist was Fritz Fischer (GER) in the 1992 relay aged 35yr 147 days. The oldest female champion was Reztsova in the 1994 relay aged 29yr 71 days. The youngest winner and medallist was Corinne Niogret (FRA) in the 1992 relay at 19yr 86 days, while the youngest male winner was Yuriy Kachkarov (URS) in the 1984 relay aged 20yr 75 days. Frank Peter Rötsch (GDR) was the youngest male medallist when he won a silver in the 20km event in 1984 aged only 19yr 298 days.

Ski Jumping

First contested in 1924 with one hill. In 1964 two hills (70m and 90m) were introduced, which were changed to 90m and 120m in 1992. The controversial 'V' style was introduced by Jan Boklev (SWE) in 1988, and was initially frowned on, and penalized, by the judges. However, by 1994 virtually all the competitors were using it. The most successful jumper has been Matti Nykänen (FIN) with 4 golds and one silver medal in 1984 and 1988, including three golds in one Games. However, his successes include the team competition, introduced in 1988. Prior to him the most successful had been Birger Ruud (NOR) with two golds and a silver medal from 1932 to 1948. He also came fourth in the Alpine Combination event of 1936, winning the downhill segment. His brother Sigmund won a silver in 1928, while a third brother, Asbjörn, was seventh in 1948. In 1994 Jens Weissflog (GER) became only the third man to win at two Games, in his case, remarkably, with a ten-year gap, having competed in four Games.

The longest jump achieved in Olympic competition was 135.5m by Espen Bredesen (NOR) in the 1994 individual event on the 120m hill. This was equalled by Jens Weissflog (GER) in the team event. The longest jump ever on the 90m hill was 118.5m by Matti Nykänen (FIN) in 1988. The oldest gold medallist was Jens Weissflog in 1994 aged 29yr 216 days, while the youngest was Toni Nieminen (FIN) in the 1992 team event aged 16yr 259 days – also the youngest ever winter Games winner. The youngest medallist was also Nieminen when he won an individual bronze 5 days earlier than his gold, while the oldest was Birger Ruud in 1948 aged 36yr 168 days. Anders Haugen (USA), whose extraordinary 50-year wait for his bronze medal is told elsewhere, was also over 36 years old. Sepp Bradl (AUT) – the first man ever to jump over 100m – competed over a period of 20 years, 1936-1956, but never won a medal.

NORDIC SKIING MEDALS TABLE

(Including Nordic Combination, Biathlon & Ski Jumping)

	Men			Women			
	G	S	B	G	S	B	Total
Norway	39	38	26	2	6	5	116
Soviet Union	22	15	19	18	17	15	106
Finland	20	26	22	8	9	10	95
Sweden	19	14	18	3	2	2	58
GDR	8	8	10	2	-	1	29
Italy	2	4	6	3	3	3	21
Germany	7	4	4	1	3	1	20
Austria	3	7	9	-	-	-	19
Czechoslovakia	1	2	5	-	1	3	12
Russia	2	1	1	4	1	1	10
Japan	3	4	1	-	-	-	8
FRG	3	3	2	-	-	-	8
Switzerland	1	3	4	-	-	-	8
France	1	1	1	1	1	1	6
Canada	-	-	-	2	-	1	3

Kazakstan	1	2	-	-	-	-	-	3
Poland	1	-	1	-	-	-	-	2
United States	-	1	1	-	-	-	-	2
Yugoslavia	-	1	1	-	-	-	-	2
Belarus	-	-	-	-	-	1	-	1
Bulgaria	-	-	1	-	-	-	-	1
Ukraine	-	-	-	-	-	-	1	1
	133	134 [1]	132	44	44	44		531

[1] *Two silvers in 1980 70m jumping*

NORDIC SKIING MEDALS — MEN

GOLD	SILVER	BRONZE

10,000 Metres Classical

	GOLD	SILVER	BRONZE
1992	Vegard Ulvang (NOR) 27:36.0	Marco Alberello (ITA) 27:55.2	Christer Majback (SWE) 27:56.4
1994	Bjorn Dählie (NOR) 24:20.1	Vladimir Smirnov (KZK) 24:38.3	Marco Alberello (ITA) 24:42.3

1924-88 Event not held

15,000 Metres

	GOLD	SILVER	BRONZE
1924 [1]	Thorleif Haug (NOR) 1h 14:31.0	Johan Gröttumsbraaten (NOR) 1h 15:51.0	Tipani Niku (FIN) 1h 26:26.0
1928 [2]	Johan Gröttumsbraaten (NOR) 1h 37:01.0	Ole Hegge (NOR) 1h 39:01.0	Reidar Odegaard (NOR) 1h 40:11.0
1932 [3]	Sven Utterström (SWE) 1h 23:07.0	Axel Wikström (SWE) 1h 25:07.0	Veli Saarinen (FIN) 1h 25:24.0
1936 [1]	Erik-August Larsson (SWE) 1h 14:38.0	Oddbjörn Hagen (NOR) 1h 15:33.0	Pekka Niemi (FIN) 1h 16:59.0
1948 [1]	Martin Lundström (SWE) 1h 13:50.0	Nils Ostensson (SWE) 1h 14:22.0	Gunnar Eriksson (SWE) 1h 16:06.6
1952 [1]	Hallgeir Brenden (NOR) 1h 1:34.0	Tapio Mäkelä (FIN) 1h 2:09.0	Paavo Lonkila (FIN) 1h 2:20.0
1956	Hallgeir Brenden (NOR) 49:39.0	Sixten Jernberg (SWE) 50:14.0	Pavel Koltschin (URS) 50:17.0
1960	Haakon Brusveen (NOR) 51:55.5	Sixten Jernberg (SWE) 51:58.6	Veikko Hakulinen (FIN) 52:03.0
1964	Eero Mäntyranta (FIN) 50:54.1	Harald Grönningen (NOR) 51:34.8	Sixten Jernberg (SWE) 51:42.2
1968	Harald Grönningen (NOR) 47:54.2	Eero Mäntyranta (FIN) 47:56.1	Gunnar Larsson (SWE) 48:33.7
1972	Sven-Ake Lundback (SWE) 45:28.24	Fedor Simaschov (URS) 46:00.84	Ivar Formo (NOR) 46:02.86
1976	Nikolai Bajukov (URS) 43:58.47	Yevgeniy Beliayev (URS) 44:01.10	Arto Koivisto (FIN) 44:19.25
1980	Thomas Wassberg (SWE) 41:57.63	Juha Mieto (FIN) 41:57.64	Ove Aunli (NOR) 42:28.62
1984	Gunde Swan (SWE) 41:25.6	Aki Karvonen (FIN) 41:34.9	Harri Kirvesniemi (FIN) 41:45.6
1988	Michael Deviatyarov (URS) 41:18.9	Pal Mikkelsplass (NOR) 41:33.4	Vladimir Smirnov (URS) 41:48.5

[1] *The distance was 18km.*
[2] *The distance was 19.7km.*
[3] *The distance was 18.2km.*
Event discontinued after 1988.

15,000 Metres Pursuit [1]

	GOLD	SILVER	BRONZE
1992	Bjorn Dählie (NOR) 1h 05:37.9	Vegard Ulvang (NOR) 1h 06:31.3	Giorgio Vanzetta (ITA) 1h 06:31.2
1994	Bjorn Dählie (NOR) 1h 00:08.8	Vladimir Smirnov (KZK) 1h 00:38.0	Silvio Fauner (ITA) 1h 01:48.6

[1] *Contestants' times are added to those achieved in 10km race*
1924-88 Event not held

30,000 Metres

	GOLD	SILVER	BRONZE
1956	Veikko Hakulinen (FIN) 1h 44:06.0	Sixten Jernberg (SWE) 1h 44:30.0	Pavel Koltschin (URS) 1h 45:45.0
1960	Sixten Jernberg (SWE) 1h 51:03.9	Rolf Rämgard (SWE) 1h 51:16.9	Nikolai Anikin (URS) 1h 52:28.2
1964	Eero Mäntyranta (FIN) 1h 30:50.7	Harald Grönningen (NOR) 1h 32:02.3	Igor Voronchikin (URS) 1h 32:15.8
1968	Franco Nones (ITA) 1h 35:29.2	Odd Martinsen (NOR) 1h 36:28.9	Eero Mäntyranta (FIN) 1h 36:55.3

1972	Vyacheslav Vedenine (URS) 1h 36:31.2	Paal Tyldum (NOR) 1h 37:25.3	Johs Harviken (NOR) 1h 37:32.4
1976	Sergey Savelyev (URS) 1h 30:29.38	William Koch (USA) 1h 30:57.84	Ivan Garanin (URS) 1h 31:09.29
1980	Nikolai Simyatov (URS) 1h 27:02.80	Vasiliy Rochev (URS) 1h 27:34.22	Ivan Lebanov (BUL) 1h 28:03.87
1984	Nikolai Simyatov (URS) 1h 28:56.3	Alexandre Zavialov (URS) 1h 29:23.3	Gunde Swan (SWE) 1h 29:35.7
1988	Alexey Prokororov (URS) 1h 24:26.3	Vladimir Smirnov (URS) 1h 24:35.1	Vegard Ulvang (NOR) 1h 25:11.6
1992	Vegard Ulvang (NOR) 1h 22:27.8	Bjorn Dählie (NOR) 1h 23:14.0	Terje Langli (NOR) 1h 23:42.5
1994	Thomas Alsgaard (NOR) 1h 12:26.4	Bjorn Dählie (NOR) 1h 13:13.6	Myka Myllyla (FIN) 1h 14:14.0

1924-52 Event not held.

50,000 Metres

1924	Thorleif Haug (NOR) 3h 44:32.0	Thoralf Strömstad (NOR) 3h 46:23.0	Johan Gröttumsbraaten (NOR) 3h 47:46.0
1928	Per Erik Hedlund (SWE) 4h 52:03.0	Gustaf Jonsson (SWE) 5h 05:30.0	Volger Andersson (SWE) 5h 05:46.0
1932	Veli Saarinen (FIN) 4h 28:00.0	Väinö Likkanen (FIN) 4h 28:20.0	Arne Rustadstuen (NOR) 4h 31:53.0
1936	Elis Wiklung (SWE) 3h 30:11.0	Axel Wikström (SWE) 3h 33:20.0	Nils-Joel Englund (SWE) 3h 34:10.0
1948	Nils Karlsson (SWE) 3h 47:48.0	Harald Eriksson (SWE) 3h 52:20.0	Benjamin Vanninen (FIN) 3h 57:28.0
1952	Veikko Hakulinen (FIN) 3h 33:33.0	Eero Kolehmainen (FIN) 3h 38:11.0	Magnar Estenstad (NOR) 3h 38:28.0
1956	Sixten Jernberg (SWE) 2h 50:27.0	Veikko Hakulinen (FIN) 2h 51:45.0	Fedor Terentyev (URS) 2h 53:32.0
1960	Kalevi Hämäläinen (FIN) 2h 59:06.3	Veikko Hakulinen (FIN) 2h 59:26.7	Rolf Rämgard (SWE) 3h 02:46.7
1964	Sixten Jernberg (SWE) 2h 43:52.6	Assar Rönnlund (SWE) 2h 44:58.2	Arto Tiainen (FIN) 2h 45:30.4
1968	Olle Ellefsaeter (NOR) 2h 28:45.8	Vyacheslav Vedenine (URS) 2h 29:02.5	Josef Haas (SUI) 2h 29:14.8
1972	Paal Tyldrum (NOR) 2h 43:14.75	Magne Myrmo (NOR) 2h 43:29.45	Vyacheslav Vedenine (URS) 2h 44:00.19
1976	Ivar Formo (NOR) 2h 37:30.50	Gert-Dietmar Klause (GDR) 2h 38:13.21	Benny Södergren (SWE) 2h 39:39.21
1980	Nikolai Simyatov (URS) 2h 27:24.60	Juha Mieto (FIN) 2h 30:20.52	Aleksandr Savyalov (URS) 2h 30:51.52
1984	Thomas Wassberg (SWE) 2h 15:55.8	Gunde Swan (SWE) 2h 16:00.7	Aki Karvonen (FIN) 2h 17:04.7
1988	Gunde Svan (SWE) 2h 04:30.9	Maurilio De Zolt (ITA) 2h 05:36.4	Andy Grünenfelder (SUI) 2h 06.01.9
1992	Bjorn Dählie (NOR) 2h 03:41.5	Maurilio de Zolt (ITA) 2h 04:39.1	Giorgio Vanzetta (ITA) 2h 06:42.1
1994	Vladimir Smirnov (KZK) 2h 07:20.0	Myka Myllyla (FIN) 2h 08:41.9	Sture Sivertsen (NOR) 2h 08:49.0

4 x 10,000 Metres Relay

1936	Finland 2h 41:33.0	Norway 2h 41:39.0	Sweden 2h 43:03.0
1948	Sweden 2h 32:08.0	Finland 2h 41:06.0	Norway 2h 44:33.0
1952	Finland 2h 20:16.0	Norway 2h 23:13.0	Sweden 2h 24:13.0
1956	Soviet Union 2h 15:30.0	Finland 2h 16:31.0	Sweden 2h 17:42.0
1960	Finland 2h 18:45.6	Norway 2h 18:46.4	Soviet Union 2h 21:21.6
1964	Sweden 2h 18:34.6	Finland 2h 18:42.4	Soviet Union 2h 18:46.9
1968	Norway 2h 08:33.5	Sweden 2h 10:13.2	Finland 2h 10:56.7
1972	Soviet Union 2h 04:47.94	Norway 2h 04:57.6	Switzerland 2h 07:00.06
1976	Finland 2h 07:59.72	Norway 2h 09:58.36	Soviet Union 2h 10:51.46
1980	Soviet Union 1h 57:03.6	Norway 1h 58:45.77	Finland 2h 00:00.18
1984	Sweden 1h 55:06.3	Soviet Union 1h 55:16.5	Finland 1h 56:31.4
1988	Sweden 1h 43:58.6	Soviet Union 1h 44:11.3	Czechoslovakia 1h 45:22.7
1992	Norway 1h 39:26.0	Italy 1h 40:52.7	Finland 1h 41:22.9
1994	Italy 1h 41:15.0	Norway 1h 41:15.4	Finland 1h 42:15.6

1924-32 Event not held.

NORDIC SKIING MEDAL RESULTS — WOMEN

	GOLD	SILVER	BRONZE

5000 Metres

1964	Klaudia Boyarskikh (URS) 17:50.5	Mirja Lehtonen (FIN) 17:52.9	Alevtina Koltschina (URS) 18:08.4
1968	Toini Gustafsson (SWE) 16:45.2	Galina Kulakova (URS) 16:48.4	Alevtina Koltschina (URS) 16:51.6
1972	Galina Kulakova (URS) 17:00.50	Marjatta Kajosmaa (FIN) 17:05.50	Helena Sikolova (TCH) 17:07.32
1976	Helena Takalo (FIN) 15:48.69	Raisa Smetanina (URS) 15:49.73	Nina Baldycheva [1] (URS) 16:12.82
1980	Raisa Semtanina (URS) 15:06.92	Hikka Riihivuori (FIN) 15:11.96	Kvetoslava Jeriova (TCH) 15:23.44
1984	Marja-Liisa Hämäläinen (FIN) 17:04.0	Berit Aunli (NOR) 17:14.1	Kvetoslava Jeriova (TCH) 17:18.3
1988	Marjo Matikainen (FIN) 15:04.0	Tamara Tikhonova (URS) 15:05.3	Vida Ventsene (URS) 15:11.1
1992	Marjut Lukkarinen (FIN) 14:13.8	Lyubov Yegorova (EUN) 14:14.7	Yelena Valbe (EUN) 14:22.7
1994	Lyubov Yegorova (RUS) 14:08.8	Manuela di Centa (ITA) 14:28.3	Marja-Liisa Kirvesniemi (FIN) 14:36.0

[1] *Galina Kulakova (URS) finished third but was disqualifed.*
1924-60 Event not held.

10,000 Metres

1952	Lydia Wideman (FIN) 41:40.0	Mirja Hietamies (FIN) 42:39.0	Siiri Rantanen (FIN) 42:50.0
1956	Lubov Kozyryeva (URS) 38:11.0	Radya Yeroschina (URS) 38:16.0	Sonja Edström (SWE) 38:23.0
1960	Maria Gusakova (URS) 39:46.6	Lubov Baranova-Kozyryeva (URS) 40:04.2	Radya Yeroschina (URS) 40:06.0
1964	Klaudia Boyarskikh (URS) 40:24.3	Yevdokia Mekshilo (URS) 40:26.6	Maria Gusakova (URS) 40:46.6
1968	Toini Gustafsson (SWE) 36:46.5	Berit Mördre (NOR) 37:54.6	Inger Aufles (NOR) 37:59.9
1972	Galina Kulakova (URS) 34:17.8	Alevtina Olunina (URS) 34:54.1	Marjatta Kajosmaa (FIN) 34:56.5
1976	Raisa Smetanina (URS) 30:13.41	Helena Takalo (FIN) 30:14.28	Galina Kulakova (URS) 30:38.61
1980	Barbara Petzold (GDR) 30:31.54	Hilkka Riihivuori (FIN) 30:35.05	Helena Takalo (FIN) 30:45.25
1984	Marja-Liisa Hämäläinen (FIN) 31:44.2	Raisa Smetanina (URS) 32:02.9	Brit Pettersen (NOR) 32:12.7
1988	Vida Ventsene (URS) 30:08.3	Raisa Smetanina (URS) 30:17.0	Marjo Matikainen (FIN) 30:20.5

1924-48 Event not held; discontinued after 1988

10,000 Metres Pursuit

1992	Lyubov Yegorova (EUN) 40:07.7	Stefania Belmondo (ITA) 40:31.8	Yelena Valbe (EUN) 40:51.7
1994	Lyubov Yegorova (RUS) 41:38.9	Manuela di Centa (ITA) 41:46.7	Stefania Belmondo (ITA) 42:21.1

15,000 Metres

1992	Lyubov Yegorova (EUN) 42:20.8	Marjut Lukkarinen (FIN) 43:29.9	Yelena Valbe (EUN) 43:42.3
1994	Manuela di Centa (ITA) 39:44.5	Lyubov Yegorova (RUS) 41:03.0	Nina Gavriluk (RUS) 41:10.4

20,000 Metres

1984	Marja-Liisa Hämäläinen (FIN) 1h 01:45.0	Raisa Smetanina (URS) 1h 02:26.7	Anne Jahren (NOR) 1h 03:13.06
1988	Tamara Tikhonova (URS) 55:53.6	Anfissa Reztsova (URS) 56:12.8	Raisa Smetanina (URS) 57:22.1
1992	Stefania Belmondo (ITA) 1h 22:30.1	Lyubov Yegorova (EUN) 1h 22:52.0	Yelena Valbe (EUN) 1h 24:13.9
1994	Manuela di Centa (ITA) 1h 25:41.6	Marit Wold (NOR) 1h 25:57.8	Marja-Liisa Kirvesniemi (FIN) 1h 26:13.6

1908–1980 Event not held; discontinued after 1988

4 [1] x 5000 Metres Relay

1956	Finland 1h 09:01.0	Soviet Union 1h 09:28.0	Sweden 1h 09:48.0
1960	Sweden 1h 04:21.4	Soviet Union 1h 05:02.6	Finland 1h 06:27.5

1964	Soviet Union 59:20.2	Sweden 1h 01:27.0	Finland 1h 02:45.1
1968	Norway 57:30.0	Sweden 57:51.0	Soviet Union 58:13.6
1972	Soviet Union 48:46.15	Finland 49:19.37	Norway 49:51.49
1976	Soviet Union 1h 07:49.75	Finland 1h 08:36.57	GDR 1h 09:57.95
1980	GDR 1h 02:11.10	Soviet Union 1h 03:18.30	Norway 1h 04:13.50
1984	Norway 1h 06:49.7	Czechoslovakia 1h 07:34.7	Finland 1h 07:36.7
1988	Soviet Union 59:51.1	Norway 1h 01:33.0	Finland 1h 01:53.8
1992	Unified Team 59:34.8	Norway 59:56.4	Italy 1h 00:25.9
1994	Russia 57:12.5	Norway 57:42.6	Italy 58:42.6

(1) *Over three stages prior to 1976.*
1924-52 Event not held.

BIATHLON MEDAL RESULTS – MEN

	GOLD	SILVER	BRONZE

10,000 Metres

1980	Frank Ullrich (GDR) 32:10.69	Vladimir Alikin (URS) 32:53.10	Anatoliy Alyabiev (URS) 33:09.16
1984	Eirik Kvalfoss (NOR) 30:53.8	Peter Angerer (FRG) 31:02.4	Matthias Jacob (GDR) 31:10.5
1988	Frank-Peter Rötsch (GDR) 25:08.1	Valeri Medvedtsev (URS) 25:23.7	Sergei Tchepikov (URS) 25:29.4
1992	Mark Kirchner (GER) 26:02.3	Ricco Gross (GER) 26:18.0	Harri Eloranta (FIN) 26:26.6
1994	Sergei Chepikov (RUS) 28:07.0	Ricco Gross (GER) 28:13.0	Sergei Tarasov (RUS) 28:27.4

1924-76 Event not held.

20,000 Metres

1960	Klas Lestander (SWE) 1h 33:21.6	Antii Tyrväinen (FIN) 1h 33:57.7	Aleksandr Privalov (URS) 1h 34:54.2
1964	Vladimir Melyanin (URS) 1h 20:26.8	Aleksandr Privalov (URS) 1h 23:42.5	Olav Jordet (NOR) 1h 24:38.8
1968	Magnar Solberg (NOR) 1h 13:45.9	Aleksandr Tikhonov (URS) 1h 14:40.4	Vladimir Gundartsev (URS) 1h 18:27.4
1972	Magnar Solberg (NOR) 1h 15:55.5	Hans-Jürg Knauthe (GDR) 1h 16:07.6	Lars Arvidsson (SWE) 1h 16:27.03
1976	Nikolai Kruglov (URS) 1h 14:12.26	Heikki Ikola (FIN) 1h 15:54.10	Aleksandr Elizarov (URS) 1h 16:05.57
1980	Anatoliy Alyabiev (URS) 1h 08:16.31	Frank Ullrich (GDR) 1h 08:27.79	Eberhard Rösch (GDR) 1h 11:11.73
1984	Peter Angerer (FRG) 1h 11:52.7	Frank-Peter Rötsch (GDR) 1h 13:21.4	Eirik Kvalfoss (NOR) 1h 14:02.4
1988	Frank-Peter Rötsch (GDR) 56:33.3	Valeri Medvedtsev (URS) 56:54.6	Johann Pasler (ITA) 57:10.1
1992	Yevgeniy Redkine (EUN) 57:34.4	Mark Kirchner (GER) 57:40.8	Mikael Lofgren (57:59.4)
1994	Sergei Tarasov (RUS) 57:25.3	Frank Luck (GER) 57:28.7	Sven Fischer (GER) 57:41.9

1924-56 Event not held.

Biathlon Relay (4 x 7500 Metres)

1968	Soviet Union 2h 13:02.4	Norway 2h 14:50.2	Sweden 2h 17:26.3
1972	Soviet Union 1h 51:44.92	Finland 1h 54:37.22	GDR 1h 54:57.67
1976	Soviet Union 1h 57:55.64	Finland 2h 01:45.58	GDR 2h 04:08.61
1980	Soviet Union 1h 34:03.27	GDR 1h 34:56.99	FRG 1h 37:30.26
1984	Soviet Union 1h 38:51.7	Norway 1h 39:03.9	FRG 1h 39:05.1
1988	Soviet Union 1h 22:30.0	FRG 1h 23:37.4	Italy 1h 23:51.5
1992	Germany 1h 24:43.5	Unified Team 1h 25:06.3	Sweden 1h 25:38.2
1994	Germany 1h 30:22.1	Russia 1h 31:23.6	France 1h 32:31.3

1924-64 Event not held.

Double biathlon gold medallist Myriam Bédard (CAN), here in the 15km event at Lillehammer (Allsport/Pascal Rondeau)

BIATHLON MEDAL RESULTS — WOMEN

GOLD	SILVER	BRONZE
7500 Metres		
1992 Anfissa Reztsova (EUN) 24:29.2	Antje Misersky (GER) 24:45.1	Yelena Belova (EUN) 24:50.8
1994 Myriam Bedard (CAN) 26:08.8	Svetlana Paramygina (BLS) 26:09.9	Valentina Tserbe (UKR) 26:10.0
1924-88 Event not held		
15,000 Metres		
1992 Antje Misersky (GER) 51:47.2	Svetlana Pecherskaya (EUN) 51:58.5	Myriam Bedard (CAN) 52:15.0
1994 Myriam Bedard (CAN) 52:06.6	Anne Briand (FRA) 52:53.3	Uschi Disl (GER) 53:15.3
1924-88 Event not held		
Biathlon Relay (4 x 7500 Metres)		
1992 [1] France 1h 15:55.6	Germany 1h 16:18.4	Unified Team 1h 16:54.6
1994 Russia 1h 47:19.5	Germany 1h 51:16.5	France 1h 52:28.1
[1] *Only three per team*		
1924-88 Event not held		

NORDIC COMBINED MEDAL RESULTS

GOLD	SILVER	BRONZE
Individual [1]		
1924 [2] Thorleif Haug (NOR)	Thoralf Strömstad (NOR)	Johan Gröttumsbraaten (NOR)
1928 [2] Johan Gröttumsbraaten (NOR)	Hans Vinjarengen (NOR)	John Snersud (NOR)
1932 Johan Gröttumsbraaten (NOR) 446.0pts	Ole Stenen (NOR) 436.05pts	Hans Vinjarengen (NOR) 434.60pts
1936 Oddbjörn Hagen (NOR) 430.30pts	Olaf Hoffsbakken (NOR) 419.80pts	Sverre Brodahl (NOR) 408.10pts
1948 Heikki Hasu (FIN) 448.80pts	Martti Huhtala (FIN) 433.65pts	Sven Israelsson (SWE) 433.40pts
1952 Simon Slöattvik (NOR) 451.621pts	Heikki Hasu (FIN) 447.50pts	Sverre Stenersen (NOR) 436.335pts
1956 Sverre Stenersen (NOR) 455.0pts	Bengt Eriksson (SWE) 437.4pts	Franciszek Gron-Gasienica (POL) 436.8pts

1960 Georg Thoma (GER) 457.952pts	Tormod Knutsen (NOR) 453.000pts	Nikolai Gusakow (URS) 452.000pts
1964 Tormod Knutson (NOR) 469.28pts	Nikolai Kiselyev (URS) 453.04pts	Georg Thoma (GER) 452.88pts
1968 Frantz Keller (FRG) 449.04pts	Alois Kälin (SUI) 447.94pts	Andreas Kunz (GDR) 444.10pts
1972 Ulrich Wehling (GDR) 413.34pts	Rauno Miettinen (FIN) 405.55pts	Karl-Heinz Luck (GDR) 398.80pts
1976 Ulrich Wehling (GDR) 423.39pts	Urban Hettich (FRG) 418.90pts	Konrad Winkler (GDR) 417.47pts
1980 Ulrich Wehling (GDR) 432.20pts	Jouko Karjalainen (FIN) 429.50pts	Konrad Winkler (GDR) 425.32pts
1984 Tom Sandberg (NOR) 422.595pts	Jouko Karjalainen (FIN) 416.900pts	Jukka Ylipulli (FIN) 410.825pts
1988 Hippolyt Kempf (SUI)	Klaus Sulzenbacher (AUT)	Allar Levandi (URS)
1992 Fabrice Guy (FRA)	Sylvain Guillaume (FRA)	Klaus Sulzenbacher (AUT)
1994 Fred Borre Lundberg (NOR)	Takanori Kono (JPN)	Bjarte Engen Vik (NOR)

[1] *From 1924–1952 distance was 18km.*

[2] *In 1924 and 1928, the scoring was decided upon a different basis from that used from 1932 onwards.*

Team

1988	FRG	Switzerland	Austria
1992	Japan	Norway	Austria
1994	Japan	Norway	Switzerland

1924-84 Event not held.

SKI JUMPING MEDAL RESULTS

GOLD	SILVER	BRONZE

Normal Hill
(1924-88 70m; from 1992 90m)

1924 [1] Jacob Tullin Thams (NOR) 18 960pts	Narve Bonna (NOR) 18 689pts	Anders Haugen (USA) 17 916pts
1928 Alf Andersen (NOR) 19 208pts	Sigmund Ruud (NOR) 18 542pts	Rudolf Burkert (TCH) 17 937pts
1932 Birger Ruud (NOR) 228.1pts	Hans Beck (NOR) 227.0pts	Kaare Wahlberg (NOR) 219.5pts
1936 Birger Ruud (NOR) 232.0pts	Sven Eriksson (SWE) 230.5pts	Reidar Andersen (NOR) 228.9pts
1948 Petter Hugsted (NOR) 228.1pts	Birger Ruud (NOR) 226.6pts	Thorleif Schjeldrup (NOR) 225.1pts
1952 Arnfinn Bergmann (NOR) 226.0pts	Torbjörn Falkanger (NOR) 221.5pts	Karl Holmström (SWE) 219.5pts
1956 Antti Hyvärinen (FIN) 227.0pts	Aulis Kallakorpi (FIN) 225.0pts	Harry Glass (GER) 224.5pts
1960 Helmut Recknagel (GER) 227.2pts	Niilo Halonen (FIN) 222.6pts	Otto Leodolter (AUT) 219.4pts
1964 Veikko Kankkonen (FIN) 229.9pts	Toralf Engan (NOR) 226.3pts	Torgeir Brandtzaeg (NOR) 222.9pts
1968 Jiri Raska (TCH) 216.5pts	Reinhold Bachler (AUT) 214.2pts	Baldur Preiml (AUT) 212.6pts
1972 Yukio Kasaya (JPN) 244.2pts	Akitsugu Konno (JPN) 234.8pts	Seiji Aochi (JPN) 229.5pts
1976 Hans-Georg Aschenbach (GDR) 252.0pts	Jochen Danneberg (GDR) 246.2pts	Karl Schnabl (AUT) 242.0pts
1980 Toni Innauer (AUT) 266.3pts	Manfred Deckert (GDR) 249.2pts Hirokazu Yagi (JPN) 249.2pts	–
1984 Jens Weissflog (GDR) 215.2pts	Matti Nykänen (FIN) 214.0pts	Jari Puikkonen (FIN) 212.8pts
1988 Matti Nykänen (FIN) 229.1pts	Pavel Ploc (TCH) 212.1pts	Jiri Malec (TCH) 211.8pts
1992 Ernst Vettori (AUT) 222.8	Martin Höllwarth (AUT) 218.1	Toni Nieminen (FIN) 217.0
1994 Espen Bredesen (NOR) 282.0	Lasse Ottesen (NOR) 268.0	Dieter Thoma (GER) 260.5

[1] *Originally Thorleif Haug (NOR) placed third due to incorrect calculations at time. Error discovered and corrected in 1974.*

Large Hill
(1964-88 90m; from 1992 120m)

1964 Toralf Engan (NOR) 230.7pts	Veikko Kankkonen (FIN) 228.9pts	Torgeir Brandtzaeg (NOR) 227.2pts
1968 Vladimir Belousov (URS) 231.3pts	Jiri Raska (TCH) 229.4pts	Lars Grini (NOR) 214.3pts
1972 Wojciech Fortuna (POL) 219.9pts	Walter Steiner (SUI) 219.8pts	Rainer Schmidt (GDR) 219.3pts
1976 Karl Schnabl (AUT) 234.8pts	Toni Innauer (AUT) 232.9pts	Henry Glass (GDR) 221.7pts
1980 Jouko Törmänen (FIN) 271.0pts	Hubert Neuper (AUT) 262.4pts	Jari Puikkonen (FIN) 248.5pts
1984 Matti Nykänen (FIN) 232.2pts	Jens Weissflog (GDR) 213.7pts	Pavel Ploc (TCH) 202.9pts
1988 Matti Nykänen (FIN) 224.0pts	Erik Johnsen (NOR) 207.9pts	Matjaz Debelak (YUG) 207.7pts

Jens Weissflog (GER) training for the 120m hill at Lillehammer which he eventually won. He had been second in 1984 at the 90m event (Allsport/Mike Powell)

1992	Toni Nieminen (FIN) 239.5	Martin Höllwarth (AUT) 227.3	Heinz Kuttin (AUT) 214.8
1994	Jens Weissflog (GER) 274.5	Espen Bredesen (NOR) 266.5	Andreas Goldberger (AUT) 255.0

1924-60 Event not held.

Large Hill – Team

1988	Finland 634.4pts	Yugoslavia 625.5pts	Norway 596.1pts
1992	Finland 644.4	Austria 642.9	Czechoslovakia 620.1
1994	Germany 970.1	Japan 956.9	Austria 918.9

1924-84 Event not held.

Speed Skating

The sport was introduced into the Olympics in 1924, with the first official events for women in 1960. There have been two major controversies over the years. In 1928 the 10km event was cancelled by the Norwegian referee due to bad weather. That caused much ill-feeling in the American camp because at the time Irving Jaffee (USA) was the surprise leader and as all the best skaters had competed the medal positions seemed assured. Despite vigorous protests by all nationalities no medals were awarded. The other occasion was in 1932 when the American 'mass start' system was used, for the only time in Olympic competition. This undoubtedly gave the Americans and Canadians a tremendous advantage as the Europeans were completely unfamiliar with the tactics involved – only two medals were won by European skaters.

Lydia Skoblikova (URS) won a record six gold medals in 1960 and 1964, which is also a record for any sport in the Winter Games for either a male or female competitor. The most by a man is five by Clas Thunberg (FIN) in 1924 and 1928, and by Eric Heiden (USA) with all five in 1980. There have been five events for men only since 1976, while a fifth event was added for women in 1988. The most medals won is eight by Karin Enke-Kania (GDR) with three golds, four silvers and a bronze from 1980 to 1988. The Winter Games record for individual events. The most by a male skater is seven by Thunberg, who added a silver and a bronze to his golds, and by Ivar Ballangrud (NOR) who won four golds, two silvers and a bronze from 1928 to 1936. Skoblikova won her four golds in 1964 on four successive days. In 1994 Bonnie Blair (USA) uniquely won the same title (500m) for the third consecutive time.

The oldest gold medallist was Thunberg aged 35yr 315

Olympic Speed Skating records

Men

500m	36.33s	Alexander Golubev (RUS)	1994
1000m	1m 12.43s	Dan Jansen (USA)	1994
1500m	1m 51.29s	Johann Olav Koss (NOR)	1994
5000m	6m 34.96s	Johann Olav Koss (NOR)	1994
10, 000m	13m 30.55s	Johann Olav Koss (NOR)	1994

Women

500m	39.10s	Bonnie Blair (USA)	1988
1000m	1m 17.65s	Christa Rothenburger (GDR)	1988
1500m	2m 00.68s	Yvonne Van Gennip (NED)	1988
3000m	4m 11.94s	Yvonne Van Gennip (NED)	1988
5000m	7m 14.13s	Yvonne Van Gennip (NED)	1988

days in the 1928 1500m. The youngest winner was Anne Henning (USA) in the 500m in 1952 aged 16yr 157 days. The youngest male champion was Igor Malkov (URS) winning the 10km in 1984 aged 19yr 9 days, while the oldest woman was Christina Baas-Kaiser (NED) who won the 3, 000m title in 1972 aged 33yr 268 days. The youngest ever medallist was Andrea Mitscherlich (later Schöne and Ehrlich) (GDR) who won the 3000m silver in 1976 when only 15yr 69 days. The youngest male medallist was Alv Gjestvang (NOR) in 1956 aged 18yr 147 days. The oldest medallist was Julius Skutnabb (FIN) in 1928 at 38yr 246 days, while the oldest female medallist was Eevi Huttunen (FIN) in the 1960 3000m aged 37yr 184 days. Frank Stack (CAN) competed over a 20 year period from 1932 to 1952 (when he was 46) winning a bronze in 1932, while Colin Coates (AUS) also competed for 20 years, in six Games 1968-1988, but his best placing was 6th in the 10km in 1976.

A number of speed skaters have found a happy affinity with cycle racing. One of the most successful at both roles has been Sheila Young (USA), who won the 500m Olympic skating title in 1976 and the world amateur sprint cycle championship in 1973 and 1976. However, Christa Rothenburger-Luding (GDR) possibly surpassed that in 1988. Having won the 1984 Olympic 500m gold and the 1986 world cycling sprint title in 1986, she then won the skating 1000m at Calgary and gained a cycling silver in Seoul, to become the first competitor to win medals at Summer and Winter Games in the same year. This achievement can no longer be equalled.

SPEED SKATING MEDALS TABLE

	Men			Women			
	G	S	B	G	S	B	Total
Norway	23	28	23	1	-	1	76
Soviet Union	12	10	9	12	7	10	60
Netherlands	6	13	13	7	4	4	47
United States	14	7	3	8	8	6	46
GDR	2	1	2	6	11	7	29
Finland	6	6	7	1	2	2	24
Germany	2	-	-	5	6	6	19
Sweden	7	4	5	-	-	-	16
Canada	2	2	6	-	2	-	12
Japan	-	2	4	-	-	2	8
Austria	-	1	2	-	-	2	6
Russia	1	1	1	1	1	1	6
FRG	2	-	-	1	-	-	3
China	-	-	-	-	2	1	3
Poland	-	-	-	-	2	1	3
Belarus	-	-	-	1	1	-	2
Korea	-	-	1	-	-	-	1
North Korea (PRK)	-	-	-	-	-	1	1
	77	77	75	43	46	41	359

SPEED SKATING MEDAL RESULTS — MEN

GOLD	SILVER	BRONZE

500 Metres

	GOLD	SILVER	BRONZE
1924	Charles Jewtraw (USA) 44.0	Oskar Olsen (NOR) 44.2	Roald Larsen (NOR) 44.8
			Clas Thunberg (FIN) 44.8
1928	Clas Thunberg (FIN) 43.4	–	John Farrell (USA) 43.6
	Bernt Evensen (NOR) 43.4		Roald Larsen (NOR) 43.6
			Jaako Friman (FIN) 43.6
1932	John Shea (USA) 43.4	Bernt Evensen (NOR) 5m	Alexander Hurd (CAN) 8m
1936	Ivar Ballangrud (NOR) 32.4	Georg Krog (NOR) 43.5	Leo Freisinger (USA) 44.0
1948	Finn Helgesen (NOR) 43.1	Kenneth Bartholomew (USA) 43.2	–
		Thomas Byberg (NOR) 43.2	
		Robert Fitzgerald (USA) 43.2	
1952	Kenneth Henry (USA) 43.2	Donald McDermott (USA) 43.9	Arne Johansen (NOR) 44.0
			Gordon Audley (CAN) 44.0
1956	Yevgeniy Grischin (URS) 40.2	Rafael Gratsch (URS) 40.8	Alv Gjestvang (NOR) 41.0
1960	Yevgeniy Grischin (URS) 40.2	William Disney (USA) 40.3	Rafael Gratsch (URS) 40.4
1964	Richard McDermott (USA) 40.1	Yevgeniy Grischin (URS) 40.6	–
		Vladimir Orlov (URS) 40.6	
		Alv Gjestvang (NOR) 40.6	
1968	Erhard Keller (FRG) 40.3	Richard McDermott (USA) 40.5	–
		Magne Thomassen (NOR) 40.5	
1972	Erhard Keller (FRG) 39.44	Hasse Borjes (SWE) 39.69	Valeriy Muratov (URS) 39.80
1976	Yevgeniy Kulikov (URS) 39.17	Valeriy Muratov (URS) 39.25	Daniel Immerfall (USA) 39.54
1980	Eric Heiden (USA) 38.03	Yevgeniy Kulikov (URS) 38.37	Lieuwe de Boer (NED) 38.48
1984	Sergey Fokitchev (URS) 38.19	Yoshihiro Kitazawa (JPN) 38.30	Gaetan Boucher (CAN) 38.39
1988	Uwe-Jens Mey (GDR) 36.45	Jan Ykema (NED) 36.76	Akira Kuroiwa (JPN) 36.77
1992	Uwe-Jens Mey (GER) 37.14	Toshiyuki Kuroiwa (JPN) 37.18	Junichi Inoue (JPN) 37.26
1994	Aleksandr Golubyev (RUS) 36.33	Sergei Klevchenya (RUS) 36.39	Manabu Horii (JPN) 36.53

1000 Metres

	GOLD	SILVER	BRONZE
1976	Peter Mueller (USA) 1:19.32	Jorn Didriksen (NOR) 1:20.45	Valeriy Muratov (URS) 1:20.57
1980	Eric Heiden (USA) 1:15.18	Gaetan Boucher (CAN) 1:16.68	Frode Rönning (NOR) 1:16.91
			Vladimir Lobanov (URS) 1:16.91
1984	Gaetan Boucher (CAN) 1:15.80	Sergey Khlebnikov (URS) 1:16.63	Kai Arne Engelstad (NOR) 1:16.75
1988	Nikolay Gouliayev (URS) 1:13.03	Uwe-Jens Mey (GDR) 1:13.11	Igor Gelezovsky (URS) 1:13.19
1992	Olaf Zinke (GER) 1:14.85	Kim Yoon-Man (KOR) 1:14.86	Yukinori Miyabe (JPN) 1:14.92
1994	Dan Jansen (USA) 1:12.43	Igor Zhelezovsky (BLS) 1:12.72	Sergei Klevchenya (RUS) 1:12.85

1924-72 Event not held

1500 Metres

	GOLD	SILVER	BRONZE
1924	Clas Thunberg (FIN) 2:20.8	Roald Larsen (NOR) 2:22.0	Sigurd Moen (NOR) 2:25.6
1928	Clas Thunberg (FIN) 2:21.1	Bernt Evensen (NOR) 2:21.9	Ivar Ballangrud (NOR) 2:22.6
1932	John Shea (USA) 2:57.5	Alexander Hurd (CAN) 5m	William Logan (CAN) 6m
1936	Charles Mathiesen (NOR) 2:19.2	Ivar Ballangrud (NOR) 2:20.2	Birger Wasenius (FIN) 2:20.9
1948	Sverre Farstad (NOR) 2:17.6	Ake Seyffarth (SWE) 2:18.1	Odd Lundberg (NOR) 2:18.9
1952	Hjalmar Andersen (NOR) 2:20.4	Willem van der Voort (NED) 2:20.6	Roald Aas (NOR) 2:21.6
1956	Yevgeniy Grischin (URS) 2:08.6	–	Tiovo Salonen (FIN) 2:09.4
	Yuriy Michailov (URS) 2:08.6		
1960	Roald Aas (NOR) 2:10.4	–	Boris Stenin (URS) 2:11.5
	Yevgeniy Grischin (URS) 2:10.4		
1964	Ants Antson (URS) 2:10.3	Cornelis Verkerk (NED) 2:10.6	Villy Haugen (NOR) 2:11.25
1968	Cornelis Verkerk (NED) 2:03.4	Ard Schenk (NED) 2:05.0	–
		Ivar Eriksen (NOR) 2:05.0	
1972	Ard Schenk (NED) 2:02.96	Roar Gronvold (NOR) 2:04.26	Goran Clässon (SWE) 2:05.89

1976	Jan Egil Storholt (NOR) 1:59.38	Yuriy Kondakov (URS) 1:59.97	Hans Van Helden (NED) 2:00.87
1980	Eric Heiden (USA) 1:55.44	Kai Stenshjemmet (NOR) 1:56.81	Jerje Andersen (NOR) 1:56.92
1984	Gaetan Boucher (CAN) 1:58.36	Sergey Khlebnikov (URS) 1:58.83	Oleg Bogiev (URS) 1:58.89
1988	Andre Hoffmann (GDR) 1:52.06	Eric Flaim (USA) 1:52.12	Michael Hadschieff (AUT) 1:52.31
1992	Johann-Olav Koss (NOR) 1:54.81	Adne Sondral (NOR) 1:54.85	Leo Visser (NED) 1:54.90
1994	Johann-Olav Koss (NOR) 1:51.29	Rintje Ritsma (NED) 1:51.99	Falko Zandstra (NED) 1:52.38

5000 Metres

1924	Clas Thunberg (FIN) 8:39.0	Julius Skutnabb (FIN) 8:48.4	Roald Larsen (NOR) 8:50.2
1928	Ivar Ballangrud (NOR) 8:50.5	Julius Skutnabb (FIN) 8:59.1	Bernt Evensen (NOR) 9:01.1
1932	Irving Jaffee (USA) 9:40.8	Edward Murphy (USA) 2m	William Logan (CAN) 4m
1936	Ivar Ballangrud (NOR) 8:19.6	Birger Wasenius (FIN) 8:23.3	Antero Ojala (FIN) 8:30.1
1948	Reidar Liaklev (NOR) 8:29.4	Odd Lundberg (NOR) 8:32.7	Göthe Hedlund (SWE) 8:34.8
1952	Hjalmar Andersen (NOR) 8:10.6	Kees Broekman (NED) 8:21.6	Sverre Haugli (NOR) 8:22.4
1956	Boris Schilkov (URS) 7:48.7	Sigvard Ericsson (SWE) 7:56.7	Oleg Gontscharenko (URS) 7:57.5
1960	Viktor Kositschkin (URS) 7:51.3	Knut Johannesen (NOR) 8:00.8	Jan Pesman (NED) 8:05.1
1964	Knut Johannesen (NOR) 7:38.4	Per Moe (NOR) 7:38.6	Anton Maier (NOR) 7:42.0
1968	Anton Maier (NOR) 7:22.4	Cornelis Verkerk (NED) 7:23.2	Petrus Nottet (NED) 7:25.5
1972	Ard Schenk (NED) 7:23.6	Roar Gronvold (NOR) 7:28.18	Sten Stensen (NOR) 7:33.39
1976	Sten Stensen (NOR) 7:24.48	Piet Kleine (NED) 7:26.47	Hans Van Helden (NED) 7:26.54
1980	Eric Heiden (USA) 7:02.29	Kai Stenshjemmet (NOR) 7:03.28	Tom Oxholm (NOR) 7:05.59
1984	Tomas Gustafson (SWE) 7:12.28	Igor Malkov (URS) 7:12.30	Rene Schoefisch (GDR) 7:17.49
1988	Tomas Gustafson (SWE) 6:44.63	Leendert Visser (NED) 6:44.98	Gerard Kemkers (NED) 6:45.92
1992	Geir Karlstad (NOR) 6:59.97	Falko Zandstra (NED) 7:02.28	Leo Visser (NED) 7:04.96
1994	Johann-Olav Koss (NOR) 6:34.96	Kjell Storelid (NOR) 6:42.68	Rintje Ritsma (NED) 6:43.94

10,000 Metres

1924	Julius Skutnabb (FIN) 18:04.8	Clas Thunberg (FIN) 18:97.8	Roald Larsen (NOR) 18:12.2
1932	Irving Jaffee (USA) 19:13.6	Ivar Ballangrud (NOR) 5m	Frank Stack (CAN) 6m
1936	Ivar Ballangrud (NOR) 17:24.3	Birger Wasenius (FIN) 17:28.2	Max Stiepl (AUT) 17:30.0
1948	Ake Seyffarth (SWE) 17:26.3	Lauri Parkkinen (FIN) 17:36.0	Pentti Lammio (FIN) 17:42.7
1952	Hjalmar Andersen (NOR) 16:45.8	Kees Broekman (NED) 17:10.6	Carl-Erik Asplund (SWE) 17:16.6

America's Bonnie Blair retained her 500m and 1000m titles in 1994, totalling five gold medals and a bronze since 1988 (Allsport/Shaun Botterill)

1956	Sigvard Ericsson (SWE) 16:35.9	Knut Johannesen (NOR) 16:36.9	Oleg Gontscharenko (URS) 16:42.3
1960	Knut Johannesen (NOR) 15:46.6	Viktor Kositschkin (URS) 15:49.2	Kjell Bäckman (SWE) 16:14.2
1964	Jonny Nilsson (SWE) 15:50.1	Anton Maier (NOR) 16:06.0	Knut Johannesen (NOR) 16:06.3
1968	Johnny Höglin (SWE) 15:23.6	Anton Maier (NOR) 15:23.9	Orjan Sandler (SWE) 15:31.8
1972	Ard Schenk (NED) 15:01.35	Cornelis Verkerk (NED) 15:04.70	Sten Stensen (NOR) 15:07.08
1976	Piet Kleine (NED) 14:50.59	Sten Stensen (NOR) 14:53.30	Hans Van Helden (NED) 15:02.02
1980	Eric Heiden (USA) 14:28.13	Piet Kleine (NED) 14:36.03	Tom Oxholm (NOR) 14:36.60
1984	Igor Malkov (URS) 14:39.90	Tomas Gustafson (SWE) 14:39.95	Rene Schoefisch (GDR) 14:46.91
1988	Tomas Gustafson (SWE) 13:48.20	Michael Hadschieff (AUT) 13:56.11	Leendert Visser (NED) 14:00.55
1992	Bart Veldkamp (NED) 14:12.12	Johann-Olav Koss (NOR) 14:14.58	Geir Karlstad (NOR) 14:18.13
1994	Johann-Olav Koss (NOR) 13:30.55	Kjell Storelid (NOR) 13:49.25	Bart Veldkamp (NED) 13:56.73

1928 Event abandoned.

DISCONTINUED EVENT

All-Round Championship
(Aggregate of placings in 500m, 1500m, 5km and 10km)

1924	Clas Thunberg (FIN) 5.5pts	Roald Larsen (NOR) 9.5pts	Julius Skutnabb (FIN) 11pts

SPEED SKATING MEDAL RESULTS — WOMEN

	GOLD	SILVER	BRONZE
500 Metres			
1960	Helga Haase (GER) 45.9	Natalya Dontschenko (URS) 46.0	Jeanne Ashworth (USA) 46.1
1964	Lydia Skoblikova (URS) 45.0	Irina Yegorova (URS) 45.4	Tatyana Sidorova (URS) 45.5
1968	Ludmila Titova (URS) 46.1	Mary Meyers (USA) 46.3	–
		Dianne Holum (USA) 46.3	
		Jennifer Fish (USA) 46.3	
1972	Anne Henning (USA) 43.33	Vera Krasnova (URS) 44.01	Ludmila Titova (URS) 44.45
1976	Sheila Young (USA) 42.76	Catherine Priestner (CAN) 43.12	Tatyana Averina (URS) 43.17
1980	Karin Enke (GDR) 41.78	Leah Poulos-Mueller (USA) 42.26	Natalya Petruseva (URS) 42.42
1984	Christa Rothenburger (GDR) 41.02	Karin Enke (GDR) 41.28	Natalya Chive (URS) 41.50
1988	Bonnie Blair (USA) 39.10	Christa Rothenburger (GDR) 39.12	Karin Enke-Kania (GDR) 39.24
1992	Bonnie Blair (USA) 40.33	Ye Qiaobo (CHN) 40.51	Christa Luding (GER) 40.57
1994	Bonnie Blair (USA) 39.25	Susan Auch (CAN) 39.61	Franziska Schenk (GER) 39.70
1000 Metres			
1960	Klara Guseva (URS) 1:34.1	Helga Haase (GER) 1:34.3	Tamara Rylova (URS) 1:34.8
1964	Lydia Skoblikova (URS) 1:33.2	Irina Yegorova (URS) 1:34.3	Kaija Mustonen (FIN) 1:34.8
1968	Carolina Geijssen (NED) 1:32.6	Ludmila Titova (URS) 1:32.9	Dianne Holum (USA) 1:33.4
1972	Monika Pflug (FRG) 1:31.40	Atje Keulen-Deelstra (NED) 1:31.61	Anne Henning (USA) 1:31.62
1976	Tatyana Averina (URS) 1:28.43	Leah Poulos (USA) 1:28.57	Shjeila Young (USA) 1:29.14
1980	Natalya Petruseva (URS) 1:24.10	Leah Poulos-Mueller (USA) 1:25.41	Sylvia Albrecht (GDR) 1:26.46
1984	Karin Enke (GDR) 1:21.61	Andrea Schöne (GDR) 1:22.83	Natalya Petruseva (URS) 1:23.21
1988	Christa Rothenburger (GDR) 1:17.65	Karin Enke-Kania (GDR) 1:17.70	Bonnie Blair (USA) 1:18.31
1992	Bonnie Blair (USA) 1:21.90	Ye Qiaobo (CHN) 1:21.92	Monique Garbrecht (GER) 1:22.10
1994	Bonnie Blair (USA) 1:18.74	Anke Baier (GER) 1:20.12	Ye Qiaobo (CHN) 1:20.22
1500 Metres			
1960	Lydia Skoblikova (URS) 2:25.2	Elvira Seroczynska (POL) 2:25.7	Helena Pilejeyk (POL) 2:27.1
1964	Lydia Skoblikova (URS) 2:22.6	Kaija Mustonen (FIN) 2:25.5	Berta Kolokoltseva (URS) 2:27.1
1968	Kaija Mustonen (FIN) 2:22.4	Carolina Geijssen (NED) 2:22.7	Christina Kaiser (NED) 2:24.5
1972	Dianne Holum (USA) 2:20.85	Christina Baas-Kaiser (NED) 2:21.05	Atje Keulen-Deelstra (NED) 2:22.05
1976	Galina Stepanskaya (URS) 2:16.58	Sheila Young (USA) 2:17.06	Tatyana Averina (URS) 2:17.96
1980	Annie Borckink (NED) 2:10.95	Ria Visser (NED) 2:12.35	Sabine Becker (GDR) 2:12.38
1984	Karin Enke (GDR) 2:03.42	Andrea Schöne (GDR) 2:05.29	Natalya Petruseva (URS) 2:05.78

1988	Yvonne Van Gennip (NED) 2:00.68	Karin Enke-Kania (GDR) 2:00.82	Andrea Schöne-Ehrig (GDR) 2:01.49
1992	Jacqueline Borner (GER) 2:05.87	Gunda Niemann (GER) 2:05.92	Seiko Hashimoto (JPN) 2:06.88
1994	Emese Hunyady (AUT) 2:02.19	Svetlana Fedotkin (RUS) 2:02.69	Gunda Niemann (GER) 2:03.41

3000 Metres

1960	Lydia Skoblikova (URS) 5:14.3	Valentina Stenina (URS) 5:16.9	Eevi Huttunen (FIN) 5:21.0
1964	Lydia Skoblikova (URS) 5:14.9	Valentina Stenina (URS) 5:18.5 Pil-Hwa Han (PRK) 5:18.5	–
1968	Johanna Schut (NED) 4:56.2	Kaija Mustonen (FIN) 5:01.0	Christina Kaiser (NED) 5:01.3
1972	Christina Baas-Kaiser (NED) 4:52.14	Dianne Holum (USA) 4:58.67	Atje Keulen-Deelstra (NED) 4:59.91
1976	Tatyana Averina (URS) 4:45.19	Andrea Mitscherlich (GDR) 4:45.23	Lisbeth Korsmo (NOR) 4:45.24
1980	Björg Eva Jensen (NOR) 4:32.13	Sabine Becker (GDR) 4:32.79	Beth Heiden (USA) 4:33.77
1984	Andrea Mitscherlich-Schöne (GDR) 4:24.79	Karin Enke (GDR) 4:26.33	Gabi Schönbrunn (GDR) 4:33.13
1988	Yvonne Van Gennip (HOL) 4:11.94	Andrea Schöne-Ehrig (GDR) 4:12.09	Gabi Schönbrunn-Zange (GDR) 4:16.92
1992	Gunda Niemann (GER) 4:19.90	Heike Warnicke (GER) 4:22.88	Emese Hunyady (AUT) 4:24.64
1994	Svetlana Bazhanova (RUS) 4:17.43	Emese Hunyady (AUT) 4:18.14	Claudia Pechstein (GER) 4:18.34

5000 Metres

1988	Yvonne Van Gennip (NED) 7:14.13	Andrea Schöne-Ehrig (GDR) 7:17.2	Gabi Schönbrunn-Zange (GDR) 7:21.61
1992	Gunda Niemann (GER) 7:31.57	Heike Warnicke (GER) 7:37.59	Claudia Pechstein (GER) 7:39.80
1994	Claudia Pechstein (GER) 7:14.37	Gunda Niemann (GER) 7:14.88	Hiromi Yamamoto (JPN) 7:19.68

1960–1984 Event not held.

Short-track Speed Skating

In 1988 short-track speed skating was a demonstration sport, and in 1992 it became a medal sport with two events each for men and women. In 1994 an extra two events were added. So far the only person to gain a medal in both styles of speed skating is Eric Flaim (USA) with silvers in the 1988 1500m and the 1994 short-track relay. The most successful competitor has been Kim Ki-Hoon (KOR) with three gold medals in 1992-94, while the best by a woman has been by Cathy Turner (USA) with 2 gold, 1 silver, 1 bronze – a record four medals in the sport. The youngest ever winner of a Winter Games gold medal was Kim Yoon-Mi (KOR) in the women's relay aged 13yr 83 days. She was also the youngest ever female Olympic winner in either winter or summer Games.

The oldest champion in short-track was Cathy Turner who won the 1994 500m title aged 31yr 320 days. The youngest male gold medallist was Jae Kun Song (KOR) aged 18yr 7 days in the 1992 relay, while the oldest was his teammate Ji Soo Mo aged 30yr 264 days. It is noteworthy that the average age of the winning Korean women's relay team in 1994 was about 15¼ yr.

SHORT-TRACK SPEED SKATING MEDAL RESULTS — MEN

	GOLD	SILVER	BRONZE
500 Metres			
1994	Chae Ji-Hoon (KOR) 43.45	Mirko Vuillermin (ITA) 43.47	Nicky Gooch (GBR) 43.68

1924-92 Event not held

1000 Metres			
1992	Kim Ki-Hoon (KOR) 1:30.76	Frederic Blackburn (CAN) 1:31.11	Lee Joon-Ho (KOR) 1:31.16
1994	Kim Ki-Hoon (KOR) 1:34.57	Chae Ji-Hoon (KOR) 1:34.92	Marc Gagnon (CAN) 1:33.03[1]

[1] *Winner of 'B' final*

1924-88 Event not held

The 1992 gold medallist Cathy Turner (USA) retains her 500m short-track title at Lillehammer (Allsport/Shaun Botterill)

5000 Metres Relay

1992	South Korea 7:14.02	Canada 7:14.06	Japan 7:18.18
1994	Italy 7:11.74	United States 7:13.37	Australia 7:13.68

1924-88 Event not held

SHORT-TRACK SPEED SKATING MEDAL RESULTS — WOMEN

500 Metres

1992	Cathy Turner (USA) 47.04	Li Yan (CHN) 47.08	Hwang Ok-Sil (PRK) 47.23
1994	Cathy Turner (USA) 45.98	Zhang Yanmei (CHN) 46.44	Amy Peterson (USA) 46.76

1924-88 Event not held

1000 Metres

1994	Chun Lee-Kyung (KOR) 1:36.87	Nathalie Lambert (CAN) 1:36.97	Kim So-Hee (KOR) 1:37.09

1924-92 Event not held

3000 Metres Relay

1992	Canada 4:36.62	United States 4:37.85	Unified Team 4:42.69
1994	Korea 4:26.64	Canada 4:32.04	United States 4:39.34

1924-88 Event not held

SHORT-TRACK SPEED SKATING MEDALS TABLE

	Men			Women			
	G	S	B	G	S	B	Total
Korea	4	1	1	2	-	1	9
United States	-	1	-	2	1	2	6
Canada	-	2	1	1	2	-	6
Italy	1	1	-	-	-	-	2

China . . . . - . . . . - . . . . - . . . . - . . . . 2 . . . . - 2
Australia . . . . - . . . . - . . . . 1 . . . . - . . . . - . . . . - 1
Great Britain . . . . - . . . . - . . . . 1 . . . . - . . . . - . . . . - 1
Japan . . . . - . . . . - . . . . 1 . . . . - . . . . - . . . . - 1
North Korea (PRK) . . . . - . . . . - . . . . - . . . . - . . . . - 1
Soviet Union . . . . - . . . . - . . . . - . . . . - 1 1
	5	5	5	5	5	5	30

Olympic short-track speed skating records

Men			
500m	43.45s	Chae Ji-Hoon (KOR)	1994
1000m	1m 30.76s	Kim Ki-Hoon (KOR)	1992
5000m Relay	7m 11.74s	Italy	1994
Women			
500m	45.98s	Cathy Turner (USA)	1994
1000m	1m 36.87s	Chun Lee-Kyung (KOR)	1994
3000m Relay	4m 26.64s	Korea	1994

DOUBLES ACROSS SPORT

There have been a number of multi-talented sports people who have won Olympic medals in different sports. The only one to win gold medals in both Summer and Winter Games was Eddie Eagan (USA) who won the 1920 light-heavyweight boxing title, and was a member of the 1932 winning 4-man bob. His closest rival has been Jacob Tullin Thams (NOR) who won the ski jump in 1924, and then took a silver in yachting in 1936. The most outstanding woman in this line of endeavour is Christa Rothenburger-Luding (GDR) who won a gold and a silver at speed skating at Calgary in 1988, and then came second in the sprint cycling at Seoul later the same year.

In the Summer Games the earliest double gold winner at two sports was Carl Schuhmann (GER), with three gymnastic events and the wrestling in 1896. At the same Games, Viggo Jensen (DEN) won a gold and silver in weightlifting, a silver and a bronze at shooting, and was fourth in the rope climb. Morris Kirksey (USA) won gold medals in the 4 x 100m relay and as a member of the American Rugby team in 1920. Daniel Norling (SWE) won

gymnastic golds in 1908 and 1912, and then an equestrian gold in 1920. John Derbyshire (GBR) and Paul Radmilovic (GBR) won golds at swimming and the allied sport of water polo in the early part of the century. Examples of women excelling in two summer Olympic sports are rare, with the most outstanding probably being Roswitha Krause (GDR) who won a 1968 silver in the 4 x 100m freestyle, and then won silver and bronze in the 1976 and 1980 handball tournaments.

One of the more unusual doubles was that of Fernand de Montigny (BEL), who won a gold, two silver and two bronze medals in fencing in five Games, 1906- 1924, and another bronze on the hockey field in 1920. However, Frank Kungler (USA) has the unique distinction of winning medals at three sports at the same Games. In 1904 he won a silver at wrestling, a bronze at tug-of-war, and two bronzes at weightlifting. Another double was by Otto Herschmann (AUT) with silvers in the 1896 100m freestyle swim and then as a member of the 1912 sabre fencing team.

*Index compiled by
Stan Greenberg*